The United Kingdom's Legal Responses To Terrorism

Yonah Alexander

and

Edgar H Brenner

Editors

Transnational Publishers, Inc / Cavendish Publishing, Ltd

Published by
Cavendish Publishing Limited
The Glass House
Wharton Street
London WC1X 9PX
United Kingdom
Tel. +44 (0) 20 7278 8000
Fax +44 (0) 20 7278 8080
info@cavendishpublishing.com
www.cavendishpublishing.com

Transnational Publishers, Inc.
410 Saw Mill River Road
United States
Tel. +1 (914) 693 5100
Fax +1 (914) 693 4430
info@transnationalpubs.com
www.transnationalpubs.com

Sold and Distributed in Europe and the Commonwealth (excluding Canada) by
Cavendish Publishing Limited.

Sold and Distributed in USA and Canada by
Transnational Publishers, Inc.

Library of Congress Cataloging-in-Publication Data on file

British Library CIP is available

ISBN 1-57105-277-1 (Transnational Publishers, Inc.)
ISBN 1-859411-787-6 (Cavendish Publishing Limited)

Printed and bound in Great Britain and the United States.

Contents

Foreword

Michael Carpenter, Esq[1]

Terrorist violence has a long history in the United Kingdom, and the legal measures adopted to counter the threat are also of long standing, even though in recent years they have been considerably expanded. For example, it was the bombing campaign by the Fenians, including the bomb attack on Clerkenwell prison in London in 1867, which led to the passing of the Explosive Substances Act 1883, an enactment which is still of the greatest importance in dealing with conspiracies to cause explosions.

Terrorist activities, such as those carried out in Northern Ireland and elsewhere in the United Kingdom, involving the causing of injury to persons or damage to property, amount to the commission of crimes, even without the enactment of specific anti-terrorist measures or the proof of any specific intent related to terrorism.[2] Apart from the question of scale, it is only the question of motivation or purpose that distinguishes these activities in any way from "ordinary" crimes, and the acts committed remain equally harmful to the victims, whatever the misguided motive. This is an important factor to recall when dealing with the so-called "political offence" exception in the extradition laws of some countries, and the tendency in some quarters to accord terrorists some special status separate from that of an offender.

Important recent legislation includes the Terrorism Act 2000 and the Anti-Terrorism, Crime and Security Act 2001. The Terrorism Act 2000 is substantially a re-enactment of the earlier Prevention of Terrorism (Temporary Provisions) Act 1989, the Northern Ireland (Emergency Provisions) Act 1996 and sections 1 to 4 of the Criminal Justice (Terrorism and Conspiracy) Act 1998, but with a number of extensions and amendments.

In the first place, the definition of terrorism in the 2000 Act has been expanded to include the use or threat of action for the purpose of advancing a religious or ideological, as well as a political, cause.[3] Secondly, the 2000 Act unlike its predecessors is not subject to a requirement of annual renewal by Parliament, although Part VII of the Act continues to provide temporary measures for Northern Ireland, which are subject to annual renewal and an overall 5

---

[1]   Counsel, European Legislation, House of Commons. (The views expressed here are entirely his own.)

[2]   Cf the offences related to the use of explosives in ss 28–30 Offences Against the Person Act 1861.

[3]   See s 1(1)(c) of the Terrorism Act 2000.

year time limit.[4] Thirdly, the 2000 Act is not limited to terrorism connected with the affairs of Northern Ireland, but applies generally to terrorism within the United Kingdom and throughout the world.[5] Accordingly, the provisions that empower the Secretary of State to proscribe an organisation if he believes it to be involved in terrorism (Part II) will now apply across the United Kingdom. Similarly, the provisions on terrorist property in Part III (which provide for the seizure of terrorist cash and other property, and the offences of fund-raising and money-laundering) will now apply to all forms of terrorism, irrespective of any connection with the affairs of Northern Ireland. The offences of providing weapons training[6] and directing a terrorist organisation[7] will also apply generally and do not require any connection with the affairs of Northern Ireland.

The Explanatory Notes to the Anti-Terrorism, Crime and Security Act 2001 indicate that the purpose of the Act is to ensure that the Government has the necessary powers to counter the threat to the UK in the light of the new situation arising from the September 11 terrorist attacks on New York and Washington. The Act contains further provisions on the freezing of terrorist property, disclosure of information, immigration and asylum as well as provisions to strengthen the current legislation on the control of chemical, nuclear and biological weapons. The Act also re-introduces the offence of failing to disclose information about acts of terrorism. Such an offence was contained in section 18 of the Prevention of Terrorism (Temporary Provisions) Act 1989 (now repealed) and applied only in Northern Ireland. The new provision (s 38B Terrorism Act 2000) applies generally throughout the UK.

Sections 22 to 23 of the 2001 Act introduce a controversial new power to detain suspected international terrorists in circumstances where it is not possible (under the European Convention on Human Rights or other inter-

---

4   Part VII continues the arrangement whereby common law offences such as murder, manslaughter, riot, kidnapping and false imprisonment and offences under statute such as those under the Offences Against the Person Act 1861, the Explosive Substances Act 1883 and offences related to hijacking, possession of firearms etc are 'scheduled' offences and therefore triable on indictment without a jury (s 75), unless the Attorney General for Northern Ireland certifies that the offence is not to be treated as a scheduled offence (in which case the trial on indictment takes place with a jury). This system has operated since the 1970s and seeks to address the problem of jury intimidation in terrorist trials.

5   Sections 62 and 63 of the 2000 Act extend jurisdiction over terrorist bombing and financing offences to acts done outside the United Kingdom. These provisions permit the UK to ratify the UN Conventions for the Suppression of Terrorist Bombings and the Suppression of Terrorist Financing.

6   Section 54.

7   Section 56.

national obligations[8]) to remove them from the UK. In December 2001, the UK notified the Council of Europe of derogation from the provisions of Article 5 ECHR (which deal with the right to liberty and security) to the extent necessary to ensure that the provisions of sections 21 to 23 are not in breach of this ECHR obligations.[9]

On July 30 2002, the Special Immigration Appeals Commission (SIAC) (which *inter alia* reviews immigration decisions involving considerations of national security) declared that these provisions of the 2001 Act were incompatible with the ECHR on grounds that they targeted non-British persons, and were therefore unlawful under Article 14 ECHR (which proibits discrimination in the application of the ECHR). The decision was reversed on appeal to the Court of Appeal in *A and Others v Secretary of State for the Home Department* (October 25, 2002).[10] The Court of Appeal did not see the closed evidence which the SIAC had seen, but nevertheless thought it obvious that the SIAC was entitled to conclude that there was an emergency threatening the life of the nation within the meaning of Article 15 ECHR. However, the Court of Appeal diagreed with the SIAC on the discrimination issue under Article 14 ECHR. The Court concluded that the Home Secretary's selection of alien terrorists for detention did not involve impermissible discrimination. The aliens who could not be deported (because of the risk of torture in the country of destination) did not, unlike British nationals, have any right to remain in the UK and therefore fell into a different class. As soon as they could be deported to a country which would not torture them, this would happen. It was only the need to protect them from torture that meant that they could not be removed for the time being. The Court thought it would be "surprising" if Article 14 (ECHR, or any international requirement not to discriminate, prevented the Home Secretary from taking the restricted action he thought necessary (in this case, detention). The Court also pointed out that the consequence of the detainees' argument on discrimination was that the Home Secretary would have to take more extensive action, applying to both national and non-nationals, than he would otherwise have thought necessary and that this result would not promote human rights but have the opposite result.

---

8   Briefly stated, the problem is that by virtue of Article 5(1)(f) of the European Convention on Human Rights a person cannot be detained under the Immigration Act 1971 unless action is being taken with a view to deportation. On the other hand, Article 3 ECHR prevents deportation to a country where there is a real risk that the person will face torture or inhuman or degrading treatment or punishment.

9   For the text of the derogation see the Human Rights Act 1998 (Amendment No 2) Order SI 2001/3644.

10   See Document No 29.

The case illustrates the significance of the ECHR as a factor in the legal context in which counter-terrorism measures operate in the United Kingdom. On the one hand, the protection of human rights is a fundamental value of a democratic society, but on the other, society itself requires protection from terrorist attack and this may necessitate some of those rights being abridged. The European Court of Human Rights has long recognised the need for a proper balance between the defence of the institutions of democracy in the common interest and the protection of human rights. It has indicated its readiness to take into account the 'special nature of terrorist crime and the exigencies of dealing with it.'[11]

The documents in this volume set out key elements of the balance between legitimate governmental interests and the protection of human rights as it is evolving in the United Kingdom.

---

[11] See *Ireland v. United Kingdom* Case A/25 (1978). For a review of ECHR jurisprudence relating to counter-terrorism measures, see Warbrick, European Human Rights Law Review, Issue 3, 2002, p 287.

Preface

Introduction

The most devastating terrorist attack ever recorded in the history of humanity occurred on September 11, 2001. Nineteen terrorists hijacked four US airplanes and crashed them into the World Trade Center towers in New York City and the Pentagon in Virginia. One plane crashed in a field in Pennsylvania. Some three thousand people were killed and thousands more injured. It is not surprising, therefore, that this carnage resulted, *inter alia*, in the proliferation of several hundred reports, studies and books on the threat of modern terrorism and what societies can, and should, do to reduce the potential risks on conventional and unconventional levels.

To be sure, the origin of *The United Kingdom's Legal Responses to Terrorism* did not stem from the horrors of September 11. The editors of this volume, and their academic and professional colleagues, have conducted relevant legal research for some four decades. Suffice it to mention earlier publications such as *Legislative Responses to Terrorism* (Martinus Nijhof, 1986), edited by Yonah Alexander and Alan S Nanes; *Cases and Materials on Terrorism: Three Nations' Response* (Kluwer Law International, 1997), edited by Michael F Noone and Yonah Alexander; *Legal Aspects of Terrorism in the United States*, Vols 1–4 (Oceana, 2000), edited by Yonah Alexander and Edgar H Brenner; *Terrorism and the Law* (Transnational, 2001), edited by Yonah Alexander and Edgar H Brenner; and *US Federal Legal Responses to Terrorism* (Transnational, 2002), edited by Yonah Alexander and Edgar H Brenner. Our academic work in this important field of public concern is expected to continue in the hope that it will contribute to national and international efforts in combating terrorism in the 21st century.

The purpose of this Preface is to provide a general overview of the threat of terrorism to the United Kingdom; to review and discuss the major legal responses included in this volume, particularly focusing on Executive Statements and Legislative Acts, International Treaties and Conventions and court cases, and also to acknowledge the support of individuals and institutions in producing this book.

Terrorism's challenge to the United Kingdom

There exists a definitional and moral confusion over what constitutes terrorism. Academic research indicates that there are some 200 definitions.[1] Indeed, every sovereign state reserves to itself the political and legal authority to define terrorism in the context of domestic and foreign affairs. It is not surprising, therefore, that for legislators, terrorism has a sufficiently precise legal meaning to enable them to enact counter-terrorism legislation.

The United Kingdom is no exception. Clearly, "English law regulating political violence has been continuously refined in the 300 years since the Glorious Revolution and has served as a paradigm for other countries that derive their jurisprudence from that experience."[2] Britain's counter-terrorism legislation reflects, therefor, perceived threats of political violence at home and abroad.

It is a truism that the United Kingdom is a victim of both domestic and international terrorism. First, it has been a principal site for terrorist activities resulting from the conflict in Northern Ireland, which is a British territory. The major challenge has been the activities of the Irish Republican Army (IRA), also known as the Provisional Irish Republican Army (PIRA). In the name of uniting the Irish Republic and Northern Ireland, the IRA resorted to bombings, assassinations, kidnappings, extortion, and robberies. The IRA has taken its fight to the streets of London and other cities in England. It attacked ordinary civilians, military personnel, police, and business centres. Militant Protestant groups in Northern Ireland have also undertaken terrorist operations resulting in 3,000 fatalities, woundings, and property damage. Despite the 1994 cease-fire and the ongoing peace process, which began under the Good Friday agreement of 1998, Catholic splinter groups, such as the Real IRA, as well as Protestant extremists opposing a political solution, continue their violent activities.

To be sure, the peace process is currently in crisis. In October 2002, the police in Northern Ireland raided the offices of Sinn Fein, the IRA's political wing. It arrested Republican activists for stealing sensitive British government documents from the offices of the parliament building at Stormont. This intelligence gathering, it was charged, could be used by terrorists. Consequently, Britain indefinitely suspended the province's local assembly in which Protestants and Catholics share power. Both the Irish Republic, which is a co-sponsor of the Good Friday agreement, and the United States, which helped to broker it,

---

[1]   See, for example, Alex P Schmidt, *Political Terrorism: A Research Guide to Concepts, Theories, Data Bases and Literature* (New Brunswick, NJ: Transaction, 1994), 103–104.

[2]   Michael F Noone and Yonah Alexander, eds. *Cases and Materials on Terrorism: Three Nations' Responses* (The Hague: Kluwer Law International, 1997), p xvi.

approved Britain's move. Nevertheless, other parts of the agreement still remain intact, including a joint Protestant-Catholic board set up to oversee policing.

In spite of this latest setback, the Northern Ireland experience indicates that the United Kingdom security and political measures, with some exceptions, generally struck a balance between maintaining democratic and legal rights and avoiding recourse to draconian responses.

Another challenge facing Britain, particularly in the past 30 years, relates to attacks in the country perpetrated by foreign terrorists. More specifically, various Middle East factions have carried their quarrels to Britain. For instance, in 1980 dissidents seized the Iranian embassy in London. It was stormed and retaken by a combination of police and special air service anti-terrorist troops. Nineteen hostages were rescued, and five terrorists killed. In 1982, members of the Palestinian Abu Nidal Organisation gravely wounded the Israeli Ambassador to the United Kingdom, Shlomo Argov. This assassination attempt triggered Israeli retaliation and the subsequent war in Lebanon.

It should be noted that Britain has been a target of many acts of terrorism abroad. British citizens traveling outside the United Kingdom have also been victims, such as the 67 nationals who were killed on September 11 at the World Trade Center. In fact, the United States House of Representatives in expressing its "sincere appreciation" of Blair's "leadership in the war on terrorism" offered in its Resolution on October 11, 2002, "deepest sympathy to the British victims of terrorism and their families," referring specifically to the September 11 victims.

Another aspect of the terrorist threat to be considered is the involvement of some British citizens in operational activities outside the United Kingdom. Two suspects are cases in point. Richard Colvin Reid, a 28 year old British national of mixed European and Jamaican descent, attempted to light a fuse to his explosive-laden shoes on American Airlines flight 63 from Paris to Miami on December 22, 2001. On January 16, 2002, Reid was charged with interfering with a flight crew, attempted use of a weapon of mass destruction, attempted homicide, placing explosive devices on an aircraft, attempted murder, attempted destruction of an aircraft, and attempted wrecking of a mass transportation vehicle. On October 3, 2002, he pleaded guilty, declaring his hatred for America and his loyalty to bin Laden.

The second case involves Ahmed Omar Saeed Sheikh, a British citizen of Pakistani origin. He attended the London School of Economics, dropping out in 1992 to become an aid worker in Bosnia. He was radicalised by his stay in Bosnia and moved to Pakistan to join the Kashmiri terrorist group Harakat ul-Muhajideen (HUM). He was captured by Indian forces in 1994 after kidnapping four Western tourists. He was released after the hijacking of an Indian Airlines jet in December 1999. Omar then joined Jaish-e-Mohammad (JEM) and was involved in the kidnapping and murder of *Wall Street Journal* journalist Daniel Pearl in February 2002. Omar was secretly indicted by the United States in November 2001 and is currently in Pakistani custody.

It is against this backdrop that the Foreign Affairs Committee of the House of Commons stated in its seventh report of Session 2001–2002 that ". . . international terrorism can only be tackled through thorough international cooperation, and not just among Britain's traditional allies. We are convinced that the government's efforts to achieve international counter-terrorism cooperation through existing international organisations, and in particular through the United Nations, are therefore an appropriate way to develop effective international cooperation against terrorism. Sufficient resources must, however, be provided to ensure that such measures succeed."[3]

The materials on the United Kingdom's legal responses to terrorism included in the volume are described as follows.

Executive Statements

The Prime Minister, three weeks after the terrorist attacks of September 11, made a statement to Parliament (and to the world), concerning "Responsibility for the Terrorist Attacks in the United States, 11 September 2001" (Document No 1). Tony Blair's presentation was based "on still-secret electronic eavesdropping, interrogations and other sensitive sources . . ." (*US News & World Report*, October 15, 2001, page 18). His remarkable support for the United States view of events asserts unequivocally that the attacks were planned and carried out by Osama bin Laden and al Qaida in alliance with the Taliban regime in Afghanistan. (Document No 1, page 4.) The Prime Minister charged bin Laden with responsibility for the 1993 attacks "on US military personnel serving in Somalia . . . the bombings of the US Embassies in Kenya and Tanzania . . . and [t]he attack on the USS Cole. . . " (page 4).

The Prime Minister closed the statement by saying "we have an absolute determination to see justice done, and this evil of mass terrorism confronted and defeated" (page 8).

Legislative Acts

The Terrorism Act 2000 (Document No 2) since its enactment is "the main source of the law relating to terrorist activity taking place within the United

---

3   House of Commons, Foreign Affairs Committee, "Foreign Policy Aspects of the War Against Terrorism," Seventh Report of Session 2001–2002. Report, together with the Proceedings of the Committee, Minutes of Evidence and Appendices (ordered by the House of Commons to be printed June 12, 2002). Published on June 20, 2002 by authority of the House of Commons (London: The Stationery Office), p 16.

Kingdom (including actions or conspiracies *within* any part of the UK to commit acts abroad—(see s 1(4) and the offences relating to weapons training under s 54 and inciting terrorism overseas under ss 59–61. . .)."[4]

The "Terrorism Act 2000 Explanatory Notes"(Document No 3, pages 87–99) provide a convenient summary of the legislation, prepared by the government department introducing the Bill. As the "Overview" sets forth, starting at page 88: Part I sets out the definition of terrorism for the purposes of the Act; Part II provides a power for the Secretary of State to proscribe organisations; Part III provides for offences relating to fund-raising and other kinds of financial support for terrorism; Part IV concerns terrorist investigations; Part V concerns counter-terrorist powers; Part VI concerns . . . ancillary offences. Part VII provides for the continuation of the system, in Northern Ireland, whereby terrorist offences may be tried without a jury (Document No 3, page 89).

The Anti-Terrorism, Crime and Security Act 2001 (Document No 4, pages 101–184) covers a variety of subjects. Part 1 concerns "terrorist property"; Part 2 "freezing orders"; Part 3 "disclosure of information"; Part 4 "immigration and asylum"; Part 5 "race and religion"; Part 6 "weapons of mass destruction"; Part 7 "security of pathogens and toxins"; Part 8 "security of nuclear industry"; Part 9 "aviation security"; Part 10 "police powers"; Part 11 "retention of communications data"; Part 12 "bribery and corruption." Part 13 concerns a variety of "miscellaneous" subjects. Part 14, "supplemental," provides in section 122(1) that "[t]he Secretary of State shall appoint a committee to conduct a review of this Act."

Part 4, Immigration and Asylum, is one of most important and controversial parts of the 2001 Act. Section 21(1) provides that the Home Secretary may issue a certificate that a person is believed by him to be a risk to national security and is suspected by him of being a terrorist. Under section 23 a person so designated may be detained "despite the fact that his removal or deportation from the United Kingdom is prevented (whether temporarily of indefinitely) by (a) a point of law . . . , or (b) a practical consideration."

Under s 25, a suspected international terrorist may appeal his certification to the previously created Special Immigration Appeals Commission (SIAC). The Commission must cancel the certification if it finds that the Home Secretary's belief or suspicion is without reasonable grounds or "that for some other reason the certificate should not have been issued."

The purpose of Part 4 was, in part, to remedy the hurdle created by the European Court of Human Rights which had concluded in *Chahal v United Kingdom* (Document No 25) that non-deportable aliens suspected of being

---

4   Private communication from Michael Carpenter, Esq. On file at the Potomac Institute for Policy Studies, Arlington, Virginia, USA.

terrorists could not be detained indefinitely and that the United Kingdom's detention review procedures did not provide an "effective remedy before a national authority" as required by Article 13 of the European Convention on Human Rights (the Convention).

However, in July 2002, the SIAC ruled that the alien detention provisions in the Anti-Terrorism, Crime and Security Act 2001 discriminated against aliens in violation of the Convention (Document No 28. This ruling was overturned on October 25, 2002. Document No 29).

The Regulation of Investigatory Powers Act of 2000 (Document No 5) is a comprehensive piece of legislation dealing with a variety of subjects related to criminal investigations. Part I concerns communications. Sub-chapters deal with interception of communications and the acquisition and disclosure of communications data. Part II concerns surveillance and covert human intelligence sources. Part III deals with investigation of electronic data protected by encryption. Part IV, and other provisions, deal with the scrutiny of investigatory powers and of the functions of the intelligence services.

In the Human Rights Act 1998 (Document No 6) the United Kingdom gave effect to the European Convention on Human Rights as substantive United Kingdom law. This means the United Kingdom courts must give effect not only to the Convention but must also take into account any "judgment, decision, declaration or advisory opinion of the European Court of Human Rights" (s 2(1)(a), pages 311–312).

International Treaties and Conventions

In the Treaty of Maastricht, Title VI, "Provisions on Cooperation in the Fields of Justice and Home Affairs" (February 12, 1992) (Document No 7), the European Community Member States agreed that they would regard as a matter of common interest "police cooperation for the purposes of preventing and combating terrorism, unlawful drug trafficking and other serious forms of international crime" (Article K.1(9), page 344).

The Treaty of Maastricht led in 1995 to "the Treaty on European Union, on the Establishment of a European Police Office (Europol Convention)" (Document No 8, pages 347–386). Among the objectives of Europol is cooperation among the Member States in "combating terrorism" (Article 2, pages 349–350).

Title VI of the Amsterdam Convention (October 2, 1997) (Document No 9) placed increased importance on police cooperation through Europol (Article K.1(9), page 388). However, it was not until after September 11, 2001, that Europol assumed its current important role in coordinating the European Union's war against terrorism.

Court Cases

We have edited the cases to delete extraneous material, or the consideration of issues unrelated to terrorism. The location of omitted text is noted.

A number of the cases mention the "Secretary of State for the Home Department." Sometimes the title is shortened to "the Secretary" or "the Secretary of State" or "the Home Secretary." In order to reduce confusion on the part of non-UK readers, we have used the title of "Home Secretary" wherever appropriate to the context.

The Queen on the Application of the Secretary of State for the Home Department v Immigration Appeal Tribunal, and *The Queen on the Application of Hwez v Secretary of State for the Home Department & an Adjudicator*, in the Supreme Court of Judicature, Queen's Bench Division (December 19, 2001) (Document No 10): this case involved passengers on an aircraft hijacked in Afghanistan, which eventually landed in the United Kingdom. Some of the passengers sought leave to enter the United Kingdom on the ground that they were refugees entitled to the protections offered by the 1951 UN Convention on the Status of Refugees. The Home Secretary denied their claim to refugee status and refused them leave to enter the United Kingdom. They appealed to the Immigration Appeal Tribunal, which adjourned the appeals indefinitely. The court held that persons refused leave to enter the United Kingdom are entitled to have the question of whether or not they are entitled to refugee status determined by the Immigration Appeal Tribunal.

In *The Queen on the Application of Louis Farrakhan*, Court of Appeal (April 30, 2002) (Document No 11): the court considered a decision by the Home Secretary to refuse Rev Farrakhan permission to enter the United Kingdom on the ground that his presence "would at the present time pose an unwelcome and significant threat to community relations and in particular to relations between the Muslim and Jewish communities . . ." (paragraph 2, page 399). The trial judge concluded that the Home Secretary had not established that there was "more than a nominal risk that community relations would be likely to be endangered . . ." if Rev Farrakhan were admitted to the United Kingdom (paragraph 33, page 410).

The appellate court reversed his decision, holding that the Home Secretary "provided sufficient explanation for a decision that turned on his personal, informed, assessment of risk to demonstrate that his decision did not involve a disproportionate interference with freedom of expression" (paragraph 81, page 423).

In *Governor of HM Prison Brixton, and Government of the United States of America v Eidarous and Abdelbary*, High Court, Queen's Bench Division, May 2, 2002 (Document No 12): Eidarous and Abdelbary sought writs of habeas corpus to challenge rulings by a magistrate in extradition proceedings based on allegations by the United States that they had conspired with Osama Bin Laden to attack US embassies in Nairobi and Dar es Salam and to murder US citizens.

The court rejected the arguments advanced by the applicants in an effort to avoid extradition to the United States. The Court held that: (1) the magistrate could rely on a statement from an anonymous witness identified only as "CS/1" (paragraph 15, page 429); (2) that the evidence met the applicable statutory tests (paragraphs 32–33, page 435); (3) that there was sufficient connection with the United States to confer jurisdiction, in particular that there was no requirement that the acts constituting the extradition crime should have taken place within the territory of the United States (paragraph 34, pages 435–436); (4) that the reasons set forth by the magistrate were adequate (paragraph 40, pages 437–438).

The case of *The Secretary of State for the Home Department v Shafiq Ur Rehman*, Court of Appeal, May 23, 2000 (Document No 13): involved Rehman's appeal of a decision by the Home Secretary to deport him on the ground that information "received from confidential sources . . ." indicated that he was "involved with an Islamic terrorist organisation Markaz Dawa al Rishad . . ." and that his continued presence in the United Kingdom "represents a danger to national security" (paragraphs 1, 2 and 3. pages 439–407).

The Special Immigration Appeals Commission (SIAC) had held on appeal that the conduct at issue "had to be directed against the United Kingdom. . ." (paragraph 33, page 450). The Court of Appeal, however, concluded that this approach was too narrow and that if Rehman's activities were directed against India's links with Kashmir, it could damage the United Kingdom's relations with India and thus could have "national security consequences" (paragraph 40, page 452).

The SIAC also concluded that the "specific allegations of serious misconduct by Mr Shafiq Ur Rehman . . . had not been proved" (paragraph 43, page 453). The Court of Appeal rejected this conclusion holding that "in any national security case the [Home Secretary] is entitled to make a decision to deport not only on the basis that the individual has in fact endangered national security but that he is a danger to national security" (paragraph 44, pages 453–454).

O'Hara v Chief Constable of the Royal Ulster Constabulary, House of Lords, December 12, 1996 (Document No 14): the case involved a question of law, namely whether in an arrest without a warrant of a person for murder in a terrorist context, the requisite "reasonable grounds" can be based on the arresting constable's briefing by a superior officer. The trial court and the Court of Appeal concluded that "reasonable grounds" could be predicated on the constable's briefing by a superior officer.

The House of Lords concluded "that the reasonable suspicion has to be in the mind of the arresting officer . . ." which in turn can be based on "the information given to the officer . . ." by a superior (page 465).

Her Majesty's Advocate v Abdelbaset Ali Mohmed Al Megrahi and Al Amin Khalifa Fhimah, the High Court of Justiciary, January 30, 2001 (Document No 15). This is the edited text of the guilty verdict against Al Megrahi of Libya in the bombing of Pan Am flight 103 over Lockerbie, Scotland on December 21, 1988. Though the court was Scottish, it heard the case sitting in the Netherlands at Camp Zeist.

Al Megrahi v HM Advocate, Appeal Court, High Court of Justiciary, March 14, 2002 (Document No 16): this is the appellate decision sustaining Al Megrahi's conviction. The Court's review of the facts has been omitted for the reason that the facts were adequately covered in the trial court decision.

The Queen (on the application of the Kurdistan Workers Party, the People's Mojahedin of Iran and Nisar Ahmed) and the Secretary of State for the Home Department. High Court, Queen's Bench Division, April 17, 2002 (Document No 17): the principal issue in this case was the procedure to be followed by an organisation challenging its proscription as a terrorist organisation pursuant to the Terrorism Act 2000. Under the Act (Document No 2 in this volume), the Home Secretary may designate an entity as a "proscribed organisation" without prior hearing. An organisation so designated may apply to the Home Secretary for "deproscription" (paragraph 7). If the application is denied, an appeal may be taken to the Proscribed Organisation Appeal Commission (POAC) (paragraph 8).

The three organisations involved in the case contended that they were entitled to immediate judicial review of their designation. The court rejected this argument holding "that challenges to an organisation's presence in the list of proscribed organisations should be brought by way of an application for deproscription and appeal to POAC" (paragraphs 82 and 92).

In paragraph 33 of the decision, the court mentions that one of the proscribed organisations relied on a United States Court of Appeals decision for the proposition that the failure to provide advance notice and a prior hearing constituted procedural unfairness. The case relied on was *National Council of Resistance of Iran v Dept of State*, 251 F3d 192 (DC Cir.2001). That case involved an organisation designated as a "foreign terrorist organisation" under the United States Antiterrorism and Effective Death Penalty of 1996 (AEDPA). Under AEDPA a designated organisation does not receive prior notice of the designation but may subsequently challenge it in the United States Court of Appeals for the District of Columbia.

In the US case, the designated organisation contended that the AEDPA procedure was unconstitutional. The Court of Appeals agreed and ordered the US Secretary of State to provide a meaningful hearing but did not lift the designation. After the hearing the same result obtained and a second appeal was taken to the Court of Appeals.

Meanwhile criminal proceedings had been bought against six individuals in a US District Court in California charging them with having supported the designated organisation. The District Court Judge concluded that the designation procedure was unconstitutional and dismissed the criminal charges. *United States of America v Roya Rahmani, et al*, Case No CRl-209 (June 21, 2002). (For a highly critical commentary on the District Court's action see: Alexander and Brenner, "Privileged Justice for Terrorists?" *The Washington Times*, July 11, 2002 page A19).

The case of *Quinlivan v Conroy*, High Court of Ireland, April 14, 2000, (Document No 18) involved efforts by Quinlivan to preclude his extradition from Ireland to England. Quinlivan had been charged with (1) conspiring "with others to murder Sir Charles Henderson Tidbury and other persons . . ."; (2) conspiring "with others to cause, by explosive substances, explosions of a nature likely to endanger life or cause serious injury to property . . ."; (3) escaping from custody in Brixton Prison "contrary to common law"; and (4) that in the process of the escape he "unlawfully and maliciously wounded . . ." a third person (pages 577–578).

Quinlivan's first argument was that the extradition should be refused because his actions were "political offences" committed on behalf of the Irish Republican Army. The "political" defence was denied because the planned use of explosives would constitute "indiscriminate attacks" and "crimes against humanity" (page 587).

As to the escape from prison and the serious wounding of a bystander, the court relied on the Extradition (European Convention on the Suppression of Terrorism) Act 1987, as precluding the "political offences" defence to extradition (pages 590–592).

Quinlivan's remaining argument that he would be prejudiced by pre-trial publicity, and that in the event he were tried and convicted he would be entitled to accelerated release under the "Good Friday Agreement," were both rejected (pages 597–601).

In re Devine, High Court of Justice in Northern Ireland, March 26, 1999 (Document No 19) involved legislation applicable only in Northern Ireland permitting certain officers of the Royal Ulster Constabulary to apply to a County Court Judge to authorise a "financial investigator" in an investigation. The financial investigator has the power to compel persons to appear before him, answer questions and produce documents (paragraph 2).

Devine also contended that the financial investigator was improperly permitted to use "the pseudonym of John Armstrong" (paragraph 5). This was done for the protection of the financial investigator in light of the violence in Northern Ireland. The court, in light of particular circumstances of the case, concluded that the use of a pseudonym by the financial investigator was proper (paragraphs 27, 28).

The case of *Martin v Conroy*, High Court of Ireland, May 1, 2001 (Document No 20) involved an unsuccessful effort by Andrew Martin to avoid extradition from Ireland to England to stand trial for terrorist acts.

Martin was charged in England with conspiracy and serious offenses involving the use of explosives occurring in 1988 (paragraph 1). Warrants issued by the Bow Street Magistrates Court in London were served on Martin in 1998 in Ireland when he was released from prison after serving a sentence on unrelated charges (paragraphs 8, 9). Consequently the time period between the alleged offences and the execution of the arrest warrants was over nine years (paragraph 10).

Martin's counsel argued that the delay of over nine years was contrary to Section 50(2)(bbb) of the Extradition Act of 1965, as amended by the Extradition (Amendment) Act of 1987, and that Martin should be released and not extradited to England (paragraph 19).

Sub-section (bbb) provides in part that a ground for release of an arrested person is "the lapse of time since the commission of the offence specified in the warrant . . . and other exceptional circumstances . . ." (paragraph 22).

The Irish Court held that the passage of time by itself was not enough in that Martin was required to make a showing of "exceptional circumstances," which he had failed to do (paragraph 61).

In *Regina v. Director of Public Prosecutions, ex parte Kebeline and Others*, House of Lords, October 28, 2001, (Document No 21): three Algerian nationals were charged with offences under section 16A of the Prevention of Terrorism (Temporary Provisions) Act 1989 (pages 634–635).

The defendants were charged with having "in their possession chemical containers, radio equipment, manuals, (documents, credit cards and sums of money in *circumstances which give rise to a reasonable suspicion that the articles were in their possession for a purpose connected with the commission, preparation or instigation of acts of terrorism*" (page 634) (emphasis added).

Section 16A of the Act provides that a person is guilty of the offence if the suspicious articles are in his possession or control, but as a defence the defendant can prove "that he did not at that time know of its presence in the premises in question, or if he did know, that he had no control over it" (page 634).

Section 19(1)(aa) of the Act of 1989 requires the consent of the Director of Public Prosecutions to initiate proceedings under the Act.

"At the close of the case for the prosecution the defence sought a ruling from the judge that section 16A of the Act reversed the legal burden of proof and was therefore in breach of Article 6(2) of the European Convention on Human Rights." Article 6(2) provides that persons criminally charged "shall be presumed innocent until proved guilty according to law" (page 635).

The trial judge ruled that section 16A was in conflict with Article 6(2). The jury was discharged, for procedural reasons, without hearing the prosecution's evidence. It was expected that a new trial date would be set.

Prior to the setting of a new trial date the three defendants applied for leave to apply for judicial review to challenge the "continuing decision" of the Director of Prosecutions to permit the case to go forward. The trial judge granted leave to apply for judicial review (page 636).

The appeal was heard by three judges in the Divisional Court, which, in an opinion by the Lord Chief Justice, held that "section 16A of *the Act* of 1989 undermines in a blatant and obvious way the presumption of innocence".

The principal issues on appeal to the House of Lords concerned the effect to be given to the Human Rights Act of 1998, which had not fully come into force, the propriety of reviewing a decision of the Director of Public Prosecutions in separate proceedings, and whether the legal burden of proof had been reversed, and if so, whether this reversal was compatible with Article 6(2) of the European Convention on Human Rights (pages 637–687).

Lord Steyn concluded that absent dishonesty or *mala fides* (which was not at issue) "the decision of the [D]irector of Public Prosecutions to consent to the prosecution . . . is not amenable to judicial review" (page 644).

Lord Cooke observed that "[on] its face section 16A of the Act of 1989 enables a person to be found guilty of a very serious offence merely on reasonable grounds of suspicion" (pages 645–646). In his view, the issue of incompatibility should be initially decided by the trial judge (page 647).

Lord Hope differed in concluding that section 16A requires "*prima facie* proof, not mere suspicion" (page 661). Whether the burden shifted to the defendant is unreasonable can only be determined when the facts are known at trial (page 662). However, he concurred with Lord Steyn that the consent of the Director of Public Prosecutions "is not amenable to judicial review" (page 649).

Lord Hobhouse concluded that any incompatibility between the Human Rights Act s 16A would "not deprive s 16A of its force and validity nor does it affect the criminal trial or any convictions resulting from the application of s 16A" (page 671). This was because section 4(6) presumes the continuing validity of any provision of an Act of Parliament in respect of which a declaration of incompatibility is made (pages 670–671).

Lord Hobhouse also stated that "[c]riminal statutes which in certain circumstances partially reverse the burden of proof are not uncommon . . . [and]

are not necessarily incompatible with the [European] Convention" on Human Rights (page 673). In his view, the issues in the case should be decided initially by the trial court.

In re Hany El Sayed El Sabaei Youseff, High Court, Queen's Bench Division, March 12, 1999 (Document No 22), involved an application for habeas corpus by an Egyptian lawyer "who represented Islamic fundamentalists in Egypt" (paragraph 1). After being tortured by Egyptian security forces, he arrived in the United Kingdom and claimed asylum.

Subsequently, he was detained under Schedule 2 to the Immigration Act of 1971 pending a decision by the Home Secretary as to whether he could be removed to Egypt. The court noted that the applicant could not be detained under the 1971 Act if he was considered to be linked to international terrorism (paragraph 22).

The court in denying the writ of habeas corpus held "that it would not be acceptable for the applicant to be kept in detention simply on the off chance that he might be able to be removed to Egypt. The Home Secretary has to be satisfied that there is a realistic prospect, which he wishes to pursue with the Egyptian authorities. Once that prospect ceases in his judgment to be realistic then the applicant should be released" (paragraph 39).

In the Matter of Ramda, in the Matter of Boutarfa, High Court, Queen's Bench Division, June 25, 1997 (Document No 23): Ramda and Boutarfa, in an effort to preclude their extradition to France, where they faced various terrorism charges, sought writs of habeas corpus (paragraph 1).

The applicants claimed that if returned to France they might be "prejudiced at . . . trial by reason of [their] race, religion, nationality or political opinions" (paragraphs 2, 3). In support of this argument they sought to "demonstrate xenophobic attitudes in France and, in particular, hostility towards immigrants from Algeria" (paragraph 6).

The applicants also claimed prejudicial pre-trial publicity and that under the French legal system the trial would be before judges with no power to stay the prosecution by virtue of prejudicial pre-trial publicity (paragraphs 9, 14). The French government denied these and other similar assertions (paragraphs 15, 16).

The court was unable to conclude, in light of all the circumstances, that "it would be unjust or oppressive to return the applicants . . . to France" (paragraph 27).

The case of *R v Samar Alami Jawad Botmeh*, Court of Appeal (Criminal Division), May 10, 1999 (Document No 24): involved the appeal by two defendants convicted of conspiracy in the London bombing of the Israeli Embassy and Balfour House in 1994 (page 693).

The two principal grounds of appeal were that the trial court refused to postpone a television program concerning a terrorist airplane hijacking incident occurring in 1977. The court concluded that prejudice was avoided when the court instructed the jurors to "try this case on what you hear and see and are told in this court, not what you see on television" (page 701).

The other ground of appeal was that a juror received a brief "approach from an Israeli journalist during the course of the trial . . ." (page 701). The juror reported the incident promptly. The journalist denied making any approach (page 702).

The court held that the trial judge was entitled to conclude that there was no possibility of bias and was entitled in his discretion to refuse to discharge [the] juror. (page 703).

Chahal v The United Kingdom and the European Court of Human Rights, November 15, 1996 (Document No 25): the case was referred to the European Court of Human Rights by the Government of the United Kingdom and by the European Commission of Human Rights to secure a ruling as to whether or not Karamjit Sing Chahal's detention in the UK pending deportation proceedings was consistent with the European Convention on Human Rights ("the Convention") (Document No 25, paragraph 1).

Chahal was a Sikh separatist believed by the Home Office to be a supporter of terrorism. The Home Office sought his deportation from Britain. Chahal applied for political asylum and claimed that he would be "subject to torture and persecution if returned to India . . ." Chahal had been held in Bedford Prison pending his deportation from August 16, 1990 to March 3, 1994 when the domestic court proceedings came to an end (paragraphs 109, 114). Thereafter, the UK government refrained from deporting him and he remained in custody until the European Court of Human Rights issued its ruling on November 15, 1996. (The total period of detention was thus almost six years.)

Chahal contended that his detention was improper because the lawfulness of his detention was not decided speedily by a court as required by Article 5, Section 4 of the Convention. He argued that the Home Secretary's reliance on national security grounds precluded the UK courts from deciding if his detention was lawful (paragraph 67).

Chahal also argued that he did not have an "effective remedy before a national authority" as required by Article 13 of the Convention. The European Court of Human Rights agreed with both arguments (at paragraphs 132, 133, 155). The ruling led to Chahal's release (Document No 26, paragraph 5).

The significance of the European Court's decision was set forth as follows in the United Kingdom's Human Rights Act of 1998 (Designated Derogation) Order 2001 (November 11, 2001). "It is well established that

Article 5(1)(f) [of the Convention] permits the detention of a person with a view to deportation only in circumstances where 'action is being taken with a view to deportation' *Chahal v United Kingdom* (1996)." The penultimate document in this volume, No 28, is a Summary of a decision by the SIAC relating to the Home Office's efforts to detain terrorists and to comply with the European Human Rights Court's decision in *Chahal v. United Kingdom* (Document No 25). The SIAC decision was set aside on October 25, 2002 (Document No 29).

R v Secretary of State for Home Department ex parte Chahal, High Court, Queen's Bench Division, November 6, 1998 (Document No 26): as a result of the decision in *Chahal v The United Kingdom*, Chahal was released from custody. Chahal unsuccessfully applied *ex parte* to the Home Office to be financially compensated for his long detention (paragraphs 12 and 14). Though Mr. Justice Tucker of the High Court of Justice referred to Chahal as "the longest serving civil detainee in this century . . ." and he dismissed Chahal's application for compensation concluding that "it has not been established that the [Home Secretary's] discretionary refusal to award compensation was irrational, or in contravention of Article 5(5) . . ." (paragraphs 4, 45, 46).

An additional aspect of the decision is worth mention. The court observed that "at no time during . . . [Chahal's] detention was there in existence a UK Court which was able to investigate and evaluate the allegation of a threat to national security that had caused the applicant to be detained during his challenge to the decision to deport him". The court continued, "[t]his defect has now been remedied by the introduction, in September 1998, of the Special Immigration Appeals Commission, presided over by a High Court Judge".

R v Hugh Thomas Jack, Court of Appeal (Criminal Division), April 7, 1998 (Document No 27): in 1995, Hugh Thomas Jack was convicted of conspiracy to cause explosions and was sentenced to 20 years' imprisonment (paragraph 1). The appellate court concluded that the circumstantial evidence against him "was very strong" and that even if they had found any merit in the three grounds for appeal, leave to appeal would not have been granted (paragraph 8).

The principal basis for appeal was the use of screens to conceal the identity of witnesses who were members of the security and intelligence services (paragraph 7, ground 1). The court approved the use of five factors to govern the exercise of the trial judge's discretion with respect to the use of screens. The court concluded that in the context of the case the trial judge properly balanced the possible prejudice to Jack against the importance of the evidence and the "risk to the witnesses . . .".

Jack's counsel claimed next that it was wrong for the prosecution not to disclose the location of a surveillance camera (paragraph 5). Doing so would have revealed the identity of the persons who permitted its location on their property, contrary to their wishes (paragraph 6). The court concluded that this ground had "no substance".

Counsel claimed finally that it was wrong to preclude cross-examination "as to the capacity of tracking devices used to monitor . . . [Jack's] movements . . ." (paragraph 5). The trial judge had considered the extent to which information could be disclosed to the jury, and that the jurors should not speculate about what they had not been told. The appellate court concluded that this was the correct approach (paragraph 7, ground 3).

Special Immigration Appeal Commission, *Summary of Conclusions*, July 30, 2002 (Document No 28): as we have seen from *ex parte Chahal* (Document No 25), and *Chahal United Kingdom* (Document No 26) prior to the Anti-Terrorism, Crime and Security Act 2001, aliens suspected of being terrorists could be detained without trial pending proceedings to remove them from the country. However, if removal became or was unrealistic within a reasonable period of time, the alien would have to be tried or released.

This presented a serious problem with respect to suspected terrorists who could not be removed to their country of origin because in the event of removal they would be subject to torture and other civil rights abuses.

To deal with this situation Part 4, sections 21 to 23 of the Anti-Terrorism, Crime and Security Act 2001 (Document No 4) provided for the detention without trial of persons the Home Secretary "has certified as threats to national security and who are suspected of being international terrorists where their removal is not possible at the present time" (Explanatory Notes to the Anti-Terrorism, Crime and Security Act 2001, paragraph 12).

Shortly after the terrorist attacks of September 11, 2001, the Home Secretary concluded that there was a "public emergency threatening the life of the nation", and filed a derogation to Article 5(1) of the European Convention on Human Rights ("the Convention") to permit suspected international terrorists deemed to constitute a risk to national security to be detained indefinitely without trial where removal or deportation is not presently possible because doing so might result in their torture, a violation of Article 3 of the Convention (Human Rights Act 1998 (Designated Derogation) Order 2001, No 3644 (November 11, 2001)).

It should be noted that these indefinite detention provisions are not applicable to UK citizens inasmuch as they cannot be removed or deported. Nor do they apply to citizens of the European Union since all Member States are parties to the Convention so that removal or deportation to any EU state would be presumed not to violate their human rights.

However, a small number of persons were categorised as suspected terrorists designated as risks to national security, who could not be removed for human rights reasons. Nine persons who had not been charged were being detained indefinitely (*The Guardian*, July 30, 2002). According to the *Summary of Conclusions* issued by the SIAC (Document No 28) it would appear that the nine persons were suspected of being "international terrorists".

On July 30, 2002, the SIAC handed down a classified "substantial document" concerning the status of the nine detainees. In addition, it published a non-classified one-page summary of its conclusions.

The most important aspects of the Commission's opinion are that the Home Secretary's derogation from Article 5 was proper because there was a continuing public emergency threatening the life of the nation, justifying the detention without trial of suspected international terrorists with ties to al Qaida.

The Commission observed that the Home Secretary had not, however, derogated from Article 14 of the Convention, which precludes discrimination against aliens in the protection of human rights. Since the Act of 2001 permits the indefinite detention only of "non-British" persons, the Commission concluded that the indefinite detention of only alien suspected terrorists was not compatible with the European Convention on Human Rights. The opinion immediately attracted considerable attention.

A and Others v Secretary of State for the Home Department, Court of Appeal, October 25, 2002 (Document No 29): this decision is the appeal from the July 30, 2002 action of the SIAC. The Court of Appeal reversed the SIAC's ruling.

The Chief Justice of the court, Lord Woolf, held that "[d]ecisions as to what was required in the interest of national security were self-evidently within the category of decisions in relation to which the court was required to show considerable deference to the Home Secretary because he was better qualified to make an assessment as to what action was called for" (page 769).

The court went on to observe that:

"[i]t was only the need to protect them [the aliens] from torture that meant for the time being they could not be removed. In those circumstances it would be surprising indeed if Art 14, or any international requirement not to discriminate, prevented the Home Secretary taking the restricted action, which he thought was necessary. . . . By limiting the number of those who were subject to the special measures, the Home Secretary was ensuring that his actions were proportionate to what was necessary" (page 770).

Justices Brook and Chadwick gave concurring judgments.

*   *   *   *   *

All twenty-nine documents that comprise this volume were downloaded from United Kingdom, Irish and European Union internet sources available to the public. The United Kingdom sources are Crown copyright, the existence of which we are pleased to acknowledge. We also acknowledge the copyright vested in the Irish sources and the European Union.

Summary

In sum, since September 11, 2001, the United Kingdom intensified its counter-terrorism efforts on all levels: legislative (the Anti-Terrorism Crime and Security Act 2001), law enforcement (the Metropolitan Police Activities), civil contingency measures (dealing with the consequences of a chemical, biological, or radiological terrorist attack), moves toward central domestic coordination, and diplomatic and military support of the United States and collation allies in the global war against terrorism. Whatever steps have been undertaken by the United Kingdom to strengthen its defence and security against the growing challenge of political violence at home and abroad, it is important to recognise that Britain has had counter-terrorism experience over some four decades.

As we have seen already, much of the pre-September 11 British legislation was designed to deal with terrorism and was focused on the situation in Northern Ireland. It prescribed penalties for a wide range of offences. Terrorism and terrorist were both defined. The possession of firearms or explosives was barred under certain circumstances. The provision of financial or material support for acts of terrorism in connection with Northern Irish affairs was designated as an offence, as was the failure to disclose information to the police which might be of assistance in preventing a terrorist attack. The IRA was proscribed, while other organisations could be added to the list. As we have seen, some of the methods adopted by the British in attempting to combat terrorism in Northern Ireland have led to criticism on civil liberties grounds. In fact, a public inquiry is currently underway into the alleged human rights abuses committed on so-called "Bloody Sunday". One witness has claimed that the soldiers shot indiscriminately at unarmed civil rights protestors.

Clearly, as events in Northern Ireland amply demonstrated, political measures by the respective communities to further the peace process are essential. In general, the British government struck a balance between maintaining democratic and legal rights and avoiding recourse to excessive military responses.

As the events of September 11 clearly demonstrate, the United Kingdom has relocated its attention to the challenge of international terrorism posed by groups such as al Qaida. The legal responses are essential in the long war against terrorism. This volume reflects some of the measures undertaken and issues faced, to deal with the threat of terrorism to the United Kingdom, and to the entire international community.

Acknowledgments

We are particularly indebted to Michael Carpenter, Esq, Counsel (European Legislation), House of Commons, for his editorial guidance and advice, as well as for his agreement to write the Foreword to this volume. We also received substantial assistance from Professor Frank Gregory, of the Department of Politics, University of Southampton, United Kingdom.

We also wish to thank the Inter-University Center for Legal Studies (International Law Institute), and the Inter-University Center for Terrorism Studies (Potomac Institute for Policy Studies). None of the aforementioned individuals or institutes bears any responsibility for our selection of materials to be included in this volume or our commentary relating to them.

We are fortunate to have sustained editorial supervision of the production of this volume by Research Associate Eric Whittington of the International Center for Terrorism Studies, Potomac Institute for Policy Studies. In addition, Research Assistant Kerrie Martin and a number of Research Interns contributed exemplary research and analysis. They include: Michelle Mendez, Melissa Brewster, Jesse Ferguson, Blaire Bingham, John M Turner, Amanda Bronsky, Jennifer Silvi, Jessica Wright, Lauren Conn, Wendy Lee, Roger Pogozelski, Tyler Richardson, Sean Corcoran, Leonard Tengco, and Joy Kolin.

Yonah Alexander
and
Edgar H Brenner

Washington, DC
October 25, 2002

EXECUTIVE ACTS

DOCUMENT NO 1

Prime Minister's Statement To Parliament "Responsibility For The Terrorist Atrocities In The United States, 11 September 2001"

October 4, 2001

Check Against Delivery

I am grateful to you for recalling Parliament on a second occasion so that the House can consider developments since it last met.

Then the scale of 11 September tragedy was still unclear. Even today we do not yet know the precise numbers of those feared dead. But a bleak picture has emerged: there are up to 7,000 feared dead, including many British victims and others from 70 different countries. Many were Muslims. It cannot be said too often: this atrocity appalled decent Muslims everywhere and is wholly contrary to the true teaching of Islam. And we condemn unreservedly racist attacks on British Muslims here, most recently at an Edinburgh Mosque.

These acts are without any justification whatever and the full force of the law will be used against those who do them.

I pay tribute again to all those in America who have been involved in dealing with the human consequences of the attacks. The rescue services and medical workers who worked tirelessly and with devotion in the most harrowing conditions imaginable. I pay tribute to our own consular staff in New York and London and the family counsellors and Metropolitan Police officers who have supported relatives of the victims. And, above all, to the relatives themselves. Those I met in New York, still uncertain finally of the fate of their loved ones, bore their grief with immense dignity which deserves the admiration of us all.

Since 11 September intensive efforts have taken place here and elsewhere to investigate these attacks and determine who is responsible. Our findings have been shared and co-ordinated with those of our allies, and are clear.

They are:

- First, it was Usama Bin Laden and Al Qaida, the terrorist network which he heads, that planned and carried out the atrocities on 11 September;
- Second, that Usama Bin Laden and Al Qaida were able to commit these atrocities because of their close alliance with the Taleban regime in Afghanistan which allows them to operate with impunity in pursuing their terrorist activity.

I will later today put in the Library of the House of Commons a document detailing the basis for our conclusions. The document covers the history of Usama Bin Laden, his relations with the Taleban, what we know of the acts of terror he has committed; and some of what we know in respect of 11 September. I enter a major caveat, much of the evidence we have is intelligence and highly sensitive. It is not possible without compromising people or security to release precise details and fresh information is daily coming in. But I hope the House will find it useful at least as an interim assessment. The Leader of the Opposition and the Leader of the Liberal Democrats have seen the full basis for the document on Privy Council terms. For myself and all other Government Ministers who have studied the full information, we have absolutely no doubt that Bin Laden and his network are responsible for the attacks on 11 September. That was also the unanimous view of the NATO members who were taken through the full facts on 2 October. Much more of the evidence in respect of earlier atrocities can be released in greater detail since it is already subject to court proceedings; and this in itself is powerful.

Indeed, there is nothing hidden about Bin Laden's agenda. He openly espouses the language of terror; has described terrorising Americans as *"a religious and logical obligation"*; and in February 1998 signed a fatwa stating that *"the killing of Americans and their civilian and military allies is a religious duty."*

As our document shows, he has been responsible for a number of terrorist outrages over the past decade.

- The attack in 1993 on US military personnel serving in Somalia—18 US military personnel killed.
- In 1998, the bombings of the US Embassies in Kenya and Tanzania. 224 people killed and over 4500 injured.
- Attempted bombings in Jordan and Los Angeles at the turn of the millennium, thankfully thwarted.
- The attack on the USS Cole nearly a year ago which left 17 crew members killed and 40 injured.

The attacks on 11 September bear all the hallmarks of a Bin Laden operation: meticulous long-term planning; a desire to inflict mass casualties; a total disregard for civilian lives (including Muslims); multiple simultaneous attacks; and the use of suicide attackers. I can now confirm that of the 19 hijackers identified from the passenger lists of the four planes hijacked on 11 September, at least three of these hijackers have already been positively identified as known associates of Bin Laden, with a track record in his camps and organisation. The others are being investigated still.

Of the three, one has also been identified as playing key roles in both the East African Embassy attacks and the USS Cole attack.

Since the attacks, we have obtained the following intelligence: shortly before 11 September, Bin Laden told associates that he had a major operation against America under preparation; a range of people were warned to return to Afghanistan because of action on or around 11 September; and most importantly, one of Bin Laden's closest lieutenants has said clearly that he helped with the planning of the 11 September attacks and has admitted the involvement of the Al Qaida organisation. There is other intelligence we cannot disclose of an even more direct nature indicating guilt. The closeness of Bin Laden's relationship with the Taleban is also plain. He provides the Taleban with troops, arms and money to fight the Northern Alliance. He is closely involved with the Taleban's military training, planning and operations. He has representatives in the Taleban's military command structure. Forces under the control of Usama Bin Laden have fought alongside the Taleban in the civil war in Afghanistan. The Taleban regime, for its part, has provided Bin Laden with a safe haven within which to operate, and allowed him to establish terrorist training camps. They jointly exploit the Afghan drugs trade. In return for active Al Qaida support the Taleban allow Al Qaida to operate freely, including planning, training and preparing for terrorist activity. In addition they provide security for the stockpiles of drugs.

Mr Speaker, in the face of this evidence, our immediate objectives are clear. We must bring Bin Laden and other Al Qaida leaders to justice and eliminate the terrorist threat they pose. And we must ensure that Afghanistan ceases to harbour and sustain international terrorism. If the Taleban regime will not comply with that objective, we must bring about change in that regime to ensure that Afghanistan's links to international terrorism are broken.

Since the House last met, we have been working ceaselessly on the diplomatic, humanitarian and military fronts.

I can confirm that we have had initial discussions with the US about a range of military capabilities with which Britain can help and have already responded positively to this. We will consider carefully any further requests and keep the House informed as appropriate, about such requests. For obvious reasons I cannot disclose the exact nature of our discussions. But I am fully satisfied they are consistent with our shared objectives. I believe the humanitarian coalition to help the people of Afghanistan to be as vital as any military action itself.

Afghanistan was in the grip of a humanitarian crisis even before the events of 11 September. Four years of drought, on top of over two decades of conflict, have forced millions of people to leave the country; and have left millions more dependent on international humanitarian aid.

Last week the United Nations launched an appeal for $584 million to meet the needs of vulnerable people in and around Afghanistan. The appeal covers the next six months. The international community has already pledged sufficient funds to meet the most immediate needs. The British Government has contributed £25 million, nearly all of which has already been allocated to UN and other agencies. We have also made available a further £11 million for support for the poorest communities in Pakistan, especially those most directly affected by the influx of refugees.

I know President Bush will shortly announce details of a major US programme of aid. I have been in detailed consultation with the UN Secretary General Kofi Annan, the UN High Commissioner for Refugees Ruud Lubbers and other leaders. Kofi Annan has now appointed Lakhdar Brahimi to be his high level coordinator for the humanitarian effort in and around Afghanistan. We will give Mr Brahimi all the support we can, to help ensure that the UN and the whole of the international community comes together to meet the humanitarian challenge.

Action is already in hand to cope with additional outflows of refugees. UNHCR are working with the governments of the region to identify sites for additional refugee camps. The first UNHCR flight of relief supplies, including tents donated by the British Government, arrived in Iran yesterday. A second flight will depart at the end of this week, carrying more tents, plastic sheeting and tarpaulins, so that we can provide essential shelter for refugees.

We are also stepping up the effort to get food into Afghanistan, before the winter snows begin. A UNICEF convoy carrying blankets and other supplies left Peshawar for Kabul on Tuesday. A World Food Programme convoy carrying over 200 tonnes of wheat arrived in Kabul on Monday. Further WFP convoys have left for Afghanistan from Pakistan and Turkmenistan.

We will do what we can to minimise the suffering of the Afghan people as a result of the conflict; and we commit ourselves to work with them afterwards inside and outside Afghanistan to ensure a better, more peaceful future free from the repression and dictatorship that is their present existence.

On the diplomatic front, over the past three weeks the Foreign Secretary and I have been in intensive contact with foreign leaders from every part of the world. In addition, the Foreign Secretary has visited the Middle East and Iran. I have visited Berlin, Paris and Washington for consultations with

Chancellor Schroeder, President Chirac and President Bush respectively. Later today I will travel to Moscow to meet with President Putin.

What we have encountered is an unprecedented level of solidarity and commitment to work together against terrorism. This is a commitment that spans all continents, cultures and religions, reinforced by attacks like the one on the Jammu and Kashmir Assembly in Srinagar which killed over 30 inno cent people.

We have already made good progress in taking forward an international agenda. Last week the United Nations Security Council unanimously adopted resolution 1373. This makes it mandatory for all states to prevent and suppress terrorist financing and requires the denial of safe haven to who finance, plan, support or commit terrorist acts. The European Union too has taken firm action. Transport, interior, finance and foreign ministers have all met to concert an ambitious and effective European response: enhancing police co-operation; speeding up extradition; putting an end to the funding of terrorism; and strengthening air security.

We are also looking closely at our national legislation. In the next few weeks, the Home Secretary intends to introduce a package of legislation to supplement existing legal powers in a number of areas. It will be a carefully-appraised set of measures: tough, but balanced and proportionate to the risk we face. It will cover the funding of terrorism. It will increase our ability to exclude and remove those whom we suspect of terrorism and who are seeking to abuse our asylum procedures. It will widen the law on incitement to include religious hatred. We will bring forward a bill to modernise our extradition law. It will not be a knee-jerk reaction. But I emphasise we do need to strengthen our laws so that, even if necessary only in a small number of cases, we have the means to protect our citizens' liberty and our national security.

We have also ensured, insofar as is possible, that every reasonable measure of internal security is being undertaken. We have in place a series of contingency plans, governing all forms of terrorism. These plans are continually reviewed and tested regularly and at all levels. In addition, we continue to monitor carefully developments in the British and International economy. Certain sectors here and around the world have inevitably been seriously affected, though I repeat the fundamentals of all the major economies, including our own, remain strong. The reduction of risk from terrorist mass action is important also to economic confidence as 11 September shows. So there is every incentive in this respect also, to close down the Bin Laden network.

Mr Speaker, three weeks on from the most appalling act of terrorism the world has ever witnessed.

The coalition is strong. Military plans are robust. The humanitarian plans are falling into place.

And the evidence against Bin Laden and his network is overwhelming. The Afghan people are not our enemy. For they have our sympathy and they will have our support.

Our enemy is Usama Bin Laden and the Al Qaida network who were responsible for the events of 11 September. The Taleban regime must yield them up or become our enemy also. We will not act for revenge. We will act because for the protection of our people and our way of life, including confidence in our economy, we need to eliminate the threat Bin Laden and his terrorism represent. We act for justice. We act with world opinion behind us. And we have an absolute determination to see justice done, and this evil of mass terrorism confronted and defeated.

LEGISLATIVE ACTS

DOCUMENT NO 2

Terrorism Act 2000

Part I
Introductory

Terrorism: Interpretation.

1. (1) In this Act "terrorism" means the use or threat of action where—
   (a) the action falls within subsection (2),
   (b) the use or threat is designed to influence the government or to intimidate the public or a section of the public, and
   (c) the use or threat is made for the purpose of advancing a political, religious or ideological cause.

   (2) Action falls within this subsection if it—
   (a) involves serious violence against a person,
   (b) involves serious damage to property,
   (c) endangers a person's life, other than that of the person committing the action,
   (d) creates a serious risk to the health or safety of the public or a section of the public, or
   (e) is designed seriously to interfere with or seriously to disrupt an electronic system.

   (3) The use or threat of action falling within subsection (2) which involves the use of firearms or explosives is terrorism whether or not subsection (1)(b) is satisfied.

   (4) In this section—
   (a) "action" includes action outside the United Kingdom,
   (b) a reference to any person or to property is a reference to any person, or to property, wherever situated,
   (c) a reference to the public includes a reference to the public of a country other than the United Kingdom, and
   (d) "the government" means the government of the United Kingdom, of a Part of the United Kingdom or of a country other than the United Kingdom.

   (5) In this Act a reference to action taken for the purposes of terrorism includes a reference to action taken for the benefit of a proscribed organisation.

Temporary Legislation.

2. (1) The following shall cease to have effect—
    (a) the Prevention of Terrorism (Temporary Provisions) Act 1989, and
    (b) the Northern Ireland (Emergency Provisions) Act 1996.
   (2) Schedule 1 (which preserves certain provisions of the 1996 Act, in some cases with amendment, for a transitional period) shall have effect.

Part II
Proscribed Organisations

Procedure Proscription.

3. (1) For the purposes of this Act an organisation is proscribed if—
    (a) it is listed in Schedule 2, or
    (b) it operates under the same name as an organisation listed in that Schedule.
   (2) Subsection (1)(b) shall not apply in relation to an organisation listed in Schedule 2 if its entry is the subject of a note in that Schedule.
   (3) The Secretary of State may by order—
    (a) add an organisation to Schedule 2;
    (b) remove an organisation from that Schedule;
    (c) amend that Schedule in some other way.
   (4) The Secretary of State may exercise his power under subsection (3)(a) in respect of an organisation only if he believes that it is concerned in terrorism.
   (5) For the purposes of subsection (4) an organisation is concerned in terrorism if it—
    (a) commits or participates in acts of terrorism,
    (b) prepares for terrorism,
    (c) promotes or encourages terrorism, or
    (d) is otherwise concerned in terrorism.

Deproscription: Application.

4. (1) An application may be made to the Secretary of State for the exercise of his power under section 3(3)(b) to remove an organisation from Schedule 2.
   (2) An application may be made by—
    (a) the organisation, or
    (b) any person affected by the organisation's proscription.

(3)   The Secretary of State shall make regulations prescribing the procedure for applications under this section.

(4)   The regulations shall, in particular—

(a)   require the Secretary of State to determine an application within a specified period of time, and

(b)   require an application to state the grounds on which it is made.

Deproscription: Appeal.

5. (1)   There shall be a commission, to be known as the Proscribed Organisations Appeal Commission.

(2)   Where an application under section 4 has been refused, the applicant may appeal to the Commission.

(3)   The Commission shall allow an appeal against a refusal to deproscribe an organisation if it considers that the decision to refuse was flawed when considered in the light of the principles applicable on an application for judicial review.

(4)   Where the Commission allows an appeal under this section by or in respect of an organisation, it may make an order under this subsection.

(5)   Where an order is made under subsection (4) the Secretary of State shall as soon as is reasonably practicable—

(a)   lay before Parliament, in accordance with section 123(4), the draft of an order under section 3(3)(b) removing the organisation from the list in Schedule 2, or

(b)   make an order removing the organisation from the list in Schedule 2 in pursuance of section 123(5).

(6)   Schedule 3 (constitution of the Commission and procedure) shall have effect.

Further Appeal.

6. (1)   A party to an appeal under section 5 which the Proscribed Organisations Appeal Commission has determined may bring a further appeal on a question of law to—

(a)   the Court of Appeal, if the first appeal was heard in England and Wales,

(b)   the Court of Session, if the first appeal was heard in Scotland, or

(c)   the Court of Appeal in Northern Ireland, if the first appeal was heard in Northern Ireland.

(2)   An appeal under subsection (1) may be brought only with the permission—

(a)   of the Commission, or

(b) where the Commission refuses permission, of the court to which the appeal would be brought.

(3) An order under section 5(4) shall not require the Secretary of State to take any action until the final determination or disposal of an appeal under this section (including any appeal to the House of Lords).

Appeal: Effect on Conviction, &c.

7. (1) This section applies where—

(a) an appeal under section 5 has been allowed in respect of an organisation,

(b) an order has been made under section 3(3)(b) in respect of the organisation in accordance with an order of the Commission under section 5(4) (and, if the order was made in reliance on section 123(5), a resolution has been passed by each House of Parliament under section 123(5)(b)),

(c) a person has been convicted of an offence in respect of the organisation under any of sections 11 to 13, 15 to 19 and 56, and

(d) the activity to which the charge referred took place on or after the date of the refusal to deproscribe against which the appeal under section 5 was brought.

(2) If the person mentioned in subsection (1)(c) was convicted on indictment—

(a) he may appeal against the conviction to the Court of Appeal, and

(b) the Court of Appeal shall allow the appeal.

(3) A person may appeal against a conviction by virtue of subsection (2) whether or not he has already appealed against the conviction.

(4) An appeal by virtue of subsection (2)—

(a) must be brought within the period of 28 days beginning with the date on which the order mentioned in subsection (1)(b) comes into force, and

(b) shall be treated as an appeal under section 1 of the Criminal Appeal Act 1968 (but does not require leave).

(5) If the person mentioned in subsection (1)(c) was convicted by a magistrates' court—

(a) he may appeal against the conviction to the Crown Court, and

(b) the Crown Court shall allow the appeal.

(6) A person may appeal against a conviction by virtue of subsection (5)—

(a) whether or not he pleaded guilty,

      (b)   whether or not he has already appealed against the conviction, and

      (c)   whether or not he has made an application in respect of the conviction under section 111 of the Magistrates' Courts Act 1980 (case stated).

  (7)   An appeal by virtue of subsection (5)—

      (a)   must be brought within the period of 21 days beginning with the date on which the order mentioned in subsection (1)(b) comes into force, and

      (b)   shall be treated as an appeal under section 108(1)(b) of the Magistrates' Courts Act 1980.

  (8)   In section 133(5) of the Criminal Justice Act 1988 (compensation for miscarriage of justice) after paragraph (b) there shall be inserted—
" or

      (c)   on an appeal under section 7 of the Terrorism Act 2000."

Section 7: Scotland and Northern Ireland.

8. (1)   In the application of section 7 to Scotland—

      (a)   for every reference to the Court of Appeal or the Crown Court substitute a reference to the High Court of Justiciary,

      (b)   in subsection (2)(b), at the end insert "and quash the conviction,"

      (c)   in subsection (4)—

          (i)   in paragraph (a), for "28 days" substitute "two weeks," and

          (ii)   in paragraph (b), for "section 1 of the Criminal Appeal Act 1968" substitute "section 106 of the Criminal Procedure (Scotland) Act 1995,"

      (d)   in subsection (5)—

          (i)   for "by a magistrates' court" substitute "in summary proceedings," and

          (ii)   in paragraph (b), at the end insert "and quash the conviction,"

      (e)   in subsection (6), paragraph (c) is omitted, and

      (f)   in subsection (7)—

          (i)   in paragraph (a) for "21 days" substitute "two weeks," and

          (ii)   for paragraph (b) substitute—

"(b) shall be by note of appeal, which shall state the ground of appeal,

      (c)   shall not require leave under any provision of Part X of the Criminal Procedure (Scotland) Act 1995, and

      (d)   shall be in accordance with such procedure as the High Court of Justiciary may, by Act of Adjournal, determine.".

(2) In the application of section 7 to Northern Ireland—

    (a) the reference in subsection (4) to section 1 of the Criminal Appeal Act 1968 shall be taken as a reference to section 1 of the Criminal Appeal (Northern Ireland) Act 1980,

    (b) references in subsection (5) to the Crown Court shall be taken as references to the county court,

    (c) the reference in subsection (6) to section 111 of the Magistrates' Courts Act 1980 shall be taken as a reference to Article 146 of the Magistrates' Courts (Northern Ireland) Order 1981, and

    (d) the reference in subsection (7) to section 108(1)(b) of the Magistrates' Courts Act 1980 shall be taken as a reference to Article 140(1)(b) of the Magistrates' Courts (Northern Ireland) Order 1981.

Human Rights Act 1998

9. (1) This section applies where rules (within the meaning of section 7 of the Human Rights Act 1998 (jurisdiction)) provide for proceedings under section 7(1) of that Act to be brought before the Proscribed Organisations Appeal Commission.

    (2) The following provisions of this Act shall apply in relation to proceedings under section 7(1) of that Act as they apply to appeals under section 5 of this Act—

        (a) section 5(4) and (5),

        (b) section 6,

        (c) section 7, and

        (d) paragraphs 4 to 8 of Schedule 3.

    (3) The Commission shall decide proceedings in accordance with the principles applicable on an application for judicial review.

    (4) In the application of the provisions mentioned in subsection (2)—

        (a) a reference to the Commission allowing an appeal shall be taken as a reference to the Commission determining that an action of the Secretary of State is incompatible with a Convention right, and

        (b) a reference to the refusal to deproscribe against which an appeal was brought shall be taken as a reference to the action of the Secretary of State which is found to be incompatible with a Convention right.

Immunity

10. (1) The following shall not be admissible as evidence in proceedings for an offence under any of sections 11 to 13, 15 to 19 and 56–

> (a) evidence of anything done in relation to an application to the Secretary of State under section 4,
>
> (b) evidence of anything done in relation to proceedings before the Proscribed Organisations Appeal Commission under section 5 above or section 7(1) of the Human Rights Act 1998,
>
> (c) evidence of anything done in relation to proceedings under section 6 (including that section as applied by section 9(2)), and
>
> (d) any document submitted for the purposes of proceedings mentioned in any of paragraphs (a) to (c).

(2) But subsection (1) does not prevent evidence from being adduced on behalf of the accused.

Offences Membership

11. (1) A person commits an offence if he belongs or professes to belong to a proscribed organisation.

(2) It is a defence for a person charged with an offence under subsection (1) to prove—

> (a) that the organisation was not proscribed on the last (or only) occasion on which he became a member or began to profess to be a member, and
>
> (b) that he has not taken part in the activities of the organisation at any time while it was proscribed.

(3) A person guilty of an offence under this section shall be liable—

> (a) on conviction on indictment, to imprisonment for a term not exceeding ten years, to a fine or to both, or
>
> (b) on summary conviction, to imprisonment for a term not exceeding six months, to a fine not exceeding the statutory maximum or to both.

(4) In subsection (2) "proscribed" means proscribed for the purposes of any of the following—

> (a) this Act;
>
> (b) the Northern Ireland (Emergency Provisions) Act 1996;
>
> (c) the Northern Ireland (Emergency Provisions) Act 1991;
>
> (d) the Prevention of Terrorism (Temporary Provisions) Act 1989;
>
> (e) the Prevention of Terrorism (Temporary Provisions) Act 1984;
>
> (f) the Northern Ireland (Emergency Provisions) Act 1978;
>
> (g) the Prevention of Terrorism (Temporary Provisions) Act 1976;
>
> (h) the Prevention of Terrorism (Temporary Provisions) Act 1974;
>
> (i) the Northern Ireland (Emergency Provisions) Act 1973.

Support

12. (1) A person commits an offence if—
    (a) he invites support for a proscribed organisation, and
    (b) the support is not, or is not restricted to, the provision of money or other property (within the meaning of section 15).

    (2) A person commits an offence if he arranges, manages or assists in arranging or managing a meeting which he knows is—
    (a) to support a proscribed organisation,
    (b) to further the activities of a proscribed organisation, or
    (c) to be addressed by a person who belongs or professes to belong to a proscribed organisation.

    (3) A person commits an offence if he addresses a meeting and the purpose of his address is to encourage support for a proscribed organisation or to further its activities.

    (4) Where a person is charged with an offence under subsection (2)(c) in respect of a private meeting it is a defence for him to prove that he had no reasonable cause to believe that the address mentioned in subsection (2)(c) would support a proscribed organisation or further its activities.

    (5) In subsections (2) to (4)—
    (a) "meeting" means a meeting of three or more persons, whether or not the public are admitted, and
    (b) a meeting is private if the public are not admitted.

    (6) A person guilty of an offence under this section shall be liable—
    (a) on conviction on indictment, to imprisonment for a term not exceeding ten years, to a fine or to both, or
    (b) on summary conviction, to imprisonment for a term not exceeding six months, to a fine not exceeding the statutory maximum or to both.

Uniform

13. (1) A person in a public place commits an offence if he—
    (a) wears an item of clothing, or
    (b) wears, carries or displays an article, in such a way or in such circumstances as to arouse reasonable suspicion that he is a member or supporter of a proscribed organisation.

    (2) A constable in Scotland may arrest a person without a warrant if he has reasonable grounds to suspect that the person is guilty of an offence under this section.

    (3) A person guilty of an offence under this section shall be liable on summary conviction to—

(a) imprisonment for a term not exceeding six months,

(b) a fine not exceeding level 5 on the standard scale, or

(c) both.

Part III
Terrorist Property

Interpretation
Terrorist Property

14. (1) In this Act "terrorist property" means—

    (a) money or other property which is likely to be used for the purposes of terrorism (including any resources of a proscribed organisation),

    (b) proceeds of the commission of acts of terrorism, and

    (c) proceeds of acts carried out for the purposes of terrorism.

  (2) In subsection (1)—

    (a) a reference to proceeds of an act includes a reference to any property which wholly or partly, and directly or indirectly, represents the proceeds of the act (including payments or other rewards in connection with its commission), and

    (b) the reference to an organisation's resources includes a reference to any money or other property which is applied or made available, or is to be applied or made available, for use by the organisation.

Offences Fund-Raising

15. (1) A person commits an offence if he—

    (a) invites another to provide money or other property, and

    (b) intends that it should be used, or has reasonable cause to suspect that it may be used, for the purposes of terrorism.

  (2) A person commits an offence if he—

    (a) receives money or other property, and

    (b) intends that it should be used, or has reasonable cause to suspect that it may be used, for the purposes of terrorism.

  (3) A person commits an offence if he—

    (a) provides money or other property, and

    (b) knows or has reasonable cause to suspect that it will or may be used for the purposes of terrorism.

  (4) In this section a reference to the provision of money or other property is a reference to its being given, lent or otherwise made available, whether or not for consideration.

Use and Possession

16. (1)   A person commits an offence if he uses money or other property for the purposes of terrorism.

   (2)   A person commits an offence if he—

     (a)   possesses money or other property, and

     (b)   intends that it should be used, or has reasonable cause to suspect that it may be used, for the purposes of terrorism.

Funding Arrangements

17. A person commits an offence if—

     (a)   he enters into or becomes concerned in an arrangement as a result of which money or other property is made available or is to be made available to another, and

     (b)   he knows or has reasonable cause to suspect that it will or may be used for the purposes of terrorism.

Money Laundering

18. (1)   A person commits an offence if he enters into or becomes concerned in an arrangement which facilitates the retention or control by or on behalf of another person of terrorist property—

     (a)   by concealment,

     (b)   by removal from the jurisdiction,

     (c)   by transfer to nominees, or

     (d)   in any other way.

   (2)   It is a defence for a person charged with an offence under subsection (1) to prove that he did not know and had no reasonable cause to suspect that the arrangement related to terrorist property.

Disclosure of Information: Duty

19. (1)   This section applies where a person—

     (a)   believes or suspects that another person has committed an offence under any of sections 15 to 18, and

     (b)   bases his belief or suspicion on information which comes to his attention in the course of a trade, profession, business or employment.

   (2)   The person commits an offence if he does not disclose to a constable as soon as is reasonably practicable—

     (a)   his belief or suspicion, and

     (b)   the information on which it is based.

(3) It is a defence for a person charged with an offence under subsection (2) to prove that he had a reasonable excuse for not making the disclosure.

(4) Where—
- (a) a person is in employment,
- (b) his employer has established a procedure for the making of disclosures of the matters specified in subsection (2), and
- (c) he is charged with an offence under that subsection, it is a defence for him to prove that he disclosed the matters specified in that subsection in accordance with the procedure.

(5) Subsection (2) does not require disclosure by a professional legal adviser of—
- (a) information which he obtains in privileged circumstances, or
- (b) a belief or suspicion based on information which he obtains in privileged circumstances.

(6) For the purpose of subsection (5) information is obtained by an adviser in privileged circumstances if it comes to him, otherwise than with a view to furthering a criminal purpose—
- (a) from a client or a client's representative, in connection with the provision of legal advice by the adviser to the client,
- (b) from a person seeking legal advice from the adviser, or from the person's representative, or
- (c) from any person, for the purpose of actual or contemplated legal proceedings.

(7) For the purposes of subsection (1)(a) a person shall be treated as having committed an offence under one of sections 15 to 18 if—
- (a) he has taken an action or been in possession of a thing, and
- (b) he would have committed an offence under one of those sections if he had been in the United Kingdom at the time when he took the action or was in possession of the thing.

(8) A person guilty of an offence under this section shall be liable—
- (a) on conviction on indictment, to imprisonment for a term not exceeding five years, to a fine or to both, or
- (b) on summary conviction, to imprisonment for a term not exceeding six months, or to a fine not exceeding the statutory maximum or to both.

Disclosure of Information: Permission

20. (1) A person may disclose to a constable—
- (a) a suspicion or belief that any money or other property is terrorist property or is derived from terrorist property;
- (b) any matter on which the suspicion or belief is based.

(2) A person may make a disclosure to a constable in the circumstances mentioned in section 19(1) and (2).

(3) Subsections (1) and (2) shall have effect notwithstanding any restriction on the disclosure of information imposed by statute or otherwise.

(4) Where—

    (a) a person is in employment, and

    (b) his employer has established a procedure for the making of disclosures of the kinds mentioned in subsection (1) and section 19(2), subsections (1) and (2) shall have effect in relation to that person as if any reference to disclosure to a constable included a reference to disclosure in accordance with the procedure.

Cooperation with Police.

21. (1) A person does not commit an offence under any of sections 15 to 18 if he is acting with the express consent of a constable.

  (2) Subject to subsections (3) and (4), a person does not commit an offence under any of sections 15 to 18 by involvement in a transaction or arrangement relating to money or other property if he discloses to a constable—

    (a) his suspicion or belief that the money or other property is terrorist property, and

    (b) the information on which his suspicion or belief is based.

  (3) Subsection (2) applies only where a person makes a disclosure—

    (a) after he becomes concerned in the transaction concerned,

    (b) on his own initiative, and

    (c) as soon as is reasonably practicable.

  (4) Subsection (2) does not apply to a person if—

    (a) a constable forbids him to continue his involvement in the transaction or arrangement to which the disclosure relates, and

    (b) he continues his involvement.

  (5) It is a defence for a person charged with an offence under any of sections 15(2) and (3) and 16 to 18 to prove that—

    (a) he intended to make a disclosure of the kind mentioned in subsections (2) and (3), and

    (b) there is reasonable excuse for his failure to do so.

  (6) Where—

    (a) a person is in employment, and

    (b) his employer has established a procedure for the making of disclosures of the same kind as may be made to a constable under subsection (2), this section shall have effect in relation to that person as if any reference to disclosure to a constable included a reference to disclosure in accordance with the procedure.

(7)   A reference in this section to a transaction or arrangement relating to money or other property includes a reference to use or possession.

Penalties

22. A person guilty of an offence under any of sections 15 to 18 shall be liable—

    (a)   on conviction on indictment, to imprisonment for a term not exceeding 14 years, to a fine or to both, or

    (b)   on summary conviction, to imprisonment for a term not exceeding six months, to a fine not exceeding the statutory maximum or to both.

Forfeiture

23. (1)   The court by or before which a person is convicted of an offence under any of sections 15 to 18 may make a forfeiture order in accordance with the provisions of this section.

    (2)   Where a person is convicted of an offence under section 15(1) or (2) or 16 the court may order the forfeiture of any money or other property—

        (a)   which, at the time of the offence, he had in his possession or under his control, and

        (b)   which, at that time, he intended should be used, or had reasonable cause to suspect might be used, for the purposes of terrorism.

    (3)   Where a person is convicted of an offence under section 15(3) the court may order the forfeiture of any money or other property—

        (a)   which, at the time of the offence, he had in his possession or under his control, and

        (b)   which, at that time, he knew or had reasonable cause to suspect would or might be used for the purposes of terrorism.

    (4)   Where a person is convicted of an offence under section 17 the court may order the forfeiture of the money or other property—

        (a)   to which the arrangement in question related, and

        (b)   which, at the time of the offence, he knew or had reasonable cause to suspect would or might be used for the purposes of terrorism.

    (5)   Where a person is convicted of an offence under section 18 the court may order the forfeiture of the money or other property to which the arrangement in question related.

(6) Where a person is convicted of an offence under any of sections 15 to 18, the court may order the forfeiture of any money or other property which wholly or partly, and directly or indirectly, is received by any person as a payment or other reward in connection with the commission of the offence.

(7) Where a person other than the convicted person claims to be the owner of or otherwise interested in anything which can be forfeited by an order under this section, the court shall give him an opportunity to be heard before making an order.

(8) A court in Scotland shall not make an order under this section except on the application of the prosecutor—

(a) in proceedings on indictment, when he moves for sentence, and

(b) in summary proceedings, before the court convicts the accused, and for the purposes of any appeal or review, an order under this section made by a court in Scotland is a sentence.

(9) Schedule 4 (which makes further provision in relation to forfeiture orders under this section) shall have effect.

Seizure of Terrorist Cash

Interpretation

24. (1) In sections 25 to 31 "authorised officer" means any of the following—

(a) a constable,

(b) a customs officer, and

(c) an immigration officer.

(2) In sections 25 to 31 "cash" means—

(a) coins and notes in any currency,

(b) postal orders,

(c) travellers' cheques,

(d) bankers' drafts, and

(e) such other kinds of monetary instrument as the Secretary of State may specify by order.

Seizure and Detention

25. (1) An authorised officer may seize and detain any cash to which this section applies if he has reasonable grounds for suspecting that—

(a) it is intended to be used for the purposes of terrorism,

(b) it forms the whole or part of the resources of a proscribed organisation, or

(c)   it is terrorist property within the meaning given in section 14(1)(b) or (c).

(2)   In subsection (1)(b) the reference to an organisation's resources includes a reference to any cash which is applied or made available, or is to be applied or made available, for use by the organisation.

(3)   This section applies to cash which—

(a)   is being imported into or exported from the United Kingdom,

(b)   is being brought to any place in the United Kingdom for the purpose of being exported from the United Kingdom,

(c)   is being brought to Northern Ireland from Great Britain, or to Great Britain from Northern Ireland,

(d)   is being brought to any place in Northern Ireland for the purpose of being brought to Great Britain, or

(e)   is being brought to any place in Great Britain for the purpose of being brought to Northern Ireland.

(4)   Subject to subsection (5), cash seized under this section shall be released not later than the end of the period of 48 hours beginning with the time when it is seized.

(5)   Where an order is made under section 26 in relation to cash seized, it may be detained during the period specified in the order.

Continued Detention

26. (1)   An authorised officer or the Commissioners of Customs and Excise may apply to a magistrates' court for an order under this section in relation to cash seized under section 25.

(2)   An order under this section—

(a)   shall authorise the further detention under section 25 of the cash to which it relates for a period specified in the order,

(b)   shall specify a period which ends not later than the end of the period of three months beginning with the date of the order, and

(c)   shall require notice to be given to the person from whom the cash was seized and to any other person who is affected by and specified in the order.

(3)   An application for an order under this section may be granted only if the court is satisfied—

(a)   that there are reasonable grounds to suspect that the cash is cash of a kind mentioned in section 25(1)(a), (b) or (c), and

(b)   that the continued detention of the cash is justified pending completion of an investigation of its origin or derivation or pending a determination whether to institute criminal proceedings (whether in the United Kingdom or elsewhere) which relate to the cash.

(4)   More than one order may be made under this section in relation to particular cash; but cash shall not be detained by virtue of an order under this section after the end of the period of two years beginning with the date when the first order under this section was made in relation to it.

(5)   In Scotland, any application under this section shall be made by the procurator fiscal to the sheriff; and in this section a reference to a magistrates' court shall be taken as a reference to the sheriff.

Detained Cash

27. (1)   Cash detained under section 25 by virtue of an order under section 26 shall, unless required as evidence of an offence, be held in an interest bearing account; and the interest accruing on the cash shall be added to it on its release or forfeiture.

(2)   Any person may apply to a magistrates' court, or in Scotland to the sheriff, for a direction that cash detained under section 25 be released.

(3)   A magistrates' court or the sheriff shall grant an application under subsection (2) if satisfied—

(a)   that section 26(3)(a) or (b) no longer applies, or

(b)   that the detention of the cash is for any other reason no longer justified.

(4)   An authorised officer, or in Scotland the procurator fiscal, may release cash detained under section 25 if—

(a)   he is satisfied that its detention is no longer justified, and

(b)   he has notified the magistrates' court or sheriff who made the order by virtue of which the cash is being detained under section 25.

(5)   Cash detained under section 25 shall not be released under this section—

(a)   while proceedings on an application for its forfeiture under section 28 have not been concluded, or

(b)   while proceedings, whether in the United Kingdom or elsewhere, which relate to the cash have not been concluded.

Forfeiture

28. (1)   An authorised officer or the Commissioners of Customs and Excise may apply to a magistrates' court, or in Scotland the procurator fiscal may apply to the sheriff, for an order forfeiting cash being detained under section 25.

(2)   A magistrates' court or the sheriff may grant an application only if satisfied on the balance of probabilities that the cash is cash of a kind mentioned in section 25(1)(a), (b) or (c).

(3) Before making an order under this section, a magistrates' court or the sheriff must give an opportunity to be heard to any person—

    (a) who is not a party to the proceedings, and

    (b) who claims to be the owner of or otherwise interested in any of the cash which can be forfeited under this section.

(4) An order may be made under this section whether or not proceedings are brought against any person for an offence with which the cash is connected.

(5) Proceedings on an application under this section to the sheriff shall be civil proceedings.

Forfeiture: Appeal

29. (1) Subject to subsection (2), any party to proceedings in which a forfeiture order is made under section 28 may appeal—

    (a) where the order is made by a magistrates' court in England and Wales, to the Crown Court,

    (b) where the order is made by the sheriff in Scotland, to the Court of Session, or

    (c) where the order is made by a magistrates' court in Northern Ireland, to the county court.

(2) An appeal under subsection (1)—

    (a) must be brought before the end of the period of 30 days beginning with the date on which the forfeiture order was made, and

    (b) may not be brought by the applicant for the forfeiture order.

(3) On an application by the appellant, a magistrates' court or the sheriff may order the release of so much of the cash to which the forfeiture order applies as it considers appropriate to enable him to meet his reasonable legal expenses in connection with the appeal.

(4) An appeal under subsection (1) shall be by way of a rehearing.

(5) If the court allows the appeal, it may order the release of—

    (a) the cash to which the forfeiture order applies together with any interest which has accrued, or

    (b) where an order has been made under subsection (3), the remaining cash to which the forfeiture order applies together with any interest which has accrued.

(6) Subsection (7) applies where a successful application for a forfeiture order relies (in whole or in part) on the fact that an organisation is proscribed, and—

    (a) a deproscription appeal under section 5 is allowed in respect of the organisation,

(b)   an order is made under section 3(3)(b) in respect of the organ-isation in accordance with an order of the Proscribed Orga-nisations Appeal Commission under section 5(4) (and, if the order is made in reliance on section 123(5), a resolution is passed by each House of Parliament under section 123(5)(b)), and

(c)   the forfeited cash was seized under section 25 on or after the date of the refusal to deproscribe against which the appeal under section 5 was brought.

(7)   Where this subsection applies an appeal under subsection (1) may be brought at any time before the end of the period of 30 days beginning with the date on which the order under section 3(3)(b) comes into force.

Treatment of Forfeited Cash

30. Any cash to which a forfeiture order under section 28 applies or accrued interest thereon shall be paid into the Consolidated Fund—

(a)   after the end of the period within which an appeal may be brought under section 29(1), or

(b)   where an appeal is brought under section 29(1), after the appeal is determined or otherwise disposed of.

Rules of Court

31. Provision may be made by rules of court about the procedure on appli-cations or appeals to any court under sections 26 to 29, and in particu-lar as to—

(a)   the giving of notice to persons affected by an application or appeal under those provisions;

(b)   the joinder, or in Scotland the sisting, of those persons as par-ties to the proceedings.

Part IV
Terrorist Investigations

Interpretation

Terrorist Investigation

32. In this Act "terrorist investigation" means an investigation of—

(a)   the commission, preparation or instigation of acts of terrorism,

(b)   an act which appears to have been done for the purposes of terrorism,

(c)   the resources of a proscribed organisation,

(d)   the possibility of making an order under section 3(3), or

(e)   the commission, preparation or instigation of an offence under this Act.

Cordons

Cordoned Areas

33. (1)   An area is a cordoned area for the purposes of this Act if it is designated under this section.

(2)   A designation may be made only if the person making it considers it expedient for the purposes of a terrorist investigation.

(3)   If a designation is made orally, the person making it shall confirm it in writing as soon as is reasonably practicable.

(4)   The person making a designation shall arrange for the demarcation of the cordoned area, so far as is reasonably practicable—

(a)   by means of tape marked with the word "police," or

(b)   in such other manner as a constable considers appropriate.

Power to Designate

34. (1)   Subject to subsection (2), a designation under section 33 may only be made—

(a)   where the area is outside Northern Ireland and is wholly or partly within a police area, by an officer for the police area who is of at least the rank of superintendent, and

(b)   where the area is in Northern Ireland, by a member of the Royal Ulster Constabulary who is of at least the rank of superintendent.

(2)   A constable who is not of the rank required by subsection (1) may make a designation if he considers it necessary by reason of urgency.

(3)   Where a constable makes a designation in reliance on subsection (2) he shall as soon as is reasonably practicable—

(a)   make a written record of the time at which the designation was made, and

(b)   ensure that a police officer of at least the rank of superintendent is informed.

(4)   An officer who is informed of a designation in accordance with subsection (3)(b)—

(a)   shall confirm the designation or cancel it with effect from such time as he may direct, and

      (b)   shall, if he cancels the designation, make a written record of the cancellation and the reason for it.

Duration

35. (1)   A designation under section 33 has effect, subject to subsections (2) to (5), during the period—

      (a)   beginning at the time when it is made, and

      (b)   ending with a date or at a time specified in the designation.

    (2)   The date or time specified under subsection (1)(b) must not occur after the end of the period of 14 days beginning with the day on which the designation is made.

    (3)   The period during which a designation has effect may be extended in writing from time to time by—

      (a)   the person who made it, or

      (b)   a person who could have made it (otherwise than by virtue of section 34(2)).

    (4)   An extension shall specify the additional period during which the designation is to have effect.

    (5)   A designation shall not have effect after the end of the period of 28 days beginning with the day on which it is made.

Police Powers

36. (1)   A constable in uniform may—

      (a)   order a person in a cordoned area to leave it immediately;

      (b)   order a person immediately to leave premises which are wholly or partly in or adjacent to a cordoned area;

      (c)   order the driver or person in charge of a vehicle in a cordoned area to move it from the area immediately;

      (d)   arrange for the removal of a vehicle from a cordoned area;

      (e)   arrange for the movement of a vehicle within a cordoned area;

      (f)   prohibit or restrict access to a cordoned area by pedestrians or vehicles.

    (2)   A person commits an offence if he fails to comply with an order, prohibition or restriction imposed by virtue of subsection (1).

    (3)   It is a defence for a person charged with an offence under subsection (2) to prove that he had a reasonable excuse for his failure.

    (4)   A person guilty of an offence under subsection (2) shall be liable on summary conviction to—

      (a)   imprisonment for a term not exceeding three months,

      (b)   a fine not exceeding level 4 on the standard scale, or

      (c)   both.

Information and Evidence Powers

37. Schedule 5 (power to obtain information, &c.) shall have effect.

Financial Information

38. Schedule 6 (financial information) shall have effect.

Disclosure of Information: duty

39. (1) Subsection (2) applies where a person knows or has reasonable cause to suspect that a constable is conducting or proposes to conduct a terrorist investigation.

(2) The person commits an offence if he—

(a) discloses to another anything which is likely to prejudice the investigation, or

(b) interferes with material which is likely to be relevant to the investigation.

(3) Subsection (4) applies where a person knows or has reasonable cause to suspect that a disclosure has been or will be made under any of sections 19 to 21.

(4) The person commits an offence if he—

(a) discloses to another anything which is likely to prejudice an investigation resulting from the disclosure under that section, or

(b) interferes with material which is likely to be relevant to an investigation resulting from the disclosure under that section.

(5) It is a defence for a person charged with an offence under subsection (2) or (4) to prove—

(a) that he did not know and had no reasonable cause to suspect that the disclosure or interference was likely to affect a terrorist investigation, or

(b) that he had a reasonable excuse for the disclosure or interference.

(6) Subsections (2) and (4) do not apply to a disclosure which is made by a professional legal adviser—

(a) to his client or to his client's representative in connection with the provision of legal advice by the adviser to the client and not with a view to furthering a criminal purpose, or

(b) to any person for the purpose of actual or contemplated legal proceedings and not with a view to furthering a criminal purpose.

(7) A person guilty of an offence under this section shall be liable—

(a) on conviction on indictment, to imprisonment for a term not exceeding five years, to a fine or to both, or

(b) on summary conviction, to imprisonment for a term not exceeding six months, to a fine not exceeding the statutory maximum or to both.

(8) For the purposes of this section—

(a) a reference to conducting a terrorist investigation includes a reference to taking part in the conduct of, or assisting, a terrorist investigation, and

(b) a person interferes with material if he falsifies it, conceals it, destroys it or disposes of it, or if he causes or permits another to do any of those things.

Part V
Counter-Terrorist Powers

Suspected Terrorists Terrorist: Interpretation

40. (1) In this Part "terrorist" means a person who—

(a) has committed an offence under any of sections 11, 12, 15 to 18, 54 and 56 to 63, or

(b) is or has been concerned in the commission, preparation or instigation of acts of terrorism.

(2) The reference in subsection (1)(b) to a person who has been concerned in the commission, preparation or instigation of acts of terrorism includes a reference to a person who has been, whether before or after the passing of this Act, concerned in the commission, preparation or instigation of acts of terrorism within the meaning given by section 1.

Arrest Without Warrant

41. (1) A constable may arrest without a warrant a person whom he reasonably suspects to be a terrorist.

(2) Where a person is arrested under this section the provisions of Schedule 8 (detention: treatment, review and extension) shall apply.

(3) Subject to subsections (4) to (7), a person detained under this section shall (unless detained under any other power) be released not later than the end of the period of 48 hours beginning—

(a) with the time of his arrest under this section, or

(b) if he was being detained under Schedule 7 when he was arrested under this section, with the time when his examination under that Schedule began.

(4) If on a review of a person's detention under Part II of Schedule 8 the review officer does not authorise continued detention, the person shall (unless detained in accordance with subsection (5) or (6) or under any other power) be released.

(5) Where a police officer intends to make an application for a warrant under paragraph 29 of Schedule 8 extending a person's detention, the person may be detained pending the making of the application.

(6) Where an application has been made under paragraph 29 or 36 of Schedule 8 in respect of a person's detention, he may be detained pending the conclusion of proceedings on the application.

(7) Where an application under paragraph 29 or 36 of Schedule 8 is granted in respect of a person's detention, he may be detained, subject to paragraph 37 of that Schedule, during the period specified in the warrant.

(8) The refusal of an application in respect of a person's detention under paragraph 29 or 36 of Schedule 8 shall not prevent his continued detention in accordance with this section.

(9) A person who has the powers of a constable in one Part of the United Kingdom may exercise the power under subsection (1) in any Part of the United Kingdom.

Search of Premises

42. (1) A justice of the peace may on the application of a constable issue a warrant in relation to specified premises if he is satisfied that there are reasonable grounds for suspecting that a person whom the constable reasonably suspects to be a person falling within section 40(1)(b) is to be found there.

(2) A warrant under this section shall authorise any constable to enter and search the specified premises for the purpose of arresting the person referred to in subsection (1) under section 41.

(3) In the application of subsection (1) to Scotland—
    (a) "justice of the peace" includes the sheriff, and
    (b) the justice of the peace or sheriff can be satisfied as mentioned in that subsection only by having heard evidence on oath.

Search of Persons

43. (1) A constable may stop and search a person whom he reasonably suspects to be a terrorist to discover whether he has in his possession anything which may constitute evidence that he is a terrorist.

(2) A constable may search a person arrested under section 41 to discover whether he has in his possession anything which may constitute evidence that he is a terrorist.

(3) A search of a person under this section must be carried out by someone of the same sex.

(4) A constable may seize and retain anything which he discovers in the

course of a search of a person under subsection (1) or (2) and which he reasonably suspects may constitute evidence that the person is a terrorist.

(5) A person who has the powers of a constable in one Part of the United Kingdom may exercise a power under this section in any Part of the United Kingdom.

Power to Stop and Search

Authorisations

44. (1) An authorisation under this subsection authorises any constable in uniform to stop a vehicle in an area or at a place specified in the authorisation and to search—

    (a) the vehicle;

    (b) the driver of the vehicle;

    (c) a passenger in the vehicle;

    (d) anything in or on the vehicle or carried by the driver or a passenger.

(2) An authorisation under this subsection authorises any constable in uniform to stop a pedestrian in an area or at a place specified in the authorisation and to search—

    (a) the pedestrian;

    (b) anything carried by him.

(3) An authorisation under subsection (1) or (2) may be given only if the person giving it considers it expedient for the prevention of acts of terrorism.

(4) An authorisation may be given—

    (a) where the specified area or place is the whole or part of a police area outside Northern Ireland other than one mentioned in paragraph (b) or (c), by a police officer for the area who is of at least the rank of assistant chief constable;

    (b) where the specified area or place is the whole or part of the metropolitan police district, by a police officer for the district who is of at least the rank of commander of the metropolitan police;

    (c) where the specified area or place is the whole or part of the City of London, by a police officer for the City who is of at least the rank of commander in the City of London police force;

    (d) where the specified area or place is the whole or part of Northern Ireland, by a member of the Royal Ulster Constabulary who is of at least the rank of assistant chief constable.

(5) If an authorisation is given orally, the person giving it shall confirm it in writing as soon as is reasonably practicable.

Exercise of Power

45. (1)   The power conferred by an authorisation under section 44(1) or (2)—

    (a)   may be exercised only for the purpose of searching for articles of a kind which could be used in connection with terrorism, and

    (b)   may be exercised whether or not the constable has grounds for suspecting the presence of articles of that kind.

  (2)   A constable may seize and retain an article which he discovers in the course of a search by virtue of section 44(1) or (2) and which he reasonably suspects is intended to be used in connection with terrorism.

  (3)   A constable exercising the power conferred by an authorisation may not require a person to remove any clothing in public except for headgear, footwear, an outer coat, a jacket or gloves.

  (4)   Where a constable proposes to search a person or vehicle by virtue of section 44(1) or (2) he may detain the person or vehicle for such time as is reasonably required to permit the search to be carried out at or near the place where the person or vehicle is stopped.

  (5)   Where—

    (a)   a vehicle or pedestrian is stopped by virtue of section 44(1) or (2), and

    (b)   the driver of the vehicle or the pedestrian applies for a written statement that the vehicle was stopped, or that he was stopped, by virtue of section 44(1) or (2), the written statement shall be provided.

  (6)   An application under subsection (5) must be made within the period of 12 months beginning with the date on which the vehicle or pedestrian was stopped.

Duration of Authorization

46. (1)   An authorisation under section 44 has effect, subject to subsections (2) to (7), during the period—

    (a)   beginning at the time when the authorisation is given, and

    (b)   ending with a date or at a time specified in the authorisation.

  (2)   The date or time specified under subsection (1)(b) must not occur after the end of the period of 28 days beginning with the day on which the authorisation is given.

  (3)   The person who gives an authorisation shall inform the Secretary of State as soon as is reasonably practicable.

  (4)   If an authorisation is not confirmed by the Secretary of State before the end of the period of 48 hours beginning with the time when it is given—

     (a)   it shall cease to have effect at the end of that period, but

     (b)   its ceasing to have effect shall not affect the lawfulness of anything done in reliance on it before the end of that period.

(5)   Where the Secretary of State confirms an authorisation he may substitute an earlier date or time for the date or time specified under subsection (1)(b).

(6)   The Secretary of State may cancel an authorisation with effect from a specified time.

(7)   An authorisation may be renewed in writing by the person who gave it or by a person who could have given it; and subsections (1) to (6) shall apply as if a new authorisation were given on each occasion on which the authorisation is renewed.

Offences

47. (1)   A person commits an offence if he—

     (a)   fails to stop a vehicle when required to do so by a constable in the exercise of the power conferred by an authorisation under section 44(1);

     (b)   fails to stop when required to do so by a constable in the exercise of the power conferred by an authorisation under section 44(2);

     (c)   wilfully obstructs a constable in the exercise of the power conferred by an authorisation under section 44(1) or (2).

(2)   A person guilty of an offence under this section shall be liable on summary conviction to—

     (a)   imprisonment for a term not exceeding six months,

     (b)   a fine not exceeding level 5 on the standard scale, or

     (c)   both.

Parking Authorisations

48. (1)   An authorisation under this section authorises any constable in uniform to prohibit or restrict the parking of vehicles on a road specified in the authorisation.

(2)   An authorisation may be given only if the person giving it considers it expedient for the prevention of acts of terrorism.

(3)   An authorisation may be given—

     (a)   where the road specified is outside Northern Ireland and is wholly or partly within a police area other than one mentioned in paragraphs (b) or (c), by a police officer for the area who is of at least the rank of assistant chief constable;

(b)   where the road specified is wholly or partly in the metropolitan police district, by a police officer for the district who is of at least the rank of commander of the metropolitan police;

(c)   where the road specified is wholly or partly in the City of London, by a police officer for the City who is of at least the rank of commander in the City of London police force;

(d)   where the road specified is in Northern Ireland, by a member of the Royal Ulster Constabulary who is of at least the rank of assistant chief constable.

(4)   If an authorisation is given orally, the person giving it shall confirm it in writing as soon as is reasonably practicable.

Exercise of Power

49. (1)   The power conferred by an authorisation under section 48 shall be exercised by placing a traffic sign on the road concerned.

(2)   A constable exercising the power conferred by an authorisation under section 48 may suspend a parking place.

(3)   Where a parking place is suspended under subsection (2), the suspension shall be treated as a restriction imposed by virtue of section 48–

(a)   for the purposes of section 99 of the Road Traffic Regulation Act 1984 (removal of vehicles illegally parked, &c.) and of any regulations in force under that section, and

(b)   for the purposes of Articles 47 and 48 of the Road Traffic Regulation (Northern Ireland) Order 1997 (in relation to Northern Ireland).

Duration of Authorization

50. (1)   An authorisation under section 48 has effect, subject to subsections (2) and (3), during the period specified in the authorisation.

(2)   The period specified shall not exceed 28 days.

(3)   An authorisation may be renewed in writing by the person who gave it or by a person who could have given it; and subsections (1) and (2) shall apply as if a new authorisation were given on each occasion on which the authorisation is renewed.

Offences

51. (1)   A person commits an offence if he parks a vehicle in contravention of a prohibition or restriction imposed by virtue of section 48.

(2)   A person commits an offence if—

      (a)   he is the driver or other person in charge of a vehicle which has been permitted to remain at rest in contravention of any prohibition or restriction imposed by virtue of section 48, and

      (b)   he fails to move the vehicle when ordered to do so by a constable in uniform.

(3)   It is a defence for a person charged with an offence under this section to prove that he had a reasonable excuse for the act or omission in question.

(4)   Possession of a current disabled person's badge shall not itself constitute a reasonable excuse for the purposes of subsection (3).

(5)   A person guilty of an offence under subsection (1) shall be liable on summary conviction to a fine not exceeding level 4 on the standard scale.

(6)   A person guilty of an offence under subsection (2) shall be liable on summary conviction to—

      (a)   imprisonment for a term not exceeding three months,

      (b)   a fine not exceeding level 4 on the standard scale, or

      (c)   both.

Interpretation

52. In sections 48 to 51–

"disabled person's badge" means a badge issued, or having effect as if issued, under any regulations for the time being in force under section 21 of the Chronically Sick and Disabled Persons Act 1970 (in relation to England and Wales and Scotland) or section 14 of the Chronically Sick and Disabled Persons (Northern Ireland) Act 1978 (in relation to Northern Ireland);

"driver" means, in relation to a vehicle which has been left on any road, the person who was driving it when it was left there;

"parking" means leaving a vehicle or permitting it to remain at rest;

"traffic sign" has the meaning given in section 142(1) of the Road Traffic Regulation Act 1984 (in relation to England and Wales and Scotland) and in Article 28 of the Road Traffic Regulation (Northern Ireland) Order 1997 (in relation to Northern Ireland);

"vehicle" has the same meaning as in section 99(5) of the Road Traffic Regulation Act 1984 (in relation to England and Wales and Scotland) and Article 47(4) of the Road Traffic Regulation (Northern Ireland) Order 1997 (in relation to Northern Ireland).

Port and Border Controls Port and Border Controls

53. (1) Schedule 7 (port and border controls) shall have effect.

   (2) The Secretary of State may by order repeal paragraph 16 of Schedule 7.

   (3) The powers conferred by Schedule 7 shall be exercisable notwithstanding the rights conferred by section 1 of the Immigration Act 1971 (general principles regulating entry into and staying in the United Kingdom).

Part VI
Miscellaneous

Terrorist Offences

Weapons Training

54. (1) A person commits an offence if he provides instruction or training in the making or use of—

   (a) firearms,

   (b) explosives, or

   (c) chemical, biological or nuclear weapons.

   (2) A person commits an offence if he receives instruction or training in the making or use of—

   (a) firearms,

   (b) explosives, or

   (c) chemical, biological or nuclear weapons.

   (3) A person commits an offence if he invites another to receive instruction or training and the receipt—

   (a) would constitute an offence under subsection (2), or

   (b) would constitute an offence under subsection (2) but for the fact that it is to take place outside the United Kingdom.

   (4) For the purpose of subsections (1) and (3)—

   (a) a reference to the provision of instruction includes a reference to making it available either generally or to one or more specific persons, and

   (b) an invitation to receive instruction or training may be either general or addressed to one or more specific persons.

   (5) It is a defence for a person charged with an offence under this section in relation to instruction or training to prove that his action or involvement was wholly for a purpose other than assisting, preparing for or participating in terrorism.

   (6) A person guilty of an offence under this section shall be liable—

      (a)   on conviction on indictment, to imprisonment for a term not exceeding ten years, to a fine or to both, or

      (b)   on summary conviction, to imprisonment for a term not exceeding six months, to a fine not exceeding the statutory maximum or to both.

(7)   A court by or before which a person is convicted of an offence under this section may order the forfeiture of anything which the court considers to have been in the person's possession for purposes connected with the offence.

(8)   Before making an order under subsection (7) a court must give an opportunity to be heard to any person, other than the convicted person, who claims to be the owner of or otherwise interested in anything which can be forfeited under that subsection.

(9)   An order under subsection (7) shall not come into force until there is no further possibility of it being varied, or set aside, on appeal (disregarding any power of a court to grant leave to appeal out of time).

Weapons Training: Interpretation

55. In section 54–

      "biological weapon" means anything to which section 1(1)(b) of the Biological Weapons Act 1974 applies,

      "chemical weapon" has the meaning given by section 1 of the Chemical Weapons Act 1996, and

      "nuclear weapon" means a weapon which contains nuclear material within the meaning of Article 1(a) and (b) of the Convention on the Physical Protection of Nuclear Material opened for signature at Vienna and New York on 3rd March 1980 (set out in the Schedule to the Nuclear Material (Offences) Act 1983).

Directing Terrorist Organization

56. (1)   A person commits an offence if he directs, at any level, the activities of an organisation which is concerned in the commission of acts of terrorism.

    (2)   A person guilty of an offence under this section is liable on conviction on indictment to imprisonment for life.

Possession for Terrorist Purposes

57. (1)   A person commits an offence if he possesses an article in circumstances which give rise to a reasonable suspicion that his possession

is for a purpose connected with the commission, preparation or instigation of an act of terrorism.

(2) It is a defence for a person charged with an offence under this section to prove that his possession of the article was not for a purpose connected with the commission, preparation or instigation of an act of terrorism.

(3) In proceedings for an offence under this section, if it is proved that an article—

(a) was on any premises at the same time as the accused, or

(b) was on premises of which the accused was the occupier or which he habitually used otherwise than as a member of the public, the court may assume that the accused possessed the article, unless he proves that he did not know of its presence on the premises or that he had no control over it.

(4) A person guilty of an offence under this section shall be liable—

(a) on conviction on indictment, to imprisonment for a term not exceeding 10 years, to a fine or to both, or

(b) on summary conviction, to imprisonment for a term not exceeding six months, to a fine not exceeding the statutory maximum or to both.

Collection of Information

58. (1) A person commits an offence if—

(a) he collects or makes a record of information of a kind likely to be useful to a person committing or preparing an act of terrorism, or

(b) he possesses a document or record containing information of that kind.

(2) In this section "record" includes a photographic or electronic record.

(3) It is a defence for a person charged with an offence under this section to prove that he had a reasonable excuse for his action or possession.

(4) A person guilty of an offence under this section shall be liable—

(a) on conviction on indictment, to imprisonment for a term not exceeding 10 years, to a fine or to both, or

(b) on summary conviction, to imprisonment for a term not exceeding six months, to a fine not exceeding the statutory maximum or to both.

(5) A court by or before which a person is convicted of an offence under this section may order the forfeiture of any document or record containing information of the kind mentioned in subsection (1)(a).

(6) Before making an order under subsection (5) a court must give an opportunity to be heard to any person, other than the convicted

person, who claims to be the owner of or otherwise interested in anything which can be forfeited under that subsection.

(7) An order under subsection (5) shall not come into force until there is no further possibility of it being varied, or set aside, on appeal (disregarding any power of a court to grant leave to appeal out of time).

Inciting Terrorism Overseas

England and Wales

59. (1) A person commits an offence if—
    (a) he incites another person to commit an act of terrorism wholly or partly outside the United Kingdom, and
    (b) the act would, if committed in England and Wales, constitute one of the offences listed in subsection (2).

(2) Those offences are—
    (a) murder,
    (b) an offence under section 18 of the Offences against the Person Act 1861 (wounding with intent),
    (c) an offence under section 23 or 24 of that Act (poison),
    (d) an offence under section 28 or 29 of that Act (explosions), and
    (e) an offence under section 1(2) of the Criminal Damage Act 1971 (endangering life by damaging property).

(3) A person guilty of an offence under this section shall be liable to any penalty to which he would be liable on conviction of the offence listed in subsection (2) which corresponds to the act which he incites.

(4) For the purposes of subsection (1) it is immaterial whether or not the person incited is in the United Kingdom at the time of the incitement.

(5) Nothing in this section imposes criminal liability on any person acting on behalf of, or holding office under, the Crown.

Northern Ireland

60. (1) A person commits an offence if—
    (a) he incites another person to commit an act of terrorism wholly or partly outside the United Kingdom, and
    (b) the act would, if committed in Northern Ireland, constitute one of the offences listed in subsection (2).

(2) Those offences are—
    (a) murder,
    (b) an offence under section 18 of the Offences against the Person Act 1861 (wounding with intent),

       (c)   an offence under section 23 or 24 of that Act (poison),

       (d)   an offence under section 28 or 29 of that Act (explosions), and

       (e)   an offence under Article 3(2) of the {/ci}Criminal Damage (Northern Ireland) Order 1977 (endangering life by damaging property).

   (3)   A person guilty of an offence under this section shall be liable to any penalty to which he would be liable on conviction of the offence listed in subsection (2) which corresponds to the act which he incites.

   (4)   For the purposes of subsection (1) it is immaterial whether or not the person incited is in the United Kingdom at the time of the incitement.

   (5)   Nothing in this section imposes criminal liability on any person acting on behalf of, or holding office under, the Crown.

Scotland

61. (1)   A person commits an offence if—

       (a)   he incites another person to commit an act of terrorism wholly or partly outside the United Kingdom, and

       (b)   the act would, if committed in Scotland, constitute one of the offences listed in subsection (2).

   (2)   Those offences are—

       (a)   murder,

       (b)   assault to severe injury, and

       (c)   reckless conduct which causes actual injury.

   (3)   A person guilty of an offence under this section shall be liable to any penalty to which he would be liable on conviction of the offence listed in subsection (2) which corresponds to the act which he incites.

   (4)   For the purposes of subsection (1) it is immaterial whether or not the person incited is in the United Kingdom at the time of the incitement.

   (5)   Nothing in this section imposes criminal liability on any person acting on behalf of, or holding office under, the Crown.

Terrorist Bombing and Finance Offences

Terrorist Bombing: Jurisdiction

62. (1)   If—

       (a)   a person does anything outside the United Kingdom as an act of terrorism or for the purposes of terrorism, and

       (b)   his action would have constituted the commission of one of the offences listed in subsection (2) if it had been done in the United Kingdom, he shall be guilty of the offence.

(2) The offences referred to in subsection (1)(b) are—

    (a) an offence under section 2, 3 or 5 of the Explosive Substances Act 1883 (causing explosions, &c.),

    (b) an offence under section 1 of the Biological Weapons Act 1974 (biological weapons), and

    (c) an offence under section 2 of the Chemical Weapons Act 1996 (chemical weapons).

Terrorist Finance: Jurisdiction

63. (1) If—

    (a) a person does anything outside the United Kingdom, and

    (b) his action would have constituted the commission of an offence under any of sections 15 to 18 if it had been done in the United Kingdom, he shall be guilty of the offence.

(2) For the purposes of subsection (1)(b), section 18(1)(b) shall be read as if for "the jurisdiction" there were substituted "a jurisdiction."

Extradition

64. (1) The Extradition Act 1989 shall be amended as follows.

(2) In section 22(2) (international conventions) after paragraph (l) insert—

"(m) the Convention for the Suppression of Terrorist Bombings, which was opened for signature at New York on 12th January 1998 ("the Terrorist Bombings Convention");

    (n) the Convention for the Suppression of the Financing of Terrorism which was opened for signature at New York on 10th January 2000 ("the Terrorist Finance Convention")."

(3) In section 22(4) (relevant offences) after paragraph (l) insert—

"(m) in relation to the Terrorist Bombings Convention, an offence, committed as an act of terrorism or for the purposes of terrorism, under—

    (i) section 2, 3 or 5 of the Explosive Substances Act 1883 (causing explosions, &c.),

    (ii) section 1 of the Biological Weapons Act 1974 (biological weapons), or

    (iii) section 2 of the Chemical Weapons Act 1996 (chemical weapons);

    (n) in relation to the Terrorist Finance Convention, an offence under any of sections 15 to 18 of the Terrorism Act 2000 (terrorist property: offences)."

(4) After section 24(4) (suppression of terrorism) insert—

"(5) Subsections (1) and (2) above shall have effect in relation to an offence to which section 22(4)(m) or (n) above applies as they have effect in relation to an offence to which section 1 of the Suppression of Terrorism Act 1978 applies.

(6) For that purpose subsection (2) applies to a country which is a party to—

(a) the Convention for the Suppression of Terrorist Bombings mentioned in section 22(2)(m) above, or

(b) the Convention for the Suppression of the Financing of Terrorism mentioned in section 22(2)(n) above."

(5) The offences to which an Order in Council under section 2 of the Extradition Act 1870 (arrangements with foreign states) can apply shall include—

(a) offences under the provisions mentioned in sections 62(2) and 63(1)(b),

(b) conspiracy to commit any of those offences, and

(c) attempt to commit any of those offences.

Part VII
Northern Ireland

Scheduled Offences
Scheduled Offence: Interpretation

65. (1) In this Part "scheduled offence" means, subject to any relevant note in Part I or III of Schedule 9, an offence specified in either of those Parts.

(2) Part II of that Schedule shall have effect in respect of offences related to those specified in Part I.

(3) The Secretary of State may by order—

(a) add an offence to Part I or II of Schedule 9;

(b) remove an offence from Part I or II of that Schedule;

(c) amend Part I or II of that Schedule in some other way.

Preliminary Inquiry

66. (1) In proceedings before a magistrates' court for a scheduled offence, if the prosecution requests the court to conduct a preliminary inquiry into the offence the court shall grant the request.

(2) In subsection (1) "preliminary inquiry" means a preliminary inquiry under the Magistrates' Courts (Northern Ireland) Order 1981.

(3) Subsection (1)—

      (a)   shall apply notwithstanding anything in Article 31 of that Order,

      (b)   shall not apply in respect of an offence where the court considers that in the interests of justice a preliminary investigation should be conducted into the offence under that Order, and

      (c)   shall not apply in respect of an extra-territorial offence (as defined in section 1(3) of the Criminal Jurisdiction Act 1975)).

(4)   Where a person charged with a scheduled offence is also charged with a non-scheduled offence, the non-scheduled offence shall be treated as a scheduled offence for the purposes of this section.

Limitation of Power to Grant Bail

67. (1)   This section applies to a person who—

      (a)   has attained the age of fourteen, and

      (b)   is charged with a scheduled offence which is neither being tried summarily nor certified by the Director of Public Prosecutions for Northern Ireland as suitable for summary trial.

(2)   Subject to subsections (6) and (7), a person to whom this section applies shall not be admitted to bail except—

      (a)   by a judge of the High Court or the Court of Appeal, or

      (b)   by the judge of the court of trial on adjourning the trial of a person charged with a scheduled offence.

(3)   A judge may, in his discretion, admit a person to whom this section applies to bail unless satisfied that there are substantial grounds for believing that the person, if released on bail (whether subject to conditions or not), would—

      (a)   fail to surrender to custody,

      (b)   commit an offence while on bail,

      (c)   interfere with a witness,

      (d)   otherwise obstruct or attempt to obstruct the course of justice, whether in relation to himself or another person, or

      (e)   fail to comply with conditions of release (if any).

(4)   In exercising his discretion in relation to a person under subsection (3) a judge shall have regard to such of the following considerations as he considers relevant (as well as to any others which he considers relevant)—

      (a)   the nature and seriousness of the offence with which the person is charged,

      (b)   the character, antecedents, associations and community ties of the person,

      (c)   the time which the person has already spent in custody and the time which he is likely to spend in custody if he is not admitted to bail, and

(d) the strength of the evidence of his having committed the offence.

(5) Without prejudice to any other power to impose conditions on admission to bail, a judge admitting a person to bail under this section may impose such conditions as he considers—

(a) likely to result in the person's appearance at the time and place required, or

(b) necessary in the interests of justice or for the prevention of crime.

(6) Subsection (7) applies where a person to whom this section applies is a serving member of—

(a) any of Her Majesty's forces, or

(b) the Royal Ulster Constabulary or the Royal Ulster Constabulary Reserve.

(7) Where this subsection applies to a person he may be admitted to bail on condition that he is held in military or police custody if the person granting bail is satisfied that suitable arrangements have been made; and—

(a) bail on that condition may be granted by a judge or a resident magistrate, and

(b) it shall be lawful for the person to be held in military or police custody in accordance with the conditions of his bail.

Bail: Legal Aid

68. (1) Where it appears to a judge of the High Court or the Court of Appeal—

(a) that a person charged with a scheduled offence intends to apply to be admitted to bail,

(b) that it is desirable in the interests of justice that he should have legal aid, and

(c) that he has not sufficient means to enable him to obtain that aid, the judge may assign to him a solicitor and counsel, or counsel only, in the application for bail.

(2) If on a question of granting a person free legal aid under this section there is a doubt—

(a) whether his means are sufficient to enable him to obtain legal aid, or

(b) whether it is desirable in the interests of justice that he should have free legal aid, the doubt shall be resolved in favour of granting him free legal aid.

(3)　Articles 32, 36 and 40 of the Legal Aid, Advice and Assistance (Northern Ireland) Order 1981 (statements, payments, rules and stamp duty) shall apply in relation to legal aid under this section as they apply in relation to legal aid under Part III of that Order as if legal aid under this section were given in pursuance of a criminal aid certificate under Article 29 of that Order.

Maximum Period of Remand in Custody

69. (1)　The period for which a person charged with a scheduled offence may be remanded in custody by a magistrates' court shall be a period of not more than 28 days beginning with the day following that on which he is remanded.

(2)　Subsection (1) has effect—
　　(a)　notwithstanding Article 47(2) and (3) of the Magistrates' Courts (Northern Ireland) Order 1981, and
　　(b)　whether or not a person is also charged with a non-scheduled offence.

Young Persons: Custody on Remand, &c

70. (1)　While a young person charged with a scheduled offence is remanded or committed for trial and not released on bail, he may be held in custody in such prison or other place as may be specified in a direction given by the Secretary of State under this section.

(2)　Subsection (1) shall have effect in respect of a person—
　　(a)　notwithstanding the provisions of any enactment, and
　　(b)　whether or not he was remanded or committed for trial at a time when this section was not in force.

(3)　The Secretary of State may give a direction under this section in respect of a person if he considers it necessary to make special arrangements as to the place at which the person is to be held in order—
　　(a)　to prevent his escape, or
　　(b)　to ensure his safety or the safety of others.

(4)　The Secretary of State may give a direction under this section at any time after the person to whom it relates has been charged.

(5)　In this section "young person" means a person who—
　　(a)　has attained the age of fourteen, and
　　(b)　has not attained the age of seventeen.

Directions Under Section 70

71. (1) A direction under section 70 shall cease to have effect at the expiry of the period specified in the direction unless—
    (a) it has previously ceased to have effect, or
    (b) it is continued in force by a further direction.

(2) The specified period shall not end after the end of the period of two months beginning with the date of the direction.

(3) Where—
    (a) a person is held in custody in a prison or other place by virtue of a direction, and
    (b) the direction ceases to have effect (whether or not by reason of the expiry or cesser of section 70), it shall be lawful for him to continue to be held in custody in that prison or place until arrangements can be made for him to be held in custody in accordance with the law then applicable to his case.

(4) Nothing in subsection (3) shall be taken as permitting the holding in custody of a person who is entitled to be released from custody.

Time Limits for Preliminary Proceedings

72. (1) The Secretary of State may by regulations make provision, in respect of a specified preliminary stage of proceedings for a scheduled offence, as to the maximum period—
    (a) to be allowed to the prosecution to complete the stage;
    (b) during which the accused may, while awaiting completion of the stage, be in the custody of a magistrates' court or the Crown Court in relation to the offence.

(2) The regulations may, in particular—
    (a) provide for a specified law about bail to apply in relation to cases to which custody or overall time limits apply (subject to any modifications which the Secretary of State considers it necessary to specify in the regulations);
    (b) provide for time limits to cease to have effect in cases where the Attorney General for Northern Ireland certifies after the institution of proceedings that an offence is not to be treated as a scheduled offence;
    (c) make such provision with respect to the procedure to be followed in criminal proceedings as the Secretary of State considers appropriate in consequence of another provision of the regulations;
    (d) make provision which has effect in relation to a non-scheduled offence where separate counts of an indictment allege a scheduled offence and a non-scheduled offence;

(e) enable the Crown Court in specified circumstances to extend or further extend a time limit at any time before it expires.

(3) Subject to subsection (4), where an overall time limit expires before the completion of the stage of proceedings to which the limit applies, the accused shall be treated for all purposes as having been acquitted of the offence to which the proceedings relate.

(4) Regulations under this section which provide for a custody time limit in relation to a preliminary stage shall have no effect where—

    (a) a person escapes from the custody of a magistrates' court or the Crown Court before the expiry of the custody time limit,

    (b) a person who has been released on bail in consequence of the expiry of a custody time limit fails to surrender himself into the custody of the court at the appointed time, or

    (c) a person who has been released on bail in consequence of the expiry of a custody time limit is arrested by a constable in connection with a breach or apprehended breach of a condition of his bail.

(5) If a person escapes from the custody of a magistrates' court or the Crown Court, the overall time limit which applies to the stage which proceedings relating to the person have reached at the time of the escape shall cease to have effect in relation to those proceedings.

(6) If a person who has been released on bail fails to surrender himself into the custody of the court at the appointed time, the overall time limit which applies to the stage which proceedings relating to the person have reached at the time of the failure shall cease to have effect in relation to those proceedings.

Time Limits: Supplementary

73. (1) Where a person is convicted of an offence, the exercise of power conferred by virtue of section 72(2)(e) in relation to proceedings for the offence shall not be called into question on an appeal against the conviction.

(2) In the application of section 72 in relation to proceedings on indictment, "preliminary stage" does not include a stage—

    (a) after the time when the case for the prosecution is opened, or

    (b) if the court accepts a plea of guilty before the case for the prosecution is opened, after the plea is accepted.

(3) In the application of section 72 in relation to summary proceedings, "preliminary stage" does not include a stage—

    (a) after the court begins to hear evidence for the prosecution at the trial,

(b)   if the court accepts a plea of guilty before it has begun to hear evidence for the prosecution, after the plea is accepted, or

(c)   after the court begins to consider whether to exercise its power under Article 44(4) of the Mental Health (Northern Ireland) Order 1986 (power to make hospital order without conviction).

(4)   In this section and section 72–

"custody of the Crown Court" includes custody to which a person is committed in pursuance of—

(a)   Article 37 or 40(4) of the Magistrates' Courts (Northern Ireland) Order 1981 (magistrates' court committing accused for trial), or

(b)   section 51(8) of the Judicature (Northern Ireland) Act 1978 (magistrates' court dealing with a person arrested under Crown Court warrant),

"custody of a magistrates' court" means custody to which a person is committed in pursuance of Article 47 or 49 of the Magistrates' Courts (Northern Ireland) Order 1981 (remand),

"custody time limit" means a time limit imposed by regulations in pursuance of section 72(1)(b) or, where a limit has been extended by the Crown Court by virtue of section 72(2)(e), the limit as extended,

"law about bail" means—

(a)   the Magistrates' Courts (Northern Ireland) Order 1981,

(b)   section 67 of this Act,

(c)   any other enactment relating to bail, and

(d)   any rule of law relating to bail, and

"overall time limit" means a time limit imposed by regulations in pursuance of section 72(1)(a) or, where a limit has been extended by the Crown Court by virtue of section 72(2)(e), the limit as extended.

(5)   For the purposes of the application of a custody time limit in relation to a person who is in the custody of a magistrates' court or the Crown Court—

(a)   all periods during which he is in the custody of a magistrates' court in respect of the same offence shall be aggregated and treated as a single continuous period; and

(b)   all periods during which he is in the custody of the Crown Court in respect of the same offence shall be aggregated and treated as a single continuous period.

Court for Trial

74. (1)   A trial on indictment of a scheduled offence shall be held only at the Crown Court sitting in Belfast, unless—

    (a)   the Lord Chancellor after consultation with the Lord Chief Justice of Northern Ireland directs that the trial, or a class of trials within which it falls, shall be held at the Crown Court sitting elsewhere, or

    (b)   the Lord Chief Justice of Northern Ireland directs that the trial, or part of it, shall be held at the Crown Court sitting elsewhere.

  (2)   A person committed for trial for a scheduled offence, or for two or more offences at least one of which is a scheduled offence, shall be committed—

    (a)   to the Crown Court sitting in Belfast, or

    (b)   where a direction has been given under subsection (1) which concerns the trial, to the Crown Court sitting at the place specified in the direction; and section 48 of the Judicature (Northern Ireland) Act 1978 (committal for trial on indictment) shall have effect accordingly.

  (3)   Where—

    (a)   a person is committed for trial to the Crown Court sitting in Belfast in accordance with subsection (2), and

    (b)   a direction is subsequently given under subsection (1), before the commencement of the trial, altering the place of trial, the person shall be treated as having been committed for trial to the Crown Court sitting at the place specified in the direction.

Mode of Trial on Indictment

75. (1)   A trial on indictment of a scheduled offence shall be conducted by the court without a jury.

  (2)   The court trying a scheduled offence on indictment under this section shall have all the powers, authorities and jurisdiction which the court would have had if it had been sitting with a jury (including power to determine any question and to make any finding which would, apart from this section, be required to be determined or made by a jury).

  (3)   A reference in an enactment to a jury, the verdict of a jury or the finding of a jury shall, in relation to a trial under this section, be construed as a reference to the court, the verdict of the court or the finding of the court.

  (4)   Where separate counts of an indictment allege a scheduled offence and a non-scheduled offence, the trial on indictment shall be con-

ducted as if all the offences alleged in the indictment were scheduled offences.

(5) Subsection (4) is without prejudice to section 5 of the Indictments Act (Northern Ireland) 1945 (orders for amendment of indictment, separate trial and postponement of trial).

(6) Without prejudice to subsection (2), where the court trying a scheduled offence on indictment—

(a) is not satisfied that the accused is guilty of the offence, but

(b) is satisfied that he is guilty of a non-scheduled offence of which a jury could have found him guilty on a trial for the scheduled offence, the court may convict him of the non-scheduled offence.

(7) Where the court trying a scheduled offence convicts the accused of that or some other offence, it shall give a judgment stating the reasons for the conviction at or as soon as is reasonably practicable after the time of conviction.

(8) A person convicted of an offence on a trial under this section without a jury may, notwithstanding anything in sections 1 and 10(1) of the Criminal Appeal (Northern Ireland) Act 1980, appeal to the Court of Appeal under Part I of that Act—

(a) against his conviction, on any ground, without the leave of the Court of Appeal or a certificate of the judge of the court of trial;

(b) against sentence passed on conviction, without that leave, unless the sentence is fixed by law.

(9) Where a person is convicted of an offence on a trial under this section, the time for giving notice of appeal under section 16(1) of that Act shall run from the date of judgment if later than the date from which it would run under that subsection.

Admission in Trial on Indictment

76. (1) This section applies to a trial on indictment for—

(a) a scheduled offence, or

(b) two or more offences at least one of which is a scheduled offence.

(2) A statement made by the accused may be given in evidence by the prosecution in so far as—

(a) it is relevant to a matter in issue in the proceedings, and

(b) it is not excluded or inadmissible (whether by virtue of subsections (3) to (5) or otherwise).

(3) Subsections (4) and (5) apply if in proceedings to which this section applies—

(a) the prosecution gives or proposes to give a statement made by the accused in evidence,

(b) prima facie evidence is adduced that the accused was subjected to torture, inhuman or degrading treatment, violence or the threat of violence in order to induce him to make the statement, and

(c) the prosecution does not satisfy the court that the statement was not obtained in the manner mentioned in paragraph (b).

(4) If the statement has not yet been given in evidence, the court shall—

(a) exclude the statement, or

(b) direct that the trial be restarted before a differently constituted court (before which the statement shall be inadmissible).

(5) If the statement has been given in evidence, the court shall—

(a) disregard it, or

(b) direct that the trial be restarted before a differently constituted court (before which the statement shall be inadmissible).

(6) This section is without prejudice to any discretion of a court to—

(a) exclude or ignore a statement, or

(b) direct a trial to be restarted, where the court considers it appropriate in order to avoid unfairness to the accused or otherwise in the interests of justice.

Possession: Onus of Proof

77. (1) This section applies to a trial on indictment for a scheduled offence where the accused is charged with possessing an article in such circumstances as to constitute an offence under any of the enactments listed in subsection (3).

(2) If it is proved that the article—

(a) was on any premises at the same time as the accused, or

(b) was on premises of which the accused was the occupier or which he habitually used otherwise than as a member of the public, the court may assume that the accused possessed (and, if relevant, knowingly possessed) the article, unless he proves that he did not know of its presence on the premises or that he had no control over it.

(3) The following are the offences mentioned in subsection (1)—

The Explosive Substances Act 1883

Section 3, so far as relating to subsection (1)(b) thereof (possessing explosive with intent to endanger life or cause serious damage to property).

Section 4 (possessing explosive in suspicious circumstances).

The Protection of the Person and Property Act (Northern Ireland) 1969

Section 2 (possessing petrol bomb, &c. in suspicious circumstances).

The Firearms (Northern Ireland) Order 1981

Article 6(1) (manufacturing, dealing in or possessing certain weapons, &c.).

Article 17 (possessing firearm or ammunition with intent to endanger life or cause serious damage to property).

Article 18(2) (possessing firearm or imitation firearm at time of committing, or being arrested for, a specified offence).

Article 22(1), (2) or (4) (possession of a firearm or ammunition by a person who has been sentenced to imprisonment, &c.).

Article 23 (possessing firearm or ammunition in suspicious circumstances).

Children: Sentence

78. (1)   This section applies where a child is convicted on indictment of a scheduled offence committed while this section is in force.

(2)   Article 45(2) of the Criminal Justice (Children) (Northern Ireland) Order 1998 (punishment for serious offence) shall have effect with the substitution for the words "14 years" of the words "five years."

(3)   In this section "child" means a person who has not attained the age of 17.

Restricted Remission

79. (1)   The remission granted under prison rules in respect of a sentence of imprisonment passed in Northern Ireland for a scheduled offence shall not, where it is for a term of five years or more, exceed one-third of the term.

(2)   Where a person is sentenced on the same occasion for two or more scheduled offences to terms which are consecutive, subsection (1) shall apply as if those terms were a single term.

(3)   Where a person is serving two or more terms which are consecutive but not all subject to subsection (1), the maximum remission granted under prison rules in respect of those terms taken together shall be arrived at by calculating the maximum remission for each term separately and aggregating the result.

(4)   In this section "prison rules" means rules made under section 13 of the Prison Act (Northern Ireland) 1953.

(5)   The Secretary of State may by order substitute a different length of sentence and a different maximum period of remission for those mentioned in subsection (1).

(6)   This section applies where—

    (a)   the scheduled offence is committed while this section is in force,

    (b)   the offence (being a scheduled offence within the meaning of the Northern Ireland (Emergency Provisions) Act 1996) was committed while section 15 of that Act was in force,

    (c)   the offence (being a scheduled offence within the meaning of the Northern Ireland (Emergency Provisions) Act 1991) was committed while section 14 of that Act was in force, or

    (d)   the offence (being a scheduled offence within the meaning of the Northern Ireland (Emergency Provisions) Act 1978) was committed while section 22 of the Prevention of Terrorism (Temporary Provisions) Act 1989 was in force.

Conviction During Remission

80. (1)   This section applies where—

    (a)   a person is sentenced to imprisonment or a term of detention in a young offenders centre for a period exceeding one year,

    (b)   he is discharged from prison or the centre in pursuance of prison rules, and

    (c)   before his sentence or term would have expired (but for the discharge) he commits, and is convicted on indictment of, a scheduled offence.

(2)   If the court before which he is convicted of the scheduled offence sentences him to imprisonment or a term of detention it shall in addition order him to be returned to prison or a young offenders centre for the period between the date of the order and the date on which the sentence or term mentioned in subsection (1) would have expired but for his discharge.

(3)   No order shall be made under subsection (2) if the sentence imposed by the court is—

    (a)   a suspended sentence,

    (b)   a sentence of life imprisonment, or

    (c)   a sentence of detention during the Secretary of State's pleasure under Article 45(1) of the Criminal Justice (Children) (Northern Ireland) Order 1998.

(4) An order made under subsection (2) shall cease to have effect if an appeal against the scheduled offence results in—

(a) the acquittal of the person concerned, or

(b) the substitution of a sentence other than imprisonment or a term of detention.

(5) The period for which a person is ordered under this section to be returned to prison or a young offenders centre—

(a) shall be taken to be a sentence of imprisonment or term of detention for the purposes of the Prison Act (Northern Ireland) 1953 and for the purposes of the Treatment of Offenders Act (Northern Ireland) 1968 other than section 26(2) (reduction for time spent in custody),

(b) shall not be subject to any provision of prison rules for discharge before expiry, and

(c) shall be served before, and be followed by, the sentence or term imposed for the scheduled offence and be disregarded in determining the appropriate length of that sentence or term.

(6) For the purposes of this section a certificate purporting to be signed by the governor or deputy governor of a prison or young offenders centre which specifies—

(a) the date on which a person was discharged from prison or a young offenders centre,

(b) the sentence or term which the person was serving at the time of his discharge, the offence in respect of which the sentence or term was imposed and the date on which he was convicted of that offence, and

(c) the date on which the person would, but for his discharge in pursuance of prison rules, have been discharged from prison or a young offenders centre, shall be evidence of the matters specified.

(7) In this section—

"prison rules" means rules made under section 13 of the Prison Act (Northern Ireland) 1953,

"sentence of imprisonment" does not include a committal in default of payment of any sum of money or for want of sufficient distress to satisfy any sum of money or for failure to do or abstain from doing anything required to be done or left undone, and

"young offenders centre" has the meaning assigned to it by section 2(a) of the Treatment of Offenders Act (Northern Ireland) 1968.

(8) For the purposes of subsection (1) consecutive terms of imprisonment or of detention in a young offenders centre shall be treated as

a single term and a sentence of imprisonment or detention in a young offenders centre includes—

    (a)   a sentence or term passed by a court in the United Kingdom or any of the Islands, and

    (b)   in the case of imprisonment, a sentence passed by a court-martial on a person found guilty of a civil offence within the meaning of the Army Act 1955, the Air Force Act 1955 and the Naval Discipline Act 1957.

(9)   The Secretary of State may by order substitute a different period for the period of one year mentioned in subsection (1).

(10)   This section applies irrespective of when the discharge from prison or a young offenders centre took place but only if—

    (a)   the scheduled offence is committed while this section is in force,

    (b)   the offence (being a scheduled offence within the meaning of the Northern Ireland (Emergency Provisions) Act 1996) was committed while section 16 of that Act was in force,

    (c)   the offence (being a scheduled offence within the meaning of the Northern Ireland (Emergency Provisions) Act 1991) was committed while section 15 of that Act was in force, or

    (d)   the offence (being a scheduled offence within the meaning of the Northern Ireland (Emergency Provisions) Act 1978) was committed while section 23 of the Prevention of Terrorism (Temporary Provisions) Act 1989 was in force.

Powers of Arrest, Search, &c

Arrest of Suspected Terrorists: Power of Entry

81. A constable may enter and search any premises if he reasonably suspects that a terrorist, within the meaning of section 40(1)(b), is to be found there.

Arrest and Seizure: Constables

82. (1)   A constable may arrest without warrant any person if he reasonably suspects that the person is committing, has committed or is about to commit—

    (a)   a scheduled offence, or

    (b)   a non-scheduled offence under this Act.

(2)   For the purpose of arresting a person under this section a constable may enter and search any premises where the person is or where the constable reasonably suspects him to be.

(3)   A constable may seize and retain anything if he reasonably suspects that it is, has been or is intended to be used in the commission of—

(a)   a scheduled offence, or

(b)   a non-scheduled offence under this Act.

Arrest and Seizure: Armed Forces

83. (1)   If a member of Her Majesty's forces on duty reasonably suspects that a person is committing, has committed or is about to commit any offence he may—

(a)   arrest the person without warrant, and

(b)   detain him for a period not exceeding four hours.

(2)   A person making an arrest under this section complies with any rule of law requiring him to state the ground of arrest if he states that he is making the arrest as a member of Her Majesty's forces.

(3)   For the purpose of arresting a person under this section a member of Her Majesty's forces may enter and search any premises where the person is.

(4)   If a member of Her Majesty's forces reasonably suspects that a person—

(a)   is a terrorist (within the meaning of Part V), or

(b)   has committed an offence involving the use or possession of an explosive or firearm,

he may enter and search any premises where he reasonably suspects the person to be for the purpose of arresting him under this section.

(5)   A member of Her Majesty's forces may seize, and detain for a period not exceeding four hours, anything which he reasonably suspects is being, has been or is intended to be used in the commission of an offence under section 93 or 94.

(6)   The reference to a rule of law in subsection (2) does not include a rule of law which has effect only by virtue of the Human Rights Act 1998.

Munitions and Transmitters

84. Schedule 10 (which confers power to search for munitions and transmitters) shall have effect.

Explosives Inspectors

85. (1)   An explosives inspector may enter and search any premises for the purpose of ascertaining whether any explosive is unlawfully there.

(2)   The power under subsection (1) may not be exercised in relation to a dwelling.

(3) An explosives inspector may stop any person in a public place and search him for the purpose of ascertaining whether he has any explosive unlawfully with him.

(4) An explosives inspector—

    (a) may seize any explosive found in the course of a search under this section unless it appears to him that it is being, has been and will be used only for a lawful purpose, and

    (b) may retain and, if necessary, destroy it.

(5) In this section "explosives inspector" means an inspector appointed under section 53 of the Explosives Act 1875.

Unlawfully Detained Persons

86. (1) If an officer reasonably believes that a person is unlawfully detained in such circumstances that his life is in danger, the officer may enter any premises for the purpose of ascertaining whether the person is detained there.

(2) In this section "officer" means—

    (a) a member of Her Majesty's forces on duty, or

    (b) a constable.

(3) A dwelling may be entered under subsection (1) only by—

    (a) a member of Her Majesty's forces authorised for the purpose by a commissioned officer of those forces, or

    (b) a constable authorised for the purpose by an officer of the Royal Ulster Constabulary of at least the rank of inspector.

Examination of Documents

87. (1) A member of Her Majesty's forces or a constable who performs a search under a provision of this Part—

    (a) may examine any document or record found in order to ascertain whether it contains information of the kind mentioned in section 58(1)(a) or 103(1)(a), and

    (b) if necessary or expedient for the purpose of paragraph (a), may remove the document or record to another place and retain it there until the examination is completed.

(2) Subsection (1) shall not permit a person to examine a document or record if he has reasonable cause to believe that it is an item subject to legal privilege (within the meaning of the Police and Criminal Evidence (Northern Ireland) Order 1989).

(3) Subject to subsections (4) and (5), a document or record may not be retained by virtue of subsection (1)(b) for more than 48 hours.

(4) An officer of the Royal Ulster Constabulary who is of at least the

rank of chief inspector may authorise a constable to retain a document or record for a further period or periods.

(5) Subsection (4) does not permit the retention of a document or record after the end of the period of 96 hours beginning with the time when it was removed for examination under subsection (1)(b).

(6) A person who wilfully obstructs a member of Her Majesty's forces or a constable in the exercise of a power conferred by this section commits an offence.

(7) A person guilty of an offence under subsection (6) shall be liable—

(a) on conviction on indictment, to imprisonment for a term not exceeding two years, to a fine or to both, or

(b) on summary conviction, to imprisonment for a term not exceeding six months, to a fine not exceeding the statutory maximum or to both.

Examination of Documents: Procedure

88. (1) Where a document or record is examined under section 87–

(a) it shall not be photographed or copied, and

(b) the person who examines it shall make a written record of the examination as soon as is reasonably practicable.

(2) The record shall—

(a) describe the document or record,

(b) specify the object of the examination,

(c) state the address of the premises where the document or record was found,

(d) where the document or record was found in the course of a search of a person, state the person's name,

(e) where the document or record was found in the course of a search of any premises, state the name of a person appearing to the person making the record to be the occupier of the premises or to have had custody or control of the document or record when it was found,

(f) where the document or record is removed for examination from the place where it was found, state the date and time when it was removed, and

(g) where the document or record was examined at the place where it was found, state the date and time of examination.

(3) The record shall identify the person by whom the examination was carried out—

(a) in the case of a constable, by reference to his police number, and

(b)   in the case of a member of Her Majesty's forces, by reference to his service number, rank and regiment.

(4)   Where a person makes a record of a search in accordance with this section, he shall as soon as is reasonably practicable supply a copy—

(a)   in a case where the document or record was found in the course of a search of a person, to that person, and

(b)   in a case where the document or record was found in the course of a search of any premises, to a person appearing to the person making the record to be the occupier of the premises or to have had custody or control of the document or record when it was found.

Power to Stop and Question

89. (1)   An officer may stop a person for so long as is necessary to question him to ascertain—

(a)   his identity and movements;

(b)   what he knows about a recent explosion or another recent incident endangering life;

(c)   what he knows about a person killed or injured in a recent explosion or incident.

(2)   A person commits an offence if he—

(a)   fails to stop when required to do so under this section,

(b)   refuses to answer a question addressed to him under this section, or

(c)   fails to answer to the best of his knowledge and ability a question addressed to him under this section.

(3)   A person guilty of an offence under this section shall be liable on summary conviction to a fine not exceeding level 5 on the standard scale.

(4)   In this section "officer" means—

(a)   a member of Her Majesty's forces on duty, or

(b)   a constable.

Power of Entry

90. (1)   An officer may enter any premises if he considers it necessary in the course of operations for the preservation of the peace or the maintenance of order.

(2)   In this section "officer" means—

(a)   a member of Her Majesty's forces on duty, or

(b)   a constable.

Taking Possession of Land, &c

91. If the Secretary of State considers it necessary for the preservation of the peace or the maintenance of order, he may authorise a person—
    (a) to take possession of land or other property;
    (b) to take steps to place buildings or other structures in a state of defence;
    (c) to detain property or cause it to be destroyed or moved;
    (d) to carry out works on land of which possession has been taken by virtue of this section;
    (e) to take any other action which interferes with a public right or with a private right of property.

Road Closure: Permission.

92. (1) If he considers it immediately necessary for the preservation of the peace or the maintenance of order, an officer may—
    (a) wholly or partly close a road;
    (b) divert or otherwise interfere with a road or the use of a road;
    (c) prohibit or restrict the exercise of a right of way;
    (d) prohibit or restrict the use of a waterway.
    (2) In this section "officer" means—
    (a) a member of Her Majesty's forces on duty,
    (b) a constable, or
    (c) a person authorised for the purposes of this section by the Secretary of State.

Sections 91 and 92: Supplementary

93. (1) A person commits an offence if he interferes with—
    (a) works executed in connection with the exercise of powers conferred by virtue of section 91 or 92, or
    (b) any apparatus, equipment or other thing used in connection with the exercise of those powers.
    (2) It is a defence for a person charged with an offence under this section to prove that he had a reasonable excuse for his interference.
    (3) A person guilty of an offence under this section shall be liable on summary conviction to—
    (a) imprisonment for a term not exceeding six months,
    (b) a fine not exceeding level 5 on the standard scale, or
    (c) both.
    (4) An authorisation to exercise powers under section 91 or 92 may authorise—

(a)   the exercise of all those powers, or

(b)   the exercise of a specified power or class of powers.

(5)   An authorisation to exercise powers under section 91 or 92 may be addressed—

(a)   to specified persons, or

(b)   to persons of a specified class.

Road Closure: Direction

94. (1)   If the Secretary of State considers it necessary for the preservation of the peace or the maintenance of order he may by order direct that a specified road—

(a)   shall be wholly closed,

(b)   shall be closed to a specified extent, or

(c)   shall be diverted in a specified manner.

(2)   A person commits an offence if he interferes with—

(a)   road closure works, or

(b)   road closure equipment.

(3)   A person commits an offence if—

(a)   he executes any bypass works within 200 metres of road closure works,

(b)   he has in his possession or under his control, within 200 metres of road closure works, materials or equipment suitable for executing bypass works, or

(c)   he knowingly permits on land occupied by him the doing or occurrence of anything which is an offence under paragraph (a) or (b).

(4)   It is a defence for a person charged with an offence under this section to prove that he had a reasonable excuse for his action, possession, control or permission.

(5)   A person guilty of an offence under this section shall be liable on summary conviction to—

(a)   imprisonment for a term not exceeding six months,

(b)   a fine not exceeding level 5 on the standard scale, or

(c)   both.

(6)   In this section—

"bypass works" means works which facilitate the bypassing by vehicles of road closure works,

"road closure equipment" means any apparatus, equipment or other thing used in pursuance of an order under this section in connection with the closure or diversion of a road, and "road closure works" means works executed in connection with the closure or diversion of a road specified in an order under this section (whether executed in pursuance of the order or in pursuance of power under an enactment to close or divert the road).

Sections 81 to 94: Supplementary

95. (1) This section applies in relation to sections 81 to 94.

   (2) A power to enter premises may be exercised by reasonable force if necessary.

   (3) A power to search premises shall, in its application to vehicles (by virtue of section 121), be taken to include—

   (a) power to stop a vehicle (other than an aircraft which is airborne), and

   (b) power to take a vehicle or cause it to be taken, where necessary or expedient, to any place for the purpose of carrying out the search.

   (4) A person commits an offence if he fails to stop a vehicle when required to do so by virtue of this section.

   (5) A person guilty of an offence under subsection (4) shall be liable on summary conviction to—

   (a) imprisonment for a term not exceeding six months,

   (b) a fine not exceeding level 5 on the standard scale, or

   (c) both.

   (6) In the application to a place or vehicle (by virtue of section 121) of a power to search premises—

   (a) a reference to the address of the premises shall be construed as a reference to the location of the place or vehicle together with its registration number (if any), and

   (b) a reference to the occupier of the premises shall be construed as a reference to the occupier of the place or the person in charge of the vehicle.

   (7) Where a search is carried out under Schedule 10 in relation to a vehicle (by virtue of section 121), the person carrying out the search may, if he reasonably believes that it is necessary in order to carry out the search or to prevent it from being frustrated—

   (a) require a person in or on the vehicle to remain with it;

   (b) require a person in or on the vehicle to go to and remain at any place to which the vehicle is taken by virtue of subsection (3)(b);

   (c) use reasonable force to secure compliance with a requirement under paragraph (a) or (b) above.

(8) Paragraphs 4(2) and (3), 8 and 9 of Schedule 10 shall apply to a requirement imposed under subsection (7) as they apply to a requirement imposed under that Schedule.

(9) Paragraph 8 of Schedule 10 shall apply in relation to the search of a vehicle which is not habitually stationary only if it is moved for the purpose of the search by virtue of subsection (3)(b); and where that paragraph does apply, the reference to the address of the premises shall be construed as a reference to the location where the vehicle is searched together with its registration number (if any).

(10) A member of Her Majesty's forces exercising any power when he is not in uniform shall, if requested to do so by any person at or about the time of exercising the power, produce to that person documentary evidence that he is a member of Her Majesty's Forces.

Miscellaneous

Preservation of the Peace: Regulations

96. (1) The Secretary of State may by regulations make provision for promoting the preservation of the peace and the maintenance of order.

(2) The regulations may authorise the Secretary of State to make orders or give directions for specified purposes.

(3) A person commits an offence if he contravenes or fails to comply with—

(a) regulations under this section, or

(b) an order or direction made or given under regulations made under this section.

(4) A person guilty of an offence under this section shall be liable on summary conviction to—

(a) imprisonment for a term not exceeding six months,

(b) a fine not exceeding level 5 on the standard scale, or

(c) both.

Port and Border Controls

97. (1) The Secretary of State may by order provide for members of Her Majesty's Forces to perform specified functions conferred on examining officers under Schedule 7.

(2) A member of Her Majesty's Forces exercising functions by virtue of subsection (1) shall be treated as an examining officer within the meaning of Schedule 7 for all purposes of this Act except for paragraphs 5 and 6 of Schedule 14.

(3) The Secretary of State may by order make provision, including provision supplementing or modifying Schedule 7, about entering or leaving Northern Ireland by land.

Independent Assessor of Military Complaints Procedures

98. (1)   The Secretary of State may appoint a person to be known as the Independent Assessor of Military Complaints Procedures in Northern Ireland.

(2)   A person may be appointed as the Independent Assessor only if—

(a)   he is not a serving member of Her Majesty's forces, and

(b)   he has not been a serving member at any time during the period of 20 years ending with the date of the appointment.

(3)   The Independent Assessor—

(a)   shall keep under review the procedures adopted by the General Officer Commanding Northern Ireland for receiving, investigating and responding to complaints to which this section applies,

(b)   shall receive and investigate any representations about those procedures,

(c)   may investigate the operation of those procedures in relation to a particular complaint or class of complaints,

(d)   may require the General Officer Commanding to review a particular case or class of cases in which the Independent Assessor considers that any of those procedures have operated inadequately, and

(e)   may make recommendations to the General Officer Commanding about inadequacies in those procedures, including inadequacies in the way in which they operate in relation to a particular complaint or class of complaints.

(4)   This section applies to complaints about the behaviour of a member of Her Majesty's forces under the command of the General Officer Commanding Northern Ireland, other than—

(a)   a complaint which is referred by the General Officer Commanding to the Royal Ulster Constabulary and which is not remitted by the Royal Ulster Constabulary to the General Officer Commanding to be dealt with by him,

(b)   a complaint about a matter in respect of which a claim for compensation has been made under Schedule 12, and

(c)   a complaint about a matter which is the subject of proceedings involving a claim for compensation which have been instituted in a court.

(5)   The General Officer Commanding Northern Ireland shall—

(a)   provide such information,

(b)   disclose such documents, and

(c)   provide such assistance, as the Independent Assessor may reasonably require for the purpose of the performance of his functions.

(6)   Schedule 11 (which makes supplementary provision about the Independent Assessor) shall have effect.

Police and Army Powers: Code of Practice

99. (1)   The Secretary of State may make codes of practice in connection with—

    (a)   the exercise by police officers of any power conferred by this Act, and

    (b)   the seizure and retention of property found by police officers when exercising powers of search conferred by any provision of this Act.

  (2)   The Secretary of State may make codes of practice in connection with the exercise by members of Her Majesty's forces of powers by virtue of this Part.

  (3)   In this section "police officer" means a member of the Royal Ulster Constabulary or the Royal Ulster Constabulary Reserve.

Video Recording: Code of Practice

100. (1)   The Secretary of State shall—

    (a)   make a code of practice about the silent video recording of interviews to which this section applies, and

    (b)   make an order requiring the silent video recording of interviews to which this section applies in accordance with the code.

  (2)   This section applies to—

    (a)   interviews by police officers of persons detained under section 41 if they take place in a police station (within the meaning of Schedule 8), and

    (b)   interviews held by police officers in such other circumstances as the Secretary of State may specify by order.

  (3)   In this section "police officer" means a member of the Royal Ulster Constabulary or the Royal Ulster Constabulary Reserve.

Codes of Practice: Supplementary

101. (1)   This section applies to a code of practice under section 99 or 100.

  (2)   Where the Secretary of State proposes to issue a code of practice he shall—

    (a)   publish a draft,

    (b)   consider any representations made to him about the draft, and

    (c)   if he thinks it appropriate, modify the draft in the light of any representations made to him.

(3) The Secretary of State shall lay a draft of the code before Parliament.

(4) When the Secretary of State has laid a draft code before Parliament he may bring it into operation by order.

(5) The Secretary of State may revise the whole or any part of a code of practice issued by him and issue the code as revised; and subsections (2) to (4) shall apply to such a revised code as they apply to an original code.

(6) A failure by a police officer to comply with a provision of a code shall not of itself make him liable to criminal or civil proceedings.

(7) A failure by a member of Her Majesty's forces to comply with a provision of a code shall not of itself make him liable to any criminal or civil proceedings other than—

    (a)   proceedings under any provision of the Army Act 1955 or the Air Force Act 1955 other than section 70 (civil offences), and

    (b)   proceedings under any provision of the Naval Discipline Act 1957 other than section 42 (civil offences).

(8) A code—

    (a)   shall be admissible in evidence in criminal or civil proceedings, and

    (b)   shall be taken into account by a court or tribunal in any case in which it appears to the court or tribunal to be relevant.

(9) In this section—

"criminal proceedings" includes proceedings in Northern Ireland before a court-martial constituted under the Army Act 1955, the Air Force Act 1955 or the Naval Discipline Act 1957 or a disciplinary court constituted under section 50 of the 1957 Act and proceedings in Northern Ireland before the Courts-Martial Appeal Court, and

"police officer" means a member of the Royal Ulster Constabulary or the Royal Ulster Constabulary Reserve.

Compensation

102. Schedule 12 (which provides for compensation to be paid for certain action taken under this Part) shall have effect.

Terrorist Information

103. (1) A person commits an offence if—

    (a)   he collects, makes a record of, publishes, communicates or attempts to elicit information about a person to whom this section applies which is of a kind likely to be useful to a person committing or preparing an act of terrorism, or

    (b)   he possesses a document or record containing information of that kind.

(2) This section applies to a person who is or has been—

    (a)   a constable,

    (b)   a member of Her Majesty's Forces,

    (c)   the holder of a judicial office,

    (d)   an officer of any court, or

    (e)   a full-time employee of the prison service in Northern Ireland.

(3) In this section "record" includes a photographic or electronic record.

(4) If it is proved in proceedings for an offence under subsection (1)(b) that a document or record—

    (a)   was on any premises at the same time as the accused, or

    (b)   was on premises of which the accused was the occupier or which he habitually used otherwise than as a member of the public, the court may assume that the accused possessed the document or record, unless he proves that he did not know of its presence on the premises or that he had no control over it.

(5) It is a defence for a person charged with an offence under this section to prove that he had a reasonable excuse for his action or possession.

(6) A person guilty of an offence under this section shall be liable—

    (a)   on conviction on indictment, to imprisonment for a term not exceeding 10 years, to a fine or to both, or

    (b)   on summary conviction, to imprisonment for a term not exceeding six months, to a fine not exceeding the statutory maximum or to both.

(7) A court by or before which a person is convicted of an offence under this section may order the forfeiture of any document or record containing information of the kind mentioned in subsection (1)(a).

(8) Before making an order under subsection (7) a court must give an opportunity to be heard to any person, other than the convicted person, who claims to be the owner of or otherwise interested in anything which can be forfeited under that subsection.

(9) An order under subsection (8) shall not come into force until there is no further possibility of it being varied, or set aside, on appeal (disregarding any power of a court to grant leave to appeal out of time).

Police Powers: Records

104. The Chief Constable of the Royal Ulster Constabulary shall make arrangements for securing that a record is made of each exercise by a constable of a power under this Part in so far as—

(a)   it is reasonably practicable to do so, and

(b)   a record is not required to be made under another enactment.

Powers

105. A power conferred on a person by virtue of this Part—

(a)   is additional to powers which he has at common law or by virtue of any other enactment, and

(b)   shall not be taken to affect those powers or Her Majesty's prerogative.

Private Security Services

106. Schedule 13 (private security services) shall have effect.

Specified Organisations

Specified Organisations: Interpretation

107. For the purposes of sections 108 to 111 an organisation is specified at a particular time if at that time—

(a)   it is specified under section 3(8) of the Northern Ireland (Sentences) Act 1998, and

(b)   it is, or forms part of, an organisation which is proscribed for the purposes of this Act.

Evidence

108. (1) This section applies where a person is charged with an offence under section 11.

(2) Subsection (3) applies where a police officer of at least the rank of superintendent states in oral evidence that in his opinion the accused—

(a)   belongs to an organisation which is specified, or

(b)   belonged to an organisation at a time when it was specified.

(3) Where this subsection applies—

(a)   the statement shall be admissible as evidence of the matter stated, but

(b)   the accused shall not be committed for trial, be found to have a case to answer or be convicted solely on the basis of the statement.

(4) In this section "police officer" means a member of—

(a)   a police force within the meaning of the Police Act 1996 or the Police (Scotland) Act 1967, or

(b)   the Royal Ulster Constabulary.

Inferences

109. (1) This section applies where a person is charged with an offence under section 11.

(2) Subsection (4) applies where evidence is given that—

    (a) at any time before being charged with the offence the accused, on being questioned under caution by a constable, failed to mention a fact which is material to the offence and which he could reasonably be expected to mention, and

    (b) before being questioned the accused was permitted to consult a solicitor.

(3) Subsection (4) also applies where evidence is given that—

    (a) on being charged with the offence or informed by a constable that he might be prosecuted for it the accused failed to mention a fact which is material to the offence and which he could reasonably be expected to mention, and

    (b) before being charged or informed the accused was permitted to consult a solicitor.

(4) Where this subsection applies—

    (a) the court, in considering any question whether the accused belongs or belonged at a particular time to a specified organisation, may draw from the failure inferences relating to that question, but

    (b) the accused shall not be committed for trial, be found to have a case to answer or be convicted solely on the basis of the inferences.

(5) Subject to any directions by the court, evidence tending to establish the failure may be given before or after evidence tending to establish the fact which the accused is alleged to have failed to mention.

Sections 108 and 109: Supplementary

110. (1) Nothing in section 108 or 109 shall—

    (a) prejudice the admissibility of evidence admissible apart from that section,

    (b) preclude the drawing of inferences which could be drawn apart from that section, or

    (c) prejudice an enactment providing (in whatever words) that an answer or evidence given by a person in specified circumstances is not admissible in evidence against him or some other person in any proceedings or class of proceedings (however described, and whether civil or criminal).

(2) In subsection (1)(c) the reference to giving evidence is a reference to giving it in any manner (whether by giving information, making discovery, producing documents or otherwise).

Forfeiture Orders

111. (1) This section applies if—

    (a) a person is convicted of an offence under section 11 or 12, and

    (b) at the time of the offence he belonged to an organisation which was a specified organisation.

  (2) The court by or before which the person is convicted may order the forfeiture of any money or other property if—

    (a) he had it in his possession or under his control at the time of the offence, and

    (b) it has been used in connection with the activities of the specified organisation or the court believes that it may be used in that connection unless it is forfeited.

  (3) Before making an order under this section the court must give an opportunity to be heard to any person, other than the convicted person, who claims to be the owner of or otherwise interested in anything which can be forfeited under this section.

  (4) A question arising as to whether subsection (1)(b) or (2)(a) or (b) is satisfied shall be determined on the balance of probabilities.

  (5) Schedule 4 shall apply (with the necessary modifications) in relation to orders under this section as it applies in relation to orders made under section 23.

Duration of Part VII

Expiry and Revival

112. (1) This Part shall (subject to subsection (2)) cease to have effect at the end of the period of one year beginning with the day on which it is brought into force.

  (2) The Secretary of State may by order provide—

    (a) that a provision of this Part which is in force (whether or not by virtue of this subsection) shall continue in force for a specified period not exceeding twelve months;

    (b) that a provision of this Part shall cease to have effect;

    (c) that a provision of this Part which is not in force (whether or not by virtue of this subsection) shall come into force and remain in force for a specified period not exceeding twelve months.

  (3) An order under subsection (2) may make provision with respect to a provision of this Part—

    (a) generally,

(b) only in so far as it concerns powers of members of Her Majesty's Forces, or

(c) except in so far as it concerns powers of members of Her Majesty's Forces.

(4) This Part shall, by virtue of this subsection, cease to have effect at the end of the period of five years beginning with the day on which it is brought into force.

(5) The following provisions shall be treated for the purposes of this section as forming part of this Part of this Act—

(a) paragraphs 36 and 37 of Schedule 4, and

(b) paragraphs 19 to 21 of Schedule 5.

Transitional Provisions

113. (1) Where a provision of sections 74 to 77 comes into force by virtue of an order under section 112(2), that shall not affect a trial on indictment where the indictment has been presented before the provision comes into force.

(2) Where a provision of sections 74 to 77 ceases to have effect (whether or not by virtue of an order under section 112(2)), that shall not affect the application of the provision to a trial on indictment where the indictment has been presented before the provision ceases to have effect.

(3) If when section 74(1) comes into force by virtue of an order under section 112(2) a person has been committed for trial for a scheduled offence and the indictment has not been presented, then on the coming into force of section 74(1) he shall, if he was committed to the Crown Court sitting elsewhere than in Belfast, be treated as having been committed—

(a) to the Crown Court sitting in Belfast, or

(b) where a direction is given under section 74(1) which affects the trial, to the Crown Court sitting at the place specified in the direction.

(4) Where section 74 ceases to have effect (whether or not by virtue of an order under section 112(2)), that shall not affect—

(a) the committal of a person for trial in accordance with that provision to the Crown Court sitting either in Belfast or elsewhere, or

(b) the committal of a person for trial which, in accordance with that provision, has taken effect as a committal for trial to the Crown Court sitting elsewhere than in Belfast, in a case where the indictment has not been presented.

(5) Where section 79 or 80 ceases to have effect (whether or not by virtue of an order under section 112(2)), that shall not affect the operation of the section in relation to an offence committed while it, or a corresponding earlier enactment, was in force.

(6) Sections 108 and 109 shall not apply to a statement made or failure occurring before 4th September 1998.

(7) Where section 108 or 109 comes into force by virtue of an order under section 112(2) it shall not apply to a statement made or failure occurring while the section was not in force.

(8) Section 111 applies where an offence is committed on or after 4th September 1998; and for this purpose an offence committed over a period of more than one day or at some time during a period of more than one day shall be taken to be committed on the last of the days in the period.

(9) Paragraph 19 of Schedule 9 shall have effect only in relation to an offence alleged to have been committed after the coming into force of that Schedule.

Part VIII
General

Police Powers

114. (1) A power conferred by virtue of this Act on a constable—
   (a) is additional to powers which he has at common law or by virtue of any other enactment, and
   (b) shall not be taken to affect those powers.

(2) A constable may if necessary use reasonable force for the purpose of exercising a power conferred on him by virtue of this Act (apart from paragraphs 2 and 3 of Schedule 7).

(3) Where anything is seized by a constable under a power conferred by virtue of this Act, it may (unless the contrary intention appears) be retained for so long as is necessary in all the circumstances.

Officers' Powers

115. Schedule 14 (which makes provision about the exercise of functions by authorised officers for the purposes of sections 25 to 31 and examining officers for the purposes of Schedule 7) shall have effect.

Powers to Stop and Search.

116. (1) A power to search premises conferred by virtue of this Act shall be taken to include power to search a container.

(2) A power conferred by virtue of this Act to stop a person includes power to stop a vehicle (other than an aircraft which is airborne).

(3) A person commits an offence if he fails to stop a vehicle when required to do so by virtue of this section.

(4) A person guilty of an offence under subsection (3) shall be liable on summary conviction to—

    (a) imprisonment for a term not exceeding six months,

    (b) a fine not exceeding level 5 on the standard scale, or

    (c) both.

Consent to Prosecution

117. (1) This section applies to an offence under any provision of this Act other than an offence under—

    (a) section 36,

    (b) section 51,

    (c) paragraph 18 of Schedule 7,

    (d) paragraph 12 of Schedule 12, or

    (e) Schedule 13.

(2) Proceedings for an offence to which this section applies—

    (a) shall not be instituted in England and Wales without the consent of the Director of Public Prosecutions, and

    (b) shall not be instituted in Northern Ireland without the consent of the Director of Public Prosecutions for Northern Ireland.

(3) Where it appears to the Director of Public Prosecutions or the Director of Public Prosecutions for Northern Ireland that an offence to which this section applies is committed for a purpose connected with the affairs of a country other than the United Kingdom—

    (a) subsection (2) shall not apply, and

    (b) proceedings for the offence shall not be instituted without the consent of the Attorney General or the Attorney General for Northern Ireland.

Defences

118. (1) Subsection (2) applies where in accordance with a provision mentioned in subsection (5) it is a defence for a person charged with an offence to prove a particular matter.

(2) If the person adduces evidence which is sufficient to raise an issue with respect to the matter the court or jury shall assume that the defence is satisfied unless the prosecution proves beyond reasonable doubt that it is not.

(3) Subsection (4) applies where in accordance with a provision mentioned in subsection (5) a court—

    (a)   may make an assumption in relation to a person charged with an offence unless a particular matter is proved, or

    (b)   may accept a fact as sufficient evidence unless a particular matter is proved.

(4) If evidence is adduced which is sufficient to raise an issue with respect to the matter mentioned in subsection (3)(a) or (b) the court shall treat it as proved unless the prosecution disproves it beyond reasonable doubt.

(5) The provisions in respect of which subsections (2) and (4) apply are—

    (a)   sections 12(4), 39(5)(a), 54, 57, 58, 77 and 103 of this Act, and

    (b)   sections 13, 32 and 33 of the Northern Ireland (Emergency Provisions) Act 1996 (possession and information offences) as they have effect by virtue of Schedule 1 to this Act.

Crown Servants, Regulators, &c

119. (1) The Secretary of State may make regulations providing for any of sections 15 to 23 and 39 to apply to persons in the public service of the Crown.

    (2) The Secretary of State may make regulations providing for section 19 not to apply to persons who are in his opinion performing or connected with the performance of regulatory, supervisory, investigative or registration functions of a public nature.

    (3) Regulations—

    (a)   may make different provision for different purposes,

    (b)   may make provision which is to apply only in specified circumstances, and

    (c)   may make provision which applies only to particular persons or to persons of a particular description.

Evidence

120. (1) A document which purports to be—

    (a)   a notice or direction given or order made by the Secretary of State for the purposes of a provision of this Act, and

(b)   signed by him or on his behalf, hall be received in evidence and shall, until the contrary is proved, be deemed to have been given or made by the Secretary of State.

(2) A document bearing a certificate which—

    (a)   purports to be signed by or on behalf of the Secretary of State, and

    (b)   states that the document is a true copy of a notice or direction given or order made by the Secretary of State for the purposes of a provision of this Act, shall be evidence (or, in Scotland, sufficient evidence) of the document in legal proceedings.

(3) In subsections (1) and (2) a reference to an order does not include a reference to an order made by statutory instrument.

(4) The Documentary Evidence Act 1868 shall apply to an authorisation given in writing by the Secretary of State for the purposes of this Act as it applies to an order made by him.

Interpretation

121. In this Act—

"act" and "action" include omission,

"article" includes substance and any other thing,

"customs officer" means an officer commissioned by the Commissioners of Customs and Excise under section 6(3) of the Customs and Excise Management Act 1979,

"dwelling" means a building or part of a building used as a dwelling, and a vehicle which is habitually stationary and which is used as a dwelling,

"explosive" means—

    (a)   an article or substance manufactured for the purpose of producing a practical effect by explosion,

    (b)   materials for making an article or substance within paragraph (a),

    (c)   anything used or intended to be used for causing or assisting in causing an explosion, and

    (d)   a part of anything within paragraph (a) or (c),

"firearm" includes an air gun or air pistol,

"immigration officer" means a person appointed as an immigration officer under paragraph 1 of Schedule 2 to the Immigration Act 1971,

"the Islands" means the Channel Islands and the Isle of Man, "organisation" includes any association or combination of persons,

"premises" includes any place and in particular includes—

(a)   a vehicle,

(b)   an offshore installation within the meaning given in section 44 of the Petroleum Act 1998, and

(c)   a tent or moveable structure,

"property" includes property wherever situated and whether real or personal, heritable or moveable, and things in action and other intangible or incorporeal property,

"public place" means a place to which members of the public have or are permitted to have access, whether or not for payment,

"road" has the same meaning as in the Road Traffic Act 1988 (in relation to England and Wales), the Roads (Scotland) Act 1984 (in relation to Scotland) and the Road Traffic Regulation (Northern Ireland) Order 1997 (in relation to Northern Ireland), and includes part of a road, and

"vehicle," except in sections 48 to 52 and Schedule 7, includes an aircraft, hovercraft, train or vessel.

Index of Defined Expressions

122. In this Act the expressions listed below are defined by the provisions specified.

Expression
Interpretation provision

Act
Section 121

Action
Section 121

Action taken for the purposes of terrorism
Section 1(5)

Article
Section 121

Authorised officer
Section 24(1)

Cash
Section 24(2)

Cordoned area
Section 33

Customs officer
Section 121

Dwelling
Section 121

Examining officer
Schedule 7, paragraph 1

Explosive
Section 121

Firearm
Section 121

Immigration officer
Section 121

The Islands
Section 121

Organisation
Section 121

Premises
Section 121

Property
Section 121

Proscribed organisation
Section 3(1)

Public place
Section 121

Road
Section 121

Scheduled offence (in Part VII)
Section 65

Terrorism
Section 1

Terrorist (in Part V)
Section 40

Terrorist investigation
Section 32

Terrorist property
Section 14

Vehicle
Section 121

Vehicle (in sections 48 to 51)
Section 52

Orders and Regulations

123. (1) An order or regulations made by the Secretary of State under this Act—
    (a)   shall be made by statutory instrument,
    (b)   may contain savings and transitional provisions, and
    (c)   may make different provision for different purposes.
   (2) Subject to subsection (3), an order or regulations under any of the following provisions shall be subject to annulment in pursuance of a resolution of either House of Parliament—
    (a)   section 4(3);
    (b)   section 24(2)(e);
    (c)   section 72;
    (d)   section 79(5);
    (e)   section 80(9);
    (f)   section 97(1) or (3);
    (g)   section 100(1)(b);
    (h)   section 119(1) or (2);
    (i)   paragraph 52(1)(a) or (b) of Schedule 4;
    (j)   paragraph 17(4) of Schedule 7;
    (k)   paragraph 3(1)(b) of Schedule 8;
    (l)   paragraph 19 of Schedule 8.
   (3) In the cases of—
    (a)   the first order to be made under paragraph 17(4) of Schedule 7, and
    (b)   the first order to be made under paragraph 19 of Schedule 8, the order shall not be made unless a draft has been laid before and approved by resolution of each House of Parliament (and subsection (2)(j) or (l) shall not apply).
   (4) An order or regulations under any of the following provisions shall not be made, subject to subsection (5), unless a draft has been laid before and approved by resolution of each House of Parliament—

(a)   section 3(3);
(b)   section 53(2);
(c)   section 65(3);
(d)   section 96;
(e)   section 101(4);
(f)   section 112(2);
(g)   paragraph 2(2) of Schedule 1;
(h)   paragraph 6(2) or 7(3) of Schedule 6;
(i)   paragraph 16 of Schedule 7;
(j)   paragraph 3(2) of Schedule 8;
(k)   paragraph 4(4) of Schedule 8;
(l)   paragraph 4(1)(e) of Schedule 14;
(m)   paragraph 7(3) of Schedule 14.

(5) An order or regulations under a provision mentioned in subsection (4), except for paragraph (b), may be made without a draft having been approved if the Secretary of State is of the opinion that it is necessary by reason of urgency; and the order—

(a)   shall contain a declaration of the Secretary of State's opinion, and

(b)   shall cease to have effect at the end of the period of 40 days beginning with the day on which the Secretary of State makes the order, unless a resolution approving the order is passed by each House during that period.

(6) For the purposes of subsection (5)—

(a)   a code of practice or revised code to which an order relates shall cease to have effect together with the order,

(b)   an order's ceasing to have effect shall be without prejudice to anything previously done or to the making of a new order (or the issue of a new code), and

(c)   the period of 40 days shall be computed in accordance with section 7(1) of the Statutory Instruments Act 1946.

(7) An order under paragraph 8(3) of Schedule 13 shall be laid before Parliament.

(8) Subsection (1)(a) does not apply to an order made—

(a)   under section 94,

(b)   by virtue of paragraph 36 of Schedule 4, or

(c)   under or by virtue of any of paragraphs 19 to 21 of Schedule 5.

(9) Subsections (1)(a) and (4)(d) do not apply to an order made under regulations made under section 96.

Directions

124. A direction given under this Act may be varied or revoked by a further direction.

Amendments and Repeals

125. (1) Schedule 15 (consequential amendments) shall have effect.
  (2) The enactments listed in Schedule 16 are hereby repealed or revoked to the extent specified.

Report to Parliamentt

126. The Secretary of State shall lay before both Houses of Parliament at least once in every 12 months a report on the working of this Act.

Money

127. The following shall be paid out of money provided by Parliament—
  (a) any expenditure of a Minister of the Crown under or by virtue of this Act, and
  (b) any increase in the sums payable out of money provided by Parliament under any other enactment.

Commencement

128. The preceding provisions of this Act, apart from sections 2(1)(b) and (2) and 118 and Schedule 1, shall come into force in accordance with provision made by the Secretary of State by order.

Transitional Provisions

129. (1) Where, immediately before the coming into force of section 2(1)(a), a person is being detained by virtue of a provision of the Prevention of Terrorism (Temporary Provisions) Act 1989–
  (a) the provisions of that Act shall continue to apply to him, in place of the corresponding provisions of this Act, until his detention comes to an end, and
  (b) nothing in paragraph 5 or 8 of Schedule 15 shall have effect in relation to him during his detention.
  (2) Where—
  (a) a person is detained by virtue of a provision of the Northern Ireland (Emergency Provisions) Act 1996 (as continued in force by virtue of Schedule 1 to this Act), and

(b)   the provision ceases to have effect, he shall be treated as lawfully detained under any corresponding provision of this Act.

(3) Where this Act repeals and re-enacts a provision of—

    (a)   the Prevention of Terrorism (Temporary Provisions) Act 1989, or

    (b)   the Northern Ireland (Emergency Provisions) Act 1996, the repeal and re-enactment shall not, unless the contrary intention appears, affect the continuity of the law.

(4) A reference in this Act or any other enactment or instrument to a provision of this Act shall (so far as the context permits) be taken to include a reference to a corresponding provision repealed by this Act.

(5) The repeal by virtue of this Act of section 14 of the Northern Ireland (Emergency Provisions) Act 1996 (young persons convicted of scheduled offences) shall not affect its operation in relation to offences committed while it was in force.

(6) Any document made, served or issued after the commencement of paragraph (a) or (b) of section 2(1) which contains a reference to an enactment repealed by that paragraph shall, so far as the context permits, be construed as referring to or (as the context may require) including a reference to the corresponding provision of this Act.

(7) Any document made, served or issued after the commencement of this Act which contains a reference to a provision of this Act shall, so far as the context permits, be construed as referring to or (as the context may require) including a reference to the corresponding provision of—

    (a)   the Prevention of Terrorism (Temporary Provisions) Act 1989, or

    (b)   the Northern Ireland (Emergency Provisions) Act 1996.

(8) Section 117 shall apply to the institution of proceedings after commencement of that section whether the offence to which the proceedings relate (which may, by virtue of subsection (4) above, be an offence under a provision repealed by this Act) is alleged to have been committed before or after commencement of that section.

Extent

130. (1) Subject to subsections (2) to (6), this Act extends to the whole of the United Kingdom.

(2) Section 59 shall extend to England and Wales only.

(3) The following shall extend to Northern Ireland only—

    (a)   section 60, and

    (b)   Part VII.

(4) Section 61 shall extend to Scotland only.

(5) In Schedule 5–

    (a)   Part I shall extend to England and Wales and Northern Ireland only, and

    (b)   Part II shall extend to Scotland only.

(6) The amendments and repeals in Schedules 15 and 16 shall have the same extent as the enactments to which they relate.

Short Title

131. This Act may be cited as the Terrorism Act 2000.

DOCUMENT NO 3

Terrorism Act 2000 Explanatory Notes

Introduction

1. These explanatory notes relate to the Terrorism Act 2000, which received Royal Assent on 20 July 2000. They have been prepared by the Home Office and the Northern Ireland Office in order to assist the reader in understanding the Act. They do not form part of the Act and have not been endorsed by Parliament.

2. The notes need to be read in conjunction with the Act. They are not, and are not meant to be, a comprehensive description of the Act. So where a section or part of a section does not seem to require any explanation or comment none is given.

Summary

3. The Act reforms and extends previous counter-terrorist legislation, and puts it largely on a permanent basis. The previous legislation concerned is:

    *   the Prevention of Terrorism (Temporary Provisions) Act 1989 (c. 4) ("the PTA");
    *   the Northern Ireland (Emergency Provisions) Act 1996 (c. 22) ("the EPA"); and
    *   sections 1 to 4 of the Criminal Justice (Terrorism and Conspiracy) Act 1998 (c. 40).

4. The Act builds on the proposals in the Government's consultation document *Legislation against terrorism* (Cm 4178), published in December 1998. The consultation document in turn responded to Lord Lloyd of Berwick's *Inquiry into legislation against terrorism* (Cm 3420), published in October 1996.

5. Previous counter-terrorist legislation provided a range of measures designed to prevent terrorism and support the investigation of terrorist crime. These fall into three broad categories: a power for the Secretary of State to proscribe terrorist organisations, backed up by a series of offences connected with such organisations (membership, fundraising etc); other specific offences connected with terrorism (such as fund-raising for terrorist purposes, training in the use of firearms for terrorist purposes, etc); and a range of police powers (powers of investigation, arrest, stop and search, detention, etc).

6. The Act repeals the PTA and re-enacts those of its provisions which remain necessary, with a number of modifications. The previous counter-terrorist legislation was subject to annual renewal by Parliament. Under the Act this will in general no longer be the case. The main provisions in the Act are to be permanent. There will, however, continue to be an annual report to Parliament on the working of the Act; this is required under section 126.

7. The EPA would have repealed itself on 24 August 2000. The consultation document expressed the Government's hope that the special provision it makes for Northern Ireland might not be needed after that date, an objective to be kept under review in the light of developments in the security situation. The Government takes the view that the time is not yet right to remove all of these provisions. Part VII of the Act therefore provides additional temporary measures for Northern Ireland only. These are subject to annual renewal and are time-limited to 5 years.

8. The previous counter-terrorist legislation was originally designed in response to terrorism connected with the affairs of Northern Ireland ("Irish terrorism"), and some of its provisions had subsequently been extended to certain categories of international terrorism. It did not apply to any other terrorism connected with UK affairs ("domestic terrorism"). Under the Act these restrictions have been lifted, so that counter-terrorist measures are to be applicable to all forms of terrorism: Irish, international, and domestic.

Overview

9. The Act's Parts and Schedules are as follows.
    *   Part I (Introductory) sets out the definition of terrorism for the purposes of the Act, repeals the PTA and, with Schedule 1, deals with the continuation of certain temporary provisions of the EPA until Part VII of the Act is brought into force.
    *   Part II (Proscribed organisations) provides a power for the Secretary of State to proscribe organisations and sets out the associated offences. Schedule 2 lists the organisations which are currently proscribed and Schedule 3 details the functions of the Proscribed Organisations Appeal Commission (POAC) which the Act sets up.
    *   Part III (Terrorist property) provides offences relating to fund-raising and other kinds of financial support for terrorism, together with power for a court to order forfeiture of any money or other property connected with the offences. Schedule 4 gives details of forfeiture procedures.
    *   Part IV (Terrorist investigations) provides the police with a power to set up cordons. Schedule 5 sets out further powers to investigate ter-

rorism by searching premises and seeking explanation of items found; and Schedule 6 provides a power to investigate terrorist finance based on an existing Northern Ireland power to investigate proceeds of crime.

- Part V (Counter-terrorist powers) provides the police with powers to arrest and detain suspected terrorists, and broader powers to stop and search vehicles and pedestrians, and to impose parking restrictions. Schedule 7 provides examination powers at ports and borders; and Schedule 8 provides for the treatment of suspects who are detained and for judicial extension of the initial period of detention.
- Part VI (Miscellaneous) provides ancillary offences of
- weapons training for terrorist purposes, including recruitment for such training,
- directing a terrorist organisation,
- possessing articles for terrorist purposes,
- possessing information for terrorist purposes, and
- incitement of overseas terrorism.

Part VI also includes provisions on extraterritorial jurisdiction and extradition which will enable the UK to ratify the UN Conventions for the Suppression of Terrorist Bombings and for the Suppression of the Financing of Terrorism.

- Part VII (Northern Ireland) provides for the system of non-jury trials in Northern Ireland for the offences listed in Schedule 9. Together with Schedules 10–13, this Part also provides additional police and Army powers for Northern Ireland, and regulates the private security industry in Northern Ireland.
- Part VIII (General) contains further technical provisions and includes a list of terms defined in the Act. Schedule 14 provides general powers for police, customs and immigration officers including powers for them to exchange information. Schedules 15 and 16 list consequential amendments and repeals.

Commentary
Part I: Introductory

Section 1: Terrorism: Interpretation

10. Under the PTA, terrorism "means the use of violence for political ends, and includes any use of violence for the purpose of putting the public or any section of the public in fear" (section 20). The definition in the PTA is limited in that the powers and offences in that Act only apply to terrorism connected with the affairs of Northern Ireland ("Irish terrorism")

or Irish and international terrorism. The Act, as suggested in the consultation document, adopts a wider definition, recognising that terrorism may have religious or ideological as well as political motivation, and covering actions which might not be violent in themselves but which can, in a modern society, have a devastating impact. These could include interfering with the supply of water or power where life, health or safety may be put at risk. *Subsection (2)(e)* covers the disrupting of key computer systems. *Subsection (3)* provides that where action involves firearms or explosives, it does not have to be designed to influence the government or to intimidate the public or a section of the public to be included in the definition. This is to ensure that, for instance, the assassination of key individuals is covered.

11. *Subsection (4)* provides for the definition to cover terrorism not only within the United Kingdom but throughout the world. This is implicit in the PTA definition but the Act makes it explicit.

Section 2: Temporary Legislation

12. *Subsection (1)* repeals the PTA and EPA. *Subsection (2)*, together with Schedule 1, preserves certain provisions of the EPA, in some cases with amendment, until the date on which Part VII (Northern Ireland) of the Act is brought into force: see further notes on Schedule 1 below.

Part II: Proscribed Organisations

13. Part II is based on Part I of the PTA (which has effect in Great Britain only) and on sections 30–31 of the EPA (which have effect in Northern Ireland only). The proscription regime under the Act differs from those it replaces as follows:

- The PTA and EPA provide separate proscription regimes for Great Britain and Northern Ireland. Under the Act proscription will no longer be specific to Northern Ireland or Great Britain, but will apply throughout the whole of the UK.
- Under the PTA and EPA proscription is only applicable to organisations concerned in Irish terrorism. Under the Act it will also be possible to proscribe organisations concerned in international or domestic terrorism.
- Under the PTA and EPA an organisation or an affected individual wishing to challenge a proscription can only do so in the UK via judicial review (no proscribed organisation has ever done this). Under the Act, organisations and individuals will be able to apply to the Secretary of State for deproscription and, if their application is refused, to appeal to the Proscribed Organisations Appeal Commission ("POAC"; see below).

Section 3: Proscription

14. Schedule 2 lists all organisations proscribed under the PTA and the EPA at the time the Act received Royal Assent. Some organisations were at that point proscribed in Northern Ireland under the EPA but not in Great Britain under the PTA. Under the Act, any organisation deemed to merit proscription will be proscribed throughout the whole of the UK. The Government is considering which organisations involved in international terrorism might be added to the Schedule.

15. The power to proscribe and deproscribe in *subsection (3)*, including deproscription following a successful appeal, will be subject to the affirmative resolution procedure.

Sections 4–6: Deproscription: Application and Appeals

16. These sections set out the route by which an organisation which thinks it should not be proscribed, or an affected individual, may seek a remedy. The first step is to ask the Secretary of State to deproscribe; the Secretary of State will be obliged to consider such applications within a period of time specified in regulations to be made under *subsection (3)* of section 4. If the Secretary of State refuses to deproscribe, then the organisation or individual may appeal to POAC as set out in section 5 and Schedule 3.

17. The grounds on which POAC will allow an appeal are set out in *subsection (3)* of section 5. The reference to "the principles applicable on an application for judicial review" allows that once the Human Rights Act 1998 (c. 42) is fully in force, it will be possible for an appellant to raise points concerning those rights under the European Convention on Human Rights which are "Convention rights" under the 1998 Act.

18. *Subsections (4)–(5)* of section 5 deal with the consequences of an appeal to POAC being successful. Where POAC makes an order, this has the effect of requiring the Secretary of State either to lay a draft deproscription order before Parliament or to make a deproscription order on the basis of the urgency procedure (see below).

19. Section 6 allows a further appeal from a decision of POAC on a question of law.

Sections 7–8: Appeal: Effect on Conviction

20. If an appeal to POAC is successful, and an order has been made deproscribing the organisation, anyone convicted of one of the offences listed in *subsection (1)(c)* in respect of the organisation, so long as the offence was committed after the date of the refusal to deproscribe, may, in England and Wales, appeal against his conviction to the Court of Appeal or Crown

Court, and the Court will allow the appeal. *Subsection (8)* ensures that he can seek compensation for the conviction. Corresponding provision is made for Scotland and Northern Ireland.

Section 9: Human Rights Act 1998

21. Since it is intended that the Lord Chancellor will make rules under section 7(2) of the Human Rights Act so that proceedings under section 7(1)(a) of that Act may be brought before POAC, this section of the Act applies provisions in the Act relating to appeals to POAC to such proceedings under the Human Rights Act.

Section 10: Immunity

22. An individual who seeks deproscription by way of application or appeal, either on behalf of the proscribed organisation or as a person affected, might be discouraged from pursuing either course, or from instituting proceedings under section 7 of the Human Rights Act, by the risk of prosecution for certain offences, for example the offence of membership of a proscribed organisation. This section therefore ensures that evidence of anything done, and any document submitted for these proceedings, cannot be relied on in criminal proceedings for such an offence except as part of the defence case.

Sections 11–12: Membership and Support

23. These offences are based on those in section 2 of the PTA and section 30 of the EPA, and have similar effect. The offence in section 12(1) is not confined to support by providing "money or other property," because that kind of support is dealt with in Part III of the Act. *Subsection (4)* of section 12 is intended to permit the arranging of genuinely benign meetings.

Section 13: Uniform

24. This section replicates the offence at section 3 of the PTA and section 31 of the EPA. The PTA version, which has effect in England and Wales and in Scotland, is summary only with a maximum custodial penalty of 6 months. The EPA version, which has effect in Northern Ireland is an either way offence with a maximum custodial penalty on indictment of 1 year. In the Act, the offence is summary only, as in the PTA. Thus in consolidating the legislation the Act aligns the situation in Northern Ireland with that in Great Britain.

Part III: Terrorist Property

25. This Part corresponds to Part III of the PTA ("Financial assistance for terrorism") and was discussed in Chapter 6 of the Government's consultation document under the heading "Terrorist finance." The name has been changed to "Terrorist property" to make it clear that in the Act—just as in the PTA—the Part III offences apply not only to money but also to other property. While Part III of the PTA applies only to Irish and certain kinds of international terrorism, Part III of the Act applies to all forms of terrorism.

26. In addition to replicating Part III of the PTA, Part III of the Act also introduces a new power for the police, customs officers and immigration officers to seize cash at borders and to seek forfeiture of the cash in civil proceedings. This is modelled on a power which already exists in Part III of the Drug Trafficking Act 1994 (c. 37).

Section 14: Terrorist Property

27. This definition comes into play in the "money laundering" offence (section 18) and the power to seize and forfeit cash at borders (sections 25 and 28). *Subsection (1)* makes it clear that terrorist property can include both property to be used for terrorism and proceeds of acts of terrorism. *Subsection (2)(a)* makes explicit that the proceeds of an act of terrorism covers not only the money stolen in, say, a terrorist robbery, but also any money paid in connection with the commission of terrorist acts. *Subsection (2)(b)* makes explicit that any resources of a proscribed organisation are covered: not only the resources they use for bomb-making, arms purchase etc but also money they have set aside for non-violent purposes such as paying rent.

Sections 15–17: Fundraising, Use, Possession and Funding arrangements

28. These sections correspond to sections 9 and 10 of the PTA. By virtue of section 1(5) of the Act the words "for the purposes of terrorism" can be taken to include "for the benefit of a proscribed organisation." As a result, the offences of fund-raising, and using and possessing money, and entering into funding arrangements for a proscribed organisation (section 10 of the PTA) are subsumed into these sections.

Section 18: Money Laundering

29. This section corresponds to section 11 of the PTA and has the same effect. Although it is entitled "money laundering" and is most likely to be used for money, it also applies to "laundering" type arrangements in respect of other property.

Section 19: Disclosure of Information: Duty

30. This section is based on section 18A of the PTA and has the same effect. It requires banks and other businesses to report any suspicion they may have that someone is laundering terrorist money or committing any of the other terrorist property offences in sections 15–18. *Subsection (1)(b)* ensures the offence is focused on suspicions which arise at work. *Subsection (5)* preserves the exemption in respect of legal advisers' privileged material.

31. Suspicions arising in home life were covered by section 18 of the PTA which the Government has decided, following Lord Lloyd, not to replicate.

Sections 20–21: Disclosure of Information: Permission; Co-operation with the Police

32. These sections correspond to section 12 of the PTA and have the same effect. Section 20 ensures that businesses can disclose information to the police without fear of breaching legal restrictions. *Subsection (1)* of section 21 allows for the activities of informants who may have to be involved with terrorist property if they are not to be found out and protects others who may innocently become involved. *Subsection (2)* makes it possible for someone involved with such property to avoid prosecution by telling the police as soon as is reasonably practicable (*subsection (3)*) and discontinuing his involvement if asked to do so by the police (*subsection (4)*).

Sections 22–23: Penalties and Forfeiture

33. Section 22 corresponds to section 13(1) of the PTA and has the same effect. Section 23 is based on section 13(2) of the PTA and has similar effect subject to one substantive modification. *Subsection (6)* allows for forfeiture of the proceeds of a terrorist property offence. This could arise in a case where an accountant prepared accounts on behalf of a proscribed organisation—thus facilitating the retention or control of the organisation's money—and was paid for doing so. The money he received in payment could not be forfeited under section 13(2) of the PTA because it was not intended or suspected for use in terrorism. It could not be confiscated under the Criminal Justice Act 1988 (c. 33) because that confis-

cation regime excludes terrorist property offences. Subsection (6) closes this loophole between the confiscation scheme in the 1988 Act and the counter-terrorist forfeiture scheme.

Sections 24–31: Seizure, Detention and Forfeiture of Terrorist Cash at Borders

34. These sections are based on sections 42–48 of the Drug Trafficking Act 1994 (c. 37) which relate to drug trafficking money imported or exported in cash. The main difference (apart from applying the powers to terrorist rather than drug trafficking cash) is that the powers in the Drug Trafficking Act only apply to cash being taken across the UK's external borders, while those in the Act also apply to cash being taken from Northern Ireland to Great Britain and vice versa. As with drug trafficking, no criminal conviction is required.

Section 24: Interpretation

35. *Subsection (1)* allows the power to seize cash to be exercised by any of the agencies operating at borders: police, customs and immigration. This is to allow for the event that a customs or immigration officer is the first to find the cash. However, it is expected that for the most part the power will be exercised by the police. The definition of cash in *subsection (2)* is intended to cover the most readily realisable monetary instruments used by terrorists; the order-making power in subsection (2)(e) will enable the Secretary of State to add further monetary instruments as the need arises.

Section 25: Seizure and Detention

36. Once cash has been seized, then under this section it can be detained for up to 48 hours. During that time the authorities must either seek continued detention or forfeiture. If neither of these occurs during the first 48 hours, the cash will be returned.

Sections 26–27: Continued Detention of Cash

37. A magistrate can allow continued detention for up to 3 months under *subsection (2)(b)* of section 26. A further application can be granted after the 3 months has expired, and so on, up to a maximum of two years (*subsection (4)*). In section 27, *subsection (1)* provides for any interest accruing on the cash, and *subsections (2)–(5)* for application to the court for a direction that the cash be released.

Sections 28–29: Forfeiture and Appeal

38. This section provides for civil forfeiture proceedings in relation to the seized cash. Evidence that the cash is terrorist property is required to the civil standard (*subsection (2)* of section 28); proceedings for a criminal offence are not needed (*subsection (4)*) and the proceedings themselves are civil as opposed to criminal. Appeals must be lodged within 30 days, and the route of appeal is in England and Wales to the Crown Court; in Northern Ireland to the county court; and in Scotland to the Court of Session. A successful appeal will result in the cash being paid back, together with any accrued interest.

39. *Subsections (6)–(7)* provide for the situation where an organisation is deproscribed following a successful appeal to POAC, and a forfeiture order has been made in reliance (in whole or in part) on the fact that the organisation was proscribed. In such cases, the person whose cash has been forfeited may appeal at any time before the end of the period of 30 days beginning with the date on which the deproscription order comes into force.

Part IV: Terrorist Investigations

Section 32: Terrorist Investigation

40. This definition applies to the power in sections 33–36 to use cordons, to the powers in Schedule 5 to obtain search warrants, production orders and explanation orders; and to the power in Schedule 6 to make financial information orders. There is also an offence in section 39 of "tipping off" in relation to a terrorist investigation.

Sections 33–36: Cordons

41. These sections make similar provision to that inserted into the PTA, at section 16C and Schedule 6A, by the Prevention of Terrorism (Additional Powers) Act 1996 (c. 7). They give the police the power for a limited period to designate and demarcate a specified area as a cordoned area for the purposes of a terrorist investigation—for instance in the wake of a bomb. They also make it an offence to breach a cordon.

Section 37: Powers

42. See notes on Schedule 5 below.

Section 38: Financial Information

43. See notes on Schedule 6 below.

Section 39: Disclosure of Information, &c.

44. This section corresponds to section 17(2)–(6) of the PTA and has similar effect. The offences it sets out, including that at *subsection (2)(a)* which
is sometimes called "tipping off," are essential to the disclosure regime
and have a powerful deterrent effect. The defence at section 39(5)(a) is
listed in section 118(5) and therefore imposes an evidential burden only
on the defendant.

Part V: Counter-Terrorist Powers

Sections 41–43: Arrest Power and Related Search Powers

45. These sections make similar provision to the arrest and detention provisions at sections 14 and 15 of the PTA. There is a special arrest power for
use in terrorist cases because experience continues to show that it is necessary to make provision for circumstances where, at the point when the
police believe an arrest should take place, there is not enough to charge
an individual with a particular offence even though there is reasonable suspicion of involvement with terrorism. Sections 42 and 43 give the police
powers to search people liable to arrest under section 41. *Subsection (9)*
of section 41 and *subsection (5)* of section 43, respectively, give constables
the power to make an arrest under section 41(1) of the Act in any Part of
the United Kingdom, and to search people under section 43 (these subsections in other words confer "cross border" powers of arrest and search).

Sections 44–47: General Powers to Stop and Search

46. These sections make similar provision to the following sections of the
PTA: section 13A (inserted by the Criminal Justice and Public Order Act
1994 (c. 33)) and section 13B (inserted by the Prevention of Terrorism
(Additional Powers) Act 1996 (c. 7)). They give the police powers to stop
and search vehicles and their occupants, and pedestrians, for the prevention of terrorism. As with the powers under the PTA, authorisations apply
to a specific area and are for a maximum of 28 days (though that period
may be renewed). The main difference is that vehicle stop and search
authorisations, as well as pedestrian authorisations, will have to be confirmed or amended by a Secretary of State within 48 hours of their being
made, or they will cease to have effect.

Sections 48–52: Parking

47. These sections make similar provision to that inserted by the Prevention of Terrorism (Additional Powers) Act 1996 (c. 7) as section 16D of the PTA. This gives the police the powers to restrict or prohibit parking for a limited period in a specified area for the prevention of terrorism and makes it an offence to park in or refuse to move from such an area.

Section 53: Port and Border Controls

48. This section brings into effect Schedule 7 on port and border controls, and by subsection (2) allows for the Secretary of State to repeal by order the provision at paragraph 16 of the Schedule, which enables him to bring in by order a requirement for passengers in the Common Travel Area to complete cards.

Part VI: Miscellaneous

49. This Part deals, among other things, with the offences which were discussed in Chapter 12 of the Government's consultation paper under the heading "Ancillary offences."

Sections 54–55: Weapons Training

50. These sections correspond to the offence at section 34 of the EPA. Whereas that offence applied only in Northern Ireland, the new version applies throughout the UK. It has also been extended to cover chemical, biological and nuclear weapons and materials as well as conventional firearms and explosives; and to cover recruitment for training (*subsection (3)*) as well as the training itself. *Subsection (5)* of section 54 provides a defence for persons who are acting for non-terrorist purposes, such as the armed forces. This defence is listed in section 118(5) and therefore imposes an evidential burden only on the defendant.

51. A further modification concerns the need for a recipient of the training. Under *subsection (1)* of section 54, by contrast with its predecessor in the EPA, no recipient is needed for the offence to be committed. This means that the offence could cover someone who makes weapons instruction for terrorist purposes generally available, for example via the Internet.

52. The definitions of chemical, biological and nuclear weapons and materials are based on other statutes.
    - Under section 1 of the Chemical Weapons Act 1996 (c. 6), "chemical weapons" are toxic chemicals and their precursors; munitions and other devices designed to cause death or harm through the toxic prop-

erties of toxic chemicals released by them; and equipment designed for use in connection with such munitions and devices.

- Section 1(1)(b) of the Biological Weapons Act 1974 (c. 6) applies to any weapon, equipment or means of delivery designed to use biological agents or toxins for hostile purposes or in armed conflict.
- The meaning of "nuclear material" set out in the Schedule to the Nuclear Material (Offences) Act 1983 (c. 18), is "plutonium except that with isotopic concentration exceeding 80% in plutonium-238; uranium-233; uranium enriched in the isotopes 235 or 233; uranium containing the mixture of isotopes as occurring in nature other than in the form of ore or ore-residue; any material containing one or more of the foregoing." The Schedule also further defines "uranium enriched in the isotopes 235 or 233."

Anti-Terrorism, Crime and Security Act 2001

Part 1
Terrorist Property

1 Forfeiture of terrorist cash
  (1) Schedule 1 (which makes provision for enabling cash which—
      (a) is intended to be used for the purposes of terrorism,
      (b) consists of resources of an organisation which is a proscribed organisation, or
      (c) is, or represents, property obtained through terrorism, to be forfeited in civil proceedings before a magistrates' court or (in Scotland) the sheriff) is to have effect.
  (2) The powers conferred by Schedule 1 are exercisable in relation to any cash whether or not any proceedings have been brought for an offence in connection with the cash.
  (3) Expressions used in this section have the same meaning as in Schedule 1.
  (4) Sections 24 to 31 of the Terrorism Act 2000 (c. 11) (seizure of terrorist cash) are to cease to have effect.
  (5) An order under section 127 bringing Schedule 1 into force may make any modifications of any code of practice then in operation under Schedule 14 to the Terrorism Act 2000 (exercise of officers' powers) which the Secretary of State thinks necessary or expedient.

2 Amendments relating to section 1
  (1) In Schedule 2 to the Access to Justice Act 1999 (c. 22) (services excluded from the Community Legal Service), paragraph 2 (exclusion of advocacy: exceptions) is amended as follows.
  (2) In paragraph 2(2) (Crown Court), after paragraph (c) insert—"or (d) which relate to an order under paragraph 6 of Schedule 1 to the Anti-terrorism, Crime and Security Act 2001," and omit the "or" at the end of paragraph (b).
  (3) In paragraph 2(3) (magistrates' courts), in paragraph (j), after "1998" insert—"or (k for an order or direction under paragraph 3, 5, 6, 9 or 10 of Schedule 1 to the Anti-terrorism, Crime and Security Act 2001," and omit the "or" at the end of paragraph (i).

(4) Schedule 14 to the Terrorism Act 2000 (exercise of officers' powers) is amended as follows.

(5) In paragraph 1—

    (a) in paragraph (a), for "section 24" substitute "the terrorist cash provisions," and

    (b) after paragraph (b) insert—

"and "the terrorist cash provisions" means Schedule 1 to the Anti-terrorism, Crime and Security Act 2001."

(6) In paragraphs 2, 3 and 6(1), at the end insert "or the terrorist cash provisions."

(7) In paragraph 5, after "Act" insert "or the terrorist cash provisions."

(8) In Part I of Schedule 1 to the Legal Aid, Advice and Assistance (Northern Ireland) Order 1981 (S.I.1981/228 (N.I.8)) (proceedings for which legal aid may be given under Part II of the Order), in paragraph 3 (courts of summary jurisdiction) after sub-paragraph (h) insert—

"(i) proceedings under paragraphs 3, 5, 6, 9 and 10 of Schedule 1 to the Anti-terrorism, Crime and Security Act 2001."

3   Terrorist property: amendments

Schedule 2 contains amendments to the Terrorism Act 2000.

Part 2
Freezing Orders

Orders

4   Power to make order

    (1) The Treasury may make a freezing order if the following two conditions are satisfied.

    (2) The first condition is that the Treasury reasonably believe that—

        (a) action to the detriment of the United Kingdom's economy (or part of it) has been or is likely to be taken by a person or persons, or

        (b) action constituting a threat to the life or property of one or more nationals of the United Kingdom or residents of the United Kingdom has been or is likely to be taken by a person or persons.

    (3) If one person is believed to have taken or to be likely to take the action the second condition is that the person is—

        (a) the government of a country or territory outside the United Kingdom, or

(b) a resident of a country or territory outside the United Kingdom.

(4) If two or more persons are believed to have taken or to be likely to take the action the second condition is that each of them falls within paragraph (a) or (b) of subsection (3); and different persons may fall within different paragraphs.

5   Contents of order

(1) A freezing order is an order which prohibits persons from making funds available to or for the benefit of a person or persons specified in the order.

(2) The order must provide that these are the persons who are prohibited—
   (a) all persons in the United Kingdom, and
   (b) all persons elsewhere who are nationals of the United Kingdom or are bodies incorporated under the law of any part of the United Kingdom or are Scottish partnerships.

(3) The order may specify the following (and only the following) as the person or persons to whom or for whose benefit funds are not to be made available—
   (a) the person or persons reasonably believed by the Treasury to have taken or to be likely to take the action referred to in section 4;
   (b) any person the Treasury reasonably believe has provided or is likely to provide assistance (directly or indirectly) to that person or any of those persons.

(4) A person may be specified under subsection (3) by—
   (a) being named in the order, or
   (b) falling within a description of persons set out in the order.

(5) The description must be such that a reasonable person would know whether he fell within it.

(6) Funds are financial assets and economic benefits of any kind.

6   Contents: further provisions

Schedule 3 contains further provisions about the contents of freezing orders.

7   Review of order

The Treasury must keep a freezing order under review.

8   Duration of order

A freezing order ceases to have effect at the end of the period of 2 years starting with the day on which it is made.

Interpretation

9   Nationals and residents

(1) A national of the United Kingdom is an individual who is—

(a) a British citizen, a British Dependent Territories citizen, a British National (Overseas) or a British Overseas citizen,

(b) a person who under the British Nationality Act 1981 (c. 61) is a British subject, or

(c) a British protected person within the meaning of that Act.

(2) A resident of the United Kingdom is—

(a) an individual who is ordinarily resident in the United Kingdom,

(b) a body incorporated under the law of any part of the United Kingdom, or

(c) a Scottish partnership.

(3) A resident of a country or territory outside the United Kingdom is—

(a) an individual who is ordinarily resident in such a country or territory, or

(b) a body incorporated under the law of such a country or territory.

(4) For the purposes of subsection (3)(b) a branch situated in a country or territory outside the United Kingdom of—

(a) a body incorporated under the law of any part of the United Kingdom, or

(b) a Scottish partnership, is to be treated as a body incorporated under the law of the country or territory where the branch is situated.

(5) This section applies for the purposes of this Part.

Orders: Procedure etc.

10 Procedure for making freezing orders

(1) A power to make a freezing order is exercisable by statutory instrument.

(2) A freezing order—

(a) must be laid before Parliament after being made;

(b) ceases to have effect at the end of the relevant period unless before the end of that period the order is approved by a resolution of each House of Parliament (but without that affecting anything done under the order or the power to make a new order).

(3) The relevant period is a period of 28 days starting with the day on which the order is made.

(4) In calculating the relevant period no account is to be taken of any time during which Parliament is dissolved or prorogued or during which both Houses are adjourned for more than 4 days.

(5) If the Treasury propose to make a freezing order in the belief that the condition in section 4(2)(b) is satisfied, they must not make the order unless they consult the Secretary of State.

11 Procedure for making certain amending orders

(1) This section applies if—

    (a) a freezing order is made specifying by description (rather than by name) the person or persons to whom or for whose benefit funds are not to be made available,

    (b) it is proposed to make a further order which amends the freezing order only so as to make it specify by name the person or persons (or any of the persons) to whom or for whose benefit funds are not to be made available, and

    (c) the Treasury reasonably believe that the person or persons named fall within the description contained in the freezing order and the further order contains a statement of the Treasury's belief.

(2) This section also applies if—

    (a) a freezing order is made specifying by name the person or persons to whom or for whose benefit funds are not to be made available,

    (b) it is proposed to make a further order which amends the freezing order only so as to make it specify by name a further person or further persons to whom or for whose benefit funds are not to be made available, and

    (c) the Treasury reasonably believe that the further person or persons fall within the same description as the person or persons specified in the freezing order and the further order contains a statement of the Treasury's belief.

(3) This section also applies if—

    (a) a freezing order is made, and

    (b) it is proposed to make a further order which amends the freezing order only so as to make it specify (whether by name or description) fewer persons to whom or for whose benefit funds are not to be made available.

(4) If this section applies, a statutory instrument containing the further order is subject to annulment in pursuance of a resolution of either House of Parliament.

12 Procedure for revoking orders

A statutory instrument containing an order revoking a freezing order (without re-enacting it) is subject to annulment in pursuance of a resolution of either House of Parliament.

13 De-hybridisation

If apart from this section an order under this Part would be treated for the purposes of the standing orders of either House of Parliament as a hybrid instrument, it is to proceed in that House as if it were not such an instrument.

14 Orders: supplementary
(1) Where this Part confers a power to make provision, different provision may be made for different purposes.
(2) An order under this Part may include supplementary, incidental, saving or transitional provisions.
(3) Nothing in this Part affects the generality of subsection (2).

Miscellaneous

15 The Crown
(1) A freezing order binds the Crown, subject to the following provisions of this section.
(2) No contravention by the Crown of a provision of a freezing order makes the Crown criminally liable; but the High Court or in Scotland the Court of Session may, on the application of a person appearing to the Court to have an interest, declare unlawful any act or omission of the Crown which constitutes such a contravention.
(3) Nothing in this section affects Her Majesty in her private capacity; and this is to be construed as if section 38(3) of the Crown Proceedings Act 1947 (c. 44) (meaning of Her Majesty in her private capacity) were contained in this Act.

16 Repeals
(1) These provisions shall cease to have effect—
    (a) section 2 of the Emergency Laws (Re-enactments and Repeals) Act 1964 (c. 60) (Treasury's power to prohibit action on certain orders as to gold etc);
    (b) section 55 of the Finance Act 1968 (c. 44) (meaning of security in section 2 of 1964 Act).
(2) Subsection (1) does not affect a reference which—
    (a) is to a provision referred to in that subsection, and
    (b) is contained in a provision made under an Act.

Part 3
Disclosure of Information

17 Extension of existing disclosure powers
(1) This section applies to the provisions listed in Schedule 4, so far as they authorise the disclosure of information.

(2) Each of the provisions to which this section applies shall have effect, in relation to the disclosure of information by or on behalf of a public authority, as if the purposes for which the disclosure of information is authorised by that provision included each of the following—

    (a) the purposes of any criminal investigation whatever which is being or may be carried out, whether in the United Kingdom or elsewhere;

    (b) the purposes of any criminal proceedings whatever which have been or may be initiated, whether in the United Kingdom or elsewhere;

    (c) the purposes of the initiation or bringing to an end of any such investigation or proceedings;

    (d) the purpose of facilitating a determination of whether any such investigation or proceedings should be initiated or brought to an end.

(3) The Treasury may by order made by statutory instrument add any provision contained in any subordinate legislation to the provisions to which this section applies.

(4) The Treasury shall not make an order under subsection (3) unless a draft of it has been laid before Parliament and approved by a resolution of each House.

(5) No disclosure of information shall be made by virtue of this section unless the public authority by which the disclosure is made is satisfied that the making of the disclosure is proportionate to what is sought to be achieved by it.

(6) Nothing in this section shall be taken to prejudice any power to disclose information which exists apart from this section.

(7) The information that may be disclosed by virtue of this section includes information obtained before the commencement of this section.

18 Restriction on disclosure of information for overseas purposes

(1) Subject to subsections (2) and (3), the Secretary of State may give a direction which—

    (a) specifies any overseas proceedings or any description of overseas proceedings; and

    (b) prohibits the making of any relevant disclosure for the purposes of those proceedings or, as the case may be, of proceedings of that description.

(2) In subsection (1) the reference, in relation to a direction, to a relevant disclosure is a reference to a disclosure authorised by any of the provisions to which section 17 applies which—

    (a) is made for a purpose mentioned in subsection (2)(a) to (d) of that section; and

     (b)   is a disclosure of any such information as is described in the direction.

(3)   The Secretary of State shall not give a direction under this section unless it appears to him that the overseas proceedings in question, or that overseas proceedings of the description in question, relate or would relate—

     (a)   to a matter in respect of which it would be more appropriate for any jurisdiction or investigation to be exercised or carried out by a court or other authority of the United Kingdom, or of a particular part of the United Kingdom;

     (b)   to a matter in respect of which it would be more appropriate for any jurisdiction or investigation to be exercised or carried out by a court or other authority of a third country; or

     (c)   to a matter that would fall within paragraph (a) or (b)—

         (i)   if it were appropriate for there to be any exercise of jurisdiction or investigation at all; and

         (ii)   if (where one does not exist) a court or other authority with the necessary jurisdiction or functions existed in the United Kingdom, in the part of the United Kingdom in question or, as the case may be, in the third country in question.

(4)   A direction under this section shall not have the effect of prohibiting—

     (a)   the making of any disclosure by a Minister of the Crown or by the Treasury; or

     (b)   the making of any disclosure in pursuance of a Community obligation.

(5)   A direction under this section—

     (a)   may prohibit the making of disclosures absolutely or in such cases, or subject to such conditions as to consent or otherwise, as may be specified in it; and

     (b)   must be published or otherwise issued by the Secretary of State in such manner as he considers appropriate for bringing it to the attention of persons likely to be affected by it.

(6)   A person who, knowing of any direction under this section, discloses any information in contravention of that direction shall be guilty of an offence and liable—

     (a)   on conviction on indictment, to imprisonment for a term not exceeding two years or to a fine or to both;

     (b)   on summary conviction, to imprisonment for a term not exceeding three months or to a fine not exceeding the statutory maximum or to both.

(7)   The following are overseas proceedings for the purposes of this section—

(a) criminal proceedings which are taking place, or will or may take place, in a country or territory outside the United Kingdom;

(b) a criminal investigation which is being, or will or may be, conducted by an authority of any such country or territory.

(8) References in this section, in relation to any proceedings or investigation, to a third country are references to any country or territory outside the United Kingdom which is not the country or territory where the proceedings are taking place, or will or may take place or, as the case may be, is not the country or territory of the authority which is conducting the investigation, or which will or may conduct it.

(9) In this section "court" includes a tribunal of any description.

19 Disclosure of information held by revenue departments

(1) This section applies to information which is held by or on behalf of the Commissioners of Inland Revenue or by or on behalf of the Commissioners of Customs and Excise, including information obtained before the coming into force of this section.

(2) No obligation of secrecy imposed by statute or otherwise prevents the disclosure, in accordance with the following provisions of this section, of information to which this section applies if the disclosure is made—

(a) for the purpose of facilitating the carrying out by any of the intelligence services of any of that service's functions;

(b) for the purposes of any criminal investigation whatever which is being or may be carried out, whether in the United Kingdom or elsewhere;

(c) for the purposes of any criminal proceedings whatever which have been or may be initiated, whether in the United Kingdom or elsewhere;

(d) for the purposes of the initiation or bringing to an end of any such investigation or proceedings; or

(e) for the purpose of facilitating a determination of whether any such investigation or proceedings should be initiated or brought to an end.

(3) No disclosure of information to which this section applies shall be made by virtue of this section unless the person by whom the disclosure is made is satisfied that the making of the disclosure is proportionate to what is sought to be achieved by it.

(4) Information to which this section applies shall not be disclosed by virtue of this section except by the Commissioners by or on whose behalf it is held or with their authority.

(5) Information obtained by means of a disclosure authorised by subsection (2) shall not be further disclosed except—

(a)   for a purpose mentioned in that subsection; and

(b)   with the consent of the Commissioners by whom or with whose authority it was initially disclosed;

and information so obtained otherwise than by or on behalf of any of the intelligence services shall not be further disclosed (with or without such consent) to any of those services, or to any person acting on behalf of any of those services, except for a purpose mentioned in paragraphs (b) to (e) of that subsection.

(6)   A consent for the purposes of subsection (5) may be given either in relation to a particular disclosure or in relation to disclosures made in such circumstances as may be specified or described in the consent.

(7)   Nothing in this section authorises the making of any disclosure which is prohibited by any provision of the Data Protection Act 1998 (c. 29).

(8)   References in this section to information which is held on behalf of the Commissioners of Inland Revenue or of the Commissioners of Customs and Excise include references to information which—

(a)   is held by a person who provides services to the Commissioners of Inland Revenue or, as the case may be, to the Commissioners of Customs and Excise; and

(b)   is held by that person in connection with the provision of those services.

(9)   In this section "intelligence service" has the same meaning as in the Regulation of Investigatory Powers Act 2000 (c. 23).

(10)   Nothing in this section shall be taken to prejudice any power to disclose information which exists apart from this section.

20 Interpretation of Part 3

(1)   In this Part—

"criminal investigation" means an investigation of any criminal conduct, including an investigation of alleged or suspected criminal conduct and an investigation of whether criminal conduct has taken place;

"information" includes—

(a)   documents; and

(b)   in relation to a disclosure authorised by a provision to which section 17 applies, anything that falls to be treated as information for the purposes of that provision;

"public authority" has the same meaning as in section 6 of the Human Rights Act 1998 (c. 42); and

"subordinate legislation" has the same meaning as in the Interpretation Act 1978 (c. 30).

(2) Proceedings outside the United Kingdom shall not be taken to be criminal proceedings for the purposes of this Part unless the conduct with which the defendant in those proceedings is charged is criminal conduct or conduct which, to a substantial extent, consists of criminal conduct.

(3) In this section—

·"conduct" includes acts, omissions and statements; and

"criminal conduct" means any conduct which—

(a) constitutes one or more criminal offences under the law of a part of the United Kingdom; or

(b) is, or corresponds to, conduct which, if it all took place in a particular part of the United Kingdom, would constitute one or more offences under the law of that part of the United Kingdom.

Part 4
Immigration and Asylum

Suspected International Terrorists

21 Suspected international terrorist: certification

(1) The Secretary of State may issue a certificate under this section in respect of a person if the Secretary of State reasonably—

(a) believes that the person's presence in the United Kingdom is a risk to national security, and

(b) suspects that the person is a terrorist.

(2) In subsection (1)(b) "terrorist" means a person who—

(a) is or has been concerned in the commission, preparation or instigation of acts of international terrorism,

(b) is a member of or belongs to an international terrorist group, or

(c) has links with an international terrorist group.

(3) A group is an international terrorist group for the purposes of subsection (2)(b) and (c) if—

(a) it is subject to the control or influence of persons outside the United Kingdom, and

(b) the Secretary of State suspects that it is concerned in the commission, preparation or instigation of acts of international terrorism.

(4) For the purposes of subsection (2)(c) a person has links with an international terrorist group only if he supports or assists it.

(5) In this Part—

"terrorism" has the meaning given by section 1 of the Terrorism Act 2000 (c. 11), and

"suspected international terrorist" means a person certified under subsection (1).

(6) Where the Secretary of State issues a certificate under subsection (1) he shall as soon as is reasonably practicable—

    (a) take reasonable steps to notify the person certified, and

    (b) send a copy of the certificate to the Special Immigration Appeals Commission.

(7) The Secretary of State may revoke a certificate issued under subsection (1).

(8) A decision of the Secretary of State in connection with certification under this section may be questioned in legal proceedings only under section 25 or 26.

(9) An action of the Secretary of State taken wholly or partly in reliance on a certificate under this section may be questioned in legal proceedings only by or in the course of proceedings under—

    (a) section 25 or 26, or

    (b) secton 2 of the Special Immigration Appeals Commission Act 1997 (c. 68) (appeal).

22 Deportation, removal, &c.

(1) An action of a kind specified in subsection (2) may be taken in respect of a suspected international terrorist despite the fact that (whether temporarily or indefinitely) the action cannot result in his removal from the United Kingdom because of—

    (a) a point of law which wholly or partly relates to an international agreement, or

    (b) a practical consideration.

(2) The actions mentioned in subsection (1) are—

    (a) refusing leave to enter or remain in the United Kingdom in accordance with provision made by or by virtue of any of sections 3 to 3B of the Immigration Act 1971 (c. 77) (control of entry to United Kingdom),

    (b) varying a limited leave to enter or remain in the United Kingdom in accordance with provision made by or by virtue of any of those sections,

    (c) recommending deportation in accordance with section 3(6) of that Act (recommendation by court),

    (d) taking a decision to make a deportation order under section 5(1) of that Act (deportation by Secretary of State),

    (e) making a deportation order under section 5(1) of that Act,

    (f) refusing to revoke a deportation order,

(g) cancelling leave to enter the United Kingdom in accordance with paragraph 2A of Schedule 2 to that Act (person arriving with continuous leave),

(h) giving directions for a person's removal from the United Kingdom under any of paragraphs 8 to 10 or 12 to 14 of Schedule 2 to that Act (control of entry to United Kingdom),

(i) giving directions for a person's removal from the United Kingdom under section 10 of the Immigration and Asylum Act 1999 (c. 33) (person unlawfully in United Kingdom), and

(j) giving notice to a person in accordance with regulations under paragraph 1 of Schedule 4 to that Act of a decision to make a deportation order against him.

(3) Action of a kind specified in subsection (2) which has effect in respect of a suspected international terrorist at the time of his certification under section 21 shall be treated as taken again (in reliance on subsection (1) above) immediately after certification.

23 Detention

(1) A suspected international terrorist may be detained under a provision specified in subsection (2) despite the fact that his removal or departure from the United Kingdom is prevented (whether temporarily or indefinitely) by—

(a) a point of law which wholly or partly relates to an international agreement, or

(b) a practical consideration.

(2) The provisions mentioned in subsection (1) are—

(a) paragraph 16 of Schedule 2 to the Immigration Act 1971 (c. 77) (detention of persons liable to examination or removal), and

(b) paragraph 2 of Schedule 3 to that Act (detention pending deportation).

24 Bail

(1) A suspected international terrorist who is detained under a provision of the Immigration Act 1971 may be released on bail.

(2) For the purpose of subsection (1) the following provisions of Schedule 2 to the Immigration Act 1971 (control on entry) shall apply with the modifications specified in Schedule 3 to the Special Immigration Appeals Commission Act 1997 (c. 68) (bail to be determined by Special Immigration Appeals Commission) and with any other necessary modifications—

(a) paragraph 22(1A), (2) and (3) (release),

(b) paragraph 23 (forfeiture),

(c) paragraph 24 (arrest), and

(d) paragraph 30(1) (requirement of Secretary of State's consent).

(3) Rules of procedure under the Special Immigration Appeals Commission Act 1997 (c. 68)—
   (a) may make provision in relation to release on bail by virtue of this section, and
   (b) subject to provision made by virtue of paragraph (a), shall apply in relation to release on bail by virtue of this section as they apply in relation to release on bail by virtue of that Act subject to any modification which the Commission considers necessary.

25 Certification: appeal
   (1) A suspected international terrorist may appeal to the Special Immigration Appeals Commission against his certification under section 21.
   (2) On an appeal the Commission must cancel the certificate if—
      (a) it considers that there are no reasonable grounds for a belief or suspicion of the kind referred to in section 21(1)(a) or (b), or
      (b) it considers that for some other reason the certificate should not have been issued.
   (3) If the Commission determines not to cancel a certificate it must dismiss the appeal.
   (4) Where a certificate is cancelled under subsection (2) it shall be treated as never having been issued.
   (5) An appeal against certification may be commenced only—
      (a) within the period of three months beginning with the date on which the certificate is issued, or
      (b) with the leave of the Commission, after the end of that period but before the commencement of the first review under section 26.

26 Certification: review
   (1) The Special Immigration Appeals Commission must hold a first review of each certificate issued under section 21 as soon as is reasonably practicable after the expiry of the period of six months beginning with the date on which the certificate is issued.
   (2) But—
      (a) in a case where before the first review would fall to be held in accordance with subsection (1) an appeal under section 25 is commenced (whether or not it is finally determined before that time) or leave to appeal is given under section 25(5)(b), the first review shall be held as soon as is reasonably practicable after the expiry of the period of six months beginning with the date on which the appeal is finally determined, and
      (b) in a case where an application for leave under section 25(5)(b) has been commenced but not determined at the time when

the first review would fall to be held in accordance with subsection (1), if leave is granted the first review shall be held as
soon as is reasonably practicable after the expiry of the period
of six months beginning with the date on which the appeal is
finally determined.

(3)   The Commission must review each certificate issued under section
21 as soon as is reasonably practicable after the expiry of the period
of three months beginning with the date on which the first review
or a review under this subsection is finally determined.

(4)   The Commission may review a certificate during a period mentioned
in subsection (1), (2) or (3) if—

(a)   the person certified applies for a review, and

(b)   the Commission considers that a review should be held because
of a change in circumstance.

(5)   On a review the Commission—

(a)   must cancel the certificate if it considers that there are no reasonable grounds for a belief or suspicion of the kind referred
to in section 21(1)(a) or (b), and

(b)   otherwise, may not make any order (save as to leave to appeal).

(6)   A certificate cancelled by order of the Commission under subsection (5) ceases to have effect at the end of the day on which the
order is made.

(7)   Where the Commission reviews a certificate under subsection (4),
the period for determining the next review of the certificate under
subsection (3) shall begin with the date of the final determination
of the review under subsection (4).

27   Appeal and review: supplementary

(1)   The following provisions of the Special Immigration Appeals
Commission Act 1997 (c. 68) shall apply in relation to an appeal or
review under section 25 or 26 as they apply in relation to an appeal
under section 2 of that Act—

(a)   section 6 (person to represent appellant's interests),

(b)   section 7 (further appeal on point of law), and

(c)   section 7A (pending appeal).

(2)   The reference in subsection (1) to an appeal or review does not
include a reference to a decision made or action taken on or in connection with—

(a)   an application under section 25(5)(b) or 26(4)(a) of this Act,
or

(b)   subsection (8) below.

(3)   Subsection (4) applies where—

(a)   a further appeal is brought by virtue of subsection (1)(b) in
connection with an appeal or review, and

    (b)   the Secretary of State notifies the Commission that in his opinion the further appeal is confined to calling into question one or more derogation matters within the meaning of section 30 of this Act.

(4)   For the purpose of the application of section 26(2) and (3) of this Act the determination by the Commission of the appeal or review in connection with which the further appeal is brought shall be treated as a final determination.

(5)   Rules under section 5 or 8 of the Special Immigration Appeals Commission Act 1997 (general procedure; and leave to appeal) may make provision about an appeal, review or application under section 25 or 26 of this Act.

(6)   Subject to any provision made by virtue of subsection (5), rules under section 5 or 8 of that Act shall apply in relation to an appeal, review or application under section 25 or 26 of this Act with any modification which the Commission considers necessary.

(7)   Subsection (8) applies where the Commission considers that an appeal or review under section 25 or 26 which relates to a person's certification under section 21 is likely to raise an issue which is also likely to be raised in other proceedings before the Commission which relate to the same person.

(8)   The Commission shall so far as is reasonably practicable—
    (a)   deal with the two sets of proceedings together, and
    (b)   avoid or minimise delay to either set of proceedings as a result of compliance with paragraph (a).

(9)   Cancellation by the Commission of a certificate issued under section 21 shall not prevent the Secretary of State from issuing another certificate, whether on the grounds of a change of circumstance or otherwise.

(10) The reference in section 81 of the Immigration and Asylum Act 1999 (c. 33) (grants to voluntary organisations) to persons who have rights of appeal under that Act shall be treated as including a reference to suspected international terrorists.

28 Review of sections 21 to 23
    (1)   The Secretary of State shall appoint a person to review the operation of sections 21 to 23.
    (2)   The person appointed under subsection (1) shall review the operation of those sections not later than—
        (a)   the expiry of the period of 14 months beginning with the day on which this Act is passed;
        (b)   one month before the expiry of a period specified in accordance with section 29(2)(b) or (c).

(3) Where that person conducts a review under subsection (2) he shall send a report to the Secretary of State as soon as is reasonably practicable.

(4) Where the Secretary of State receives a report under subsection (3) he shall lay a copy of it before Parliament as soon as is reasonably practicable.

(5) The Secretary of State may make payments to a person appointed under subsection (1).

29 Duration of sections 21 to 23

(1) Sections 21 to 23 shall, subject to the following provisions of this section, expire at the end of the period of 15 months beginning with the day on which this Act is passed.

(2) The Secretary of State may by order—

(a) repeal sections 21 to 23;

(b) revive those sections for a period not exceeding one year;

(c) provide that those sections shall not expire in accordance with subsection (1) or an order under paragraph (b) or this paragraph, but shall continue in force for a period not exceeding one year.

(3) An order under subsection (2)—

(a) must be made by statutory instrument, and

(b) may not be made unless a draft has been laid before and approved by resolution of each House of Parliament.

(4) An order may be made without compliance with subsection (3)(b) if it contains a declaration by the Secretary of State that by reason of urgency it is necessary to make the order without laying a draft before Parliament; in which case the order—

(a) must be laid before Parliament, and

(b) shall cease to have effect at the end of the period specified in subsection (5) unless the order is approved during that period by resolution of each House of Parliament.

(5) The period referred to in subsection (4)(b) is the period of 40 days—

(a) beginning with the day on which the order is made, and

(b) ignoring any period during which Parliament is dissolved or prorogued or during which both Houses are adjourned for more than four days.

(6) The fact that an order ceases to have effect by virtue of subsection (4)—

(a) shall not affect the lawfulness of anything done before the order ceases to have effect, and

(b) shall not prevent the making of a new order.

(7) Sections 21 to 23 shall by virtue of this subsection cease to have effect at the end of 10th November 2006.

30 Legal proceedings: derogation

(1) In this section "derogation matter" means—

(a) a derogation by the United Kingdom from Article 5(1) of the Convention on Human Rights which relates to the detention of a person where there is an intention to remove or deport him from the United Kingdom, or

(b) the designation under section 14(1) of the Human Rights Act 1998 (c. 42) of a derogation within paragraph (a) above.

(2) A derogation matter may be questioned in legal proceedings only before the Special Immigration Appeals Commission; and the Commission—

(a) is the appropriate tribunal for the purpose of section 7 of the Human Rights Act 1998 in relation to proceedings all or part of which call a derogation matter into question; and

(b) may hear proceedings which could, but for this subsection, be brought in the High Court or the Court of Session.

(3) In relation to proceedings brought by virtue of subsection (2)—

(a) section 6 of the Special Immigration Appeals Commission Act 1997 (c. 68) (person to represent appellant's interests) shall apply with the reference to the appellant being treated as a reference to any party to the proceedings,

(b) rules under section 5 or 8 of that Act (general procedure; and leave to appeal) shall apply with any modification which the Commission considers necessary, and

(c) in the case of proceedings brought by virtue of subsection (2)(b), the Commission may do anything which the High Court may do (in the case of proceedings which could have been brought in that court) or which the Court of Session may do (in the case of proceedings which could have been brought in that court).

(4) The Commission's power to award costs (or, in Scotland, expenses) by virtue of subsection (3)(c) may be exercised only in relation to such part of proceedings before it as calls a derogation matter into question.

(5) In relation to proceedings brought by virtue of subsection (2)(a) or (b)—

(a) an appeal may be brought to the appropriate appeal court (within the meaning of section 7 of the Special Immigration Appeals Commission Act 1997 (c. 68)) with the leave of the Commission or, if that leave is refused, with the leave of the appropriate appeal court, and

(b) the appropriate appeal court may consider and do only those things which it could consider and do in an appeal brought from the High Court or the Court of Session in proceedings for judicial review.

(6) In relation to proceedings which are entertained by the Commission under subsection (2) but are not brought by virtue of subsection (2)(a) or (b), subsection (4) shall apply in so far as the proceedings call a derogation matter into question.

(7) In this section "the Convention on Human Rights" has the meaning given to "the Convention" by section 21(1) of the Human Rights Act 1998 (c. 42).

31 Interpretation

A reference in section 22, 23 or 24 to a provision of the Immigration Act 1971 (c. 77) includes a reference to that provision as applied by—

(a) another provision of that Act, or

(b) another Act.

32 Channel Islands and Isle of Man

Her Majesty may by Order in Council direct that sections 21 to 31 shall extend, with such modifications as appear to Her Majesty to be appropriate, to any of the Channel Islands or the Isle of Man.

Refugee Convention

33 Certificate that Convention does not apply

(1) This section applies to an asylum appeal before the Special Immigration Appeals Commission where the Secretary of State issues a certificate that—

(a) the appellant is not entitled to the protection of Article 33(1) of the Refugee Convention because Article 1(F) or 33(2) applies to him (whether or not he would be entitled to protection if that Article did not apply), and

(b) the removal of the appellant from the United Kingdom would be conducive to the public good.

(2) In this section—

"asylum appeal" means an appeal under section 2 of the Special Immigration Appeals Commission Act 1997 (c. 68) in which the appellant makes a claim for asylum (within the meaning given by section 167(1) of the Immigration and Asylum Act 1999 (c. 33)), and

"the Refugee Convention" has the meaning given by that section.

(3) Where this section applies the Commission must begin its substantive deliberations on the asylum appeal by considering the statements in the Secretary of State's certificate.

(4)   If the Commission agrees with those statements it must dismiss such part of the asylum appeal as amounts to a claim for asylum (before considering any other aspect of the case).

(5)   If the Commission does not agree with those statements it must quash the decision or action against which the asylum appeal is brought.

(6)   Where a decision or action is quashed under subsection (5)—

    (a)   the quashing shall not prejudice any later decision or action, whether taken on the grounds of a change of circumstance or otherwise, and

    (b)   the claim for asylum made in the course of the asylum appeal shall be treated for the purposes of section 15 of the Immigration and Asylum Act 1999 (interim protection from removal) as undecided until it has been determined whether to take a new decision or action of the kind quashed.

(7)   The Secretary of State may revoke a certificate issued under subsection (1).

(8)   No court may entertain proceedings for questioning—

    (a)   a decision or action of the Secretary of State in connection with certification under subsection (1),

    (b)   a decision of the Secretary of State in connection with a claim for asylum (within the meaning given by section 167(1) of the Immigration and Asylum Act 1999) in a case in respect of which he issues a certificate under subsection (1) above, or

    (c)   a decision or action of the Secretary of State taken as a consequence of the dismissal of all or part of an asylum appeal in pursuance of subsection (4).

(9)   Subsection (8) shall not prevent an appeal under section 7 of the Special Immigration Appeals Commission Act 1997 (appeal on point of law).

(10) Her Majesty may by Order in Council direct that this section shall extend, with such modifications as appear to Her Majesty to be appropriate, to any of the Channel Islands or the Isle of Man.

34 Construction

(1)   Articles 1(F) and 33(2) of the Refugee Convention (exclusions: war criminals, national security, &c.) shall not be taken to require consideration of the gravity of—

    (a)   events or fear by virtue of which Article 1(A) would or might apply to a person if Article 1(F) did not apply, or

    (b)   a threat by reason of which Article 33(1) would or might apply to a person if Article 33(2) did not apply.

(2)   In this section "the Refugee Convention" means the Convention relating to the Status of Refugees done at Geneva on 28th July 1951 and the Protocol to the Convention.

Special Immigration Appeals Commission

35 Status of Commission

At the end of section 1 of the Special Immigration Appeals Commission Act 1997 (c. 68) insert—

(3) The Commission shall be a superior court of record.

(4) A decision of the Commission shall be questioned in legal proceedings only in accordance with—

(a) section 7, or

(b) section 30(5)(a) of the Anti-terrorism, Crime and Security Act 2001 (derogation)."

Fingerprints

36 Destruction of fingerprints

(1) In section 143 of the Immigration and Asylum Act 1999 (c. 33) (destruction of fingerprints)—

(a) subsections (3) to (8) (requirement to destroy fingerprints on resolution of asylum and immigration cases) shall cease to have effect,

(b) in subsection (9) (dependants) after "F" insert "(within the meaning of section 141(7))," and

(c) subsection (14) (interpretation) shall cease to have effect.

(2) Subsection (1)—

(a) shall have effect in relation to fingerprints whether taken before or after the coming into force of this section, and

(b) in relation to fingerprints which before the coming into force of this section were required by section 143 to be destroyed, shall be treated as having had effect before the requirement arose.

Part 5
Race and Religion

37 Meaning of racial hatred

In section 17 of the Public Order Act 1986 (c. 64) (racial hatred defined by reference to a group of persons in Great Britain) omit the words "in Great Britain."

38 Meaning of fear and hatred

In Article 8 of the Public Order (Northern Ireland) Order 1987 (S.I. 1987/463 (N.I. 7)) in the definition of fear and the definition of hatred (fear and hatred defined by reference to a group of persons in Northern Ireland) omit the words "in Northern Ireland."

39 Religiously aggravated offences
   (1)   Part 2 of the Crime and Disorder Act 1998 (c. 37) is amended as
         set out in subsections (2) to (6).
   (2)   In the cross-heading preceding section 28 for "Racially-aggravated"
         substitute "Racially or religiously aggravated."
   (3)   In section 28 (meaning of racially aggravated)—
         (a)   in the sidenote and subsection (1) for "racially aggravated"
               substitute "racially or religiously aggravated";
         (b)   in subsections (1) and (2) for "racial group" substitute "racial
               or religious group";
         (c)   in subsection (3) for the words from "on" to the end of the
               subsection substitute "on any other factor not mentioned in
               that paragraph."
   (4)   In section 28 after subsection (4) insert—

         "(5) In this section "religious group" means a group of persons
         defined by reference to religious belief or lack of religious belief."

   (5)   In each of the provisions listed in subsection (6)—
         (a)   in the sidenote for "Racially-aggravated" substitute "Racially
               or religiously aggravated";
         (b)   in subsection (1) for "racially aggravated" substitute "racially
               or religiously aggravated."
   (6)   The provisions are—
         (a)   section 29 (assaults);
         (b)   section 30 (criminal damage);
         (c)   section 31 (public order offences);
         (d)   section 32 (harassment etc.).
   (7)   In section 153 of the Powers of Criminal Courts (Sentencing) Act
         2000 (c. 6) (increase in sentences for racial aggravation)—
         (a)   in the sidenote for "racial aggravation" substitute "racial or
               religious aggravation";
         (b)   in subsection (1) for the words from "racially-aggravated
               assaults" to the end of the subsection substitute "racially or
               religiously aggravated assaults, criminal damage, public order
               offences and harassment etc).";
         (c)   in subsections (2) and (3) for "racially aggravated" substitute
               "racially or religiously aggravated."
   (8)   In section 24(2) of the Police and Criminal Evidence Act 1984 (c.
         60) (arrestable offences) in paragraph (p) (offences falling within
         section 32(1)(a) of the Crime and Disorder Act 1998) for "racially-
         aggravated" substitute "racially or religiously aggravated."
40 Racial hatred offences: penalties

In section 27(3) of the Public Order Act 1986 (c. 64) (penalties for racial hatred offences) for "two years" substitute "seven years."

41 Hatred and fear offences: penalties
   In Article 16(1) of the Public Order (Northern Ireland) Order 1987 (S.I. 1987/ 463 (N.I. 7)) (penalties for offences involving stirring up hatred or arousing fear) for "2 years" substitute "7 years."

42 Saving
   This Part does not apply to anything done before it comes into force.

Part 6
Weapons of Mass Destruction

Amendment of the Biological Weapons Act 1974 and the Chemical Weapons Act 1996

43 Transfers of biological agents and toxins

In section 1 of the Biological Weapons Act 1974 (c. 6) (restriction on development etc. of certain biological agents and toxins and of biological weapons), after subsection (1) insert—

"(1A) A person shall not—

(a) transfer any biological agent or toxin to another person or enter into an agreement to do so, or

(b) make arrangements under which another person transfers any biological agent or toxin or enters into an agreement with a third person to do so,

if the biological agent or toxin is likely to be kept or used (whether by the transferee or any other person) otherwise than for prophylactic, protective or other peaceful purposes and he knows or has reason to believe that that is the case."

44 Extraterritorial application of biological weapons offences

After section 1 of the Biological Weapons Act 1974 insert—

"1A Extraterritorial application of section 1

(1) Section 1 applies to acts done outside the United Kingdom, but only if they are done by a United Kingdom person.

(2) Proceedings for an offence committed under section 1 outside the United Kingdom may be taken, and the offence may for incidental purposes be treated as having been committed, in any place in the United Kingdom.

(3)   Her Majesty may by Order in Council extend the application of section 1, so far as it applies to acts done outside the United Kingdom, to bodies incorporated under the law of any of the Channel Islands, the Isle of Man or any colony.

(4)   In this section "United Kingdom person" means a United Kingdom national, a Scottish partnership or a body incorporated under the law of a part of the United Kingdom.

(5)   For this purpose a United Kingdom national is an individual who is—

(a)   a British citizen, a British Dependent Territories citizen, a British National (Overseas) or a British Overseas citizen;

(b)   a person who under the British Nationality Act 1981 (c. 61) is a British subject; or

(c)   a British protected person within the meaning of that Act.

(6)   Nothing in this section affects any criminal liability arising otherwise than under this section."

45   Customs and Excise prosecutions for biological weapons offences

Before section 2 of the Biological Weapons Act 1974 (c. 6) insert—

"1B Customs and Excise prosecutions

(1)   Proceedings for a biological weapons offence may be instituted by order of the Commissioners of Customs and Excise if it appears to them that the offence has involved—

(a)   the development or production outside the United Kingdom of any thing mentioned in section 1(1)(a) or (b) above;

(b)   the movement of any such thing into or out of any country or territory;

(c)   any proposal or attempt to do anything falling within paragraph (a) or (b) above.

(2)   In this section "biological weapons offence" means an offence under section 1 of this Act or section 50 of the Anti-terrorism, Crime and Security Act 2001 (including an offence of aiding, abetting, counselling, procuring or inciting the commission of, or attempting or conspiring to commit, such an offence).

(3)   Any proceedings for an offence which are instituted under subsection (1) above shall be commenced in the name of an officer, but may be continued by another officer.

(4)   Where the Commissioners of Customs and Excise investigate, or propose to investigate, any matter with a view to determining—

(a)   whether there are grounds for believing that a biological weapons offence has been committed, or

(b)   whether a person should be prosecuted for such an offence, that matter shall be treated as an assigned matter within the meaning of the Customs and Excise Management Act 1979.

(5) Nothing in this section affects any power of any person (including any officer) apart from this section.

(6) In this section "officer" means a person commissioned by the Commissioners of Customs and Excise.

(7) This section does not apply to the institution of proceedings in Scotland."

46 Customs and Excise prosecutions for chemical weapons offences

Before section 31 of the Chemical Weapons Act 1996 (c. 6) insert—

"30A Customs and Excise prosecutions

(1) Proceedings for a chemical weapons offence may be instituted by order of the Commissioners of Customs and Excise if it appears to them that the offence has involved—

   (a) the development or production outside the United Kingdom of a chemical weapon;

   (b) the movement of a chemical weapon into or out of any country or territory;

   (c) any proposal or attempt to do anything falling within paragraph (a) or (b).

(2) In this section "chemical weapons offence" means an offence under section 2 above or section 50 of the Anti-terrorism, Crime and Security Act 2001 (including an offence of aiding, abetting, counselling, procuring or inciting the commission of, or attempting or conspiring to commit, such an offence).

(3) Any proceedings for an offence which are instituted under subsection (1) shall be commenced in the name of an officer, but may be continued by another officer.

(4) Where the Commissioners of Customs and Excise investigate, or propose to investigate, any matter with a view to determining—

   (a) whether there are grounds for believing that a chemical weapons offence has been committed, or

   (b) whether a person should be prosecuted for such an offence, that matter shall be treated as an assigned matter within the meaning of the Customs and Excise Management Act 1979.

(5) Nothing in this section affects any power of any person (including any officer) apart from this section.

(6) In this section "officer" means a person commissioned by the Commissioners of Customs and Excise.

(7) This section does not apply to the institution of proceedings in Scotland."

Nuclear Weapons

47 Use etc. of nuclear weapons

   (1) A person who—

   (a) knowingly causes a nuclear weapon explosion;

   (b) develops or produces, or participates in the development or production of, a nuclear weapon;

   (c) has a nuclear weapon in his possession;

   (d) participates in the transfer of a nuclear weapon; or

   (e) engages in military preparations, or in preparations of a military nature, intending to use, or threaten to use, a nuclear weapon, is guilty of an offence.

   (2) Subsection (1) has effect subject to the exceptions and defences in sections 48 and 49.

   (3) For the purposes of subsection (1)(b) a person participates in the development or production of a nuclear weapon if he does any act which—

   (a) facilitates the development by another of the capability to produce or use a nuclear weapon, or

   (b) facilitates the making by another of a nuclear weapon, knowing or having reason to believe that his act has (or will have) that effect.

   (4) For the purposes of subsection (1)(d) a person participates in the transfer of a nuclear weapon if—

   (a) he buys or otherwise acquires it or agrees with another to do so;

   (b) he sells or otherwise disposes of it or agrees with another to do so; or

   (c) he makes arrangements under which another person either acquires or disposes of it or agrees with a third person to do so.

   (5) A person guilty of an offence under this section is liable on conviction on indictment to imprisonment for life.

   (6) In this section "nuclear weapon" includes a nuclear explosive device that is not intended for use as a weapon.

   (7) This section applies to acts done outside the United Kingdom, but only if they are done by a United Kingdom person.

   (8) Nothing in subsection (7) affects any criminal liability arising otherwise than under that subsection.

   (9) Paragraph (a) of subsection (1) shall cease to have effect on the coming into force of the Nuclear Explosions (Prohibition and Inspections) Act 1998 (c. 7).

48 Exceptions

   (1) Nothing in section 47 applies—

   (a) to an act which is authorised under subsection (2); or

  (b)   to an act done in the course of an armed conflict.
(2)   The Secretary of State may—
    (a)   authorise any act which would otherwise contravene section 47 in such manner and on such terms as he thinks fit; and
    (b)   withdraw or vary any authorisation given under this subsection.
(3)   Any question arising in proceedings for an offence under section 47 as to whether anything was done in the course of an armed conflict shall be determined by the Secretary of State.
(4)   A certificate purporting to set out any such determination and to be signed by the Secretary of State shall be received in evidence in any such proceedings and shall be presumed to be so signed unless the contrary is shown.

49   Defences
(1)   In proceedings for an offence under section 47(1)(c) or (d) relating to an object it is a defence for the accused to show that he did not know and had no reason to believe that the object was a nuclear weapon.
(2)   But he shall be taken to have shown that fact if—
    (a)   sufficient evidence is adduced to raise an issue with respect to it; and
    (b)   the contrary is not proved by the prosecution beyond reasonable doubt.
(3)   In proceedings for such an offence it is also a defence for the accused to show that he knew or believed that the object was a nuclear weapon but, as soon as reasonably practicable after he first knew or believed that fact, he took all reasonable steps to inform the Secretary of State or a constable of his knowledge or belief.

Assisting or inducing weapons-related acts overseas

50   Assisting or inducing certain weapons-related acts overseas
(1)   A person who aids, abets, counsels or procures, or incites, a person who is not a United Kingdom person to do a relevant act outside the United Kingdom is guilty of an offence.
(2)   For this purpose a relevant act is an act that, if done by a United Kingdom person, would contravene any of the following provisions—
    (a)   section 1 of the Biological Weapons Act 1974 (offences relating to biological agents and toxins);
    (b)   section 2 of the Chemical Weapons Act 1996 (offences relating to chemical weapons); or
    (c)   section 47 above (offences relating to nuclear weapons).
(3)   Nothing in this section applies to an act mentioned in subsection (1) which—

  (a) relates to a relevant act which would contravene section 47; and

  (b) is authorised by the Secretary of State;

and section 48(2) applies for the purpose of authorising acts that would otherwise constitute an offence under this section.

(4) A person accused of an offence under this section in relation to a relevant act which would contravene a provision mentioned in subsection (2) may raise any defence which would be open to a person accused of the corresponding offence ancillary to an offence under that provision.

(5) A person convicted of an offence under this section is liable on conviction on indictment to imprisonment for life.

(6) This section applies to acts done outside the United Kingdom, but only if they are done by a United Kingdom person.

(7) Nothing in this section prejudices any criminal liability existing apart from this section.

Supplemental Provisions Relating to Sections 47 and 50

51 Extraterritorial application

(1) Proceedings for an offence committed under section 47 or 50 outside the United Kingdom may be taken, and the offence may for incidental purposes be treated as having been committed, in any part of the United Kingdom.

(2) Her Majesty may by Order in Council extend the application of section 47 or 50, so far as it applies to acts done outside the United Kingdom, to bodies incorporated under the law of any of the Channel Islands, the Isle of Man or any colony.

52 Powers of entry

(1) If—

  (a) a justice of the peace is satisfied on information on oath that there are reasonable grounds for suspecting that evidence of the commission of an offence under section 47 or 50 is to be found on any premises; or

  (b) in Scotland the sheriff is satisfied by evidence on oath as mentioned in paragraph (a), he may issue a warrant authorising an authorised officer to enter the premises, if necessary by force, at any time within one month from the time of the issue of the warrant and to search them.

(2) The powers of a person who enters the premises under the authority of the warrant include power—

  (a) to take with him such other persons and such equipment as appear to him to be necessary;

    (b)   to inspect, seize and retain any substance, equipment or document found on the premises;

    (c)   to require any document or other information which is held in electronic form and is accessible from the premises to be produced in a form—

        (i)   in which he can read and copy it; or

        (ii)   from which it can readily be produced in a form in which he can read and copy it;

    (d)   to copy any document which he has reasonable cause to believe may be required as evidence for the purposes of proceedings in respect of an offence under section 47 or 50.

(3)   A constable who enters premises under the authority of a warrant or by virtue of subsection (2)(a) may—

    (a)   give such assistance as an authorised officer may request for the purpose of facilitating the exercise of any power under this section; and

    (b)   search or cause to be searched any person on the premises who the constable has reasonable cause to believe may have in his possession any document or other thing which may be required as evidence for the purposes of proceedings in respect of an offence under section 47 or 50.

(4)   No constable shall search a person of the opposite sex.

(5)   The powers conferred by a warrant under this section shall only be exercisable, if the warrant so provides, in the presence of a constable.

(6)   A person who—

    (a)   wilfully obstructs an authorised officer in the exercise of a power conferred by a warrant under this section; or

    (b)   fails without reasonable excuse to comply with a reasonable request made by an authorised officer or a constable for the purpose of facilitating the exercise of such a power, is guilty of an offence.

(7)   A person guilty of an offence under subsection (6) is liable—

    (a)   on summary conviction, to a fine not exceeding the statutory maximum; and

    (b)   on conviction on indictment, to imprisonment for a term not exceeding two years or a fine (or both).

(8)   In this section "authorised officer" means an authorised officer of the Secretary of State.

53 Customs and Excise prosecutions

(1)   Proceedings for a nuclear weapons offence may be instituted by order of the Commissioners of Customs and Excise if it appears to them that the offence has involved—

    (a)   the development or production outside the United Kingdom of a nuclear weapon;

    (b)   the movement of a nuclear weapon into or out of any country or territory;

    (c)   any proposal or attempt to do anything falling within paragraph (a) or (b).

(2)   In this section "nuclear weapons offence" means an offence under section 47 or 50 (including an offence of aiding, abetting, counselling, procuring or inciting the commission of, or attempting or conspiring to commit, such an offence).

(3)   Any proceedings for an offence which are instituted under subsection (1) shall be commenced in the name of an officer, but may be continued by another officer.

(4)   Where the Commissioners of Customs and Excise investigate, or propose to investigate, any matter with a view to determining—

    (a)   whether there are grounds for believing that a nuclear weapons offence has been committed, or

    (b)   whether a person should be prosecuted for such an offence, that matter shall be treated as an assigned matter within the meaning of the Customs and Excise Management Act 1979 (c. 2).

(5)   Nothing in this section affects any powers of any person (including any officer) apart from this section.

(6)   In this section "officer" means a person commissioned by the Commissioners of Customs and Excise.

(7)   This section does not apply to the institution of proceedings in Scotland.

54 Offences

(1)   A person who knowingly or recklessly makes a false or misleading statement for the purpose of obtaining (or opposing the variation or withdrawal of) authorisation for the purposes of section 47 or 50 is guilty of an offence.

(2)   A person guilty of an offence under subsection (1) is liable—

    (a)   on summary conviction, to a fine of an amount not exceeding the statutory maximum;

    (b)   on conviction on indictment, to imprisonment for a term not exceeding two years or a fine (or both).

(3)   Where an offence under section 47, 50 or subsection (1) above committed by a body corporate is proved to have been committed with the consent or connivance of, or to be attributable to any neglect on the part of—

    (a)   a director, manager, secretary or other similar officer of the body corporate; or

      (b)   any person who was purporting to act in any such capacity, he as well as the body corporate shall be guilty of that offence and shall be liable to be proceeded against and punished accordingly.

    (4)   In subsection (3) "director," in relation to a body corporate whose affairs are managed by its members, means a member of the body corporate.

55 Consent to prosecutions

Proceedings for an offence under section 47 or 50 shall not be instituted—

      (a)   in England and Wales, except by or with the consent of the Attorney General;

      (b)   in Northern Ireland, except by or with the consent of the Attorney General for Northern Ireland.

56 Interpretation of Part 6

    (1)   In this Part "United Kingdom person" means a United Kingdom national, a Scottish partnership or a body incorporated under the law of a part of the United Kingdom.

    (2)   For this purpose a United Kingdom national is an individual who is—

      (a)   a British citizen, a British Dependent Territories citizen, a British National (Overseas) or a British Overseas citizen;

      (b)   a person who under the British Nationality Act 1981 (c. 61) is a British subject; or

      (c)   a British protected person within the meaning of that Act.

Extension of Part 6 to Dependencies

57 Power to extend Part 6 to dependencies

Her Majesty may by Order in Council direct that any of the provisions of this Part shall extend, with such exceptions and modifications as appear to Her Majesty to be appropriate, to any of the Channel Islands, the Isle of Man or to any British overseas territory.

Part 7
Security of Pathogens and Toxins

58 Pathogens and toxins in relation to which requirements under Part 7 apply

    (1)   Schedule 5 (which lists the pathogens and toxins in relation to which the requirements of this Part apply) has effect.

    (2)   The Secretary of State may by order modify any provision of Schedule 5 (including the notes).

(3) The Secretary of State may not add any pathogen or toxin to that Schedule unless he is satisfied that the pathogen or toxin could be used in an act of terrorism to endanger life or cause serious harm to human health.

(4) In this Part "dangerous substance" means—

    (a) anything which consists of or includes a substance for the time being mentioned in Schedule 5; or

    (b) anything which is infected with or otherwise carries any such substance.

(5) But something otherwise falling within subsection (4) is not to be regarded as a dangerous substance if—

    (a) it satisfies prescribed conditions; or

    (b) it is kept or used in prescribed circumstances.

59 Duty to notify Secretary of State before keeping or using dangerous substances

(1) The occupier of any premises must give a notice to the Secretary of State before any dangerous substance is kept or used there.

(2) Subsection (1) does not apply to premises in respect of which a notice has previously been given under that subsection (unless it has been withdrawn).

(3) The occupier of any premises in respect of which a notice has been given may withdraw the notice if no dangerous substance is kept or used there.

(4) A notice under this section must—

    (a) identify the premises in which the substance is kept or used;

    (b) identify any building or site of which the premises form part; and

    (c) contain such other particulars (if any) as may be prescribed.

(5) The occupier of any premises in which any dangerous substance is kept or used on the day on which this section comes into force must give a notice under this section before the end of the period of one month beginning with that day.

(6) Where—

    (a) a substance which is kept or used in any premises becomes a dangerous substance by virtue of a modification of Schedule 5, but

    (b) no other dangerous substance is kept or used there, the occupier of the premises must give a notice under this section before the end of the period of one month beginning with the day on which that modification comes into force.

60 Information about security of dangerous substances

(1) A constable may give to the occupier of any relevant premises a

notice requiring him to give the chief officer of police such information as is specified or described in the notice by a time so specified and in a form and manner so specified.

(2) The required information must relate to—

    (a) any dangerous substance kept or used in the premises; or

    (b) the measures taken (whether by the occupier or any other person) to ensure the security of any such substance.

(3) In this Part references to measures taken to ensure the security of any dangerous substance kept or used in any relevant premises include—

    (a) measures taken to ensure the security of any building or site of which the premises form part; and

    (b) measures taken for the purpose of ensuring access to the substance is given only to those whose activities require access and only in circumstances that ensure the security of the substance.

(4) In this Part "relevant premises" means any premises—

    (a) in which any dangerous substance is kept or used, or

    (b) in respect of which a notice under section 59 is in force.

61 Information about persons with access to dangerous substances

(1) A police officer of at least the rank of inspector may give to the occupier of any relevant premises a notice requiring him to give the chief officer of police a list of—

    (a) each person who has access to any dangerous substance kept or used there;

    (b) each person who, in such circumstances as are specified or described in the notice, has access to such part of the premises as is so specified or described;

    (c) each person who, in such circumstances as are specified or described in the notice, has access to the premises; or

    (d) each person who, in such circumstances as are specified or described in the notice, has access to any building or site of which the premises form part.

(2) A list under subsection (1) must be given before the end of the period of one month beginning with the day on which the notice is given.

(3) Where a list under subsection (1) is given, the occupier of the premises for the time being—

    (a) must secure that only the persons mentioned in the list are given the access identified in the list relating to them; but

    (b) may give a supplementary list to the chief officer of police of other persons to whom it is proposed to give access.

(4) Where a supplementary list is given under subsection (3)(b), the occupier of the premises for the time being must secure that

persons mentioned in that list do not have the proposed access relating to them until the end of the period of 30 days beginning with the day on which that list is given.

(5) The chief officer of police may direct that a person may have such access before the end of that period.

(6) The Secretary of State may by order modify the period mentioned in subsection (4).

(7) Any list under this section must—

  (a) identify the access which the person has, or is proposed to have;

  (b) state the full name of that person, his date of birth, his address and his nationality; and

  (c) contain such other matters (if any) as may be prescribed.

62 Directions requiring security measures

(1) A constable may give directions to the occupier of any relevant premises requiring him to take such measures to ensure the security of any dangerous substance kept or used there as are specified or described in the directions by a time so specified.

(2) The directions may—

  (a) specify or describe the substances in relation to the security of which the measures relate; and

  (b) require the occupier to give a notice to the chief officer of police before any other dangerous substance specified or described in the directions is kept or used in the premises.

63 Directions requiring disposal of dangerous substances

(1) Where the Secretary of State has reasonable grounds for believing that adequate measures to ensure the security of any dangerous substance kept or used in any relevant premises are not being taken and are unlikely to be taken, he may give a direction to the occupier of the premises requiring him to dispose of the substance.

(2) The direction must—

  (a) specify the manner in which, and time by which, the dangerous substance must be disposed of; or

  (b) require the occupier to produce the dangerous substance to a person specified or described in the notice in a manner and by a time so specified for him to dispose of.

64 Directions requiring denial of access

(1) The Secretary of State may give directions to the occupier of any relevant premises requiring him to secure that the person identified in the directions—

  (a) is not to have access to any dangerous substance kept or used there;

(b) is not to have, in such circumstances (if any) as may be specified or described in the directions, access to such part of the premises as is so specified or described;

(c) is not to have, in such circumstances (if any) as may be specified or described in the directions, access to the premises; or

(d) is not to have, in such circumstances (if any) as may be specified or described in the directions, access to any building or site of which the premises form part.

(2) The directions must be given under the hand of the Secretary of State.

(3) The Secretary of State may not give the directions unless he believes that they are necessary in the interests of national security.

65 Powers of entry

(1) A constable may, on giving notice under this section, enter any relevant premises, or any building or site of which the premises form part, at a reasonable time for the purpose of assessing the measures taken to ensure the security of any dangerous substance kept or used in the premises.

(2) The notice must be given to the occupier of the premises, or (as the case may be) the occupier of the building or site of which the premises form part, at least 2 working days before the proposed entry.

(3) The notice must set out the purpose mentioned in subsection (1).

(4) A constable who has entered any premises, building or site by virtue of subsection (1) may for the purpose mentioned in that subsection—

(a) search the premises, building or site;

(b) require any person who appears to the constable to be in charge of the premises, building or site to facilitate any such inspection; and

(c) require any such person to answer any question.

(5) The powers of a constable under this section include power to take with him such other persons as appear to him to be necessary.

66 Search warrants

(1) If, in England and Wales or Northern Ireland, on an application made by a constable a justice of the peace is satisfied that there are reasonable grounds for believing—

(a) that a dangerous substance is kept or used in any premises but that no notice under section 59 is in force in respect of the premises, or

(b) that the occupier of any relevant premises is failing to comply with any direction given to him under section 62 or 63, and that any of the conditions mentioned in subsection (4) apply, he may issue a warrant authorising a constable to enter the premises, if necessary by force, and to search them.

(2) If, in Scotland, on an application made by the procurator fiscal the sheriff is satisfied as mentioned in subsection (1), he may issue a warrant authorising a constable to enter the premises, if necessary by force, and to search them.

(3) A constable may seize and retain anything which he believes is or contains a dangerous substance.

(4) The conditions mentioned in subsection (1) are—

    (a) that it is not practicable to communicate with any person entitled to grant entry to the premises;

    (b) that it is practicable to communicate with a person entitled to grant entry to the premises but it is not practicable to communicate with any person entitled to grant access to any substance which may be a dangerous substance;

    (c) that entry to the premises will not be granted unless a warrant is produced;

    (d) that the purpose of a search may be frustrated or seriously prejudiced unless a constable arriving at the premises can secure immediate entry to them.

67 Offences

(1) An occupier who fails without reasonable excuse to comply with any duty or direction imposed on him by or under this Part is guilty of an offence.

(2) A person who, in giving any information to a person exercising functions under this Part, knowingly or recklessly makes a statement which is false or misleading in a material particular is guilty of an offence.

(3) A person guilty of an offence under this section is liable—

    (a) on conviction on indictment, to imprisonment for a term not exceeding five years or a fine (or both); and

    (b) on summary conviction, to imprisonment for a term not exceeding six months or a fine not exceeding the statutory maximum (or both).

68 Bodies corporate

(1) If an offence under this Part committed by a body corporate is shown to have been committed with the consent or connivance of, or to be attributable to any neglect on the part of—

    (a) any officer, or

    (b) any other employee of the body corporate who is in charge of any relevant premises or the access to any dangerous substance kept or used there, he, as well as the body corporate, is guilty of the offence and liable to be proceeded against and punished accordingly.

(2) In this section "officer," in relation to a body corporate, means—
   (a) any director, manager, secretary or other similar officer of the body corporate; or
   (b) any person purporting to act in any such capacity.

(3) Where the affairs of a body corporate are managed by its members, this section applies in relation to the acts and defaults of a member in connection with his functions of management as if he were a director of the body corporate.

69 Partnerships and unincorporated associations
   (1) Proceedings for an offence alleged to have been committed by a partnership or an unincorporated association must be brought in the name of the partnership or association (and not in that of any of its members).

   (2) A fine imposed on the partnership or association on its conviction of an offence is to be paid out of the funds of the partnership or association.

   (3) Rules of court relating to the service of documents are to have effect as if the partnership or association were a body corporate.

   (4) In proceedings for an offence brought against the partnership or association—
      (a) section 33 of the Criminal Justice Act 1925 (c. 86) and Schedule 3 to the Magistrates' Courts Act 1980 (c. 43) (procedure) apply as they do in relation to a body corporate;
      (b) sections 70 and 143 of the Criminal Procedure (Scotland) Act 1995 (c. 46) (procedure) apply as they do in relation to a body corporate;
      (c) section 18 of the Criminal Justice (Northern Ireland) Act 1945 (c. 15 (N.I.)) and Schedule 4 to the Magistrates' Courts (Northern Ireland) Order 1981 (S.I. 1981/1675 (N.I. 26)) (procedure) apply as they do in relation to a body corporate.

   (5) If an offence under this Part committed by a partnership is shown to have been committed with the consent or connivance of, or to be attributable to any neglect on the part of—
      (a) a partner or a person purporting to act as a partner, or
      (b) any employee of the partnership who is in charge of any relevant premises or the access to any dangerous substance kept or used there, he, as well as the partnership, is guilty of the offence and liable to be proceeded against and punished accordingly.

   (6) If an offence under this Part committed by an unincorporated association is shown to have been committed with the consent or connivance of, or to be attributable to any neglect on the part of—
      (a) any officer, or

(b)   any employee of the association who is in charge of any relevant premises or the access to any dangerous substance kept or used there, he, as well as the association, is guilty of the offence and liable to be proceeded against and punished accordingly.

(7)   In subsection (6) "officer," in relation to any association, means—

    (a)   any officer of the association or any member of its governing body; or

    (b)   any person purporting to act in such a capacity.

70   Denial of access: appeals

(1)   There shall be a commission, to be known as the Pathogens Access Appeal Commission.

(2)   Any person aggrieved by directions given under section 64 may appeal to the Commission.

(3)   The Commission must allow an appeal if it considers that the decision to give the directions was flawed when considered in the light of the principles applicable on an application for judicial review.

(4)   A party to any appeal under this section which the Commission has determined may bring a further appeal on a question of law to—

    (a)   the Court of Appeal, if the first appeal was heard in England and Wales;

    (b)   the Court of Session, if the first appeal was heard in Scotland; or

    (c)   the Court of Appeal in Northern Ireland, if the first appeal was heard in Northern Ireland.

(5)   An appeal under subsection ( ) may be brought only with the permission of—

    (a)   the Commission; or

    (b)   where the Commission refuses permission, the court to which the appeal would be brought.

(6)   Schedule 6 (constitution of the Commission and procedure) has effect.

71   Other appeals

(1)   Any person who is required to do any act in response to—

    (a)   any notice under section 60, or

    (b)   any directions under section 62 or 63,

may appeal to a magistrates' court against the requirement on the ground that, having regard to all the circumstances of the case, it is unreasonable to be required to do that act.

(2)   An appeal may not be brought after the end of the period of one month beginning with the day on which the notice or directions were given.

(3)   If the magistrates' court allows the appeal, it may—

       (a)   direct that the required act need not be done; or

       (b)   make such modification of the requirement as it considers appropriate.

  (4)   An appeal shall lie to the Crown Court against any decision of the magistrates' court.

  (5)   Subsections (1) to (3) apply to Scotland with the substitution for references to the magistrates' court of references to the sheriff.

  (6)   The appeal to the sheriff is by way of summary application.

  (7)   A further appeal shall lie—

       (a)   to the sheriff principal from the decision of the sheriff; and

       (b)   with the leave of the sheriff principal, to the Court of Session from the decision of the sheriff principal.

  (8)   In the application of this section to Northern Ireland references to a magistrates' court are to a court of summary jurisdiction.

72 Giving of directions or notices

Any direction or notice under this Part may be given by post.

73 Orders and regulations

  (1)   The power to make an order or regulations under this Part is exercisable by statutory instrument.

  (2)   A statutory instrument containing an order under section 58 shall not be made unless a draft of it has been laid before and approved by a resolution of each House of Parliament.

  (3)   A statutory instrument containing—

       (a)   an order under section 61, or

       (b)   regulations under section 58, 59 or 61,

shall be subject to annulment in pursuance of a resolution of either House of Parliament.

74 Interpretation of Part 7

  (1)   In this Part—

"act of terrorism" has the same meaning as in the Terrorism Act 2000 (c. 11);

"chief officer of police" means—

       (a)   in relation to any premises in Great Britain, the chief officer of police for the area in which the premises are situated; and

       (b)   in relation to any premises in Northern Ireland, the Chief Constable of the Police Service of Northern Ireland;

"dangerous substance" has the meaning given in section 58;

"direction" means a direction in writing;

"notice" means a notice in writing;

"occupier" includes a partnership or unincorporated association and, in relation to premises that are unoccupied, means any person entitled to occupy the premises;

"prescribed" means prescribed in regulations made by the Secretary of State; and

"relevant premises" has the meaning given in section 60.

(2) In this Part references to measures taken to ensure the security of any dangerous substance are to be construed in accordance with section 60.

75 Power to extend Part 7 to animal or plant pathogens, pests or toxic chemicals

(1) The Secretary of State may, in relation to anything to which this section applies, make an order applying, or making provision corresponding to, any provision of this Part, with or without modifications.

(2) This section applies to—

   (a) toxic chemicals (within the meaning of the Chemical Weapons Act 1996 (c. 6));

   (b) animal pathogens;

   (c) plant pathogens; and

   (d) pests.

(3) The power under this section may be exercised in relation to any chemical only if the Secretary of State is satisfied that the chemical could be used in an act of terrorism to endanger life or cause serious harm to human health.

(4) The power under this section may be exercised in relation to any pathogen or pest only if the Secretary of State is satisfied that there is a risk that the pathogen or pest is of a description that could be used in an act of terrorism to cause—

   (a) widespread damage to property;

   (b) significant disruption to the public; or

   (c) significant alarm to the public.

(5) An order under this section may—

   (a) provide for any reference in the order to an instrument or other document to take effect as a reference to that instrument or document as revised or re-issued from time to time;

   (b) make different provision for different purposes; and

   (c) make such incidental, supplementary and transitional provision as the Secretary of State thinks fit.

(6) A statutory instrument containing an order under this section shall not be made unless a draft of it has been laid before and approved by a resolution of each House of Parliament.

Part 8
Security of Nuclear Industry

76 Atomic Energy Authority special constables
   (1)   Section 3 of the Special Constables Act 1923 (c. 11) shall have effect
         as if all nuclear sites that are not for the time being designated under
         subsection (2) were premises under the control of the United
         Kingdom Atomic Energy Authority.
   (2)   The Secretary of State may by order made by statutory instrument
         designate any nuclear sites which appear to him to be used wholly
         or mainly for defence purposes as premises to which subsection (1)
         does not apply.
   (3)   An AEA constable shall have the powers and privileges (and be liable
         to the duties and responsibilities) of a constable anywhere within 5
         kilometres of the limits of the nuclear sites to which subsection (1)
         applies.
   (4)   An AEA constable shall have the powers and privileges (and be liable
         to the duties and responsibilities) of a constable anywhere it appears
         to him expedient to go—
         (a)   in order to safeguard any nuclear material which is being car-
               ried (or being trans-shipped or stored incidentally to its car-
               riage) before its delivery at its final destination; or
         (b)   in order to pursue, arrest, place in the custody of the police, or
               take to any premises within which the constable was appointed
               to act, a person who the constable reasonably believes has (or
               has attempted to) unlawfully remove or interfere with any
               nuclear material being safeguarded by the constable.
   (5)   An AEA constable shall have the powers and privileges (and be liable
         to the duties and responsibilities) of a constable at any place at which
         he reasonably believes a particular consignment of nuclear material
         will be trans-shipped or stored incidentally to its carriage, in order
         to ensure the security of the nuclear material on its arrival at that
         place.
   (6)   This section has effect in United Kingdom waters adjacent to Great
         Britain as it applies in Great Britain.
   (7)   In this section—
         "AEA constable" means a person appointed on the nomination of
         the United Kingdom Atomic Energy Authority to be a special con-
         stable under section 3 of the Special Constables Act 1923;
         "nuclear material" means—

(a) any fissile material in the form of uranium metal, alloy or chemical compound, or of plutonium metal, alloy or chemical compound; or

(b) any other fissile material which may be prescribed by regulations made by the Secretary of State;

"nuclear site" means premises in respect of which a nuclear site licence (within the meaning of the Nuclear Installations Act 1965 (c. 57)) is for the time being in force; and

"United Kingdom waters" means waters within the seaward limits of the territorial sea.

(8) An order under subsection (2) shall be laid before Parliament after being made.

(9) The power to make regulations under subsection (7) is exercisable by statutory instrument subject to annulment in pursuance of a resolution of either House of Parliament.

77 Regulation of security of civil nuclear industry

(1) The Secretary of State may make regulations for the purpose of ensuring the security of—

(a) nuclear sites and other nuclear premises;

(b) nuclear material used or stored on nuclear sites or other nuclear premises and equipment or software used or stored on such sites or premises in connection with activities involving nuclear material;

(c) other radioactive material used or stored on nuclear sites and equipment or software used or stored on nuclear sites in connection with activities involving other radioactive material;

(d) sensitive nuclear information which is in the possession or control of anyone who is (or is expected to be) involved in activities on, or in relation to, any nuclear site or other nuclear premises;

(e) nuclear material which is being (or is expected to be)—

(i) transported within the United Kingdom or its territorial sea;

(ii) transported (outside the United Kingdom and its territorial sea) to or from any nuclear site or other nuclear premises in the United Kingdom; or

(iii) carried on board a United Kingdom ship;

(f) information relating to the security of anything mentioned in paragraphs (a) to (e).

(2) The regulations may, in particular—

(a) require a person to produce for the approval of the Secretary of State a plan for ensuring the security of anything mentioned in subsection (1) and to comply with the plan as approved by the Secretary of State;

(b) require compliance with any directions given by the Secretary of State;

(c) impose requirements in relation to any activities by reference to the approval of the Secretary of State;

(d) create summary offences or offences triable either way;

(e) make provision for the purposes mentioned in subsection (1) corresponding to any provision which may be made for the general purposes of Part 1 of the Health and Safety at Work etc. Act 1974 (c. 37) by virtue of section 15(2), (3)(c) and (4) to (8) of that Act (health and safety regulations);

(f) make provision corresponding to any provision which may be made by virtue of section 43(2) to (5), (8) and (9) of that Act (fees), in connection with the performance by or on behalf of the Secretary of State or any other specified body or person of functions under the regulations; and

(g) apply (with or without modifications), or make provision corresponding to, any provision contained in sections 19 to 42 and 44 to 47 of that Act.

(3) An offence under the regulations may be made punishable—

(a) in the case of an offence triable either way—

(i) on conviction on indictment, with imprisonment for a term not exceeding two years or a fine (or both); and

(ii) on summary conviction, with imprisonment for a term not exceeding six months or a fine not exceeding the statutory maximum (or both); or

(b) in the case of a summary offence, with imprisonment for a term not exceeding six months or a fine not exceeding level 5 on the standard scale (or both).

(4) The regulations may make—

(a) provision applying to acts done outside the United Kingdom by United Kingdom persons;

(b) different provision for different purposes; and

(c) such incidental, supplementary and transitional provision as the Secretary of State considers appropriate.

(5) Before making the regulations the Secretary of State shall consult—

(a) the Health and Safety Commission; and

(b) such other persons as he considers appropriate.

(6) The power to make the regulations is exercisable by statutory instrument subject to annulment in pursuance of a resolution of either House of Parliament.

(7) In this section—

"nuclear material" and "nuclear site" have the same meaning as in section 76;

"other nuclear premises" means premises other than a nuclear site on which nuclear material is used or stored;

"sensitive nuclear information" means—

(a) information relating to, or capable of use in connection with, any treatment of uranium that increases the proportion of the isotope 235 contained in the uranium; or

(b) information relating to activities carried out on or in relation to nuclear sites or other nuclear premises which appears to the Secretary of State to be information which needs to be protected in the interests of national security;

"United Kingdom ship" means a ship registered in the United Kingdom under Part 2 of the Merchant Shipping Act 1995 (c. 21)

(8) Any sums received by virtue of provision made under subsection (2)(f) shall be paid into the Consolidated Fund.

78 Repeals relating to security of civil nuclear installations

(1) In Schedule 1 to the Nuclear Installations Act 1965 (c. 57) (security provisions applicable by order under section 2 of that Act), paragraphs 5 and 6 shall cease to have effect.

(2) In section 19(1) of the Atomic Energy Authority Act 1971 (c. 11) (application of certain security provisions to designated companies), for "Paragraphs 4 to 6" and "they apply" substitute respectively "Paragraph 4" and "it applies."

79 Prohibition of disclosures relating to nuclear security

(1) A person is guilty of an offence if he discloses any information or thing the disclosure of which might prejudice the security of any nuclear site or of any nuclear material—

(a) with the intention of prejudicing that security; or

(b) being reckless as to whether the disclosure might prejudice that security.

(2) The reference in subsection (1) to nuclear material is a reference to—

(a) nuclear material which is being held on any nuclear site, or

(b) nuclear material anywhere in the world which is being transported to or from a nuclear site or carried on board a British ship, (including nuclear material which is expected to be so held, transported or carried).

(3) A person guilty of an offence under subsection (1) is liable—

    (a)   on conviction on indictment, to imprisonment for a term not exceeding seven years or a fine (or both); and

    (b)   on summary conviction, to imprisonment for a term not exceeding six months or a fine not exceeding the statutory maximum (or both).

(4)   In this section—

"British ship" means a ship (including a ship belonging to Her Majesty) which is registered in the United Kingdom;

"disclose" and "disclosure," in relation to a thing, include parting with possession of it;

"nuclear material" has the same meaning as in section 76; and

"nuclear site" means a site in the United Kingdom (including a site occupied by or on behalf of the Crown) which is (or is expected to be) used for any purpose mentioned in section 1(1) of the Nuclear Installations Act 1965 (c. 57).

(5)   This section applies to acts done outside the United Kingdom, but only if they are done by a United Kingdom person.

(6)   Proceedings for an offence committed outside the United Kingdom may be taken, and the offence may for incidental purposes be treated as having been committed, in any place in the United Kingdom.

(7)   Nothing in subsection (5) affects any criminal liability arising otherwise than under that subsection.

80 Prohibition of disclosures of uranium enrichment technology

(1)   This section applies to—

    (a)   any information about the enrichment of uranium; or

    (b)   any information or thing which is, or is likely to be, used in connection with the enrichment of uranium;

and for this purpose "the enrichment of uranium" means any treatment of uranium that increases the proportion of the isotope 235 contained in the uranium.

(2)   The Secretary of State may make regulations prohibiting the disclosure of information or things to which this section applies.

(3)   A person who contravenes a prohibition is guilty of an offence and liable—

    (a)   on conviction on indictment, to imprisonment for a term not exceeding seven years or a fine (or both); and

    (b)   on summary conviction, to imprisonment for a term not exceeding six months or a fine not exceeding the statutory maximum (or both).

(4)   The regulations may, in particular, provide for—

     (a)   a prohibition to apply, or not to apply—
        (i)   to such information or things; and
        (ii) in such cases or circumstances,

        as may be prescribed;

     (b)   the authorisation by the Secretary of State of disclosures that would otherwise be prohibited; and

     (c)   defences to an offence under subsection (3) relating to any prohibition.

(5)   The regulations may—

     (a)   provide for any prohibition to apply to acts done outside the United Kingdom by United Kingdom persons;

     (b)   make different provision for different purposes; and

     (c)   make such incidental, supplementary and transitional provision as the Secretary of State thinks fit.

(6)   The power to make the regulations is exercisable by statutory instrument.

(7)   The regulations shall not be made unless a draft of the regulations has been laid before and approved by each House of Parliament.

(8)   In this section—

"disclosure," in relation to a thing, includes parting with possession of it;

"information" includes software; and

"prescribed" means specified or described in the regulations.

81   Part 8: supplementary

(1)   Proceedings for an offence under section 79 or 80 shall not be instituted—

     (a)   in England and Wales, except by or with the consent of the Attorney General; or

     (b)   in Northern Ireland, except by or with the consent of the Attorney General for Northern Ireland.

(2)   In this Part "United Kingdom person" means a United Kingdom national, a Scottish partnership or a body incorporated under the law of any part of the United Kingdom.

(3)   For this purpose a United Kingdom national is an individual who is—

     (a)   a British citizen, a British Dependent Territories citizen, a British National (Overseas) or a British Overseas citizen;

     (b)   a person who under the British Nationality Act 1981 (c. 61) is a British subject; or

     (c)   a British protected person within the meaning of that Act.

Part 9
Aviation Security

82 Arrest without warrant

(1) At the end of section 24(2) of the Police and Criminal Evidence Act 1984 (c. 60) (arrest without warrant: particular offences) insert—

"(u) an offence under section 21C(1) or 21D(1) of the Aviation Security Act 1982 (c. 36) (unauthorised presence in restricted zone or on aircraft);

(v) an offence under section 39(1) of the Civil Aviation Act 1982 (c. 16) (trespass on aerodrome)."

(2) At the end of Article 26(2) of the Police and Criminal Evidence (Northern Ireland) Order 1989 (S.I. 1989/1341 (N.I. 12)) (arrest without warrant: particular offences) insert—

"(j) an offence under section 21C(1) or 21D(1) of the Aviation Security Act 1982 (unauthorised presence in restricted zone or on aircraft);

(k) an offence under section 39(1) of the Civil Aviation Act 1982 (trespass on aerodrome)."

(3) Where, in Scotland, a constable has reasonable grounds for suspecting that a person has committed—

(a) an offence under section 21C(1) or 21D(1) of the Aviation Security Act 1982 (unauthorised presence in restricted zone or on aircraft);

(b) an offence under section 39(1) of the Civil Aviation Act 1982 (trespass on aerodrome),

he may arrest that person without warrant.

(4) This section shall have effect in relation to an offence committed or alleged to have been committed after the end of the period of two months beginning with the day on which this Act is passed.

83 Trespass on aerodrome: penalty

(1) In section 39(1) of the Civil Aviation Act 1982 (trespass on aerodrome) for "level 1 on the standard scale" substitute "level 3 on the standard scale."

(2) This section shall have effect in relation to an offence committed after the end of the period of two months beginning with the day on which this Act is passed.

84 Removal of intruder

(1) At the end of section 21C of the Aviation Security Act 1982 (unauthorised presence in aerodrome) add—

"(4) A constable, the manager of an aerodrome or a person acting on his behalf may use reasonable force to remove a person who fails to comply with a request under subsection (.1)(b) above."

(2) At the end of section 21D of that Act (unauthorised presence on aircraft) add—

"(3) A constable, the operator of an aircraft or a person acting on his behalf may use reasonable force to remove a person who fails to comply with a request under subsection (1)(b) above."

85 Aviation security services

After section 20 of the Aviation Security Act 1982 (c. 36) (security directions: inspection) insert—

"20A Aviation security services: approved providers

(1) In this section "aviation security service" means a process or activity carried out for the purpose of—
  (a) complying with a requirement of a direction under any of sections 12 to 14, or
  (b) facilitating a person's compliance with a requirement of a direction under any of those sections.

(2) Regulations may provide for the Secretary of State to maintain a list of persons who are approved by him for the provision of a particular aviation security service.

(3) The regulations may—
  (a) prohibit the provision of an aviation security service by a person who is not listed in respect of that service;
  (b) prohibit the use or engagement for the provision of an aviation security service of a person who is not listed in respect of that service;
  (c) create a criminal offence;
  (d) make provision about application for inclusion in the list (including provision about fees);
  (e) make provision about the duration and renewal of entries on the list (including provision about fees);
  (f) make provision about training or qualifications which persons who apply to be listed or who are listed are required to undergo or possess;
  (g) make provision about removal from the list which shall include provision for appeal;
  (h) make provision about the inspection of activities carried out by listed persons;
  (i) confer functions on the Secretary of State or on a specified person;

(j)   confer jurisdiction on a court.

(4)   Regulations under subsection (3)(c)—

    (a)   may not provide for a penalty on summary conviction greater than a fine not exceeding the statutory maximum,

    (b)   may not provide for a penalty of imprisonment on conviction on indictment greater than imprisonment for a term not exceeding two years (whether or not accompanied by a fine), and

    (c)   may create a criminal offence of purporting, with intent to deceive, to do something as a listed person or of doing something, with intent to deceive, which purports to be done by a listed person.

(5)   A direction under any of sections 12 to 14 may—

    (a)   include a requirement to use a listed person for the provision of an aviation security service;

    (b)   provide for all or part of the direction not to apply or to apply with modified effect where a listed person provides an aviation security service.

(6)   Regulations under this section—

    (a)   may make different provision for different cases,

    (b)   may include incidental, supplemental or transitional provision,

    (c)   shall be made by the Secretary of State by statutory instrument,

    (d)   shall not be made unless the Secretary of State has consulted organisations appearing to him to represent persons affected by the regulations, and

    (e)   shall be subject to annulment in pursuance of a resolution of either House of Parliament."

86 Detention of aircraft

    (1)   After section 20A of the Aviation Security Act 1982 (c. 36) (aviation security services) (inserted by section 85)) insert—

    "Detention of aircraft

20B   Detention direction

    (1)   An authorised person may give a detention direction in respect of an aircraft if he is of the opinion that—

    (a)   a person has failed to comply or is likely to fail to comply with a requirement of a direction under section 12 or 14 of this Act in respect of the aircraft,

    (b)   a person has failed to comply with a requirement of an enforcement notice in respect of the aircraft,

    (c)   a threat has been made to commit an act of violence against the aircraft or against any person or property on board the aircraft, or

        (d)   an act of violence is likely to be committed against the aircraft or against any person or property on board the aircraft.

(2)   A detention direction in respect of an aircraft—

        (a)   shall be given in writing to the operator of the aircraft, and

        (b)   shall require him to take steps to ensure that the aircraft does not fly while the direction is in force.

(3)   An authorised person who has given a detention direction in respect of an aircraft may do anything which he considers necessary or expedient for the purpose of ensuring that the aircraft does not fly while the direction is in force; in particular, the authorised person may—

        (a)   enter the aircraft;

        (b)   arrange for another person to enter the aircraft;

        (c)   arrange for a person or thing to be removed from the aircraft;

        (d)   use reasonable force;

        (e)   authorise the use of reasonable force by another person.

(4)   The operator of an aircraft in respect of which a detention direction is given may object to the direction in writing to the Secretary of State.

(5)   On receipt of an objection to a detention direction under subsection (4) the Secretary of State shall—

        (a)   consider the objection,

        (b)   allow the person making the objection and the authorised person who gave the direction an opportunity to make written or oral representations to the Secretary of State or to a person appointed by him,

        (c)   confirm, vary or cancel the direction, and

        (d)   give notice of his decision in writing to the person who made the objection and to the authorised person who gave the direction.

(6)   A detention direction in respect of an aircraft shall continue in force until—

        (a)   an authorised person cancels it by notice in writing to the operator of the aircraft, or

        (b)   the Secretary of State cancels it under subsection (5)(c).

(7)   A person commits an offence if—

        (a)   without reasonable excuse he fails to comply with a requirement of a detention direction, or

        (b)   he intentionally obstructs a person acting in accordance with subsection (3).

(8)   A person who is guilty of an offence under subsection (7) shall be liable—

        (a)   on summary conviction, to a fine not exceeding the statutory maximum, or

    (b)   on conviction on indictment, to a fine, to imprisonment for a
           term not exceeding two years or to both.
    (9)   A detention direction may be given in respect of—
           (a)   any aircraft in the United Kingdom, and
           (b)   any aircraft registered or operating in the United Kingdom.
    (10)   A detention direction may be given in respect of a class of aircraft;
           and for that purpose—
           (a)   a reference to "the aircraft" in subsection (1) shall be treated
                  as a reference to all or any of the aircraft within the class, and
           (b)   subsections (2) to (9) shall apply as if the direction were given
                  in respect of each aircraft within the class."
    (2)   In section 23 of the Aviation Security Act 1982 (c. 36) (annual
           report)—
           (a)   in subsection (1) after "enforcement notices" insert "and
                  detention directions," and
           (b)   in subsection (2) for "and enforcement notices" substitute
                  "enforcement notices and detention directions."
    (3)   At the end of section 24 of that Act add—
    "(9) Subsections (6) to (8) above shall apply to a detention direction as
    they apply to an enforcement notice."

87 Air cargo agent: documents

    After section 21F of the Aviation Security Act 1982 (air cargo agents)
    insert—

    "21F A Air cargo agents: documents

    (1)   A person commits an offence if with intent to deceive he issues a
           document which purports to be issued by a person on a list of
           approved air cargo agents maintained under section 21F(2)(a) of
           this Act.
    (2)   A person guilty of an offence under subsection (1) shall be liable on
           summary conviction to imprisonment for a term not exceeding six
           months or to a fine not exceeding level 5 on the standard scale or
           to both."

88 Extent outside United Kingdom

    (1)   The powers in section 108(1) and (2) of the Civil Aviation Act 1982
           (c. 16) (extension outside United Kingdom) apply to provisions of
           this Part which amend that Act.
    (2)   The powers in section 39(3) of the Aviation Security Act 1982
           (extension outside United Kingdom) apply to provisions of this Part
           which amend that Act.

Part 10
Police Powers

Identification

89 Fingerprinting of terrorist suspects

(1) Schedule 8 to the Terrorism Act 2000 (c. 11) (persons detained under terrorism provisions) is amended as follows.

(2) In paragraph 10, at the beginning of sub-paragraph (6) (grounds on which officer may authorise fingerprinting or taking of sample), insert "Subject to sub-paragraph (6A)"; and after that sub-paragraph insert—

"(6A) An officer may also give an authorisation under sub-paragraph (4)(a) for the taking of fingerprints if—

(a) he is satisfied that the fingerprints of the detained person will facilitate the ascertainment of that person's identity; and

(b) that person has refused to identify himself or the officer has reasonable grounds for suspecting that that person is not who he claims to be.

(6B) In this paragraph references to ascertaining a person's identity include references to showing that he is not a particular person."

(3) In paragraph 20(2), for the subsection (2) substituted by way of modification of section 18 of the Criminal Procedure (Scotland) Act 1995 (c. 46) substitute—

"'(2) Subject to subsection (2A), a constable may take from a detained person or require a detained person to provide relevant physical data only if—

(a) in the case of a person detained under section 41 of the Terrorism Act 2000, he reasonably suspects that the person has been involved in an offence under any of the provisions mentioned in section 40(1)(a) of that Act and he reasonably believes that the relevant physical data will tend to confirm or disprove his involvement; or

(b) in any case, he is satisfied that it is necessary to do so in order to assist in determining whether the person falls within section 40(1)(b).

(2A) A constable may also take fingerprints from a detained person or require him to provide them if—

(a) he is satisfied that the fingerprints of that person will facilitate the ascertainment of that person's identity; and

(b) that person has refused to identify himself or the constable has reasonable grounds for suspecting that that person is not who he claims to be.

(2B) In this section references to ascertaining a person's identity include references to showing that he is not a particular person.'"

(4) For paragraph 20(3) substitute—

"(3) Subsections (3) to (5) shall not apply, but any relevant physical data or sample taken in pursuance of section 18 as applied by this paragraph may be retained but shall not be used by any person except for the purposes of a terrorist investigation or for purposes related to the prevention or detection of crime, the investigation of an offence or the conduct of a prosecution.

(4) In this paragraph—

(a) a reference to crime includes a reference to any conduct which—
   (i) constitutes one or more criminal offences (whether under the law of a part of the United Kingdom or of a country or territory outside the United Kingdom); or
   (ii) is, or corresponds to, any conduct which, if it all took place in any one part of the United Kingdom, would constitute one or more criminal offences; and

(b) the references to an investigation and to a prosecution include references, respectively, to any investigation outside the United Kingdom of any crime or suspected crime and to a prosecution brought in respect of any crime in a country or territory outside the United Kingdom."

90 Searches, examinations and fingerprinting: England and Wales

(1) After section 54 of the Police and Criminal Evidence Act 1984 (c. 60) (searches of detained persons) insert—

"54A Searches and examination to ascertain identity

(1) If an officer of at least the rank of inspector authorises it, a person who is detained in a police station may be searched or examined, or both—

(a) for the purpose of ascertaining whether he has any mark that would tend to identify him as a person involved in the commission of an offence; or

(b) for the purpose of facilitating the ascertainment of his identity.

(2) An officer may only give an authorisation under subsection (1) for the purpose mentioned in paragraph (a) of that subsection if—

(a) the appropriate consent to a search or examination that would reveal whether the mark in question exists has been withheld; or

(b) it is not practicable to obtain such consent.

(3)   An officer may only give an authorisation under subsection (1) in a case in which subsection (2) does not apply if—

(a)   the person in question has refused to identify himself; or

(b)   the officer has reasonable grounds for suspecting that that person is not who he claims to be.

(4)   An officer may give an authorisation under subsection (1) orally or in writing but, if he gives it orally, he shall confirm it in writing as soon as is practicable.

(5)   Any identifying mark found on a search or examination under this section may be photographed—

(a)   with the appropriate consent; or

(b)   if the appropriate consent is withheld or it is not practicable to obtain it, without it.

(6)   Where a search or examination may be carried out under this section, or a photograph may be taken under this section, the only persons entitled to carry out the search or examination, or to take the photograph, are—

(a)   constables; and

(b)   persons who (without being constables) are designated for the purposes of this section by the chief officer of police for the police area in which the police station in question is situated;

and section 117 (use of force) applies to the exercise by a person falling within paragraph (b) of the powers conferred by the preceding provisions of this section as it applies to the exercise of those powers by a constable.

(7)   A person may not under this section carry out a search or examination of a person of the opposite sex or take a photograph of any part of the body of a person of the opposite sex.

(8)   An intimate search may not be carried out under this section.

(9)   A photograph taken under this section—

(a)   may be used by, or disclosed to, any person for any purpose related to the prevention or detection of crime, the investigation of an offence or the conduct of a prosecution; and

(b)   after being so used or disclosed, may be retained but may not be used or disclosed except for a purpose so related.

(10) In subsection—-

(a)   the reference to crime includes a reference to any conduct which—

(i)   constitutes one or more criminal offences (whether under the law of a part of the United Kingdom or of a country or territory outside the United Kingdom); or

   (ii)   is, or corresponds to, any conduct which, if it all took place in any one part of the United Kingdom, would constitute one or more criminal offences;

and

   (b)   the references to an investigation and to a prosecution include references, respectively, to any investigation outside the United Kingdom of any crime or suspected crime and to a prosecution brought in respect of any crime in a country or territory outside the United Kingdom.

(11)   In this section—

   (a)   references to ascertaining a person's identity include references to showing that he is not a particular person; and

   (b)   references to taking a photograph include references to using any process by means of which a visual image may be produced, and references to photographing a person shall be construed accordingly.

(12)   In this section "mark" includes features and injuries; and a mark is an identifying mark for the purposes of this section if its existence in any person's case facilitates the ascertainment of his identity or his identification as a person involved in the commission of an offence."

(2)   In section 61(4) of that Act (grounds on which fingerprinting of person detained at a police station may be authorised)—

   (a)   in paragraph (b), after "his involvement" insert "or will facilitate the ascertainment of his identity (within the meaning of section 54A), or both";

   (b)   after that paragraph insert—

"but an authorisation shall not be given for the purpose only of facilitating the ascertainment of that person's identity except where he has refused to identify himself or the officer has reasonable grounds for suspecting that he is not who he claims to be."

91   Searches, examinations and fingerprinting: Northern Ireland

(1)   After Article 55 of the Police and Criminal Evidence (Northern Ireland) Order 1989 (S.I. 1989/1341 (N.I. 12)) (searches of detained persons) insert—

"55A   Searches and examination to ascertain identity

(1)   If an officer of at least the rank of inspector authorises it, a person who is detained in a police station may be searched or examined, or both—

   (a)   for the purpose of ascertaining whether he has any mark that would tend to identify him as a person involved in the commission of an offence; or

    (b)   for the purpose of facilitating the ascertainment of his identity.

(2)   An officer may only give an authorisation under paragraph (1) for the purpose mentioned in sub-paragraph (a) of that paragraph if—

    (a)   the appropriate consent to a search or examination that would reveal whether the mark in question exists has been withheld; or

    (b)   it is not practicable to obtain such consent.

(3)   An officer may only give an authorisation under paragraph (1) in a case in which paragraph (2) does not apply if—

    (a)   the person in question has refused to identify himself; or

    (b)   the officer has reasonable grounds for suspecting that that person is not who he claims to be.

(4)   An officer may give an authorisation under paragraph (1) orally or in writing but, if he gives it orally, he shall confirm it in writing as soon as is practicable.

(5)   Any identifying mark found on a search or examination under this Article may be photographed—

    (a)   with the appropriate consent; or

    (b)   if the appropriate consent is withheld or it is not practicable to obtain it, without it.

(6)   Where a search or examination may be carried out under this Article, or a photograph may be taken under this Article, the only persons entitled to carry out the search or examination, or to take the photograph, are—

    (a)   constables; and

    (b)   persons who (without being constables) are designated for the purposes of this Article by the Chief Constable;

and Article 88 (use of force) applies to the exercise by a person falling within sub-paragraph (b) of the powers conferred by the preceding provisions of this Article as it applies to the exercise of those powers by a constable.

(7)   A person may not under this Article carry out a search or examination of a person of the opposite sex or take a photograph of any part of the body of a person of the opposite sex.

(8)   An intimate search may not be carried out under this Article.

(9)   A photograph taken under this Article—

    (a)   may be used by, or disclosed to, any person for any purpose related to the prevention or detection of crime, the investigation of an offence or the conduct of a prosecution; and

    (b)   after being so used or disclosed, may be retained but may not be used or disclosed except for a purpose so related.

(10) In paragraph (9)—

    (a)   the reference to crime includes a reference to any conduct which—

(i)   constitutes one or more criminal offences (whether under the law of a part of the United Kingdom or of a country or territory outside the United Kingdom); or

(ii) is, or corresponds to, any conduct which, if it all took place in any one part of the United Kingdom, would constitute one or more criminal offences;

and

(b)   the references to an investigation and to a prosecution include references, respectively, to any investigation outside the United Kingdom of any crime or suspected crime and to a prosecution brought in respect of any crime in a country or territory outside the United Kingdom.

(11) In this Article
(a)   references to ascertaining a person's identity include references to showing that he is not a particular person; and

(b)   references to taking a photograph include references to using any process by means of which a visual image may be produced, and references to photographing a person shall be construed accordingly.

(12) In this Article "mark" includes features and injuries; and a mark is an identifying mark for the purposes of this Article if its existence in any person's case facilitates the ascertainment of his identity or his identification as a person involved in the commission of an offence."

(2)   In Article 61(4) of that Order (grounds on which fingerprinting of person detained at a police station may be authorised)—
(a)   in sub-paragraph (b), after "his involvement" insert "or will facilitate the ascertainment of his identity (within the meaning of Article 55A), or both"; and

(b)   after that sub-paragraph insert—

"but an authorisation shall not be given for the purpose only of facilitating the ascertainment of that person's identity except where he has refused to identify himself or the officer has reasonable grounds for suspecting that he is not who he claims to be."

92 Photographing of suspects etc.: England and Wales

After section 64 of the Police and Criminal Evidence Act 1984 (c. 60) insert—

"64A Photographing of suspects etc.

(1)   A person who is detained at a police station may be photographed—
(a)   with the appropriate consent; or

(b)   if the appropriate consent is withheld or it is not practicable to obtain it, without it.

(2)   A person proposing to take a photograph of any person under this section—

   (a)   may, for the purpose of doing so, require the removal of any item or substance worn on or over the whole or any part of the head or face of the person to be photographed; and

   (b)   if the requirement is not complied with, may remove the item or substance himself.

(3)   Where a photograph may be taken under this section, the only persons entitled to take the photograph are—

   (a)   constables; and

   (b)   persons who (without being constables) are designated for the purposes of this section by the chief officer of police for the police area in which the police station in question is situated;

and section 117 (use of force) applies to the exercise by a person falling within paragraph (b) of the powers conferred by the preceding provisions of this section as it applies to the exercise of those powers by a constable.

(4)   A photograph taken under this section—

   (a)   may be used by, or disclosed to, any person for any purpose related to the prevention or detection of crime, the investigation of an offence or the conduct of a prosecution; and

   (b)   after being so used or disclosed, may be retained but may not be used or disclosed except for a purpose so related.

(5)   In subsection (4)—

   (a)   the reference to crime includes a reference to any conduct which—

      (i)   constitutes one or more criminal offences (whether under the law of a part of the United Kingdom or of a country or territory outside the United Kingdom); or

      (ii)   is, or corresponds to, any conduct which, if it all took place in any one part of the United Kingdom, would constitute one or more criminal offences;

   and

   (b)   the references to an investigation and to a prosecution include references, respectively, to any investigation outside the United Kingdom of any crime or suspected crime and to a prosecution brought in respect of any crime in a country or territory outside the United Kingdom.

(6)   References in this section to taking a photograph include references to using any process by means of which a visual image may be pro-

duced; and references to photographing a person shall be construed accordingly."

93 Photographing of suspects etc.: Northern Ireland

After Article 64 of the Police and Criminal Evidence (Northern Ireland) Order 1989 (S.I. 1989/1341 (N.I. 12)) insert—

"64A Photographing of suspects etc.

(1) A person who is detained at a police station may be photographed—
   (a) with the appropriate consent; or
   (b) if the appropriate consent is withheld or it is not practicable to obtain it, without it.

(2) A person proposing to take a photograph of any person under this Article—
   (a) may, for the purpose of doing so, require the removal of any item or substance worn on or over the whole or any part of the head or face of the person to be photographed; and
   (b) if the requirement is not complied with, may remove the item or substance himself.

(3) Where a photograph may be taken under this Article, the only persons entitled to take the photograph are—
   (a) constables; and
   (b) persons who (without being constables) are designated for the purposes of this Article by the Chief Constable;

and Article 88 (use of force) applies to the exercise by a person falling within sub-paragraph (b) of the powers conferred by the preceding provisions of this Article as it applies to the exercise of those powers by a constable.

(4) A photograph taken under this Article—
   (a) may be used by, or disclosed to, any person for any purpose related to the prevention or detection of crime, the investigation of an offence or the conduct of a prosecution; and
   (b) after being so used or disclosed, may be retained but may not be used or disclosed except for a purpose so related.

(5) In paragraph (4)—
   (a) the reference to crime includes a reference to any conduct which—
      (i) constitutes one or more criminal offences (whether under the law of a part of the United Kingdom or of a country or territory outside the United Kingdom); or
      (ii) is, or corresponds to, any conduct which, if it all took place in any one part of the United Kingdom, would constitute one or more criminal offences;and

    (b)   the references to an investigation and to a prosecution include references, respectively, to any investigation outside the United Kingdom of any crime or suspected crime and to a prosecution brought in respect of any crime in a country or territory outside the United Kingdom.

(6)   References in this Article to taking a photograph include references to using any process by means of which a visual image may be produced; and references to photographing a person shall be construed accordingly."

94 Powers to require removal of disguises: England and Wales

    (1)   After section 60 of the Criminal Justice and Public Order Act 1994 (c. 33) insert—

"60AA Powers to require removal of disguises

(1)   Where—

    (a)   an authorisation under section 60 is for the time being in force in relation to any locality for any period, or

    (b)   an authorisation under subsection (3) that the powers conferred by subsection (2) shall be exercisable at any place in a locality is in force for any period, those powers shall be exercisable at any place in that locality at any time in that period.

(2)   This subsection confers power on any constable in uniform—

    (a)   to require any person to remove any item which the constable reasonably believes that person is wearing wholly or mainly for the purpose of concealing his identity;

    (b)   to seize any item which the constable reasonably believes any person intends to wear wholly or mainly for that purpose.

(3)   If a police officer of or above the rank of inspector reasonably believes—

    (a)   that activities may take place in any locality in his police area that are likely (if they take place) to involve the commission of offences, and

    (b)   that it is expedient, in order to prevent or control the activities, to give an authorisation under this subsection,

he may give an authorisation that the powers conferred by this section shall be exercisable at any place within that locality for a specified period not exceeding twenty-four hours.

(4)   If it appears to an officer of or above the rank of superintendent that it is expedient to do so, having regard to offences which—

    (a)   have been committed in connection with the activities in respect of which the authorisation was given, or

(b)   are reasonably suspected to have been so committed, he may direct that the authorisation shall continue in force for a further twenty-four hours.

(5)   If an inspector gives an authorisation under subsection, he must, as soon as it is practicable to do so, cause an officer of or above the rank of superintendent to be informed.

(6)   Any authorisation under this section—
    (a)   shall be in writing and signed by the officer giving it; and
    (b)   shall specify—
        (i)   the grounds on which it is given;
        (ii)   the locality in which the powers conferred by this section are exercisable;
        (iii)   the period during which those powers are exercisable;

and a direction under subsection (4) shall also be given in writing or, where that is not practicable, recorded in writing as soon as it is practicable to do so.

(7)   A person who fails to remove an item worn by him when required to do so by a constable in the exercise of his power under this section shall be liable, on summary conviction, to imprisonment for a term not exceeding one month or to a fine not exceeding level 3 on the standard scale or both.

(8)   The preceding provisions of this section, so far as they relate to an authorisation by a member of the British Transport Police Force (including one who for the time being has the same powers and privileges as a member of a police force for a police area), shall have effect as if references to a locality or to a locality in his police area were references to any locality in or in the vicinity of any policed premises, or to the whole or any part of any such premises.

(9)   In this section "British Transport Police Force" and "policed premises" each has the same meaning as in section 60.

(10)   The powers conferred by this section are in addition to, and not in derogation of, any power otherwise conferred.

(11)   This section does not extend to Scotland."

(2)   In section 60A(1) of that Act (retention of things seized under section 60), after "section 60" insert "or 60AA."

(3)   In section 24(2) of the Police and Criminal Evidence Act 1984 (c. 60) (arrestable offences), in paragraph (o), for "section 60(8)(b)" substitute "section 60AA(7)."

95   Powers to require removal of disguises: Northern Ireland

(1)   In Part 5 of the Public Order (Northern Ireland) Order 1987 (S.I. 1987/463 (N.I. 7)), before Article 24 insert—

"Temporary powers to deal with activities in a locality

23A Powers to require removal of disguises

(1) Where—

    (a)   an authorisation under paragraph (3) that the powers conferred by paragraph (2) shall be exercisable at any place in a locality is in force for any period, or

    (b)   an authorisation under Article 23B is for the time being in force in relation to any locality for any period, those powers shall be exercisable at any place in that locality at any time in that period.

(2) This paragraph confers power on any constable in uniform—

    (a)   to require any person to remove any item which the constable reasonably believes that person is wearing wholly or mainly for the purpose of concealing his identity;

    (b)   to seize any item which the constable reasonably believes any person intends to wear wholly or mainly for that purpose.

(3) If a police officer of or above the rank of inspector reasonably believes—

    (a)   that activities may take place in any locality that are likely (if they take place) to involve the commission of offences, and

    (b)   that it is expedient, in order to prevent or control the activities, to give an authorisation under this paragraph, he may give an authorisation that the powers conferred by this Article shall be exercisable at any place within that locality for a specified period not exceeding twenty-four hours.

(4) If it appears to an officer of or above the rank of superintendent that it is expedient to do so, having regard to offences which—

    (a)   have been committed in connection with the activities in respect of which the authorisation was given, or

    (b)   are reasonably suspected to have been so committed, he may direct that the authorisation shall continue in force for a further twenty-four hours.

(5) If an officer below the rank of superintendent gives an authorisation under paragraph, he must, as soon as it is practicable to do so, cause an officer of or above that rank to be informed.

(6) Any authorisation under this Article—

    (a)   shall be in writing and signed by the officer giving it; and

    (b)   shall specify—

    (i)   the grounds on which it is given;

    (ii)   the locality in which the powers conferred by this Article are exercisable;

    (iii)   the period during which those powers are exercisable;

and a direction under paragraph (4) shall also be given in writing or, where that is not practicable, recorded in writing as soon as it is practicable to do so.

(7) A person who fails to remove an item worn by him when required to do so by a constable in the exercise of his power under this Article shall be liable, on summary conviction, to imprisonment for a term not exceeding one month or to a fine not exceeding level 3 on the standard scale or both.

(8) The powers conferred by this Article are in addition to, and not in derogation of, any power otherwise conferred."

(2) In Article 26(2) of the Police and Criminal Evidence (Northern Ireland) Order 1989 (S.I. 1989/1341 (N.I. 12)) (arrestable offences), after sub-paragraph (i) insert—

"(ia) an offence under Article 23A(7) of the Public Order (Northern Ireland) Order 1987 (S.I. 1987/463 (N.I. 7)) (failing to comply to requirement to remove disguise)."

Powers of stop, search and seizure in Northern Ireland

96 Power to stop and search in anticipation of violence

In the Public Order (Northern Ireland) Order 1987 (S.I. 1987/463 (N.I. 7)), after Article 23A (which is inserted by section 95) insert—

"23B Powers to stop and search in anticipation of violence

(1) If a police officer of or above the rank of inspector reasonably believes—
   (a) that incidents involving serious violence may take place in any locality, and that it is expedient to give an authorisation under this Article to prevent or control their occurrence, or
   (b) that persons are carrying dangerous instruments or offensive weapons in any locality without good reason,

he may give an authorisation that the powers conferred by this Article are to be exercisable at any place within that locality for a specified period not exceeding twenty-four hours.

(2) This Article confers power on any constable in uniform—
   (a) to stop any pedestrian and search him or anything carried by him for offensive weapons or dangerous instruments;
   (b) to stop any vehicle and search the vehicle, its driver and any passenger for offensive weapons or dangerous instruments;

and a constable may in the exercise of those powers stop any person or vehicle and make any search he thinks fit whether or not he has any grounds for suspecting that the person or vehicle is carrying weapons or dangerous instruments.

(3) If it appears to an officer of or above the rank of superintendent that it is expedient to do so, having regard to offences which—

(a) have been committed in connection with the activities in respect of which the authorisation was given, or

(b) are reasonably suspected to have been so committed,

he may direct that the authorisation shall continue in force for a further twenty-four hours.

(4) If an officer below the rank of superintendent gives an authorisation under paragraph ( ) he must, as soon as it is practicable to do so, cause an officer of or above that rank to be informed.

(5) If in the course of a search under this Article a constable discovers a dangerous instrument or an article which he has reasonable grounds for suspecting to be an offensive weapon, he may seize it.

(6) This Article applies (with the necessary modifications) to ships, aircraft and hovercraft as it applies to vehicles.

(7) A person who fails to stop or (as the case may be) fails to stop a vehicle when required to do so by a constable in the exercise of his powers under this Article shall be liable on summary conviction to imprisonment for a term not exceeding one month or to a fine not exceeding level 3 on the standard scale or both.

(8) Any authorisation under this Article—

(a) shall be in writing and signed by the officer giving it; and

(b) shall specify—

(i) the grounds on which it is given;

(ii) the locality in which the powers conferred by this Article are exercisable;

(iii) the period during which those powers are exercisable;

and a direction under paragraph ( ) shall also be given in writing or, where that is not practicable, recorded in writing as soon as it is practicable to do so.

(9) Where a vehicle is stopped by a constable under this Article the driver shall be entitled to obtain a written statement that the vehicle was stopped under the powers conferred by this Article if he applies for such a statement not later than the end of the period of 12 months from the day on which the vehicle was stopped.

(10) A person who is searched by a constable under this Article shall be entitled to obtain a written statement that he was searched under the powers conferred by this Article if he applies for such a statement not later than the end of the period of 12 months from the day on which he was searched.

(11) The powers conferred by this Article are in addition to, and not in derogation of, any power otherwise conferred.

(12) For the purposes of this Article, a person carries a dangerous instrument or an offensive weapon if he has it in his possession.

(13) In this Article—

"caravan" has the meaning given by section 25(1) of the Caravans Act (Northern Ireland) 1963 (N.I. c. 17);

"dangerous instrument" means an instrument which has a blade or is sharply pointed;

"offensive weapon" has the meaning given by Article 22(1);

"vehicle" includes a caravan."

97 Seized articles

In the Public Order (Northern Ireland) Order 1987 (S.I. 1987/463 (N.I. 7)), after Article 23B insert—

"23C Retention and disposal of things seized under Article 23A and 23B

(1) Anything seized by a constable under Article 23A or 23B may be retained in accordance with regulations made by the Secretary of State under this Article.

(2) The Secretary of State may make regulations regulating the retention and safe keeping, and the disposal and destruction in prescribed circumstances, of such things.

(3) Regulations made under this Article shall be subject to annulment in pursuance of a resolution of either House of Parliament in like manner as a statutory instrument and section 5 of the Statutory Instruments Act 1946 (c. 36) shall apply accordingly."

MoD and Transport Police

98 Jurisdiction of MoD police

(1) Section 2 of the Ministry of Defence Police Act 1987 (c. 4) (jurisdiction of members of the Ministry of Defence Police) is amended as follows.

(2) In subsection (2) (places where members of Ministry of Defence Police have powers and privileges of constables), omit paragraph (d) (which is superseded by the amendment made by subsection (4) of this section).

(3) In subsection (3) (circumstances in which members of Ministry of Defence Police have powers and privileges of constables in places in United Kingdom not mentioned in subsection (2)), after paragraph (b) insert—

"(ba) in connection with offences against persons within paragraph (b) above, with the incitement of such persons to commit offences and with offences under the Prevention of Corruption Acts 1889 to 1916 in relation to such persons;".

(4) After that subsection insert—

"(3A) Where a member of the Ministry of Defence Police has been requested by a constable of—

(a) the police force for any police area;
(b) the Police Service of Northern Ireland;
(c) the British Transport Police Force; or
(d) the United Kingdom Atomic Energy Authority Constabulary,

to assist him in the execution of his duties in relation to a particular incident, investigation or operation, members of the Ministry of Defence Police shall have the powers and privileges of constables for the purposes of that incident, investigation or operation but subject to subsection (3B) below.

(3B) Members of the Ministry of Defence Police have the powers and privileges of constables for the purposes of an incident, investigation or operation by virtue of subsection (3A) above—

(a) if the request was made under paragraph (a) of that subsection by a constable of the police force for a police area, only in that police area;
(b) if it was made under paragraph (b) of that subsection, only in Northern Ireland;
(c) if it was made under paragraph (c) of that subsection, only to the extent that those powers and privileges would in the circumstances be exercisable for those purposes by a constable of the British Transport Police Force by virtue of subsection (1A) or, in Scotland, subsection (4) of section 53 of the British Transport Commission Act 1949 (c. xxix); or
(d) if it was made under paragraph (d) of that subsection, only to the extent that those powers and privileges would in the circumstances be exercisable for those purposes by a constable of the United Kingdom Atomic Energy Authority Constabulary.

(3C) Members of the Ministry of Defence Police shall have in any police area the same powers and privileges as constables of the police force for that police area, and in Northern Ireland the same powers and privileges as constables of the Police Service of Northern Ireland,—

(a) in relation to persons whom they suspect on reasonable grounds of having committed, being in the course of committing or being about to commit an offence; or
(b) if they believe on reasonable grounds that they need those powers and privileges in order to save life or to prevent or minimise personal injury.

(3D) But members of the Ministry of Defence Police have powers and privileges by virtue of subsection (3C) above only if—

    (a)   they are in uniform or have with them documentary evidence that they are members of the Ministry of Defence Police; and

    (b)   they believe on reasonable grounds that a power of a constable which they would not have apart from that subsection ought to be exercised and that, if it cannot be exercised until they secure the attendance of or a request under subsection (3A) above by a constable who has it, the purpose for which they believe it ought to be exercised will be frustrated or seriously prejudiced."

(5)   In subsection (4) (territorial waters)—

    (a)   for "to (3)" substitute "to (3D)," and

    (b)   for "subsections (1) and (3)" substitute "those subsections."

(6)   In subsection (5)—

    (a)   after the definition of "appropriate Gazette" insert—

"British Transport Police Force" means the constables appointed under section 53 of the British Transport Commission Act 1949 (c. xxix);", and

    (b)   after the definition of "service authorities" insert—

"United Kingdom Atomic Energy Authority Constabulary" means the special constables appointed under section 3 of the Special Constables Act 1923 (c. 11) on the nomination of the United Kingdom Atomic Energy Authority;".

99 Provision of assistance by MoD police

After section 2 of the Ministry of Defence Police Act 1987 (c. 4) insert

"2A Provision of assistance to other forces

(1)   The Chief Constable of the Ministry of Defence Police may, on the application of the chief officer of any relevant force, provide constables or other assistance for the purpose of enabling that force to meet any special demand on its resources.

(2)   Where a member of the Ministry of Defence Police is provided for the assistance of a relevant force under this section—

    (a)   he shall be under the direction and control of the chief officer of that force; and

    (b)   he shall have the same powers and privileges as a member of that force.

(3)   Constables are not to be regarded as provided for the assistance of a relevant force under this section in a case where assistance is provided under section 2 above.

(4) In this section—

"British Transport Police Force" has the same meaning as in section 2 above;

"chief officer" means—

(a) the chief officer of the police force for any police area;
(b) the Chief Constable of the Police Service of Northern Ireland;
(c) the Chief Constable of the British Transport Police Force; or
(d) the Chief Constable of the United Kingdom Atomic Energy Authority Constabulary;"

relevant force" means—

(a) the police force for any police area;
(b) the Police Service of Northern Ireland;
(c) the British Transport Police Force; or
(d) the United Kingdom Atomic Energy Authority Constabulary; and

"United Kingdom Atomic Energy Authority Constabulary" has the same meaning as in section 2 above."

100 Jurisdiction of transport police

(1) Where a member of the British Transport Police Force has been requested by a constable of—

(a) the police force for any police area,
(b) the Ministry of Defence Police, or
(c) the United Kingdom Atomic Energy Authority Constabulary,

("the requesting force") to assist him in the execution of his duties in relation to a particular incident, investigation or operation, members of the British Transport Police Force have for the purposes of that incident, investigation or operation the same powers and privileges as constables of the requesting force.

(2) Members of the British Transport Police Force have in any police area the same powers and privileges as constables of the police force for that police area—

(a) in relation to persons whom they suspect on reasonable grounds of having committed, being in the course of committing or being about to commit an offence, or
(b) if they believe on reasonable grounds that they need those powers and privileges in order to save life or to prevent or minimise personal injury.

(3) But members of the British Transport Police Force have powers and privileges by virtue of subsection (2) only if—

(a) they are in uniform or have with them documentary evidence that they are members of that Force, and

(b) they believe on reasonable grounds that a power of a constable which they would not have apart from that subsection ought to be exercised and that, if it cannot be exercised until they secure the attendance of or a request under subsection (1) by a constable who has it, the purpose for which they believe it ought to be exercised will be frustrated or seriously prejudiced.

(4) In this section—

"British Transport Police Force" means the constables appointed under section 53 of the British Transport Commission Act 1949 (c. xxix), and

"United Kingdom Atomic Energy Authority Constabulary" means the special constables appointed under section 3 of the Special Constables Act 1923 (c. 11) on the nomination of the United Kingdom Atomic Energy Authority.

101 Further provisions about transport police and MoD police

Schedule 7 contains amendments relating to the British Transport Police Force and the Ministry of Defence Police.

Part 11
Retention of Communications Data

102 Codes and agreements about the retention of communications data

(1) The Secretary of State shall issue, and may from time to time revise, a code of practice relating to the retention by communications providers of communications data obtained by or held by them.

(2) The Secretary of State may enter into such agreements as he considers appropriate with any communications provider about the practice to be followed by that provider in relation to the retention of communications data obtained by or held by that provider.

(3) A code of practice or agreement under this section may contain any such provision as appears to the Secretary of State to be necessary—

(a) for the purpose of safeguarding national security; or

(b) for the purposes of prevention or detection of crime or the prosecution of offenders which may relate directly or indirectly to national security.

(4) A failure by any person to comply with a code of practice or agreement under this section which is for the time being in force shall not of itself render him liable to any criminal or civil proceedings.

(5) A code of practice or agreement under this section which is for the time being in force shall be admissible in evidence in any legal proceedings in which the question arises whether or not the retention of any communications data is justified on the grounds that a failure to retain the data would be likely to prejudice national security, the prevention or detection of crime or the prosecution of offenders.

103 Procedure for codes of practice

(1) Before issuing the code of practice under section 102 the Secretary of State shall—

(a) prepare and publish a draft of the code; and

(b) consider any representations made to him about the draft; and the Secretary of State may incorporate in the code finally issued any modifications made by him to the draft after its publication.

(2) Before publishing a draft of the code the Secretary of State shall consult with—

(a) the Information Commissioner; and

(b) the communications providers to whom the code will apply.

(3) The Secretary of State may discharge his duty under subsection (2) to consult with any communications providers by consulting with a person who appears to him to represent those providers.

(4) The Secretary of State shall lay before Parliament the draft code of practice under section 102 that is prepared and published by him under this section.

(5) The code of practice issued by the Secretary of State under section 102 shall not be brought into force except in accordance with an order made by the Secretary of State by statutory instrument.

(6) An order under subsection (5) may contain such transitional provisions and savings as appear to the Secretary of State to be necessary or expedient in connection with the coming into force of the code to which the order relates.

(7) The Secretary of State shall not make an order under this section unless a draft of the order has been laid before Parliament and approved by resolution of each House.

(8) The Secretary of State may from time to time—

(a) revise the whole or any part of the code issued under section 102; and

(b) issue the revised code.

(9) The preceding provisions of this section shall apply (with appropriate modifications) in relation to the issue of any revised code under section 102 as they apply in relation to the first issuing of the code.

(10) Subsection (9) shall not, in the case of a draft of a revised code, require the Secretary of State to consult under subsection (2) with

any communications providers who would not be affected by the proposed revisions.

104 Directions about retention of communications data

   (1) If, after reviewing the operation of any requirements contained in the code of practice and any agreements under section 102, it appears to the Secretary of State that it is necessary to do so, he may by order made by statutory instrument authorise the giving of directions under this section for purposes prescribed in section 102(3).

   (2) Where any order under this section is in force, the Secretary of State may give such directions as he considers appropriate about the retention of communications data—

      (a) to communications providers generally;

      (b) to communications providers of a description specified in the direction; or

      (c) to any particular communications providers or provider.

   (3) An order under this section must specify the maximum period for which a communications provider may be required to retain communications data by any direction given under this section while the order is in force.

   (4) Before giving a direction under this section the Secretary of State shall consult—

      (a) with the communications provider or providers to whom it will apply; or

      (b) except in the case of a direction confined to a particular provider, with the persons appearing to the Secretary of State to represent the providers to whom it will apply.

   (5) A direction under this section must be given or published in such manner as the Secretary of State considers appropriate for bringing it to the attention of the communications providers or provider to whom it applies.

   (6) It shall be the duty of a communications provider to comply with any direction under this section that applies to him.

   (7) The duty imposed by subsection (6) shall be enforceable by civil proceedings by the Secretary of State for an injunction, or for specific performance of a statutory duty under section 45 of the Court of Session Act 1988 (c. 36), or for any other appropriate relief.

   (8) The Secretary of State shall not make an order under this section unless a draft of it has been laid before Parliament and approved by a resolution of each House.

105 Lapsing of powers in section 104

   (1) Section 104 shall cease to have effect at the end of the initial period unless an order authorising the giving of directions is made under that section before the end of that period.

(2) Subject to subsection (3), the initial period is the period of two years beginning with the day on which this Act is passed.

(3) The Secretary of State may by order made by statutory instrument extend, or (on one or more occasions) further extend the initial period.

(4) An order under subsection (3)—

    (a) must be made before the time when the initial period would end but for the making of the order; and

    (b) shall have the effect of extending, or further extending, that period for the period of two years beginning with that time.

(5) The Secretary of State shall not make an order under subsection (3) unless a draft of it has been laid before Parliament and approved by a resolution of each House.

106 Arrangements for payments

(1) It shall be the duty of the Secretary of State to ensure that such arrangements are in force as he thinks appropriate for authorising or requiring, in such cases as he thinks fit, the making to communications providers of appropriate contributions towards the costs incurred by them—

    (a) in complying with the provisions of any code of practice, agreement or direction under this Part, or

    (b) as a consequence of the retention of any communications data in accordance with any such provisions.

(2) For the purpose of complying with his duty under this section, the Secretary of State may make arrangements for the payments to be made out of money provided by Parliament.

107 Interpretation of Part 11

(1) In this Part—

"communications data" has the same meaning as in Chapter 2 of Part 1 of the Regulation of Investigatory Powers Act 2000 (c. 23);

"communications provider" means a person who provides a postal service or a telecommunications service;

"legal proceedings," "postal service" and "telecommunications service" each has the same meaning as in that Act;

and any reference in this Part to the prevention or detection of crime shall be construed as if contained in Chapter 2 of Part 1 of that Act.

(2) References in this Part, in relation to any code of practice, agreement or direction, to the retention by a communications provider of any communications data include references to the retention of any data obtained by that provider before the time when the code was issued, the agreement made or the direction given, and to data already held by that provider at that time.

Part 12
Bribery and Corruption

108 Bribery and corruption: foreign officers etc.

(1) For the purposes of any common law offence of bribery it is immaterial if the functions of the person who receives or is offered a reward have no connection with the United Kingdom and are carried out in a country or territory outside the United Kingdom.

(2) In section 1 of the Prevention of Corruption Act 1906 (c. 34) (corrupt transactions with agents) insert this subsection after subsection (3)—

"(4) For the purposes of this Act it is immaterial if—

(a) the principal's affairs or business have no connection with the United Kingdom and are conducted in a country or territory outside the United Kingdom;

(b) the agent's functions have no connection with the United Kingdom and are carried out in a country or territory outside the United Kingdom."

(3) In section 7 of the Public Bodies Corrupt Practices Act 1889 (c. 69) (interpretation relating to corruption in office) in the definition of "public body" for "but does not include any public body as above defined existing elsewhere than in the United Kingdom" substitute "and includes any body which exists in a country or territory outside the United Kingdom and is equivalent to any body described above."

(4) In section 4(2) of the Prevention of Corruption Act 1916 (c. 64) (in the 1889 and 1916 Acts public body includes local and public authorities of all descriptions) after "descriptions" insert "(including authorities existing in a country or territory outside the United Kingdom)."

109 Bribery and corruption committed outside the UK

(1) This section applies if—

(a) a national of the United Kingdom or a body incorporated under the law of any part of the United Kingdom does anything in a country or territory outside the United Kingdom, and

(b) the act would, if done in the United Kingdom, constitute a corruption offence (as defined below).

(2) In such a case—

(a) the act constitutes the offence concerned, and

(b) proceedings for the offence may be taken in the United Kingdom.

(3) These are corruption offences—

    (a)   any common law offence of bribery;

    (b)   the offences under section 1 of the Public Bodies Corrupt Practices Act 1889 (c. 69) (corruption in office);

    (c)   the first two offences under section 1 of the Prevention of Corruption Act 1906 (c. 34) (bribes obtained by or given to agents).

(4) A national of the United Kingdom is an individual who is—

    (a)   a British citizen, a British Dependent Territories citizen, a British National (Overseas) or a British Overseas citizen,

    (b)   a person who under the British Nationality Act 1981 (c. 61) is a British subject, or

    (c)   a British protected person within the meaning of that Act.

110   Presumption of corruption not to apply

Section 2 of the Prevention of Corruption Act 1916 (c. 64) (presumption of corruption in certain cases) is not to apply in relation to anything which would not be an offence apart from section 108 or section 109.

Part 13
Miscellaneous

Third Pillar of the European Union

111   Implementation of the third pillar

(1) At any time before 1st July 2002, an authorised Minister may by regulations make provision—

    (a)   for the purpose of implementing any obligation of the United Kingdom created or arising by or under any third pillar measure or enabling any such obligation to be implemented,

    (b)   for the purpose of enabling any rights enjoyed or to be enjoyed by the United Kingdom under or by virtue of any third pillar measure to be exercised, or

    (c)   for the purpose of dealing with matters arising out of or related to any such obligation or rights.

(2) For the purposes of subsection (1), the following are third pillar measures—

    (a)   the 1995 Convention drawn up on the basis of Article K.3 of the Treaty on European Union on Simplified Extradition Procedure between the Member States of the European Union,

    (b)   the 1996 Convention drawn up on the basis of Article K.3 of the Treaty on European Union relating to Extradition between the Member States of the European Union,

(c) any framework decision adopted under Article 34 of the Treaty on European Union on the execution in the European Union of orders freezing property or evidence, on joint investigation teams, or on combatting terrorism, and

(d) the Convention on Mutual Assistance in Criminal Matters between the Member States of the European Union, and the Protocol to that Convention, established in accordance with Article 34 of the Treaty on European Union.

(3) The provision that may be made under subsection (1) includes, subject to subsection (4), any such provision (of any such extent) as might be made by Act of Parliament.

(4) The powers conferred by subsection (1) do not include power—

(a) to make any provision imposing or increasing taxation,

(b) to make any provision taking effect from a date earlier than that of the making of the instrument containing the provision,

(c) to confer any power to legislate by means of orders, rules, regulations or other subordinate instrument, other than rules of procedure for a court or tribunal, or

(d) to create, except in accordance with subsection (6), a criminal offence which is punishable—

(i) on conviction on indictment, with imprisonment for more than two years,

(ii) on summary conviction, with imprisonment for more than three months,

(iii) on summary conviction, with a fine (not calculated on a daily basis) of more than level 5 on the standard scale or (for an offence triable either way) more than the statutory maximum, or

(iv) on summary conviction, with a fine of more than £100 a day.

(5) Subsection (4)(c) does not preclude the modification of a power to legislate conferred otherwise than under subsection (1), or the extension of any such power to purposes of the like nature as those for which it was conferred, and a power to give directions as to matters of administration is not to be regarded as a power to legislate within the meaning of subsection (4)(c).

(6) Subsection (4)(d) does not preclude the creation of an offence punishable on conviction on indictment with imprisonment for a term of any length if—

(a) the offence is one for which a term of that length, a term of at least that length, or a term within a range of lengths including that length, is required for the offence by an obligation created or arising by or under any third pillar measure,

(b)   the offence, if committed in particular circumstances, would be an offence falling within paragraph (a), or

(c)   the offence is not committed in the United Kingdom but would, if committed in the United Kingdom, or a part of the United Kingdom, be punishable on conviction on indictment with imprisonment for a term of that length.

112   Third pillar: supplemental

(1) "Authorised Minister" in section 111(1) has the meaning given by subsections (2) and (3).

(2) The Scottish Ministers are authorised Ministers for any purpose for which powers under section 111(1) are exercisable within devolved competence (within the meaning of the Scotland Act 1998 (c. 46)).

(3) For any other purpose, the following are authorised Ministers—

(a)   the Secretary of State,

(b)   the Lord Chancellor,

(c)   the Treasury,

(d)   the National Assembly for Wales, if designated under subsection (4),

(e)   the First Minister and deputy First Minister acting jointly, a Northern Ireland Minister or a Northern Ireland department, if the Ministers are, or the Minister or the department is, designated under subsection (4).

(4) A designation under this subsection may be made by Order in Council in relation to any matter or for any purpose, and is subject to any restriction or condition specified in the Order.

(5) An Order in Council under subsection (4) is subject to annulment in pursuance of a resolution of either House of Parliament.

(6) The power to make regulations under section 111(1)—

(a)   in the case of the First Minister and deputy First Minister acting jointly, a Northern Ireland Minister or a Northern Ireland Department, is exercisable by statutory rule for the purposes of the Statutory Rules (Northern Ireland) Order 1979 (S.I.1979/1573 (N.I. 12)),

(b)   in any other case, is exercisable by statutory instrument.

(7) No regulations may be made under section 111(1) unless a draft of the regulations has been laid before and approved by a resolution of each House of Parliament.

(8) Subsection (7) has effect, so far as it relates to the exercise of powers under section 111(1) by the Scottish Ministers, as if the reference to each House of Parliament were a reference to the Scottish Parliament.

(9) Subsection (7) does not apply to a statutory instrument containing

regulations made by the National Assembly for Wales unless the statutory instrument contains regulations—

(a) made by the Secretary of State, the Lord Chancellor or the Treasury (whether or not jointly with the Assembly),

(b) relating to an English border area, or

(c) relating to a cross-border body (and not relating only to the exercise of functions, or the carrying on of activities, by the body in or with respect to Wales or a part of Wales);

and in this subsection expressions used in the Government of Wales Act 1998 (c. 38) have the same meaning as in that Act.

(10) Subsection (7) has effect, so far as it relates to the exercise of powers under section 111(1) by the First Minister and deputy First Minister acting jointly, a Northern Ireland Minister or a Northern Ireland department, as if the reference to each House of Parliament were a reference to the Northern Ireland Assembly.

Dangerous Substances

113 Use of noxious substances or things to cause harm and intimidate

(1) A person who takes any action which—

(a) involves the use of a noxious substance or other noxious thing;

(b) has or is likely to have an effect falling within subsection (2); and

(c) is designed to influence the government or to intimidate the public or a section of the public,is guilty of an offence.

(2) Action has an effect falling within this subsection if it—

(a) causes serious violence against a person anywhere in the world;

(b) causes serious damage to real or personal property anywhere in the world;

(c) endangers human life or creates a serious risk to the health or safety of the public or a section of the public; or

(d) induces in members of the public the fear that the action is likely to endanger their lives or create a serious risk to their health or safety;

but any effect on the person taking the action is to be disregarded.

(3) A person who—

(a) makes a threat that he or another will take any action which constitutes an offence under subsection (1); and

(b) intends thereby to induce in a person anywhere in the world the fear that the threat is likely to be carried out,

is guilty of an offence.

(4) A person guilty of an offence under this section is liable—

(a) on summary conviction, to imprisonment for a term not exceeding six months or a fine not exceeding the statutory maximum (or both); and

    (b)   on conviction on indictment, to imprisonment for a term not exceeding fourteen years or a fine (or both).

(5) In this section—

"the government" means the government of the United Kingdom, of a part of the United Kingdom or of a country other than the United Kingdom; and

"the public" includes the public of a country other than the United Kingdom.

114 Hoaxes involving noxious substances or things

    (1) A person is guilty of an offence if he—

        (a)   places any substance or other thing in any place; or

        (b)   sends any substance or other thing from one place to another (by post, rail or any other means whatever);
with the intention of inducing in a person anywhere in the world a belief that it is likely to be (or contain) a noxious substance or other noxious thing and thereby endanger human life or create a serious risk to human health.

    (2) A person is guilty of an offence if he communicates any information which he knows or believes to be false with the intention of inducing in a person anywhere in the world a belief that a noxious substance or other noxious thing is likely to be present (whether at the time the information is communicated or later) in any place and thereby endanger human life or create a serious risk to human health.

    (3) A person guilty of an offence under this section is liable—

        (a)   on summary conviction, to imprisonment for a term not exceeding six months or a fine not exceeding the statutory maximum (or both); and

        (b)   on conviction on indictment, to imprisonment for a term not exceeding seven years or a fine (or both).

115 Sections 113 and 114: supplementary

    (1) For the purposes of sections 113 and 114 "substance" includes any biological agent and any other natural or artificial substance (whatever its form, origin or method of production).

    (2) For a person to be guilty of an offence under section 113(3) or 114 it is not necessary for him to have any particular person in mind as the person in whom he intends to induce the belief in question.

Intelligence Services Act 1994

116 Amendments of Intelligence Services Act 1994

    (1) In section 7 of the Intelligence Services Act 1994 (c. 13) (authorisation of acts outside the British Islands), in subsection (3)—

(a) in paragraphs (a) and (b)(i), after "the Intelligence Service" insert, in each case, "or GCHQ"; and

(b) in paragraph (c), after "2(2)(a)" insert "or 4(2)(a)."

(2) After subsection (8) of that section insert—

"(9) For the purposes of this section the reference in subsection (1) to an act done outside the British Islands includes a reference to any act which—

(a) is done in the British Islands; but

(b) is or is intended to be done in relation to apparatus that is believed to be outside the British Islands, or in relation to anything appearing to originate from such apparatus; and in this subsection "apparatus" has the same meaning as in the Regulation of Investigatory Powers Act 2000 (c. 23)."

(3) In section 11(1A) of that Act (prevention and detection of crime to have the same meaning as in Chapter 1 of Part 1 of the Regulation of Investigatory Powers Act 2000), for the words from "for the purposes of this Act" to the end of the subsection substitute—

"(a) for the purposes of section 3 above, as it applies for the purposes of Chapter 1 of Part 1 of that Act; and

(b) for the other purposes of this Act, as it applies for the purposes of the provisions of that Act not contained in that Chapter."

Terrorism Act 2000

117 Information about acts of terrorism

(1) The Terrorism Act 2000 (c. 11) is amended as follows.

(2) After section 38 insert—

"38B Information about acts of terrorism

(1) This section applies where a person has information which he knows or believes might be of material assistance—

(a) in preventing the commission by another person of an act of terrorism, or

(b) in securing the apprehension, prosecution or conviction of another person, in the United Kingdom, for an offence involving the commission, preparation or instigation of an act of terrorism.

(2) The person commits an offence if he does not disclose the information as soon as reasonably practicable in accordance with subsection (3).

(3) Disclosure is in accordance with this subsection if it is made—

(a) in England and Wales, to a constable,

(b) in Scotland, to a constable, or

    (c)   in Northern Ireland, to a constable or a member of Her Majesty's forces.

(4) It is a defence for a person charged with an offence under subsection (2) to prove that he had a reasonable excuse for not making the disclosure.

(5) A person guilty of an offence under this section shall be liable—

    (a)   on conviction on indictment, to imprisonment for a term not exceeding five years, or to a fine or to both, or

    (b)   on summary conviction, to imprisonment for a term not exceeding six months, or to a fine not exceeding the statutory maximum or to both.

(6) Proceedings for an offence under this section may be taken, and the offence may for the purposes of those proceedings be treated as having been committed, in any place where the person to be charged is or has at any time been since he first knew or believed that the information might be of material assistance as mentioned in subsection (1)."

(3) In section 39(3) (disclosure of information etc.), after "21" insert "or 38B."

118 Port and airport controls for domestic travel

(1) Schedule 7 to the Terrorism Act 2000 (port and border controls) is amended as follows.

(2) In paragraph 2(2)(b), at the end insert "or his travelling by air within Great Britain or within Northern Ireland."

(3) In paragraph 2(3), for "in Great Britain or Northern Ireland." substitute "at any place in Great Britain or Northern Ireland (whether from within or outside Great Britain or Northern Ireland)."

(4) For paragraph 9(2) substitute—

"(2) This paragraph applies to—

    (a)   goods which have arrived in or are about to leave Great Britain or Northern Ireland on a ship or vehicle, and

    (b)   goods which have arrived at or are about to leave any place in Great Britain or Northern Ireland on an aircraft (whether the place they have come from or are going to is within or outside Great Britain or Northern Ireland)."

119 Passenger information

(1) Paragraph 17 of Schedule 7 to the Terrorism Act 2000 (c. 11) (port and border controls: passenger information) is amended as follows.

(2) For sub-paragraph (1) substitute—

"(1) This paragraph applies to a ship or aircraft which—

(a)   arrives or is expected to arrive in any place in the United Kingdom (whether from another place in the United Kingdom or from outside the United Kingdom), or

(b)   leaves or is expected to leave the United Kingdom."

(3) In sub-paragraph (4)—

(a)   omit the "or" at the end of paragraph (b), and

(b)   after paragraph (c) add—," or

(d)   to goods."

120 Weapons training for terrorists

(1) In section 54(1) and (2) of the Terrorism Act 2000 (weapons training for terrorists), after paragraph (a) insert—

"(aa) radioactive material or weapons designed or adapted for the discharge of any radioactive material,".

(2) In section 55 of that Act (definitions)—

(a)   for the definition of "biological weapon" substitute—

"biological weapon" means a biological agent or toxin (within the meaning of the Biological Weapons Act 1974) in a form capable of use for hostile purposes or anything to which section 1(1)(b) of that Act applies,";

(b)   after the definition of "chemical weapon" insert—

"radioactive material" means radioactive material capable of endangering life or causing harm to human health,"; and

(c)   the definition of "nuclear weapon" shall cease to have effect.

121 Crown Court judges: Northern Ireland

(1) The Terrorism Act 2000 (c. 11) is amended as follows.

(2) In paragraph 18 of Schedule 5 (terrorist investigations: application to Northern Ireland)—

(a)   omit paragraph (e);

(b)   in paragraph (g) for "county court judge" substitute "Crown Court judge."

(3) In paragraph 20 of that Schedule (powers of Secretary of State), in sub-paragraphs (2) and (3)(a) for "county court judge" substitute "Crown Court judge."

(4) In paragraph 3(c) of Schedule 6 (persons by whom financial information orders may be made) for "county court judge" substitute "Crown Court judge."

Part 14
Supplemental

122 Review of Act
    (1) The Secretary of State shall appoint a committee to conduct a review of this Act.
    (2) He must seek to secure that at any time there are not fewer than seven members of the committee.
    (3) A person may be a member of the committee only if he is a member of the Privy Council.
    (4) The committee shall complete the review and send a report to the Secretary of State not later than the end of two years beginning with the day on which this Act is passed.
    (5) The Secretary of State shall lay a copy of the report before Parliament as soon as is reasonably practicable.
    (6) The Secretary of State may make payments to persons appointed as members of the committee.

123 Effect of report
    (1) A report under section 122(4) may specify any provision of this Act as a provision to which this section applies.
    (2) Subject to subsection (3), any provision specified under subsection (1) ceases to have effect at the end of the period of 6 months beginning with the day on which the report is laid before Parliament under section 122(5).
    (3) Subsection (2) does not apply if before the end of that period a motion has been made in each House of Parliament considering the report.

124 Consequential and supplementary provision
    (1) A Minister of the Crown may by order make such incidental, consequential, transitional or supplemental provision as he thinks necessary or expedient for the general purposes, or any particular purpose, of this Act or in consequence of any provision made by or under this Act or for giving full effect to this Act or any such provision.
    (2) An order under this section may, in particular, make provision—
        (a) for applying (with or without modifications) or amending, repealing or revoking any provision of or made under an Act passed before this Act or in the same Session,
        (b) for making savings, or additional savings, from the effect of any repeal or revocation made by or under this Act.
    (3) Amendments made under this section are in addition, and without prejudice, to those made by or under any other provision of this Act.

(4) No other provision of this Act restricts the powers conferred by this section.

(5) An order under this section may make different provision for different purposes.

(6) An order under this section shall be made by statutory instrument which shall be subject to annulment in pursuance of a resolution of either House of Parliament.

(7) In this Part, "Minister of the Crown" has the same meaning as in the Ministers of the Crown Act 1975 (c. 26).

125 Repeals and revocation

The enactments mentioned in Schedule 8 are repealed or revoked to the extent specified in the second column of that Schedule.

126 Expenses

There shall be paid out of money provided by Parliament—

(a) any expenditure incurred by a Minister of the Crown by virtue of this Act, and

(b) any increase attributable to this Act in the sums payable out of money so provided under any other enactment.

127 Commencement

(1) Except as provided in subsections (2) to (4), this Act comes into force on such day as the Secretary of State may appoint by order.

(2) The following provisions come into force on the day on which this Act is passed—

(a) Parts 2 to 6,

(b) Part 8, except section 78,

(c) Part 9, except sections 84 and 87,

(d) sections 89 to 97,

(e) sections 98 to 100, except so far as they extend to Scotland,

(f) section 101 and Schedule 7, except so far as they relate to the entries in respect of the Police (Scotland) Act 1967,

(g) Part 11,

(h) Part 13, except section 121,

(i) this Part, except section 125 and Schedule 8 so far as they relate to the entries—

(i) in Part 1 of Schedule 8,

(ii) in Part 5 of Schedule 8, in respect of the Nuclear Installations Act 1965,

(iii) in Part 6 of Schedule 8, in respect of the British Transport Commission Act 1962 and the Ministry of Defence Police Act 1987, so far as those entries extend to Scotland,

        (iv) in Part 7 of Schedule 8, in respect of Schedule 5 to the Terrorism Act 2000.

(3) The following provisions come into force at the end of the period of two months beginning with the day on which this Act is passed—

        (a)   section 84,

        (b)   section 87.

(4) The following provisions come into force on such day as the Secretary of State and the Scottish Ministers, acting jointly, may appoint by order—

        (a)   sections 98 to 100, so far as they extend to Scotland,

        (b)   section 101 and Schedule 7, so far as they relate to the entries in respect of the Police (Scotland) Act 1967, and

        (c)   section 125 and Schedule 8, so far as they relate to the entries in Part 6 of Schedule 8 in respect of the British Transport Commission Act 1962 and the Ministry of Defence Police Act 1987, so far as those entries extend to Scotland.

(5) Different days may be appointed for different provisions and for different purposes.

(6) An order under this section—

        (a)   must be made by statutory instrument, and

        (b)   may contain incidental, supplemental, consequential or transitional provision.

128 Extent

(1) The following provisions do not extend to Scotland—

        (a)   Part 5,

        (b)   Part 12,

        (c)   in Part 6 of Schedule 8, the repeals in the Criminal Justice and Police Order Act 1994 and in the Crime and Disorder Act 1998.

(2) The following provisions do not extend to Northern Ireland—

        (a)   section 76,

        (b)   section 100.

(3) Except as provided in subsections (1) and (2), an amendment, repeal or revocation in this Act has the same extent as the enactment amended, repealed or revoked.

129 Short title

This Act may be cited as the Anti-terrorism, Crime and Security Act 2001.

Regulation of Investigatory Powers Act of 2000

Part I: Communications

Chapter I: Interception

Unlawful and authorised interception

Unlawful interception.

1. (1) It shall be an offence for a person intentionally and without lawful authority to intercept, at any place in the United Kingdom, any communication in the course of its transmission by means of—
   (a) a public postal service; or
   (b) a public telecommunication system.

   (2) It shall be an offence for a person—
   (a) intentionally and without lawful authority, and
   (b) otherwise than in circumstances in which his conduct is excluded by subsection (6) from criminal liability under this subsection, to intercept, at any place in the United Kingdom, any communication in the course of its transmission by means of a private telecommunication system.

   (3) Any interception of a communication which is carried out at any place in the United Kingdom by, or with the express or implied consent of, a person having the right to control the operation or the use of a private telecommunication system shall be actionable at the suit or instance of the sender or recipient, or intended recipient, of the communication if it is without lawful authority and is either—
   (a) an interception of that communication in the course of its transmission by means of that private system; or
   (b) an interception of that communication in the course of its transmission, by means of a public telecommunication system, to or from apparatus comprised in that private telecommunication system.

   (4) Where the United Kingdom is a party to an international agreement which—
   (a) relates to the provision of mutual assistance in connection with, or in the form of, the interception of communications,

(b)   requires the issue of a warrant, order or equivalent instrument in cases in which assistance is given, and

(c)   is designated for the purposes of this subsection by an order made by the Secretary of State, it shall be the duty of the Secretary of State to secure that no request for assistance in accordance with the agreement is made on behalf of a person in the United Kingdom to the competent authorities of a country or territory outside the United Kingdom except with lawful authority.

(5)   Conduct has lawful authority for the purposes of this section if, and only if—

(a)   it is authorised by or under section 3 or 4;

(b)   it takes place in accordance with a warrant under section 5 ("an interception warrant"); or

(c)   it is in exercise, in relation to any stored communication, of any statutory power that is exercised (apart from this section) for the purpose of obtaining information or of taking possession of any document or other property; and conduct (whether or not prohibited by this section) which has lawful authority for the purposes of this section by virtue of paragraph (a) or (b) shall also be taken to be lawful for all other purposes.

(6)   The circumstances in which a person makes an interception of a communication in the course of its transmission by means of a private telecommunication system are such that his conduct is excluded from criminal liability under subsection (2) if—

(a)   he is a person with a right to control the operation or the use of the system; or

(b)   he has the express or implied consent of such a person to make the interception.

(7)   A person who is guilty of an offence under subsection (1) or (2) shall be liable—

(a)   on conviction on indictment, to imprisonment for a term not exceeding two years or to a fine, or to both;

(b)   on summary conviction, to a fine not exceeding the statutory maximum.

(8)   No proceedings for any offence which is an offence by virtue of this section shall be instituted—

(a)   in England and Wales, except by or with the consent of the Director of Public Prosecutions;

(b)   in Northern Ireland, except by or with the consent of the Director of Public Prosecutions for Northern Ireland.

Meaning and location of "interception" etc.

2. (1) In this Act-

"postal service" means any service which—

(a) consists in the following, or in any one or more of them, namely, the collection, sorting, conveyance, distribution and delivery (whether in the United Kingdom or elsewhere) of postal items; and

(b) is offered or provided as a service the main purpose of which, or one of the main purposes of which, is to make available, or to facilitate, a means of transmission from place to place of postal items containing communications;

"private telecommunication system" means any telecommunication system which, without itself being a public telecommunication system, is a system in relation to which the following conditions are satisfied—

(a) it is attached, directly or indirectly and whether or not for the purposes of the communication in question, to a public telecommunication system; and

(b) there is apparatus comprised in the system which is both located in the United Kingdom and used (with or without other apparatus) for making the attachment to the public telecommunication system;

"public postal service" means any postal service which is offered or provided to, or to a substantial section of, the public in any one or more parts of the United Kingdom;

"public telecommunications service" means any telecommunications service which is offered or provided to, or to a substantial section of, the public in any one or more parts of the United Kingdom;

"public telecommunication system" means any such parts of a telecommunication system by means of which any public telecommunications service is provided as are located in the United Kingdom;

"telecommunications service" means any service that consists in the provision of access to, and of facilities for making use of, any telecommunication system (whether or not one provided by the person providing the service); and

"telecommunication system" means any system (including the apparatus comprised in it) which exists (whether wholly or partly in the United Kingdom or elsewhere) for the purpose of facilitating the transmission of communications by any means involving the use of electrical or electro-magnetic energy.

(2) For the purposes of this Act, but subject to the following provisions of this section, a person intercepts a communication in the course of its transmission by means of a telecommunication system if, and only if, he—
   (a) so modifies or interferes with the system, or its operation,
   (b) so monitors transmissions made by means of the system, or
   (c) so monitors transmissions made by wireless telegraphy to or from apparatus comprised in the system, as to make some or all of the contents of the communication available, while being transmitted, to a person other than the sender or intended recipient of the communication.

(3) References in this Act to the interception of a communication do not include references to the interception of any communication broadcast for general reception.

(4) For the purposes of this Act the interception of a communication takes place in the United Kingdom if, and only if, the modification, interference or monitoring or, in the case of a postal item, the interception is effected by conduct within the United Kingdom and the communication is either—
   (a) intercepted in the course of its transmission by means of a public postal service or public telecommunication system; or
   (b) intercepted in the course of its transmission by means of a private telecommunication system in a case in which the sender or intended recipient of the communication is in the United Kingdom.

(5) References in this Act to the interception of a communication in the course of its transmission by means of a postal service or telecommunication system do not include references to—
   (a) any conduct that takes place in relation only to so much of the communication as consists in any traffic data comprised in or attached to a communication (whether by the sender or otherwise) for the purposes of any postal service or telecommunication system by means of which it is being or may be transmitted; or
   (b) any such conduct, in connection with conduct falling within paragraph (a), as gives a person who is neither the sender nor the intended recipient only so much access to a communication as is necessary for the purpose of identifying traffic data so comprised or attached.

(6) For the purposes of this section references to the modification of a telecommunication system include references to the attachment of any apparatus to, or other modification of or interference with—

    (a)   any part of the system; or

    (b)   any wireless telegraphy apparatus used for making transmissions to or from apparatus comprised in the system.

(7)   For the purposes of this section the times while a communication is being transmitted by means of a telecommunication system shall be taken to include any time when the system by means of which the communication is being, or has been, transmitted is used for storing it in a manner that enables the intended recipient to collect it or otherwise to have access to it.

(8)   For the purposes of this section the cases in which any contents of a communication are to be taken to be made available to a person while being transmitted shall include any case in which any of the contents of the communication, while being transmitted, are diverted or recorded so as to be available to a person subsequently.

(9)   In this section "traffic data," in relation to any communication, means—

    (a)   any data identifying, or purporting to identify, any person, apparatus or location to or from which the communication is or may be transmitted,

    (b)   any data identifying or selecting, or purporting to identify or select, apparatus through which, or by means of which, the communication is or may be transmitted,

    (c)   any data comprising signals for the actuation of apparatus used for the purposes of a telecommunication system for effecting (in whole or in part) the transmission of any communication, and

    (d)   any data identifying the data or other data as data comprised in or attached to a particular communication, but that expression includes data identifying a computer file or computer program access to which is obtained, or which is run, by means of the communication to the extent only that the file or program is identified by reference to the apparatus in which it is stored.

(10) In this section—

    (a)   references, in relation to traffic data comprising signals for the actuation of apparatus, to a telecommunication system by means of which a communication is being or may be transmitted include references to any telecommunication system in which that apparatus is comprised; and

    (b)   references to traffic data being attached to a communication include references to the data and the communication being logically associated with each other;

    and in this section "data," in relation to a postal item, means anything written on the outside of the item.

(11) In this section "postal item" means any letter, postcard or other such thing in writing as may be used by the sender for imparting information to the recipient, or any packet or parcel.

Lawful interception without an interception warrant.

3. (1) Conduct by any person consisting in the interception of a communication is authorised by this section if the communication is one which, or which that person has reasonable grounds for believing, is both—

    (a) a communication sent by a person who has consented to the interception; and

    (b) a communication the intended recipient of which has so consented.

(2) Conduct by any person consisting in the interception of a communication is authorised by this section if—

    (a) the communication is one sent by, or intended for, a person who has consented to the interception; and

    (b) surveillance by means of that interception has been authorised under Part II.

(3) Conduct consisting in the interception of a communication is authorised by this section if—

    (a) it is conduct by or on behalf of a person who provides a postal service or a telecommunications service; and

    (b) it takes place for purposes connected with the provision or operation of that service or with the enforcement, in relation to that service, of any enactment relating to the use of postal services or telecommunications services.

(4) Conduct by any person consisting in the interception of a communication in the course of its transmission by means of wireless telegraphy is authorised by this section if it takes place—

    (a) with the authority of a designated person under section 5 of the Wireless Telegraphy Act 1949 (misleading messages and interception and disclosure of wireless telegraphy messages); and

    (b) for purposes connected with anything falling within subsection (5).

(5) Each of the following falls within this subsection—

    (a) the issue of licences under the Wireless Telegraphy Act 1949;

    (b) the prevention or detection of anything which constitutes intergfference with wireless telegraphy; and

    (c) the enforcement of any enactment contained in that Act or of any enactment not so contained that relates to such interference.

Power to provide for lawful interception.

4. (1) Conduct by any person ("the interceptor") consisting in the interception of a communication in the course of its transmission by means of a telecommunication system is authorised by this section if—

   (a) the interception is carried out for the purpose of obtaining information about the communications of a person who, or who the interceptor has reasonable grounds for believing, is in a country or territory outside the United Kingdom;

   (b) the interception relates to the use of a telecommunications service provided to persons in that country or territory which is either—

      (i) a public telecommunications service; or

      (ii) a telecommunications service that would be a public telecommunications service if the persons to whom it is offered or provided were members of the public in a part of the United Kingdom;

   (c) the person who provides that service (whether the interceptor or another person) is required by the law of that country or territory to carry out, secure or facilitate the interception in question;

   (d) the situation is one in relation to which such further conditions as may be prescribed by regulations made by the Secretary of State are required to be satisfied before conduct may be treated as authorised by virtue of this subsection; and

   (e) the conditions so prescribed are satisfied in relation to that situation.

(2) Subject to subsection (3), the Secretary of State may by regulations authorise any such conduct described in the regulations as appears to him to constitute a legitimate practice reasonably required for the purpose, in connection with the carrying on of any business, of monitoring or keeping a record of—

   (a) communications by means of which transactions are entered into in the course of that business; or

   (b) other communications relating to that business or taking place in the course of its being carried on.

(3) Nothing in any regulations under subsection (2) shall authorise the interception of any communication except in the course of its transmission using apparatus or services provided by or to the person carrying on the business for use wholly or partly in connection with that business.

(4) Conduct taking place in a prison is authorised by this section if it is conduct in exercise of any power conferred by or under any rules

made under section 47 of the Prison Act 1952, section 39 of the Prisons (Scotland) Act 1989 or section 13 of the Prison Act (Northern Ireland) 1953 (prison rules).

(5) Conduct taking place in any hospital premises where high security psychiatric services are provided is authorised by this section if it is conduct in pursuance of, and in accordance with, any direction given under section 17 of the National Health Service Act 1977 (directions as to the carrying out of their functions by health bodies) to the body providing those services at those premises.

(6) Conduct taking place in a state hospital is authorised by this section if it is conduct in pursuance of, and in accordance with, any direction given to the State Hospitals Board for Scotland under section 2(5) of the National Health Service (Scotland) Act 1978 (regulations and directions as to the exercise of their functions by health boards) as applied by Article 5(1) of and the Schedule to The State Hospitals Board for Scotland Order 1995 (which applies certain provisions of that Act of 1978 to the State Hospitals Board).

(7) In this section references to a business include references to any activities of a government department, of any public authority or of any person or office holder on whom functions are conferred by or under any enactment.

(8) In this section—

"government department" includes any part of the Scottish Administration, a Northern Ireland department and the National Assembly for Wales;

"high security psychiatric services" has the same meaning as in the National Health Service Act 1977;

"hospital premises" has the same meaning as in section 4(3) of that Act; and

"state hospital" has the same meaning as in the National Health Service (Scotland) Act 1978.

(9) In this section "prison" means—
  (a) any prison, young offender institution, young offenders centre or remand centre which is under the general superintendence of, or is provided by, the Secretary of State under the Prison Act 1952 or the Prison Act (Northern Ireland) 1953, or
  (b) any prison, young offenders institution or remand centre which is under the general superintendence of the Scottish Ministers under the Prisons (Scotland) Act 1989,
    and includes any contracted out prison, within the meaning of Part IV of the Criminal Justice Act 1991 or section 106(4)

of the Criminal Justice and Public Order Act 1994, and any legalised police cells within the meaning of section 14 of the Prisons (Scotland) Act 1989.

Interception with a warrant.

5. (1) Subject to the following provisions of this Chapter, the Secretary of State may issue a warrant authorising or requiring the person to whom it is addressed, by any such conduct as may be described in the warrant, to secure any one or more of the following—

   (a) the interception in the course of their transmission by means of a postal service or telecommunication system of the communications described in the warrant;

   (b) the making, in accordance with an international mutual assistance agreement, of a request for the provision of such assistance in connection with, or in the form of, an interception of communications as may be so described;

   (c) the provision, in accordance with an international mutual assistance agreement, to the competent authorities of a country or territory outside the United Kingdom of any such assistance in connection with, or in the form of, an interception of communications as may be so described;

   (d) the disclosure, in such manner as may be so described, of intercepted material obtained by any interception authorised or required by the warrant, and of related communications data.

   (2) The Secretary of State shall not issue an interception warrant unless he believes—

   (a) that the warrant is necessary on grounds falling within subsection (3); and

   (b) that the conduct authorised by the warrant is proportionate to what is sought to be achieved by that conduct.

   (3) Subject to the following provisions of this section, a warrant is necessary on grounds falling within this subsection if it is necessary—

   (a) in the interests of national security;

   (b) for the purpose of preventing or detecting serious crime;

   (c) for the purpose of safeguarding the economic well-being of the United Kingdom; or

   (d) for the purpose, in circumstances appearing to the Secretary of State to be equivalent to those in which he would issue a warrant by virtue of paragraph (b), of giving effect to the provisions of any international mutual assistance agreement.

   (4) The matters to be taken into account in considering whether the requirements of subsection (2) are satisfied in the case of any warrant shall include whether the information which it is thought nec-

essary to obtain under the warrant could reasonably be obtained by other means.

(5) A warrant shall not be considered necessary on the ground falling within subsection (3)(c) unless the information which it is thought necessary to obtain is information relating to the acts or intentions of persons outside the British Islands.

(6) The conduct authorised by an interception warrant shall be taken to include—

    (a) all such conduct (including the interception of communications not identified by the warrant) as it is necessary to undertake in order to do what is expressly authorised or required by the warrant;

    (b) conduct for obtaining related communications data; and

    (c) conduct by any person which is conduct in pursuance of a requirement imposed by or on behalf of the person to whom the warrant is addressed to be provided with assistance with giving effect to the warrant.

Interception warrants

Application for issue of an interception warrant.

6. (1) An interception warrant shall not be issued except on an application made by or on behalf of a person specified in subsection (2).

(2) Those persons are—

    (a) the Director-General of the Security Service;

    (b) the Chief of the Secret Intelligence Service;

    (c) the Director of GCHQ;

    (d) the Director General of the National Criminal Intelligence Service;

    (e) the Commissioner of Police of the Metropolis;

    (f) the Chief Constable of the Royal Ulster Constabulary;

    (g) the chief constable of any police force maintained under or by virtue of section 1 of the Police (Scotland) Act 1967;

    (h) the Commissioners of Customs and Excise;

    (i) the Chief of Defence Intelligence;

    (j) a person who, for the purposes of any international mutual assistance agreement, is the competent authority of a country or territory outside the United Kingdom.

(3) An application for the issue of an interception warrant shall not be made on behalf of a person specified in subsection (2) except by a person holding office under the Crown.

Issue of warrants.

7. (1) An interception warrant shall not be issued except—

      (a)   under the hand of the Secretary of State; or

      (b)   in a case falling within subsection (2), under the hand of a senior official.

(2)   Those cases are—

      (a)   an urgent case in which the Secretary of State has himself expressly authorised the issue of the warrant in that case; and

      (b)   a case in which the warrant is for the purposes of a request for assistance made under an international mutual assistance agreement by the competent authorities of a country or territory outside the United Kingdom and either—

           (i)   it appears that the interception subject is outside the United Kingdom; or

           (ii)   the interception to which the warrant relates is to take place in relation only to premises outside the United Kingdom.

(3)   An interception warrant—

      (a)   must be addressed to the person falling within section 6(2) by whom, or on whose behalf, the application for the warrant was made; and

      (b)   in the case of a warrant issued under the hand of a senior official, must contain, according to whatever is applicable—

           (i)   one of the statements set out in subsection (4); and

           (ii)   if it contains the statement set out in subsection (4)(b), one of the statements set out in subsection (5).

(4)   The statements referred to in subsection (3)(b)(i) are—

      (a)   a statement that the case is an urgent case in which the Secretary of State has himself expressly authorised the issue of the warrant;

      (b)   a statement that the warrant is issued for the purposes of a request for assistance made under an international mutual assistance agreement by the competent authorities of a country or territory outside the United Kingdom.

(5)   The statements referred to in subsection (3)(b)(ii) are—

      (a)   a statement that the interception subject appears to be outside the United Kingdom;

      (b)   a statement that the interception to which the warrant relates is to take place in relation only to premises outside the United Kingdom.

Contents of warrants.

8. (1)   An interception warrant must name or describe either—

      (a)   one person as the interception subject; or

(b)   a single set of premises as the premises in relation to which the interception to which the warrant relates is to take place.

(2)   The provisions of an interception warrant describing communications the interception of which is authorised or required by the warrant must comprise one or more schedules setting out the addresses, numbers, apparatus or other factors, or combination of factors, that are to be used for identifying the communications that may be or are to be intercepted.

(3)   Any factor or combination of factors set out in accordance with subsection (2) must be one that identifies communications which are likely to be or to include—

    (a)   communications from, or intended for, the person named or described in the warrant in accordance with subsection (1); or

    (b)   communications originating on, or intended for transmission to, the premises so named or described.

(4)   Subsections (1) and (2) shall not apply to an interception warrant if—

    (a)   the description of communications to which the warrant relates confines the conduct authorised or required by the warrant to conduct falling within subsection (5); and

    (b)   at the time of the issue of the warrant, a certificate applicable to the warrant has been issued by the Secretary of State certifying—

        (i)   the descriptions of intercepted material the examination of which he considers necessary; and

        (ii)   that he considers the examination of material of those descriptions necessary as mentioned in section 5(3)(a), (b) or (c).

(5)   Conduct falls within this subsection if it consists in—

    (a)   the interception of external communications in the course of their transmission by means of a telecommunication system; and

    (b)   any conduct authorised in relation to any such interception by section 5(6).

(6)   A certificate for the purposes of subsection (4) shall not be issued except under the hand of the Secretary of State.

Duration, cancellation and renewal of warrants.

9. (1)   An interception warrant—

    (a)   shall cease to have effect at the end of the relevant period; but

    (b)   may be renewed, at any time before the end of that period, by an instrument under the hand of the Secretary of State or, in a case falling within section 7(2)(b), under the hand of a senior official.

(2) An interception warrant shall not be renewed under subsection (1) unless the Secretary of State believes that the warrant continues to be necessary on grounds falling within section 5(3).

(3) The Secretary of State shall cancel an interception warrant if he is satisfied that the warrant is no longer necessary on grounds falling within section 5(3).

(4) The Secretary of State shall cancel an interception warrant if, at any time before the end of the relevant period, he is satisfied in a case in which—

(a) the warrant is one which was issued containing the statement set out in section 7(5)(a) or has been renewed by an instrument containing the statement set out in subsection (5)(b)(i) of this section, and

(b) the latest renewal (if any) of the warrant is not a renewal by an instrument under the hand of the Secretary of State, that the person named or described in the warrant as the interception subject is in the United Kingdom.

(5) An instrument under the hand of a senior official that renews an interception warrant must contain—

(a) a statement that the renewal is for the purposes of a request for assistance made under an international mutual assistance agreement by the competent authorities of a country or territory outside the United Kingdom; and

(b) whichever of the following statements is applicable—

(i) a statement that the interception subject appears to be outside the United Kingdom;

(ii) a statement that the interception to which the warrant relates is to take place in relation only to premises outside the United Kingdom.

(6) In this section "the relevant period"—

(a) in relation to an unrenewed warrant issued in a case falling within section 7(2)(a) under the hand of a senior official, means the period ending with the fifth working day following the day of the warrant's issue;

(b) in relation to a renewed warrant the latest renewal of which was by an instrument endorsed under the hand of the Secretary of State with a statement that the renewal is believed to be necessary on grounds falling within section 5(3)(a) or (c), means the period of six months beginning with the day of the warrant's renewal; and

    (c)   in all other cases, means the period of three months beginning with the day of the warrant's issue or, in the case of a warrant that has been renewed, of its latest renewal.

Modification of warrants and certificates.

10. (1)   The Secretary of State may at any time—

    (a)   modify the provisions of an interception warrant; or

    (b)   modify a section 8(4) certificate so as to include in the certified material any material the examination of which he considers to be necessary as mentioned in section 5(3)(a), (b) or (c).

(2)   If at any time the Secretary of State considers that any factor set out in a schedule to an interception warrant is no longer relevant for identifying communications which, in the case of that warrant, are likely to be or to include communications falling within section 8(3)(a) or (b), it shall be his duty to modify the warrant by the deletion of that factor.

(3)   If at any time the Secretary of State considers that the material certified by a section 8(4) certificate includes any material the examination of which is no longer necessary as mentioned in any of paragraphs (a) to (c) of section 5(3), he shall modify the certificate so as to exclude that material from the certified material.

(4)   Subject to subsections (5) to (8), a warrant or certificate shall not be modified under this section except by an instrument under the hand of the Secretary of State or of a senior official.

(5)   Unscheduled parts of an interception warrant shall not be modified under the hand of a senior official except in an urgent case in which—

    (a)   the Secretary of State has himself expressly authorised the modification; and

    (b)   a statement of that fact is endorsed on the modifying instrument.

(6)   Subsection (4) shall not authorise the making under the hand of either—

    (a)   the person to whom the warrant is addressed, or

    (b)   any person holding a position subordinate to that person, of any modification of any scheduled parts of an interception warrant.

(7)   A section 8(4) certificate shall not be modified under the hand of a senior official except in an urgent case in which—

    (a)   the official in question holds a position in respect of which he is expressly authorised by provisions contained in the certificate to modify the certificate on the Secretary of State's behalf; or

(b)   the Secretary of State has himself expressly authorised the modification and a statement of that fact is endorsed on the modifying instrument.

(8)   Where modifications in accordance with this subsection are expressly authorised by provision contained in the warrant, the scheduled parts of an interception warrant may, in an urgent case, be modified by an instrument under the hand of—

(a)   the person to whom the warrant is addressed; or

(b)   a person holding any such position subordinate to that person as may be identified in the provisions of the warrant.

(9)   Where—

(a)   a warrant or certificate is modified by an instrument under the hand of a person other than the Secretary of State, and

(b)   a statement for the purposes of subsection (5)(b) or (7)(b) is endorsed on the instrument, or the modification is made under subsection (8), that modification shall cease to have effect at the end of the fifth working day following the day of the instrument's issue.

(10)   For the purposes of this section—

(a)   the scheduled parts of an interception warrant are any provisions of the warrant that are contained in a schedule of identifying factors comprised in the warrant for the purposes of section 8(2); and

(b)   the modifications that are modifications of the scheduled parts of an interception warrant include the insertion of an additional such schedule in the warrant; and references in this section to unscheduled parts of an interception warrant, and to their modification, shall be construed accordingly.

Implementation of warrants.

11. (1)   Effect may be given to an interception warrant either—

(a)   by the person to whom it is addressed; or

(b)   by that person acting through, or together with, such other persons as he may require (whether under subsection (2) or otherwise) to provide him with assistance with giving effect to the warrant.

(2)   For the purpose of requiring any person to provide assistance in relation to an interception warrant the person to whom it is addressed may—

(a)   serve a copy of the warrant on such persons as he considers may be able to provide such assistance; or

(b)   make arrangements under which a copy of it is to be or may be so served.

(3) The copy of an interception warrant that is served on any person under subsection (2) may, to the extent authorised—

(a) by the person to whom the warrant is addressed, or

(b) by the arrangements made by him for the purposes of that subsection, omit any one or more of the schedules to the warrant.

(4) Where a copy of an interception warrant has been served by or on behalf of the person to whom it is addressed on—

    (a) a person who provides a postal service,

    (b) a person who provides a public telecommunications service, or

    (c) a person not falling within paragraph (b) who has control of the whole or any part of a telecommunication system located wholly or partly in the United Kingdom, it shall (subject to subsection (5)) be the duty of that person to take all such steps for giving effect to the warrant as are notified to him by or on behalf of the person to whom the warrant is addressed.

(5) A person who is under a duty by virtue of subsection (4) to take steps for giving effect to a warrant shall not be required to take any steps which it is not reasonably practicable for him to take.

(6) For the purposes of subsection (5) the steps which it is reasonably practicable for a person to take in a case in which obligations have been imposed on him by or under section 12 shall include every step which it would have been reasonably practicable for him to take had he complied with all the obligations so imposed on him.

(7) A person who knowingly fails to comply with his duty under subsection (4) shall be guilty of an offence and liable—

    (a) on conviction on indictment, to imprisonment for a term not exceeding two years or to a fine, or to both;

    (b) on summary conviction, to imprisonment for a term not exceeding six months or to a fine not exceeding the statutory maximum, or to both.

(8) A person's duty under subsection (4) to take steps for giving effect to a warrant shall be enforceable by civil proceedings by the Secretary of State for an injunction, or for specific performance of a statutory duty under section 45 of the Court of Session Act 1988, or for any other appropriate relief.

(9) For the purposes of this Act the provision of assistance with giving effect to an interception warrant includes any disclosure to the person to whom the warrant is addressed, or to persons acting on his behalf, of intercepted material obtained by any interception authorised or required by the warrant, and of any related communications data.

Interception capability and costs

Maintenance of interception capability.

12. (1) The Secretary of State may by order provide for the imposition by
him on persons who—

    (a) are providing public postal services or public telecommunica-
tions services, or

    (b) are proposing to do so, of such obligations as it appears to
him reasonable to impose for the purpose of securing that it
is and remains practicable for requirements to provide assistance in relation to interception warrants to be imposed and
complied with.

  (2) The Secretary of State's power to impose the obligations provided
for by an order under this section shall be exercisable by the giving,
in accordance with the order, of a notice requiring the person who
is to be subject to the obligations to take all such steps as may be
specified or described in the notice.

  (3) Subject to subsection (11), the only steps that may be specified or
described in a notice given to a person under subsection (2) are
steps appearing to the Secretary of State to be necessary for securing that that person has the practical capability of providing any
assistance which he may be required to provide in relation to relevant interception warrants.

  (4) A person shall not be liable to have an obligation imposed on him
in accordance with an order under this section by reason only that
he provides, or is proposing to provide, to members of the public
a telecommunications service the provision of which is or, as the
case may be, will be no more than—

    (a) the means by which he provides a service which is not a
telecommunications service; or

    (b) necessarily incidental to the provision by him of a service which
is not a telecommunications service.

  (5) Where a notice is given to any person under subsection (2) and otherwise than by virtue of subsection (6)(c), that person may, before
the end of such period as may be specified in an order under this
section, refer the notice to the Technical Advisory Board.

  (6) Where a notice given to any person under subsection (2) is referred
to the Technical Advisory Board under subsection (5)—

    (a) there shall be no requirement for that person to comply, except
in pursuance of a notice under paragraph (c)(ii), with any obligations imposed by the notice;

    (b) the Board shall consider the technical requirements and the
financial consequences, for the person making the reference,

of the notice referred to them and shall report their conclusions on those matters to that person and to the Secretary of State; and

(c) the Secretary of State, after considering any report of the Board relating to the notice, may either—

(i) withdraw the notice; or

(ii) give a further notice under subsection (2) confirming its effect, with or without modifications.

(7) It shall be the duty of a person to whom a notice is given under subsection (2) to comply with the notice; and that duty shall be enforceable by civil proceedings by the Secretary of State for an injunction, or for specific performance of a statutory duty under section 45 of the Court of Session Act 1988, or for any other appropriate relief.

(8) A notice for the purposes of subsection (2) must specify such period as appears to the Secretary of State to be reasonable as the period within which the steps specified or described in the notice are to be taken.

(9) Before making an order under this section the Secretary of State shall consult with—

(a) such persons appearing to him to be likely to be subject to the obligations for which it provides,

(b) the Technical Advisory Board,

(c) such persons representing persons falling within paragraph (a), and

(d) such persons with statutory functions in relation to persons falling within that paragraph, as he considers appropriate.

(10) The Secretary of State shall not make an order under this section unless a draft of the order has been laid before Parliament and approved by a resolution of each House.

(11) For the purposes of this section the question whether a person has the practical capability of providing assistance in relation to relevant interception warrants shall include the question whether all such arrangements have been made as the Secretary of State considers necessary—

(a) with respect to the disclosure of intercepted material;

(b) for the purpose of ensuring that security and confidentiality are maintained in relation to, and to matters connected with, the provision of any such assistance; and

(c) for the purpose of facilitating the carrying out of any functions in relation to this Chapter of the Interception of Communications Commissioner; but before determining for the purposes of the making of any order, or the imposition of any obligation, under this section what arrangements he considers necessary for the purpose mentioned in paragraph (c) the Secretary of State shall consult that Commissioner.

(12) In this section "relevant interception warrant"—

    (a) in relation to a person providing a public postal service, means an interception warrant relating to the interception of communications in the course of their transmission by means of that service; and

    (b) in relation to a person providing a public telecommunications service, means an interception warrant relating to the interception of communications in the course of their transmission by means of a telecommunication system used for the purposes of that service.

Technical Advisory Board.

13. (1) There shall be a Technical Advisory Board consisting of such number of persons appointed by the Secretary of State as he may by order provide.

  (2) The order providing for the membership of the Technical Advisory Board must also make provision which is calculated to ensure—

    (a) that the membership of the Technical Advisory Board includes persons likely effectively to represent the interests of the persons on whom obligations may be imposed under section 12;

    (b) that the membership of the Board includes persons likely effectively to represent the interests of the persons by or on whose behalf applications for interception warrants may be made;

    (c) that such other persons (if any) as the Secretary of State thinks fit may be appointed to be members of the Board; and

    (d) that the Board is so constituted as to produce a balance between the representation of the interests mentioned in paragraph (a) and the representation of those mentioned in paragraph (b).

  (3) The Secretary of State shall not make an order under this section unless a draft of the order has been laid before Parliament and approved by a resolution of each House.

Grants for interception costs.

14. (1) It shall be the duty of the Secretary of State to ensure that such arrangements are in force as are necessary for securing that a person who provides—

    (a) a postal service, or

    (b) a telecommunications service, receives such contribution as is, in the circumstances of that person's case, a fair contribution towards the costs incurred, or likely to be incurred, by that person in consequence of the matters mentioned in subsection (2).

(2) Those matters are—

   (a) in relation to a person providing a postal service, the issue of interception warrants relating to communications transmitted by means of that postal service;

   (b) in relation to a person providing a telecommunications service, the issue of interception warrants relating to communications transmitted by means of a telecommunication system used for the purposes of that service;

   (c) in relation to each description of person, the imposition on that person of obligations provided for by an order under section 12.

(3) For the purpose of complying with his duty under this section, the Secretary of State may make arrangements for payments to be made out of money provided by Parliament.

Restrictions on use of intercepted material etc.

General safeguards.

15. (1) Subject to subsection (6), it shall be the duty of the Secretary of State to ensure, in relation to all interception warrants, that such arrangements are in force as he considers necessary for securing—

   (a) that the requirements of subsections (2) and (3) are satisfied in relation to the intercepted material and any related communications data; and

   (b) in the case of warrants in relation to which there are section 8(4) certificates, that the requirements of section 16 are also satisfied.

(2) The requirements of this subsection are satisfied in relation to the intercepted material and any related communications data if each of the following—

   (a) the number of persons to whom any of the material or data is disclosed or otherwise made available,

   (b) the extent to which any of the material or data is disclosed or otherwise made available,

   (c) the extent to which any of the material or data is copied, and

   (d) the number of copies that are made, is limited to the minimum that is necessary for the authorised purposes.

(3) The requirements of this subsection are satisfied in relation to the intercepted material and any related communications data if each copy made of any of the material or data (if not destroyed earlier) is destroyed as soon as there are no longer any grounds for retaining it as necessary for any of the authorised purposes.

(4) For the purposes of this section something is necessary for the authorised purposes if, and only if—

    (a) it continues to be, or is likely to become, necessary as mentioned in section 5(3);

    (b) it is necessary for facilitating the carrying out of any of the functions under this Chapter of the Secretary of State;

    (c) it is necessary for facilitating the carrying out of any functions in relation to this Part of the Interception of Communications Commissioner or of the Tribunal;

    (d) it is necessary to ensure that a person conducting a criminal prosecution has the information he needs to determine what is required of him by his duty to secure the fairness of the prosecution; or

    (e) it is necessary for the performance of any duty imposed on any person by the Public Records Act 1958 or the Public Records Act (Northern Ireland) 1923.

(5) The arrangements for the time being in force under this section for securing that the requirements of subsection (2) are satisfied in relation to the intercepted material or any related communications data must include such arrangements as the Secretary of State considers necessary for securing that every copy of the material or data that is made is stored, for so long as it is retained, in a secure manner.

(6) Arrangements in relation to interception warrants which are made for the purposes of subsection (1)—

    (a) shall not be required to secure that the requirements of subsections (2) and (3) are satisfied in so far as they relate to any of the intercepted material or related communications data, or any copy of any such material or data, possession of which has been surrendered to any authorities of a country or territory outside the United Kingdom; but

    (b) shall be required to secure, in the case of every such warrant, that possession of the intercepted material and data and of copies of the material or data is surrendered to authorities of a country or territory outside the United Kingdom only if the requirements of subsection (7) are satisfied.

(7) The requirements of this subsection are satisfied in the case of a warrant if it appears to the Secretary of State—

    (a) that requirements corresponding to those of subsections (2) and (3) will apply, to such extent (if any) as the Secretary of State thinks fit, in relation to any of the intercepted material or related communications data possession of which, or of any copy of which, is surrendered to the authorities in question; and

(b)   that restrictions are in force which would prevent, to such extent (if any) as the Secretary of State thinks fit, the doing of anything in, for the purposes of or in connection with any proceedings outside the United Kingdom which would result in such a disclosure as, by virtue of section 17, could not be made in the United Kingdom.

(8)   In this section "copy," in relation to intercepted material or related communications data, means any of the following (whether or not in documentary form)—

(a)   any copy, extract or summary of the material or data which identifies itself as the product of an interception, and

(b)   any record referring to an interception which is a record of the identities of the persons to or by whom the intercepted material was sent, or to whom the communications data relates, and "copied" shall be construed accordingly.

Extra safeguards in the case of certificated warrants.

16. (1)   For the purposes of section 15 the requirements of this section, in the case of a warrant in relation to which there is a section 8(4) certificate, are that the intercepted material is read, looked at or listened to by the persons to whom it becomes available by virtue of the warrant to the extent only that it—

(a)   has been certified as material the examination of which is necessary as mentioned in section 5(3)(a), (b) or (c); and

(b)   falls within subsection (2).

(2)   Subject to subsections (3) and (4), intercepted material falls within this subsection so far only as it is selected to be read, looked at or listened to otherwise than according to a factor which—

(a)   is referable to an individual who is known to be for the time being in the British Islands; and

(b)   has as its purpose, or one of its purposes, the identification of material contained in communications sent by him, or intended for him.

(3)   Intercepted material falls within subsection (2), notwithstanding that it is selected by reference to any such factor as is mentioned in paragraph (a) and (b) of that subsection, if—

(a)   it is certified by the Secretary of State for the purposes of section 8(4) that the examination of material selected according to factors referable to the individual in question is necessary as mentioned in subsection 5(3)(a), (b) or (c); and

(b)   the material relates only to communications sent during a period of not more than three months specified in the certificate.

(4) Intercepted material also falls within subsection (2), notwithstanding that it is selected by reference to any such factor as is mentioned in paragraph (a) and (b) of that subsection, if—

   (a) the person to whom the warrant is addressed believes, on reasonable grounds, that the circumstances are such that the material would fall within that subsection; or

   (b) the conditions set out in subsection (5) below are satisfied in relation to the selection of the material.

(5) Those conditions are satisfied in relation to the selection of intercepted material if—

   (a) it has appeared to the person to whom the warrant is addressed that there has been such a relevant change of circumstances as, but for subsection (4)(b), would prevent the intercepted material from falling within subsection (2);

   (b) since it first so appeared, a written authorisation to read, look at or listen to the material has been given by a senior official; and

   (c) the selection is made before the end of the first working day after the day on which it first so appeared to that person.

(6) References in this section to its appearing that there has been a relevant change of circumstances are references to its appearing either—

   (a) that the individual in question has entered the British Islands; or

   (b) that a belief by the person to whom the warrant is addressed in the individual's presence outside the British Islands was in fact mistaken.

Exclusion of matters from legal proceedings.

17. (1) Subject to section 18, no evidence shall be adduced, question asked, assertion or disclosure made or other thing done in, for the purposes of or in connection with any legal proceedings which (in any manner)—

   (a) discloses, in circumstances from which its origin in anything falling within subsection (2) may be inferred, any of the contents of an intercepted communication or any related communications data; or

   (b) tends (apart from any such disclosure) to suggest that anything falling within subsection (2) has or may have occurred or be going to occur.

(2) The following fall within this subsection—

   (a) conduct by a person falling within subsection (3) that was or would be an offence under section 1(1) or (2) of this Act or under section 1 of the Interception of Communications Act 1985;

   (b) a breach by the Secretary of State of his duty under section 1(4) of this Act;

    (c)   the issue of an interception warrant or of a warrant under the Interception of Communications Act 1985;

    (d)   the making of an application by any person for an interception warrant, or for a warrant under that Act;

    (e)   the imposition of any requirement on any person to provide assistance with giving effect to an interception warrant.

(3)   The persons referred to in subsection (2)(a) are—

    (a)   any person to whom a warrant under this Chapter may be addressed;

    (b)   any person holding office under the Crown;

    (c)   any member of the National Criminal Intelligence Service;

    (d)   any member of the National Crime Squad;

    (e)   any person employed by or for the purposes of a police force;

    (f)   any person providing a postal service or employed for the purposes of any business of providing such a service; and

    (g)   any person providing a public telecommunications service or employed for the purposes of any business of providing such a service.

(4)   In this section "intercepted communication" means any communication intercepted in the course of its transmission by means of a postal service or telecommunication system.

Exceptions to section 17.

18. (1)   Section 17(1) shall not apply in relation to—

    (a)   any proceedings for a relevant offence;

    (b)   any civil proceedings under section 11(8);

    (c)   any proceedings before the Tribunal;

    (d)   any proceedings on an appeal or review for which provision is made by an order under section 67(8);

    (e)   any proceedings before the Special Immigration Appeals Commission or any proceedings arising out of proceedings before that Commission; or

    (f)   any proceedings before the Proscribed Organisations Appeal Commission or any proceedings arising out of proceedings before that Commission.

(2)   Subsection (1) shall not, by virtue of paragraph (e) or (f), authorise the disclosure of anything—

    (a)   in the case of any proceedings falling within paragraph (e), to—

        (i)   the appellant to the Special Immigration Appeals Commission; or

        (ii)   any person who for the purposes of any proceedings so falling (but otherwise than by virtue of an appointment under section 6 of the Special Immigration Appeals Commission Act 1997) represents that appellant;

or

(b) in the case of proceedings falling within paragraph (f), to—
  (i) the applicant to the Proscribed Organisations Appeal Commission;
  (ii) the organisation concerned (if different);
  (iii) any person designated under paragraph 6 of Schedule 3 to the Terrorism Act 2000 to conduct proceedings so falling on behalf of that organisation; or
  (iv) any person who for the purposes of any proceedings so falling (but otherwise than by virtue of an appointment under paragraph 7 of that Schedule) represents that applicant or that organisation.

(3) Section 17(1) shall not prohibit anything done in, for the purposes of, or in connection with, so much of any legal proceedings as relates to the fairness or unfairness of a dismissal on the grounds of any conduct constituting an offence under section 1(1) or (2), 11(7) or 19 of this Act, or section 1 of the Interception of Communications Act 1985.

(4) Section 17(1)(a) shall not prohibit the disclosure of any of the contents of a communication if the interception of that communication was lawful by virtue of section 1(5)(c), 3 or 4.

(5) Where any disclosure is proposed to be or has been made on the grounds that it is authorised by subsection (4), section 17(1) shall not prohibit the doing of anything in, or for the purposes of, so much of any legal proceedings as relates to the question whether that disclosure is or was so authorised.

(6) Section 17(1)(b) shall not prohibit the doing of anything that discloses any conduct of a person for which he has been convicted of an offence under section 1(1) or (2), 11(7) or 19 of this Act, or section 1 of the Interception of Communications Act 1985.

(7) Nothing in section 17(1) shall prohibit any such disclosure of any information that continues to be available for disclosure as is confined to—
  (a) a disclosure to a person conducting a criminal prosecution for the purpose only of enabling that person to determine what is required of him by his duty to secure the fairness of the prosecution; or
  (b) a disclosure to a relevant judge in a case in which that judge has ordered the disclosure to be made to him alone.

(8) A relevant judge shall not order a disclosure under subsection (7)(b)

except where he is satisfied that the exceptional circumstances of the case make the disclosure essential in the interests of justice.

(9) Subject to subsection (10), where in any criminal proceedings—

(a) a relevant judge does order a disclosure under subsection (7)(b), and

(b) in consequence of that disclosure he is of the opinion that there are exceptional circumstances requiring him to do so, he may direct the person conducting the prosecution to make for the purposes of the proceedings any such admission of fact as that judge thinks essential in the interests of justice.

(10) Nothing in any direction under subsection (9) shall authorise or require anything to be done in contravention of section 17(1).

(11) In this section "a relevant judge" means—

(a) any judge of the High Court or of the Crown Court or any Circuit judge;

(b) any judge of the High Court of Justiciary or any sheriff;

(c) in relation to a court-martial, the judge advocate appointed in relation to that court-martial under section 84B of the Army Act 1955, section 84B of the Air Force Act 1955 or section 53B of the Naval Discipline Act 1957; or

(d) any person holding any such judicial office as entitles him to exercise the jurisdiction of a judge falling within paragraph (a) or (b).

(12) In this section "relevant offence" means—

(a) an offence under any provision of this Act;

(b) an offence under section 1 of the Interception of Communications Act 1985;

(c) an offence under section 5 of the Wireless Telegraphy Act 1949;

(d) an offence under section 45 of the Telegraph Act 1863, section 20 of the Telegraph Act 1868 or section 58 of the Post Office Act 1953;

(e) an offence under section 45 of the Telecommunications Act 1984;

(f) an offence under section 4 of the Official Secrets Act 1989 relating to any such information, document or article as is mentioned in subsection (3)(a) of that section;

(g) an offence under section 1 or 2 of the Official Secrets Act 1911 relating to any sketch, plan, model, article, note, document or information which incorporates or relates to the contents of any intercepted communication or any related communications data or tends to suggest as mentioned in section 17(1)(b) of this Act;

(h) perjury committed in the course of any proceedings mentioned in subsection (1) or (3) of this section;

(i) attempting or conspiring to commit, or aiding, abetting, counselling or procuring the commission of, an offence falling within any of the preceding paragraphs; and

(j) contempt of court committed in the course of, or in relation to, any proceedings mentioned in subsection (1) or (3) of this section.

(13) In subsection (12) "intercepted communication" has the same meaning as in section 17.

Offence for unauthorised disclosures.

19. (1) Where an interception warrant has been issued or renewed, it shall be the duty of every person falling within subsection (2) to keep secret all the matters mentioned in subsection (3).

(2) The persons falling within this subsection are—

(a) the persons specified in section 6(2);

(b) every person holding office under the Crown;

(c) every member of the National Criminal Intelligence Service;

(d) every member of the National Crime Squad;

(e) every person employed by or for the purposes of a police force;

(f) persons providing postal services or employed for the purposes of any business of providing such a service;

(g) persons providing public telecommunications services or employed for the purposes of any business of providing such a service;

(h) persons having control of the whole or any part of a telecommunication system located wholly or partly in the United Kingdom.

(3) Those matters are—

(a) the existence and contents of the warrant and of any section 8(4) certificate in relation to the warrant;

(b) the details of the issue of the warrant and of any renewal or modification of the warrant or of any such certificate;

(c) the existence and contents of any requirement to provide assistance with giving effect to the warrant;

(d) the steps taken in pursuance of the warrant or of any such requirement; and

(e) everything in the intercepted material, together with any related communications data.

(4) A person who makes a disclosure to another of anything that he is required to keep secret under this section shall be guilty of an offence and liable—

(a) on conviction on indictment, to imprisonment for a term not exceeding five years or to a fine, or to both;

(b) on summary conviction, to imprisonment for a term not exceeding six months or to a fine not exceeding the statutory maximum, or to both.

(5) In proceedings against any person for an offence under this section in respect of any disclosure, it shall be a defence for that person to show that he could not reasonably have been expected, after first becoming aware of the matter disclosed, to take steps to prevent the disclosure.

(6) In proceedings against any person for an offence under this section in respect of any disclosure, it shall be a defence for that person to show that—

(a) the disclosure was made by or to a professional legal adviser in connection with the giving, by the adviser to any client of his, of advice about the effect of provisions of this Chapter; and

(b) the person to whom or, as the case may be, by whom it was made was the client or a representative of the client.

(7) In proceedings against any person for an offence under this section in respect of any disclosure, it shall be a defence for that person to show that the disclosure was made by a legal adviser—

(a) in contemplation of, or in connection with, any legal proceedings; and

(b) for the purposes of those proceedings.

(8) Neither subsection (6) nor subsection (7) applies in the case of a disclosure made with a view to furthering any criminal purpose.

(9) In proceedings against any person for an offence under this section in respect of any disclosure, it shall be a defence for that person to show that the disclosure was confined to a disclosure made to the Interception of Communications Commissioner or authorised—

(a) by that Commissioner;

(b) by the warrant or the person to whom the warrant is or was addressed;

(c) by the terms of the requirement to provide assistance; or

(d) by section 11(9).

Interpretation of Chapter I

Interpretation of Chapter I.

20. In this Chapter—

"certified," in relation to a section 8(4) certificate, means of a description certified by the certificate as a description of material the examination of which the Secretary of State considers necessary;

"external communication" means a communication sent or received outside the British Islands;

"intercepted material," in relation to an interception warrant, means the contents of any communications intercepted by an interception to which the warrant relates;

"the interception subject," in relation to an interception warrant, means the person about whose communications information is sought by the interception to which the warrant relates;

"international mutual assistance agreement" means an international agreement designated for the purposes of section 1(4);

"related communications data," in relation to a communication intercepted in the course of its transmission by means of a postal service or telecommunication system, means so much of any communications data (within the meaning of Chapter II of this Part) as—

(a) is obtained by, or in connection with, the interception; and

(b) relates to the communication or to the sender or recipient, or intended recipient, of the communication;

"section 8(4) certificate" means any certificate issued for the purposes of section 8(4).

Chapter II: Acquisition and Disclosure of Communications Data

Lawful acquisition and disclosure of communications data.

21. (1) This Chapter applies to—

(a) any conduct in relation to a postal service or telecommunication system for obtaining communications data, other than conduct consisting in the interception of communications in the course of their transmission by means of such a service or system; and

(b) the disclosure to any person of communications data.

(2) Conduct to which this Chapter applies shall be lawful for all purposes if—

(a) it is conduct in which any person is authorised or required to engage by an authorisation or notice granted or given under this Chapter; and

(b) the conduct is in accordance with, or in pursuance of, the authorisation or requirement.

(3) A person shall not be subject to any civil liability in respect of any conduct of his which—

(a) is incidental to any conduct that is lawful by virtue of subsection (2); and

    (b)   is not itself conduct an authorisation or warrant for which is capable of being granted under a relevant enactment and might reasonably have been expected to have been sought in the case in question.

(4)   In this Chapter "communications data" means any of the following—

    (a)   any traffic data comprised in or attached to a communication (whether by the sender or otherwise) for the purposes of any postal service or telecommunication system by means of which it is being or may be transmitted;

    (b)   any information which includes none of the contents of a communication (apart from any information falling within paragraph (a)) and is about the use made by any person—

        (i)   of any postal service or telecommunications service; or

        (ii)   in connection with the provision to or use by any person of any telecommunications service, of any part of a telecommunication system;

    (c)   any information not falling within paragraph (a) or (b) that is held or obtained, in relation to persons to whom he provides the service, by a person providing a postal service or telecommunications service.

(5)   In this section "relevant enactment" means—

    (a)   an enactment contained in this Act;

    (b)   section 5 of the Intelligence Services Act 1994 (warrants for the intelligence services); or

    (c)   an enactment contained in Part III of the Police Act 1997 (powers of the police and of customs officers).

(6)   In this section "traffic data," in relation to any communication, means—

    (a)   any data identifying, or purporting to identify, any person, apparatus or location to or from which the communication is or may be transmitted,

    (b)   any data identifying or selecting, or purporting to identify or select, apparatus through which, or by means of which, the communication is or may be transmitted,

    (c)   any data comprising signals for the actuation of apparatus used for the purposes of a telecommunication system for effecting (in whole or in part) the transmission of any communication, and

    (d)   any data identifying the data or other data as data comprised in or attached to a particular communication, but that expression includes data identifying a computer file or computer program access to which is obtained, or which is run, by means of the communication to the extent only that the file or program is identified by reference to the apparatus in which it is stored.

(7) In this section—

    (a) references, in relation to traffic data comprising signals for the actuation of apparatus, to a telecommunication system by means of which a communication is being or may be transmitted include references to any telecommunication system in which that apparatus is comprised; and

    (b) references to traffic data being attached to a communication include references to the data and the communication being logically associated with each other; and in this section "data," in relation to a postal item, means anything written on the outside of the item.

Obtaining and disclosing communications data.

22. (1) This section applies where a person designated for the purposes of this Chapter believes that it is necessary on grounds falling within subsection (2) to obtain any communications data.

    (2) It is necessary on grounds falling within this subsection to obtain communications data if it is necessary—

        (a) in the interests of national security;

        (b) for the purpose of preventing or detecting crime or of preventing disorder;

        (c) in the interests of the economic well-being of the United Kingdom;

        (d) in the interests of public safety;

        (e) for the purpose of protecting public health;

        (f) for the purpose of assessing or collecting any tax, duty, levy or other imposition, contribution or charge payable to a government department;

        (g) for the purpose, in an emergency, of preventing death or injury or any damage to a person's physical or mental health, or of mitigating any injury or damage to a person's physical or mental health; or

        (h) for any purpose (not falling within paragraphs (a) to (g)) which is specified for the purposes of this subsection by an order made by the Secretary of State.

    (3) Subject to subsection (5), the designated person may grant an authorisation for persons holding offices, ranks or positions with the same relevant public authority as the designated person to engage in any conduct to which this Chapter applies.

    (4) Subject to subsection (5), where it appears to the designated person that a postal or telecommunications operator is or may be in

possession of, or be capable of obtaining, any communications data, the designated person may, by notice to the postal or telecommunications operator, require the operator—

    (a)   if the operator is not already in possession of the data, to obtain the data; and

    (b)   in any case, to disclose all of the data in his possession or subsequently obtained by him.

(5)   The designated person shall not grant an authorisation under subsection (3), or give a notice under subsection (4), unless he believes that obtaining the data in question by the conduct authorised or required by the authorisation or notice is proportionate to what is sought to be achieved by so obtaining the data.

(6)   It shall be the duty of the postal or telecommunications operator to comply with the requirements of any notice given to him under subsection (4).

(7)   A person who is under a duty by virtue of subsection (6) shall not be required to do anything in pursuance of that duty which it is not reasonably practicable for him to do.

(8)   The duty imposed by subsection (6) shall be enforceable by civil proceedings by the Secretary of State for an injunction, or for specific performance of a statutory duty under section 45 of the Court of Session Act 1988, or for any other appropriate relief.

(9)   The Secretary of State shall not make an order under subsection (2)(h) unless a draft of the order has been laid before Parliament and approved by a resolution of each House.

Form and duration of authorisations and notices.

23. (1)   An authorisation under section 22(3)—

    (a)   must be granted in writing or (if not in writing) in a manner that produces a record of its having been granted;

    (b)   must describe the conduct to which this Chapter applies that is authorised and the communications data in relation to which it is authorised;

    (c)   must specify the matters falling within section 22(2) by reference to which it is granted; and

    (d)   must specify the office, rank or position held by the person granting the authorisation.

(2)   A notice under section 22(4) requiring communications data to be disclosed or to be obtained and disclosed—

    (a)   must be given in writing or (if not in writing) must be given in a manner that produces a record of its having been given;

    (b)   must describe the communications data to be obtained or disclosed under the notice;

(c)   must specify the matters falling within section 22(2) by reference to which the notice is given;

(d)   must specify the office, rank or position held by the person
giving it; and

(e)   must specify the manner in which any disclosure required by
the notice is to be made.

(3)   A notice under section 22(4) shall not require the disclosure of data
to any person other than—

(a)   the person giving the notice; or

(b)   such other person as may be specified in or otherwise identified by, or in accordance with, the provisions of the notice;
but the provisions of the notice shall not specify or otherwise
identify a person for the purposes of paragraph (b) unless he
holds an office, rank or position with the same relevant public authority as the person giving the notice.

(4)   An authorisation under section 22(3) or notice under section
22(4)—

(a)   shall not authorise or require any data to be obtained after the
end of the period of one month beginning with the date on
which the authorisation is granted or the notice given; and

(b)   in the case of a notice, shall not authorise or require any disclosure after the end of that period of any data not in the possession of, or obtained by, the postal or telecommunications
operator at a time during that period.

(5)   An authorisation under section 22(3) or notice under section 22(4)
may be renewed at any time before the end of the period of one
month applying (in accordance with subsection (4) or subsection
(7)) to that authorisation or notice.

(6)   A renewal of an authorisation under section 22(3) or of a notice
under section 22(4) shall be by the grant or giving, in accordance
with this section, of a further authorisation or notice.

(7)   Subsection (4) shall have effect in relation to a renewed authorisation or renewal notice as if the period of one month mentioned in
that subsection did not begin until the end of the period of one
month applicable to the authorisation or notice that is current at
the time of the renewal.

(8)   Where a person who has given a notice under subsection (4) of section 22 is satisfied—

(a)   that it is no longer necessary on grounds falling within subsection (2) of that section for the requirements of the notice
to be complied with, or

(b)   that the conduct required by the notice is no longer proportionate to what is sought to be achieved by obtaining com-

municaitons data to which the notice relates, he shall cancel the notice.

(9)   The Secretary of State may by regulations provide for the person by whom any duty imposed by subsection (8) is to be performed in a case in which it would otherwise fall on a person who is no longer available to perform it; and regulations under this subsection may provide for the person on whom the duty is to fall to be a person appointed in accordance with the regulations.

Arrangements for payments.

24. (1)   It shall be the duty of the Secretary of State to ensure that such arrangements are in force as he thinks appropriate for requiring or authorising, in such cases as he thinks fit, the making to postal and telecommunications operators of appropriate contributions towards the costs incurred by them in complying with notices under section 22(4).

(2)   For the purpose of complying with his duty under this section, the Secretary of State may make arrangements for payments to be made out of money provided by Parliament.

Interpretation of Chapter II.

25. (1)   In this Chapter—

"communications data" has the meaning given by section 21(4);

"designated" shall be construed in accordance with subsection (2);

"postal or telecommunications operator" means a person who provides a postal service or telecommunications service;

"relevant public authority" means (subject to subsection (4)) any of the following—

(a)   a police force;

(b)   the National Criminal Intelligence Service;

(c)   the National Crime Squad;

(d)   the Commissioners of Customs and Excise;

(e)   the Commissioners of Inland Revenue;

(f)   any of the intelligence services;

(g)   any such public authority not falling within paragraphs (a) to (f) as may be specified for the purposes of this subsection by an order made by the Secretary of State.

(2)   Subject to subsection (3), the persons designated for the purposes of this Chapter are the individuals holding such offices, ranks or positions with relevant public authorities as are prescribed for the purposes of this subsection by an order made by the Secretary of State.

(3) The Secretary of State may by order impose restrictions—

    (a) on the authorisations and notices under this Chapter that may be granted or given by any individual holding an office, rank or position with a specified public authority; and

    (b) on the circumstances in which, or the purposes for which, such authorisations may be granted or notices given by any such individual.

(4) The Secretary of State may by order remove any person from the list of persons who are for the time being relevant public authorities for the purposes of this Chapter.

(5) The Secretary of State shall not make an order under this section that adds any person to the list of persons who are for the time being relevant public authorities for the purposes of this Chapter unless a draft of the order has been laid before Parliament and approved by a resolution of each House.

Part II: Surveillance and Covert Human Intelligence Sources

Introductory

Conduct to which Part II applies.

26. (1) This Part applies to the following conduct—

    (a) directed surveillance;

    (b) intrusive surveillance; and

    (c) the conduct and use of covert human intelligence sources.

(2) Subject to subsection (6), surveillance is directed for the purposes of this Part if it is covert but not intrusive and is undertaken—

    (a) for the purposes of a specific investigation or a specific operation;

    (b) in such a manner as is likely to result in the obtaining of private information about a person (whether or not one specifically identified for the purposes of the investigation or operation); and

    (c) otherwise than by way of an immediate response to events or circumstances the nature of which is such that it would not be reasonably practicable for an authorisation under this Part to be sought for the carrying out of the surveillance.

(3) Subject to subsections (4) to (6), surveillance is intrusive for the purposes of this Part if, and only if, it is covert surveillance that—

    (a) is carried out in relation to anything taking place on any residential premises or in any private vehicle; and

(b)   involves the presence of an individual on the premises or in the vehicle or is carried out by means of a surveillance device.

(4)   For the purposes of this Part surveillance is not intrusive to the extent that—

   (a)   it is carried out by means only of a surveillance device designed or adapted principally for the purpose of providing information about the location of a vehicle; or

   (b)   it is surveillance consisting in any such interception of a communication as falls within section 48(4).

(5)   For the purposes of this Part surveillance which—

   (a)   is carried out by means of a surveillance device in relation to anything taking place on any residential premises or in any private vehicle, but

   (b)   is carried out without that device being present on the premises or in the vehicle, is not intrusive unless the device is such that it consistently provides information of the same quality and detail as might be expected to be obtained from a device actually present on the premises or in the vehicle.

(6)   For the purposes of this Part surveillance which—

   (a)   is carried out by means of apparatus designed or adapted for the purpose of detecting the installation or use in any residential or other premises of a television receiver (within the meaning of section 1 of the Wireless Telegraphy Act 1949), and

   (b)   is carried out from outside those premises exclusively for that purpose, is neither directed nor intrusive.

(7)   In this Part—

   (a)   references to the conduct of a covert human intelligence source are references to any conduct of such a source which falls within any of paragraphs (a) to (c) of subsection (8), or is incidental to anything falling within any of those paragraphs; and

   (b)   references to the use of a covert human intelligence source are references to inducing, asking or assisting a person to engage in the conduct of such a source, or to obtain information by means of the conduct of such a source.

(8)   For the purposes of this Part a person is a covert human intelligence source if—

   (a)   he establishes or maintains a personal or other relationship with a person for the covert purpose of facilitating the doing of anything falling within paragraph (b) or (c);

   (b)   he covertly uses such a relationship to obtain information or to provide access to any information to another person; or

   (c)   he covertly discloses information obtained by the use of such a relationship, or as a consequence of the existence of such a relationship.

(9) For the purposes of this section—

    (a) surveillance is covert if, and only if, it is carried out in a manner that is calculated to ensure that persons who are subject to the surveillance are unaware that it is or may be taking place;

    (b) a purpose is covert, in relation to the establishment or maintenance of a personal or other relationship, if and only if the relationship is conducted in a manner that is calculated to ensure that one of the parties to the relationship is unaware of the purpose; and

    (c) a relationship is used covertly, and information obtained as mentioned in subsection (8)(c) is disclosed covertly, if and only if it is used or, as the case may be, disclosed in a manner that is calculated to ensure that one of the parties to the relationship is unaware of the use or disclosure in question.

(10) In this section "private information," in relation to a person, includes any information relating to his private or family life.

(11) References in this section, in relation to a vehicle, to the presence of a surveillance device in the vehicle include references to its being located on or under the vehicle and also include references to its being attached to it.

Authorisation of surveillance and human intelligence sources

Lawful surveillance etc.

27. (1) Conduct to which this Part applies shall be lawful for all purposes if—

    (a) an authorisation under this Part confers an entitlement to engage in that conduct on the person whose conduct it is; and

    (b) his conduct is in accordance with the authorisation.

(2) A person shall not be subject to any civil liability in respect of any conduct of his which—

    (a) is incidental to any conduct that is lawful by virtue of subsection (1); and

    (b) is not itself conduct an authorisation or warrant for which is capable of being granted under a relevant enactment and might reasonably have been expected to have been sought in the case in question.

(3) The conduct that may be authorised under this Part includes conduct outside the United Kingdom.

(4) In this section "relevant enactment" means—

    (a) an enactment contained in this Act;

    (b)   section 5 of the Intelligence Services Act 1994 (warrants for the intelligence services); or

    (c)   an enactment contained in Part III of the Police Act 1997 (powers of the police and of customs officers).

Authorisation of directed surveillance.

28. (1)   Subject to the following provisions of this Part, the persons designated for the purposes of this section shall each have power to grant authorisations for the carrying out of directed surveillance.

    (2)   A person shall not grant an authorisation for the carrying out of directed surveillance unless he believes—

    (a)   that the authorisation is necessary on grounds falling within subsection (3); and

    (b)   that the authorised surveillance is proportionate to what is sought to be achieved by carrying it out.

    (3)   An authorisation is necessary on grounds falling within this subsection if it is necessary—

    (a)   in the interests of national security;

    (b)   for the purpose of preventing or detecting crime or of preventing disorder;

    (c)   in the interests of the economic well-being of the United Kingdom;

    (d)   in the interests of public safety;

    (e)   for the purpose of protecting public health;

    (f)   for the purpose of assessing or collecting any tax, duty, levy or other imposition, contribution or charge payable to a government department; or

    (g)   for any purpose (not falling within paragraphs (a) to (f)) which is specified for the purposes of this subsection by an order made by the Secretary of State.

    (4)   The conduct that is authorised by an authorisation for the carrying out of directed surveillance is any conduct that—

    (a)   consists in the carrying out of directed surveillance of any such description as is specified in the authorisation; and

    (b)   is carried out in the circumstances described in the authorisation and for the purposes of the investigation or operation specified or described in the authorisation.

    (5)   The Secretary of State shall not make an order under subsection (3)(g) unless a draft of the order has been laid before Parliament and approved by a resolution of each House.

Authorisation of covert human intelligence sources.

29. (1)   Subject to the following provisions of this Part, the persons designated for the purposes of this section shall each have power to grant

authorisations for the conduct or the use of a covert human intelligence source.

(2) A person shall not grant an authorisation for the conduct or the use of a covert human intelligence source unless he believes—

    (a) that the authorisation is necessary on grounds falling within subsection (3);

    (b) that the authorised conduct or use is proportionate to what is sought to be achieved by that conduct or use; and

    (c) that arrangements exist for the source's case that satisfy the requirements of subsection (5) and such other requirements as may be imposed by order made by the Secretary of State.

(3) An authorisation is necessary on grounds falling within this subsection if it is necessary—

    (a) in the interests of national security;

    (b) for the purpose of preventing or detecting crime or of preventing disorder;

    (c) in the interests of the economic well-being of the United Kingdom;

    (d) in the interests of public safety;

    (e) for the purpose of protecting public health;

    (f) for the purpose of assessing or collecting any tax, duty, levy or other imposition, contribution or charge payable to a government department; or

    (g) for any purpose (not falling within paragraphs (a) to (f)) which is specified for the purposes of this subsection by an order made by the Secretary of State.

(4) The conduct that is authorised by an authorisation for the conduct or the use of a covert human intelligence source is any conduct that—

    (a) is comprised in any such activities involving conduct of a covert human intelligence source, or the use of a covert human intelligence source, as are specified or described in the authorisation;

    (b) consists in conduct by or in relation to the person who is so specified or described as the person to whose actions as a covert human intelligence source the authorisation relates; and

    (c) is carried out for the purposes of, or in connection with, the investigation or operation so specified or described.

(5) For the purposes of this Part there are arrangements for the source's case that satisfy the requirements of this subsection if such arrangements are in force as are necessary for ensuring—

    (a) that there will at all times be a person holding an office, rank or position with the relevant investigating authority who will have day-to-day responsibility for dealing with the source on behalf of that authority, and for the source's security and welfare;

(b) that there will at all times be another person holding an office, rank or position with the relevant investigating authority who will have general oversight of the use made of the source;

(c) that there will at all times be a person holding an office, rank or position with the relevant investigating authority who will have responsibility for maintaining a record of the use made of the source;

(d) that the records relating to the source that are maintained by the relevant investigating authority will always contain particulars of all such matters (if any) as may be specified for the purposes of this paragraph in regulations made by the Secretary of State; and

(e) that records maintained by the relevant investigating authority that disclose the identity of the source will not be available to persons except to the extent that there is a need for access to them to be made available to those persons.

(6) The Secretary of State shall not make an order under subsection (3)(g) unless a draft of the order has been laid before Parliament and approved by a resolution of each House.

(7) The Secretary of State may by order—

(a) prohibit the authorisation under this section of any such conduct or uses of covert human intelligence sources as may be described in the order; and

(b) impose requirements, in addition to those provided for by subsection (2), that must be satisfied before an authorisation is granted under this section for any such conduct or uses of covert human intelligence sources as may be so described.

(8) In this section "relevant investigating authority," in relation to an authorisation for the conduct or the use of an individual as a covert human intelligence source, means (subject to subsection (9)) the public authority for whose benefit the activities of that individual as such a source are to take place.

(9) In the case of any authorisation for the conduct or the use of a covert human intelligence source whose activities are to be for the benefit of more than one public authority, the references in subsection (5) to the relevant investigating authority are references to one of them (whether or not the same one in the case of each reference).

Persons entitled to grant authorisations under ss. 28 and 29.

30.
- (1) Subject to subsection (3), the persons designated for the purposes of sections 28 and 29 are the individuals holding such offices, ranks or positions with relevant public authorities as are prescribed for the purposes of this subsection by an order under this section.
- (2) For the purposes of the grant of an authorisation that combines—
  - (a) an authorisation under section 28 or 29, and
  - (b) an authorisation by the Secretary of State for the carrying out of intrusive surveillance, the Secretary of State himself shall be a person designated for the purposes of that section.
- (3) An order under this section may impose restrictions—
  - (a) on the authorisations under sections 28 and 29 that may be granted by any individual holding an office, rank or position with a specified public authority; and
  - (b) on the circumstances in which, or the purposes for which, such authorisations may be granted by any such individual.
- (4) A public authority is a relevant public authority for the purposes of this section—
  - (a) in relation to section 28 if it is specified in Part I or II of Schedule 1; and
  - (b) in relation to section 29 if it is specified in Part I of that Schedule.
- (5) An order under this section may amend Schedule 1 by—
  - (a) adding a public authority to Part I or II of that Schedule;
  - (b) removing a public authority from that Schedule;
  - (c) moving a public authority from one Part of that Schedule to the other;
  - (d) making any change consequential on any change in the name of a public authority specified in that Schedule.
- (6) Without prejudice to section 31, the power to make an order under this section shall be exercisable by the Secretary of State.
- (7) The Secretary of State shall not make an order under subsection (5) containing any provision for—
  - (a) adding any public authority to Part I or II of that Schedule, or
  - (b) moving any public authority from Part II to Part I of that Schedule, unless a draft of the order has been laid before Parliament and approved by a resolution of each House.

Orders under s. 30 for Northern Ireland.

31. (1) Subject to subsections (2) and (3), the power to make an order under section 30 for the purposes of the grant of authorisations for

conduct in Northern Ireland shall be exercisable by the Office of the First Minister and deputy First Minister in Northern Ireland (concurrently with being exercisable by the Secretary of State).

(2) The power of the Office of the First Minister and deputy First Minister to make an order under section 30 by virtue of subsection (1) or (3) of that section shall not be exercisable in relation to any public authority other than—

(a) the Food Standards Agency;

(b) the Intervention Board for Agricultural Produce;

(c) an authority added to Schedule 1 by an order made by that Office;

(d) an authority added to that Schedule by an order made by the Secretary of State which it would (apart from that order) have been within the powers of that Office to add to that Schedule for the purposes mentioned in subsection (1) of this section.

(3) The power of the Office of the First Minister and deputy First Minister to make an order under section 30—

(a) shall not include power to make any provision dealing with an excepted matter;

(b) shall not include power, except with the consent of the Secretary of State, to make any provision dealing with a reserved matter.

(4) The power of the Office of the First Minister and deputy First Minister to make an order under section 30 shall be exercisable by statutory rule for the purposes of the Statutory Rules (Northern Ireland) Order 1979.

(5) A statutory rule containing an order under section 30 which makes provision by virtue of subsection (5) of that section for—

(a) adding any public authority to Part I or II of Schedule 1, or

(b) moving any public authority from Part II to Part I of that Schedule, shall be subject to affirmative resolution (within the meaning of section 41(4) of the Interpretation Act (Northern Ireland) 1954).

(6) A statutory rule containing an order under section 30 (other than one to which subsection (5) of this section applies) shall be subject to negative resolution (within the meaning of section 41(6) of the Interpretation Act (Northern Ireland) 1954).

(7) An order under section 30 made by the Office of the First Minister and deputy First Minister may—

(a) make different provision for different cases;

(b) contain such incidental, supplemental, consequential and transitional provision as that Office thinks fit.

(8)   The reference in subsection (2) to an addition to Schedule 1 being within the powers of the Office of the First Minister and deputy First Minister includes a reference to its being within the powers exercisable by that Office with the consent for the purposes of subsection (3)(b) of the Secretary of State.

(9)   In this section "excepted matter" and "reserved matter" have the same meanings as in the Northern Ireland Act 1998; and, in relation to those matters, section 98(2) of that Act (meaning of "deals with") applies for the purposes of this section as it applies for the purposes of that Act.

Authorisation of intrusive surveillance.

32. (1)   Subject to the following provisions of this Part, the Secretary of State and each of the senior authorising officers shall have power to grant authorisations for the carrying out of intrusive surveillance.

(2)   Neither the Secretary of State nor any senior authorising officer shall grant an authorisation for the carrying out of intrusive surveillance unless he believes—

(a)   that the authorisation is necessary on grounds falling within subsection (3); and

(b)   that the authorised surveillance is proportionate to what is sought to be achieved by carrying it out.

(3)   Subject to the following provisions of this section, an authorisation is necessary on grounds falling within this subsection if it is necessary—

(a)   in the interests of national security;

(b)   for the purpose of preventing or detecting serious crime; or

(c)   in the interests of the economic well-being of the United Kingdom.

(4)   The matters to be taken into account in considering whether the requirements of subsection (2) are satisfied in the case of any authorisation shall include whether the information which it is thought necessary to obtain by the authorised conduct could reasonably be obtained by other means.

(5)   The conduct that is authorised by an authorisation for the carrying out of intrusive surveillance is any conduct that—

(a)   consists in the carrying out of intrusive surveillance of any such description as is specified in the authorisation;

(b)   is carried out in relation to the residential premises specified or described in the authorisation or in relation to the private vehicle so specified or described; and

(c)   is carried out for the purposes of, or in connection with, the investigation or operation so specified or described.

(6)   For the purposes of this section the senior authorising officers are—

    (a)   the chief constable of every police force maintained under section 2 of the Police Act 1996 (police forces in England and Wales outside London);

    (b)   the Commissioner of Police of the Metropolis and every Assistant Commissioner of Police of the Metropolis;

    (c)   the Commissioner of Police for the City of London;

    (d)   the chief constable of every police force maintained under or by virtue of section 1 of the Police (Scotland) Act 1967 (police forces for areas in Scotland);

    (e)   the Chief Constable of the Royal Ulster Constabulary and the Deputy Chief Constable of the Royal Ulster Constabulary;

    (f)   the Chief Constable of the Ministry of Defence Police;

    (g)   the Provost Marshal of the Royal Navy Regulating Branch;

    (h)   the Provost Marshal of the Royal Military Police;

    (i)   the Provost Marshal of the Royal Air Force Police;

    (j)   the Chief Constable of the British Transport Police;

    (k)   the Director General of the National Criminal Intelligence Service;

    (l)   the Director General of the National Crime Squad and any person holding the rank of assistant chief constable in that Squad who is designated for the purposes of this paragraph by that Director General; and

    (m)   any customs officer designated for the purposes of this paragraph by the Commissioners of Customs and Excise.

Police and customs authorisations

Rules for grant of authorisations.

33. (1)   A person who is a designated person for the purposes of section 28 or 29 by reference to his office, rank or position with a police force, the National Criminal Intelligence Service or the National Crime Squad shall not grant an authorisation under that section except on an application made by a member of the same force, Service or Squad.

    (2)   A person who is designated for the purposes of section 28 or 29 by reference to his office, rank or position with the Commissioners of Customs and Excise shall not grant an authorisation under that section except on an application made by a customs officer.

    (3)   A person who is a senior authorising officer by reference to a police force, the National Criminal Intelligence Service or the National Crime Squad shall not grant an authorisation for the carrying out of intrusive surveillance except—

    (a)   on an application made by a member of the same force, Service or Squad; and

    (b)   in the case of an authorisation for the carrying out of intrusive surveillance in relation to any residential premises, where those premises are in the area of operation of that force, Service or Squad.

(4)   A person who is a senior authorising officer by virtue of a designation by the Commissioners of Customs and Excise shall not grant an authorisation for the carrying out of intrusive surveillance except on an application made by a customs officer.

(5)   A single authorisation may combine both—

    (a)   an authorisation granted under this Part by, or on the application of, an individual who is a member of a police force, the National Criminal Intelligence Service or the National Crime Squad, or who is a customs officer; and

    (b)   an authorisation given by, or on the application of, that individual under Part III of the Police Act 1997; but the provisions of this Act or that Act that are applicable in the case of each of the authorisations shall apply separately in relation to the part of the combined authorisation to which they are applicable.

(6)   For the purposes of this section—

    (a)   the area of operation of a police force maintained under section 2 of the Police Act 1996, of the metropolitan police force, of the City of London police force or of a police force maintained under or by virtue of section 1 of the Police (Scotland) Act 1967 is the area for which that force is maintained;

    (b)   the area of operation of the Royal Ulster Constabulary is Northern Ireland;

    (c)   residential premises are in the area of operation of the Ministry of Defence Police if they are premises where the members of that police force, under section 2 of the Ministry of Defence Police Act 1987, have the powers and privileges of a constable;

    (d)   residential premises are in the area of operation of the Royal Navy Regulating Branch, the Royal Military Police or the Royal Air Force Police if they are premises owned or occupied by, or used for residential purposes by, a person subject to service discipline;

    (e)   the area of operation of the British Transport Police and also of the National Criminal Intelligence Service is the United Kingdom;

    (f)   the area of operation of the National Crime Squad is England and Wales; and references in this section to the United

Kingdom or to any part or area of the United Kingdom include any adjacent waters within the seaward limits of the territorial waters of the United Kingdom.

(7) For the purposes of this section a person is subject to service discipline—

(a) in relation to the Royal Navy Regulating Branch, if he is subject to the Naval Discipline Act 1957 or is a civilian to whom Parts I and II of that Act for the time being apply by virtue of section 118 of that Act ;

(b) in relation to the Royal Military Police, if he is subject to military law or is a civilian to whom Part II of the Army Act 1955 for the time being applies by virtue of section 209 of that Act; and

(c) in relation to the Royal Air Force Police, if he is subject to air-force law or is a civilian to whom Part II of the Air Force Act 1955 for the time being applies by virtue of section 209 of that Act.

Grant of authorisations in the senior officer's absence.

34. (1) This section applies in the case of an application for an authorisation for the carrying out of intrusive surveillance where—

(a) the application is one made by a member of a police force, of the National Criminal Intelligence Service or of the National Crime Squad or by a customs officer; and

(b) the case is urgent.

(2) If—

(a) it is not reasonably practicable, having regard to the urgency of the case, for the application to be considered by any person who is a senior authorising officer by reference to the force, Service or Squad in question or, as the case may be, by virtue of a designation by the Commissioners of Customs and Excise, and

(b) it also not reasonably practicable, having regard to the urgency of the case, for the application to be considered by a person (if there is one) who is entitled, as a designated deputy of a senior authorising officer, to exercise the functions in relation to that application of such an officer, the application may be made to and considered by any person who is entitled under subsection (4) to act for any senior authorising officer who would have been entitled to consider the application.

(3) A person who considers an application under subsection (1) shall have the same power to grant an authorisation as the person for whom he is entitled to act.

(4) For the purposes of this section—

    (a)   a person is entitled to act for the chief constable of a police force maintained under section 2 of the Police Act 1996 if he holds the rank of assistant chief constable in that force;

    (b)   a person is entitled to act for the Commissioner of Police of the Metropolis, or for an Assistant Commissioner of Police of the Metropolis, if he holds the rank of commander in the metropolitan police force;

    (c)   a person is entitled to act for the Commissioner of Police for the City of London if he holds the rank of commander in the City of London police force;

    (d)   a person is entitled to act for the chief constable of a police force maintained under or by virtue of section 1 of the Police (Scotland) Act 1967 if he holds the rank of assistant chief constable in that force;

    (e)   a person is entitled to act for the Chief Constable of the Royal Ulster Constabulary, or for the Deputy Chief Constable of the Royal Ulster Constabulary, if he holds the rank of assistant chief constable in the Royal Ulster Constabulary;

    (f)   a person is entitled to act for the Chief Constable of the Ministry of Defence Police if he holds the rank of deputy or assistant chief constable in that force;

    (g)   a person is entitled to act for the Provost Marshal of the Royal Navy Regulating Branch if he holds the position of assistant Provost Marshal in that Branch;

    (h)   a person is entitled to act for the Provost Marshal of the Royal Military Police or the Provost Marshal of the Royal Air Force Police if he holds the position of deputy Provost Marshal in the police force in question;

    (i)   a person is entitled to act for the Chief Constable of the British Transport Police if he holds the rank of deputy or assistant chief constable in that force;

    (j)   a person is entitled to act for the Director General of the National Criminal Intelligence Service if he is a person designated for the purposes of this paragraph by that Director General;

    (k)   a person is entitled to act for the Director General of the National Crime Squad if he is designated for the purposes of this paragraph by that Director General as a person entitled so to act in an urgent case;

    (l)   a person is entitled to act for a person who is a senior authorising officer by virtue of a designation by the Commissioners of Customs and Excise, if he is designated for the purposes of this paragraph by those Commissioners as a person entitled so to act in an urgent case.

(5)   A police member of the National Criminal Intelligence Service or the National Crime Squad appointed under section 9(1)(b) or 55(1)(b) of the Police Act 1997 (police members) may not be designated under subsection (4)(j) or (k) unless he holds the rank of assistant chief constable in that Service or Squad.

(6)   In this section "designated deputy"—

(a)   in relation to a chief constable, means a person holding the rank of assistant chief constable who is designated to act under section 12(4) of the Police Act 1996 or section 5(4) of the Police (Scotland) Act 1967;

(b)   in relation to the Commissioner of Police for the City of London, means a person authorised to act under section 25 of the City of London Police Act 1839;

(c)   in relation to the Director General of the National Criminal Intelligence Service or the Director General of the National Crime Squad, means a person designated to act under section 8 or, as the case may be, section 54 of the Police Act 1997.

Notification of authorisations for intrusive surveillance.

35. (1)   Where a person grants or cancels a police or customs authorisation for the carrying out of intrusive surveillance, he shall give notice that he has done so to an ordinary Surveillance Commissioner.

(2)   A notice given for the purposes of subsection (1)—

(a)   must be given in writing as soon as reasonably practicable after the grant or, as the case may be, cancellation of the authorisation to which it relates;

(b)   must be given in accordance with any such arrangements made for the purposes of this paragraph by the Chief Surveillance Commissioner as are for the time being in force; and

(c)   must specify such matters as the Secretary of State may by order prescribe.

(3)   A notice under this section of the grant of an authorisation shall, as the case may be, either—

(a)   state that the approval of a Surveillance Commissioner is required by section 36 before the grant of the authorisation will take effect; or

(b)   state that the case is one of urgency and set out the grounds on which the case is believed to be one of urgency.

(4)   Where a notice for the purposes of subsection (1) of the grant of an authorisation has been received by an ordinary Surveillance Commissioner, he shall, as soon as practicable—

(a)   scrutinise the authorisation; and

(b)   in a case where notice has been given in accordance with sub-section (3)(a), decide whether or not to approve the authorisation.

(5)   Subject to subsection (6), the Secretary of State shall not make an order under subsection (2)(c) unless a draft of the order has been laid before Parliament and approved by a resolution of each House.

(6)   Subsection (5) does not apply in the case of the order made on the first occasion on which the Secretary of State exercises his power to make an order under subsection (2)(c).

(7)   The order made on that occasion shall cease to have effect at the end of the period of forty days beginning with the day on which it was made unless, before the end of that period, it has been approved by a resolution of each House of Parliament.

(8)   For the purposes of subsection (7)—

(a)   the order's ceasing to have effect shall be without prejudice to anything previously done or to the making of a new order; and

(b)   in reckoning the period of forty days no account shall be taken of any period during which Parliament is dissolved or prorogued or during which both Houses are adjourned for more than four days.

(9)   Any notice that is required by any provision of this section to be given in writing may be given, instead, by being transmitted by electronic means.

(10) In this section references to a police or customs authorisation are references to an authorisation granted by—

(a)   a person who is a senior authorising officer by reference to a police force, the National Criminal Intelligence Service or the National Crime Squad;

(b)   a person who is a senior authorising officer by virtue of a designation by the Commissioners of Customs and Excise; or

(c)   a person who for the purposes of section 34 is entitled to act for a person falling within paragraph (a) or for a person falling within paragraph (b).

Approval required for authorisations to take effect.

36. (1)   This section applies where an authorisation for the carrying out of intrusive surveillance has been granted on the application of—

(a)   a member of a police force;

(b)   a member of the National Criminal Intelligence Service;

(c)   a member of the National Crime Squad; or

(d)   a customs officer.

(2) Subject to subsection (3), the authorisation shall not take effect until such time (if any) as—

    (a) the grant of the authorisation has been approved by an ordinary Surveillance Commissioner; and

    (b) written notice of the Commissioner's decision to approve the grant of the authorisation has been given, in accordance with subsection (4), to the person who granted the authorisation.

(3) Where the person who grants the authorisation—

    (a) believes that the case is one of urgency, and

    (b) gives notice in accordance with section 35(3)(b), subsection (2) shall not apply to the authorisation, and the authorisation shall have effect from the time of its grant.

(4) Where subsection (2) applies to the authorisation—

    (a) a Surveillance Commissioner shall give his approval under this section to the authorisation if, and only if, he is satisfied that there are reasonable grounds for believing that the requirements of section 32(2)(a) and (b) are satisfied in the case of the authorisation; and

    (b) a Surveillance Commissioner who makes a decision as to whether or not the authorisation should be approved shall, as soon as reasonably practicable after making that decision, give written notice of his decision to the person who granted the authorisation.

(5) If an ordinary Surveillance Commissioner decides not to approve an authorisation to which subsection (2) applies, he shall make a report of his findings to the most senior relevant person.

(6) In this section "the most senior relevant person" means—

    (a) where the authorisation was granted by the senior authorising officer with any police force who is not someone's deputy, that senior authorising officer;

    (b) where the authorisation was granted by the Director General of the National Criminal Intelligence Service or the Director General of the National Crime Squad, that Director General;

    (c) where the authorisation was granted by a senior authorising officer with a police force who is someone's deputy, the senior authorising officer whose deputy granted the authorisation;

    (d) where the authorisation was granted by the designated deputy of the Director General of the National Criminal Intelligence Service or a person entitled to act for him by virtue of section 34(4)(j), that Director General;

    (c) where the authorisation was granted by the designated deputy of the Director General of the National Crime Squad or by a person designated by that Director General for the purposes of section 32(6)(l) or 34(4)(k), that Director General;

(f)   where the authorisation was granted by a person entitled to act for a senior authorising officer under section 34(4)(a) to (i), the senior authorising officer in the force in question who is not someone's deputy; and

(g)   where the authorisation was granted by a customs officer, the customs officer for the time being designated for the purposes of this paragraph by a written notice given to the Chief Surveillance Commissioner by the Commissioners of Customs and Excise.

(7)   The references in subsection (6) to a person's deputy are references to the following—

    (a)   in relation to—

        (i)   a chief constable of a police force maintained under section 2 of the Police Act 1996,

        (ii)   the Commissioner of Police for the City of London, or

        (iii)   a chief constable of a police force maintained under or by virtue of section 1 of the Police (Scotland) Act 1967, to his designated deputy;

    (b)   in relation to the Commissioner of Police of the Metropolis, to an Assistant Commissioner of Police of the Metropolis; and

    (c)   in relation to the Chief Constable of the Royal Ulster Constabulary, to the Deputy Chief Constable of the Royal Ulster Constabulary; and in this subsection and that subsection "designated deputy" has the same meaning as in section 34.

(8)   Any notice that is required by any provision of this section to be given in writing may be given, instead, by being transmitted by electronic means.

Quashing of police and customs authorisations etc.

37. (1)   This section applies where an authorisation for the carrying out of intrusive surveillance has been granted on the application of—

    (a)   a member of a police force;

    (b)   a member of the National Criminal Intelligence Service;

    (c)   a member of the National Crime Squad; or

    (d)   a customs officer.

(2)   Where an ordinary Surveillance Commissioner is at any time satisfied that, at the time when the authorisation was granted or at any time when it was renewed, there were no reasonable grounds for believing that the requirements of section 32(2)(a) and (b) were satisfied, he may quash the authorisation with effect, as he thinks

fit, from the time of the grant of the authorisation or from the time of any renewal of the authorisation.

(3)   If an ordinary Surveillance Commissioner is satisfied at any time while the authorisation is in force that there are no longer any reasonable grounds for believing that the requirements of section 32(2)(a) and (b) are satisfied in relation to the authorisation, he may cancel the authorisation with effect from such time as appears to him to be the time from which those requirements ceased to be so satisfied.

(4)   Where, in the case of any authorisation of which notice has been given in accordance with section 35(3)(b), an ordinary Surveillance Commissioner is at any time satisfied that, at the time of the grant or renewal of the authorisation to which that notice related, there were no reasonable grounds for believing that the case was one of urgency, he may quash the authorisation with effect, as he thinks fit, from the time of the grant of the authorisation or from the time of any renewal of the authorization.

(5)   Subject to subsection (7), where an ordinary Surveillance Commissioner quashes an authorisation under this section, he may order the destruction of any records relating wholly or partly to information obtained by the authorised conduct after the time from which his decision takes effect.

(6) Subject to subsection (7), where—

   (a)   an authorisation has ceased to have effect (otherwise than by virtue of subsection (2) or (4)), and

   (b)   an ordinary Surveillance Commissioner is satisfied that there was a time while the authorisation was in force when there were no reasonable grounds for believing that the requirements of section 32(2)(a) and (b) continued to be satisfied in relation to the authorisation, he may order the destruction of any records relating, wholly or partly, to information obtained at such a time by the authorised conduct.

(7)   No order shall be made under this section for the destruction of any records required for pending criminal or civil proceedings.

(8)   Where an ordinary Surveillance Commissioner exercises a power conferred by this section, he shall, as soon as reasonably practicable, make a report of his exercise of that power, and of his reasons for doing so—

   (a)   to the most senior relevant person (within the meaning of section 36); and

   (b)   to the Chief Surveillance Commissioner.

(9)   Where an order for the destruction of records is made under this section, the order shall not become operative until such time (if any) as—

(a)   the period for appealing against the decision to make the order has expired; and

(b)   any appeal brought within that period has been dismissed by the Chief Surveillance Commissioner.

(10) No notice shall be required to be given under section 35(1) in the case of a cancellation under subsection (3) of this section.

Appeals against decisions by Surveillance Commissioners.

38. (1)   Any senior authorising officer may appeal to the Chief Surveillance Commissioner against any of the following—

(a)   any refusal of an ordinary Surveillance Commissioner to approve an authorisation for the carrying out of intrusive surveillance;

(b)   any decision of such a Commissioner to quash or cancel such an authorisation;

(c)   any decision of such a Commissioner to make an order under section 37 for the destruction of records.

(2)   In the case of an authorisation granted by the designated deputy of a senior authorising office or by a person who for the purposes of section 34 is entitled to act for a senior authorising officer, that designated deputy or person shall also be entitled to appeal under this section.

(3)   An appeal under this section must be brought within the period of seven days beginning with the day on which the refusal or decision appealed against is reported to the appellant.

(4)   Subject to subsection (5), the Chief Surveillance Commissioner, on an appeal under this section, shall allow the appeal if—

(a)   he is satisfied that there were reasonable grounds for believing that the requirements of section 32(2)(a) and (b) were satisfied in relation to the authorisation at the time in question; and

(b)   he is not satisfied that the authorisation is one of which notice was given in accordance with section 35(3)(b) without there being any reasonable grounds for believing that the case was one of urgency.

(5)   If, on an appeal falling within subsection (1)(b), the Chief Surveillance Commissioner—

(a)   is satisfied that grounds exist which justify the quashing or cancellation under section 37 of the authorisation in question, but

(b)   considers that the authorisation should have been quashed or cancelled from a different time from that from which it was quashed or cancelled by the ordinary Surveillance Commissioner against whose decision the appeal is brought, he may modify that Commissioner's decision to quash or cancel the authorisation, and any related decision for the destruction of records, so as to give effect to the decision under section 37 that he considers should have been made.

(6) Where, on an appeal under this section against a decision to quash or cancel an authorisation, the Chief Surveillance Commissioner allows the appeal he shall also quash any related order for the destruction of records relating to information obtained by the authorised conduct.

(7) In this section "designated deputy" has the same meaning as in section 34.

Appeals to the Chief Surveillance Commissioner: supplementary.

39. (1) Where the Chief Surveillance Commissioner has determined an appeal under section 38, he shall give notice of his determination to both—

(a) the person by whom the appeal was brought; and

(b) the ordinary Surveillance Commissioner whose decision was appealed against.

(2) Where the determination of the Chief Surveillance Commissioner on an appeal under section 38 is a determination to dismiss the appeal, the Chief Surveillance Commissioner shall make a report of his findings—

(a) to the persons mentioned in subsection (1); and

(b) to the Prime Minister.

(3) Subsections (3) and (4) of section 107 of the Police Act 1997 (reports to be laid before Parliament and exclusion of matters from the report) apply in relation to any report to the Prime Minister under subsection (2) of this section as they apply in relation to any report under subsection (2) of that section.

(4) Subject to subsection (2) of this section, the Chief Surveillance Commissioner shall not give any reasons for any determination of his on an appeal under section 38.

Information to be provided to Surveillance Commissioners.

40. It shall be the duty of—

(a) every member of a police force,

(b) every member of the National Criminal Intelligence Service,

(c) every member of the National Crime Squad, and

(d) every customs officer, to comply with any request of a Surveillance Commissioner for documents or information required by that Commissioner for the purpose of enabling him to carry out the functions of such a Commissioner under sections 35 to 39.

Other authorisations

Secretary of State authorisations.

41. (1)   The Secretary of State shall not grant an authorisation for the carrying out of intrusive surveillance except on an application made by—

(a)   a member of any of the intelligence services;

(b)   an official of the Ministry of Defence;

(c)   a member of Her Majesty's forces;

(d)   an individual holding an office, rank or position with any such public authority as may be designated for the purposes of this section as an authority whose activities may require the carrying out of intrusive surveillance.

(2)   Section 32 shall have effect in relation to the grant of an authorisation by the Secretary of State on the application of an official of the Ministry of Defence, or of a member of Her Majesty's forces, as if the only matters mentioned in subsection (3) of that section were—

(a)   the interests of national security; and

(b)   the purpose of preventing or detecting serious crime.

(3)   The designation of any public authority for the purposes of this section shall be by order made by the Secretary of State.

(4)   The Secretary of State may by order provide, in relation to any public authority, that an application for an authorisation for the carrying out of intrusive surveillance may be made by an individual holding an office, rank or position with that authority only where his office, rank or position is one prescribed by the order.

(5)   The Secretary of State may by order impose restrictions—

(a)   on the authorisations for the carrying out of intrusive surveillance that may be granted on the application of an individual holding an office, rank or position with any public authority designated for the purposes of this section; and

(b)   on the circumstances in which, or the purposes for which, such authorisations may be granted on such an application.

(6)   The Secretary of State shall not make a designation under subsection (3) unless a draft of the order containing the designation has been laid before Parliament and approved by a resolution of each House

(7)   References in this section to a member of Her Majesty's forces do not include references to any member of Her Majesty's forces who is a member of a police force by virtue of his service with the Royal Navy Regulating Branch, the Royal Military Police or the Royal Air Force Police.

Intelligence services authorisations.

42. (1) The grant by the Secretary of State on the application of a member of one of the intelligence services of any authorisation under this Part must be made by the issue of a warrant.

(2) A single warrant issued by the Secretary of State may combine both—

(a) an authorisation under this Part; and

(b) an intelligence services warrant; but the provisions of this Act or the Intelligence Services Act 1994 that are applicable in the case of the authorisation under this Part or the intelligence services warrant shall apply separately in relation to the part of the combined warrant to which they are applicable.

(3) Intrusive surveillance in relation to any premises or vehicle in the British Islands shall be capable of being authorised by a warrant issued under this Part on the application of a member of the Secret Intelligence Service or GCHQ only if the authorisation contained in the warrant is one satisfying the requirements of section 32(2)(a) otherwise than in connection with any functions of that intelligence service in support of the prevention or detection of serious crime.

(4) Subject to subsection (5), the functions of the Security Service shall include acting on behalf of the Secret Intelligence Service or GCHQ in relation to—

(a) the application for and grant of any authorisation under this Part in connection with any matter within the functions of the Secret Intelligence Service or GCHQ; and

(b) the carrying out, in connection with any such matter, of any conduct authorised by such an authorisation.

(5) Nothing in subsection (4) shall authorise the doing of anything by one intelligence service on behalf of another unless—

(a) it is something which either the other service or a member of the other service has power to do; and

(b) it is done otherwise than in connection with functions of the other service in support of the prevention or detection of serious crime.

(6) In this section "intelligence services warrant" means a warrant under section 5 of the Intelligence Services Act 1994.

Grant, renewal and duration of authorisations

General rules about grant, renewal and duration.

43. (1) An authorisation under this Part—

(a) may be granted or renewed orally in any urgent case in which the entitlement to act of the person granting or renewing it is not confined to urgent cases; and

(b) in any other case, must be in writing.

(2) A single authorisation may combine two or more different authorisations under this Part; but the provisions of this Act that are applicable in the case of each of the authorisations shall apply separately in relation to the part of the combined authorisation to which they are applicable.

(3) Subject to subsections (4) and (8), an authorisation under this Part shall cease to have effect at the end of the following period—

    (a) in the case of an authorisation which—

        (i) has not been renewed and was granted either orally or by a person whose entitlement to act is confined to urgent cases, or

        (ii) was last renewed either orally or by such a person, the period of seventy-two hours beginning with the time when the grant of the authorisation or, as the case may be, its latest renewal takes effect;

    (b) in a case not falling within paragraph (a) in which the authorisation is for the conduct or the use of a covert human intelligence source, the period of twelve months beginning with the day on which the grant of the authorisation or, as the case may be, its latest renewal takes effect; and

    (c) in any case not falling within paragraph (a) or (b), the period of three months beginning with the day on which the grant of the authorisation or, as the case may be, its latest renewal takes effect.

(4) Subject to subsection (6), an authorisation under this Part may be renewed, at any time before the time at which it ceases to have effect, by any person who would be entitled to grant a new authorisation in the same terms.

(5) Sections 28 to 41 shall have effect in relation to the renewal of an authorisation under this Part as if references to the grant of an authorisation included references to its renewal.

(6) A person shall not renew an authorisation for the conduct or the use of a covert human intelligence source, unless he—

    (a) is satisfied that a review has been carried out of the matters mentioned in subsection (7); and

    (b) has, for the purpose of deciding whether he should renew the authorisation, considered the results of that review.

(7) The matters mentioned in subsection (6) are—

    (a) the use made of the source in the period since the grant or, as the case may be, latest renewal of the authorisation; and

    (b) the tasks given to the source during that period and the information obtained from the conduct or the use of the source.

(8) The Secretary of State may by order provide in relation to authorisations of such descriptions as may be specified in the order that subsection (3) is to have effect as if the period at the end of which an authorisation of a description so specified is to cease to have effect were such period shorter than that provided for by that subsection as may be fixed by or determined in accordance with that order.

(9) References in this section to the time at which, or the day on which, the grant or renewal of an authorisation takes effect are references—

    (a) in the case of the grant of an authorisation to which paragraph (c) does not apply, to the time at which or, as the case may be, day on which the authorisation is granted;

    (b) in the case of the renewal of an authorisation to which paragraph (c) does not apply, to the time at which or, as the case may be, day on which the authorisation would have ceased to have effect but for the renewal; and

    (c) in the case of any grant or renewal that takes effect under subsection (2) of section 36 at a time or on a day later than that given by paragraph (a) or (b), to the time at which or, as the case may be, day on which the grant or renewal takes effect in accordance with that subsection.

(10) In relation to any authorisation granted by a member of any of the intelligence services, and in relation to any authorisation contained in a warrant issued by the Secretary of State on the application of a member of any of the intelligence services, this section has effect subject to the provisions of section 44.

Special rules for intelligence services authorisations.

44. (1) Subject to subsection (2), a warrant containing an authorisation for the carrying out of intrusive surveillance—

    (a) shall not be issued on the application of a member of any of the intelligence services, and

    (b) if so issued shall not be renewed, except under the hand of the Secretary of State.

(2) In an urgent case in which—

    (a) an application for a warrant containing an authorisation for the carrying out of intrusive surveillance has been made by a member of any of the intelligence services, and

    (b) the Secretary of State has himself expressly authorised the issue of the warrant in that case, the warrant may be issued (but not renewed) under the hand of a senior official.

(3) Subject to subsection (6), a warrant containing an authorisation for the carrying out of intrusive surveillance which—

(a)   was issued, on the application of a member of any of the intelligence services, under the hand of a senior official, and

(b)   has not been renewed under the hand of the Secretary of State,

shall cease to have effect at the end of the second working day following the day of the issue of the warrant, instead of at the time provided for by section 43(3).

(4)   Subject to subsections (3) and (6), where any warrant for the carrying out of intrusive surveillance which is issued or was last renewed on the application of a member of any of the intelligence services, the warrant (unless renewed or, as the case may be, renewed again) shall cease to have effect at the following time, instead of at the time provided for by section 43(3), namely—

    (a)   in the case of a warrant that has not been renewed, at the end of the period of six months beginning with the day on which it was issued; and

    (b)   in any other case, at the end of the period of six months beginning with the day on which it would have ceased to have effect if not renewed again.

(5)   Subject to subsection (6), where—

    (a)   an authorisation for the carrying out of directed surveillance is granted by a member of any of the intelligence services, and

    (b)   the authorisation is renewed by an instrument endorsed under the hand of the person renewing the authorisation with a statement that the renewal is believed to be necessary on grounds falling within section 32(3)(a) or (c), the authorisation (unless renewed again) shall cease to have effect at the end of the period of six months beginning with the day on which it would have ceased to have effect but for the renewal, instead of at the time provided for by section 43(3).

(6)   The Secretary of State may by order provide in relation to authorisations of such descriptions as may be specified in the order that subsection (3), (4) or (5) is to have effect as if the period at the end of which an authorisation of a description so specified is to cease to have effect were such period shorter than that provided for by that subsection as may be fixed by or determined in accordance with that order.

(7)   Notwithstanding anything in section 43(2), in a case in which there is a combined warrant containing both—

    (a)   an authorisation for the carrying out of intrusive surveillance, and

    (b)   an authorisation for the carrying out of directed surveillance, the reference in subsection (4) of this section to a warrant for the carrying out of intrusive surveillance is a reference to the warrant so far as it confers both authorisations.

Cancellation of authorisations.

45. (1) The person who granted or, as the case may be, last renewed an authorisation under this Part shall cancel it if—

(a) he is satisfied that the authorisation is one in relation to which the requirements of section 28(2)(a) and (b), 29(2)(a) and (b) or, as the case may be, 32(2)(a) and (b) are no longer satisfied; or

(b) in the case of an authorisation under section 29, he is satisfied that arrangements for the source's case that satisfy the requirements mentioned in subsection (2)(c) of that section no longer exist.

(2) Where an authorisation under this Part was granted or, as the case may be, last renewed—

(a) by a person entitled to act for any other person, or

(b) by the deputy of any other person, that other person shall cancel the authorisation if he is satisfied as to either of the matters mentioned in subsection (1).

(3) Where an authorisation under this Part was granted or, as the case may be, last renewed by a person whose deputy had power to grant it, that deputy shall cancel the authorisation if he is satisfied as to either of the matters mentioned in subsection (1).

(4) The Secretary of State may by regulations provide for the person by whom any duty imposed by this section is to be performed in a case in which it would otherwise fall on a person who is no longer available to perform it.

(5) Regulations under subsection (4) may provide for the person on whom the duty is to fall to be a person appointed in accordance with the regulations.

(6) The references in this section to a person's deputy are references to the following—(a) in relation to—

(i) a chief constable of a police force maintained under section 2 of the Police Act 1996,

(ii) the Commissioner of Police for the City of London, or

(iii) a chief constable of a police force maintained under or by virtue of section 1 of the Police (Scotland) Act 1967, to his designated deputy;

(b) in relation to the Commissioner of Police of the Metropolis, to an Assistant Commissioner of Police of the Metropolis;

(c) in relation to the Chief Constable of the Royal Ulster Constabulary, to the Deputy Chief Constable of the Royal Ulster Constabulary;

(d) in relation to the Director General of the National Criminal Intelligence Service, to his designated deputy; and

(e)   in relation to the Director General of the National Crime Squad, to any person designated by him for the purposes of section 32(6)(l) or to his designated deputy.

(7)   In this section "designated deputy" has the same meaning as in section 34.

Scotland

Restrictions on authorisations extending to Scotland.

46. (1)   No person shall grant or renew an authorisation under this Part for the carrying out of any conduct if it appears to him—

    (a)   that the authorisation is not one for which this Part is the relevant statutory provision for all parts of the United Kingdom; and

    (b)   that all the conduct authorised by the grant or, as the case may be, renewal of the authorisation is likely to take place in Scotland.

(2)   In relation to any authorisation, this Part is the relevant statutory provision for all parts of the United Kingdom in so far as it—

    (a)   is granted or renewed on the grounds that it is necessary in the interests of national security or in the interests of the economic well-being of the United Kingdom;

    (b)   is granted or renewed by or on the application of a person holding any office, rank or position with any of the public authorities specified in subsection (3);

    (c)   authorises conduct of a person holding an office, rank or position with any of the public authorities so specified;

    (d)   authorises conduct of an individual acting as a covert human intelligence source for the benefit of any of the public authorities so specified; or

    (e)   authorises conduct that is surveillance by virtue of section 48(4).

(3)   The public authorities mentioned in subsection (2) are—

    (a)   each of the intelligence services;

    (b)   Her Majesty's forces;

    (c)   the Ministry of Defence;

    (d)   the Ministry of Defence Police;

    (e)   the Commissioners of Customs and Excise; and

    (f)   the British Transport Police.

(4)   For the purposes of so much of this Part as has effect in relation to any other public authority by virtue of—

    (a)   the fact that it is a public authority for the time being specified in Schedule 1, or

(b)   an order under subsection (1)(d) of section 41 designating that authority for the purposes of that section, the authorities specified in subsection (3) of this section shall be treated as including that authority to the extent that the Secretary of State by order directs that the authority is a relevant public authority or, as the case may be, is a designated authority for all parts of the United Kingdom.

Supplemental provision for Part II

Power to extend or modify authorisation provisions.

47. (1)   The Secretary of State may by order do one or both of the following—

(a)   apply this Part, with such modifications as he thinks fit, to any such surveillance that is neither directed nor intrusive as may be described in the order;

(b)   provide for any description of directed surveillance to be treated for the purposes of this Part as intrusive surveillance.

(2)   No order shall be made under this section unless a draft of it has been laid before Parliament and approved by a resolution of each House.

Interpretation of Part II.

48. (1)   In this Part—

"covert human intelligence source" shall be construed in accordance with section 26(8);

"directed" and "intrusive," in relation to surveillance, shall be construed in accordance with section 26(2) to (6);

"private vehicle" means (subject to subsection (7)(a)) any vehicle which is used primarily for the private purposes of the person who owns it or of a person otherwise having the right to use it;

"residential premises" means (subject to subsection (7)(b)) so much of any premises as is for the time being occupied or used by any person, however temporarily, for residential purposes or otherwise as living accommodation (including hotel or prison accommodation that is so occupied or used);

"senior authorising officer" means a person who by virtue of subsection (6) of section 32 is a senior authorising officer for the purposes of that section;

"surveillance" shall be construed in accordance with subsections (2) to (4);

"surveillance device" means any apparatus designed or adapted for use in surveillance.

(2)   Subject to subsection (3), in this Part "surveillance" includes—

(a)   monitoring, observing or listening to persons, their movements, their conversations or their other activities or communications;

(b)   recording anything monitored, observed or listened to in the course of surveillance; and

(c)   surveillance by or with the assistance of a surveillance device.

(3)   References in this Part to surveillance do not include references to—

(a)   any conduct of a covert human intelligence source for obtaining or recording (whether or not using a surveillance device) any information which is disclosed in the presence of the source;

(b)   the use of a covert human intelligence source for so obtaining or recording information; or

(c)   any such entry on or interference with property or with wireless telegraphy as would be unlawful unless authorised under—

(i)   section 5 of the Intelligence Services Act 1994 (warrants for the intelligence services); or

(ii)   Part III of the Police Act 1997 (powers of the police and of customs officers).

(4)   References in this Part to surveillance include references to the interception of a communication in the course of its transmission by means of a postal service or telecommunication system if, and only if—

(a)   the communication is one sent by or intended for a person who has consented to the interception of communications sent by or to him; and

(b)   there is no interception warrant authorising the interception.

(5)   References in this Part to an individual holding an office or position with a public authority include references to any member, official or employee of that authority.

(6)   For the purposes of this Part the activities of a covert human intelligence source which are to be taken as activities for the benefit of a particular public authority include any conduct of his as such a source which is in response to inducements or requests made by or on behalf of that authority.

(7)   In subsection (1)—

(a)   the reference to a person having the right to use a vehicle does not, in relation to a motor vehicle, include a reference to a person whose right to use the vehicle derives only from his having paid, or undertaken to pay, for the use of the vehicle and its driver for a particular journey; and

(b)   the reference to premises occupied or used by any person for residential purposes or otherwise as living accommodation does not include a reference to so much of any premises as constitutes any common area to which he has or is allowed access in connection with his use or occupation of any accommodation.

(8)   In this section—

"premises" includes any vehicle or moveable structure and any other place whatever, whether or not occupied as land;

"vehicle" includes any vessel, aircraft or hovercraft.

Part III Investigation of Electronic Data Protected by Encryption Etc.

Power to require disclosure

Notices requiring disclosure.

49. (1)   This section applies where any protected information—

(a)   has come into the possession of any person by means of the exercise of a statutory power to seize, detain, inspect, search or otherwise to interfere with documents or other property, or is likely to do so;

(b)   has come into the possession of any person by means of the exercise of any statutory power to intercept communications, or is likely to do so;

(c)   has come into the possession of any person by means of the exercise of any power conferred by an authorisation under section 22(3) or under Part II, or as a result of the giving of a notice under section 22(4), or is likely to do so;

(d)   has come into the possession of any person as a result of having been provided or disclosed in pursuance of any statutory duty (whether or not one arising as a result of a request for information), or is likely to do so; or

(e)   has, by any other lawful means not involving the exercise of statutory powers, come into the possession of any of the intelligence services, the police or the customs and excise, or is likely so to come into the possession of any of those services, the police or the customs and excise.

(2)   If any person with the appropriate permission under Schedule 2 believes, on reasonable grounds—

    (a)   that a key to the protected information is in the possession of any person,

    (b)   that the imposition of a disclosure requirement in respect of the protected information is—

        (i)   necessary on grounds falling within subsection (3), or

        (ii)   necessary for the purpose of securing the effective exercise or proper performance by any public authority of any statutory power or statutory duty,

    (c)   that the imposition of such a requirement is proportionate to what is sought to be achieved by its imposition, and

    (d)   that it is not reasonably practicable for the person with the appropriate permission to obtain possession of the protected information in an intelligible form without the giving of a notice under this section, the person with that permission may, by notice to the person whom he believes to have possession of the key, impose a disclosure requirement in respect of the protected information.

(3)   A disclosure requirement in respect of any protected information is necessary on grounds falling within this subsection if it is necessary—

    (a)   in the interests of national security;

    (b)   for the purpose of preventing or detecting crime; or

    (c)   in the interests of the economic well-being of the United Kingdom.

(4)   A notice under this section imposing a disclosure requirement in respect of any protected information—

    (a)   must be given in writing or (if not in writing) must be given in a manner that produces a record of its having been given;

    (b)   must describe the protected information to which the notice relates;

    (c)   must specify the matters falling within subsection (2)(b)(i) or (ii) by reference to which the notice is given;

    (d)   must specify the office, rank or position held by the person giving it;

    (e)   must specify the office, rank or position of the person who for the purposes of Schedule 2 granted permission for the giving of the notice or (if the person giving the notice was entitled to give it without another person's permission) must set out the circumstances in which that entitlement arose;

    (f)   must specify the time by which the notice is to be complied with; and

    (g)   must set out the disclosure that is required by the notice and the form and manner in which it is to be made; and the time specified for the purposes of paragraph (f) must allow a period for compliance which is reasonable in all the circumstances.

(5) Where it appears to a person with the appropriate permission—

    (a)   that more than one person is in possession of the key to any protected information,

    (b)   that any of those persons is in possession of that key in his capacity as an officer or employee of any body corporate, and

    (c)   that another of those persons is the body corporate itself or another officer or employee of the body corporate, a notice under this section shall not be given, by reference to his possession of the key, to any officer or employee of the body corporate unless he is a senior officer of the body corporate or it appears to the person giving the notice that there is no senior officer of the body corporate and (in the case of an employee) no more senior employee of the body corporate to whom it is reasonably practicable to give the notice.

(6) Where it appears to a person with the appropriate permission—

    (a)   that more than one person is in possession of the key to any protected information,

    (b)   that any of those persons is in possession of that key in his capacity as an employee of a firm, and

    (c)   that another of those persons is the firm itself or a partner of the firm, a notice under this section shall not be given, by reference to his possession of the key, to any employee of the firm unless it appears to the person giving the notice that there is neither a partner of the firm nor a more senior employee of the firm to whom it is reasonably practicable to give the notice.

(7) Subsections (5) and (6) shall not apply to the extent that there are special circumstances of the case that mean that the purposes for which the notice is given would be defeated, in whole or in part, if the notice were given to the person to whom it would otherwise be required to be given by those subsections.

(8) A notice under this section shall not require the making of any disclosure to any person other than—

    (a)   the person giving the notice; or

    (b)   such other person as may be specified in or otherwise identified by, or in accordance with, the provisions of the notice.

(9) A notice under this section shall not require the disclosure of any key which—

    (a)   is intended to be used for the purpose only of generating electronic signatures; and

    (b)   has not in fact been used for any other purpose.

(10) In this section "senior officer," in relation to a body corporate, means a director, manager, secretary or other similar officer of the body corporate; and for this purpose "director," in relation to a body corporate whose affairs are managed by its members, means a member of the body corporate.

(11) Schedule 2 (definition of the appropriate permission) shall have effect.

Effect of notice imposing disclosure requirement.

50. (1) Subject to the following provisions of this section, the effect of a section 49 notice imposing a disclosure requirement in respect of any protected information on a person who is in possession at a relevant time of both the protected information and a means of obtaining access to the information and of disclosing it in an intelligible form is that he—

    (a) shall be entitled to use any key in his possession to obtain access to the information or to put it into an intelligible form; and

    (b) shall be required, in accordance with the notice imposing the requirement, to make a disclosure of the information in an intelligible form.

(2) A person subject to a requirement under subsection (1)(b) to make a disclosure of any information in an intelligible form shall be taken to have complied with that requirement if—

    (a) he makes, instead, a disclosure of any key to the protected information that is in his possession; and

    (b) that disclosure is made, in accordance with the notice imposing the requirement, to the person to whom, and by the time by which, he was required to provide the information in that form.

(3) Where, in a case in which a disclosure requirement in respect of any protected information is imposed on any person by a section 49 notice—

    (a) that person is not in possession of the information,

    (b) that person is incapable, without the use of a key that is not in his possession, of obtaining access to the information and of disclosing it in an intelligible form, or

    (c) the notice states, in pursuance of a direction under section 51, that it can be complied with only by the disclosure of a key to the information, the effect of imposing that disclosure requirement on that person is that he shall be required, in accordance with the notice imposing the requirement, to make a disclosure of any key to the protected information that is in his possession at a relevant time.

(4) Subsections (5) to (7) apply where a person ("the person given notice")—

    (a) is entitled or obliged to disclose a key to protected information for the purpose of complying with any disclosure requirement imposed by a section 49 notice; and

    (b) is in possession of more than one key to that information.

(5) It shall not be necessary, for the purpose of complying with the requirement, for the person given notice to make a disclosure of any keys in addition to those the disclosure of which is, alone, sufficient to enable the person to whom they are disclosed to obtain access to the information and to put it into an intelligible form.

(6) Where—

    (a) subsection (5) allows the person given notice to comply with a requirement without disclosing all of the keys in his possession, and

    (b) there are different keys, or combinations of keys, in the possession of that person the disclosure of which would, under that subsection, constitute compliance, the person given notice may select which of the keys, or combination of keys, to disclose for the purpose of complying with that requirement in accordance with that subsection.

(7) Subject to subsections (5) and (6), the person given notice shall not be taken to have complied with the disclosure requirement by the disclosure of a key unless he has disclosed every key to the protected information that is in his possession at a relevant time.

(8) Where, in a case in which a disclosure requirement in respect of any protected information is imposed on any person by a section 49 notice—

    (a) that person has been in possession of the key to that information but is no longer in possession of it,

    (b) if he had continued to have the key in his possession, he would have been required by virtue of the giving of the notice to disclose it, and

    (c) he is in possession, at a relevant time, of information to which subsection (9) applies, the effect of imposing that disclosure requirement on that person is that he shall be required, in accordance with the notice imposing the requirement, to disclose all such information to which subsection (9) applies as is in his possession and as he may be required, in accordance with that notice, to disclose by the person to whom he would have been required to disclose the key.

(9) This subsection applies to any information that would facilitate the

obtaining or discovery of the key or the putting of the protected information into an intelligible form.

(10) In this section "relevant time," in relation to a disclosure requirement imposed by a section 49 notice, means the time of the giving of the notice or any subsequent time before the time by which the requirement falls to be complied with.

Cases in which key required.

51. (1) A section 49 notice imposing a disclosure requirement in respect of any protected information shall not contain a statement for the purposes of section 50(3)(c) unless—

    (a) the person who for the purposes of Schedule 2 granted the permission for the giving of the notice in relation to that information, or

    (b) any person whose permission for the giving of a such a notice in relation to that information would constitute the appropriate permission under that Schedule, has given a direction that the requirement can be complied with only by the disclosure of the key itself.

(2) A direction for the purposes of subsection (1) by the police, the customs and excise or a member of Her Majesty's forces shall not be given—

    (a) in the case of a direction by the police or by a member of Her Majesty's forces who is a member of a police force, except by or with the permission of a chief officer of police;

    (b) in the case of a direction by the customs and excise, except by or with the permission of the Commissioners of Customs and Excise; or

    (c) in the case of a direction by a member of Her Majesty's forces who is not a member of a police force, except by or with the permission of a person of or above the rank of brigadier or its equivalent.

(3) A permission given for the purposes of subsection (2) by a chief officer of police, the Commissioners of Customs and Excise or a person of or above any such rank as is mentioned in paragraph (c) of that subsection must be given expressly in relation to the direction in question.

(4) A person shall not give a direction for the purposes of subsection (1) unless he believes—

    (a) that there are special circumstances of the case which mean that the purposes for which it was believed necessary to impose the requirement in question would be defeated, in whole or in part, if the direction were not given; and

      (b)   that the giving of the direction is proportionate to what is sought to be achieved by prohibiting any compliance with the requirement in question otherwise than by the disclosure of the key itself.

(5)   The matters to be taken into account in considering whether the requirement of subsection (4)(b) is satisfied in the case of any direction shall include—

      (a)   the extent and nature of any protected information, in addition to the protected information in respect of which the disclosure requirement is imposed, to which the key is also a key; and

      (b)   any adverse effect that the giving of the direction might have on a business carried on by the person on whom the disclosure requirement is imposed.

(6)   Where a direction for the purposes of subsection (1) is given by a chief officer of police, by the Commissioners of Customs and Excise or by a member of Her Majesty's forces, the person giving the direction shall give a notification that he has done so—(a) in a case where the direction is given—

          (i)   by a member of Her Majesty's forces who is not a member of a police force, and

          (ii)   otherwise than in connection with activities of members of Her Majesty's forces in Northern Ireland, to the Intelligences Services Commissioner; and

      (b)   in any other case, to the Chief Surveillance Commissioner.

(7)   A notification under subsection (6)—

      (a)   must be given not more than seven days after the day of the giving of the direction to which it relates; and

      (b)   may be given either in writing or by being transmitted to the Commissioner in question by electronic means.

Contributions to costs

Arrangements for payments for disclosure.

52. (1)   It shall be the duty of the Secretary of State to ensure that such arrangements are in force as he thinks appropriate for requiring or authorising, in such cases as he thinks fit, the making to persons to whom section 49 notices are given of appropriate contributions towards the costs incurred by them in complying with such notices.

      (2)   For the purpose of complying with his duty under this section, the Secretary of State may make arrangements for payments to be made out of money provided by Parliament.

Offences

Failure to comply with a notice.

53. (1) A person to whom a section 49 notice has been given is guilty of an offence if he knowingly fails, in accordance with the notice, to make the disclosure required by virtue of the giving of the notice.

(2) In proceedings against any person for an offence under this section, if it is shown that that person was in possession of a key to any protected information at any time before the time of the giving of the section 49 notice, that person shall be taken for the purposes of those proceedings to have continued to be in possession of that key at all subsequent times, unless it is shown that the key was not in his possession after the giving of the notice and before the time by which he was required to disclose it.

(3) For the purposes of this section a person shall be taken to have shown that he was not in possession of a key to protected information at a particular time if—

(a) sufficient evidence of that fact is adduced to raise an issue with respect to it; and

(b) the contrary is not proved beyond a reasonable doubt.

(4) In proceedings against any person for an offence under this section it shall be a defence for that person to show—

(a) that it was not reasonably practicable for him to make the disclosure required by virtue of the giving of the section 49 notice before the time by which he was required, in accordance with that notice, to make it; but

(b) that he did make that disclosure as soon after that time as it was reasonably practicable for him to do so.

(5) A person guilty of an offence under this section shall be liable—

(a) on conviction on indictment, to imprisonment for a term not exceeding two years or to a fine, or to both;

(b) on summary conviction, to imprisonment for a term not exceeding six months or to a fine not exceeding the statutory maximum, or to both.

Tipping-off.

54. (1) This section applies where a section 49 notice contains a provision requiring—

(a) the person to whom the notice is given, and

(b) every other person who becomes aware of it or of its contents,

to keep secret the giving of the notice, its contents and the things done in pursuance of it.

(2) A requirement to keep anything secret shall not be included in a section 49 notice except where—

(a) it is included with the consent of the person who for the purposes of Schedule 2 granted the permission for the giving of the notice; or

(b) the person who gives the notice is himself a person whose permission for the giving of such a notice in relation to the information in question would have constituted appropriate permission under that Schedule.

(3) A section 49 notice shall not contain a requirement to keep anything secret except where the protected information to which it relates—

(a) has come into the possession of the police, the customs and excise or any of the intelligence services, or

(b) is likely to come into the possession of the police, the customs and excise or any of the intelligence services, by means which it is reasonable, in order to maintain the effectiveness of any investigation or operation or of investigatory techniques generally, or in the interests of the safety or well-being of any person, to keep secret from a particular person.

(4) A person who makes a disclosure to any other person of anything that he is required by a section 49 notice to keep secret shall be guilty of an offence and liable—

(a) on conviction on indictment, to imprisonment for a term not exceeding five years or to a fine, or to both;

(b) on summary conviction, to imprisonment for a term not exceeding six months or to a fine not exceeding the statutory maximum, or to both.

(5) In proceedings against any person for an offence under this section in respect of any disclosure, it shall be a defence for that person to show that—

(a) the disclosure was effected entirely by the operation of software designed to indicate when a key to protected information has ceased to be secure; and

(b) that person could not reasonably have been expected to take steps, after being given the notice or (as the case may be) becoming aware of it or of its contents, to prevent the disclosure.

(6) In proceedings against any person for an offence under this section in respect of any disclosure, it shall be a defence for that person to show that—

(a) the disclosure was made by or to a professional legal adviser in connection with the giving, by the adviser to any client of his, of advice about the effect of provisions of this Part; and

       (b)   the person to whom or, as the case may be, by whom it was made was the client or a representative of the client.

  (7)   In proceedings against any person for an offence under this section in respect of any disclosure, it shall be a defence for that person to show that the disclosure was made by a legal adviser—

       (a)   in contemplation of, or in connection with, any legal proceedings; and

       (b)   for the purposes of those proceedings.

  (8)   Neither subsection (6) nor subsection (7) applies in the case of a disclosure made with a view to furthering any criminal purpose.

  (9)   In proceedings against any person for an offence under this section in respect of any disclosure, it shall be a defence for that person to show that the disclosure was confined to a disclosure made to a relevant Commissioner or authorised—

       (a)   by such a Commissioner;

       (b)   by the terms of the notice;

       (c)   by or on behalf of the person who gave the notice; or

       (d)   by or on behalf of a person who—

          (i)   is in lawful possession of the protected information to which the notice relates; and

         (ii)   came into possession of that information as mentioned in section 49(1).

 (10)   In proceedings for an offence under this section against a person other than the person to whom the notice was given, it shall be a defence for the person against whom the proceedings are brought to show that he neither knew nor had reasonable grounds for suspecting that the notice contained a requirement to keep secret what was disclosed.

 (11)   In this section "relevant Commissioner" means the Interception of Communications Commissioner, the Intelligence Services Commissioner or any Surveillance Commissioner or Assistant Surveillance Commissioner.

Safeguards

General duties of specified authorities.

55. (1)   This section applies to—

       (a)   the Secretary of State and every other Minister of the Crown in charge of a government department;

       (b)   every chief officer of police;

       (c)   the Commissioners of Customs and Excise; and

       (d)   every person whose officers or employees include persons with duties that involve the giving of section 49 notices.

(2) It shall be the duty of each of the persons to whom this section applies to ensure that such arrangements are in force, in relation to persons under his control who by virtue of this Part obtain possession of keys to protected information, as he considers necessary for securing—

   (a) that a key disclosed in pursuance of a section 49 notice is used for obtaining access to, or putting into an intelligible form, only protected information in relation to which power to give such a notice was exercised or could have been exercised if the key had not already been disclosed;

   (b) that the uses to which a key so disclosed is put are reasonable having regard both to the uses to which the person using the key is entitled to put any protected information to which it relates and to the other circumstances of the case;

   (c) that, having regard to those matters, the use and any retention of the key are proportionate to what is sought to be achieved by its use or retention;

   (d) that the requirements of subsection (3) are satisfied in relation to any key disclosed in pursuance of a section 49 notice;

   (e) that, for the purpose of ensuring that those requirements are satisfied, any key so disclosed is stored, for so long as it is retained, in a secure manner;

   (f) that all records of a key so disclosed (if not destroyed earlier) are destroyed as soon as the key is no longer needed for the purpose of enabling protected information to be put into an intelligible form.

(3) The requirements of this subsection are satisfied in relation to any key disclosed in pursuance of a section 49 notice if—

   (a) the number of persons to whom the key is disclosed or otherwise made available, and

   (b) the number of copies made of the key, are each limited to the minimum that is necessary for the purpose of enabling protected information to be put into an intelligible form.

(4) Subject to subsection (5), where any relevant person incurs any loss or damage in consequence of—

   (a) any breach by a person to whom this section applies of the duty imposed on him by subsection (2), or

   (b) any contravention by any person whatever of arrangements made in pursuance of that subsection in relation to persons under the control of a person to whom this section applies, the breach or contravention shall be actionable against the person to whom this section applies at the suit or instance of the relevant person.

(5) A person is a relevant person for the purposes of subsection (4) if he is—

    (a) a person who has made a disclosure in pursuance of a section 49 notice; or

    (b) a person whose protected information or key has been disclosed in pursuance of such a notice; and loss or damage shall be taken into account for the purposes of that subsection to the extent only that it relates to the disclosure of particular protected information or a particular key which, in the case of a person falling with paragraph (b), must be his information or key.

(6) For the purposes of subsection (5)—

    (a) information belongs to a person if he has any right that would be infringed by an unauthorised disclosure of the information; and

    (b) a key belongs to a person if it is a key to information that belongs to him or he has any right that would be infringed by an unauthorised disclosure of the key.

(7) In any proceedings brought by virtue of subsection (4), it shall be the duty of the court to have regard to any opinion with respect to the matters to which the proceedings relate that is or has been given by a relevant Commissioner.

(8) In this section "relevant Commissioner" means the Interception of Communications Commissioner, the Intelligence Services Commissioner, the Investigatory Powers Commissioner for Northern Ireland or any Surveillance Commissioner or Assistant Surveillance Commissioner.

Interpretation of Part III

Interpretation of Part III.

56. (1) In this Part—

"chief officer of police" means any of the following—

    (a) the chief constable of a police force maintained under or by virtue of section 2 of the Police Act 1996 or section 1 of the Police (Scotland) Act 1967;

    (b) the Commissioner of Police of the Metropolis;

    (c) the Commissioner of Police for the City of London;

    (d) the Chief Constable of the Royal Ulster Constabulary;

    (e) the Chief Constable of the Ministry of Defence Police;

    (f) the Provost Marshal of the Royal Navy Regulating Branch;

    (g) the Provost Marshal of the Royal Military Police;

    (h) the Provost Marshal of the Royal Air Force Police;

(i)   the Chief Constable of the British Transport Police;

(j)   the Director General of the National Criminal Intelligence Service;

(k)   the Director General of the National Crime Squad;

"the customs and excise" means the Commissioners of Customs and Excise or any customs officer;

"electronic signature" means anything in electronic form which—

(a)   is incorporated into, or otherwise logically associated with, any electronic communication or other electronic data;

(b)   is generated by the signatory or other source of the communication or data; and

(c)   is used for the purpose of facilitating, by means of a link between the signatory or other source and the communication or data, the establishment of the authenticity of the communication or data, the establishment of its integrity, or both;

"key," in relation to any electronic data, means any key, code, password, algorithm or other data the use of which (with or without other keys)—

(a)   allows access to the electronic data, or

(b)   facilitates the putting of the data into an intelligible form;

"the police" means—

(a)   any constable;

(b)   the Commissioner of Police of the Metropolis or any Assistant Commissioner of Police of the Metropolis; or

(c)   the Commissioner of Police for the City of London;

"protected information" means any electronic data which, without the key to the data—

(a)   cannot, or cannot readily, be accessed, or

(b)   cannot, or cannot readily, be put into an intelligible form;

"section 49 notice" means a notice under section 49;

"warrant" includes any authorisation, notice or other instrument (however described) conferring a power of the same description as may, in other cases, be conferred by a warrant.

(2)   References in this Part to a person's having information (including a key to protected information) in his possession include references—

(a)   to its being in the possession of a person who is under his control so far as that information is concerned;

(b)   to his having an immediate right of access to it, or an immediate right to have it transmitted or otherwise supplied to him; and

(c)   to its being, or being contained in, anything which he or a person under his control is entitled, in exercise of any statutory power and without otherwise taking possession of it, to detain, inspect or search.

(3)   References in this Part to something's being intelligible or being put into an intelligible form include references to its being in the condition in which it was before an encryption or similar process was applied to it or, as the case may be, to its being restored to that condition.

(4)   In this section—

(a)   references to the authenticity of any communication or data are references to any one or more of the following—

(i)   whether the communication or data comes from a particular person or other source;

(ii)   whether it is accurately timed and dated;

(iii) whether it is intended to have legal effect;

and

(b)   references to the integrity of any communication or data are references to whether there has been any tampering with or other modification of the communication or data.

Part IV
Scrutiny etc. of Investigatory Powers and of the Functions of the Intelligence Services

Commissioners

Interception of Communications Commissioner.

57. (1)   The Prime Minister shall appoint a Commissioner to be known as the Interception of Communications Commissioner.

(2)   Subject to subsection (4), the Interception of Communications Commissioner shall keep under review—

(a)   the exercise and performance by the Secretary of State of the powers and duties conferred or imposed on him by or under sections 1 to 11;

(b)   the exercise and performance, by the persons on whom they are conferred or imposed, of the powers and duties conferred or imposed by or under Chapter II of Part I;

(c)   the exercise and performance by the Secretary of State in relation to information obtained under Part I of the powers and duties conferred or imposed on him by or under Part III; and

    (d)   the adequacy of the arrangements by virtue of which—

        (i)   the duty which is imposed on the Secretary of State by section 15, and

        (ii)   so far as applicable to information obtained under Part I, the duties imposed by section 55, are sought to be discharged.

(3)   The Interception of Communications Commissioner shall give the Tribunal all such assistance (including his opinion as to any issue falling to be determined by the Tribunal) as the Tribunal may require—

    (a)   in connection with the investigation of any matter by the Tribunal; or

    (b)   otherwise for the purposes of the Tribunal's consideration or determination of any matter.

(4)   It shall not be the function of the Interception of Communications Commissioner to keep under review the exercise of any power of the Secretary of State to make, amend or revoke any subordinate legislation.

(5)   A person shall not be appointed under this section as the Interception of Communications Commissioner unless he holds or has held a high judicial office (within the meaning of the Appellate Jurisdiction Act 1876).

(6)   The Interception of Communications Commissioner shall hold office in accordance with the terms of his appointment; and there shall be paid to him out of money provided by Parliament such allowances as the Treasury may determine.

(7)   The Secretary of State, after consultation with the Interception of Communications Commissioner, shall—

    (a)   make such technical facilities available to the Commissioner, and

    (b)   subject to the approval of the Treasury as to numbers, provide the Commissioner with such staff, as are sufficient to secure that the Commissioner is able properly to carry out his functions.

(8)   On the coming into force of this section the Commissioner holding office as the Commissioner under section 8 of the Interception of Communications Act 1985 shall take and hold office as the Interception of Communications Commissioner as if appointed under this Act—

    (a)   for the unexpired period of his term of office under that Act; and

    (b)   otherwise, on the terms of his appointment under that Act.

Co-operation with and reports by s. 57 Commissioner.

58. (1)   It shall be the duty of—

(a)   every person holding office under the Crown,

(b)   every member of the National Criminal Intelligence Service,

(c)   every member of the National Crime Squad,

(d)   every person employed by or for the purposes of a police force,

(e)   every person required for the purposes of section 11 to provide assistance with giving effect to an interception warrant,

(f)   every person on whom an obligation to take any steps has been imposed under section 12,

(g)   every person by or to whom an authorisation under section 22(3) has been granted,

(h)   every person to whom a notice under section 22(4) has been given,

(i)   every person to whom a notice under section 49 has been given in relation to any information obtained under Part I, and

(j)   every person who is or has been employed for the purposes of any business of a person falling within paragraph (e), (f), (h) or (i), to disclose or provide to the Interception of Communications Commissioner all such documents and information as he may require for the purpose of enabling him to carry out his functions under section 57.

(2)   If it at any time appears to the Interception of Communications Commissioner—

(a)   that there has been a contravention of the provisions of this Act in relation to any matter with which that Commissioner is concerned, and

(b)   that the contravention has not been the subject of a report made to the Prime Minister by the Tribunal, he shall make a report to the Prime Minister with respect to that contravention.

(3)   If it at any time appears to the Interception of Communications Commissioner that any arrangements by reference to which the duties imposed by sections 15 and 55 have sought to be discharged have proved inadequate in relation to any matter with which the Commissioner is concerned, he shall make a report to the Prime Minister with respect to those arrangements.

(4)   As soon as practicable after the end of each calendar year, the Interception of Communications Commissioner shall make a report to the Prime Minister with respect to the carrying out of that Commissioner's functions.

(5)   The Interception of Communications Commissioner may also, at any time, make any such other report to the Prime Minister on any matter relating to the carrying out of the Commissioner's functions as the Commissioner thinks fit.

(6) The Prime Minister shall lay before each House of Parliament a copy of every annual report made by the Interception of Communications Commissioner under subsection (4), together with a statement as to whether any matter has been excluded from that copy in pursuance of subsection (7).

(7) If it appears to the Prime Minister, after consultation with the Interception of Communications Commissioner, that the publication of any matter in an annual report would be contrary to the public interest or prejudicial to—

(a) national security,

(b) the prevention or detection of serious crime,

(c) the economic well-being of the United Kingdom, or

(d) the continued discharge of the functions of any public authority whose activities include activities that are subject to review by that Commissioner, the Prime Minister may exclude that matter from the copy of the report as laid before each House of Parliament.

Intelligence Services Commissioner.

59. (1) The Prime Minister shall appoint a Commissioner to be known as the Intelligence Services Commissioner.

(2) Subject to subsection (4), the Intelligence Services Commissioner shall keep under review, so far as they are not required to be kept under review by the Interception of Communications Commissioner—

(a) the exercise by the Secretary of State of his powers under sections 5 to 7 of the Intelligence Services Act 1994 (warrants for interference with wireless telegraphy, entry and interference with property etc.);

(b) the exercise and performance by the Secretary of State, in connection with or in relation to—

(i) the activities of the intelligence services, and

(ii) the activities in places other than Northern Ireland of the officials of the Ministry of Defence and of members of Her Majesty's forces, of the powers and duties conferred or imposed on him by Parts II and III of this Act;

(c) the exercise and performance by members of the intelligence services of the powers and duties conferred or imposed on them by or under Parts II and III of this Act;

(d) the exercise and performance in places other than Northern Ireland, by officials of the Ministry of Defence and by members of Her Majesty's forces, of the powers and duties conferred or imposed on such officials or members of Her Majesty's forces by or under Parts II and III; and

(e) the adequacy of the arrangements by virtue of which the duty imposed by section 55 is sought to be discharged—

    (i) in relation to the members of the intelligence services; and

    (ii) in connection with any of their activities in places other than Northern Ireland, in relation to officials of the Ministry of Defence and members of Her Majesty's forces.

(3) The Intelligence Services Commissioner shall give the Tribunal all such assistance (including his opinion as to any issue falling to be determined by the Tribunal) as the Tribunal may require—

    (a) in connection with the investigation of any matter by the Tribunal; or

    (b) otherwise for the purposes of the Tribunal's consideration or determination of any matter.

(4) It shall not be the function of the Intelligence Services Commissioner to keep under review the exercise of any power of the Secretary of State to make, amend or revoke any subordinate legislation.

(5) A person shall not be appointed under this section as the Intelligence Services Commissioner unless he holds or has held a high judicial office (within the meaning of the Appellate Jurisdiction Act 1876).

(6) The Intelligence Services Commissioner shall hold office in accordance with the terms of his appointment; and there shall be paid to him out of money provided by Parliament such allowances as the Treasury may determine.

(7) The Secretary of State shall, after consultation with the Intelligence Services Commissioner and subject to the approval of the Treasury as to numbers, provide him with such staff as the Secretary of State considers necessary for the carrying out of the Commissioner's functions.

(8) Section 4 of the Security Service Act 1989 and section 8 of the Intelligence Services Act 1994 (Commissioners for the purposes of those Acts) shall cease to have effect.

(9) On the coming into force of this section the Commissioner holding office as the Commissioner under section 8 of the Intelligence Services Act 1994 shall take and hold office as the Intelligence Services Commissioner as if appointed under this Act—

    (a) for the unexpired period of his term of office under that Act; and

    (b) otherwise, on the terms of his appointment under that Act.

(10) Subsection (7) of section 41 shall apply for the purposes of this section as it applies for the purposes of that section.

Co-operation with and reports by s. 59 Commissioner.

60. (1) It shall be the duty of—
    (a) every member of an intelligence service,
    (b) every official of the department of the Secretary of State, and
    (c) every member of Her Majesty's forces, to disclose or provide to the Intelligence Services Commissioner all such documents and information as he may require for the purpose of enabling him to carry out his functions under section 59.

(2) As soon as practicable after the end of each calendar year, the Intelligence Services Commissioner shall make a report to the Prime Minister with respect to the carrying out of that Commissioner's functions.

(3) The Intelligence Services Commissioner may also, at any time, make any such other report to the Prime Minister on any matter relating to the carrying out of the Commissioner's functions as the Commissioner thinks fit.

(4) The Prime Minister shall lay before each House of Parliament a copy of every annual report made by the Intelligence Services Commissioner under subsection (2), together with a statement as to whether any matter has been excluded from that copy in pursuance of subsection (5).

(5) If it appears to the Prime Minister, after consultation with the Intelligence Services Commissioner, that the publication of any matter in an annual report would be contrary to the public interest or prejudicial to—
    (a) national security,
    (b) the prevention or detection of serious crime,
    (c) the economic well-being of the United Kingdom, or
    (d) the continued discharge of the functions of any public authority whose activities include activities that are subject to review by that Commissioner, the Prime Minister may exclude that matter from the copy of the report as laid before each House of Parliament.

(6) Subsection (7) of section 41 shall apply for the purposes of this section as it applies for the purposes of that section.

Investigatory Powers Commissioner for Northern Ireland.

61. (1) The Prime Minister, after consultation with the First Minister and deputy First Minister in Northern Ireland, shall appoint a Commissioner to be known as the Investigatory Powers Commissioner for Northern Ireland.

(2) The Investigatory Powers Commissioner for Northern Ireland shall keep under review the exercise and performance in Northern Ireland, by the persons on whom they are conferred or imposed, of any pow-

ers or duties under Part II which are conferred or imposed by virtue of an order under section 30 made by the Office of the First Minister and deputy First Minister in Northern Ireland.

(3) The Investigatory Powers Commissioner for Northern Ireland shall give the Tribunal all such assistance (including his opinion as to any issue falling to be determined by the Tribunal) as the Tribunal may require—

    (a) in connection with the investigation of any matter by the Tribunal; or

    (b) otherwise for the purposes of the Tribunal's consideration or determination of any matter.

(4) It shall be the duty of—

    (a) every person by whom, or on whose application, there has been given or granted any authorisation the function of giving or granting which is subject to review by the Investigatory Powers Commissioner for Northern Ireland,

    (b) every person who has engaged in conduct with the authority of such an authorisation,

    (c) every person who holds or has held any office, rank or position with the same public authority as a person falling within paragraph (a), and

    (d) every person who holds or has held any office, rank or position with any public authority for whose benefit (within the meaning of Part II) activities which are or may be subject to any such review have been or may be carried out, to disclose or provide to that Commissioner all such documents and information as he may require for the purpose of enabling him to carry out his functions.

(5) As soon as practicable after the end of each calendar year, the Investigatory Powers Commissioner for Northern Ireland shall make a report to the First Minister and deputy First Minister in Northern Ireland with respect to the carrying out of that Commissioner's functions.

(6) The First Minister and deputy First Minister in Northern Ireland shall lay before the Northern Ireland Assembly a copy of every annual report made by the Investigatory Powers Commissioner for Northern Ireland under subsection (5), together with a statement as to whether any matter has been excluded from that copy in pursuance of subsection (7).

(7) If it appears to the First Minister and deputy First Minister in Northern Ireland, after consultation with the Investigatory Powers Commissioner for Northern Ireland, that the publication of any

matter in an annual report would be contrary to the public interest or prejudicial to—

(a) the prevention or detection of serious crime, or

(b) the continued discharge of the functions of any public authority whose activities include activities that are subject to review by that Commissioner, they may exclude that matter from the copy of the report as laid before the Northern Ireland Assembly.

(8) A person shall not be appointed under this section as the Investigatory Powers Commissioner for Northern Ireland unless he holds or has held office in Northern Ireland—

(a) in any capacity in which he is or was the holder of a high judicial office (within the meaning of the Appellate Jurisdiction Act 1876); or

(b) as a county court judge.

(9) The Investigatory Powers Commissioner for Northern Ireland shall hold office in accordance with the terms of his appointment; and there shall be paid to him out of the Consolidated Fund of Northern Ireland such allowances as the Department of Finance and Personnel may determine.

(10) The First Minister and deputy First Minister in Northern Ireland shall, after consultation with the Investigatory Powers Commissioner for Northern Ireland, provide him with such staff as they consider necessary for the carrying out of his functions.

Additional functions of Chief Surveillance Commissioner.

62. (1) The Chief Surveillance Commissioner shall (in addition to his functions under the Police Act 1997) keep under review, so far as they are not required to be kept under review by the Interception of Communications Commissioner, the Intelligence Services Commissioner or the Investigatory Powers Commissioner for Northern Ireland—

(a) the exercise and performance, by the persons on whom they are conferred or imposed, of the powers and duties conferred or imposed by or under Part II;

(b) the exercise and performance, by any person other than a judicial authority, of the powers and duties conferred or imposed, otherwise than with the permission of such an authority, by or under Part III; and

(c) the adequacy of the arrangements by virtue of which the duties imposed by section 55 are sought to be discharged in relation to persons whose conduct is subject to review under paragraph (b).

(2) It shall not by virtue of this section be the function of the Chief Surveillance Commissioner to keep under review the exercise of any

power of the Secretary of State to make, amend or revoke any subordinate legislation.

(3) In this section "judicial authority" means—

    (a) any judge of the High Court or of the Crown Court or any Circuit Judge;

    (b) any judge of the High Court of Justiciary or any sheriff;

    (c) any justice of the peace;

    (d) any county court judge or resident magistrate in Northern Ireland;

    (e) any person holding any such judicial office as entitles him to exercise the jurisdiction of a judge of the Crown Court or of a justice of the peace.

Assistant Surveillance Commissioners.

63. (1) The Prime Minister may, after consultation with the Chief Surveillance Commissioner as to numbers, appoint as Assistant Surveillance Commissioners such number of persons as the Prime Minister considers necessary (in addition to the ordinary Surveillance Commissioners) for the purpose of providing the Chief Surveillance Commissioner with assistance under this section.

(2) A person shall not be appointed as an Assistant Surveillance Commissioner unless he holds or has held office as—

    (a) a judge of the Crown Court or a Circuit judge;

    (b) a sheriff in Scotland; or

    (c) a county court judge in Northern Ireland.

(3) The Chief Surveillance Commissioner may—

    (a) require any ordinary Surveillance Commissioner or any Assistant Surveillance Commissioner to provide him with assistance in carrying out his functions under section 62(1); or

    (b) require any Assistant Surveillance Commissioner to provide him with assistance in carrying out his equivalent functions under any Act of the Scottish Parliament in relation to any provisions of such an Act that are equivalent to those of Part II of this Act.

(4) The assistance that may be provided under this section includes—

    (a) the conduct on behalf of the Chief Surveillance Commissioner of the review of any matter; and

    (b) the making of a report to the Chief Surveillance Commissioner about the matter reviewed.

(5) Subsections (3) to (8) of section 91 of the Police Act 1997 (Commissioners) apply in relation to a person appointed under this section as they apply in relation to a person appointed under that section.

Delegation of Commissioners' functions.

64. (1) Anything authorised or required by or under any enactment or any provision of an Act of the Scottish Parliament to be done by a relevant Commissioner may be done by any member of the staff of that Commissioner who is authorised for the purpose (whether generally or specifically) by that Commissioner.

(2) In this section "relevant Commissioner" means the Interception of Communications Commissioner, the Intelligence Services Commissioner, the Investigatory Powers Commissioner for Northern Ireland or any Surveillance Commissioner or Assistant Surveillance Commissioner.

The Tribunal

The Tribunal.

65. (1) There shall, for the purpose of exercising the jurisdiction conferred on them by this section, be a tribunal consisting of such number of members as Her Majesty may by Letters Patent appoint.

(2) The jurisdiction of the Tribunal shall be—

(a) to be the only appropriate tribunal for the purposes of section 7 of the Human Rights Act 1998 in relation to any proceedings under subsection (1)(a) of that section (proceedings for actions incompatible with Convention rights) which fall within subsection (3) of this section;

(b) to consider and determine any complaints made to them which, in accordance with subsection (4), are complaints for which the Tribunal is the appropriate forum;

(c) to consider and determine any reference to them by any person that he has suffered detriment as a consequence of any prohibition or restriction, by virtue of section 17, on his relying in, or for the purposes of, any civil proceedings on any matter; and

(d) to hear and determine any other such proceedings falling within subsection (3) as may be allocated to them in accordance with provision made by the Secretary of State by order.

(3) Proceedings fall within this subsection if—

(a) they are proceedings against any of the intelligence services;

(b) they are proceedings against any other person in respect of any conduct, or proposed conduct, by or on behalf of any of those services;

(c) they are proceedings brought by virtue of section 55(4); or

(d) they are proceedings relating to the taking place in any challengeable circumstances of any conduct falling within subsection (5).

(4) The Tribunal is the appropriate forum for any complaint if it is a complaint by a person who is aggrieved by any conduct falling within subsection (5) which he believes—

   (a) to have taken place in relation to him, to any of his property, to any communications sent by or to him, or intended for him, or to his use of any postal service, telecommunications service or telecommunication system; and

   (b) to have taken place in challengeable circumstances or to have been carried out by or on behalf of any of the intelligence services.

(5) Subject to subsection (6), conduct falls within this subsection if (whenever it occurred) it is—

   (a) conduct by or on behalf of any of the intelligence services;

   (b) conduct for or in connection with the interception of communications in the course of their transmission by means of a postal service or telecommunication system;

   (c) conduct to which Chapter II of Part I applies;

   (d) conduct to which Part II applies;

   (e) the giving of a notice under section 49 or any disclosure or use of a key to protected information;

   (f) any entry on or interference with property or any interference with wireless telegraphy.

(6) For the purposes only of subsection (3), nothing mentioned in paragraph (d) or (f) of subsection (5) shall be treated as falling within that subsection unless it is conduct by or on behalf of a person holding any office, rank or position with—

   (a) any of the intelligence services;

   (b) any of Her Majesty's forces;

   (c) any police force;

   (d) the National Criminal Intelligence Service;

   (e) the National Crime Squad; or

   (f) the Commissioners of Customs and Excise; and section 48(5) applies for the purposes of this subsection as it applies for the purposes of Part II.

(7) For the purposes of this section conduct takes place in challengeable circumstances if—

   (a) it takes place with the authority, or purported authority, of anything falling within subsection (8); or

   (b) the circumstances are such that (whether or not there is such authority) it would not have been appropriate for the conduct to take place without it, or at least without proper consideration having been given to whether such authority should be sought; but conduct does not take place in challengeable circumstances to the extent that it is authorised by, or takes place with the permission of, a judicial authority.

(8) The following fall within this subsection—

    (a) an interception warrant or a warrant under the Interception of Communications Act 1985;

    (b) an authorisation or notice under Chapter II of Part I of this Act;

    (c) an authorisation under Part II of this Act or under any enactment contained in or made under an Act of the Scottish Parliament which makes provision equivalent to that made by that Part;

    (d) a permission for the purposes of Schedule 2 to this Act;

    (e) a notice under section 49 of this Act; or

    (f) an authorisation under section 93 of the Police Act 1997.

(9) Schedule 3 (which makes further provision in relation to the Tribunal) shall have effect.

(10) In this section—

    (a) references to a key and to protected information shall be construed in accordance with section 56;

    (b) references to the disclosure or use of a key to protected information taking place in relation to a person are references to such a disclosure or use taking place in a case in which that person has had possession of the key or of the protected information; and

    (c) references to the disclosure of a key to protected information include references to the making of any disclosure in an intelligible form (within the meaning of section 56) of protected information by a person who is or has been in possession of the key to that information; and the reference in paragraph (b) to a person's having possession of a key or of protected information shall be construed in accordance with section 56.

(11) In this section "judicial authority" means—

    (a) any judge of the High Court or of the Crown Court or any Circuit Judge;

    (b) any judge of the High Court of Justiciary or any sheriff;

    (c) any justice of the peace;

    (d) any county court judge or resident magistrate in Northern Ireland;

    (e) any person holding any such judicial office as entitles him to exercise the jurisdiction of a judge of the Crown Court or of a justice of the peace.

Orders allocating proceedings to the Tribunal.

66. (1) An order under section 65(2)(d) allocating proceedings to the Tribunal—

(a)   may provide for the Tribunal to exercise jurisdiction in relation to that matter to the exclusion of the jurisdiction of any court or tribunal; but

(b)   if it does so provide, must contain provision conferring a power on the Tribunal, in the circumstances provided for in the order, to remit the proceedings to the court or tribunal which would have had jurisdiction apart from the order.

(2)   In making any provision by an order under section 65(2)(d) the Secretary of State shall have regard, in particular, to—

(a)   the need to secure that proceedings allocated to the Tribunal are properly heard and considered; and

(b)   the need to secure that information is not disclosed to an extent, or in a manner, that is contrary to the public interest or prejudicial to national security, the prevention or detection of serious crime, the economic well-being of the United Kingdom or the continued discharge of the functions of any of the intelligence services.

(3)   The Secretary of State shall not make an order under section 65(2)(d) unless a draft of the order has been laid before Parliament and approved by a resolution of each House.

Exercise of the Tribunal's jurisdiction.

67. (1)   Subject to subsections (4) and (5), it shall be the duty of the Tribunal—

(a)   to hear and determine any proceedings brought before them by virtue of section 65(2)(a) or (d); and

(b)   to consider and determine any complaint or reference made to them by virtue of section 65(2)(b) or (c).

(2)   Where the Tribunal hear any proceedings by virtue of section 65(2)(a), they shall apply the same principles for making their determination in those proceedings as would be applied by a court on an application for judicial review.

(3)   Where the Tribunal consider a complaint made to them by virtue of section 65(2)(b), it shall be the duty of the Tribunal—

(a)   to investigate whether the persons against whom any allegations are made in the complaint have engaged in relation to—

(i)   the complainant,

(ii)   any of his property,

(iii)   any communications sent by or to him, or intended for him, or

(iv)   his use of any postal service, telecommunications service or telecommunication system, in any conduct falling within section 65(5);

(b)   to investigate the authority (if any) for any conduct falling within section 65(5) which they find has been so engaged in; and

(c)   in relation to the Tribunal's findings from their investigations, to determine the complaint by applying the same principles as would be applied by a court on an application for judicial review.

(4)   The Tribunal shall not be under any duty to hear, consider or determine any proceedings, complaint or reference if it appears to them that the bringing of the proceedings or the making of the complaint or reference is frivolous or vexatious.

(5)   Except where the Tribunal, having regard to all the circumstances, are satisfied that it is equitable to do so, they shall not consider or determine any complaint made by virtue of section 65(2)(b) if it is made more than one year after the taking place of the conduct to which it relates.

(6)   Subject to any provision made by rules under section 69, where any proceedings have been brought before the Tribunal or any reference made to the Tribunal, they shall have power to make such interim orders, pending their final determination, as they think fit.

(7)   Subject to any provision made by rules under section 69, the Tribunal on determining any proceedings, complaint or reference shall have power to make any such award of compensation or other order as they think fit; and, without prejudice to the power to make rules under section 69(2)(h), the other orders that may be made by the Tribunal include—

(a)   an order quashing or cancelling any warrant or authorisation; and

(b)   an order requiring the destruction of any records of information which—

(i)   has been obtained in exercise of any power conferred by a warrant or authorisation; or

(ii)   is held by any public authority in relation to any person.

(8)   Except to such extent as the Secretary of State may by order otherwise provide, determinations, awards, orders and other decisions of the Tribunal (including decisions as to whether they have jurisdiction) shall not be subject to appeal or be liable to be questioned in any court.

(9)   It shall be the duty of the Secretary of State to secure that there is at all times an order under subsection (8) in force allowing for an appeal to a court against any exercise by the Tribunal of their jurisdiction under section 65(2)(c) or (d).

(10) The provision that may be contained in an order under subsection (8) may include—

    (a) provision for the establishment and membership of a tribunal or body to hear appeals;

    (b) the appointment of persons to that tribunal or body and provision about the remuneration and allowances to be payable to such persons and the expenses of the tribunal;

    (c) the conferring of jurisdiction to hear appeals on any existing court or tribunal; and

    (d) any such provision in relation to an appeal under the order as corresponds to provision that may be made by rules under section 69 in relation to proceedings before the Tribunal, or to complaints or references made to the Tribunal.

(11) The Secretary of State shall not make an order under subsection (8) unless a draft of the order has been laid before Parliament and approved by a resolution of each House.

(12) The Secretary of State shall consult the Scottish Ministers before making any order under subsection (8); and any such order shall be laid before the Scottish Parliament.

Tribunal procedure.

68. (1) Subject to any rules made under section 69, the Tribunal shall be entitled to determine their own procedure in relation to any proceedings, complaint or reference brought before or made to them.

    (2) The Tribunal shall have power—

        (a) in connection with the investigation of any matter, or

        (b) otherwise for the purposes of the Tribunal's consideration or determination of any matter, to require a relevant Commissioner appearing to the Tribunal to have functions in relation to the matter in question to provide the Tribunal with all such assistance (including that Commissioner's opinion as to any issue falling to be determined by the Tribunal) as the Tribunal think fit.

    (3) Where the Tribunal hear or consider any proceedings, complaint or reference relating to any matter, they shall secure that every relevant Commissioner appearing to them to have functions in relation to that matter—

        (a) is aware that the matter is the subject of proceedings, a complaint or a reference brought before or made to the Tribunal; and

        (b) is kept informed of any determination, award, order or other decision made by the Tribunal with respect to that matter.

    (4) Where the Tribunal determine any proceedings, complaint or reference brought before or made to them, they shall give notice to

the complainant which (subject to any rules made by virtue of section 69(2)(i)) shall be confined, as the case may be, to either—

(a) a statement that they have made a determination in his favour; or

(b) a statement that no determination has been made in his favour.

(5) Where—

(a) the Tribunal make a determination in favour of any person by whom any proceedings have been brought before the Tribunal or by whom any complaint or reference has been made to the Tribunal, and

(b) the determination relates to any act or omission by or on behalf of the Secretary of State or to conduct for which any warrant, authorisation or permission was issued, granted or given by the Secretary of State, they shall make a report of their findings to the Prime Minister.

(6) It shall be the duty of the persons specified in subsection (7) to disclose or provide to the Tribunal all such documents and information as the Tribunal may require for the purpose of enabling them—

(a) to exercise the jurisdiction conferred on them by or under section 65; or

(b) otherwise to exercise or perform any power or duty conferred or imposed on them by or under this Act.

(7) Those persons are—

(a) every person holding office under the Crown;

(b) every member of the National Criminal Intelligence Service;

(c) every member of the National Crime Squad;

(d) every person employed by or for the purposes of a police force;

(e) every person required for the purposes of section 11 to provide assistance with giving effect to an interception warrant;

(f) every person on whom an obligation to take any steps has been imposed under section 12;

(g) every person by or to whom an authorisation under section 22(3) has been granted;

(h) every person to whom a notice under section 22(4) has been given;

(i) every person by whom, or on whose application, there has been granted or given any authorisation under Part II of this Act or under Part III of the Police Act 1997;

(j) every person who holds or has held any office, rank or position with the same public authority as a person falling within paragraph (i);

(k) every person who has engaged in any conduct with the authority of an authorisation under section 22 or Part II of this Act or under Part III of the Police Act 1997;

(l)   every person who holds or has held any office, rank or position with a public authority for whose benefit any such authorisation has been or may be given;

(m)   every person to whom a notice under section 49 has been given; and

(n)   every person who is or has been employed for the purposes of any business of a person falling within paragraph (e), (f), (h) or (m).

(8)   In this section "relevant Commissioner" means the Interception of Communications Commissioner, the Intelligence Services Commissioner, the Investigatory Powers Commissioner for Northern Ireland or any Surveillance Commissioner or Assistant Surveillance Commissioner.

Tribunal rules.

69. (1)   The Secretary of State may make rules regulating—

(a)   the exercise by the Tribunal of the jurisdiction conferred on them by or under section 65; and

(b)   any matters preliminary or incidental to, or arising out of, the hearing or consideration of any proceedings, complaint or reference brought before or made to the Tribunal.

(2)   Without prejudice to the generality of subsection (1), rules under this section may—

(a)   enable the jurisdiction of the Tribunal to be exercised at any place in the United Kingdom by any two or more members of the Tribunal designated for the purpose by the President of the Tribunal;

(b)   enable different members of the Tribunal to carry out functions in relation to different complaints at the same time;

(c)   prescribe the form and manner in which proceedings are to be brought before the Tribunal or a complaint or reference is to be made to the Tribunal;

(d)   require persons bringing proceedings or making complaints or references to take such preliminary steps, and to make such disclosures, as may be specified in the rules for the purpose of facilitating a determination of whether—

(i)   the bringing of the proceedings, or

(ii)   the making of the complaint or reference, is frivolous or vexatious;

(e)   make provision about the determination of any question as to whether a person by whom—

(i)   any proceedings have been brought before the Tribunal, or

        (ii)   any complaint or reference has been made to the Tribunal, is a person with a right to bring those proceedings or make that complaint or reference;

(f)   prescribe the forms of hearing or consideration to be adopted by the Tribunal in relation to particular proceedings, complaints or references (including a form that requires any proceedings brought before the Tribunal to be disposed of as if they were a complaint or reference made to the Tribunal);

(g)   prescribe the practice and procedure to be followed on, or in connection with, the hearing or consideration of any proceedings, complaint or reference (including, where applicable, the mode and burden of proof and the admissibility of evidence);

(h)   prescribe orders that may be made by the Tribunal under section 67(6) or (7);

(i)   require information about any determination, award, order or other decision made by the Tribunal in relation to any proceedings, complaint or reference to be provided (in addition to any statement under section 68(4)) to the person who brought the proceedings or made the complaint or reference, or to the person representing his interests.

(3)   Rules under this section in relation to the hearing or consideration of any matter by the Tribunal may provide—

(a)   for a person who has brought any proceedings before or made any complaint or reference to the Tribunal to have the right to be legally represented;

(b)   for the manner in which the interests of a person who has brought any proceedings before or made any complaint or reference to the Tribunal are otherwise to be represented;

(c)   for the appointment in accordance with the rules, by such person as may be determined in accordance with the rules, of a person to represent those interests in the case of any proceedings, complaint or reference.

(4)   The power to make rules under this section includes power to make rules—

(a)   enabling or requiring the Tribunal to hear or consider any proceedings, complaint or reference without the person who brought the proceedings or made the complaint or reference having been given full particulars of the reasons for any conduct which is the subject of the proceedings, complaint or reference;

(b)   enabling or requiring the Tribunal to take any steps in exercise of their jurisdiction in the absence of any person (including the person bringing the proceedings or making the complaint or reference and any legal representative of his);

(c)   enabling or requiring the Tribunal to give a summary of any evidence taken in his absence to the person by whom the proceedings were brought or, as the case may be, to the person who made the complaint or reference;

(d)   enabling or requiring the Tribunal to exercise their jurisdiction, and to exercise and perform the powers and duties conferred or imposed on them (including, in particular, in relation to the giving of reasons), in such manner provided for in the rules as prevents or limits the disclosure of particular matters.

(5)   Rules under this section may also include provision—

(a)   enabling powers or duties of the Tribunal that relate to matters preliminary or incidental to the hearing or consideration of any proceedings, complaint or reference to be exercised or performed by a single member of the Tribunal; and

(b)   conferring on the Tribunal such ancillary powers as the Secretary of State thinks necessary for the purposes of, or in connection with, the exercise of the Tribunal's jurisdiction, or the exercise or performance of any power or duty conferred or imposed on them.

(6)   In making rules under this section the Secretary of State shall have regard, in particular, to—

(a)   the need to secure that matters which are the subject of proceedings, complaints or references brought before or made to the Tribunal are properly heard and considered; and

(b)   the need to secure that information is not disclosed to an extent, or in a manner, that is contrary to the public interest or prejudicial to national security, the prevention or detection of serious crime, the economic well-being of the United Kingdom or the continued discharge of the functions of any of the intelligence services.

(7)   Rules under this section may make provision by the application, with or without modification, of the provision from time to time contained in specified rules of court.

(8)   Subject to subsection (9), no rules shall be made under this section unless a draft of them has first been laid before Parliament and approved by a resolution of each House.

(9)   Subsection (8) does not apply in the case of the rules made on the first occasion on which the Secretary of State exercises his power to make rules under this section.

(10)   The rules made on that occasion shall cease to have effect at the end of the period of forty days beginning with the day on which they were made unless, before the end of that period, they have been approved by a resolution of each House of Parliament.

(11) For the purposes of subsection (10)—

    (a) the rules' ceasing to have effect shall be without prejudice to anything previously done or to the making of new rules; and

    (b) in reckoning the period of forty days no account shall be taken of any period during which Parliament is dissolved or prorogued or during which both Houses are adjourned for more than four days.

(12) The Secretary of State shall consult the Scottish Ministers before making any rules under this section; and any rules so made shall be laid before the Scottish Parliament.

Abolition of jurisdiction in relation to complaints.

70. (1) The provisions set out in subsection (2) (which provide for the investigation etc. of certain complaints) shall not apply in relation to any complaint made after the coming into force of this section.

    (2) Those provisions are—

        (a) section 5 of, and Schedules 1 and 2 to, the Security Service Act 1989 (investigation of complaints about the Security Service made to the Tribunal established under that Act);

        (b) section 9 of, and Schedules 1 and 2 to, the Intelligence Services Act 1994 (investigation of complaints about the Secret Intelligence Service or GCHQ made to the Tribunal established under that Act); and

        (c) section 102 of, and Schedule 7 to, the Police Act 1997 (investigation of complaints made to the Surveillance Commissioners).

Codes of practice

Issue and revision of codes of practice.

71. (1) The Secretary of State shall issue one or more codes of practice relating to the exercise and performance of the powers and duties mentioned in subsection (2).

    (2) Those powers and duties are those (excluding any power to make subordinate legislation) that are conferred or imposed otherwise than on the Surveillance Commissioners by or under—

        (a) Parts I to III of this Act;

        (b) section 5 of the Intelligence Services Act 1994 (warrants for interference with property or wireless telegraphy for the purposes of the intelligence services); and

        (c) Part III of the Police Act 1997 (authorisation by the police or customs and excise of interference with property or wireless telegraphy).

    (3) Before issuing a code of practice under subsection (1), the Secretary of State shall—

(a)   prepare and publish a draft of that code; and

(b)   consider any representations made to him about the draft; and the Secretary of State may incorporate in the code finally issued any modifications made by him to the draft after its publication.

(4)   The Secretary of State shall lay before both Houses of Parliament every draft code of practice prepared and published by him under this section.

(5)   A code of practice issued by the Secretary of State under this section shall not be brought into force except in accordance with an order made by the Secretary of State.

(6)   An order under subsection (5) may contain such transitional provisions and savings as appear to the Secretary of State to be necessary or expedient in connection with the bringing into force of the code brought into force by that order.

(7)   The Secretary of State may from time to time—

(a)   revise the whole or any part of a code issued under this section; and

(b)   issue the revised code.

(8)   Subsections (3) to (6) shall apply (with appropriate modifications) in relation to the issue of any revised code under this section as they apply in relation to the first issue of such a code.

(9)   The Secretary of State shall not make an order containing provision for any of the purposes of this section unless a draft of the order has been laid before Parliament and approved by a resolution of each House.

Effect of codes of practice.

72. (1)   A person exercising or performing any power or duty in relation to which provision may be made by a code of practice under section 71 shall, in doing so, have regard to the provisions (so far as they are applicable) of every code of practice for the time being in force under that section.

(2)   A failure on the part of any person to comply with any provision of a code of practice for the time being in force under section 71 shall not of itself render him liable to any criminal or civil proceedings.

(3)   A code of practice in force at any time under section 71 shall be admissible in evidence in any criminal or civil proceedings.

(4)   If any provision of a code of practice issued or revised under section 71 appears to—

(a)   the court or tribunal conducting any civil or criminal proceedings,

(b)   the Tribunal,

(c)   a relevant Commissioner carrying out any of his functions under this Act,

(d)   a Surveillance Commissioner carrying out his functions under this Act or the Police Act 1997, or

(e)   any Assistant Surveillance Commissioner carrying out any functions of his under section 63 of this Act, to be relevant to any question arising in the proceedings, or in connection with the exercise of that jurisdiction or the carrying out of those functions, in relation to a time when it was in force, that provision of the code shall be taken into account in determining that question.

(5)   In this section "relevant Commissioner" means the Interception of Communications Commissioner, the Intelligence Services Commissioner or the Investigatory Powers Commissioner for Northern Ireland.

Part V
Miscellaneous and Supplemental

Miscellaneous

Conduct in relation to wireless telegraphy.

73. (1)   Section 5 of the Wireless Telegraphy Act 1949 (misleading messages and interception and disclosure of wireless telegraphy messages) shall become subsection (1) of that section.

(2)   In paragraph (b) of that subsection—

(a)   for the words from "under the authority of" to "servant of the Crown," there shall be substituted "under the authority of a designated person"; and

(b)   in sub-paragraph (i), for the words from "which neither" to the end of the sub-paragraph there shall be substituted "of which neither the person using the apparatus nor a person on whose behalf he is acting is an intended recipient,".

(3)   In that section, after that subsection there shall be inserted—"(2) The conduct in relation to which a designated person may give a separate authority for the purposes of this section shall not, except where he believes the conduct to be necessary on grounds falling within subsection (5) of this section, include—

(a)   any conduct which, if engaged in without lawful authority, constitutes an offence under section 1(1) or (2) of the Regulation of Investigatory Powers Act 2000;

  (b) any conduct which, if engaged in without lawful authority, is actionable under section 1(3) of that Act;

  (c) any conduct which is capable of being authorised by an authorisation or notice granted by any person under Chapter II of Part I of that Act (communications data);

  (d) any conduct which is capable of being authorised by an authorisation granted by any person under Part II of that Act (surveillance etc.).

(3) A designated person shall not exercise his power to give a separate authority for the purposes of this section except where he believes—

  (a) that the giving of his authority is necessary on grounds falling within subsection (4) or (5) of this section; and

  (b) that the conduct authorised by him is proportionate to what is sought to be achieved by that conduct.

(4) A separate authority for the purposes of this section is necessary on grounds falling within this subsection if it is necessary—

  (a) in the interests of national security;

  (b) for the purpose of preventing or detecting crime (within the meaning of the Regulation of Investigatory Powers Act 2000) or of preventing disorder;

  (c) in the interests of the economic well-being of the United Kingdom;

  (d) in the interests of public safety;

  (e) for the purpose of protecting public health;

  (f) for the purpose of assessing or collecting any tax, duty, levy or other imposition, contribution or charge payable to a government department; or

  (g) for any purpose (not falling within paragraphs (a) to (f)) which is specified for the purposes of this subsection by regulations made by the Secretary of State.

(5) A separate authority for the purposes of this section is necessary on grounds falling within this subsection if it is not necessary on grounds falling within subsection (4)(a) or (c) to (g) but is necessary for purposes connected with—

  (a) the issue of licences under this Act;

  (b) the prevention or detection of anything which constitutes interference with wireless telegraphy; or

  (c) the enforcement of any enactment contained in this Act or of any enactment not so contained that relates to such interference.

(6) The matters to be taken into account in considering whether the requirements of subsection (3) of this section are satisfied in the case of the giving of any separate authority for the purposes of this section shall include whether what it is thought necessary to achieve

by the authorised conduct could reasonably be achieved by other means.

(7) A separate authority for the purposes of this section must be in writing and under the hand of—

    (a) the Secretary of State;

    (b) one of the Commissioners of Customs and Excise; or

    (c) a person not falling within paragraph (a) or (b) who is designated for the purposes of this subsection by regulations made by the Secretary of State.

(8) A separate authority for the purposes of this section may be general or specific and may be given—

    (a) to such person or persons, or description of persons,

    (b) for such period, and

    (c) subject to such restrictions and limitations, as the designated person thinks fit.

(9) No regulations shall be made under subsection (4)(g) unless a draft of them has first been laid before Parliament and approved by a resolution of each House.

(10) For the purposes of this section the question whether conduct is capable of being authorised under Chapter II of Part I of the Regulation of Investigatory Powers Act 2000 or under Part II of that Act shall be determined without reference—

    (a) to whether the person whose conduct it is is a person on whom any power or duty is or may be conferred or imposed by or under Chapter II of Part I or Part II of that Act; or

    (b) to whether there are grounds for believing that the requirements for the grant of an authorisation or the giving of a notice under Chapter II of Part I or Part II of that Act are satisfied.

(11) References in this section to a separate authority for the purposes of this section are references to any authority for the purposes of this section given otherwise than by way of the issue or renewal of a warrant, authorisation or notice under Part I or II of the Regulation of Investigatory Powers Act 2000.

(12) In this section "designated person" means—

    (a) the Secretary of State;

    (b) the Commissioners of Customs and Excise; or

    (c) any other person designated for the purposes of this section by regulations made by the Secretary of State." (4) In section 16(2) of that Act (regulations and orders), after "the said powers" there shall be inserted "other than one containing regulations a draft of which has been approved for the purposes of section 5(9),".

Warrants under the Intelligence Services Act 1994.

74. (1)   In subsection (2) of section 5 of the Intelligence Services Act 1994 (the circumstances in which the Secretary of State may issue a warrant authorising interference with property or wireless telegraphy)—

    (a)   in paragraph (a), for "on the ground that it is likely to be of substantial value in" there shall be substituted "for the purpose of"; and

    (b)   for paragraph (b) there shall be substituted-"(b) is satisfied that the taking of the action is proportionate to what the action seeks to achieve;"

(2)   After that subsection, there shall be inserted— "(2A) The matters to be taken into account in considering whether the requirements of subsection (2)(a) and (b) are satisfied in the case of any warrant shall include whether what it is thought necessary to achieve by the conduct authorised by the warrant could reasonably be achieved by other means."

(3)   In each of sections 6(1)(b) and 7(5)(b) of that Act (warrants issued under the hand of a senior official of the Secretary of State's department), the words "of his department" shall be omitted.

(4)   In section 11 of that Act (interpretation), for paragraph (1)(d) there shall be substituted "(d) "senior official" has the same meaning as in the Regulation of Investigatory Powers Act 2000;".

Authorisations under Part III of the Police Act 1997.

75. (1)   Section 93 of the Police Act 1997 (authorisations to interfere with property etc.) shall be amended as follows.

(2)   In subsection (1) (the action that the authorising officer may authorise), for "or" at the end of paragraph (a) there shall be substituted— "(ab) the taking of such action falling within subsection (1A), in respect of property outside the relevant area, as he may specify, or."

(3)   After that subsection there shall be inserted—"(1A) The action falling within this subsection is action for maintaining or retrieving any equipment, apparatus or device the placing or use of which in the relevant area has been authorised under this Part or Part II of the Regulation of Investigatory Powers Act 2000 or under any enactment contained in or made under an Act of the Scottish Parliament which makes provision equivalent to that made by Part II of that Act of 2000. (1B) Subsection (1) applies where the authorising officer is a customs officer with the omission of—

    (a)   the words "in the relevant area," in each place where they occur; and

    (b)   paragraph (ab)."

(4) In subsection (2) (the grounds on which action may be authorised)—

    (a) in paragraph (a), for the words from "on the ground" to "detection of" there shall be substituted "for the purpose of preventing or detecting"; and

    (b) for paragraph (b) there shall be substituted—

"(b) that the taking of the action is proportionate to what the action seeks to achieve."

(5) After subsection (2) there shall be inserted— "(2A) Subsection (2) applies where the authorising officer is the Chief Constable or the Deputy Chief Constable of the Royal Ulster Constabulary as if the reference in subsection (2)(a) to preventing or detecting serious crime included a reference to the interests of national security. (2B) The matters to be taken into account in considering whether the requirements of subsection (2) are satisfied in the case of any authorisation shall include whether what it is thought necessary to achieve by the authorised action could reasonably be achieved by other means."

(6) In subsection (5) (the meaning of authorising officer)—

    (a) after paragraph (e) there shall be inserted—

"(ea) the Chief Constable of the Ministry of Defence Police;
(eb) the Provost Marshal of the Royal Navy Regulating Branch;
(ec) the Provost Marshal of the Royal Military Police;
(ed) the Provost Marshal of the Royal Air Force Police;
(ee) the Chief Constable of the British Transport Police;";

    (b) in paragraph (g), after "National Crime Squad" there shall be inserted "or any person holding the rank of assistant chief constable in that Squad who is designated for the purposes of this paragraph by that Director General"; and

    (c) in paragraph (h), for the word "the," in the first place where it occurs, there shall be substituted "any."

(7) In subsection (6) (the meaning of relevant area), after paragraph (c) there shall be inserted—

"(ca) in relation to a person within paragraph (ea), means any place where, under section 2 of the Ministry of Defence Police Act 1987, the members of the Ministry of Defence Police have the powers and privileges of a constable;

(cb) in relation to a person within paragraph (ee), means the United Kingdom;".

(8) After that subsection there shall be inserted— "(6A) For the purposes of any authorisation by a person within paragraph (eb), (ec) or (ed) of subsection (5) property is in the relevant area or action

in respect of wireless telegraphy is taken in the relevant area if, as the case may be—

(a)   the property is owned, occupied, in the possession of or being used by a person subject to service discipline; or

(b)   the action is taken in relation to the use of wireless telegraphy by such a person. (6B) For the purposes of this section a person is subject to service discipline—

(a)   in relation to the Royal Navy Regulating Branch, if he is subject to the Naval Discipline Act 1957 or is a civilian to whom Parts I and II of that Act for the time being apply by virtue of section 118 of that Act ;

(b)   in relation to the Royal Military Police, if he is subject to military law or is a civilian to whom Part II of the Army Act 1955 for the time being applies by virtue of section 209 of that Act; and

(c)   in relation to the Royal Air Force Police, if he is subject to airforce law or is a civilian to whom Part II of the Air Force Act 1955 for the time being applies by virtue of section 209 of that Act."

Surveillance etc. operations beginning in Scotland.

76. (1)   Subject to subsection (2), where—

(a)   an authorisation under the relevant Scottish legislation has the effect of authorising the carrying out in Scotland of the conduct described in the authorisation,

(b)   the conduct so described is or includes conduct to which Part II of this Act applies, and

(c)   circumstances arise by virtue of which some or all of the conduct so described can for the time being be carried out only outwith Scotland, section 27 of this Act shall have effect for the purpose of making lawful the carrying out outwith Scotland of the conduct so described as if the authorisation, so far as is it relates to conduct to which that Part applies, were an authorisation duly granted under that Part.

(2)   Where any such circumstances as are mentioned in paragraph (c) of subsection (1) so arise as to give effect outwith Scotland to any authorisation granted under the relevant Scottish legislation, that authorisation shall not authorise any conduct outwith Scotland at any time after the end of the period of three weeks beginning with the time when the circumstances arose.

(3)   Subsection (2) is without prejudice to the operation of subsection (1) in relation to any authorisation on the second or any subsequent occasion on which any such circumstances as are mentioned in subsection (1)(c) arise while the authorisation remains in force.

(4) In this section "the relevant Scottish legislation" means an enact-ment contained in or made under an Act of the Scottish Parliament which makes provision, corresponding to that made by Part II, for the authorisation of conduct to which that Part applies.

Supplemental

Ministerial expenditure etc.

77. There shall be paid out of money provided by Parliament—

(a) any expenditure incurred by the Secretary of State for or in connection with the carrying out of his functions under this Act; and

(b) any increase attributable to this Act in the sums which are payable out of money so provided under any other Act.

Orders, regulations and rules.

78. (1) This section applies to any power of the Secretary of State to make any order, regulations or rules under any provision of this Act.

(2) The powers to which this section applies shall be exercisable by statu-tory instrument.

(3) A statutory instrument which contains any order made in exercise of a power to which this section applies (other than the power to appoint a day under section 83(2)) but which contains neither—

(a) an order a draft of which has been approved for the purposes of section 12(10), 13(3), 22(9), 25(5), 28(5), 29(6), 30(7), 35(5), 41(6), 47(2), 66(3), 67(11) or 71(9), nor

(b) the order to which section 35(7) applies, shall be subject to annulment in pursuance of a resolution of either House of Parliament.

(4) A statutory instrument containing any regulations made in exercise of a power to which this section applies shall be subject to annul-ment in pursuance of a resolution of either House of Parliament.

(5) Any order, regulations or rules made in exercise of a power to which this section applies may—

(a) make different provisions for different cases;

(b) contain such incidental, supplemental, consequential and tran-sitional provision as the Secretary of State thinks fit.

Criminal liability of directors etc.

79. (1) Where an offence under any provision of this Act other than a pro-vision of Part III is committed by a body corporate and is proved to have been committed with the consent or connivance of, or to be attributable to any neglect on the part of—

(a) a director, manager, secretary or other similar officer of the body corporate, or

(b) any person who was purporting to act in any such capacity, he (as well as the body corporate) shall be guilty of that offence and liable to be proceeded against and punished accordingly.

(2) Where an offence under any provision of this Act other than a provision of Part III—

(a) is committed by a Scottish firm, and

(b) is proved to have been committed with the consent or connivance of, or to be attributable to any neglect on the part of, a partner of the firm, he (as well as the firm) shall be guilty of that offence and liable to be proceeded against and punished accordingly.

(3) In this section "director," in relation to a body corporate whose affairs are managed by its members, means a member of the body corporate.

General saving for lawful conduct.

80. Nothing in any of the provisions of this Act by virtue of which conduct of any description is or may be authorised by any warrant, authorisation or notice, or by virtue of which information may be obtained in any manner, shall be construed—

(a) as making it unlawful to engage in any conduct of that description which is not otherwise unlawful under this Act and would not be unlawful apart from this Act;

(b) as otherwise requiring—

(i) the issue, grant or giving of such a warrant, authorisation or notice, or

(ii) the taking of any step for or towards obtaining the authority of such a warrant, authorisation or notice, before any such conduct of that description is engaged in; or

(c) as prejudicing any power to obtain information by any means not involving conduct that may be authorised under this Act.

General interpretation.

81. (1) In this Act—

"apparatus" includes any equipment, machinery or device and any wire or cable;

"Assistant Commissioner of Police of the Metropolis" includes the Deputy Commissioner of Police of the Metropolis;

"Assistant Surveillance Commissioner" means any person holding office under section 63;

"civil proceedings" means any proceedings in or before any court or tribunal that are not criminal proceedings;

"communication" includes—

(a) (except in the definition of "postal service" in section 2(1)) anything transmitted by means of a postal service;

(b) anything comprising speech, music, sounds, visual images or data of any description; and

(c) signals serving either for the impartation of anything between persons, between a person and a thing or between things or for the actuation or control of any apparatus;

"criminal," in relation to any proceedings or prosecution, shall be construed in accordance with subsection (4);

"customs officer" means an officer commissioned by the Commissioners of Customs and Excise under section 6(3) of the Customs and Excise Management Act 1979;

"document" includes a map, plan, design, drawing, picture or other image;

"enactment" includes—

(a) an enactment passed after the passing of this Act; and

(b) an enactment contained in Northern Ireland legislation;

"GCHQ" has the same meaning as in the Intelligence Services Act 1994;

"Her Majesty's forces" has the same meaning as in the Army Act 1955;

"intelligence service" means the Security Service, the Secret Intelligence Service or GCHQ;

"interception" and cognate expressions shall be construed (so far as it is applicable) in accordance with section 2;

"interception warrant" means a warrant under section 5;

"legal proceedings" means civil or criminal proceedings in or before any court or tribunal;

"modification" includes alterations, additions and omissions, and cognate expressions shall be construed accordingly;

"ordinary Surveillance Commissioner" means a Surveillance Commissioner other than the Chief Surveillance Commissioner;

"person" includes any organisation and any association or combination of persons;

"police force" means any of the following—

(a) any police force maintained under section 2 of the Police Act 1996 (police forces in England and Wales outside London);

(b) the metropolitan police force;

(c) the City of London police force;

(d) any police force maintained under or by virtue of section 1 of the Police (Scotland) Act 1967

(e) the Royal Ulster Constabulary;

(f) the Ministry of Defence Police;

(g) the Royal Navy Regulating Branch;

(h) the Royal Military Police;

(i) the Royal Air Force Police;

(j) the British Transport Police;

"postal service" and "public postal service" have the meanings given by section 2(1);

"private telecommunication system," "public telecommunications service" and "public telecommunication system" have the meanings given by section 2(1);

"public authority" means any public authority within the meaning of section 6 of the Human Rights Act 1998 (acts of public authorities) other than a court or tribunal;

"senior official" means, subject to subsection (7), a member of the Senior Civil Service or a member of the Senior Management Structure of Her Majesty's Diplomatic Service;

"statutory," in relation to any power or duty, means conferred or imposed by or under any enactment or subordinate legislation;

"subordinate legislation" means any subordinate legislation (within the meaning of the Interpretation Act 1978) or any statutory rules (within the meaning of the Statutory Rules (Northern Ireland) Order 1979);

"Surveillance Commissioner" means a Commissioner holding office under section 91 of the Police Act 1997 and "Chief Surveillance Commissioner" shall be construed accordingly;

"telecommunication system" and "telecommunications service" have the meanings given by section 2(1);

"the Tribunal" means the tribunal established under section 65;

"wireless telegraphy" has the same meaning as in the Wireless Telegraphy Act 1949 and, in relation to wireless telegraphy, "interfere" has the same meaning as in that Act;

"working day" means any day other than a Saturday, a Sunday, Christmas Day, Good Friday or a day which is a bank holiday under the Banking and Financial Dealings Act 1971 in any part of the United Kingdom.

(2)   In this Act—

   (a)   references to crime are references to conduct which constitutes one or more criminal offences or is, or corresponds to, any conduct which, if it all took place in any one part of the United Kingdom would constitute one or more criminal offences; and

   (b)   references to serious crime are references to crime that satisfies the test in subsection (3)(a) or (b).

(3)   Those tests are—

   (a)   that the offence or one of the offences that is or would be constituted by the conduct is an offence for which a person who has attained the age of twenty-one and has no previous convictions could reasonably be expected to be sentenced to imprisonment for a term of three years or more;

   (b)   that the conduct involves the use of violence, results in substantial financial gain or is conduct by a large number of persons in pursuit of a common purpose.

(4)   In this Act "criminal proceedings" includes—

   (a)   proceedings in the United Kingdom or elsewhere before—

      (i)   a court-martial constituted under the Army Act 1955, the Air Force Act 1955 or the Naval Discipline Act 1957; or

      (ii)   a disciplinary court constituted under section 50 of the Act of 1957;

   (b)   proceedings before the Courts-Martial Appeal Court; and

   (c)   proceedings before a Standing Civilian Court;

   and references in this Act to criminal prosecutions shall be construed accordingly.

(5)   For the purposes of this Act detecting crime shall be taken to include—

   (a)   establishing by whom, for what purpose, by what means and generally in what circumstances any crime was committed; and

   (b)   the apprehension of the person by whom any crime was committed; and any reference in this Act to preventing or detecting serious crime shall be construed accordingly, except that, in Chapter I of Part I, it shall not include a reference to gathering evidence for use in any legal proceedings.

(6)   In this Act—

   (a)   references to a person holding office under the Crown include references to any servant of the Crown and to any member of Her Majesty's forces; and

   (b)   references to a member of a police force, in relation to the Royal Navy Regulating Branch, the Royal Military Police or the Royal Air Force Police, do not include references to any member of that Branch or Force who is not for the time being attached to or serving either with the Branch or Force of which he is a member or with another of those police forces.

(7)   If it appears to the Secretary of State that it is necessary to do so in consequence of any changes to the structure or grading of the home civil service or diplomatic service, he may by order make such amendments of the definition of "senior official" in subsection (1) as appear to him appropriate to preserve, so far as practicable, the effect of that definition.

Amendments, repeals and savings etc.

82. (1)   The enactments specified in Schedule 4 (amendments consequential on the provisions of this Act) shall have effect with the amendments set out in that Schedule.

(2)   The enactments mentioned in Schedule 5 are hereby repealed to the extent specified in the third column of that Schedule.

(3)   For the avoidance of doubt it is hereby declared that nothing in this Act (except paragraphs 1 and 2 of Schedule 4) affects any power conferred on the Post Office by or under any enactment to open, detain or delay any postal packet or to deliver any such packet to a person other than the person to whom it is addressed.

(4)   Where any warrant under the Interception of Communications Act 1985 is in force under that Act at the time when the repeal by this Act of section 2 of that Act comes into force, the conduct authorised by that warrant shall be deemed for the period which—
(a)   begins with that time, and
(b)   ends with the time when that warrant would (without being renewed) have ceased to have effect under that Act, as if it were conduct authorised by an interception warrant issued in accordance with the requirements of Chapter I of Part I of this Act.

(5)   In relation to any such warrant, any certificate issued for the purposes of section 3(2) of the Interception of Communications Act 1985 shall have effect in relation to that period as if it were a certificate issued for the purposes of section 8(4) of this Act.

(6)   Sections 15 and 16 of this Act shall have effect as if references to interception warrants and to section 8(4) certificates included references, respectively, to warrants under section 2 of the Interception of Communications Act 1985 and to certificates under section 3(2) of that Act; and references in sections 15 and 16 of this Act to intercepted or certified material shall be construed accordingly.

Short title, commencement and extent.

83. (1) This Act may be cited as the Regulation of Investigatory Powers Act 2000.

(2) The provisions of this Act, other than this section, shall come into force on such day as the Secretary of State may by order appoint; and different days may be appointed under this subsection for different purposes.

(3) This Act extends to Northern Ireland.

SCHEDULE 1
RELEVANT PUBLIC AUTHORITIES

Part I
Relevant Authorities for the Purposes of SS. 28 and 29

Police forces etc.
1. Any police force.
2. The National Criminal Intelligence Service.
3. The National Crime Squad.
4. The Serious Fraud Office.

The intelligence services
5. Any of the intelligence services.

The armed forces
6. Any of Her Majesty's forces.

The revenue departments
7. The Commissioners of Customs and Excise.
8. The Commissioners of Inland Revenue.

Government departments
9. The Ministry of Agriculture, Fisheries and Food.
10. The Ministry of Defence.
11. The Department of the Environment, Transport and the Regions.
12. The Department of Health.
13. The Home Office.
14. The Department of Social Security.
15. The Department of Trade and Industry.

The National Assembly for Wales
16. The National Assembly for Wales.

Local authorities
17. Any local authority (within the meaning of section 1 of the Local Government Act 1999).

Other bodies
18. The Environment Agency.
19. The Financial Services Authority.
20. The Food Standards Agency.
21. The Intervention Board for Agricultural Produce.
22. The Personal Investment Authority.
23. The Post Office.

Part II
Relevant Authorities for the Purposes Only of S. 28

The Health and Safety Executive
24. The Health and Safety Executive.

NHS bodies in England and Wales
25. A Health Authority established under section 8 of the National Health Service Act 1977.
26. A Special Health Authority established under section 11 of the National Health Service Act 1977.
27. A National Heath Service trust established under section 5 of the National Health Service and Community Care Act 1990.

The Royal Pharmaceutical Society of Great Britain
28. The Royal Pharmaceutical Society of Great Britain.

SCHEDULE 2
PERSONS HAVING THE APPROPRIATE PERMISSION

Requirement that appropriate permission is granted by a judge

1. (1) Subject to the following provisions of this Schedule, a person has the appropriate permission in relation to any protected information if, and only if, written permission for the giving of section 49 notices in relation to that information has been granted—
   (a) in England and Wales, by a Circuit judge;
   (b) in Scotland, by a sheriff; or
   (c) in Northern Ireland, by a county court judge.

   (2) Nothing in paragraphs 2 to 5 of this Schedule providing for the manner in which a person may be granted the appropriate permission in relation to any protected information without a grant under this paragraph shall be construed as requiring any further permission to be obtained in a case in which permission has been granted under this paragraph.

Data obtained under warrant etc.

2. (1) This paragraph applies in the case of protected information falling within section 49(1)(a), (b) or (c) where the statutory power in question is one exercised, or to be exercised, in accordance with—

    (a) a warrant issued by the Secretary of State or a person holding judicial office; or

    (b) an authorisation under Part III of the Police Act 1997 (authorisation of otherwise unlawful action in respect of property).

(2) Subject to sub-paragraphs (3) to (5) and paragraph 6(1), a person has the appropriate permission in relation to that protected information (without any grant of permission under paragraph 1) if—

    (a) the warrant or, as the case may be, the authorisation contained the relevant authority's permission for the giving of section 49 notices in relation to protected information to be obtained under the warrant or authorisation; or

    (b) since the issue of the warrant or authorisation, written permission has been granted by the relevant authority for the giving of such notices in relation to protected information obtained under the warrant or authorisation.

(3) Only persons holding office under the Crown, the police and customs and excise shall be capable of having the appropriate permission in relation to protected information obtained, or to be obtained, under a warrant issued by the Secretary of State.

(4) Only a person who—

    (a) was entitled to exercise the power conferred by the warrant, or

    (b) is of the description of persons on whom the power conferred by the warrant was, or could have been, conferred, shall be capable of having the appropriate permission in relation to protected information obtained, or to be obtained, under a warrant issued by a person holding judicial office.

(5) Only the police and the customs and excise shall be capable of having the appropriate permission in relation to protected information obtained, or to be obtained, under an authorisation under Part III of the Police Act 1997.

(6) In this paragraph "the relevant authority"—

    (a) in relation to a warrant issued by the Secretary of State, means the Secretary of State;

    (b) in relation to a warrant issued by a person holding judicial office, means any person holding any judicial office that would have entitled him to issue the warrant; and

    (c) in relation to protected information obtained under an authorisation under Part III of the Police Act 1997, means (subject to sub-paragraph (7)) an authorising officer within the meaning of section 93 of that Act.

(7)   Section 94 of the Police Act 1997 (power of other persons to grant authorisations in urgent cases) shall apply in relation to—

    (a)   an application for permission for the giving of section 49 notices in relation to protected information obtained, or to be obtained, under an authorisation under Part III of that Act, and

    (b)   the powers of any authorising officer (within the meaning of section 93 of that Act) to grant such a permission, as it applies in relation to an application for an authorisation under section 93 of that Act and the powers of such an officer under that section.

(8)   References in this paragraph to a person holding judicial office are references to—

    (a)   any judge of the Crown Court or of the High Court of Justiciary;

    (b)   any sheriff;

    (c)   any justice of the peace;

    (d)   any resident magistrate in Northern Ireland; or

    (e)   any person holding any such judicial office as entitles him to exercise the jurisdiction of a judge of the Crown Court or of a justice of the peace.

(9)   Protected information that comes into a person's possession by means of the exercise of any statutory power which—

    (a)   is exercisable without a warrant, but

    (b)   is so exercisable in the course of, or in connection with, the exercise of another statutory power for which a warrant is required, shall not be taken, by reason only of the warrant required for the exercise of the power mentioned in paragraph (b), to be information in the case of which this paragraph applies.

Data obtained by the intelligence services under statute but without a warrant

3.   (1)   This paragraph applies in the case of protected information falling within section 49(1)(a), (b) or (c) which—

    (a)   has come into the possession of any of the intelligence services or is likely to do so; and

    (b)   is not information in the case of which paragraph 2 applies.

   (2)   Subject to paragraph 6(1), a person has the appropriate permission in relation to that protected information (without any grant of permission under paragraph 1) if written permission for the giving of

section 49 notices in relation to that information has been granted by the Secretary of State.

(3) Sub-paragraph (2) applies where the protected information is in the possession, or (as the case may be) is likely to come into the possession, of both—

    (a) one or more of the intelligence services, and

    (b) a public authority which is not one of the intelligence services, as if a grant of permission under paragraph 1 were unnecessary only where the application to the Secretary of State for permission under that sub-paragraph is made by or on behalf of a member of one of the intelligence services.

Data obtained under statute by other persons but without a warrant

4. (1) This paragraph applies—

    (a) in the case of protected information falling within section 49(1)(a), (b) or (c) which is not information in the case of which paragraph 2 or 3 applies; and

    (b) in the case of protected information falling within section 49(1)(d) which is not information also falling within section 49(1)(a), (b) or (c) in the case of which paragraph 3 applies.

(2) Subject to paragraph 6, where—

    (a) the statutory power was exercised, or is likely to be exercised, by the police, the customs and excise or a member of Her Majesty's forces, or

    (b) the information was provided or disclosed, or is likely to be provided or disclosed, to the police, the customs and excise or a member of Her Majesty's forces, or

    (c) the information is in the possession of, or is likely to come into the possession of, the police, the customs and excise or a member of Her Majesty's forces, the police, the customs and excise or, as the case may be, members of Her Majesty's forces have the appropriate permission in relation to the protected information, without any grant of permission under paragraph 1.

(3) In any other case a person shall not have the appropriate permission by virtue of a grant of permission under paragraph 1 unless he is a person falling within sub-paragraph (4).

(4) A person falls within this sub-paragraph if, as the case may be—

    (a) he is the person who exercised the statutory power or is of the description of persons who would have been entitled to exercise it;

    (b) he is the person to whom the protected information was provided or disclosed, or is of a description of person the provision or disclosure of the information to whom would have discharged the statutory duty; or

> (c) he is a person who is likely to be a person falling within paragraph (a) or (b) when the power is exercised or the protected information provided or disclosed.

Data obtained without the exercise of statutory powers

5. (1) This paragraph applies in the case of protected information falling within section 49(1)(e).

 (2) Subject to paragraph 6, a person has the appropriate permission in relation to that protected information (without any grant of permission under paragraph 1) if—

> (a) the information is in the possession of any of the intelligence services, or is likely to come into the possession of any of those services; and
>
> (b) written permission for the giving of section 49 notices in relation to that information has been granted by the Secretary of State.

 (3) Sub-paragraph (2) applies where the protected information is in the possession, or (as the case may be) is likely to come into the possession, of both—

> (a) one or more of the intelligence services, and
>
> (b) the police or the customs and excise, as if a grant of permission under paragraph 1 were unnecessary only where the application to the Secretary of State for permission under that sub-paragraph is made by or on behalf of a member of one of the intelligence services.

General requirements relating to the appropriate permission

6. (1) A person does not have the appropriate permission in relation to any protected information unless he is either—

> (a) a person who has the protected information in his possession or is likely to obtain possession of it; or
>
> (b) a person who is authorised (apart from this Act) to act on behalf of such a person.

 (2) Subject to sub-paragraph (3), a constable does not by virtue of paragraph 1, 4 or 5 have the appropriate permission in relation to any protected information unless—

> (a) he is of or above the rank of superintendent; or
>
> (b) permission to give a section 49 notice in relation to that information has been granted by a person holding the rank of superintendent, or any higher rank.

 (3) In the case of protected information that has come into the police's possession by means of the exercise of powers conferred by—

> (a) section 44 of the Terrorism Act 2000 (power to stop and search), or

(b)　section 13A or 13B of the Prevention of Terrorism (Temporary Provisions) Act 1989 (which had effect for similar purposes before the coming into force of section 44 of the Terrorism Act 2000), the permission required by sub-paragraph (2) shall not be granted by any person below the rank mentioned in section 44(4) of that Act of 2000 or, as the case may be, section 13A(1) of that Act of 1989.

(4)　A person commissioned by the Commissioners of Customs and Excise does not by virtue of paragraph 1, 4 or 5 have the appropriate permission in relation to any protected information unless permission to give a section 49 notice in relation to that information has been granted—

(a)　by those Commissioners themselves; or

(b)　by an officer of their department of or above such level as they may designate for the purposes of this sub-paragraph.

(5)　A member of Her Majesty's forces does not by virtue of paragraph 1, 4 or 5 have the appropriate permission in relation to any protected information unless—

(a)　he is of or above the rank of lieutenant colonel or its equivalent; or

(b)　permission to give a section 49 notice in relation to that information has been granted by a person holding the rank of lieutenant colonel or its equivalent, or by a person holding a rank higher than lieutenant colonel or its equivalent.

Duration of permission

7.　(1)　A permission granted by any person under any provision of this Schedule shall not entitle any person to give a section 49 notice at any time after the permission has ceased to have effect.

(2)　Such a permission, once granted, shall continue to have effect (notwithstanding the cancellation, expiry or other discharge of any warrant or authorisation in which it is contained or to which it relates) until such time (if any) as it—

(a)　expires in accordance with any limitation on its duration that was contained in its terms; or

(b)　is withdrawn by the person who granted it or by a person holding any office or other position that would have entitled him to grant it.

Formalities for permissions granted by the Secretary of State

8.　A permission for the purposes of any provision of this Schedule shall not be granted by the Secretary of State except—

(a) under his hand; or

(b) in an urgent case in which the Secretary of State has expressly authorised the grant of the permission, under the hand of a senior official.

SCHEDULE 3
THE TRIBUNAL

Membership of the Tribunal

1. (1) A person shall not be appointed as a member of the Tribunal unless he is—

(a) a person who holds or has held a high judicial office (within the meaning of the Appellate Jurisdiction Act 1876);

(b) a person who has a ten year general qualification, within the meaning of section 71 of the Courts and Legal Services Act 1990;

(c) an advocate or solicitor in Scotland of at least ten years' standing; or

(d) a member of the Bar of Northern Ireland or solicitor of the Supreme Court of Northern Ireland of at least ten years' standing.

(2) Subject to the following provisions of this paragraph, the members of the Tribunal shall hold office during good behaviour.

(3) A member of the Tribunal shall vacate office at the end of the period of five years beginning with the day of his appointment, but shall be eligible for reappointment.

(4) A member of the Tribunal may be relieved of office by Her Majesty at his own request.

(5) A member of the Tribunal may be removed from office by Her Majesty on an Address presented to Her by both Houses of Parliament.

(6) If the Scottish Parliament passes a resolution calling for the removal of a member of the Tribunal, it shall be the duty of the Secretary of State to secure that a motion for the presentation of an Address to Her Majesty for the removal of that member, and the resolution of the Scottish Parliament, are considered by each House of Parliament.

President and Vice-President

2. (1) Her Majesty may by Letters Patent appoint as President or Vice-President of the Tribunal a person who is, or by virtue of those Letters will be, a member of the Tribunal.

(2)   A person shall not be appointed President of the Tribunal unless he holds or has held a high judicial office (within the meaning of the Appellate Jurisdiction Act 1876).

(3)   If at any time—

(a)   the President of the Tribunal is temporarily unable to carry out any functions conferred on him by this Schedule or any rules under section 69, or

(b)   the office of President of the Tribunal is for the time being vacant, the Vice-President shall carry out those functions.

(4)   A person shall cease to be President or Vice-President of the Tribunal if he ceases to be a member of the Tribunal.

Members of the Tribunal with special responsibilities

3.   (1)   The President of the Tribunal shall designate one or more members of the Tribunal as the member or members having responsibilities in relation to matters involving the intelligence services.

(2)   It shall be the duty of the President of the Tribunal, in exercising any power conferred on him by rules under section 69 to allocate the members of the Tribunal who are to consider or hear any complaint, proceedings, reference or preliminary or incidental matter, to exercise that power in a case in which the complaint, proceedings or reference relates to, or to a matter involving—

(a)   an allegation against any of the intelligence services or any member of any of those services, or

(b)   conduct by or on behalf of any of those services or any member of any of those services, in such manner as secures that the allocated members consist of, or include, one or more of the members for the time being designated under sub-paragraph (1).

Salaries and expenses

4.   (1)   The Secretary of State shall pay to the members of the Tribunal out of money provided by Parliament such remuneration and allowances as he may with the approval of the Treasury determine.

(2)   Such expenses of the Tribunal as the Secretary of State may with the approval of the Treasury determine shall be defrayed by him out of money provided by Parliament.

Officers

5.   (1)   The Secretary of State may, after consultation with the Tribunal and with the approval of the Treasury as to numbers, provide the Tribunal with such officers as he thinks necessary for the proper discharge of their functions.

(2)   The Tribunal may authorise any officer provided under this paragraph to obtain any documents or information on the Tribunal's behalf.

Parliamentary disqualification

6. In Part II of Schedule 1 to the House of Commons Disqualification Act 1975 and in Part II of Schedule 1 to the Northern Ireland Assembly Disqualification Act 1975 (bodies whose members are disqualified) there shall be inserted (at the appropriate places) the following entry— The Tribunal established under section 65 of the Regulation of Investigatory Powers Act 2000."

SCHEDULE 4
CONSEQUENTIAL AMENDMENTS

The Post Office Act 1953 (c. 36)

1. In section 58(1) of the Post Office Act 1953 (opening or delaying of postal packets by officers of Post Office), after "the Interception of Communications Act 1985" there shall be inserted "or under the authority of an interception warrant under section 5 of the Regulation of Investigatory Powers Act 2000."

The Post Office Act 1969 (c. 48)

2. In paragraph 1(1) of Schedule 5 to the Post Office Act 1969 (repair of minor deficiencies in certain Acts), for the words from "in obedience" to the end of the sub-paragraph there shall be substituted "under the authority of an interception warrant under section 5 of the Regulation of Investigatory Powers Act 2000, under section 11(9) of that Act or in pursuance of a requirement imposed by the Interception of Communications Commissioner under section 58(1) of that Act or imposed by section 68(6) of that Act or by or in accordance with any rules under section 69 of that Act."

The Telecommunications Act 1984 (c. 12)

3. In section 45 of the Telecommunications Act 1984 (offence of disclosing of messages and use of telecommunication system), for subsections (2) and (3) there shall be substituted—"(2) Subsection (1) above does not apply to any disclosure made—
    (a) in accordance with the order of any court or for the purposes of any criminal proceedings;
    (b) in accordance with any warrant, authorisation or notice issued, granted or given under any provision of the Regulation of Investigatory Powers Act 2000;
    (c) in compliance with any requirement imposed (apart from that Act) in consequence of the exercise by any person of any statutory power exercisable by him for the purpose of obtaining any document or other information; or

      (d)   in pursuance of any duty under that Act of 2000, or under Part III of the Police Act 1997, to provide information or produce any document to the Interception of Communications Commissioner or to the tribunal established under section 65 of that Act of 2000.

  (3)   In subsection (2) above "criminal proceedings" and "statutory power" have the same meanings as in the Regulation of Investigatory Powers Act 2000."

The Security Service Act 1989 (c. 5)

4. (1)   In section 1 of the Security Service Act 1989 (functions of the Security Service), after subsection (4) there shall be inserted—"(5) Section 81(5) of the Regulation of Investigatory Powers Act 2000 (meaning of "prevention" and "detection"), so far as it relates to serious crime, shall apply for the purposes of this Act as it applies for the purposes of the provisions of that Act not contained in Chapter I of Part I."

  (2)   In section 2(2)(a) of that Act (duty of Director General to secure that information not disclosed except for authorised purposes), for "preventing or detecting" there shall be substituted "the prevention or detection of."

The Official Secrets Act 1989 (c. 6)

5. In section 4(3)(a) of the Official Secrets Act 1989 (offence of disclosing interception information), after "1985" there shall be inserted "or under the authority of an interception warrant under section 5 of the Regulation of Investigatory Powers Act 2000."

The Intelligence Services Act 1994 (c. 13)

6. In section 11 of the Intelligence Services Act 1994 (interpretation), after subsection (1) there shall be inserted—"(1A) Section 81(5) of the Regulation of Investigatory Powers Act 2000 (meaning of "prevention" and "detection"), so far as it relates to serious crime, shall apply for the purposes of this Act as it applies for the purposes of Chapter I of Part I of that Act."

The Criminal Procedure and Investigations Act 1996 (c. 25)

7. (1)   In each of sections 3(7), 7(6), 8(6) and 9(9) of the Criminal Procedure and Investigations Act 1996 (exceptions for interceptions from obligations to make disclosures to the defence), for paragraphs (a) and (b) there shall be substituted "it is material the disclosure of which is prohibited by section 17 of the Regulation of Investigatory Powers Act 2000."

  (2)   In section 23(6) of that Act (code of practice not to apply to material intercepted under the Interception of Communications Act

1985), after "1985" there shall be inserted "or under the authority of an interception warrant under section 5 of the Regulation of Investigatory Powers Act 2000."

The Police Act 1997 (c. 50)

8. (1) In section 91(9) of the Police Act 1997 (staff for Surveillance Commissioners)—

    (a) after "Chief Commissioner" there shall be inserted "and subject to the approval of the Treasury as to numbers"; and

    (b) after "Commissioners" there shall be inserted "and any Assistant Surveillance Commissioners holding office under section 63 of the Regulation of Investigatory Powers Act 2000."

    (2) In section 93(3) of that Act (persons who may make an application to an authorising officer within section 93(5))—

    (a) in paragraph (a), for "(e)" there shall be substituted "(ea) or (ee)"; and

    (b) after that paragraph there shall be inserted—"(aa) if the authorising officer is within subsection (5)(eb) to (ed), by a member, as the case may be, of the Royal Navy Regulating Branch, the Royal Military Police or the Royal Air Force Police;".

    (3) In section 94(1) of that Act (circumstances in which authorisations may be given in absence of authorising officer), in paragraph (b), for "(f), (g) or (h)" there shall be substituted "or (f)," and after that paragraph there shall be inserted"or (c) if the authorising officer is within paragraph (g) of section 93(5), it is also not reasonably practicable for the application to be considered either—

    (i) by any other person designated for the purposes of that paragraph; or

    (ii) by the designated deputy of the Director General of the National Crime Squad."

    (4) In section 94(2) of that Act (persons who may act in absence of the authorising officer)—

    (a) after paragraph (d), there shall be inserted—

"(da) where the authorising officer is within paragraph (ea) of that subsection, by a person holding the rank of deputy or assistant chief constable in the Ministry of Defence Police;

(db) where the authorising officer is within paragraph (eb) of that subsection, by a person holding the position of assistant Provost Marshal in the Royal Navy Regulating Branch;

(dc) where the authorising officer is within paragraph (ec) or (ed) of that subsection, by a person holding the position of deputy Provost Marshal in the Royal Military Police or, as the case may be, in the Royal Air Force Police;

(dd) where the authorising officer is within paragraph (ee) of that subsection, by a person holding the rank of deputy or assistant chief constable in the British Transport Police;";

(b) in paragraph (e), the words "or (g)" and "or, as the case may be, of the National Crime Squad" shall be omitted; and

(c) after that paragraph, there shall be inserted—

"(ea) where the authorising officer is within paragraph (g) of that subsection, by a person designated for the purposes of this paragraph by the Director General of the National Crime Squad as a person entitled to act in an urgent case;".

(5) In section 94(3) of that Act (rank of police members of the National Crime Intelligence Squad and National Crime Squad entitled to act), after "(2)(e)" there shall be inserted "or (2)(ea)."

(6) In section 95 of that Act (authorisations: form and duration etc.)—

(a) in each of subsections (4) and (5), for the words from "the action" onwards there shall be substituted "the authorisation is one in relation to which the requirements of paragraphs (a) and (b) of section 93(2) are no longer satisfied."; and

(b) in subsection (6), for "or (e)" there shall be substituted "(e) or (g)."

(7) In section 97 of that Act (authorisations requiring approval), in subsection (6), the words from "(and paragraph 7" onwards shall be omitted, and after that subsection there shall be inserted—"(6A) The reference in subsection (6) to the authorising officer who gave the authorisation or in whose absence it was given shall be construed, in the case of an authorisation given by or in the absence of a person within paragraph (b), (e) or (g) of section 93(5), as a reference to the Commissioner of Police, Chief Constable or, as the case may be, Director General mentioned in the paragraph concerned."

(8) In section 103(7) of that Act (quashing authorisations), for the words from "and paragraph 7" onwards there shall be substituted "and subsection (6A) of section 97 shall apply for the purposes of this subsection as it applies for the purposes of subsection (6) of that section."

(9) In section 105 of that Act (appeals by authorising officers: supplementary), in subsection (1)(a), the word "and" shall be inserted at the end of sub-paragraph (i), and sub-paragraph (iii) and the word "and" immediately preceding it shall be omitted.

(10) In section 107 of that Act—

(a) in subsection (2) (report of Chief Surveillance Commissioner on the discharge of his functions under Part III of that Act)—

(i)   for "the discharge of functions under this Part" there shall be substituted "the matters with which he is concerned"; and

(ii)   for "any matter relating to those functions" there shall be substituted "anything relating to any of those matters";

(b)   in subsection (4) (matters that may be excluded from a report), for "the prevention or detection of serious crime or otherwise" there shall be substituted "any of the purposes for which authorisations may be given or granted under this Part of this Act or Part II of the Regulation of Investigatory Powers Act 2000 or under any enactment contained in or made under an Act of the Scottish Parliament which makes provision equivalent to that made by Part II of that Act of 2000 or"; and

(c)   after subsection (5) (duty to co-operate with the Chief Surveillance Commissioner) there shall be inserted the subsections set out in sub-paragraph (11).

(11)   The subsections inserted after subsection (5) of section 107 of that Act are as follows "(5A) It shall be the duty of-

(a)   every person by whom, or on whose application, there has been given or granted any authorisation the function of giving or granting which is subject to review by the Chief Commissioner,

(b)   every person who has engaged in conduct with the authority of such an authorisation,

(c)   every person who holds or has held any office, rank or position with the same public authority as a person falling within paragraph (a),

(d)   every person who holds or has held any office, rank or position with any public authority for whose benefit (within the meaning of Part II of the Regulation of Investigatory Powers Act 2000) activities which are or may be subject to any such review have been or may be carried out, and

(e)   every person to whom a notice under section 49 of the Regulation of Investigatory Powers Act 2000 (notices imposing a disclosure requirement in respect of information protected by a key) has been given in relation to any information obtained by conduct to which such an authorisation relates, to disclose or provide to the Chief Commissioner all such documents and information as he may require for the purpose of enabling him to carry out his functions.

(5B)   It shall be the duty of every Commissioner to give the tribunal established under section 65 of the Regulation of Investigatory Powers

Act 2000 all such assistance (including his opinion as to any issue falling to be determined by that tribunal) as that tribunal may require—

(a)   in connection with the investigation of any matter by that tribunal; or

(b)   otherwise for the purposes of that tribunal's consideration or determination of any matter.

(5C) In this section "public authority" means any public authority within the meaning of section 6 of the Human Rights Act 1998 (acts of public authorities) other than a court or tribunal."

(12) In section 108(1) of that Act after "In this Part—"there shall be inserted—" "Assistant Commissioner of Police of the Metropolis" includes the Deputy Commissioner of Police of the Metropolis;".

(13) In Part VII of that Act, before section 134 there shall be inserted— "Meaning of "prevention" and "detection."   133A. Section 81(5) of the Regulation of Investigatory Powers Act 2000 (meaning of "prevention" and "detection") shall apply for the purposes of this Act as it applies for the purposes of the provisions of that Act not contained in Chapter I of Part I."

The Northern Ireland Act 1998 (c. 47)

9.   In paragraph 17(b) of Schedule 2 to the Northern Ireland Act 1998 (excepted matters), for "the Interception of Communications Act 1985" there shall be substituted "Chapter I of Part I of the Regulation of Investigatory Powers Act 2000."

The Electronic Communications Act 2000 (c. 7)

10. In section 4(2) of the Electronic Communications Act 2000 (exception to rules restricting disclosure of information obtained under Part I of that Act), for the word "or" at the end of paragraph (e) there shall be substituted—

"(ea) for the purposes of any proceedings before the tribunal established under section 65 of the Regulation of Investigatory Powers Act 2000; or."

The Financial Services and Markets Act 2000 (c. 8)

11. In section 394(7) of the Financial Services and Markets Act 2000 (exclusion of material from material of the Authority to which a person must be allowed access), for paragraphs (a) and (b) there shall be substituted—

"(a) is material the disclosure of which for the purposes of or in connection with any legal proceedings is prohibited by section 17 of the Regulation of Investigatory Powers Act 2000; or"

The Terrorism Act 2000 (c. 11)

12. (1)   In section 9(2)(d) of the Terrorism Act 2000 (proceedings under

the Human Rights Act 1998), for "8" there shall be substituted "7."

(2) In each of paragraphs 6(3) and 7(5) of Schedule 3 to that Act (references to an organisation and representative in paragraphs 5 and 8 of that Schedule), for "paragraphs 5 and 8" there shall be substituted "paragraph 5."

SCHEDULE 5
REPEALS

Chapter	Short title	Extent of repeal

1975 c. 24.

The House of Commons Disqualification Act 1975.

In Part II of Schedule 1, the words "The Tribunal established under the Interception of Communications Act 1985," "The Tribunal established under the Security Service Act 1989," and "The Tribunal established under section 9 of the Intelligence Services Act 1994."

1975 c. 25.

The Northern Ireland Assembly Disqualification Act 1975.

In Part II of Schedule 1, the words "The Tribunal established under the Interception of Communications Act 1985," "The Tribunal established under the Security Service Act 1989," and "The Tribunal established under section 9 of the Intelligence Services Act 1994."

1985 c. 56.

The Interception of Communications Act 1985.

Sections 1 to 10.

Section 11(3) to (5).

Schedule 1.

1989 c. 5.

The Security Service Act 1989.

Sections 4 and 5.

Schedules 1 and 2.

1989 c. 6.

The Official Secrets Act 1989.

In Schedule 1, paragraph 3.

1990 c. 41.

The Courts and Legal Services Act 1990.

In Schedule 10, paragraphs 62 and 74.

1994 c. 13.

The Intelligence Services Act 1994.
In section 6(1)(b), the words "of his department."
In section 7(5)(b), the words "of his department."
Sections 8 and 9.
In section 11(1), paragraph (b).
Schedules 1 and 2.

1997 c. 50.
The Police Act 1997.
In section 93(6), paragraph (f) and the word "and" immediately preceding it.
In section 94(1), the word "or" at the end of paragraph (a).
In section 94(2)(e), the words "or (g)" and "or, as the case may be, of the National Crime Squad."
In section 94(4)—
    (a)   the words "in his absence," in each place where they occur; and
    (b)   paragraph (d) and the word "and" immediately preceding it.

In section 97(6), the words from "(and paragraph 7" onwards.

Sections 101 and 102.

In section 104—
    (a)   in subsection (1), paragraph (g);
    (b)   in each of subsections (4), (5) and (6), paragraph (b) and the word "or" immediately preceding it;
    (c)   in subsection (8), paragraph (b) and the word "and" immediately preceding it.

In section 105(1)(a), sub-paragraph (iii) and the word "and" immediately preceding it.

Section 106.
Section 107(6).
Schedule 7.

1997 c. 68.
The Special Immigration Appeals Commission Act 1997.
Section 5(7).

1998 c. 37.
The Crime and Disorder Act 1998.
Section 113(1) and (3).

2000 c. 11.
The Terrorism Act 2000.
In Schedule 3, paragraph 8.

DOCUMENT NO 6

Human Rights Act 1998

An Act to give further effect to rights and freedoms guaranteed under the European Convention on Human Rights; to make provision with respect to holders of certain judicial offices who become judges of the European Court of Human Rights; and for connected purposes.

9th November 1998

BE IT ENACTED by the Queen's most Excellent Majesty, by and with the advice and consent of the Lords Spiritual and Temporal, and Commons, in this present Parliament assembled, and by the authority of the same, as follows:—

Introduction

The Convention Rights.

1. (1) In this Act "the Convention rights" means the rights and fundamental freedoms set out in—

   (a) Articles 2 to 12 and 14 of the Convention,

   (b) Articles 1 to 3 of the First Protocol, and

   (c) Articles 1 and 2 of the Sixth Protocol, as read with Articles 16 to 18 of the Convention.

   (2) Those Articles are to have effect for the purposes of this Act subject to any designated derogation or reservation (as to which see sections 14 and 15).

   (3) The Articles are set out in Schedule 1.

   (4) The Secretary of State may by order make such amendments to this Act as he considers appropriate to reflect the effect, in relation to the United Kingdom, of a protocol.

   (5) In subsection (4) "protocol" means a protocol to the Convention—

   (a) which the United Kingdom has ratified; or

   (b) which the United Kingdom has signed with a view to ratification.

   (6) No amendment may be made by an order under subsection (4) so as to come into force before the protocol concerned is in force in relation to the United Kingdom.

Interpretation of Convention rights.

2. (1) A court or tribunal determining a question which has arisen in connection with a Convention right must take into account any—

(a)   judgment, decision, declaration or advisory opinion of the European Court of Human Rights,

(b)   opinion of the Commission given in a report adopted under Article 31 of the Convention,

(c)   decision of the Commission in connection with Article 26 or 27(2) of the Convention, or

(d)   decision of the Committee of Ministers taken under Article 46 of the Convention, whenever made or given, so far as, in the opinion of the court or tribunal, it is relevant to the proceedings in which that question has arisen.

(2)   Evidence of any judgment, decision, declaration or opinion of which account may have to be taken under this section is to be given in proceedings before any court or tribunal in such manner as may be provided by rules.

(3)   In this section "rules" means rules of court or, in the case of proceedings before a tribunal, rules made for the purposes of this section—

(a)   by the Lord Chancellor or the Secretary of State, in relation to any proceedings outside Scotland;

(b)   by the Secretary of State, in relation to proceedings in Scotland; or

(c)   by a Northern Ireland department, in relation to proceedings before a tribunal in Northern Ireland—

(i)   which deals with transferred matters; and

(ii)   for which no rules made under paragraph (a) are in force.

Legislation

Interpretation of legislation.

3.   (1)   So far as it is possible to do so, primary legislation and subordinate legislation must be read and given effect in a way which is compatible with the Convention rights.

(2)   This section—

(a)   applies to primary legislation and subordinate legislation whenever enacted;

(b)   does not affect the validity, continuing operation or enforcement of any incompatible primary legislation; and

(c)   does not affect the validity, continuing operation or enforcement of any incompatible subordinate legislation if (disregarding any possibility of revocation) primary legislation prevents removal of the incompatibility.

Declaration of incompatibility.

4. (1) Subsection (2) applies in any proceedings in which a court determines whether a provision of primary legislation is compatible with a Convention right.

   (2) If the court is satisfied that the provision is incompatible with a Convention right, it may make a declaration of that incompatibility.

   (3) Subsection (4) applies in any proceedings in which a court determines whether a provision of subordinate legislation, made in the exercise of a power conferred by primary legislation, is compatible with a Convention right.

   (4) If the court is satisfied—
       (a) that the provision is incompatible with a Convention right, and
       (b) that (disregarding any possibility of revocation) the primary legislation concerned prevents removal of the incompatibility, it may make a declaration of that incompatibility.

   (5) In this section "court" means—
       (a) the House of Lords;
       (b) the Judicial Committee of the Privy Council;
       (c) the Courts-Martial Appeal Court;
       (d) in Scotland, the High Court of Justiciary sitting otherwise than as a trial court or the Court of Session;
       (e) in England and Wales or Northern Ireland, the High Court or the Court of Appeal.

   (6) A declaration under this section ("a declaration of incompatibility")—
       (a) does not affect the validity, continuing operation or enforcement of the provision in respect of which it is given; and
       (b) is not binding on the parties to the proceedings in which it is made.

Right of Crown to intervene.

5. (1) Where a court is considering whether to make a declaration of incompatibility, the Crown is entitled to notice in accordance with rules of court.

   (2) In any case to which subsection (1) applies—
       (a) a Minister of the Crown (or a person nominated by him),
       (b) a member of the Scottish Executive,
       (c) a Northern Ireland Minister,
       (d) a Northern Ireland department, is entitled, on giving notice in accordance with rules of court, to be joined as a party to the proceedings.

   (3) Notice under subsection (2) may be given at any time during the proceedings.

(4) A person who has been made a party to criminal proceedings (other than in Scotland) as the result of a notice under subsection (2) may, with leave, appeal to the House of Lords against any declaration of incompatibility made in the proceedings.

(5) In subsection (4)—

"criminal proceedings" includes all proceedings before the Courts-Martial Appeal Court; and

"leave" means leave granted by the court making the declaration of incompatibility or by the House of Lords.

Public authorities

Acts of public authorities.

6. (1) It is unlawful for a public authority to act in a way which is incompatible with a Convention right.

(2) Subsection (1) does not apply to an act if—

(a) as the result of one or more provisions of primary legislation, the authority could not have acted differently; or

(b) in the case of one or more provisions of, or made under, primary legislation which cannot be read or given effect in a way which is compatible with the Convention rights, the authority was acting so as to give effect to or enforce those provisions.

(3) In this section "public authority" includes—

(a) a court or tribunal, and

(b) any person certain of whose functions are functions of a public nature, but does not include either House of Parliament or a person exercising functions in connection with proceedings in Parliament.

(4) In subsection (3) "Parliament" does not include the House of Lords in its judicial capacity.

(5) In relation to a particular act, a person is not a public authority by virtue only of subsection (3)(b) if the nature of the act is private.

(6) "An act" includes a failure to act but does not include a failure to—

(a) introduce in, or lay before, Parliament a proposal for legislation; or

(b) make any primary legislation or remedial order.

Proceedings.

7. (1) A person who claims that a public authority has acted (or proposes to act) in a way which is made unlawful by section 6(1) may—

(a) bring proceedings against the authority under this Act in the appropriate court or tribunal, or

(b) rely on the Convention right or rights concerned in any legal proceedings, but only if he is (or would be) a victim of the unlawful act.

(2) In subsection (1)(a) "appropriate court or tribunal" means such court or tribunal as may be determined in accordance with rules; and proceedings against an authority include a counterclaim or similar proceeding.

(3) If the proceedings are brought on an application for judicial review, the applicant is to be taken to have a sufficient interest in relation to the unlawful act only if he is, or would be, a victim of that act.

(4) If the proceedings are made by way of a petition for judicial review in Scotland, the applicant shall be taken to have title and interest to sue in relation to the unlawful act only if he is, or would be, a victim of that act.

(5) Proceedings under subsection (1)(a) must be brought before the end of—
(a) the period of one year beginning with the date on which the act complained of took place; or
(b) such longer period as the court or tribunal considers equitable having regard to all the circumstances, but that is subject to any rule imposing a stricter time limit in relation to the procedure in question.

(6) In subsection (1)(b) "legal proceedings" includes—
(a) proceedings brought by or at the instigation of a public authority; and
(b) an appeal against the decision of a court or tribunal.

(7) For the purposes of this section, a person is a victim of an unlawful act only if he would be a victim for the purposes of Article 34 of the Convention if proceedings were brought in the European Court of Human Rights in respect of that act.

(8) Nothing in this Act creates a criminal offence.

(9) In this section "rules" means—
(a) in relation to proceedings before a court or tribunal outside Scotland, rules made by the Lord Chancellor or the Secretary of State for the purposes of this section or rules of court,
(b) in relation to proceedings before a court or tribunal in Scotland, rules made by the Secretary of State for those purposes,
(c) in relation to proceedings before a tribunal in Northern Ireland—
(i) which deals with transferred matters; and
(ii) for which no rules made under paragraph (a) are in force, rules made by a Northern Ireland department for those

purposes, and includes provision made by order under section 1 of the Courts and Legal Services Act 1990.

(10) In making rules, regard must be had to section 9.

(11) The Minister who has power to make rules in relation to a particular tribunal may, to the extent he considers it necessary to ensure that the tribunal can provide an appropriate remedy in relation to an act (or proposed act) of a public authority which is (or would be) unlawful as a result of section 6(1), by order add to—

(a) the relief or remedies which the tribunal may grant; or

(b) the grounds on which it may grant any of them.

(12) An order made under subsection (11) may contain such incidental, supplemental, consequential or transitional provision as the Minister making it considers appropriate.

(13) "The Minister" includes the Northern Ireland department concerned.

Judicial remedies.

8. (1) In relation to any act (or proposed act) of a public authority which the court finds is (or would be) unlawful, it may grant such relief or remedy, or make such order, within its powers as it considers just and appropriate.

(2) But damages may be awarded only by a court which has power to award damages, or to order the payment of compensation, in civil proceedings.

(3) No award of damages is to be made unless, taking account of all the circumstances of the case, including—

(a) any other relief or remedy granted, or order made, in relation to the act in question (by that or any other court), and

(b) the consequences of any decision (of that or any other court) in respect of that act, the court is satisfied that the award is necessary to afford just satisfaction to the person in whose favour it is made.

(4) In determining—

(a) whether to award damages, or

(b) the amount of an award, the court must take into account the principles applied by the European Court of Human Rights in relation to the award of compensation under Article 41 of the Convention.

(5) A public authority against which damages are awarded is to be treated—

(a) in Scotland, for the purposes of section 3 of the Law Reform (Miscellaneous Provisions) (Scotland) Act 1940 as if the award were made in an action of damages in which the authority has been found liable in respect of loss or damage to the person to whom the award is made;

(b)   for the purposes of the Civil Liability (Contribution) Act 1978 as liable in respect of damage suffered by the person to whom the award is made.

(6)   In this section—

"court" includes a tribunal;

"damages" means damages for an unlawful act of a public authority; and

"unlawful" means unlawful under section 6(1).

Judicial acts.

9. (1)   Proceedings under section 7(1)(a) in respect of a judicial act may be brought only—
     (a)   by exercising a right of appeal;
     (b)   on an application (in Scotland a petition) for judicial review; or
     (c)   in such other forum as may be prescribed by rules.

(2)   That does not affect any rule of law which prevents a court from being the subject of judicial review.

(3)   In proceedings under this Act in respect of a judicial act done in good faith, damages may not be awarded otherwise than to compensate a person to the extent required by Article 5(5) of the Convention.

(4)   An award of damages permitted by subsection (3) is to be made against the Crown; but no award may be made unless the appropriate person, if not a party to the proceedings, is joined.

(5)   In this section—

"appropriate person" means the Minister responsible for the court concerned, or a person or government department nominated by him;

"court" includes a tribunal;

"judge" includes a member of a tribunal, a justice of the peace and a clerk or other officer entitled to exercise the jurisdiction of a court;

"judicial act" means a judicial act of a court and includes an act done on the instructions, or on behalf, of a judge; and

"rules" has the same meaning as in section 7(9).

Remedial action

Power to take remedial action.

10. (1)   This section applies if—
     (a)   a provision of legislation has been declared under section 4 to be incompatible with a Convention right and, if an appeal lies—

        (i)   all persons who may appeal have stated in writing that they do not intend to do so;

        (ii)   the time for bringing an appeal has expired and no appeal has been brought within that time; or

        (iii) an appeal brought within that time has been determined or abandoned; or

    (b)   it appears to a Minister of the Crown or Her Majesty in Council that, having regard to a finding of the European Court of Human Rights made after the coming into force of this section in proceedings against the United Kingdom, a provision of legislation is incompatible with an obligation of the United Kingdom arising from the Convention.

(2)   If a Minister of the Crown considers that there are compelling reasons for proceeding under this section, he may by order make such amendments to the legislation as he considers necessary to remove the incompatibility.

(3)   If, in the case of subordinate legislation, a Minister of the Crown considers—

    (a)   that it is necessary to amend the primary legislation under which the subordinate legislation in question was made, in order to enable the incompatibility to be removed, and

    (b)   that there are compelling reasons for proceeding under this section, he may by order make such amendments to the primary legislation as he considers necessary.

(4)   This section also applies where the provision in question is in subordinate legislation and has been quashed, or declared invalid, by reason of incompatibility with a Convention right and the Minister proposes to proceed under paragraph 2(b) of Schedule 2.

(5)   If the legislation is an Order in Council, the power conferred by subsection (2) or (3) is exercisable by Her Majesty in Council.

(6)   In this section "legislation" does not include a Measure of the Church Assembly or of the General Synod of the Church of England.

(7)   Schedule 2 makes further provision about remedial orders.

Other rights and proceedings

Safeguard for existing human rights.

11. A person's reliance on a Convention right does not restrict—

    (a)   any other right or freedom conferred on him by or under any law having effect In any part of the United Kingdom; or

    (b)   his right to make any claim or bring any proceedings which he could make or bring apart from sections 7 to 9.

Freedom of expression.

12. (1) This section applies if a court is considering whether to grant any relief which, if granted, might affect the exercise of the Convention right to freedom of expression.

(2) If the person against whom the application for relief is made ("the respondent") is neither present nor represented, no such relief is to be granted unless the court is satisfied—

(a) that the applicant has taken all practicable steps to notify the respondent; or

(b) that there are compelling reasons why the respondent should not be notified.

(3) No such relief is to be granted so as to restrain publication before trial unless the court is satisfied that the applicant is likely to establish that publication should not be allowed.

(4) The court must have particular regard to the importance of the Convention right to freedom of expression and, where the proceedings relate to material which the respondent claims, or which appears to the court, to be journalistic, literary or artistic material (or to conduct connected with such material), to—

(a) the extent to which—

(i) the material has, or is about to, become available to the public; or

(ii) it is, or would be, in the public interest for the material to be published;

(b) any relevant privacy code.

(5) In this section—

"court" includes a tribunal; and

"relief" includes any remedy or order (other than in criminal proceedings).

Freedom of thought, conscience and religion.

13. (1) If a court's determination of any question arising under this Act might affect the exercise by a religious organisation (itself or its members collectively) of the Convention right to freedom of thought, conscience and religion, it must have particular regard to the importance of that right.

(2) In this section "court" includes a tribunal.

Derogations and Reservations

Derogations.

14. (1) In this Act "designated derogation" means—

  (a) the United Kingdom's derogation from Article 5(3) of the Convention; and

  (b) any derogation by the United Kingdom from an Article of the Convention, or of any protocol to the Convention, which is designated for the purposes of this Act in an order made by the Secretary of State.

(2) The derogation referred to in subsection (1)(a) is set out in Part I of Schedule 3.

(3) If a designated derogation is amended or replaced it ceases to be a designated derogation.

(4) But subsection (3) does not prevent the Secretary of State from exercising his power under subsection (1)(b) to make a fresh designation order in respect of the Article concerned.

(5) The Secretary of State must by order make such amendments to Schedule 3 as he considers appropriate to reflect—

  (a) any designation order; or

  (b) the effect of subsection (3).

(6) A designation order may be made in anticipation of the making by the United Kingdom of a proposed derogation.

Reservations.

15. (1) In this Act "designated reservation" means—

  (a) the United Kingdom's reservation to Article 2 of the First Protocol to the Convention; and

  (b) any other reservation by the United Kingdom to an Article of the Convention, or of any protocol to the Convention, which is designated for the purposes of this Act in an order made by the Secretary of State.

(2) The text of the reservation referred to in subsection (1)(a) is set out in Part II of Schedule 3.

(3) If a designated reservation is withdrawn wholly or in part it ceases to be a designated reservation.

(4) But subsection (3) does not prevent the Secretary of State from exercising his power under subsection (1)(b) to make a fresh designation order in respect of the Article concerned.

(5) The Secretary of State must by order make such amendments to this Act as he considers appropriate to reflect—

  (a) any designation order; or

  (b) the effect of subsection (3).

Period for which designated derogations have effect.

16. (1) If it has not already been withdrawn by the United Kingdom, a designated derogation ceases to have effect for the purposes of this Act—

(a)   in the case of the derogation referred to in section 14(1)(a), at the end of the period of five years beginning with the date on which section 1(2) came into force;

(b)   in the case of any other derogation, at the end of the period of five years beginning with the date on which the order designating it was made.

(2)   At any time before the period—

    (a)   fixed by subsection (1)(a) or (b), or

    (b)   extended by an order under this subsection, comes to an end, the Secretary of State may by order extend it by a further period of five years.

(3)   An order under section 14(1)(b) ceases to have effect at the end of the period for consideration, unless a resolution has been passed by each House approving the order.

(4)   Subsection (3) does not affect—

    (a)   anything done in reliance on the order; or

    (b)   the power to make a fresh order under section 14(1)(b).

(5)   In subsection (3) "period for consideration" means the period of forty days beginning with the day on which the order was made.

(6)   In calculating the period for consideration, no account is to be taken of any time during which—

    (a)   Parliament is dissolved or prorogued; or

    (b)   both Houses are adjourned for more than four days.

(7)   If a designated derogation is withdrawn by the United Kingdom, the Secretary of State must by order make such amendments to this Act as he considers are required to reflect that withdrawal.

Periodic review of designated reservations.

17. (1)   The appropriate Minister must review the designated reservation referred to in section 15(1)(a)—

    (a)   before the end of the period of five years beginning with the date on which section 1(2) came into force; and

    (b)   if that designation is still in force, before the end of the period of five years beginning with the date on which the last report relating to it was laid under subsection (3).

(2)   The appropriate Minister must review each of the other designated reservations (if any)—

    (a)   before the end of the period of five years beginning with the date on which the order designating the reservation first came into force; and

    (b)   if the designation is still in force, before the end of the period of five years beginning with the date on which the last report relating to it was laid under subsection (3).

(3) The Minister conducting a review under this section must prepare a report on the result of the review and lay a copy of it before each House of Parliament.

Judges of the European Court of Human Rights

Appointment to European Court of Human Rights.

18. (1) In this section "judicial office" means the office of—
    (a) Lord Justice of Appeal, Justice of the High Court or Circuit judge, in England and Wales;
    (b) judge of the Court of Session or sheriff, in Scotland;
    (c) Lord Justice of Appeal, judge of the High Court or county court judge, in Northern Ireland.

(2) The holder of a judicial office may become a judge of the European Court of Human Rights ("the Court") without being required to relinquish his office.

(3) But he is not required to perform the duties of his judicial office while he is a judge of the Court.

(4) In respect of any period during which he is a judge of the Court—
    (a) a Lord Justice of Appeal or Justice of the High Court is not to count as a judge of the relevant court for the purposes of section 2(1) or 4(1) of the Supreme Court Act 1981 (maximum number of judges) nor as a judge of the Supreme Court for the purposes of section 12(1) to (6) of that Act (salaries etc.);
    (b) a judge of the Court of Session is not to count as a judge of that court for the purposes of section 1(1) of the Court of Session Act 1988 (maximum number of judges) or of section 9(1)(c) of the Administration of Justice Act 1973 ("the 1973 Act") (salaries etc.);
    (c) a Lord Justice of Appeal or judge of the High Court in Northern Ireland is not to count as a judge of the relevant court for the purposes of section 2(1) or 3(1) of the Judicature (Northern Ireland) Act 1978 (maximum number of judges) nor as a judge of the Supreme Court of Northern Ireland for the purposes of section 9(1)(d) of the 1973 Act (salaries etc.);
    (d) a Circuit judge is not to count as such for the purposes of section 18 of the Courts Act 1971 (salaries etc.);
    (e) a sheriff is not to count as such for the purposes of section 14 of the Sheriff Courts (Scotland) Act 1907 (salaries etc.);
    (f) a county court judge of Northern Ireland is not to count as such for the purposes of section 106 of the County Courts Act Northern Ireland) 1959 (salaries etc.).

(5) If a sheriff principal is appointed a judge of the Court, section 11(1) of the Sheriff Courts (Scotland) Act 1971 (temporary appointment of sheriff principal) applies, while he holds that appointment, as if his office is vacant.

(6) Schedule 4 makes provision about judicial pensions in relation to the holder of a judicial office who serves as a judge of the Court.

(7) The Lord Chancellor or the Secretary of State may by order make such transitional provision (including, in particular, provision for a temporary increase in the maximum number of judges) as he considers appropriate in relation to any holder of a judicial office who has completed his service as a judge of the Court.

Parliamentary Procedure

Statements of compatibility.

19. (1) A Minister of the Crown in charge of a Bill in either House of Parliament must, before Second Reading of the Bill—

    (a) make a statement to the effect that in his view the provisions of the Bill are compatible with the Convention rights ("a statement of compatibility"); or

    (b) make a statement to the effect that although he is unable to make a statement of compatibility the government nevertheless wishes the House to proceed with the Bill.

(2) The statement must be in writing and be published in such manner as the Minister making it considers appropriate.

Supplemental

Orders etc. under this Act.

20. (1) Any power of a Minister of the Crown to make an order under this Act is exercisable by statutory instrument.

(2) The power of the Lord Chancellor or the Secretary of State to make rules (other than rules of court) under section 2(3) or 7(9) is exercisable by statutory instrument.

(3) Any statutory instrument made under section 14, 15 or 16(7) must be laid before Parliament.

(4) No order may be made by the Lord Chancellor or the Secretary of State under section 1(4), 7(11) or 16(2) unless a draft of the order has been laid before, and approved by, each House of Parliament.

(5) Any statutory instrument made under section 18(7) or Schedule 4, or to which subsection (2) applies, shall be subject to annulment in pursuance of a resolution of either House of Parliament.

(6) The power of a Northern Ireland department to make—
  (a) rules under section 2(3)(c) or 7(9)(c), or
  (b) an order under section 7(11), is exercisable by statutory rule for the purposes of the Statutory Rules (Northern Ireland) Order 1979.

(7) Any rules made under section 2(3)(c) or 7(9)(c) shall be subject to negative resolution; and section 41(6) of the Interpretation Act Northern Ireland) 1954 (meaning of "subject to negative resolution") shall apply as if the power to make the rules were conferred by an Act of the Northern Ireland Assembly.

(8) No order may be made by a Northern Ireland department under section 7(11) unless a draft of the order has been laid before, and approved by, the Northern Ireland Assembly.

Interpretation, etc.

21. (1) In this Act—

"amend" includes repeal and apply (with or without modifications);

"the appropriate Minister" means the Minister of the Crown having charge of the appropriate authorised government department (within the meaning of the Crown Proceedings Act 1947);

"the Commission" means the European Commission of Human Rights;

"the Convention" means the Convention for the Protection of Human Rights and Fundamental Freedoms, agreed by the Council of Europe at Rome on 4th November 1950 as it has effect for the time being in relation to the United Kingdom;

"declaration of incompatibility" means a declaration under section 4;

"Minister of the Crown" has the same meaning as in the Ministers of the Crown Act 1975;

"Northern Ireland Minister" includes the First Minister and the deputy First Minister in Northern Ireland;

"primary legislation" means any—
  (a) public general Act;
  (b) local and personal Act;
  (c) private Act;
  (d) Measure of the Church Assembly;
  (e) Measure of the General Synod of the Church of England;
  (f) Order in Council—
    (i) made in exercise of Her Majesty's Royal Prerogative;
    (ii) made under section 38(1)(a) of the Northern Ireland Constitution Act 1973 or the corresponding provision of the Northern Ireland Act 1998; or

(iii)   amending an Act of a kind mentioned in paragraph (a), (b) or (c);

and includes an order or other instrument made under primary legislation (otherwise than by the National Assembly for Wales, a member of the Scottish Executive, a Northern Ireland Minister or a Northern Ireland department) to the extent to which it operates to bring one or more provisions of that legislation into force or amends any primary legislation;

"the First Protocol" means the protocol to the Convention agreed at Paris on 20th March 1952;

"the Sixth Protocol" means the protocol to the Convention agreed at Strasbourg on 28th April 1983;

"the Eleventh Protocol" means the protocol to the Convention (restructuring the control machinery established by the Convention) agreed at Strasbourg on 11th May 1994;

"remedial order" means an order under section 10;

"subordinate legislation" means any—

(a)   Order in Council other than one—
    (i)   made in exercise of Her Majesty's Royal Prerogative;
    (ii)   made under section 38(1)(a) of the Northern Ireland Constitution Act 1973 or the corresponding provision of the Northern Ireland Act 1998; or
    (iii) amending an Act of a kind mentioned in the definition of primary legislation;

(b)   Act of the Scottish Parliament;

(c)   Act of the Parliament of Northern Ireland;

(d)   Measure of the Assembly established under section 1 of the Northern Ireland Assembly Act 1973;

(e)   Act of the Northern Ireland Assembly;

(f)   order, rules, regulations, scheme, warrant, byelaw or other instrument made under primary legislation (except to the extent to which it operates to bring one or more provisions of that legislation into force or amends any primary legislation);

(g)   order, rules, regulations, scheme, warrant, byelaw or other instrument made under legislation mentioned in paragraph (b), (c), (d) or (e) or made under an Order in Council applying only to Northern Ireland;

(h)   order, rules, regulations, scheme, warrant, byelaw or other instrument made by a member of the Scottish Executive, a

> Northern Ireland Minister or a Northern Ireland department in exercise of prerogative or other executive functions of Her Majesty which are exercisable by such a person on behalf of Her Majesty;
>
> "transferred matters" has the same meaning as in the Northern Ireland Act 1998; and "tribunal" means any tribunal in which legal proceedings may be brought.

(2)   The references in paragraphs (b) and (c) of section 2(1) to Articles are to Articles of the Convention as they had effect immediately before the coming into force of the Eleventh Protocol.

(3)   The reference in paragraph (d) of section 2(1) to Article 46 includes a reference to Articles 32 and 54 of the Convention as they had effect immediately before the coming into force of the Eleventh Protocol.

(4)   The references in section 2(1) to a report or decision of the Commission or a decision of the Committee of Ministers include references to a report or decision made as provided by paragraphs 3, 4 and 6 of Article 5 of the Eleventh Protocol (transitional provisions).

(5)   Any liability under the Army Act 1955, the Air Force Act 1955 or the Naval Discipline Act 1957 to suffer death for an offence is replaced by a liability to imprisonment for life or any less punishment authorised by those Acts; and those Acts shall accordingly have effect with the necessary modifications.

Short title, commencement, application and extent.

22. (1)   This Act may be cited as the Human Rights Act 1998.

(2)   Sections 18, 20 and 21(5) and this section come into force on the passing of this Act.

(3)   The other provisions of this Act come into force on such day as the Secretary of State may by order appoint; and different days may be appointed for different purposes.

(4)   Paragraph (b) of subsection (1) of section 7 applies to proceedings brought by or at the instigation of a public authority whenever the act in question took place; but otherwise that subsection does not apply to an act taking place before the coming into force of that section.

(5)   This Act binds the Crown.

(6)   This Act extends to Northern Ireland.

(7)   Section 21(5), so far as it relates to any provision contained in the Army Act 1955, the Air Force Act 1955 or the Naval Discipline Act 1957, extends to any place to which that provision extends.

SCHEDULES
Schedule 1

THE ARTICLES
PART I

THE CONVENTION
RIGHTS AND FREEDOMS

ARTICLE 2
RIGHT TO LIFE

1. Everyone's right to life shall be protected by law. No one shall be deprived of his life intentionally save in the execution of a sentence of a court following his conviction of a crime for which this penalty is provided by law.
2. Deprivation of life shall not be regarded as inflicted in contravention of this Article when it results from the use of force which is no more than absolutely necessary:
   (a) in defence of any person from unlawful violence;
   (b) in order to effect a lawful arrest or to prevent the escape of a person lawfully detained;
   (c) in action lawfully taken for the purpose of quelling a riot or insurrection.

ARTICLE 3
PROHIBITION OF TORTURE

No one shall be subjected to torture or to inhuman or degrading treatment or punishment.

ARTICLE 4
PROHIBITION OF SLAVERY AND FORCED LABOUR

1. No one shall be held in slavery or servitude.
2. No one shall be required to perform forced or compulsory labour.
3. For the purpose of this Article the term "forced or compulsory labour" shall not include:

(a) any work required to be done in the ordinary course of detention imposed according to the provisions of Article 5 of this Convention or during conditional release from such detention;

(b) any service of a military character or, in case of conscientious objectors in countries where they are recognised, service exacted instead of compulsory military service;

(c) any service exacted in case of an emergency or calamity threatening the life or well-being of the community;

(d) any work or service which forms part of normal civic obligations.

ARTICLE 5
RIGHT TO LIBERTY AND SECURITY

1. Everyone has the right to liberty and security of person. No one shall be deprived of his liberty save in the following cases and in accordance with a procedure prescribed by law:

(a) the lawful detention of a person after conviction by a competent court;

(b) the lawful arrest or detention of a person for non-compliance with the lawful order of a court or in order to secure the fulfilment of any obligation prescribed by law;

(c) the lawful arrest or detention of a person effected for the purpose of bringing him before the competent legal authority on reasonable suspicion of having committed an offence or when it is reasonably considered necessary to prevent his committing an offence or fleeing after having done so;

(d) the detention of a minor by lawful order for the purpose of educational supervision or his lawful detention for the purpose of bringing him before the competent legal authority;

(e) the lawful detention of persons for the prevention of the spreading of infectious diseases, of persons of unsound mind, alcoholics or drug addicts or vagrants;

(f) the lawful arrest or detention of a person to prevent his effecting an unauthorised entry into the country or of a person against whom action is being taken with a view to deportation or extradition.

2. Everyone who is arrested shall be informed promptly, in a language which he understands, of the reasons for his arrest and of any charge against him.

3. Everyone arrested or detained in accordance with the provisions of paragraph 1(c) of this Article shall be brought promptly before a judge or other officer authorised by law to exercise judicial power and shall be entitled to trial within a reasonable time or to release pending trial. Release may be conditioned by guarantees to appear for trial.

4. Everyone who is deprived of his liberty by arrest or detention shall be entitled to take proceedings by which the lawfulness of his detention shall be decided speedily by a court and his release ordered if the detention is not lawful.

5. Everyone who has been the victim of arrest or detention in contravention of the provisions of this Article shall have an enforceable right to compensation.

ARTICLE 6
RIGHT TO A FAIR TRIAL

1. In the determination of his civil rights and obligations or of any criminal charge against him, everyone is entitled to a fair and public hearing within a reasonable time by an independent and impartial tribunal established by law. Judgment shall be pronounced publicly but the press and public may be excluded from all or part of the trial in the interest of morals, public order or national security in a democratic society, where the interests of juveniles or the protection of the private life of the parties so require, or to the extent strictly necessary in the opinion of the court in special circumstances where publicity would prejudice the interests of justice.

2. Everyone charged with a criminal offence shall be presumed innocent until proved guilty according to law.

3. Everyone charged with a criminal offence has the following minimum rights:
    (a)   to be informed promptly, in a language which he understands and in detail, of the nature and cause of the accusation against him;
    (b)   to have adequate time and facilities for the preparation of his defence;
    (c)   to defend himself in person or through legal assistance of his own choosing or, if he has not sufficient means to pay for legal assistance, to be given it free when the interests of justice so require;
    (d)   to examine or have examined witnesses against him and to obtain the attendance and examination of witnesses on his behalf under the same conditions as witnesses against him;
    (e)   to have the free assistance of an interpreter if he cannot understand or speak the language used in court.

ARTICLE 7
NO PUNISHMENT WITHOUT LAW

1. No one shall be held guilty of any criminal offence on account of any act or omission which did not constitute a criminal offence under national or international law at the time when it was committed. Nor shall a heavier

penalty be imposed than the one that was applicable at the time the criminal offence was committed.

2. This Article shall not prejudice the trial and punishment of any person for any act or omission which, at the time when it was committed, was criminal according to the general principles of law recognised by civilised nations.

ARTICLE 8
RIGHT TO RESPECT FOR PRIVATE AND FAMILY LIFE

1. Everyone has the right to respect for his private and family life, his home and his correspondence.

2. There shall be no interference by a public authority with the exercise of this right except such as is in accordance with the law and is necessary in a democratic society in the interests of national security, public safety or the economic well-being of the country, for the prevention of disorder or crime, for the protection of health or morals, or for the protection of the rights and freedoms of others.

ARTICLE 9
FREEDOM OF THOUGHT, CONSCIENCE AND RELIGION

1. Everyone has the right to freedom of thought, conscience and religion; this right includes freedom to change his religion or belief and freedom, either alone or in community with others and in public or private, to manifest his religion or belief, in worship, teaching, practice and observance.

2. Freedom to manifest one's religion or beliefs shall be subject only to such limitations as are prescribed by law and are necessary in a democratic society in the interests of public safety, for the protection of public order, health or morals, or for the protection of the rights and freedoms of others.

ARTICLE 10
FREEDOM OF EXPRESSION

1. Everyone has the right to freedom of expression. This right shall include freedom to hold opinions and to receive and impart information and ideas without interference by public authority and regardless of frontiers. This Article shall not prevent States from requiring the licensing of broadcasting, television or cinema enterprises.

2. The exercise of these freedoms, since it carries with it duties and responsibilities, may be subject to such formalities, conditions, restrictions or

penalties as are prescribed by law and are necessary in a democratic society, in the interests of national security, territorial integrity or public safety, for the prevention of disorder or crime, for the protection of health or morals, for the protection of the reputation or rights of others, for preventing the disclosure of information received in confidence, or for maintaining the authority and impartiality of the judiciary.

ARTICLE 11
FREEDOM OF ASSEMBLY AND ASSOCIATION

1. Everyone has the right to freedom of peaceful assembly and to freedom of association with others, including the right to form and to join trade unions for the protection of his interests.

2. No restrictions shall be placed on the exercise of these rights other than such as are prescribed by law and are necessary in a democratic society in the interests of national security or public safety, for the prevention of disorder or crime, for the protection of health or morals or for the protection of the rights and freedoms of others. This Article shall not prevent the imposition of lawful restrictions on the exercise of these rights by members of the armed forces, of the police or of the administration of the State.

ARTICLE 12
RIGHT TO MARRY

Men and women of marriageable age have the right to marry and to found a family, according to the national laws governing the exercise of this right.

ARTICLE 14
PROHIBITION OF DISCRIMINATION

The enjoyment of the rights and freedoms set forth in this Convention shall be secured without discrimination on any ground such as sex, race, colour, language, religion, political or other opinion, national or social origin, association with a national minority, property, birth or other status.

ARTICLE 16
RESTRICTIONS ON POLITICAL ACTIVITY OF ALIENS

Nothing in Articles 10, 11 and 14 shall be regarded as preventing the High Contracting Parties from imposing restrictions on the political activity of aliens.

ARTICLE 17
PROHIBITION OF ABUSE OF RIGHTS

Nothing in this Convention may be interpreted as implying for any State, group or person any right to engage in any activity or perform any act aimed at the destruction of any of the rights and freedoms set forth herein or at their limitation to a greater extent than is provided for in the Convention.

ARTICLE 18
LIMITATION ON USE OF RESTRICTIONS ON RIGHTS

The restrictions permitted under this Convention to the said rights and freedoms shall not be applied for any purpose other than those for which they have been prescribed.

PART II
THE FIRST PROTOCOL

ARTICLE 1
PROTECTION OF PROPERTY

Every natural or legal person is entitled to the peaceful enjoyment of his possessions. No one shall be deprived of his possessions except in the public interest and subject to the conditions provided for by law and by the general principles of international law.

The preceding provisions shall not, however, in any way impair the right of a State to enforce such laws as it deems necessary to control the use of property in accordance with the general interest or to secure the payment of taxes or other contributions or penalties.

ARTICLE 2
RIGHT TO EDUCATION

No person shall be denied the right to education. In the exercise of any functions which it assumes in relation to education and to teaching, the State shall respect the right of parents to ensure such education and teaching in conformity with their own religious and philosophical convictions.

ARTICLE 3
RIGHT TO FREE ELECTIONS

The High Contracting Parties undertake to hold free elections at reasonable intervals by secret ballot, under conditions which will ensure the free expression of the opinion of the people in the choice of the legislature.

PART III
THE SIXTH PROTOCOL

ARTICLE 1
ABOLITION OF THE DEATH PENALTY

The death penalty shall be abolished. No one shall be condemned to such penalty or executed.

ARTICLE 2
DEATH PENALTY IN TIME OF WAR

A State may make provision in its law for the death penalty in respect of acts committed in time of war or of imminent threat of war; such penalty shall be applied only in the instances laid down in the law and in accordance with its provisions. The State shall communicate to the Secretary General of the Council of Europe the relevant provisions of that law.

Schedule 2
REMEDIAL ORDERS

Orders

1. (1)   A remedial order may—
    (a)   contain such incidental, supplemental, consequential or transitional provision as the person making it considers appropriate;
    (b)   be made so as to have effect from a date earlier than that on which it is made;
    (c)   make provision for the delegation of specific functions;
    (d)   make different provision for different cases.
    (2)   The power conferred by sub-paragraph (1)(a) includes—
    (a)   power to amend primary legislation (including primary legislation other than that which contains the incompatible provision); and

(b)   power to amend or revoke subordinate legislation (including subordinate legislation other than that which contains the incompatible provision).

(3)   A remedial order may be made so as to have the same extent as the legislation which it affects.

(4)   No person is to be guilty of an offence solely as a result of the retrospective effect of a remedial order.

Procedure

2.   No remedial order may be made unless—

(a)   a draft of the order has been approved by a resolution of each House of Parliament made after the end of the period of 60 days beginning with the day on which the draft was laid; or

(b)   it is declared in the order that it appears to the person making it that, because of the urgency of the matter, it is necessary to make the order without a draft being so approved.

Orders laid in draft

3.   (1)   No draft may be laid under paragraph 2(a) unless—

(a)   the person proposing to make the order has laid before Parliament a document which contains a draft of the proposed order and the required information; and

(b)   the period of 60 days, beginning with the day on which the document required by this sub-paragraph was laid, has ended.

(2)   If representations have been made during that period, the draft laid under paragraph 2(a) must be accompanied by a statement containing—

(a)   a summary of the representations; and

(b)   if, as a result of the representations, the proposed order has been changed, details of the changes.

Urgent cases

4.   (1)   If a remedial order ("the original order") is made without being approved in draft, the person making it must lay it before Parliament, accompanied by the required information, after it is made.

(2)   If representations have been made during the period of 60 days beginning with the day on which the original order was made, the person making it must (after the end of that period) lay before Parliament a statement containing—

(a)   a summary of the representations; and

(b)   if, as a result of the representations, he considers it appropriate to make changes to the original order, details of the changes.

(3) If sub-paragraph (2)(b) applies, the person making the statement must—

   (a) make a further remedial order replacing the original order; and

   (b) lay the replacement order before Parliament.

(4) If, at the end of the period of 120 days beginning with the day on which the original order was made, a resolution has not been passed by each House approving the original or replacement order, the order ceases to have effect (but without that affecting anything previously done under either order or the power to make a fresh remedial order).

Definitions

5. In this Schedule—

"representations" means representations about a remedial order (or proposed remedial order) made to the person making (or proposing to make) it and includes any relevant Parliamentary report or resolution; and

"required information" means—

   (a) an explanation of the incompatibility which the order (or proposed order) seeks to remove, including particulars of the relevant declaration, finding or order; and

   (b) a statement of the reasons for proceeding under section 10 and for making an order in those terms.

Calculating periods

6. In calculating any period for the purposes of this Schedule, no account is to be taken of any time during which—

   (a) Parliament is dissolved or prorogued; or

   (b) both Houses are adjourned for more than four days.

Schedule 3
DEROGATION AND RESERVATION

PART I
DEROGATION

The 1988 notification

The United Kingdom Permanent Representative to the Council of Europe presents his compliments to the Secretary General of the Council, and has the honour to convey the following information in order to ensure compliance with the obligations of Her Majesty's Government in the United Kingdom under Article 15(3) of the Convention for the Protection of Human Rights and Fundamental Freedoms signed at Rome on 4 November 1950.

There have been in the United Kingdom in recent years campaigns of organised terrorism connected with the affairs of Northern Ireland which have manifested themselves in activities which have included repeated murder, attempted murder, maiming, intimidation and violent civil disturbance and in bombing and fire raising which have resulted in death, injury and widespread destruction of property. As a result, a public emergency within the meaning of Article 15(1) of the Convention exists in the United Kingdom.

The Government found it necessary in 1974 to introduce and since then, in cases concerning persons reasonably suspected of involvement in terrorism connected with the affairs of Northern Ireland, or of certain offences under the legislation, who have been detained for 48 hours, to exercise powers enabling further detention without charge, for periods of up to five days, on the authority of the Secretary of State. These powers are at present to be found in Section 12 of the Prevention of Terrorism (Temporary Provisions) Act 1984, Article 9 of the Prevention of Terrorism (Supplemental Temporary Provisions) Order 1984 and Article 10 of the Prevention of Terrorism (Supplemental Temporary Provisions) (Northern Ireland) Order 1984.

Section 12 of the Prevention of Terrorism (Temporary Provisions) Act 1984 provides for a person whom a constable has arrested on reasonable grounds of suspecting him to be guilty of an offence under Section 1, 9 or 10 of the Act, or to be or to have been involved in terrorism connected with the affairs of Northern Ireland, to be detained in right of the arrest for up to 48 hours and thereafter, where the Secretary of State extends the detention period, for up to a further five days. Section 12 substantially re-enacted Section 12 of the Prevention of Terrorism (Temporary Provisions) Act 1976 which, in turn, substantially re-enacted Section 7 of the Prevention of Terrorism (Temporary Provisions) Act 1974.

Article 10 of the Prevention of Terrorism (Supplemental Temporary Provisions) (Northern Ireland) Order 1984 (SI 1984/417) and Article 9 of the Prevention of Terrorism (Supplemental Temporary Provisions) Order 1984 (SI 1984/418) were both made under Sections 13 and 14 of and Schedule 3 to the 1984 Act and substantially re-enacted powers of detention in Orders made under the 1974 and 1976 Acts. A person who is being examined under Article 4 of either Order on his arrival in, or on seeking to leave, Northern Ireland or Great Britain for the purpose of determining whether he is or has been involved in terrorism connected with the affairs of Northern Ireland, or whether there are grounds for suspecting that he has committed an offence under Section 9 of the 1984 Act, may be detained under Article 9 or 10, as appropriate, pending the conclusion of his examination. The period of this examination may exceed 12 hours if an examining officer has reasonable grounds for suspecting him to be or to have been involved in acts of terrorism connected with the affairs of Northern Ireland.

Where such a person is detained under the said Article 9 or 10 he may be detained for up to 48 hours on the authority of an examining officer and thereafter, where the Secretary of State extends the detention period, for up to a further five days.

In its judgment of 29 November 1988 in the Case of Brogan and Others, the European Court of Human Rights held that there had been a violation of Article 5(3) in respect of each of the applicants, all of whom had been detained under Section 12 of the 1984 Act. The Court held that even the shortest of the four periods of detention concerned, namely four days and six hours, fell outside the constraints as to time permitted by the first part of Article 5(3). In addition, the Court held that there had been a violation of Article 5(5) in the case of each applicant.

Following this judgment, the Secretary of State for the Home Department informed Parliament on 6 December 1988 that, against the background of the terrorist campaign, and the over-riding need to bring terrorists to justice, the Government did not believe that the maximum period of detention should be reduced. He informed Parliament that the Government were examining the matter with a view to responding to the judgment. On 22 December 1988, the Secretary of State further informed Parliament that it remained the Government's wish, if it could be achieved, to find a judicial process under which extended detention might be reviewed and where appropriate authorised by a judge or other judicial officer. But a further period of reflection and consultation was necessary before the Government could bring forward a firm and final view.

Since the judgment of 29 November 1988 as well as previously, the Government have found it necessary to continue to exercise, in relation to terrorism connected with the affairs of Northern Ireland, the powers described above enabling further detention without charge for periods of up to 5 days, on the authority of the Secretary of State, to the extent strictly required by the exigencies of the situation to enable necessary enquiries and investigations properly to be completed in order to decide whether criminal proceedings should be instituted. To the extent that the exercise of these powers may be inconsistent with the obligations imposed by the Convention the Government has availed itself of the right of derogation conferred by Article 15(1) of the Convention and will continue to do so until further notice.

Dated 23 December 1988.

The 1989 notification

The United Kingdom Permanent Representative to the Council of Europe presents his compliments to the Secretary General of the Council, and has the honour to convey the following information.

In his communication to the Secretary General of 23 December 1988, reference was made to the introduction and exercise of certain powers under section 12 of the Prevention of Terrorism (Temporary Provisions) Act 1984, Article 9 of the Prevention of Terrorism (Supplemental Temporary Provisions) Order 1984 and Article 10 of the Prevention of Terrorism (Supplemental Temporary Provisions) (Northern Ireland) Order 1984.

These provisions have been replaced by section 14 of and paragraph 6 of Schedule 5 to the Prevention of Terrorism (Temporary Provisions) Act 1989, which make comparable provision. They came into force on 22 March 1989. A copy of these provisions is enclosed.

The United Kingdom Permanent Representative avails himself of this opportunity to renew to the Secretary General the assurance of his highest consideration.

23 March 1989.

PART II
RESERVATION

At the time of signing the present (First) Protocol, I declare that, in view of certain provisions of the Education Acts in the United Kingdom, the principle affirmed in the second sentence of Article 2 is accepted by the United Kingdom only so far as it is compatible with the provision of efficient instruction and training, and the avoidance of unreasonable public expenditure.

Dated 20 March 1952

Made by the United Kingdom Permanent Representative to the Council of Europe.

Schedule 4
JUDICIAL PENSIONS

Duty to make orders about pensions

1. (1) The appropriate Minister must by order make provision with respect to pensions payable to or in respect of any holder of a judicial office who serves as an ECHR judge.

    (2) A pensions order must include such provision as the Minister making it considers is necessary to secure that—

    (a) an ECHR judge who was, immediately before his appointment as an ECHR judge, a member of a judicial pension scheme is entitled to remain as a member of that scheme;

    (b) the terms on which he remains a member of the scheme are those which would have been applicable had he not been appointed as an ECHR judge; and

    (c) entitlement to benefits payable in accordance with the scheme continues to be determined as if, while serving as an ECHR judge, his salary was that which would (but for section 18(4)) have been payable to him in respect of his continuing service as the holder of his judicial office.

Contributions

2. A pensions order may, in particular, make provision—

    (a) for any contributions which are payable by a person who remains a member of a scheme as a result of the order, and which would otherwise be payable by deduction from his salary, to be made otherwise than by deduction from his salary as an ECHR judge; and

    (b) for such contributions to be collected in such manner as may be determined by the administrators of the scheme.

Amendments of other enactments

3. A pensions order may amend any provision of, or made under, a pensions Act in such manner and to such extent as the Minister making the order considers necessary or expedient to ensure the proper administration of any scheme to which it relates.

Definitions

4. In this Schedule—

    "appropriate Minister" means—

    (a) in relation to any judicial office whose jurisdiction is exercisable exclusively in relation to Scotland, the Secretary of State;

and

(b)   otherwise, the Lord Chancellor;

"ECHR judge" means the holder of a judicial office who is serving as a judge of the Court;

"judicial pension scheme" means a scheme established by and in accordance with a pensions Act;

"pensions Act" means—

(a)   the County Courts Act Northern Ireland) 1959;

(b)   the Sheriffs' Pensions (Scotland) Act 1961;

(c)   the Judicial Pensions Act 1981; or

(d)   the Judicial Pensions and Retirement Act 1993; and

"pensions order" means an order made under paragraph 1.

INTERNATIONAL TREATIES
AND CONVENTIONS

DOCUMENT NO 7

The Treaty of Maastricht

TITLE VI: PROVISIONS ON COOPERATION IN THE FIELDS OF JUSTICE AND HOME AFFAIRS

February 12, 1992

ARTICLE K

Cooperation in the fields of justice and home affairs shall be governed by the following provisions.

ARTICLE K.1

For the purposes of achieving the objectives of the Union, in particular the free movement of persons, and without prejudice to the powers of the European Community, Member States shall regard the following areas as matters of common interest:

1. asylum policy;
2. rules governing the crossing by persons of the external borders of the Member States and the exercise of controls thereon;
3. immigration policy and policy regarding nationals of third countries;
   (a) conditions of entry and movement by nationals of third countries on the territory of Member States;
   (b) conditions of residence by nationals of third countries on the territory of Member States, including family reunion and access to employment;
   (c) combating unauthorized immigration, residence and work by nationals of third countries on the territory of Member States;
4. combating drug addiction in so far as this is not covered by 7 to 9;
5. combating fraud on an international scale in so far as this is not covered by 7 to 9;
6. judicial cooperation in civil matters;
7. judicial cooperation in criminal matters;
8. customs cooperation;

9. police cooperation for the purposes of preventing and combating terrorism, unlawful drug trafficking and other serious forms of international crime, including if necessary certain aspects of customs cooperation, in connection with the organization of a Union-wide system for exchanging information within a European Police Office (Europol).

ARTICLE K.2

1) The matters referred to in Article K.1 shall be dealt with in compliance with the European Convention for the Protection of Human Rights and Fundamental Freedoms of 4 November 1950 and the Convention relating to the Status of Refugees of 28 July 1951 and having regard to the protection afforded by Member States to persons persecuted on political grounds.

2) This Title shall not affect the exercise of the responsibilities incumbent upon Member States with regard to the maintenance of law and order and the safeguarding of internal security.

ARTICLE K.3

1) In the areas referred to in Article K.1, Member States shall inform and consult one another within the Council with a view to coordinating their action. To that end, they shall establish collaboration between the relevant departments of their administrations.

2) The Council may:
    —   on the initiative of any Member State of the Commission, in the areas referred to in Article K.1(1) to (6);
    —   on the initiative of any Member State, in the areas referred to Article K1(7) to (9):
    a) adopt joint positions and promote, using the appropriate form and procedures, any cooperation contributing to the pursuit of the objectives of the Union;
    b) adopt joint action in so far as the objectives of the Union can be attained better by joint action than by the Member States acting individually on account of the scale or effects of the action envisaged; it may decide that measures implementing joint action are to be adopted by a qualified majority;
    c) without prejudice to Article 220 of the Treaty establishing the European Community, draw up conventions which it shall recommend to the Member States for adoption in accordance with their respective constitutional requirements. Unless otherwise provided by such conventions, measures implementing them shall be adopted within the Council by a majority of two-thirds of the High Contracting Parties.

Such conventions may stipulate that the Court of Justice shall have jurisdiction to interpret their provisions and to rule on any disputes regarding their application, in accordance with such arrangements as they may lay down.

ARTICLE K.4

1) A Coordinating Committee shall be set up consisting of senior officials. In additions to its coordinating role, it shall be the task of the Committee to;
   — give opinions for the attention of the Council, either at the Councils request or on its own initiative.
   — contribute, without prejudice to Article 151 of the Treaty establishing the European Community, to the preparation of the Council's discussions in the areas referred to in Article K.1 and, in accordance with the conditions laid down in Article 100d of the Treaty establishing the European Community, in the areas referred to in Article 100c of that Treaty.

2) The Commission shall be fully associated with the work in the areas referred to in this Title.

3) The Council shall act unanimously, except on matters of procedure and in cases where Article K.3 expressly provides for other voting rules. Where the Council is required to act by a qualified majority, the votes of its members shall be weighted as laid down in Article 148(2) of the Treaty establishing the European Community, and for their adoption, acts of the Council shall require at least fifty-four votes in favour, cast by at least eight members.

ARTICLE K.5

Within international organizations and at international conferences in which they take part, Member States shall defend the common positions adopted under the provisions of this Title.

ARTICLE K.6

The Presidency and the Commission shall regularly inform the European Parliament of discussions in the areas covered by this Title.

The Presidency shall consult the European Parliament on the principal aspects of activities in the areas referred to in this Title and shall ensure that the views of the European Parliament are duly taken into consideration.

The European Parliament may ask questions of the Council or make recommendations to it. Each year, it shall hold a debate on the progress made in implementation of the areas referred to in this Title.

ARTICLE K.7

The provisions of this Title shall not prevent the establishment or development of closer cooperation between two or more Member States in so far as such cooperation does not conflict with, or impede, that provided for in this Title.

ARTICLE K.8

1) The provisions referred to in Article 137,138,139 top 142, 146, 147, 150 to 153, 157 to 163 and 217 of the Treaty establishing the European Community shall apply to the provisions relating to the areas referred to in this Title.

2) Administrative expenditure which the provisions relating to the areas referred to in this Title entail for the institutions shall be charged to the budget of European Communities.

The Council may also:

— either decide unanimously that operational expenditure to which the implementation of those provisions gives rise is to be charged to the budget of the European Communities; in that event, the budgetary procedure laid down in the treaty establishing the European Community shall be applicable;

— or determine that such expenditure shall be charged to the Member States, where appropriate in accordance with a scale to be decided.

ARTICLE K.9

The Council, acting unanimously on the initiative of the Commission or a Member State, may decide to apply Article 100c of the Treaty establishing the European Community to action in areas referred to in Article K.1(1) to (6), and at the same time determine the relevant voting conditions relating to it. It shall recommend the Member States to adopt that decision in accordance with their respective constitutional requirements

DOCUMENT NO 8

The Treaty on European Union, on the Establishment of A European Police Office (EUROPOL Convention)

July 18, 1995

Subject: Council Act drawing up the Convention based on Article K.3 of the Treaty on European Union, on the establishment of a European Police Office (Europol Convention) Delegations will find attached the above text, as finalized by the Legal/Linguistic Experts' Working Party.

Council Act of ...... drawing up the Convention based on Article K.3 of the Treaty on European Union, on the establishment of a European Police Office (Europol Convention)

The Council of the European Union,

HAVING REGARD to the Treaty on European Union, and in particular Article K.3(2)(c) and Article K.1(9) thereof,

WHEREAS for the purposes of achieving the objectives of the Union the Member States regard the establishment of a European Police Office as a matter of common interest;

HAS DECIDED on the drawing up of the Convention, the text of which is annexed, which has been signed today by the Representatives of the Governments of the Member States of the Union;

RECOMMENDS that it be adopted by the Member States in accordance with their respective constitutional requirements.

Done at For the Council The President

ANNEX
CONVENTION BASED ON

ARTICLE K.3 OF THE TREATY ON EUROPEAN UNION, ON THE ESTABLISHMENT OF A EUROPEAN POLICE OFFICE (EUROPOL CONVENTION)

THE HIGH CONTRACTING PARTIES to the present Convention, Member States of the European Union,

REFERRING to the Council act of the twenty-sixth day of July in the year one thousand nine hundred and ninety-five;

AWARE of the urgent problems arising from terrorism, unlawful drug trafficking and other serious forms of international crime;

WHEREAS there is a need for progress in solidarity and co-operation between the Member States of the European Union, particularly through an improvement in police cooperation between the Member States;

WHEREAS such progress should enable the protection of security and public order to be further improved;

WHEREAS the establishment of a European Police Office (Europol) was agreed in the Treaty on European Union of 7 February 1992;

IN VIEW of the decision of the European Council of 29 October 1993 that Europol should be established in the Netherlands and have its seat in The Hague;

MINDFUL of the common objective of improving police cooperation in the field of terrorism, unlawful drug trafficking and other serious forms of international crime through a constant, confidential and intensive exchange of information between Europol and Member States' national units;

ON THE UNDERSTANDING that the forms of cooperation laid down in this Convention should not affect other forms of bilateral or multilateral cooperation;

CONVINCED that in the field of police co-operation, particular attention must be paid to the protection of the rights of individuals, and in particular to the protection of their personal data;

WHEREAS the activities of Europol under this Convention are without prejudice to the powers of the European Communities; whereas Europol and the Communities have a mutual interest, in the framework of the European Union, in establishing types of cooperation enabling each of them to perform their respective tasks as effectively as possible,

HAVE AGREED as follows:

TITLE I: ESTABLISHMENT AND TASKS

ARTICLE 1: ESTABLISHMENT

1. The Member States of the European Union, hereinafter referred to as "Member States", hereby establish a European Police Office, hereinafter referred to as "Europol".
2. Europol shall liaise with a single national unit in each Member State, to be established or designated in accordance with Article 4.

ARTICLE 2: OBJECTIVE

1. The objective of Europol shall be, within the framework of cooperation between the Member States pursuant to Article K.1(9) of the Treaty on European Union, to improve, by means of the measures referred to in this Convention, the effectiveness and cooperation of the competent authorities in the Member States in preventing and combating terrorism, unlawful drug trafficking and other serious forms of international crime where there are factual indications that an organized criminal structure is involved and two or more Member States are affected by the forms of crime in question in such a way as to require a common approach by the Member States owing to the scale, significance and consequences of the offences concerned.
2. In order to achieve progressively the objective mentioned in paragraph 1, Europol shall initially act to prevent and combat unlawful drug trafficking, trafficking in nuclear and radioactive substances, illegal immigrant smuggling, trade in human beings and motor vehicle crime. Within two years at the latest following the entry into force of this Convention, Europol shall also deal with crimes committed or likely to be committed in the course of terrorist activities against life, limb, personal freedom or property. The Council, acting unanimously in accordance with the procedure laid down in Title VI of the Treaty on European Union, may decide to instruct Europol to deal with such terrorist activities before that period has expired. The Council, acting unanimously in accordance with the procedure laid down in Title VI of the Treaty on European Union, may decide to instruct Europol to deal with other forms of crime listed in the Annex to this Convention or specific manifestations thereof. Before acting, the Council shall instruct the Management Board to prepare its decision and in particular to set out the budgetary and staffing implications for Europol.

3.   Europol's competence as regards a form of crime or specific manifestations thereof shall cover both:

1)   illegal money-laundering activities in connection with these forms of crime or specific manifestations thereof;

2)   related criminal offences. The following shall be regarded as related and shall be taken into account in accordance with the procedures set out in Articles 8 and 10:

   —   criminal offences committed in order to procure the means for perpetrating acts within the sphere of competence of Europol;

   —   criminal offences committed in order to facilitate or carry out acts within the sphere of competence of Europol;

   —   criminal offences committed to ensure the impunity of acts within the sphere of competence of Europol.

4.   For the purposes of this Convention, "competent authorities" means all public bodies existing in the Member States which are responsible under national law for preventing and combating criminal offences.

5.   For the purposes of paragraphs 1 and 2, "unlawful drug trafficking" means the criminal offences listed in Article 3(1) of the United Nations Convention of 20 December 1988 against Illicit Traffic in Narcotic Drugs and Psychotropic Substances and in the provisions amending or replacing that Convention.

ARTICLE 3: TASKS

1.   In the framework of its objective pursuant to Article 2(1), Europol shall have the following principal tasks:

1)   to facilitate the exchange of information between the Member States;

2)   to obtain, collate and analyse information and intelligence;

3)   to notify the competent authorities of the Member States without delay via the national units referred to in Article 4 of information concerning them and of any connections identified between criminal offences;

4)   to aid investigations in the Member States by forwarding all relevant information to the national units;

5)   to maintain a computerized system of collected information containing data in accordance with Articles 8, 10 and 11.

2.   In order to improve the cooperation and effectiveness of the competent authorities in the Member States through the national units with a view to fulfilling the objective set out in Article 2(1), Europol shall furthermore have the following additional tasks:

1) to develop specialist knowledge of the investigative procedures of the competent authorities in the Member States and to provide advice on investigations;
2) to provide strategic intelligence to assist with and promote the efficient and effective use of the resources available at national level for operational activities;
3) to prepare general situation reports.

3. In the context of its objective under Article 2(1) Europol may, in addition, in accordance with its staffing and the budgetary resources at its disposal and within the limits set by the Management Board, assist Member States through advice and research in the following areas:
1) training of members of their competent authorities;
2) organization and equipment of those authorities;
3) crime prevention methods;
4) technical and forensic police methods and investigative procedures.

ARTICLE 4: NATIONAL UNITS

1. Each Member State shall establish or designate a national unit to carry out the tasks listed in this Article.
2. The national unit shall be the only liaison body between Europol and the competent national authorities. Relationships between the national unit and the competent authorities shall be governed by national law, and, in particular the relevant national constitutional requirements.
3. Member States shall take the necessary measures to ensure that the national units are able to fulfil their tasks and, in particular, have access to relevant national data.
4. It shall be the task of the national units to:
1) supply Europol on their own initiative with the information and intelligence necessary for it to carry out its tasks;
2) respond to Europol's requests for information, intelligence and advice;
3) keep information and intelligence up to date;
4) evaluate information and intelligence in accordance with national law for the competent authorities and transmit this material to them;
5) issue requests for advice, information, intelligence and analysis to Europol;
6) supply Europol with information for storage in the computerized system;

7) ensure compliance with the law in every exchange of information between themselves and Europol.

5. Without prejudice to the exercise of the responsibilities incumbent upon Member States as set out in Article K.2(2) of the Treaty on European Union, a national unit shall not be obliged in a particular case to supply the information and intelligence provided for in paragraph 4, points 1, 2 and 6 and in Articles 7 and 10 if this would mean:

1) harming essential national security interests; or

2) jeopardizing the success of a current investigation or the safety of individuals;

3) involving information pertaining to organizations or specific intelligence activities in the field of State security.

6. The costs incurred by the national units for communications with Europol shall be borne by the Member States and, apart from the costs of connection, shall not be charged to Europol.

7. The Heads of national units shall meet as necessary to assist Europol by giving advice.

ARTICLE 5: LIAISON OFFICERS

1. Each national unit shall second at least one liaison officer to Europol. The number of liaison officers who may be sent by Member States to Europol shall be laid down by unanimous decision of the Management Board; the decision may be altered at any time by unanimous decision of the Management Board. Except as otherwise stipulated in specific provisions of this Convention, liaison officers shall be subject to the national law of the seconding Member State.

2. The liaison officers shall be instructed by their national units to represent the interests of the latter within Europol in accordance with the national law of the seconding Member State and in compliance with the provisions applicable to the administration of Europol.

3. Without prejudice to Article 4(4) and (5), the liaison officers shall, within the framework of the objective laid down in Article 2(1), assist in the exchange of information between the national units which have seconded them and Europol, in particular by:

1) providing Europol with information from the seconding national unit;

2) forwarding information from Europol to the seconding national unit; and

3) cooperating with the officials of Europol by providing information and giving advice as regards analysis of the information concerning the seconding Member State.

4. At the same time, the liaison officers shall assist in the exchange of information from their national units and the coordination of the resulting measures in accordance with their national law and within the framework of the objective laid down in Article 2(1).

5. To the extent necessary for the performance of the tasks under paragraph 3 above, the liaison officers shall have the right to consult the various files in accordance with the appropriate provisions specified in the relevant Articles.

6. Article 25 shall apply mutatis mutandis to the activity of the liaison officers.

7. Without prejudice to the other provisions of this Convention, the rights and obligations of liaison officers in relation to Europol shall be determined unanimously by the Management Board.

8. Liaison officers shall enjoy the privileges and immunities necessary for the performance of their tasks in accordance with Article 41(2).

9. Europol shall provide Member States free of charge with the necessary premises in the Europol building for the activity of their liaison officers. All other costs which arise in connection with seconding liaison officers shall be borne by the seconding Member State; this shall also apply to the costs of equipment for liaison officers, to the extent that the Management Board does not unanimously recommend otherwise in a specific case when drawing up the budget of Europol.

ARTICLE 6: COMPUTERIZED SYSTEM OF COLLECTED INFORMATION

1. Europol shall maintain a computerized system of collected information consisting of the following components:

    1) an information system as referred to in Article 7 with a restricted and precisely defined content which allows rapid reference to the information available to the Member States and Europol;

    2) work files as referred to in Article 10 established for variable periods of time for the purposes of analysis and containing comprehensive information and

    3) an index system containing certain particulars from the analysis files referred to in point 2, in accordance with the arrangements laid down in Article 11.

2. The computerized system of collected information operated by Europol must under no circumstances be linked to other automated processing systems, except for the automated processing systems of the national units.

TITLE II: INFORMATION SYSTEM

ARTICLE 7: ESTABLISHMENT OF THE INFORMATION SYSTEM

1. In order to perform its tasks, Europol shall establish and maintain a computerized information system. The information system, into which Member States, represented by their national units and liaison officers, may directly input data in compliance with their national procedures, and into which Europol may directly input data supplied by third States and third bodies and analysis data, shall be directly accessible for consultation by national units, liaison officers, the Director, the Deputy Directors and duly empowered Europol officials.

    Direct access by the national units to the information system in respect of the persons referred to in Article 8(1), point 2 shall be restricted solely to the details of identity listed in Article 8(2). If needed for a specific enquiry, the full range of data shall be accessible to them via the liaison officers.

1. Europol shall:
    1) have the task of ensuring compliance with the provisions governing cooperation on and operation of the information system, and
    2) be responsible for the proper working of the information system in technical and operational respects. Europol shall in particular take all necessary measures to ensure that the measures referred to in Articles 21 and 25 regarding the information system are properly implemented.
2. The national unit in each Member State shall be responsible for communication with the information system. It shall, in particular, be responsible for the security measures referred to in Article 25 in respect of the data-processing equipment used within the territory of the Member State in question, for the review in accordance with Article 21 and, insofar as required under the laws, regulations, administrative provisions and procedures of that Member State, for the proper implementation of this Convention in other respects.

ARTICLE 8: CONTENT OF THE INFORMATION SYSTEM

1. The information system may be used to store, modify and utilize only the data necessary for the performance of Europol's tasks, with the exception of data concerning related criminal offences as referred to in the second subparagraph of Article 2(3). Data entered shall relate to:
    1) persons who, in accordance with the national law of the Member State concerned, are suspected of having committed or having taken part in a criminal offence for which Europol

is competent under Article 2 or who have been convicted of such an offence;

2) persons who there are serious grounds under national law for believing will commit criminal offences for which Europol is competent under Article 2.

2. Personal data as referred to in paragraph 1 may include only the following details:

1) surname, maiden name, given names and any alias or assumed name;

2) date and place of birth;

3) nationality;

4) sex, and

5) where necessary, other characteristics likely to assist in identification, including any specific objective physical characteristics not subject to change.

3. In addition to the data referred to in paragraph 2 and data on Europol or the inputting national unit, the information system may also be used to store, modify and utilize the following details concerning the persons referred to in paragraph 1:

1) criminal offences, alleged crimes and when and where they were committed;

2) means which were or may be used to commit the crimes;

3) departments handling the case and their filing references;

4) suspected membership of a criminal organization;

5) convictions, where they relate to criminal offences for which Europol is competent under Article 2. These data may also be input when they do not yet contain any references to persons. Where Europol inputs the data itself, as well as giving its filing reference it shall also indicate whether the data were provided by a third party or are the result of its own analyses.

4. Additional information held by Europol or national units concerning the groups of persons referred to in paragraph 1 may be communicated to any national unit or Europol should either so request. National units shall do so in compliance with their national law. Where the additional information concerns one or more related criminal offences as defined in the second subparagraph of Article 2(3), the data stored in the information system shall be marked accordingly to enable national units and Europol to exchange information on the related criminal offences.

5. If proceedings against the person concerned are dropped or if that person is acquitted, the data relating to either decision shall be deleted.

ARTICLE 9: RIGHT OF ACCESS TO THE INFORMATION SYSTEM

1. Only national units, liaison officers, and the Director, Deputy Directors or duly empowered Europol officials shall have the right to input data directly into the information system and retrieve it therefrom. Data may be retrieved where this is necessary for the performance of Europol's tasks in a particular case; retrieval shall be effected in accordance with the laws, regulations, administrative provisions and procedures of the retrieving unit, subject to any additional provisions contained in this Convention.

2. Only the unit which entered the data may modify, correct or delete such data. Where a unit has reason to believe that data as referred to in Article 8(2) are incorrect or wishes to supplement them, it shall immediately inform the inputting unit; the latter shall examine such notification without delay and if necessary modify, supplement, correct or delete the data immediately. Where the system contains data as referred to in Article 8(3) concerning a person any unit may enter additional data as referred to in Article 8(3). Where there is an obvious contradiction between the data input, the units concerned shall consult each other and reach agreement. Where a unit intends to delete altogether data as referred to in Article 8(2) which is has input on a person and where data as referred to in Article 8(3) are held on the same person but input by other units, responsibility in terms of data protection legislation pursuant to Article 15(1) and the right to modify, supplement, correct and delete such data pursuant to Article 8(2) shall be transferred to the next unit to have entered data as referred to in Article 8(3) on that person. The unit intending to delete shall inform the unit to which responsibility in terms of data protection is transferred of its intention.

3. Responsibility for the permissibility of retrieval from, input into and modifications within the information system shall lie with the retrieving, inputting or modifying unit; it must be possible to identify that unit. The communication of information between national units and the competent authorities in the Member States shall be governed by national law.

TITLE III: WORK FILES FOR THE PURPOSES OF ANALYSIS

ARTICLE 10: COLLECTION, PROCESSING AND UTILIZATION OF PERSONAL DATA

1. Where this is necessary to achieve the objective laid down in Article 2(1), Europol, in addition to data of a non-personal nature, may store, modify, and utilize in other files data on criminal offences for which Europol

is competent under Article 2(2), including data on the related criminal offences provided for in the second subparagraph of Article 2(3) which are intended for specific analyses, and concerning:

1) persons as referred to in Article 8(1);
2) persons who might be called on to testify in investigations in connection with the offences under consideration or in subsequent criminal proceedings;
3) persons who have been the victims of one of the offences under consideration or with regard to whom certain facts give reason for believing that they could be the victims of such an offence;
4) contacts and associates, and
5) persons who can provide information on the criminal offences under consideration. The collection, storage and processing of the data listed in the first sentence of Article 6 of the Council of Europe Convention of 28 January 1981 with regard to Automatic Processing of Personal Data shall not be permitted unless strictly necessary for the purposes of the file concerned and unless such data supplement other personal data already entered in that file. It shall be prohibited to select a particular group of persons solely on the basis of the data listed in the first sentence of Article 6 of the Council of Europe Convention of 28 January 1981 in breach of the aforementioned rules with regard to purpose. The Council, acting unanimously, in accordance with the procedure laid down in Title VI of the Treaty on European Union, shall adopt implementing rules for data files prepared by the Management Board containing additional details, in particular with regard to the categories of personal data referred to in this Article and the provisions concerning the security of the data concerned and the internal supervision of their use.

2. Such files shall be opened for the purposes of analysis defined as the assembly, processing or utilization of data with the aim of helping a criminal investigation. Each analysis project shall entail the establishment of an analysis group closely associating the following participants in accordance with the tasks defined in Article 3(1) and (2) and Article 5(3):
   1) analysts and other Europol officials designated by the Europol Directorate: only analysts shall be authorized to enter data into and retrieve data from the file concerned;
   2) the liaison officers and/or experts of the Member States supplying the information or concerned by the analysis within the meaning of paragraph 6.

3. At the request of Europol or on their own initiative, national units shall, subject to Article 4(5), communicate to Europol all the information which it may require for the performance of its tasks under Article 3(1), point

2. The Member States shall communicate such data only where processing thereof for the purposes of preventing, analysing or combating offences is also authorized by their national law. Depending on their degree of sensitivity, data from national units may be routed directly and by whatever means may be appropriate to the analysis groups, whether via the liaison officers concerned or not.

4. If, in addition to the data referred to in paragraph 3, it would seem justified for Europol to have other information for the performance of tasks under Article 3(1), point 2, Europol may request that:

   1) the European Communities and bodies governed by public law established under the Treaties establishing those Communities;

   2) other bodies governed by public law established in the framework of the European Union;

   3) bodies which are based on an agreement between two or more Member States of the European Union;

   4) third States;

   5) international organizations and their subordinate bodies governed by public law;

   6) other bodies governed by public law which are based on an agreement between two or more States, and

   7) the International Criminal Police Organization, forward the relevant information to it by whatever means may be appropriate. It may also, under the same conditions and by the same means, accept information provided by those various bodies on their own initiative. The Council, acting unanimously in accordance with the procedure laid down in Title VI of the Treaty on European Union and after consulting the Management Board, shall draw up the rules to be observed by Europol in this respect.

5. Insofar as Europol is entitled under other Conventions to gain computerized access to data from other information systems, Europol may retrieve personal data by such means if this is necessary for the performance of its tasks pursuant to Article 3(1), point 2.

6. If an analysis is of a general nature and of a strategic type, all Member States, through liaison officers and/or experts, shall be fully associated in the findings thereof, in particular through the communication of reports drawn up by Europol. If the analysis bears on specific cases not concerning all Member States and has a direct operational aim, representatives of the following Member States shall participate therein:

   1) Member States which were the source of the information giving rise to the decision to open the analysis file, or those which are directly concerned by that information and Member States subsequently invited by the analysis group to take part in the analysis because they are also becoming concerned;

2) Member States which learn from consulting the index system that they need to be informed and assert that need to know under the conditions laid down in paragraph 7.

7. The need to be informed may be claimed by authorized liaison officers. Each Member State shall nominate and authorize a limited number of such liaison officers. It shall forward the list thereof to the Management Board. A liaison officer shall claim the need to be informed as defined in paragraph 6 by means of a written reasoned statement approved by the authority to which he is subordinate in his Member State and forwarded to all the participants in the analysis. He shall then be automatically associated in the analysis in progress. If an objection is raised in the analysis group, automatic association shall be deferred until completion of a conciliation procedure, which may comprise three stages as follows:

1) the participants in the analysis shall endeavour to reach agreement with the liaison officer claiming the need to be informed; they shall have no more than eight days for that purpose;

2) if no agreement is reached, the heads of the national units concerned and the Directorate of Europol shall meet within three days;

3) if the disagreement persists, the representatives of the parties concerned on the Management Board shall meet within eight days. If the Member State concerned does not waive its need to be informed, automatic association of that Member State shall be decided by consensus.

8. The Member State communicating an item of data to Europol shall be the sole judge of the degree of its sensitivity and variations thereof. Any dissemination or operational use of analysis data shall be decided on in consultation with the participants in the analysis. A Member State joining an analysis in progress may not, in particular, disseminate or use the data without the prior agreement of the Member States initially concerned.

ARTICLE 11: INDEX SYSTEM

1. An index system shall be created by Europol for the data stored on the files referred to in Article 10(1).

2. The Director, Deputy Directors and duly empowered officials of Europol and liaison officers shall have the right to consult the index system. The index system shall be such that it is clear to the liaison officer consulting it, from the data being consulted, that the files referred to in Article 6(1), point 2 and Article 10(1) contain data concerning the seconding Member State. Access by liaison officers shall be defined in such a way that it is possible to determine whether or not an item of information is stored, but that it is not possible to establish connections or further conclusions regarding the content of the files.

3. The detailed procedures for the design of the index system shall be defined by the Management Board acting unanimously.

ARTICLE 12: ORDER OPENING A DATA FILE

1. For every computerized data file containing personal data operated by Europol for the purpose of performing its tasks referred to in Article 10, Europol shall specify in an order opening the file, which shall require the approval of the Management Board:
    1)   the file name;
    2)   the purpose of the file;
    3)   the groups of persons on whom data are stored;
    4)   the nature of the data to be stored, and any of the data listed in the first sentence of Article 6 of the Council of Europe Convention of 28 January 1981 which are strictly necessary;
    5)   the type of personal data used to open the file;
    6)   the supply or input of the data to be stored;
    7)   the conditions under which the personal data stored in the file may be communicated, to which recipients and under what procedure;
    8)   the time-limits for examination and duration of storage;
    9)   the method of establishing the audit log. The joint supervisory body provided for in Article 24 shall immediately be advised by the Director of Europol of the plan to order the opening of such a data file and shall receive the dossier so that it may address any comments it deems necessary to the Management Board.

2. If the urgency of the matter is such as to preclude obtaining the approval of the Management Board as required under paragraph 1, the Director, on his own initiative or at the request of the Member States concerned, may by a reasoned decision, order the opening of a data file. At the same time he shall inform the members of the Management Board of his decision. The procedure pursuant to paragraph 1 shall then be set in motion without delay and completed as soon as possible.

TITLE IV: COMMON PROVISIONS ON INFORMATION PROCESSING

ARTICLE 13: DUTY TO NOTIFY

Europol shall promptly notify the national units and also their liaison officers if the national units so request, of any information concerning their Member State and of connections identified between criminal offences for which Europol is competent under Article 2. Information and intelligence concerning other serious criminal offences, of which Europol becomes aware in the course of its duties, may also be communicated.

ARTICLE 14: STANDARD OF DATA PROTECTION

1. By the time of the entry into force of this Convention at the latest, each Member State shall, under its national legislation, take the necessary measures in relation to the processing of personal data in data files in the framework of this Convention to ensure a standard of data protection which at least corresponds to the standard resulting from the implementation of the principles of the Council of Europe Convention of 28 January 1981, and, in doing so, shall take account of Recommendation No R(87) 15 of the Committee of Ministers of the Council of Europe of 17 September 1987 concerning the use of personal data in the police sector.

2. The communication of personal data provided for in this Convention may not begin until the data protection rules laid down in paragraph 1 above have entered into force on the territory of each of the Member States involved in such communication.

3. In the collection, processing and utilization of personal data Europol shall take account of the principles of the Council of Europe Convention of 28 January 1981 and of Recommendation No R(87) 15 of the Committee of Ministers of the Council of Europe of 17 September 1987. Europol shall also observe these principles in respect of non-automated data held in the form of data files, i.e. any structured set of personal data accessible in accordance with specific criteria.

ARTICLE 15: RESPONSIBILITY IN DATA PROTECTION MATTERS

1. Subject to other provisions in this Convention, the responsibility for data stored at Europol, in particular as regards the legality of the collection, the transmission to Europol and the input of data, as well as their accuracy, their up-to-date nature and verification of the storage time-limits, shall lie with:
    1) the Member State which input or otherwise communicated the data;
    2) Europol in respect of data communicated to Europol by third parties or which result from analyses conducted by Europol.

2. In addition, subject to other provisions in this Convention, Europol shall be responsible for all data received by Europol and processed by it, whether such data be in the information system referred to in Article 8, in the data files opened for the purposes of analysis referred to in Article 10, or in the index system referred to in Article 11, or in the data files referred to in Article 14(3).

3. Europol shall store data in such a way that it can be established by which Member State or third party the data were transmitted or whether they are the result of an analysis by Europol.

ARTICLE 16: PROVISIONS ON THE DRAWING UP OF REPORTS

On average, Europol shall draw up reports for at least one in ten retrievals of personal data—and for each retrieval made within the information system referred to in Article 7—in order to check whether they are permissible under law. The data contained in the reports shall only be used for that purpose by Europol and the supervisory bodies referred to in Articles 23 and 24 and shall be deleted after six months, unless the data are further required for ongoing control. The details shall be decided upon by the Management Board following consultation with the joint supervisory body.

ARTICLE 17: RULES ON THE USE OF DATA

1. Personal data retrieved from the information system, the index system or data files opened for the purposes of analysis and data communicated by any other appropriate means, may be transmitted or utilized only by the competent authorities of the Member States in order to prevent and combat crimes falling within the competence of Europol and to combat other serious forms of crime. The data referred to in the first paragraph shall be utilized in compliance with the law of the Member State responsible for the authorities which utilized the data. Europol may utilize the data referred to in paragraph 1 only for the performance of its tasks as referred to in Article 3.

2. If, in the case of certain data, the communicating Member State or the communicating third State or third body as referred to in Article 10(4) stipulates particular restrictions on use to which such data is subject in that Member State or by third parties, such restrictions shall also be complied with by the user of the data except in the specific case where national law lays down that the restrictions on use be waived for judicial authorities, legislative bodies or any other independent body set up under the law and made responsible for supervising the national competent authorities within the meaning of Article 2(4). In such cases, the data may only be used after prior consultation of the communicating Member State whose interests and opinions must be taken into account as far as possible.

3. Use of the data for other purposes or by authorities other than those referred to in Article 2 of this Convention shall be possible only after prior consultation of the Member State which transmitted the data insofar as the national law of that Member State permits.

ARTICLE 18: COMMUNICATION OF DATA TO THIRD STATES AND THIRD BODIES

1. Europol may under the conditions laid down in paragraph 4 communicate personal data which it holds to third states and third bodies within the meaning of Article 10(4), where:
    1)   this is necessary in individual cases for the purposes of preventing or combating criminal offences for which Europol is competent under Article 2;
    2)   an adequate level of data protection is ensured in that State or that body, and
    3)   this is permissible under the general rules within the meaning of paragraph 2.

2. In accordance with the procedure in Title VI of the Treaty on European Union, and taking into account the circumstances referred to in paragraph 3, the Council, acting unanimously, shall determine the general rules for the communication of personal data by Europol to the third States and third bodies within the meaning of Article 10(4). The Management Board shall prepare the Council decision and consult the joint supervisory body referred to in Article 24.

3. The adequacy of the level of data protection afforded by third States and third bodies within the meaning of Article 10(4) shall be assessed taking into account all the circumstances which play a part in the communication of personal data; in particular, the following shall be taken into account:
    1)   the nature of the data;
    2)   the purpose for which the data is intended;
    3)   the duration of the intended processing, and
    4)   the general or specific provisions applying to the third States and third bodies within the meaning of Article 10(4).

4. If the data referred to have been communicated to Europol by a Member State, Europol may communicate them to third States and third bodies only with the Member State's consent. The Member State may give its prior consent, in general or other terms, to such communication; that consent may be withdrawn at any time. If the data have not been communicated by a Member State, Europol shall satisfy itself that communication of those data is not liable to:
    1)   obstruct the proper performance of the tasks falling within a Member State's sphere of competence;
    2)   jeopardize the security and public order of a Member State or otherwise prejudice its general welfare.

5. Europol shall be responsible for the legality of the authorizing communication. Europol shall keep a record of communications of data and of the grounds for such communications. The communication of data shall be authorized only if the recipient gives an undertaking that the data will be used only for the purpose for which it was communicated. This shall not apply to the communication of personal data required for a Europol inquiry.

6. Where the communication provided for in paragraph 1 concerns information subject to the requirement of confidentiality, it shall be permissible only insofar as an agreement on confidentiality exists between Europol and the recipient.

ARTICLE 19: RIGHT OF ACCESS

1. Any individual wishing to exercise his right of access to data relating to him which have been stored within Europol or to have such data checked may make a request to that effect free of charge to the national competent authority in any Member State he wishes, and that authority shall refer it to Europol without delay and inform the enquirer that Europol will reply to him directly.

2. The request must be fully dealt with by Europol within three months following its receipt by the national competent authority of the Member State concerned.

3. The right of any individual to have access to data relating to him or to have such data checked shall be exercised in accordance with the law of the Member State where the right is claimed, taking into account the following provisions: Where the law of the Member State applied to provides for a communication concerning data, such communication shall be refused if such refusal is necessary to:
   1) enable Europol to fulfil its duties properly;
   2) protect security and public order in the Member States or to prevent crime;
   3) protect the rights and freedoms of third parties, considerations which it follows cannot be overridden by the interests of the person concerned by the communication of the information.

4. The right to communication of information in accordance with paragraph 3 shall be exercised according to the following procedures:
   1) as regards data entered within the information system defined in Article 8, a decision to communicate such data cannot be taken unless the Member State which entered the data and the Member States directly concerned by communication of such data have first had the opportunity of stating their position, which may extend to

a refusal to communicate the data. The data which may be communicated and the arrangements for communicating such data shall be indicated by the Member State which entered the data;

2) as regards data entered within the information system by Europol, the Member States directly concerned by communication of such data must first have had the opportunity of stating their position, which may extend to a refusal to communicate the data;

3) as regards data entered within the work files for the purposes of analysis as defined in Article 10, the communication of such data shall be conditional upon the consensus of Europol and the Member States participating in the analysis, within the meaning of Article 10(2), and the consensus of the Member State(s) directly concerned by the communication of such data. Should one or more Member State or Europol have objected to a communication concerning data, Europol shall notify the person concerned that it has carried out the checks, without giving any information which might reveal to him whether or not he is known.

5. The right to the checking of information shall be exercised in accordance with the following procedures: Where the national law applicable makes no provision for a communication concerning data or in the case of a simple request for a check, Europol, in close cooperation with the national authorities concerned, shall carry out the checks and notify the enquirer that it has done so without giving any information which might reveal to him whether or not he is known.

6. In its reply to a request for a check or for access to data, Europol shall inform the enquirer that he may appeal to the joint supervisory body if he is not satisfied with the decision. The latter may also refer the matter to the joint supervisory body if there has been no response to his request within the time-limits laid down in this Article.

7. If the enquirer lodges an appeal to the joint supervisory body provided for in Article 24, the appeal shall be examined by that body. Where the appeal relates to a communication concerning data entered by a Member State in the information system, the joint supervisory body shall take its decision in accordance with the national law of the Member State in which the application was made. The joint supervisory body shall first consult the national supervisory body or the competent judicial body in the Member State which was the source of the data. Either national body shall make the necessary checks, in particular to establish whether the decision to refuse was taken in accordance with paragraphs 3 and 4(1) of this Article. On confirmation of that, the decision, which may extend to a refusal to communicate any information, shall be taken by the joint supervisory body in close cooperation with the national supervisory body or competent judicial body.

Where the appeal relates to a communication concerning data entered by Europol in the information system or data stored in the work files for the purposes of analysis, the joint supervisory body, in the event of persistent objections from Europol or a Member State, may not overrule such objections unless by a majority of two-thirds of its members after having heard Europol or the Member State concerned. If there is no such majority, the joint supervisory body shall notify the enquirer that it has carried out the checks, without giving any information which might reveal to him whether or not he is known.

Where the appeal concerns the checking of data entered by a Member State in the information system, the joint supervisory body shall ensure that the necessary checks have been carried out correctly in close cooperation with the national supervisory body of the Member State which entered the data. The joint supervisory body shall notify the enquirer that it has carried out the checks, without giving any information which might reveal to him whether or not he is known.

Where the appeal concerns the checking of data entered by Europol in the information system or of data stored in the work files for the purposes of analysis, the joint supervisory body shall ensure that the necessary checks have been carried out by Europol. The joint supervisory body shall notify the enquirer that it has carried out the checks, without giving any information which might reveal to him whether or not he is known.

8. The above provisions shall apply mutatis mutandis to non-automated data held by Europol in the form of data files, i.e. any structured set of personal data accessible in accordance with specific criteria.

ARTICLE 20: CORRECTION AND DELETION OF DATA

1. If it emerges that data held by Europol which have been communicated to it by third States or third bodies or which are the result of its own analyses are incorrect or that their input or storage contravenes this Convention, Europol shall correct or delete such data.

2. If data that are incorrect or that contravene this Convention have been passed directly to Europol by Member States, they shall be obliged to correct or delete them in collaboration with Europol. If incorrect data are transmitted by another appropriate means or if the errors in the data supplied by Member States are due to faulty transmission or have been transmitted in breach of the provisions of this Convention or if they result from their being entered, taken over or stored in an incorrect manner or in breach of the provisions of this Convention by Europol, Europol shall be obliged to correct them or delete them in collaboration with the Member States concerned.

3. In the cases referred to in paragraphs 1 and 2, the Member States which are recipients of the data shall be notified forthwith. The recipient Member States shall also correct or delete those data.

4. Any person shall have the right to ask Europol to correct or delete incorrect data concerning him. Europol shall inform the enquirer that data concerning him have been corrected or deleted. If the enquirer is not satisfied with Europol's reply or if he has received no reply within three months, he may refer the matter to the joint supervisory body.

ARTICLE 21: TIME LIMITS FOR THE STORAGE AND DELETION OF DATA FILES

1. Data in data files shall be held by Europol only for as long as is necessary for the performance of its tasks. The need for continued storage shall be reviewed no later than three years after the input of data. Review of data stored in the information system and its deletion shall be carried out by the inputting unit. Review of data stored in other Europol data files and their deletion shall be carried out by Europol. Europol shall automatically inform the Member States three months in advance of the expiry of the time limits for reviewing the storage of data.

2. During the review, the units referred to in the third and fourth sentences of paragraph 1 above may decide on continued storage of data until the next review if this is still necessary for the performance of Europol's tasks. If no decision is taken on the continued storage of data, those data shall automatically be deleted.

3. Storage of personal data relating to individuals as referred to in point 1 of the first subparagraph of Article 10(1) may not exceed a total of three years. Each time limit shall begin to run afresh on the date on which an event leading to the storage of data relating to that individual occurs. The need for continued storage shall be reviewed annually and the review documented.

4. Where a Member State deletes from its national data files data communicated to Europol which are stored in other Europol data files, it shall inform Europol accordingly. In such cases, Europol shall delete the data unless it has further interest in them, based on intelligence that is more extensive than that possessed by the communicating Member State. Europol shall inform the Member State concerned of the continued storage of such data.

5. Deletion shall not occur if it would damage the interests of the data subject which require protection. In such cases, the data may be used only with the consent of the data subject.

ARTICLE 22: CORRECTION AND STORAGE OF DATA IN PAPER FILES

1. If it emerges that an entire paper file or data included in that file held by Europol are no longer necessary for the performance of Europol's tasks, or if the information concerned is overall in contravention of this Convention, the paper file or data concerned shall be destroyed. The paper file or data concerned must be marked as not for use until they have been effectively destroyed.

   Destruction may not take place if there are grounds for assuming that the legitimate interests of the data subject would otherwise be prejudiced. In such cases, the paper file must bear the same note prohibiting all use.

2. If it emerges that data contained in the Europol paper files are incorrect, Europol shall be obliged to correct them.

3. Any person covered by a Europol paper file may claim the right vis-à-vis Europol to c correction or destruction of paper files or the inclusion of a note. Article 20(4) and Article 24(2) and (7) shall be applicable.

ARTICLE 23: NATIONAL SUPERVISORY BODY

1. Each Member State shall designate a national supervisory body, the task of which shall be to monitor independently, in accordance with its respective national law, the permissibility of the input, the retrieval and any communication to Europol of personal data by the Member State concerned and to examine whether this violates the rights of the data subject. For this purpose, the supervisory body shall have access at the national unit or at the liaison officers' premises to the data entered by the Member State in the information system and in the index system in accordance with the relevant national procedures.

   For their supervisory purposes, national supervisory bodies shall have access to the offices and documents of their respective liaison officers at Europol.

   In addition, in accordance with the relevant national procedures, the national supervisory bodies shall supervise the activities of national units under Article 4(4) and the activities of liaison officers under Article 5(3), points 1 and 3 and Article 5(4) and (5), insofar as such activities are of relevance to the protection of personal data.

1. Each individual shall have the right to request the national supervisory body to ensure that the entry or communication of data concerning him to Europol in any form and the consultation of the data by the Member State concerned are lawful. This right shall be exercised in accordance with the national law of the Member State to the national supervisory body of which the request is made.

ARTICLE 24: JOINT SUPERVISORY BODY

1. An independent joint supervisory body shall be set up, which shall have the task of reviewing, in accordance with this Convention, the activities of Europol in order to ensure that the rights of the individual are not violated by the storage, processing and utilization of the data held by Europol. In addition, the joint supervisory body shall monitor the permissibility of the transmission of data originating from Europol. The joint supervisory body shall be composed of not more than two members or representatives (where appropriate assisted by alternates) of each of the national supervisory bodies guaranteed to be independent and having the necessary abilities, and appointed for five years by each Member State. Each delegation shall be entitled to one vote. The joint supervisory body shall appoint a chairman from among its members. In the performance of their duties, the members of the joint supervisory body shall not receive instructions from any other body.

2. Europol must assist the joint supervisory body in the performance of the latter's tasks. In doing so, it shall, in particular:
   1) supply the information it requests, give it access to all documents and paper files as well as access to the data stored in the system, and
   2) allow it free access at any time to all its premises.
   3) carry out the joint supervisory body's decisions on appeals in accordance with the provisions of Articles 19(7) and 20(4).

3. The joint supervisory body shall also be competent for the examination of questions relating to implementation and interpretation in connection with Europol's activities as regards the processing and utilization of personal data, for the examination of questions relating to checks carried out independently by the national supervisory bodies of the Member States or relating to the exercise of the right to information, as well as for drawing up harmonized proposals for common solutions to existing problems.

4. Each individual shall have the right to request the joint supervisory body to ensure that the manner in which his personal data have been collected, stored, processed and utilized by Europol is lawful and accurate.

5. If the joint supervisory body notes any violations of the provisions of this Convention in the storage, processing or utilization of personal data, it shall make any complaints it deems necessary to the Director of Europol and shall request him to reply within a time limit to be determined by it. The Director shall keep the Management Board informed of the entire procedure. In the event of any difficulty, the joint supervisory body shall refer the matter to the Management Board.

6. The joint supervisory body shall draw up activity reports at regular intervals. In accordance with the procedure laid down in Title VI of the Treaty

on European Union, these shall be forwarded to the Council; the Management Board shall first have the opportunity to deliver an opinion, which shall be attached to the reports. The joint supervisory body shall decide whether or not to publish its activity report, and, if it decides to do so, determine how it should be published.

7. The joint supervisory body shall unanimously adopt its rules of procedure, which shall be submitted for the unanimous approval of the Council. It shall set up internally a committee comprising one qualified representative from each Member State with entitlement to a vote. The committee shall have the task of examining the appeals provided for in Articles 19(7) and 20(4) by all appropriate means. Should they so request, the parties, assisted by their advisers if they so wish, shall be heard by the committee. The decisions taken in this context shall be final as regards all the parties concerned.

8. It may also set up one or more other committees.

9. It shall be consulted on that part of the budget which concerns it. Its opinion shall be annexed to the draft budget in question.

10. It shall be assisted by a secretariat, the tasks of which shall be defined in the rules of procedure.

ARTICLE 25: DATA SECURITY

1. Europol shall take the necessary technical and organizational measures to ensure the implementation of this Convention. Measures shall only be necessary where the effort they involve is proportionate to the objective they are designed to achieve in terms of protection.

2. In respect of automated data processing at Europol each Member State and Europol shall implement measures designed to:
    1) deny unauthorized persons access to data processing equipment used for processing personal data (equipment access control);
    2) prevent the unauthorized reading, copying, modification or removal of data media (data media control);
    3) prevent the unauthorized input of data and the unauthorized inspection, modification or deletion of stored personal data (storage control);
    4) prevent the use of automated data processing systems by unauthorized persons using data communication equipment (user control);
    5) ensure that persons authorized to use an automated data processing system only have access to the data covered by their access authorization (data access control);
    6) ensure that it is possible to verify and establish to which bodies personal data may be transmitted using data communication equipment (communication control);

7) ensure that it is subsequently possible to verify and establish which personal data have been input into automated data processing systems and when and by whom the data were input (input control);

8) prevent unauthorized reading, copying, modification or deletion of personal data during transfers of personal data or during transportation of data media (transport control);

9) ensure that installed systems may, in case of interruption, be immediately restored (recovery);

10) ensure that the functions of the system perform without fault, that the appearance of faults in the functions is immediately reported (reliability) and that stored data cannot be corrupted by means of a malfunctioning of the system (integrity).

TITLE V: LEGAL STATUS, ORGANIZATION AND FINANCIAL PROVISIONS

ARTICLE 26: LEGAL CAPACITY

1. Europol shall have legal personality.

2. Europol shall enjoy in each Member State the most extensive legal and contractual capacity available to legal persons under that State's law. Europol may in particular acquire and dispose of movable or immovable property and be a party to legal proceedings.

3. Europol shall be empowered to conclude a headquarters agreement with the Kingdom of the Netherlands and to conclude with third States and third bodies within the meaning of Article 10(4) the necessary confidentiality agreements pursuant to Article 18(6) as well as other arrangements in the framework of the rules laid down unanimously by the Council on the basis of this Convention and of Title VI of the Treaty on European Union.

ARTICLE 27: ORGANS OF EUROPOL

The organs of Europol shall be:
1) the Management Board;
2) the Director;
3) the Financial Controller;
4) the Financial Committee.

ARTICLE 28: MANAGEMENT BOARD

1. Europol shall have a Management Board. The Management Board:

1) shall take part in the extension of Europol's objective (Article 2(2));
2) shall define unanimously liaison officers' rights and obligations towards Europol (Article 5);
3) shall decide unanimously on the number of liaison officers the Member States may send to Europol (Article 5);
4) shall prepare the implementing rules governing data files (Article 10);
5) shall take part in the adoption of rules governing Europol's relations with third States and third bodies within the meaning of Article 10(4) (Articles 10, 18 and 42);
6) shall unanimously decide on details concerning the design of the index system (Article 11);
7) shall approve by a two-thirds majority orders opening data files (Article 12);
8) may deliver opinions on the comments and reports of the joint supervisory body (Article 24);
9) shall examine problems which the joint supervisory body brings to is attention (Article 24(5));
10) shall decide on the details of the procedure for checking the legal character of retrievals in the information system (Article 16);
11) shall take part in the appointment and dismissal of the Director and Deputy Directors (Article 29);
12) shall oversee the proper performance of the Director's duties (Articles 7 and 29);
13) shall take part in the adoption of staff regulations (Article 30);
14) shall take part in the preparation of agreements on confidentiality and the adoption of provisions on the protection of confidentiality (Articles 18 and 31);
15) shall take part in the drawing up of the budget, including the establishment plan, the auditing and the discharge to be given to the Director (Articles 35 and 36);
16) shall adopt unanimously the five-year financing plan (Article 35);
17) shall appoint unanimously the financial controller and oversee the performance of his duties (Article 35);
18) shall take part in the adoption of the financial regulation (Article 35);
19) shall unanimously approve the conclusion of the headquarters agreement (Article 37);
20) shall adopt unanimously the rules for the security clearance of Europol officials;
21) shall act by a two-thirds majority in disputes between a Member State and Europol or between Member States concerning compensation paid under the liability for unauthorized or incorrect processing of data (Article 38);

22) shall take part in any amendment of this Convention (Article 43);

23) shall be responsible for any other tasks assigned to it by the Council particularly in provisions for the implementation of this Convention.

2. The Management Board shall be composed of one representative of each Member State. Each member of the Management Board shall have one vote.

3. Each member of the Management Board may be represented by an alternate member; in the absence of the full member, the alternate member may exercise his right to vote.

4. The Commission of the European Communities shall be invited to attend meetings of the Management Board with non-voting status. However, the Management Board may decide to meet without the Commission representative.

5. The members or alternate members shall be entitled to be accompanied and advised by experts from their respective Member States at meetings of the Management Board.

6. The Management Board shall be chaired by the representative of the Member State holding the Presidency of the Council.

7. The Management Board shall unanimously adopt its rules of procedure.

8. Abstentions shall not prevent the Management Board from adopting decisions which must be taken unanimously.

9. The Management Board shall meet at least twice a year.

10. The Management Board shall adopt unanimously each year:

    1) a general report on Europol's activities during the previous year;

    2) a report on Europol's future activities taking into account Member States' operational requirements and budgetary and staffing implications for Europol. These reports shall be submitted to the Council in accordance with the procedure laid down in Title VI of the Treaty on European Union.

ARTICLE 29: DIRECTOR

1. Europol shall be headed by a Director appointed by the Council, acting unanimously in accordance with the procedure laid down in Title VI of the Treaty on European Union after obtaining the opinion of the Management Board, for a four-year period renewable once.

2. The Director shall be assisted by a number of Deputy Directors as determined by the Council and appointed for a four-year period renewable once, in accordance with the procedure laid down in paragraph 1. Their tasks shall be defined in greater detail by the Director.

3. The Director shall be responsible for:
   1) performance of the tasks assigned to Europol;
   2) day-to-day administration;
   3) personnel management;
   4) proper preparation and implementation of the Management Board's decisions;
   5) preparing the draft budget, draft establishment plan and draft five-year financing plan and implementing Europol's budget;
   6) all other tasks assigned to him in this Convention or by the Management Board.

4. The Director shall be accountable to the Management Board in respect of the performance of his duties. He shall attend its meetings.

5. The Director shall be Europol's legal representative.

6. The Director and the Deputy Directors may be dismissed by a decision of the Council, to be taken in accordance with the procedure laid down in Title VI of the Treaty on European Union by a two-thirds majority of the Member States, after obtaining the opinion of the Management Board.

7. Notwithstanding paragraphs 1 and 2, the first term of office after entry into force of this Convention shall be five years for the Director, four years for his immediate Deputy and three years for the second Deputy Director.

ARTICLE 30: STAFF

1. The Director, Deputy Directors and the employees of Europol shall be guided in their actions by the objectives and tasks of Europol and shall not take or seek orders from any government, authority, organization or person outside Europol, save as otherwise provided in this Convention and without prejudice to Title VI of the Treaty on European Union.

2. The Director shall be in charge of the Deputy Directors and employees of Europol. He shall engage and dismiss employees. In selecting employees, in addition to having regard to personal suitability and professional qualifications, he shall take into account the need to ensure the adequate representation of nationals of all Member States and of the official languages of the European Union.

3. Detailed arrangements shall be laid down in staff regulations which the Council shall, after obtaining the opinion of the Management Board, adopt unanimously in accordance with the procedure laid down in Title VI of the Treaty on European Union.

ARTICLE 31: CONFIDENTIALITY

1. Europol and the Member States shall take appropriate measures to protect information subject to the requirement of confidentiality which is obtained by or exchanged with Europol on the basis of this Convention. To this end the Council shall unanimously adopt appropriate rules on confidentiality prepared by the Management Board and submitted to the Council in accordance with the procedure laid down in Title VI of the Treaty on European Union.

2. Where Europol has entrusted persons with a sensitive activity, Member States shall undertake to arrange, at the request of the Director of Europol, for security screening of their own nationals to be carried out in accordance with their national provisions and to provide each other with mutual assistance for the purpose. The relevant authority under national provisions shall inform Europol only of the results of the security screening, which shall be binding on Europol.

3. Each Member State and Europol may entrust with the processing of data at Europol, only those persons who have had special training and undergone security screening.

ARTICLE 32: OBLIGATION OF DISCRETION AND CONFIDENTIALITY

1. Europol organs, their members, the Deputy Directors, employees of Europol and liaison officers shall refrain from any action and any expression of opinion which might be harmful to Europol or prejudice its activities.

2. Europol organs, their members, the Deputy Directors, employees of Europol and liaison officers, as well as any other person under a particular obligation of discretion or confidentiality, shall be bound not to disclose any facts or information which come to their knowledge in the performance of their duties or the exercise of their activities to any unauthorized person or to the public. This shall not apply to facts or information too insignificant to require confidentiality. The obligation of discretion and confidentiality shall apply even after leaving office or employment, or after termination of activities. The particular obligation laid down in the first sentence shall be notified by Europol, and a warning given of the legal consequences of any infringement; a written record shall be drawn up of such notification.

3. Europol organs, their members, the Deputy Directors, employees of Europol and liaison officers, as well as persons under the obligation provided for in paragraph 2, may not give evidence in or outside court or make any statements on any facts or information which come to their

knowledge in the performance of their duties or the exercise of their activities, without reference to the Director or, in the case of the Director himself, to the Management Board.

The Director or Management Board, depending on the case, shall approach the judicial body or any other competent body with a view to taking the necessary measures under the national law applicable to the body approached; such measures may either be to adjust the procedures for giving evidence in order to ensure the confidentiality of the information, or, provided that the national law concerned so permits, to refuse to make any communication concerning data insofar as is vital for the protection of the interests of Europol or of a Member State.

Where a Member State's legislation provides for the right to refuse to give evidence, persons asked to give evidence must obtain permission to do so. Permission shall be granted by the Director and, as regards evidence to be given by the Director, by the Management Board. Where a liaison officer is asked to give evidence concerning information he receives from Europol, such permission shall be given after the agreement of the Member State responsible for the officer concerned has been obtained.

Furthermore, if the possibility exists that the evidence may extend to information and knowledge which a Member State has communicated to Europol or which clearly involve a Member State, the position of that Member State concerning the evidence must be sought before permission is given.

Permission to give evidence may be refused only insofar as this is necessary to protect overriding interests of Europol or of a Member State or States that need protection.

This obligation shall apply even after leaving office or employment or after termination of activities.

4. Each Member State shall treat any infringement of the obligation of discretion or confidentiality laid down in paragraphs 2 and 3 as a breach of the obligations imposed by its law on official or professional secrets or its provisions for the protection of confidential material.

Where appropriate, each Member State shall introduce, no later than the date of entry into force of this Convention, the rules under national law or the provisions required to proceed against breaches of the obligations of discretion or confidentiality referred to in paragraphs 2 and 3. It shall ensure that the rules and provisions concerned apply also to its own employees who have contact with Europol in the course of their work.

ARTICLE 33: LANGUAGES

1. Reports and all other papers and documentation placed before the Management Board shall be submitted in all official languages of the European Union; the working languages of the Management Board shall be the official languages of the European Union.

2. The translations required for Europol's work shall be provided by the translation centre of the European Union institutions.

ARTICLE 34: INFORMING THE EUROPEAN PARLIAMENT

1. The Council Presidency shall each year forward a special report to the European Parliament on the work of Europol. The European Parliament shall be consulted should this Convention be amended in any way.

2. The Council Presidency or its representative appointed by the Presidency shall, with respect to the European Parliament, take into account the obligations of discretion and confidentiality.

3. The obligations laid down in this Article shall be without prejudice to the rights of national parliaments, to Article K.6 of the Treaty on European Union and to the general principles applicable to relations with the European Parliament pursuant to Title VI of the Treaty on European Union.

ARTICLE 35: BUDGET

1. Estimates shall be drawn up of all of Europol's income and expenditure including all costs of the joint supervisory body and of the secretariat set up by it under Article 22 for each financial year and these items entered in the budget; an establishment plan shall be appended to the budget. The financial year shall begin on 1 January and end on 31 December.

   The income and expenditure shown in the budget shall be in balance. A five-year financing plan shall be drawn up together with the budget.

2. The budget shall be financed from Member States' contributions and by other incidental income. Each Member State's financial contribution shall be determined according to the proportion of its gross national product to the sum total of the gross national products of the Member States for the year preceding the year in which the budget is drawn up. For the purposes of this paragraph, "gross national product" shall mean gross national product as determined in accordance with Council Directive 89/130/EEC, Euratom of 13 February 1989 on the harmonization of the compilation of gross national product at market prices.

3. By 31 March each year at the latest, the Director shall draw up the draft budget and draft establishment plan for the following financial year and

shall submit them, after examination by the Financial Committee, to the Management Board together with the draft five-year financing plan.

4. The Management Board shall take a decision on the five-year financing plan. It shall act unanimously.

5. After obtaining the opinion of the Management Board, the Council shall, in accordance with the procedure laid down in Title VI of the Treaty on European Union, adopt Europol's budget by 30 June of the year preceding the financial year at the latest. It shall act unanimously. The adoption of the budget by the Council shall entail the obligation for each Member State to make available promptly the financial contribution due from it .

6. The Director shall implement the budget in accordance with the financial regulation provided for in paragraph 9.

7. Monitoring of the commitment and disbursement of expenditure and of the establishment and collection of income shall be carried out by a financial controller from an official audit body of one of the Member States who shall be appointed by the Management Board, acting unanimously, and shall be accountable to it. The financial regulation may make provision for ex-post monitoring by the financial controller in the case of certain items of income or expenditure.

8. The Financial Committee shall be composed of one budgetary representative from each Member State. Its task shall be to prepare for discussions on budgetary and financial matters.

9. The Council shall, in accordance with the procedure laid down in Title VI of the Treaty on European Union, unanimously adopt the financial regulation, specifying in particular the detailed rules for drawing up, amending and implementing the budget and for monitoring its implementation as well as for the manner of payment of financial contributions by the Member States.

ARTICLE 36: AUDITING

1. The accounts in respect of all income and expenditure entered in the budget together with the balance sheet showing Europol's assets and liabilities shall be subject to an annual audit in accordance with the financial regulation. For this purpose the Director shall submit a report on the annual accounts by 31 May of the following year at the latest.

2. The audit shall be carried out by a joint audit committee composed of three members, appointed by the Court of Auditors of the European Communities on a proposal from its President. The term of office of the members shall be three years; these shall alternate in such a way that each

year the member who has been on the audit committee for three years shall be replaced. Notwithstanding the provisions of the second sentence, the term of office of the member that, after drawing lots:
— is first, shall be two years;
— is second, shall be three years;
— is third, shall be four years, in the initial composition of the joint audit committee after Europol has begun to operate. Any costs arising from the audit shall be charged to the budget provided for in Article 35.

3. The joint audit committee shall in accordance with the procedure laid down in Title VI of the Treaty on European Union submit to the Council an audit report on the annual accounts; prior thereto the Director and Financial Controller shall be given an opportunity to express an opinion on the audit report and the report shall be discussed by the Management Board.

4. The Europol Director shall provide the members of the joint audit committee with all information and every assistance which they require in order to perform their task.

5. A decision on the discharge to be given to the Director in respect of budget implementation for the financial year in question shall be taken by the Council, after examination of the report on the annual accounts.

6. The detailed rules for performing audits shall be laid down in the Financial Regulation.

ARTICLE 37: HEADQUARTERS AGREEMENT

The necessary arrangements concerning the accommodation to be provided for Europol in the headquarters State and the facilities to be made available by that State as well as the particular rules applicable in the Europol headquarters State to members of Europol's organs, its Deputy Directors, employees and members of their families shall be laid down in a headquarters agreement between Europol and the Kingdom of the Netherlands to be concluded after obtaining the unanimous approval of the Management Board.

TITLE VI: LIABILITY AND LEGAL PROTECTION

ARTICLE 38: LIABILITY FOR UNAUTHORIZED OR INCORRECT DATA PROCESSING

1. Each Member State shall be liable, in accordance with its national law, for any damage caused to an individual as a result of legal or factual errors in data stored or processed at Europol. Only the Member State in which the

event which gave rise to the damage occurred may be the subject of an action for compensation on the part of the injured party, who shall apply to the courts having jurisdiction under the national law of the Member State involved. A Member State may not plead that another Member State had transmitted inaccurate data in order to avoid its liability under its national legislation vis-à-vis an injured party.

2. If these legal or factual errors occurred as a result of data erroneously communicated or of failure to comply with the obligations laid down in this Convention on the part of one or more Member States or as a result of unauthorized or incorrect storage or processing by Europol, Europol or the other Member State in question shall be bound to repay, on request, the amounts paid as compensation unless the data were used by the Member State in the territory of which the damage was caused in breach of this Convention.

3. Any dispute between that Member State and Europol or another Member State over the principle or amount of the repayment must be referred to the Management Board, which shall settle the matter by a two-thirds majority.

ARTICLE 39: OTHER LIABILITY

1. Europol's contractual liability shall be governed by the law applicable to the contract in question.

2. In the case of non-contractual liability, Europol shall be obliged, independently of any liability under Article 38, to make good any damage caused through the fault of its organs, of its Deputy Directors or of its employees in the performance of their duties, insofar as it may be imputed to them and regardless of the different procedures for claiming damages which exist under the law of the Member States.

3. The injured party shall have the right to demand that Europol refrain from or drop any action.

4. The national courts of the Member States competent to deal with disputes involving Europol's liability as referred to in this Article shall be determined by reference to the relevant provisions of the Brussels Convention of 27 September 1968 on Jurisdiction and the Enforcement of Judgments in Civil and Commercial Matters, as later amended by Accession Agreements.

ARTICLE 40: SETTLEMENT OF DISPUTES

1. Disputes between Member States on the interpretation or application of this Convention shall in an initial stage be discussed by the Council in

accordance with the procedure set out in Title VI of the Treaty on European Union with the aim of finding a settlement.

2. When such disputes are not so settled within six months, the Member States who are parties to the dispute shall decide, by agreement among themselves, the modalities according to which they shall be settled.

3. The provisions on appeals referred to in the rules relating to the conditions of employment applicable to temporary and auxiliary staff of the European Communities shall apply, mutatis mutandis, to Europol staff.

ARTICLE 41: PRIVILEGES AND IMMUNITIES

1. Europol, the members of its organs and the Deputy Directors and employees of Europol shall enjoy the privileges and immunities necessary for the performance of their tasks in accordance with a Protocol setting out the rules to be applied in all Member States.

2. The Kingdom of the Netherlands and the other Member States shall agree in the same terms that liaison officers seconded from the other Member States as well as members of their families shall enjoy those privileges and immunities necessary for the proper performance of the tasks of the liaison officers at Europol.

3. The Protocol referred to in paragraph 1 shall be adopted by the Council acting unanimously in accordance with the procedure laid down in Title VI of the Treaty on European Union and approved by the Member States in accordance with their respective constitutional requirements.

TITLE VII: FINAL PROVISIONS

ARTICLE 42: RELATIONS WITH THIRD STATES AND THIRD BODIES

1. Insofar as is relevant for the performance of the tasks described in Article 3, Europol shall establish and maintain cooperative relations with third bodies within the meaning of Article 10(4), points 1 to 3. The Management Board shall unanimously draw up rules governing such relations. This provision shall be without prejudice to Article 10(4) and (5) and Article 18(2); exchanges of personal data shall take place only in accordance with the provisions of Titles II to IV of this Convention.

2. Insofar as is required for the performance of the tasks described in Article 3, Europol may also establish and maintain relations with third States and third bodies within the meaning of Article 10(4), points 4, 5, 6 and 7. Having obtained the opinion of the Management Board, the Council, acting unanimously in accordance with the procedure laid down in Title

VI of the Treaty on European Union, shall draw up rules governing the relations referred to in the first sentence. The third sentence of paragraph 1 shall apply mutatis mutandis.

ARTICLE 43: AMENDMENT OF THE CONVENTION

1. In accordance with the procedure laid down in Title VI of the Treaty on European Union, the Council, acting on a proposal from a Member State and, after consulting the Management Board, shall unanimously decide, within the framework of Article K.1(9) of the Treaty on European Union, on any amendments to this Convention which it shall recommend to the Member States for adoption in accordance with their respective constitutional requirements.

2. The amendments shall enter into force in accordance with Article 45(2) of this Convention.

3. However, the Council, acting unanimously in accordance with the procedure laid down in Title VI of the Treaty on European Union, may decide, on the initiative of a Member State and after the Management Board has discussed the matter, to amplify, amend or supplement the definitions of forms of crime contained in the Annex. It may in addition decide to introduce new definitions of the forms of crime listed in the Annex.

4. The Secretary-General of the Council of the European Union shall notify all Member States of the date of entry into force of the amendments.

ARTICLE 44: RESERVATIONS

Reservations shall not be permissible in respect of this Convention.

ARTICLE 45: ENTRY INTO FORCE

1. This Convention shall be subject to adoption by the Member States in accordance with their respective constitutional requirements.

2. Member States shall notify the depositary of the completion of their constitutional requirements for adopting this Convention.

3. This Convention shall enter into force on the first day of the month following the expiry of a three-month period after the notification, referred to in paragraph 2, by the Member State which, being a member of the European Union on the date of adoption by the Council of the act drawing up this Convention, is the last to fulfil that formality.

4. Without prejudice to paragraph 2, Europol shall not take up its activities under this Convention until the last of the acts provided for in Articles 5(7), 10(1), 24(7), 30(3), 31(1), 35(9), 37 and 41(1) and (2) enters into force.

5. When Europol takes up its activities, the activities of the Europol Drugs Unit under the joint action concerning the Europol Drugs Unit of 10 March 1995 shall come to an end. At the same time, all equipment financed from the Europol Drugs Unit joint budget, developed or produced by the Europol Drugs Unit or placed at its disposal free of charge by the headquarters State for its permanent use, together with that Unit's entire archives and independently administered data files shall become the property of Europol.

6. Once the Council has adopted the act drawing up this Convention, Member States, acting either individually or in common, shall take all preparatory measures under their national law which are necessary for the commencement of Europol activities.

ARTICLE 46: ACCESSION BY NEW MEMBER STATES

1. This Convention shall be open to accession by any State that becomes a member of the European Union.

2. The text of this Convention in the language of the acceding State, drawn up by the Council of the European Union, shall be authentic.

3. Instruments of accession shall be deposited with the depositary.

4. This Convention shall enter into force with respect to any State that accedes to it on the first day of the month following expiry of a three-month period following the date of deposit of its instrument of accession or on the date of entry into force of the Convention if it has not already entered into force at the time of expiry of the said period.

ARTICLE 47: DEPOSITARY

1. The Secretary-General of the Council of the European Union shall act as depositary of this Convention.

2. The depositary shall publish in the Official Journal of the European Communities the notifications, instruments or communications concerning this Convention.

IN WITNESS WHEREOF the undersigned Plenipotentiaries have signed this Convention.

DONE at Brussels, this twenty-sixth day of July in the year one thousand nine hundred and ninety-five, in a single original in the Danish, Dutch, English, Finnish, French, German, Greek, Irish, Italian, Portuguese, Spanish and Swedish languages, each text being equally authentic; it shall be deposited with the Secretary-General of the Council of the European Union, which shall transmit a certified copy to each of the Member States.

ANNEX REFERRED TO IN ARTICLE 2

List of other serious forms of international crime which Europol could deal with in addition to those already provided for in Article 2(2) in compliance with Europol's objective as set out in Article 2(1).

Against life, limb or personal freedom:
— murder, grievous bodily injury—illicit trade in human organs and tissue—kidnapping, illegal restraint and hostage-taking—racism and xenophobia Against property or public goods including fraud:
— organized robbery—illicit trafficking in cultural goods, including antiquities and works of art—swindling and fraud—racketeering and extortion—counterfeiting and product piracy—forgery of administrative documents and trafficking therein—forgery of money and means of payment—computer crime—corruption illegal trading and harm to the environment:
— illicit trafficking in arms, ammunition and explosives—illicit trafficking in endangered animal species—illicit trafficking in endangered plant species and varieties—environmental crime—illicit trafficking in hormonal substances and other growth promoters.

In addition, in accordance with Article 2(2), the act of instructing Europol to deal with one of the forms of crime listed above implies that it is also competent to deal with the related money-laundering activities and the related criminal offences.

With regard to the forms of crime listed in Article 2(2) for the purposes of this Convention:
— "crime connected with nuclear and radioactive substances" means the criminal offences listed in Article 7(1) of the Convention on the Physical Protection of Nuclear Material, signed at Vienna and New York on 3 March 1980, and relating to the nuclear and/or radioactive materials defined in Article 197 of the Euratom Treaty and Directive 80/836 Euratom of 15 July 1980;
— "illegal immigrant smuggling" means activities intended deliberately to facilitate, for financial gain, the entry into, residence or employment in the territory of the Member States of the European Union, contrary to the rules and conditions applicable in the Member States;
— "traffic in human beings" means subjection of a person to the real and illegal sway of other persons by using violence or menaces or by abuse of authority or intrigue with a view to the exploitation of prostitution, forms of sexual exploitation and assault of minors or trade in abandoned children;
— "motor vehicle crime" means the theft or misappropriation of motor vehicles, lorries, semi-trailers, the loads of lorries or semi-trailers,

buses, motorcycles, caravans and agricultural vehicles, works vehicles, and the spare parts for such vehicles, and the receiving and concealing of such objects;

— "illegal money-laundering activities" means the criminal offences listed in Article 6(1) to (3) of the Council of Europe Convention on Laundering, Search, Seizure and Confiscation of the Proceeds from Crime, signed at Strasbourg on 8 November 1990. The forms of crime referred to in Article 2 and in this Annex shall be assessed by the competent national authorities in accordance with the national law of the Member States to which they belong.

DECLARATIONS

Re Article 10(1) of the Convention "The Federal Republic of Germany and the Republic of Austria will continue to ensure that the following principle is affirmed when drafting the implementing provisions concerning Article 10(1):

Data on persons referred to in point 1 of the first sentence of Article 10(1), other than those listed in Article 8(2) and (3) may be stored only if there are reasons to suspect, because of the nature of the act or of its perpetration, or any other intelligence, that criminal proceedings need to be taken against such persons for criminal offences for which Europol is competent under Article 2."

Re Article 14(1) and (3), Article 15(2) and Article 19(8) of the Convention

1. "The Federal Republic of Germany, the Republic of Austria and the Kingdom of the Netherlands will transmit data under this Convention on the understanding that, for the non-automated processing and use of such data, Europol and the Member States will comply with the spirit of the data protection provisions of this Convention."

2. "The Council declares that, having regard to Articles 14(1) and (3), 15(2) and 19(8) of the Convention, with regard to compliance with the level of protection of data exchanged between Member States and Europol in the case of non-automated data processing, Europol will—three years after its inception and with the participation of the joint supervisory authority and national control authorities each acting within its sphere of competence—draw up a report, which will be submitted to the Council for examination after consideration by the Management Board."

Article 40(2)

"The following Member States agree that in such cases they will systematically submit the dispute in question to the Court of Justice of the European Communities:
— Kingdom of Belgium—Kingdom of Denmark—Federal Republic of Germany—Hellenic Republic—Kingdom of Spain—French Republic—Ireland—Italian Republic—Grand Duchy of Luxembourg—Kingdom of the Netherlands—Republic of Austria—Portuguese Republic—Republic of Finland—Kingdom of Sweden".

Article 42

"The Council declares that Europol should as a matter of priority establish relations with the competent bodies of those States with which the European Communities and their Member States have established a structured dialogue."

DOCUMENT NO 9

Title VI of The Treaty on European Union: Provisions on Cooperation in the Fields of Justice and Home Affairs as Amended by the Treaty of Amsterdam

October 2, 1997

ARTICLE K

Cooperation in the fields of justice and home affairs shall be governed by the following provisions.

ARTICLE K.1

For the purposes of achieving the objectives of the Union, in particular the free movement of persons, and without prejudice to the powers of the European Community, Member States shall regard the following areas as matters of common interest:

1. asylum policy;
2. rules governing the crossing by persons of the external borders of the Member States and the exercise of controls thereon;
3. immigration policy and policy regarding nationals of third countries; (a) conditions of entry and movement by nationals of third countries on the territory of Member States;
    (b) conditions of residence by nationals of third countries on the territory of Member States, including family reunion and access to employment;
    (c) combatting unauthorized immigration, residence and work by nationals of third countries on the territory of Member States;
4. combating drug addiction in so far as this is not covered by 7 to 9;
5. combating fraud on an international scale in so far as this is not covered by 7 to 9;
6. judicial cooperation in civil matters;
7. judicial cooperation in criminal matters;

8. customs cooperation;

9. police cooperation for the purposes of preventing and combating terrorism, unlawful drug trafficking and other serious forms of international crime, including if necessary certain aspects of customs cooperation, in connection with the organization of a Union-wide system for exchanging information within a European Police Office (Europol).

ARTICLE K.2

1. The matters referred to in Article K.1 shall be dealt with in compliance with the European Convention for the Protection of Human Rights and Fundamental Freedoms of 4 November 1950 and the Convention relating to the Status of Refugees of 28 July 1951 and having regard to the protection afforded by Member States to persons persecuted on political grounds.

2. This Title shall not affect the exercise of the responsibilities incumbent upon Member States with regard to the maintenance of law and order and the safeguarding of internal security.

ARTICLE K.3

1. In the areas referred to in Article K.1, Member States shall inform and consult one another within the Council with a view to coordinating their action. To that end, they shall establish collaboration between the relevant departments of their administrations.

2. The Council may:
    *   on the initiative of any Member State of the Commission, in the areas referred to in Article K.1(1) to (6);
    *   on the initiative of any Member State, in the areas referred to Article K1(7) to (9):
        (a) adopt joint positions and promote, using the appropriate form and procedures, any cooperation contributing to the pursuit of the objectives of the Union;
        (b) adopt joint action in so far as the objectives of the Union can be attained better by joint action than by the Member States acting individually on account of the scale or effects of the action envisaged; it may decide that measures implementing joint action are to be adopted by a qualified majority;
        (c) without prejudice to Article 220 of the Treaty establishing the European Community, draw up conventions which it shall recommend to the Member States for adoption in accordance with their respective constitutional requirements. Unless otherwise

provided by such conventions, measures implementing them shall be adopted within the Council by a majority of two-thirds of the High Contracting Parties. Such conventions may stipulate that the Court of Justice shall have jurisdiction to interpret their provisions and to rule on any disputes regarding their application, in accordance with such arrangements as they may lay down.

ARTICLE K.4

1. A Coordinating Committee shall be set up consisting of senior officials. In additions to its coordinating role, it shall be the task of the Committee to;
   * give opinions for the attention of the Council, either at the Councils request or on its own initiative.
   * contribute, without prejudice to Article 151 of the Treaty establishing the European Community, to the preparation of the Council's discussions in the areas referred to in Article K.1 and, in accordance with the conditions laid down in Article 100d of the Treaty establishing the European Community, in the areas referred to in Article 100c of that Treaty.

2. The Commission shall be fully associated with the work in the areas referred to in this Title.

3. The Council shall act unanimously, except on matters of procedure and in cases where Article K.3 expressly provides for other voting rules. Where the Council is required to act by a qualified majority, the votes of its members shall be weighted as laid down in Article 148(2) of the Treaty establishing the European Community, and for their adoption, acts of the Council shall require at least fifty-four votes in favour, cast by at least eight members.

ARTICLE K.5

Within international organizations and at international conferences in which they take part, Member States shall defend the common positions adopted under the provisions of this Title.

ARTICLE K.6

The Presidency and the Commission shall regularly inform the European Parliament of discussions in the areas covered by this Title.

The Presidency shall consult the European Parliament on the principal aspects of activities in the areas referred to in this Title and shall ensure that the views of the European Parliament are duly taken into consideration.

The European Parliament may ask questions of the Council or make recommendations to it. Each year, it shall hold a debate on the progress made in implementation of the areas referred to in this Title.

ARTICLE K.7

The provisions of this Title shall not prevent the establishment or development of closer cooperation between two or more Member States in so far as such cooperation does not conflict with, or impede, that provided for in this Title.

ARTICLE K.8

1. The provisions referred to in Article 137,138,139 top 142, 146, 147, 150 to 153, 157 to 163 and 217 of the Treaty establishing the European Community shall apply to the provisions relating to the areas referred to in this Title.

2. Administrative expenditure which the provisions relating to the areas referred to in this Title entail for the institutions shall be charged to the budget of European Communities. The Council may also:
    *   either decide unanimously that operational expenditure to which the implementation of those provisions gives rise is to be charged to the budget of the European Communities; in that event, the budgetary procedure laid down in the treaty establishing the European Community shall be applicable;
    *   or determine that such expenditure shall be charged to the Member States, where appropriate in accordance with a scale to be decided.

ARTICLE K.9

The Council, acting unanimously on the initiative of the Commission or a Member State, may decide to apply Article 100c of the Treaty establishing the European Community to action in areas referred to in Article K.1(1) to (6), and at the same time determine the relevant voting conditions relating to it. It shall recommend the Member States to adopt that decision in accordance with their respective constitutional requirements.

COURT CASES

The Queen on the Application of the Secretary of State for the Home Department -V- Immigration Appeal Tribunal (Co/2090/01)

v

The Queen on the Application of Hwez -V- Secretary of State for the Home Department & An Adjudicator (Co/2405/01)

In the Supreme Court of Judicature Queen's Bench Division

December 19, 2001
(Edited Text)

Lord Justice SCHIEMANN:

1. This is the judgment of the Court.

2. In February of last year there landed at an airport in the United Kingdom an aeroplane which had been hijacked on an internal flight in Afghanistan. On board were a number of passengers who sought leave to enter the United Kingdom on the basis that they were refugees and thus entitled to the protection of the Refugee Convention. Their claim to be refugees was rejected by the Secretary of State for the Home Department and they were refused leave to enter. They appealed to a panel of adjudicators who dismissed their appeals. They appealed to the Immigration Appeal Tribunal ("IAT") which decided to adjourn their appeals indefinitely. Before the

court is an application by the Secretary of State for judicial review of that decision to adjourn. He submits that the IAT should have decided the cases one way or another. Broadly speaking his application, which strictly only relates to one of the passengers, no. 19, is supported by all those whose appeals have been adjourned.

3. The facts were unusual in that, although he refused leave to enter, the Secretary of State neither initiated removal or granted nor granted exceptional leave to remain. He chose a middle course. He indicated that he intended to remove the passengers when circumstances permitted but had instructed the immigration officers not to set directions for their removal until he had given further consideration to wider issues.

4. The appeals were pursuant to section 8(1) of the Asylum and Immigration Appeals Act 1993 ("the 1993 Act). The section was repealed by the Immigration and Asylum Act 1999 ("the 1999 Act") but continues to apply to the present appeal. It provides

    "A person who is refused leave to enter the UK under the 1971 Act may appeal against that refusal to an adjudicator on the ground that his removal in consequence of the refusal would be contrary to the [Refugee] Convention."

5. The IAT adjourned the hearing of the appeals despite the wishes of all concerned that the hearings should proceed. It did so because of the view it formed of the task of an appellate tribunal hearing an appeal under section 8(1) in the light of the decision of this court in *Massaquoi v Secretary of State for the Home Department* [2001] Imm AR 309.

6. The IAT relied on two separate strands of reasoning to support its conclusion. The first is set out in subparagraphs 1–7 below and the second in sub-paragraphs 8–13.

    a. In *Massaquoi* the Court of Appeal clearly rejected the submission that the IAT could deal with asylum status if there was to be no deportation.

    b. That principle applies if there is a grant of Exceptional Leave to Remain ("ELR") following a refusal of leave since the refusal then disappears.

    c. Therefore the appellate authority is not concerned to determine status where there is not a continuing refusal of leave to enter

    d. It follows that the supposed advantages, whether to the appellants or to the respondent, of having a decision whether or not an appellant is a refugee cannot weigh in deciding whether these appeals should go ahead.

    e. Since the right of appeal, albeit against the immigration decision to refuse leave to enter, is based on the obligation not to "refoule" contrary to Article 33, it follows that if there is to be no removal the appeal becomes academic.

f.   In the present case the evidence indicated that the Secretary of State did intend to remove at some point. In those circumstances, since the appellant would, once removal directions were given, have no further right to appeal, it would be unfair to the refugee claimant to dismiss his appeal now.

g.   Since the IAT was not empowered to consider an appeal limited to status and since it would be unfair to dismiss the appeal at present the appeal should be adjourned.

h.   A person refused leave to enter is not lawfully in the territory of the United Kingdom: see *In re Musisi* [1987] A.C.514. A person refused leave to enter is thus, even if he be a refugee, not protected by Article 32 of the Convention, and his being required to leave the United Kingdom is not of itself capable of amounting to a breach of Convention. His 'removal in consequence of the refusal' of leave to enter will be in breach of the Convention if, and (for present purposes) only if, it contravenes Article 33.

i.   A claimant who is able to establish (by reference to his country of nationality) that he is a refugee within the definition of Article 1A (2) is therefore not necessarily protected from removal from the United Kingdom. If he is not here lawfully, he is protected only from removal to a place where he would be at risk either of persecution or of refoulement to another place where he would be at risk of persecution. In order to succeed in an appeal, an appellant under section 8 (1) needs to establish that his removal 'in consequence of the refusal' of leave to enter would be removal to such a place. If he is not in a position to do that, it cannot make any difference whether he is able or unable to establish that he is a refugee.

j.   An appellant cannot be expected to deal with the effect of all possible removal directions. He is entitled to be told, clearly, what is the case that he needs to establish. Until he is told, clearly and irrevocably, the destination to which his removal is envisaged, it is not fair to expect him to argue his case against removal.

k.   It was wrong on the facts to assume that Afghanistan would be the country to which the Afghanis would be removed.

l.   The appellant's task in these proceedings as they stand is impossible. If he cannot establish that (if he were a refugee) his removal would contravene Article 33, then the question whether he is a refugee is immaterial to the outcome of the appeal. But it would be grossly unfair, while the respondent declines to specify the place to which he is to be removed, to require him to establish that the place is a place to which he cannot be removed in compliance with the

Convention. On the other hand, to allow him simply to establish that he is a refugee, regardless of any actual or proposed removal, would be an excess of jurisdiction as it would be an appeal not within section 8 of 1993 Act.

m.   It follows that, while the projected removal destination remains open, it is not possible for this appeal to be determined justly or effectively. The Tribunal therefore adjourned the appeal until such time as the proposed removal destination was indicated by the Secretary of State .

7.   The IAT was represented before us by Miss Dinah Rose who made it clear that, as one might expect, the tribunal was not pressing for any particular interpretation of the legislation. She supported the reasoning which we have set out in the preceding paragraph although she laid more emphasis on the first strand than on the second.

8.   We were sitting as a division of the Court of Appeal in *Osorio and others v Secretary of State for the Home Department* when the present application to the Administrative Court was drawn to our attention. It was suggested that the Secretary of State was arguing two incompatible positions in the two cases. It was clear that in any event the two cases covered very much the same ground and, having reserved our judgement in *Osorio*, we decided to sit as the Administrative Court and hear the submissions in the present case before delivering judgement in *Osorio*. The parties in *Osorio* were invited to be represented at the hearing of the present case and to advance any further argument should they be so minded in the light of the submissions in the present case. We then reserved judgement in the present case.

9.   We express our indebtedness to the careful argument of Mr John Howell, Q.C. who appeared on behalf of the Secretary of State in the present case. He put forward the following submissions.

a.   A person may appeal against a refusal of leave to enter on the ground that his removal in consequence of the refusal *would be* contrary to the United Kingdom's obligations under the Refugee Convention. If his removal would be contrary to those obligations, his appeal is entitled to succeed even if the Secretary of State has no current ability or intention to remove him. By contrast, his removal would not be contrary to the Convention if he is not a refugee. Accordingly his appeal must be dismissed if he is not a refugee. However, if he is a refugee, his removal to a country in respect of which he is a refugee would generally be contrary to the Convention. Accordingly, in such a case, if the Secretary of State does not indicate another country ('a third country') to which a refugee can be removed without infringing Article 33 of the Refugee Convention, the refugee's appeal should be allowed. If the Secretary of State does indicate a third country, however, then the appellant must show that his removal to that country would be contrary to the United Kingdom's obligation under the Convention.

b. In this case, therefore, if no. 19 is not a refugee (as the panel of adjudicators held), his appeal should be dismissed. However, if he is a refugee then, since the Secretary of State had not indicated any third country to which he could be removed, no. 19's appeal should be allowed. There was thus no reason for any adjournment.

c. The IAT's approach of adjourning the cases *sine die* benefits those claimants who are not refugees, whose appeals should be dismissed, and penalises any claimant who may be a refugee by postponing the determination of his appeal unnecessarily.

d. When a person makes a claim for asylum he may not know whether the Secretary of State is able, or intends, to remove him either (a) to a country in relation to which he claims to be a refugee or (b) to any other country. But that does not mean that he cannot make a claim for asylum. To make good his claim to asylum a person must first show that he is a refugee. Admittedly, his asylum claim also necessarily contains the assertion that there is no safe third country to which he can be removed. But the Secretary of State accepts that, if a refugee's asylum claim is to be rejected, the onus is on the Secretary of State to indicate to which third country the claimant can be removed. It would then be for the claimant to show that his removal to that country would be contrary to the Convention. It would be unreasonable to expect, and Parliament cannot have intended, that a refugee must also prove when making a claim for asylum that he would not be admitted to, or that his life and liberty would be threatened in, each and every other country in the world.

e. If the IAT were correct, however, a claim for asylum would have to be refused if the Secretary of State had no current ability and intention to remove an asylum claimant, since the claimant could not establish his claim. The claimant's appeal against any consequent refusal of leave to enter would have to be dismissed since the claimant could not establish his ground of appeal. But, as the IAT recognised, the claimant would have no further right to appeal a subsequent decision based on the original refusal of leave to enter. Accordingly, on the IAT's reasoning, a claim for asylum and an appeal by a person whom the Secretary of State wrongly considered was not a refugee could fail, and that person could be subsequently removed, without having his appeal that his removal would be in breach of the United Kingdom's obligations considered on the merits. Such a result cannot have been intended by Parliament.

f. Since leave to enter had been refused in the present cases, *Massaquoi* was distinguishable and there was jurisdiction to hear the appeals. The IAT should have first considered whether the claimants were refugees—only once it is determined that the claimant is a refugee can the question arise whether it would be in breach of the United Kingdom's obligations under the Convention to remove him in consequence of the refusal of leave. The IAT should have dismissed their appeals if they were not refugees in the IAT's view. If however the IAT took the view that they were refugees then, in the absence of any indication by the Secretary of State of an appropriate safe third country the tribunal should have allowed the appeal and not adjourned it.

g. To suggest that before an appeal can be effective there must be removal directions is to fly in the face of paragraph 28 of the Second Schedule to the Immigration Act 1971 which provides that pending an appeal any removal directions shall be of no effect.

10. It is apparent from our judgment in *Osorio* that the Immigration Appeal Tribunal in the present case took an understandable but in our view erroneous view of the scope of the decision in *Massaquoi*. For the reasons which we there set out, that case should not be regarded as authority for the proposition that an appellate authority has no jurisdiction to hear an appeal under section 8(1) once ELR has been granted. Once there has been a refusal of leave to enter then the refugee claimant has a right under that subsection to appeal and that right is not taken away by any subsequent grant of ELR still less by a statement by the Secretary of State that he has no intention to remove him in the immediate future.

11. In the light of our reasoning in *Osorio* we accept the submissions of the Secretary of State in the present case. On that basis the injustice against which the Immigration Appeal Tribunal was rightly trying to guard is avoided. The refugee claimant is entitled to have the question, whether or not he is a refugee determined by the appellate authorities. In these circumstances the argument in favour of adjourning the case indefinitely disappears.

12. We therefore grant the Secretary of State's application for judicial review and quash the decision of the IAT adjourning no. 19's appeal. As we understand it, all parties agree that in those circumstances the appropriate relief is that the decision of the IAT to adjourn be quashed and the matter be remitted to the IAT. We think that is the right course to follow.

13. We also add by way of postscript that we heard some argument in the case of Mr. Hwez but it was agreed that that case should be adjourned for reconsideration in the light of our decision on this application.

DOCUMENT NO 11

The Queen on the Application Of Louis Farrakhan

v

Secretary of State for the Home Department
Court of Appeal

April 30, 2002
(Edited Text)

This is the judgment of the Court

Introduction

1. Louis Farrakhan is a United States citizen who is based in Chicago. He is an African-American. He is the spiritual leader of the Nation of Islam, a religious, social and political movement whose aims include 'the regeneration of black self-esteem, dignity and self discipline.' A branch of the Nation of Islam has been established in the United Kingdom. Mr Farrakhan has long been anxious to come to address his followers in this country and they have been keen to receive a visit from him. Thus far, he has never been permitted to enter the country. This appeal concerns the most recent decision of the Secretary of State for the Home Department refusing him admission.

2. That decision was contained in a letter dated 20 November 2000. The reasons given for excluding Mr Farrakhan included the following:

    "[He] has given close attention to the current tensions in the Middle East and to the potential impact on community relations in the United Kingdom. He has concluded that a visit to the United Kingdom by [Mr Farrakhan], or the lifting of his exclusion generally, would at the present time pose an unwelcome and significant threat to community relations and in particular to relations between the Muslim and Jewish communities here and a potential threat to public order for that reason. Further, the Home Secretary remains concerned that the profile of [Mr Farrakhan's] visit would create a risk of public disorder at those meetings."

3. Mr Farrakhan applied to Turner J. for an order quashing the decision of the Secretary of State. His application succeeded. In a judgment dated 1 October 2001 Turner J. held that the Secretary of State was required to demonstrate objective justification for excluding Mr Farrakhan from this country and that this he had failed to do.

4. The Secretary of State applied to Sedley L.J. for permission to appeal to this Court. Sedley L.J. granted his application, but in his reasons indicated that he did not consider that the appeal had a realistic prospect of success. The reason that he gave permission to appeal was because the issues raised by this case would be relevant on the next occasion that Mr Farrakhan applied to enter this country. As to these, Sedley L.J. commented:

"There is no issue about the primacy of the Home Secretary's judgment; nor about the need for it to be within the law. The main issues in my view are:
a. To what extent Art.16 limits the applicability of Art. 10 to the Home Secretary's exercise of his power to exclude a foreign national from the UK on public good grounds.
b. To what extent the licence for local intolerance given by the Otto Preminger decision ought to affect judicial review of executive decisions in this country. Whatever the answers, the Home Secretary will still have to face up to the exiguousness of the grounds for his decision."

The nature of the challenge

5. Mr Blake, QC, on behalf of Mr Farrakhan, described the challenge made to the decision of the Secretary of State as a 'reasons challenge.' The Secretary of State had explained the policy that he had applied when considering whether Mr Farrakhan should be admitted to this country. He had failed, however, to give the reasons why the application of that policy had led to the exclusion of Mr Farrakhan. The consequence of the quashing of his decision was not that he was obliged to admit Mr Farrakhan, but that, if he decided to continue to exclude him, he would have to provide adequate reasons for so doing.

6. It is correct that the judgment of Turner J. is redolent with statements that the Secretary of State had given inadequate reasons for his decision. But the basis upon which his decision was quashed is encapsulated in the following sentence from paragraph 48 of the judgment:

"The inference which a court is bound to draw in the absence of a sufficiency of justification (reasons) is that there are none which will support the conclusion reached, or decision made, as being properly within the 'discretionary area of judgment.'

7. We do not believe that, under established principles of judicial review, the absence of reasons gives rise to the inference that none exists. Turner J. did not, however, rest on the inference to which he referred. He held, in paragraphs 41 and 42, that it was appropriate to carry out a rigorous review of the 'reasons provided and of the underlying circumstances' in order to decide whether the Secretary of State had reached a conclusion which was not open to a reasonable decision maker. In considering whether there was a basis for the supposition that a likelihood or risk that disorder would occur if Mr Farrakhan were to be admitted to this country, it was necessary to look at the history and at the nature of Mr Farrakhan's teachings.

8. Turner J. performed that exercise and concluded that it had not been shown that there was more than a 'nominal risk' that community relations would be harmed if Mr Farrakhan visited this country. It was on that basis that he ordered that the Secretary of State's decision should be quashed.

9. Turner J's decision was pronounced on 31 July 2001, but his reasoned judgment was handed down on 1 October. The events of September 11 had intervened. We suspect that it was with those events particularly in mind that Turner J., on October 1, emphasised that his judgment had regard to the state of affairs pertaining on 31 July and that nothing in his judgment could prejudge what decision might have been taken if other domestic political or international circumstances had prevailed.

10. Before us Mr Blake emphasised the point, which was plainly correct, that if we were to uphold Turner J's judgment, the Secretary of State would have to consider afresh, in the light of the circumstances prevailing at the time, any renewed application by Mr Farrakhan, to enter this country. The only practical significance of this judgment lies in any guidance that it may afford to the Secretary of State should he have to undertake that task.

The legislative framework.

11. The position of persons seeking to enter this country from abroad is governed by a complex patchwork of statutory rules and regulations. Section 1 of the Immigration Act 1971 empowers the Secretary of State to lay down rules for regulating the entry into the United Kingdom of persons not having a right of abode here, including visitors. Section 3 of that Act provides that a person who is not a British citizen shall not enter the United Kingdom unless given leave to do so in accordance with the provisions of, or made under, the Act.

12. Lengthy Immigration Rules (HC395) have been made pursuant to ss. 1, 3(2) of the 1971 Act. Rule 41 lays down requirements for leave to enter

as a visitor with which Mr Farrakhan would have complied. Rule 320(6) provides, however, that grounds for refusing leave to enter include:

"Where the Secretary of State has personally directed that the exclusion of a person from the United Kingdom is conducive to the public good."

13. Section 59 of the Immigration and Asylum Act 1999 makes provision for an appeal to an adjudicator against the refusal of leave to enter the United Kingdom. Section 60(9) of that Act provides, however, that:

"Section 59 does not entitle a person to appeal against a refusal of leave to enter, or against a refusal of an entry clearance, if—

(a) the Secretary of State certifies that directions have been given by the Secretary of State (and not by a person acting under his authority) for the appellant not to be given entry to the United Kingdom on the ground that his exclusion is conducive to the public good; or

(b) the leave to enter, or entry clearance, was refused in compliance with any such directions."

The history of the exclusion of Mr Farrakhan

14. Mr Farrakhan is a charismatic and a controversial figure. On various occasions, none of which was later than 1998, his public pronouncements in the United States embraced accusations, in extreme language, that those who had been guilty of exploiting the black people included wealthy Jews. More recently he has emphasised the need for black people to establish self-esteem, dignity and self-discipline.

15. On 16 January 1986, the then Home Secretary, Mr Douglas Hurd, gave his personal direction that Mr Farrakhan should be excluded from the United Kingdom on the ground that his presence would not be conducive to the public good. He expressed the belief that Mr Farrakhan's public statements in the United States gave reasonable cause to believe that, if he came to the United Kingdom, he would be likely to cause racial dishar-mony and possibly commit the offence of inciting racial hatred.

16. No attempt to challenge Mr Farrakhan's exclusion appears to have been made until 1997. In September of that year the late Mr Bernie Grant MP invited Mr Jack Straw, who was then Home Secretary, to reconsider Mr Farrakhan's continued exclusion. Mr Straw replied on the 30 October 1997 as follows:

"As in all cases where individuals have been excluded from the United Kingdom the need for Mr Farrakhan's continued exclusion is the subject of regular review. The most recent review was carried out in July this year at an official level. Other Government Departments were consulted and all representations made, whether they were in support of Mr Farrakhan's admission or against it, were taken into consideration at the time. My

Department were advised at the time that it was possible that some of Mr Farrakhan's public statements could, if repeated in the United Kingdom, contravene the Public Order Act 1996. It was concluded that the threat Mr Farrakhan posed to the maintenance of racial harmony in the United Kingdom remained. The exclusion was therefore maintained.

In the light of your letter I have decided personally to conduct a full review of the decision. The exclusion will stand until I have reached a final conclusion, and you will understand that my review of this case does not in any way pre-empt the final conclusion I may reach.

The balance between the need to preserve the freedom of speech and the undesirability of giving a platform here to those espousing views which would be deeply offensive to the public or large sections of the community is, of course, a very delicate one."

17. On 9 June 1998, while Mr Straw's review was in progress, the British Vice-Consul in Chicago wrote to Mr Farrakhan, inviting him to sign an undertaking. The letter stated that this document, once signed, would be submitted to the Secretary of State for a final decision on Mr Farrakhan's exclusion. Mr Farrakhan signed the undertaking, which was in the following terms:

"I understand that Britain is a diverse multi-cultural society which places a high value on the maintenance of good relations between the different communities. I confirm that I would not engage in conduct during any visit which would jeopardise those good relations.

In particular I will ensure that I do not say anything during any visit which would vilify any group within the United Kingdom or which would otherwise incite discord in the community. I understand that the long standing right to freedom of speech which is enjoyed in Britain must be exercised with due care to the rights of others to live in a society where abusive and threatening behaviour is not tolerated.

I am aware that Britain has legislation which makes it a criminal offence to incite racial hatred. I understand that under the Public Order Act 1986 it is a criminal offence in Great Britain to use threatening, abusive or insulting words or behaviour with the intention or likelihood of thereby stirring up racial hatred. I understand that the same test also applies to the display of written material; the publication or distribution of written material; the distribution, showing or playing of a recording; and the possession of racially inflammatory material. I understand that in this context "racial hatred" means hatred against a group of persons in Great Britain defined by reference to colour, race, nationality (including citizenship) or ethnic or national origins. I understand that similar offences exist in Northern Ireland. During any visit I will abide by this legislation.

I understand that should I breach this undertaking on any visit the question of my exclusion from the United Kingdom at the personal direction of the Secretary of State for the Home Department will be reconsidered."

The Secretary of State has proffered no explanation of why Mr Farrakhan was invited to sign this document.

18. On 29 June there was a highly publicised disturbance outside the building where the Stephen Lawrence Inquiry was being held. Three members of the Nation of Islam were arrested and charged, two with obstructing the police in the execution of their duty and one with affray contrary to the Public Order Act 1986.

19. On 6 July 1998 an official in the Asylum and Appeals Policy Directorate wrote to Mr Farrakhan to inform him that the Secretary of State was minded to maintain his exclusion from the United Kingdom on the grounds that his presence here 'would not be conducive to the public good for reasons of race relations and the maintenance of public order.' Early in the letter the writer explained:

"The Home Secretary is able personally to exclude from the United Kingdom any individual whose presence here would not be conducive to the public good. An individual who holds views which are deeply offensive to large sections of the population would not normally be excluded unless the Home Secretary was also satisfied that that individual posed a threat to the public order here or was likely to commit criminal offences here, in particular under the racial hatred provisions of the Public Order Act 1986."

20. The letter referred to a number of matters considered by the Secretary of State, which weighed in favour of admitting Mr Farrakhan. It also referred to a number of anti-Semitic remarks said to have been made by Mr Farrakhan. It referred to conflicting reactions of two different groups of consultees:

"He has also formally consulted several groups representing the black and Muslim population in the United Kingdom and has considered their views. All these groups expressed the basic sentiment that refusing to allow you into the United Kingdom without any firm evidence that your presence would lead to racial disturbance ran counter to the liberal and tolerant traditions of this country.

. . . .

The Home Secretary has received numerous representations against the lifting of your exclusion from Members of Parliament here and from Jewish representative bodies. They have suggested that your views are bigoted and racially divisive; that they exceed the right to freedom of speech and that the spreading of such views incites anti-Semitism. In the circumstances the Home Secretary considers there is a serious concern that you would, whilst in the United Kingdom, use language which would constitute an offence under the public Order Act 1986 of stirring up racial hatred."

21. The letter then referred to the disturbance at the Stephen Lawrence Inquiry and to a sequel to this:

"The Home Secretary considers that the actions taken at this Inquiry by members of the Nation of Islam undermine your claims that if permitted to enter the United Kingdom you would not come to stir racial or religious tension. Furthermore, the incident gives rise to serious concern that any visit by you would pose a serious threat to public order as a result of the actions taken by Nation of Islam members here and the raising of racial tension."

22. The letter ended with the following provisional decision:

"The Home Secretary accordingly remains of the view that your presence here would be deeply offensive to large sections of the population. He has considered your application with great care, taking account of your representations and your willingness to sign an undertaking. But the issue before him is whether he can be satisfied that the undertaking is sufficient to ensure that the damage to race relations and the risk of serious disorder caused by your presence here is acceptably low. In the light of all the information he has received during the review he cannot be so satisfied and is therefore minded to maintain your exclusion from the United Kingdom."

It invited further representations before a final decision was taken.

23. On 23 July 1999 the Immigration and Nationality Directorate wrote to Mr Farrakhan's solicitors in the following terms:

"This is to inform you that, after very careful consideration of all the circumstances of his case, the Home Secretary has now decided that Mr Farrakhan should continue to be excluded form the United Kingdom. In reaching his decision the Home Secretary took into account, inter alia, the racist and offensive views Mr Farrakhan had expressed whilst in the United States and the threat to public order in the United Kingdom posed by some of his supporters, as evidenced by the behaviour of some members of the Nation of Islam at the Stephen Lawrence Inquiry on 29 June last year.

You asked for details of the review process culminating in the Home Secretary's decision. On 24 November 1997 the Immigration and Nationality Directorate informed Mr Farrakhan that the Home Secretary had decided personally to review his exclusion. Mr Farrakhan was invited to submit representations and the views of a range of groups representing ethnic minority communities were sought. I can confirm that the Home Secretary received and considered views from Mr Farrakhan, his representative, Minister Ava Muhammad and the groups mentioned above. He also received a large number of unsolicited letters from other bodies, members of the public and from Members of Parliament, both for and against maintaining the exclusion. I am afraid that we are not prepared to disclose to you which groups he consulted or the content of the representations they made but I can assure you that the Home Secretary took great care to ensure that a broad range of views was canvassed.

The review process was nearing its completion when the Home Secretary learnt of the events at the Stephen Lawrence Inquiry. On 6 July last year the Immigration and Nationality Directorate wrote to Mr Farrakhan to inform him that the Home Secretary was minded to maintain the decision to exclude him and inviting a further response from Mr Farrakhan. After very careful consideration of the response sent on Mr Farrakhan's behalf by Ms Muhammad and other representations he received over this period, the Home Secretary decided, for the reasons given above, that Mr Farrakhan should continue to be excluded. I am directed to inform you that there is no right of appeal against this decision."

24. This led Mr Farrakhan's solicitors to write, on 25 August, seeking particulars of Mr Farrakhan's "racist and offensive views" and details of the "threat to public order in the United Kingdom" perceived by the Home Secretary. The Directorate replied on 14 October 1999, annexing a schedule of "anti-Semitic and racially divisive views" which Mr Farrakhan was alleged to have expressed. The letter explained:

". . . . the Secretary of State is of the view that a visit to the United Kingdom by Minister Farrakhan poses an unacceptable risk that, as a result of the words and behaviour of the Minster, racial tension will be increased to a point where supporters of the National of Islam would commit public order offences or others would be provoked to commit such offences, as evidenced by the events of 29 July 1998 at the Stephen Lawrence Inquiry, however contrary to the wishes of the Minister this might be."

25. Mr Farrakhan's solicitors replied at great length to this letter on 8 March 2000. They gave details of the seven day visit that Mr Farrakhan wished to make to the United Kingdom. This would include meetings with community leaders and local community groups to promote 'positive, crime-free, drug-free and socially responsible behaviour within the community' and a public speech on 'Atonement, Reconciliation and Responsibility.' The letter addressed the suggestion that the behaviour of members of the Nation of Islam outside the Stephen Lawrence Inquiry was cause for concern, tracing the subsequent prosecution of one member for affray and the vigorous criticism of this course by Otton LJ in the Court of Appeal. The letter contended that apparently offensive comments said to have been made by Mr Farrakhan had been taken out of context and that two

of these had been wrongly attributed to him.

26. We have set out at the beginning of this judgment the most significant passage from the Secretary of State's decision letter of 20 November 2000. Because of the attack that has been made on the adequacy of the reasons given by him, it is right that we should set out the earlier part of that letter:

"The Home Secretary has carried out a personal review of the exclusion, taking into careful account all the circumstances and the points raised in your letters.

He has attached particular weight to the following points which you raise:

(a) Copies of many of Mr Farrakhan's speeches are in free circulation within the United Kingdom and have not been the subject of legal proceedings.

(b) A dialogue between the Nation of Islam and certain Jewish groups has been opened in the USA.

(c) The Nation of Islam has a reputation for advocating social responsibility.

(d) Apart from the incident at the Stephen Lawrence inquiry on 29 June 1998, there is no record of violent disorder associated with the group in the UK.

The Secretary of State has also taken into account, as matters favourable to Mr Farrakhan, the following:

a. Mr Farrakhan is not excluded from any other country.

b. The Secretary of State finds nothing objectionable in Mr Farrakhan's conduct during his visit to Australia, Canada and Israel.

c. Mr Farrakhan has signed assurances as to his behaviour should he be allowed to visit the United Kingdom.

d. Mr Farrakhan's current message of reconciliation.

The Secretary of State has also taken into account that freedom of expression is a fundamental right, recognised both by the common law and by the European Convention on Human rights. It encompasses not only ideas that are favourably received but also those that offend shock or disturb. Any restrictions of this freedom must be prescribed by law and be necessary in a democratic society. And any restrictions must pursue a legitimate aim and be proportionate. It is, however, permissible to impose greater restrictions on the political activity of aliens than of a State's own citizens.

The Home Secretary nevertheless remains satisfied that Mr Farrakhan has expressed anti-Semitic and racially divisive views, notwithstanding the explanations offered in relation to the particular examples in the correspondence. For example, the tenor of the remarks by Mr Farrakhan listed in paragraphs 5 to 9 of the appendix to your letter of 8 March 2000 indicate that Mr Farrakhan apparently believes in an extensive Jewish conspiracy. Further, the Home Secretary is aware that sections of the community, in particular the Jewish community, clearly associate Mr Farrakhan with anti-Semitic views. The Home Secretary does not consider this perception to be without foundation."

The decision of Turner J.

27. Turner J noted that the decision letter referred inferentially to the following Articles of the European Convention on Human Rights:

"Article 10

Freedom of expression

28. Everyone has the right to freedom of expression. This right shall include freedom to hold opinions and to receive and impart information and ideas without interference by public authority and regardless of frontiers. This Article shall not prevent States from requiring the licensing of broadcasting, television or cinema enterprises.

29. The exercise of these freedoms, since it carries with it duties and responsibilities, may be subject to such formalities, conditions, restrictions or penalties as are prescribed by law and are necessary in a democratic society, in the interests of national security, territorial integrity or public safety, for the prevention of disorder or crime, for the protection of health or morals, for the protection of the reputation or rights of others for preventing the disclosure of information received in confidence, or for maintaining the authority and impartiality of the judiciary.

Article 16

Restrictions on political activity of aliens

Nothing in Articles 10, 11 and 14 shall be regarded as preventing the High Contracting Parties from imposing restrictions on the political activity of aliens."

He commented at paragraph 16 that the court had to review the decision in accordance with the approach to review of restrictions on Convention rights and that the question was whether the interference with the right both to impart and to receive information could be justified in a democratic society.

30. Turner J. set out at length the contentions advanced on behalf of Mr Farrakhan. These focussed on Article 10 of the Convention. While it was conceded that this did not, of itself, confer a right of entry on an alien, it was contended that if, as in the case of Mr Farrakhan, the only identifiable reason for maintaining the refusal of entry was restriction of free-

dom of expression, the Home Secretary had to justify that restriction under Article 10.2. Furthermore the freedom of expression that was engaged was not merely that of Mr Farrakhan, but also that of his followers in the United Kingdom who wished to hear what he had to say.

31. For the Home Secretary, Turner J. recorded the concession that freedom of speech could only be restricted if it was necessary in a democratic society, as identified in Article 10.2. It was contended that in the case of an alien seeking to enter the United Kingdom, the Home Secretary retained a broad area of discretion and that Mr Farrakhan had been refused entry into the United Kingdom in the interests of the community in the exercise of proper immigration considerations and his right to freedom of speech could not override these.

32. Turner J. went on to conduct a 'rigorous review' of whether there were reasonable grounds to suppose that admitting Mr Farrakhan to this country would involve a significant risk of civil disorder. The extent of his analysis of the background evidence is apparent from the following list of factors which he considered to be indicative of the context and probable content of the pronouncements that Mr Farrakhan was likely to make:

(a) NOI developed in the United States among the Afro-American communities, which have historically faced discrimination, from among others, Jewish-Americans, who in their turn have also faced discrimination.

(b) The teaching of NOI concerns the need for self-reliance, self-discipline and the observance of religious, as well as national laws. The need to develop responsibility among that part of society which has, or has felt itself to have been culturally or economically disadvantaged.

(c) Disapproval of violence, drugs and crime.

(d) In 1998, a march was organised in Trafalgar Square by NOI in which more than 10,000 people took part. It passed off without incident.

(e) The only recorded incident which might have indicated a propensity to violence or disorder was that at the Stephen Lawrence Inquiry, as to which, see above.

(f) The terms of the first three paragraphs of the undertaking of June 1998, above, the integrity of which have never been the subject of challenge or doubt.

(g) The outline programme contained in section 2 of the claimant's solicitors' letter of application dated 8 March 2000.

(h) The fact that the claimant has been set on a path of reconciliation with Jewish leaders in the United States.

(i) There is no evidence to support the position upon which the Home Secretary relied in July 1998 (bundle p.42) as still applying in 2001.

(j) The fact that the entry was for a limited period and limited purpose.

(k) There was no history of violence or public disorder in relation to any public gathering associated with the Claimant in the United States or elsewhere, including most importantly, Israel.

(l) The mere recital of grounds which might have supported maintenance of the ban on the claimant could not support the Home Secretary's decision which had to demonstrate that he had in fact engaged with the complete circumstances of the application."

33. Turner J. then considered the jurisprudence on the approach to be adopted by the court when reviewing an executive decision that interfered with a fundamental right. He concluded at paragraph 48 that the effect of this was that the terms of the Home Secretary's decision had to demonstrate that he had properly found and identified 'substantial objective justification' for his decision. His conclusions appear in the following passage from paragraph 53 of his judgment:

33. "The claimant is, and only holds himself out to be a Black Muslim. Insofar as his pronouncements have touched upon the relations between Jews and Muslims, they have been so restricted, particularly those in the United States of America. Historically, the claimant's statements relating to Jews were directed in the main to the inequality which existed between Jews and Black Muslims both of whom were and are racial minorities in the United States. The time when those pronouncements were made and which reached a state of great hyperbole and rhetoric has effectively now passed. The contemporary, and undisputed, evidence before the court, and so far as is disclosed in the decision letter also before the Home Secretary, was that in the more recent past the claimant has endeavoured to follow a path of reconciliation between Jews and Black Muslims as well as teaching the latter the virtues of self discipline and respect. Apart from the incident at the Stephen Lawrence Inquiry, which was successfully dealt with by NOI as an internal disciplinary matter, there is no history in this country or abroad of meetings or gatherings of NOI leading to any form of disturbance. Indeed two high profile marches in the United States, to one at least, of which Jews were invited to, and did, take part, passed off without incident. There is a complete absence of evidence before the Court of racial, religious or ethnic tension between the Black Muslim and Jewish communities in the United Kingdom existing at the date of the decision letter. Of course it might be the case that this was due to the policy of exclusion of religious zealots of whom the claimant may be one. But it is in my judgment simply not made out, as it must if the Home Secretary is to be successful in this case, that there was more than a nominal risk that community relations would be likely to be endangered if the ban on the claimant's entry to the United Kingdom for the limited purposes and duration which he has sought were to be relaxed."

Is Article 10 of the Convention engaged?

34. Mr Pannick, QC, who appeared for the Secretary of State before Turner J., had conceded that the facts of the case engaged Article 10 of the Convention. We gave advance warning to Counsel that we wished to hear submissions as to why this was so. This led Miss Carss-Frisk, QC, who appeared for the Secretary of State before us, to submit that Article 10 was not in fact engaged. Mr Farrakhan had been refused entry because his presence in this country was not desirable. In those circumstances Article 10 gave him no right to demand entry in order to exercise his freedom of speech within this country.

35. Before the hearing of this appeal we had entertained doubts as to whether Article 10 was engaged where the authorities of a State refused entry to an alien, even if their sole reason for doing so was that they did not wish him to exercise a freedom to express his opinions within their territory. Article 10 requires the authorities of a State to permit those within its boundaries freely to express their views, even if these are deeply offensive to the majority of the community. It did not seem to us to follow that those authorities should be obliged to allow into the State a person bent on giving its citizens such offence.

36. It is a remarkable fact that almost all the Articles of the Convention which permit, for specified purposes, restrictions on the freedoms that they guarantee, do not include in those purposes the exercise of control of immigration. This strongly suggests to us that those who negotiated the Convention only envisaged that its obligations would apply to the treatment of individuals who were within the territory of the Member State concerned. This impression is enhanced by the fact that, under Article 5.1(f) an exception to the right to liberty is 'the lawful arrest or detention of a person to prevent his effecting an unauthorised entry into the country.' The Convention is, however, a living instrument and, in accordance with the requirement of section 2 of the Human Rights Act 1998, we must have regard to the Strasbourg jurisprudence when considering whether Article 10 imposes obligations in relation to an alien who is seeking admission to a Member State. In this context we should record that, for the purposes of this case, the Secretary of State was prepared to accept that the fact that an individual was neither a citizen of a Member State nor within the territory of a Member State did not, of itself, preclude the application of the Convention. We have proceeded on the basis of that concession without examining whether or not it is correctly made.

37. A similar issue to that with which we are concerned arose in relation to Article 8 of the Convention in Abdulaziz and Others v United Kingdom (1985) 7 EHRR 471. The applicants were women settled in the United Kingdom who complained that their rights to respect for family life were

infringed because their husbands were refused permission to enter in order to join them. The Government argued that Article 8 did not apply to immigration control. Both the Commission and the Court rejected this submission, holding—see paragraph 59—that immigration controls had to be exercised consistently with Convention obligations and the exclusion of a person from a State where members of his family were living might raise an issue under Article 8.

38. The Court observed in the next paragraph that the applicants were not the husbands but the wives, who were complaining not of being refused leave to enter, but as persons lawfully settled in the country of being deprived of the society of their spouses there. However, in paragraph 67 the Court observed:

". . . . in the area now under consideration, the extent of a State's obligation to admit to its territory relatives of settled immigrants will vary according to the particular circumstances of the persons involved. Moreover, the Court cannot ignore that the present case is concerned not only with family life but also with immigration and that, as a matter of well-established international law and subject to its treaty obligations, a State has the right to control the entry of non-nationals into its territory."

39. In Article 8 cases the Court has been reluctant to override decisions taken in the interests of immigration control on the ground that they interfere with respect for family life. The jurisprudence of the Court was accurately summarised by the Commission in Poku v United Kingdom (1996) 22 EHRR CD 94 at CD 97-8, and in particular in the following passage:

"Whether removal or exclusion of a family member from a contracting states [sic] is incompatible with the requirements of article 8 will depend on a number of factors; the extent to which family life is effectively ruptured, whether there are insurmountable obstacles in the way of the family living in the country of origin of one or more of them, whether there are factors of immigration control (eg history of breaches of immigration law) or considerations of public order (eg serious or persistent offences) weighing in favour of exclusion."

40. It is apparent, however, that an immigration decision can bring Article 8 into play. Furthermore, we have no doubt that if a State were to refuse entry with the motive of preventing the enjoyment of family life because, for instance, of a policy of opposing the intermarriage of its citizens with aliens, the Court would hold that Article 8 was infringed.

41. We turn to decisions involving Article 10, of which there are very few. Miss Carss-Frisk relied heavily on the decision of the Commission in Agee v United Kingdom (1976) 7 D & R 164. The Secretary of State had made a deportation order against the applicant, who was a United States citi-

zen, on grounds which included that he had maintained regular contacts harmful to the security of the United Kingdom with foreign intelligence officers. He complained that this infringed a number of his Convention rights, including Article 10. The Commission held that this complaint was manifestly ill-founded, observing at paragraph 19:

"Art 10(1) of the Convention provides inter alia that everyone has the right to freedom of expression and that this right includes freedom 'to receive and impart information and ideas without interference by public authority. . . .'

However, Art 10 does not in itself grant a right of asylum or a right for an alien to stay in a given country. Deportation on security grounds does not therefore as such constitute an interference with the rights guaranteed by Art 10. It follows that an alien's rights under Art 10 are independent of his right to stay in the country and do not protect this latter right. In the present case the applicant has not, whilst in the jurisdiction of the United Kingdom, been subjected to any restrictions on his rights to receive and impart information. Nor has it been shown that the deportation decision in reality constituted a penalty imposed on the applicant for having exercised his rights under Art 10 of the Convention, rather than a proper exercise on security grounds of the discretionary power of deportation reserved to States."

42. We observe that it is implicit in this passage that the Commission might have considered the complaint well-founded if the reason for Mr Agee's deportation had been the manner in which he exercised freedom of speech.

43. Mr Blake submitted that there was a decision of the Court which demonstrated that Article 10 could be engaged in the context of a refusal to permit an alien to enter the territory of a Member State. Piermont v France (19950 20 EHRR 301 involved an application by a German MEP. She entered French Polynesia at a time when an election campaign was in progress at the invitation of the leader of the Liberation Front. She took part in a public meeting and subsequently in a demonstration at which she denounced nuclear testing and the French presence in the Pacific. The High Commissioner made an order expelling her for attacking French policy. She was then excluded from entry to New Caledonia by the High Commissioner for reasons that included his belief that her presence there during an election campaign was likely to cause public disorder. She complained that Article 10 of the Convention was infringed on both occasions, contending that neither lawful entry nor lawful residence was necessary for Article 10 to apply.

44. The French Government sought to rely on Article 16. The Court held that the fact that the applicant was a national of a Member State of the

European Union and a member of the European Parliament meant that Article 16 could not be raised against her.

45. So far as the expulsion from Polynesia was concerned, both the Commission and the Court upheld the applicant's complaint. They held that a fair balance had not been struck between, on the one hand, the public interest requiring the prevention of disorder and territorial integrity and, on the other, the applicant's freedom of expression.

46. So far as the refusal to admit the applicant into New Caledonia was concerned, the view of the Commission differed from that of the Court. The Commission held that the fact that the applicant was unable to exercise certain rights, particularly the right to freedom of expression, in New Caledonia was a consequence of the refusal to allow her to enter the territory, which was a measure that was compatible with the Convention. Accordingly there was no violation of Article 10.

47. The Court was divided 5 to 4. The minority agreed with the Commission. The majority held, however, that:

"The exclusion order made by the High Commissioner of the Republic amounted to an interference with the exercise of the right secured by Article 10 as, having been detained at the airport, the applicant had not been able to come into contact with the politicians who had invited her or to express her ideas on the spot."

48. The Court went on to consider whether the interference with the applicant's freedom of expression was justified. In so doing it simply considered whether the exceptions of necessity in the interests of prevention of disorder or territorial integrity provided for by Article 10.2 justified the interference. It held that they did not as the interference was disproportionate to these legitimate aims.

49. After the hearing of the appeal, we identified two further decisions of the Commission, which we considered to be relevant and we gave the parties the opportunity to make written submissions in relation to these. The first was Swami Omkarananda and the Divine Light Zentrum v Switzerland (1997) 25 D & R 105. The first applicant was an Indian citizen. The second applicant, DLZ, was a religious and philosophical institution that he had helped to found. Disturbances between DLZ and citizens of the Canton of Zurich led the State Council to order his expulsion, an order extended by the Federal authorities to cover all the territory of the State. Before the order was carried out criminal proceedings were instituted against the first applicant which ultimately resulted in his being sentenced to 14 years imprisonment and 15 years expulsion from Swiss territory. He complained that the order for his expulsion infringed, among others, Articles 9, 10 and 11 of the Convention. The Commission ruled his application inadmissible.

50. The following passages of the decision of the Commission are of relevance:

    (a)   . . . This provision does not in itself grant a right for an alien to stay in a given country. Deportation does not therefore as such constitute an interference with the rights guaranteed by Article 9 (see, mutatis mutandis, decision on Application No. 7729/76, Agee v the United Kingdom, Decisions and Reports 7, pp.164, 174), unless it can be established that the measure was designed to repress the exercise of such rights and stifle the spreading of the religion or philosophy of the followers.

    (b)   In the present case, the first applicant has not, whilst in the jurisdiction of Switzerland, been subjected by the authorities to any restriction on his rights to manifest his religion, in particular in teaching and worship. The question has been raised nevertheless whether at the time of the expulsion order complained of there were obvious reasons of public order to justify the measure or whether it must be suspected that the main purpose sought was to remove the source of an unwanted faith and dismantle the group of his followers.

        The Commission notes however that the expulsion order issued by the cantonal authorities and later extended by the Federal authorities to cover all the territory of the State was never carried out. If the first applicant is ever expelled it will be in pursuance of the judgment of the Federal Criminal Court sentencing him to fourteen years' imprisonment and fifteen years' expulsion from Swiss territory.

        Such decision, based on obvious reasons of public order, constitutes an exercise of the discretionary power of deportation reserved to States.

    . . .

    (c)   The above considerations under Article 9 of the Convention also apply to both applicants' claims under Articles 10 and 11 of the Convention."

51. The other decision, Adams and Benn v United Kingdom (1997) 88A D & R, 137 involved a complaint arising out of an exclusion order made against Mr Gerry Adams, the President of Sinn Fein, an Irish citizen resident in Northern Ireland, under the Prevention of Terrorism Act 1989. This excluded him from Great Britain and prevented him from accepting an invitation from Mr Tony Benn to speak to Members of Parliament and a number of journalists in the Grand Committee Room at the House of Commons. Both complained of violation of their Article 10 rights of freedom of expression—the former of the right to impart information and ideas; the latter of the right to receive them.

52. The Commission held at p.144 that Article 10 was engaged:

"The Commission recalls that the exclusion order imposed on the first applicant prevented him from attending a specific meeting in the House of Commons to which he had been invited by the second applicant. In these circumstances, the first applicant has been subject to a restriction on his freedom of expression and to impart information and ideas, and the second applicant to a restriction on his right to receive information and ideas, within the meaning of the first paragraph of Article 10."

53. The Commission went on at p.145 to consider whether the restriction could be justified under Article 10.2, and decided that it could:

"In the present case, the restriction complained of prevented the first applicant from attending a specific meeting in London. The Commission notes in that context that the United Kingdom is not a party to Protocol No. 4 to the Convention, which in Article 2 guarantees freedom of movement within the territory of a State. It remained open to the first applicant to express his views by other means or in Northern Ireland and for the second applicant to receive those views. The limitation was thus narrowly confined in its scope in so far as it affected the freedom to receive and impart information. The Commission recalls the sensitive and complex issues arising in the context of Northern Ireland, where there have been ongoing efforts to establish a peace process acceptable to the various communities and parties involved and where the threat of renewed incidents of violence remains real and continuous. It also notes that the exclusion order was lifted following the announcement of a cease-fire by the IRA. In these circumstances, the Commission finds that the decision of the Secretary of State to impose an exclusion order which prevented the first applicant from attending a meeting in London was not disproportionate to the aim of protecting national security and preventing disorder and crime and that it could be regarded as necessary in a democratic society for those purposes."

Discussion

54. We have drawn the following conclusions from the Strasbourg jurisprudence.

55. The right under international law of a State to control the entry of non-nationals into its territory is one which is recognised by the Strasbourg Court. Where entry is refused or an alien is expelled for reasons which are wholly independent of the exercise by the alien of Convention rights, the fact that this carries the consequence that he cannot exercise those rights in the territory from which he is excluded will not constitute a violation of the Convention.

56. In exceptional circumstances the obligation to protect Convention rights can override the right of a State to control the entry into its territory or presence within its territory of aliens. This is clear from the cases involving Article 8.

57. Where the authorities of a State refuse entry or expel an alien from its territory solely for the purpose of preventing the alien from exercising a Convention right within the territory, or by way of sanction for the exercise of a Convention right, the Convention will be directly engaged. This proposition is implicit in the observations of the Commission in Agee and Omkarananda and is expressly supported by the decision of the Court in Piermont and by the reasoning of the Commission in Adams and Benn. The fact that, in the latter two cases, the complainants were not, or not treated as being, in precisely the same position as aliens for immigration purposes does not detract from the relevance of those decisions.

58. Thus, where the authorities of a State refuse entry to an alien solely to prevent his expressing opinions within its territory, Article 10 will be engaged. In such a situation the application of the provisions of Article 10.2 will determine whether or not the interference with the alien's freedom of expression is justified.

Why has Mr Farrakhan been excluded?

59. In order to see how the principles that we have derived from the Strasbourg jurisprudence apply to the facts of the present case, it is necessary to determine why it is that the Secretary of State has excluded Mr Farrakhan. In considering this question it is not right to have regard solely to the terms of the decision letter of 20 November 2000. That letter was the last of a series written on behalf of the Home Secretary in relation to the application for Mr Farrakhan's admission and must be considered in the context of the earlier letters. Thus it is necessary to have regard to the fact that the Home Secretary carried out the consultation described in the letter of 23 July 1999 and to the large number of unsolicited letters for and against maintaining the exclusion of Mr Farrakhan that he received.

60. The Home Secretary stated in his decision letter that he had taken into account the undertaking signed by Mr Farrakhan and the fact that his current message was one of reconciliation. In these circumstances we do not consider that the reason why the Home Secretary excluded him was simply, or even predominantly, in order to prevent him exercising the right of freedom of expression in this country. We suggested to Miss Carss-Frisk, and she agreed, that, on the evidence, the reason for Mr Farrakhan's exclusion was the risk that his presence in this country might prove a catalyst for disorder. The Home Secretary has advanced as part of the explanation

for this risk the fact that 'sections of the community, in particular the Jewish community, clearly associate Mr Farrakhan with anti-semitic views' and that this perception is not without foundation.

61. At paragraph 50 of his judgment, Turner J. remarked that, on a superficial level, this case might appear to bear a striking resemblance to Otto-Preminger Institute v Austria (1949) 19EHRR 34. In granting permission to appeal Sedley LJ stated that, in his view, one of the main issues was 'to what extent the licence for local intolerance given by the Otto Preminger decision ought to affect judicial review of executive decisions in this country.'

62. In Otto Preminger the Strasbourg Court upheld the decision of the Innsbruck provincial court to order the seizure and forfeiture of a film on the ground that its subject matter amounted to an abusive attack on the Roman Catholic religion. The decision has been attacked by some commentators on the basis that it went too far in censoring freedom of expression within a Member State and it is apparent that it is not a decision which finds favour with Sedley LJ. Turner J. considered the resemblance of that case to the present to be superficial because, in Otto Preminger there was evidence before the court of the effect that the film would have on the religious majority in the Tyrol, whereas in the present case the Secretary of State has advanced no evidence to justify his decision.

63. If the Home Secretary had excluded Mr Farrakhan simply on the grounds that his character or views made him a person whom a large section of the community would not wish to see within their country, Otto Preminger might have been invoked in support of an argument that this did not violate the Convention. But that is not this case. The Home Secretary did not exclude Mr Farrakhan simply because he held views that would be offensive to many. He excluded him because of the effect that he considered that his admission would have on community relations and the risk that meetings attended by him would be the occasion for disorder. For this reason, which is not the same as that of Turner J, we agree that any resemblance between this case and Otto Preminger is superficial.

64. Although preventing Mr Farrakhan from expressing his views was not the primary object of his exclusion, the fact remains that the Home Secretary did not wish him to address meetings in this country because he considered that such meetings might prove the occasion for disorder. To this extent, one object of his exclusion can be said to have been to prevent him exercising the right of freedom of expression in this country. In these circumstances, which are not precisely covered by the Strasbourg authorities to which we have referred, we consider that Article 10 of the Convention was in play. The Home Secretary was correct to recognise this in his decision letter, which also recognised the importance that is accorded to freedom of speech by the common law.

The approach to judicial review

65. The Home Secretary made it plain that he was balancing the importance of freedom of speech against the risk of disorder that might ensue if Mr Farrakhan were admitted into this country. That was an appropriate approach, for Article 10.2 recognises that the prevention of disorder is one of the legitimate aims that can justify placing restrictions on freedom of expression. Much argument before Turner J and before us was directed to the approach in such circumstances to judicial review of the Secretary of State's decision.

66. Before the Human Rights Act 1998 came into force, the approach to judicial review in this country involved the application of the test in Associated Picture Houses Ltd v Wednesbury Corporation [1948] 1 KB 223. It was only appropriate for the court to overturn an administrative decision if it was one which no reasonable decision maker could have reached. Using the language of the Strasbourg jurisprudence, this test left a very wide margin of appreciation to the decision maker. Indeed, the margin was far too wide to accommodate the demands of the Convention. In deciding whether restriction of a Convention right can be justified, it is necessary to apply the doctrine of proportionality. In applying that doctrine, the width of the margin of appreciation that must be accorded to the decision maker will vary, depending upon the right that is in play and the facts of the particular case. Applying a margin of appreciation is a flexible approach; the Wednesbury approach is not.

67. For this reason, in cases involving Convention rights, the courts have moved from the Wednesbury test towards the application of the principle of proportionality, via the stepping stone of the judgment of Sir Thomas Bingham MR in R v Ministry of Defence, Ex parte Smith [1996] QB 517 at 554. The following passage in the speech of Lord Steyn in R(Daly) v Home Secretary [2001] 2AC 532 at 547 is now generally accepted as the best source of guidance in judicial review cases where human rights are in play:

"The contours of the principle of proportionality are familiar. In de Freitas v Permanent Secretary of Ministry of Agriculture, Fisheries, Lands and Housing [1999] 1 AC 69 the Privy Council adopted a three-stage test. Lord Clyde observed, at p80, that in determining whether a limitation (by an act, rule or decision) is arbitrary or excessive the court should ask itself:

'Whether: (i) the legislative objective is sufficiently important to justify limiting a fundamental right; (ii) the measures designed to meet the legislative objective are rationally connected to it; and (iii) the means used to impair the right or freedom are no more than is necessary to accomplish the objective."

Clearly, these criteria are more precise and more sophisticated than the traditional grounds of review. What is the difference for the disposal of concrete cases? Academic public lawyers have in remarkably similar terms elucidated the difference between the traditional grounds of review and the proportionality approach: see Professor Jeffrey Jowell QC, "Beyond the Rule of Law: Towards Constitutional Judicial Review" [2000] PL 671; Professor Paul Craig, Administrative Law, 4th ed (1999), pp 561-563; Professor David Feldman, "Proportionality and the Human Rights Act 1998," essay in The Principle of Proportionality in the Laws of Europe edited by Evelyn Ellis (1999), pp 117, 127 et seq. The starting point is that there is an overlap between the traditional grounds of review and the approach of proportionality. Most cases would be decided in the same way whichever approach is adopted. But the intensity of review is somewhat greater under the proportionality approach. Making due allowance for important structural differences between various convention rights, which I do not propose to discuss, a few generalisations are perhaps permissible. I would mention three concrete differences without suggesting that my statement is exhaustive. First, the doctrine of proportionality may require the reviewing court to assess the balance which the decision maker has struck, not merely whether it is within the range of rational or reasonable decisions. Secondly, the proportionality test may go further than the traditional grounds of review inasmuch as it may require attention to be directed to the relative weight accorded to interests and considerations. Thirdly, even the heightened scrutiny test developed in R v Ministry of Defence, Ex p Smith [1996] QB 517, 554 is not necessarily appropriate to the protection of human rights."

68. In the same case at p.549 Lord Cooke of Thorndon, who agreed with Lord Steyn, suggested that it was not merely in cases involving fundamental rights that the Wednesbury test should be replaced with a more flexible approach:

"I think that the day will come when it will be more widely recognised that Associated Provincial Picture Houses Ltd v Wednesbury Corpn [1948] 1 KB 223 was an unfortunately retrogressive decision in English administrative law, in so far as it suggested that there are degrees of unreasonableness and that only a very extreme degree can bring an administrative decision within the legitimate scope of judicial invalidation. The depth of judicial review and the deference due to administrative discretion vary with the subject matter. It may well be, however, that the law can never be satisfied in any administrative field merely by a finding that the decision under review is not capricious or absurd."

69. When applying a test of proportionality, the margin of appreciation or discretion accorded to the decision maker is all important, for it is only

by recognising the margin of discretion that the court avoids substituting its own decision for that of the decision maker. In the context of considering the margin of discretion in the present case, it is necessary to deal with the other matter which Sedley LJ considered to be a major issue in this case, the effect of Article 16

Article 16

70. Article 16 provides: 'Nothing in Articles 10,11 and 14 shall be regarded as preventing the High Contracting Parties from imposing restrictions on the political activity of aliens.' The Secretary of State referred inferentially to Article 16 in his decision letter. There is almost no reference to it in the Strasbourg jurisprudence. In Piermont the Commission made the following comments about it:

"The Commission observes that in placing this article in the Convention those who drafted it were subscribing to a concept that was then prevalent in international law, under which a general, unlimited restriction of the political activities of aliens was thought legitimate.

The Commission reiterates, however, that the Convention is a living instrument, which must be interpreted in the light of present day conditions, and the evolution of modern society."

71. As we have noted, the Commission and the Court held that, having regard to the status of Mrs Piermont, the Article had no application.

72. Mr Blake submitted that Article 16 is, by its terms, directed at permissible restrictions on the political rights of aliens in the host country and seems designed to preclude a discrimination challenge where less favourable treatment is accorded to aliens than others after admission. We agree that this conclusion is consistent with the wording of Article 16 and of Article 1 of the Convention. On this basis this Article appears something of an anachronism half a century after the agreement of the Convention. We do not consider that it has direct impact in the present case.

The margin of discretion

73. Miss Carss-Frisk submitted that there were factors in the present case which made it appropriate to accord a particularly wide margin of discretion to the Secretary of State. We agree. We would identify these factors as follows. First and foremost is the fact that this case concerns an immigration decision. As we have pointed out, the Strasbourg Court attaches considerable weight to the right under international law of a State to control immigration into its territory. And the weight that this carries in the present case is the greater because the Secretary of State is not moti-

vated by the wish to prevent Mr Farrakhan from expressing his views, but by concern for public order within the United Kingdom.

74. The second factor is the fact that the decision in question is the personal decision of the Secretary of State. Nor is it a decision that he has taken lightly. The history that we have set out at the beginning of this judgment demonstrates the very detailed consideration, involving widespread consultation, that the Secretary of State has given to his decision.

75. The third factor is that the Secretary of State is far better placed to reach an informed decision as to the likely consequences of admitting Mr Farrakhan to this country than is the Court.

76. The fourth factor is that the Secretary of State is democratically accountable for this decision. This is underlined by the fact that s.60(9) of the 1999 Act precludes any right of appeal where the Secretary of State has certified that he has personally directed the exclusion of a person on the ground that this is conducive to the public good. Mr Blake submitted that the absence of a right of appeal required a particularly rigorous scrutiny under the process of judicial review. This submission appeared to us tantamount to negating the effect of s.60(9). There is no doubt that the Secretary of State's decision is subject to review, but we consider that the effect of the legislative scheme is legitimately to require the Court to confer a wide margin of discretion upon the Minister.

77. These conclusions gain support from the approach of the House of Lords to the discretion of the Secretary of State to deport a person on grounds of national security in SHDD v Rehman [2001] 3WLR 877.

78. Miss Carss-Frisk submitted that these considerations were not reflected in the judgment of Turner J., but that he had replaced his own evaluation of the relevant facts for that of the Minister. We consider that there is force in this submission.

79. The other factor of great relevance to the test of proportionality is the very limited extent to which the right of freedom of expression of Mr Farrakhan was restricted. The reality is that it was a particular forum which was denied to him rather than the freedom to express his views. Furthermore, no restriction was placed on his disseminating information or opinions within the United Kingdom by any means of communication other than his presence within the country. In making this observation we do not ignore the fact that freedom of expression extends to receiving as well as imparting views and information and that those within this country were not able to receive these from Mr Farrakhan face to face.

80. Sedley LJ described the grounds for excluding Mr Farrakhan as exiguous. We have already indicated that to ascertain the reasons for Mr Farrakhan's exclusion it is appropriate to have regard to all the correspondence on the

subject written by or on behalf of the Secretary of State. The Home Secretary's decision had turned upon his evaluation of risk—the risk that because of his notorious opinions a visit by Mr Farrakhan to this country might provoke disorder. In evaluating that risk the Home Secretary had had regard to tensions in the Middle East current at the time of his decision. He had also had regard to the fruits of widespread consultation and to sources of information available to him that are not available to the Court. He had not chosen to describe his sources of information or the purport of that information. We can see that he may have had good reason for not disclosing his sources but feel that it would have been better had he been less diffident about explaining the nature of the information and advice that he had received.

81. We consider that the merits of this appeal are finely balanced, but have come to the conclusion that the Secretary of State provided sufficient explanation for a decision that turned on his personal, informed, assessment of risk to demonstrate that his decision did not involve a disproportionate interference with freedom of expression. The Secretary of State exercised a power expressly conferred upon him by Immigration Rule 320(6), whose terms are reflected in s.60(9) of the 1999 Act. He did so for the purpose of the prevention of disorder, which is a legitimate aim under Article 10.2 of the Convention. His decision struck a proportionate balance between that aim and freedom of expression, to the extent to which that was in play on the facts of this case. This appeal will, accordingly be allowed

DOCUMENT NO 12

Governor of H.M. Prison Brixton, and Government of the United States of America

V

Eidarous And Abdelbary
High Court, Queen's Bench Division

May 2, 2001
(Edited Text)

Lord Justice Kennedy:

1. These are applications for writs of Habeas Corpus made in the context of extradition proceedings. On 7th August 1998 bombs were exploded at 2 United States embassies. As a result of the explosion in Nairobi 213 people died and 4500 were injured. As a result of the explosion in Dar es Salam 11 people died. The government of the United States contends that the bombings were but two overt acts committed in furtherance of a prolonged conspiracy to cause explosions and to murder United States citizens, including diplomats and other internationally protected persons, and that these applicants were active members of that conspiracy, in which a key figure was Usama Bin Laden. They were arrested at their London homes on 23rd September 1998 but were released without charge four days later. They were then held in relation to immigration matters until 9th July 1999. A man named Al Fawwaz, who was arrested on the same day, was kept in custody, and extradition proceedings were commenced against him. On 11th July 1999 the present applicants were arrested on a provisional arrest warrant, and were brought before the Metropolitan Magistrate at Bow Street Magistrates' Court. Since that date they have remained in custody.

2. On 8th September 1999 the Magistrate committed Al Fawwaz to await the decision of the Secretary of State as to his return to the United States. An application for a writ of Habeas Corpus was made arising out of that

decision, and on 30th November 2000, this court, differently constituted, dismissed that application. On 21st September 1999 the Secretary of State instructed the Magistrate to proceed in respect of the present applicants, and on 25th April 2000 the Magistrate committed them in custody to await the decision of the Secretary of State on a charge which reads—

"That you between the 1st January 1993 and the 27th September 1998 agreed with Usama Bin Laden and others that a course of conduct would be pursued, namely:

1.   That citizens of the United States of America would be murdered in the United States of America and elsewhere;
2.   That bombs would be planted and exploded in American embassies and other American installations;
3.   That American officials would be killed in the Middle East and Africa;
4.   That American diplomats and other internationally protected persons would be murdered;
      which course of conduct would necessarily involve the commission of the offence of murder within the jurisdiction of the United States of America."

Scheme of the Act

3.   Extradition from the United Kingdom to the United States is governed by the Extradition Act 1989. Section 1(3) of that Act causes schedule I of the Act to apply where there is in force in relation to a foreign state an Order in Council giving effect to the terms of a relevant treaty. That is the position with the United States. The result is that when the Secretary of State orders the magistrate to proceed the order specifies the offence or offences which it appears to the Secretary of State are constituted by equivalent conduct had it occurred in the United Kingdom. The magistrate then conducts an enquiry into the offence or offences which the Secretary of State has specified to establish whether the evidence before him would make a case requiring an answer by the prisoner if the proceedings were for the trial in England and Wales of an information for that crime or those crimes (see paragraph 7(1) of schedule I to the 1989 Act). If that proves to be the case the magistrate commits the prisoner or prisoners as happened in the present case.

Issues

4.   Before us Mr Mansfield QC for Eidarous and Mr Emmerson QC and Mr Knowles for Abdelbary have developed submissions as to—

1. Whether the magistrate was right to accept and admit as part of the government's case a statement from a witness whose identity was at that stage not revealed. He was simply referred to as CS/1.
2. Whether the evidence before the magistrate was sufficient to meet the statutory test, properly applied.
3. Whether the matter under consideration was sufficiently connected with the United States to found jurisdiction.
4. Whether the magistrate's reasons, especially in relation to the issues of sufficiency, were adequate."

Admissibility of CS/1

5. CS/1 was an important source of background information. His statement reveals that from about 1989 to 1996 he was a member of Al Qaeda, an organisation founded by Bin Laden and that, like other members, he took an oath of allegiance or bayat pledging his loyalty to Bin Laden and Al Qaeda. he explained that at the relevant time—

   "The primary goal of Al Qaeda was to oppose through violence those governments that did not follow the group's view of Islam, including most notably the United States. To further this goal, Bin Laden would make use of front companies and organisations which he would use to conceal the activities of the group."

6. He also explained the command structure of Al Qaeda which included a Fatwah committee issuing Islamic law rulings, known as Fatwahs as to whether particular conduct was permitted or required under Islamic law. A source of concern to Bin Laden and Al Qaeda was the United States military presence in Saudi Arabia and the Horn of Africa, including Somalia, and some Fatwahs called for a Jihad, or holy war, against Americans in those regions.

7. According to CS/1, Bin Laden and Al Qaeda did not only exhort. Al Qaeda used Port Sudan to import weapons and explosives, many of them under cover of Bin Laden's companies, and there were also attempts to obtain components for nuclear and chemical weapons.

8. Also, according to CS/1, Bin Laden on behalf of Al Qaeda formed a close operational relationship with other groups, one of which was Egyptian Islamic Jihad (EIJ) led by Ayman Al Zawahiri, and there was talk of attacking US forces in Saudi Arabia, Yemen and the Horn of Africa.

9. CS/1 had personal knowledge of the fact that Al Fawwaz made bayat to Al Qaeda and Bin Laden, and was a prominent figure in the organisation. Bin Laden put Al Fawwaz in charge of the body he created in London called the Advice and Reformation Committee, and faxes were then sent to him in London so that he could pass on orders and messages on behalf

of Bin laden, including Fatwahs, one of which declared a Jihad based on Bin Laden's belief that for religious reasons it was unacceptable for US forces to be occupying the same land as the two Muslim holy places in Saudi Arabia. It thus became the obligation of faithful recipients of the Fatwah to remove the Americans by death or other means.

10. A different affidavit from CS/1 was tendered by the United States government in support of the application for the extradition of Al Fawwaz, and it was said then that it was necessary to omit the real name and place of residence of CS/1 in order to protect his/her identity and preserve his/her safety and that of his /her family because Al Qaeda may seek to cause harm to him/her for co-operating with the United States government. The magistrate admitted the affidavit in its anonymised form.

11. Neither affidavit from CS/1 referred to either of the present applicants by name, and by the time that the magistrate was considering the admissibility of the affidavit of CS/1 in these proceedings the United States government had been able to decide and confirm that the identity of CS/1 would be disclosed at the trial in the United States. It was clear from his affidavit that he had pleaded guilty to terrorism charges, and the magistrate concluded that "there must be a real risk of danger to CS/1 and any members of CS/1's family." The magistrate did not consider that there was any real risk of prejudice to the defence in proceedings before him in not knowing the true identity of CS/1 and that information would be available at trial in the event of extradition.

12. In R v Taylor (Gary) 17th August 1994 Times Law Reports the Court of Appeal Criminal Division set out 5 factors it considered relevant to the exercise of a judge's discretion to deny a defendant the right to see and know the identity of his accusers. Those factors were—

    1. There must be real grounds for fear of the consequences if the evidence were given and the identity of the witness revealed.
    2. The evidence must be sufficiently relevant and important to make it unfair to make the Crown proceed without it.
    3. The Crown must satisfy the court that the credit worthiness of the witness had been fully investigated and disclosed.
    4. The court must be satisfied that there would be no undue prejudice to the accused, although some prejudice was inevitable, even if it was only the qualification placed on the right to confront a witness as accuser.
    5. The court could balance the need for protection of the witness, including the extent of that protection, against unfairness or the appearance of unfairness."

13. In the present case the magistrate referred to those principles, applying them so far as possible to the field of extradition. As he said, "they are

not ideally suited for an extradition committal hearing at which there can be no cross-examination of a foreign witness whose evidence is by affidavit." The magistrate also referred to authorities pointing out the importance of magistrates in committal proceedings and extradition proceedings not, in the interest of fairness, attempting to shut out evidence which, if it is to be excluded at all, should be excluded at a later stage by a trial judge. The magistrate then ruled the evidence of CS/1 to be admissible. He had made a similar ruling in the case of Al Fawwaz, and that was challenged unsuccessfully in this court. As Mr Emmerson points out, the challenge in that case was on the basis that the second Taylor criterion was mandatory, and the conclusions of the magistrate were irrational. In the present case Mr Emmerson submits that at least the first Taylor criterion must be mandatory—the person whose identity is being concealed must be shown to be at risk, and in this case it is now apparent that at all material times CS/1 had the benefit of the United States Witness Protection Scheme. That, Mr Emmerson contends, is something that should have been revealed, together with information as to the extent of the risk and the extent of the protection provided.

14. In my judgment it is unnecessary to enter into the question of what needs to be disclosed in extradition proceedings because, as Mr Hardy for the government submits, on the facts it would have been remarkable if CS/1 had not been afforded witness protection, and it is common knowledge that even that form of protection cannot guarantee security. If anything the information now relied upon tends to support rather than undermine the magistrate's decision. As Buxton LJ said in this court in Al Fawwaz (paragraph 55)—

"In extradition proceedings it would not avail Mr Al Fawwaz simply to produce evidence that casts doubt on CS/1's credit worthiness. Investigation of that question is a matter for the trial, and for cross-examination there. The only material that could assist Mr Al Fawwaz before the magistrate is material that showed that, because of previous contradictory statements or behaviour by (CS/1) his evidence was worthless. . . . It will be noted that that is a much more demanding test than the test of whether, there is material that casts doubts on the witness's creditability."

15. If one substitutes "these applicants" for the references to Mr Al Fawwaz that passage, in my judgment, clearly represents the position in this case. The magistrate was fully entitled, on the evidence before him, to take the view that the statement of CS/1 was not shown to be worthless, and that is still the position even though, as Mr Knowles pointed out in reply, it is now clear from what has apparently been said by CS/1 when giving evidence in the United States, that not only does he enjoy witness protection but also he has made a plea bargain, has received a loan to restart

his life, and has an added reason for requiring witness protection in that he took a significant amount of money from Bin Laden which he has not repaid. He may have also have had difficulty recognising Bin Laden's military commander in a photograph. Those are no doubt all useful points for cross-examination, but they do not even start to cross the threshold to which Buxton LJ referred. It was also suggested in this case, as it was in the case of Al Fawwaz that the admissions of the evidence of CS/1 contravened the provisions of articles 5 and 6 of the European Convention on Human Rights. As to that I am content simply to adopt what was said by Buxton LJ in paragraphs 58 to 62 of his judgment. Accordingly, in my judgment, the attack upon the magistrate's decision to admit the statement of CS/1 fails.

Sufficiency of evidence

16. I can now turn to the question of sufficiency of evidence on the basis that the statement of CS/1 was part of the evidence which the magistrate was entitled to consider. In his decision in Al Fawwaz the magistrate identified two questions in relation to sufficiency of evidence and that approach (which is referred to in the judgment of the Divisional Court) although not precisely reflected in the decision by the magistrate in the present case, is useful. He asked himself first whether the evidence established a case to answer that there was an agreement between Bin Laden and others to pursue the course of conduct alleged in the charge. In the case of Al Fawwaz the answer to that first question was not really in issue. In the present case Mr Mansfield did make some submissions in relation to it, inviting us to have regard to the shifting nature of dissident Arab alliances, and as to a certain readiness to make statements containing threats which were never carried out, but in reality the statement of CS/1, supported as it is by the evidence of the American investigators and by documentary evidence, is quite sufficient to provide proof to the requisite standard of the existence of the conspiracy alleged. The requisite standard is that as set out by the magistrate in paragraph 14 and 15 of his ruling, namely whether a jury properly directed could reach that conclusion, and although there was initially a suggestion that the magistrate applied the wrong test, that was not pursued. So the vital question in relation to sufficiency of evidence in the present case, as in the case of Al Fawwaz, was what was there identified as the second question, namely whether the evidence established a case to answer that each applicant was a party to the agreement. As was said in ex parte Osman [1990] 1 WLR 277 at 299H it was the magistrate's duty to consider the evidence as a whole, and to reject any evidence he considered worthless—

"In that sense it was his duty to weigh up the evidence. But it was not his duty to weigh the evidence. He was neither entitled nor obliged to determine the amount of weight to be attached to any evidence, or to compare one witness with another. That would be for the jury at the trial. It follows that the magistrate was not concerned with the inconsistencies or contradictions in (a given witness's) evidence, unless they were such as to justify rejecting or eliminating his evidence altogether."

That passage was cited by Buxton LJ in Al Fawwaz, but it bears repetition.

17. The resolution to establish the London office of Al Qaeda—the Advice and Reform Committee—with Al Fawwaz as director, was signed by Bin Laden in 1994. That is apparent from one of the many documents recovered at the time when the present applicants were originally arrested, and most of the information to which I will now refer comes from the same general source. Sometimes the precise origin of the document is significant and where that is the case I will say so.

18. On 25th May 1996 Al Zawahiri of EIJ put Abdelbary in charge of the London Cell and on 23rd August 1996 Bin Laden issued a bellicose Jihad requiring the faithful to expel Americans from the Arabian peninsular. At the time of the arrests copies of that Jihad were found at Abdelbary's house and at the office at 1A Beethoven Street, which both applicants used, together with Al Fawwaz, who with Abdelbary signed the lease. As Mr Mansfield points out, that Jihad was published, but what the applicants had was not simply the published material.

19. Still in 1996, on 31st October someone calling themselves Khaleel purchased a satellite telephone in the United States, and the government was able to show how over the next two years both applicants and Al Fawwaz were linked to the International use of that telephone from Afghanistan, where Al Qaeda were based. In 1996 CS/1 ceased to be member of Al Qaeda but the organisation seems to have continued in the same vein. From the home of Abdelbary there was recovered a fax dated 29th July 1997 addressed to Abdelbary from one of Bin Laden's assistants in Afghanistan which referred to a financial statement sent by Abdelbary to Al Zawahiri and to the operation of the media office. It questions whether that office ran according to a policy agreed upon by Al Zawahiri, and asked what are the office security precautions. The question is raised of whether another individual is suspected of working for the Americans. Many questions are asked and the recipient of the fax is told to write down the answers and he will be told a fax number to which he can transmit the answers. The document is, to say the least, consistent with the existence with a conspiracy to which the recipient is a party.

20. One of the documents found in the boot Eidarous' car was a fax from Al Zawahiri in Kandahar dated 18th January 1998. It is addressed to more

than one recipient, and refers to having "arrived at a good draft agreement with our friend here." The government submits that the friend was Bin Laden and the draft agreement was the Fatwah, which came into existence soon afterwards. A copy of that Fatwah signed by Bin Laden and Al Zawahiri and others was found in Eidarous' car. That copy is dated 31st January 1998 and the government submits that it was another draft. The document contends that the activities of the "Jewish Christian Alliance" and in particular the United States, constitute a declaration of war on God and His messenger and the Muslims. It states—

"Killing the Americans and their allies civilians or military men is a personal duty on every Muslim. This is possible to him in every country in which this can be done, and this till the grand mosque of Jerusalem (Al Aqsa) is liberated and so the holy mosques of Mecca (Al Kaba) are liberated. . . ."

21. The government contends that the reference to the two mosques is significant, and can be linked with what happened later in Nairobi and Dar es Salam. A later part of the document reads—

"We in the name of God call every Muslim who believes in God and who desires His rewards to abide by the order of God in killing the Americans and looting their wealth in every where he finds them at every time that he can do that. We also call the Muslims learned men and their eternal leaders and their youths and their believing soldiers to launch a raid. . . ."

22. A copy of that Fatwah dated 12th February 1998 was found at 1A Beethoven Street and another copy was found at the home of Abdelbary. In due course on 23rd February 1998 the Fatwah was published in the Arab publication Al Quds. Another item found in the possession of Eidarous was a fax dated 4th May 1998, addressed to him, which enclosed "the Lufthansa Shipping receipt for the satellite telephone" The author continues "it should reach you in two days. Mr Yousif was listed as the recipient." The government did not in the end contend that what was being transmitted was the satellite phone to which I have already referred. However, satellite phone movement by air is evidenced by another weigh bill, found in Eidarous' car, from Afghan Airlines dated 23rd July 1998 describing the goods to which it relates as "said to contain telephone." It relates to carriage from Sharjah to Kandahar in Afghanistan.

23. On 28th June 1998 Al Zawahiri by fax confirmed that Eidarous "is the one in charge in London" and required Abdelbary to mend his ways. That fax was recovered from Eidarous' car, with a copy of Abdelbary's reply giving the necessary assurances.

24. Another item found in Eidarous' car was a copy of an interview given by Al Zawahiri to an Egyptian newspaper published on 9th July 1998 making the point that the threat to American interests was serious. Also found

in the boot of Eidarous' car was a document which, amongst other things, gave warning of the ability of the United States and other western nations to spy on cell telephones and communications systems worked by satellite.

25. On 4th August 1998 the public office of EIJ issued a declaration relating to the capture of three of "our brothers" who had allegedly been participating in Jihad. Part of the declaration reads—

"It is important for us to inform the Americans in brief that their letter was received, and the reply is being prepared, which we hope they will read very carefully, because by God's will, we are writing it in the language that they understand."

26. The government contend that in the light of subsequent events that can be seen to be a clear threat of retaliation and the fax containing that threat was found at 1A Beethoven Street where both appellants worked and where it had been copied.

27. The explosions at Nairobi and Dar es Salam occurred at about 10.30 am local time, 7.30 am GMT and from 1A Beethoven Street were recovered two faxes headed Aug 07 0445 am. They are both headed "The Islamic Army for the Liberation of the Holy Places" and are in identical terms, save that one headed "Operation Blessed Kaaba" claims responsibility for the Nairobi bombing, and the other headed "Operation Aqsa Mosque" claims responsibility for the Tanzania bombing. The names of the two operations are the names of the two Mosques referred to in the Fatwah of February 1998. If the faxes claiming responsibility were sent before the explosions occurred it would be surprising if they were sent to 1A Beethoven Street even via the shop known as the Grapevine unless those at Beethoven Street were parties to the conspiracy, but, as Mr Mansfield points out, the sender's time may not have been GMT. Even if the faxes were sent after the explosions the question remains as to why they were sent to that address, why they were collected from the Grapevine and taken to 1A Beethoven Street and why the fingerprints of both applicants appear upon them. As Mr Lewis points out, the contents of the faxes suggest familiarity with what went on in Africa, and the reasons for it. And if they were really no more than unsolicited mail why did those at 1A Beethoven Street react as they did?

28. On 8th August 1998 faxes were sent from Formosa Street post office, near to Beethoven Street, to Radio France and others. The numbers to which the faxes were sent were in an Eidarous diary, and a claim of responsibility fax was later recovered in France. Mr Mansfield takes the point that there is no admissible evidence that it was recovered from Radio France.

29. I have referred to a number of documents recovered when the applicants were arrested, but there were many more. There was evidence to show

that Eidarous was on the founding council of EIJ and diary evidence to show that he had the telephone numbers of the other members of that council. Abdelbary also had an address book showing founding council members, and there was evidence of the involvement of Eidarous in the forging of passports. And of course both of these applicants were in close contact with, and worked with Al Fawwaz, who was arrested at the same time. There was evidence from telephone records of close contacts between all three men and Al Zawahiri, and there was also evidence of the use by those at Beethoven Street of cloned credit cards to make anonymous telephone calls.

30. After the arrest of these applicants, on 22nd September 1998 Bin Laden signed a minute directing the closure of the London office partly, it would seem, because of the threat presented by new anti-terrorist legislation.

31. As the magistrate said this is a complex matter, and the outline which I have given is no more than an outline. There is a wealth of material which was before the magistrate, and the amount is substantial even when reduced for the purposes of this court. The magistrate referred to some of the material, including the defence points about the time of the faxes claiming responsibility, and then said—

"Nevertheless, I am satisfied that a jury, properly directed, could conclude, on the totality of the evidence that the claims were sent before the bombings. Similarly a jury could conclude, regardless of whether they conclude the claims were sent before or after the bombings, that they were genuine. Similarly a jury could conclude that both defendants played a part in the dissemination of the claims to the international media. Further a jury could conclude that Bin Laden was the moving force behind the bombings and played a central part in the conspiracy to cause the explosions

I have carefully re-read all the written submissions and my notes and considered those matters afresh. It does not seem to me to be either sensible or desirable that I should deal with each point in turn. Any review of my decision would necessitate those conducting the review to come to their own conclusion on whether there is a case to answer, rather than deciding whether or not there are flaws in my approach or reasoning. I am satisfied that the facts taken as a whole are capable of enabling this court (or a jury properly directed) to come to the conclusion that the only reasonable inference to be drawn from this is that each defendant is guilty of the proposed charge. Thus each has a case to answer."

Mr Mansfield and Mr Emmerson are critical of that conclusion. Mr Mansfield points out that those who carried out the bombings in Nairobi and Dar es Salam have never been identified. He suggests that if the applicants were conspirators they would not have used the Grapevine to receive incoming faxes. He points out that the Fatwahs were not secret, they were intended to be published, and that the declaration of Jihad emanated from Egypt. It was not signed by Bin Laden or Al Qaeda nor do they feature on the faxes claiming responsibility for events for which they might be expected to claim "credit." As already noted, Mr Mansfield draws a distinction between exhortation and action. There were, he points out, no recorded telephone calls to Tanzania or Kenya for six and a half months prior to the bombings, and he submits that the detail in the faxes claiming responsibility was not such as to show that the author had personal knowledge of what had occurred. It is not, he says, unknown for dissident groups to claim responsibility for atrocities. He points out that there is no evidence to show that either applicant collected faxes from the Grapevine, or sent faxes from Formosa Street post office. Or that Eidarous was anything other than a genuine businessman. In reply Mr Mansfield submitted that there must be basic facts proved from which inferences can be drawn, and here, he submitted, the whole case is based on assertions, innuendo and inadmissible material. Mr Emmerson and Mr Knowles made submissions to the same effect.

32. In Osman (supra) Lloyd J at 301 H cited what he had said in ex parte Blair as to the jurisdiction of this court when considering the decision of a magistrate in extradition proceedings—

"The question for us is not whether there was sufficient evidence to send Mr Blair for trial if these offences had been committed in England. That was a question for the Chief Magistrate not for us. The question for us is whether there was any evidence on which the Chief Magistrate could so find. The discretion in the matter was his not ours. For the same reason, it is not for us to say whether, in our view, the inference is irresistible that there was here reliance. The question for us is whether the Chief Magistrate could lawfully reach that view; whether, in other words, it was within the range of views that a reasonable magistrate, directing himself properly and in accordance with the law, could reach."

33. In my judgment, the magistrate in the present case was clearly entitled to decide as he did. As he said, it was his duty to look at the facts as a whole and when taken as a whole they are capable of enabling a court to come to the conclusion that each defendant is guilty of the proposed charge.

U.S. jurisdiction

34. The two remaining items I can deal with quite briefly. When dealing with Al Fawwaz this court accepted the argument of the applicant that in cases governed by schedule I of the 1989 Act the extradition crime has to be committed within the territory of the requesting state (see paragraph 32

of the judgment). We were invited to reconsider that decision, but I find it unnecessary to do so in this case because, as this court in Al Fawwaz went on to say, there is clear evidence of overt acts committed in the United States in furtherance of the alleged conspiracy, and the conspiracy to which the court was addressing itself in Al Fawwaz is the conspiracy with which we are concerned. Furthermore, the evidence relied upon is the same. The purchase of the satellite telephone system and the issuing of Fatwahs and Jihads are two such overt acts, as explained in paragraph 39 of the judgment in Al Fawwaz.

35. As Mr Lewis points out, the satellite telephone purchased in the United States was much used. Minutes and accessories were also purchased in the United States, and from Afghanistan that telephone made 1080 outgoing calls, 143 of which were to Al Fawwaz, 89 of which were to Eidarous and 7 of which were to Abdelbary. In addition there were four calls to Kenya and 30 incoming calls from London public phones, made, the government submit, by the applicants using cloned cards.

36. Turning to the Fatwahs and Jihads, the government case is that the conspirators wanted them published to further their conspiracy, so the publication in Al Quds, which is published in the United States, constituted a second activity in furtherance of the conspiracy within the relevant jurisdiction, and, as was made clear in DPP v Doot [1973] AC 807, part performance of the conspiracy within the jurisdiction is all that is required for the purposes of establishing jurisdiction (see Lord Pearson at 827 E). In Al Fawwaz there was also reliance on him setting up and operating a secure telephone line in the United States through an organisation called MCI. That evidence was not before the magistrate in the present case and I need say no more about it.

Reasons

37. It is right to say that in this case the magistrate did not rehearse the evidence in any detail when dealing with the submission that there was insufficient evidence to constitute a case to answer. He explained the nature and aims of the alleged conspiracy, and the position taken by each applicant in relation to it. He referred to the bombings in Nairobi and Dar es Salam and to the "threat" and "claims of responsibility" faxes and posed a number of questions. Mr Mansfield makes no complaint of the questions, but he submits that the magistrate failed to answer them. The magistrate then continued—

"As can be seen from the written representations there is no agreement between the parties as to how I should approach my task. There is no direct evidence to prove the alleged conspiracy. The prosecution can prove hundreds of facts by direct evidence e.g. the bombings and the faxes. There are several gaps in the continuity evidence (e.g. dissemination of claims of responsibility to France etc) but for which various events could be proved by direct evidence. From the totality of the facts proved, either directly or by inference, the court is invited to conclude that there is a proper basis on which a jury could infer guilt on the proposed charge."

38. The magistrate then indicated his acceptance of the prosecution approach, referred to the defence submissions in relation to the timing of the faxes, and expressed the conclusion set out earlier in this judgment.

39. I confess that I would have found it helpful if the magistrate had gone a bit further, because, as Lloyd LJ explained in Osman, it is not our conclusion as to whether there is a case to answer which matters. We simply have to consider whether there was evidence on which the magistrate could reach his conclusion. Furthermore, as both Mr Mansfield and Mr Emmerson have pointed out, there is a growing expectation that when decisions are taken by legally qualified tribunals reasons will be given, but in Rey [1999] 1 AC 54 Lord Steyn, sitting in the Privy Council, said at 66F—

"Despite a growing practice in England of stipendiary magistrates to give reasons in extradition proceedings it has not been held that magistrates are under a legal duty to do so. And the legal position in England is perhaps justified by the right of the fugitive to apply for habeas corpus to the Divisional Court if the decision of the stipendiary magistrate goes against him: see section 11 of the Extradition Act 1989. ...In these circumstances their Lordships are not prepared to hold that there is a general implied duty upon magistrates to give reasons in respect of all disputed issues of fact and law in extradition proceedings. But their Lordships must enter a cautionary note: it is unnecessary in the present case to consider whether in the great diversity of cases which come before magistrates in extradition proceedings the principle of fairness may in particular circumstances require a magistrate to give reasons."

40. Mr Mansfield and Mr Emmerson submit that in this case we should give effect to the cautionary note because the particular circumstances were such that the principle of fairness required the magistrate to give reasons. I do not accept that submission. The magistrate did explain his approach, and it can be said that he was being realistic. Even if he had attempted to explain in more detail the case which he decided required an answer it is overwhelmingly likely that we would have still been required to carry out the exercise performed in this court. Accordingly I do not accept that in law his reasons were inadequate, and even if I were able to accept that

submission I cannot see that it would afford any basis for relief given that, in reality, in my judgment there were good reasons for the magistrate deciding as he did.

Conclusion

41. I would therefore dismiss these applications.

Mr Justice Garland: I agree.

DOCUMENT NO 13

The Secretary of State for the Home Department
v
Shafiq Ur Rehman

Court of Appeal

May 23, 2000
(Edited Text)

Lord Woolf MR:

1. This is a judgment of the court on the first appeal from a decision of the Special Immigration Appeals Commission ("SIAC"). SIAC was established by the Special Immigration Appeals Commission Act 1997. The decision of SIAC was given on 7 September 1999. The SIAC allowed an appeal by Mr Shafiq Ur Rehman against the decision of the Secretary of State for the Home Department to refuse his application for indefinite leave to remain in the United Kingdom and to make a deportation order. In a letter of 9 December 1998, the Secretary of State wrote to the respondent giving his decision in these terms:

"Application for Indefinite Leave to Remain

I am writing with reference to your application for indefinite leave to remain in the United Kingdom on the basis that you have spent a continuous period of four years in the United Kingdom as a Minister of Religion.

The Secretary of State is satisfied that you have completed the requisite period in permit free employment and has therefore gone on to consider your application in the light of all the known circumstances. I must therefore inform you that the Secretary of State is satisfied, on the basis of the information he has received from confidential sources, that you are involved with an Islamic terrorist organisation Markaz Dawa al Rishad (MDI). He is satisfied that in the light of your association with the MDI it is undesirable to permit you to remain and that your continued presence in this country represents a danger to national security. In these circumstances, the Secretary of State has decided to refuse your application for indefinite leave to remain in accordance with Paragraph 322(5) of the immigration rules (HC395).

Notice of intention to make a Deportation Order

The Secretary of State has decided that your deportation from the United Kingdom would be conducive to the public good in the interests of national security because of your association with Islamic terrorist groups. Accordingly, he has decided to make a deportation order against you by virtue of Section 3(5)(b) of the Immigration Act 1971, requiring you to leave the United Kingdom and prohibiting you from returning while the order remains in force. He proposes to give directions for your removal to Pakistan, the country of which you are a national or which most recently provided you with a travel document.

By virtue of Section 2(1)(c) of the Special Immigration Appeals Commission Act 1997 you are entitled to appeal against the decision to make a deportation order against you on the grounds that your presence in this country is not conducive to the public good in the interests of national security. At any such appeal hearing the Special Immigration Appeals Commission would be provided with details of the security case against you."

2. By letter of 17 February 1999 the Secretary of State corrected his previous letter. In that letter he indicated that he had been in error in informing the respondent that he had a right of appeal in relation to the refusal of his application for indefinite leave to remain because the application was out of time and subsequently withdrawn when the respondent travelled out of the United Kingdom in October 1997. The Secretary of State did however reiterate that the respondent had a right of appeal against his decision that the respondent be deported.

3. The respondent appealled the decision to deport and it was in respect of that appeal that SIAC gave its decision which gives rise to the appeal to this court.

The Legislation

4. In order to understand the role of SIAC, it is necessary initially to start with the Immigration Act 1971 ("the 1971 Act"). S.3 of the 1971 Act contains the general provisions for regulation and control of immigration. S.3(5) identifies who is liable to deportation. There are three categories of individuals who can be liable for deportation. The power which is relevant is contained in s.3(5)(b). The provision reads:

1. A person who is not [a British Citizen] shall be liable to deportation from the United Kingdom . . .

2.   if the Secretary of State deems his deportation to be conducive to the public good; or. . . ."

5.   If the Secretary of State is proposing to make a deportation order, the first step is to make a decision to deport. The decision to deport is one in relation to which there is normally an appeal under s.15 of the 1971 Act. S.15(1)(a) states:

    (a)   Subject to the provisions of this Part of this Act, a person may appeal to an adjudicator against—

    (b)   a decision of the Secretary of State to make a deportation order against him by virtue of section.3(5) above; or . . ."

6.   S.15(2) prevents a deportation order being made against the person by virtue of S.3(5) so long as an appeal is being brought against the decision to make it. This underlines the two-stage process. First the decision to make a deportation order and then, if there is no successful appeal, the deportation order. Once a deportation order has been made, there can be an appeal against a refusal to revoke the deportation. There are however limitations both with regard to who is entitled to appeal against a decision to make a deportation order and who can appeal against a decision to refuse to revoke a deportation order.

7.   Here we are concerned with a decision to make a deportation order. The limitation on such an appeal is expressed in these terms:

"15(3) A person shall not be entitled to appeal against a decision to make a deportation order against him if the ground of the decision was that his deportation is conducive to the public good as being in the interests of national security or of the relations between the United Kingdom and any other country or for other reasons of a political nature."

8.   Although s.15(3) refers to three specific grounds why deportation can be conducive to the public good, s.3(5) does not refer to those grounds. S.3(5) is silent as to the circumstances which need to exist to make a deportation because it is conducive to the public good to do so. The Secretary of State is however required to give his reasons why he considers deportation to be conducive to the public good and if he relies on "interests of national security" etc. he brings into play s.15(3).

9.   Although there was no appeal under the Immigration Act 1971 in s.15(3) cases, there was a non-statutory advisory procedure which enabled those to whom the section applied to appear before "the Three Advisors" and then make representations to them. They then advised the Secretary of State as to whether he should adhere to his decision. The question of whether this non-statutory protection complied with the standards of the European Convention on Human Rights was considered by the European Court of Human Rights in *Chahal v The UK* [1997] 23 EHRR 413. In

that case it was held that the procedures did not do so as the advisory panel was not a "court" within the meaning of Article 5 (4) ECHR and judicial review, where national security was involved, did not provide an "effective remedy" within the meaning of Article 13. The court however recognised that the use of confidential material may be unavoidable where national security is at stake and the European Court of Human Rights was impressed by the fact that in Canada a more effective form of judicial control had been developed for cases of this type.

10. The response of the government was to introduce the Special Immigration Appeals Commission Act 1997 ("the 1997 Act"). The Act was clearly designed to bring the United Kingdom into a position where it complied with its obligations under the European Convention and to provide greater protection for individuals who it is intending to deport on national security grounds.

11. S.1 of the 1997 Act establishes the Commission. Its membership is of significance. One member has to have held high judicial office. One is or has to have been the Chief Adjudicator or a legally qualified member of the Immigration Appeal Tribunal. While there is no statutory restriction as to who is to be the third member, in fact it has been indicated that the third person will be someone who has experience of national security matters.

12. S.2 deals with the jurisdiction of the Commission. One situation in which the jurisdiction exists is where a person would have been entitled to appeal but for s.15(3). SIAC's task in relation to determining appeals is set out in s.4(1) and (2) of the 1997 Act. S.4 so far as relevant provides:
   1.   The Special Immigration Appeals Commission on an appeal to it under this Act—
       1.   shall allow the appeal if it considers—
           1.   that the decision or action against which the appeal is brought was not in accordance with the law or with any immigration rules applicable to the case, or
           2.   where the decision or action involved the exercise of a discretion by the Secretary of State or an officer, that the discretion should have been exercised differently, and
       2.   in any other case, shall dismiss the appeal.

   (2) Where an appeal is allowed, the Commission shall give such directions for giving effect to the determination as it thinks requisite, and may also make recommendations with respect to any other action which it considers should be taken in the case under the Immigration Act 1971; and it shall be the duty of the Secretary of State and of any officer to whom directions are given under this subsection to comply with them."

13. There are virtually identical provisions to the provisions of s.4(1) in S.19(1) of the Immigration Act 1971. S.19 of the 1971 Act deals with appeals to

adjudicators, inter alia, in those cases where s.15(3) does not apply. S.19 of the 1971 Act differs from s.4 of the 1997 Act in that the former expressly sets out the powers of an adjudicator on an appeal under the 1971 Act to review a question of fact and deals with cases where the Secretary of State is asked to depart from the rules. This is not reproduced in s.4. This difference is of no relevance here. However, it is not in issue that SIAC can review questions of fact.

14. S.5 of the 1997 Act gives the Lord Chancellor wide powers to make rules for regulating the exercise of the rights of appeal. The rule making power enables the Lord Chancellor to make the most satisfactory arrangements practical to deal with the tension which will inevitably arise in cases involving national security between the rights of the individual and the need to maintain the confidentiality of security information. The 1997 Act provides for the appointment of a special advocate in accordance with s.6. He is able to represent the appellant before SIAC during those parts of the proceedings from which the appellant and his legal representatives are excluded. In order to perform this purpose, the special advocate will usually be present during the entire proceedings and not only the closed sessions. This means that in practice an appellant will have two sets of legal representatives. Those of his own choice can represent him during open sessions and in private sessions, that is sessions during which the public are excluded but not the appellant, and the special advocate in closed sessions, where the information is of a category which it is necessary to keep confidential from the appellant, and the appellant is not present.

15. S.7 of the 1997 Act gives *"any party"* the right to bring a further appeal *"on any question of law material"* to SIAC's determination. The appeal is either with the leave of SIAC or the Court of Appeal. In the case of the present appeal SIAC refused leave to appeal and Sir Anthony McCowan gave leave.

16. The rules which it was anticipated by the 1997 Act would be made have been made. They are the Special Immigration Appeals Commission (Procedure) Rules 1998 ("the Rules"). It is not necessary to refer to any of the provisions of the Rules. It is, however, Rule 7 which places restriction upon what the Special Advocate can communicate to an appellant who is appealing to SIAC.

The Decision of SIAC

17. Mr Shafiq Ur Rehman's appeal was heard by Mr Justice Potts, His Honour Judge Pearl and Sir Brian Barder KCMG. The members of SIAC who heard the appeal were singularly well-qualified to do so. Potts J is a judge of very broad experience. Judge Pearl until fairly recently was the Chief

Immigration Adjudicator. Sir Brian has considerable experience of security matters.

The Facts

18. The factual background of this appeal is succinctly summarised by SIAC in its ruling and I gratefully adopt this account.

"The Appellant is a Pakistani national, born on 2 June 1971 in Mian Channu, Pakistan. He is married to Hashmad Bibi by whom he has two children both born in the United Kingdom. The Appellant's father and mother came to the United Kingdom in 1988; both hold British citizenship. His father is a Minister of Religion at the Halifax Mosque, Halifax, Yorkshire.

Other members of his immediate family all live in the United Kingdom. The Appellant matriculated from Rawalpindi Board in Pakistan in 1988. He studied at the Jamiah Salsiah, Islamabad, Pakistan until March 1992, when he was awarded a Masters Degree in Islamic Studies. Thereafter he taught at Jamiah Salsiah until January 1993. The Appellant originally applied to come to the United Kingdom in 1990 as a dependant of his father. However, as he was over the age of 18, his entry clearance application was refused. He was subsequently issued with an entry clearance on 17 January 1993 to enable him to work as a Minister of Religion with the Jamait Ahele-e-Hadith (JAH) in Oldham. He arrived in the United Kingdom on the 9 February 1993. He was subsequently granted further leave to remain until 9 February 1997 in order to complete four years as a Minister. On 3 March 1997, the Appellant made an out-of-time application for indefinite leave to remain in the United Kingdom. In October 1997, the Appellant was granted leave to remain until 7 January 1998 to enable him and his family to travel to Pakistan on holiday. On his return to the United Kingdom on 4 December 1997 at Manchester Airport he was detained and was interviewed by Special Branch Officers and seen by an Officer of the Security Service.

By letter dated 9 December 1998 the Appellant's application for indefinite leave to remain in the United Kingdom was refused."

19. The appellant gave notice of appeal on 10 December 1998.

20. For the purpose of the appeal the Secretary of State made an "open" statement of his case in accordance with rule 10(1) of the Rules. I refer to the relevant parts of that statement as amended by counsel for SIAC at the conclusion of the evidence. It alleged that Shafiq Ur Rehman is the United Kingdom point of contact of "Markaz Dawa Al Irshad" ("MDI"). MDI is an Islamic extremist organisation whose mujahidin fighters are known as the "Lashkar Taiyyaba" ("LT"). On MDI's behalf, Ur Rehman has been involved in the recruitment of British Muslims to undergo mil-

itary training and in fund-raising for LT. Ur Rehman is a personal contact of Mohammad Saeed, the world-wide leader of MDI and LT. It was the security service assessment that Ur Reham's activities directly support a terrorist organisation. The statement continued:

"The Security Service assesses that while Ur Rehman and his United Kingdom based followers are unlikely to carry out any acts of violence in this country, his activities directly support terrorism in the Indian sub-continent and are likely to continue unless he is deported. Ur Rehman has only been partly responsible for an increase in the number of Muslims in the United Kingdom who have undergone some form of military training, including indoctrination into extremist beliefs and at least some basic weapons handling. The Security Service is concerned that the presence of returned jihad trainees in the UK may encourage the radicalisation of the British Muslim community. His activities in the United Kingdom are intended to further the cause of terrorist organisation abroad. For this reason, the Secretary of State considers both that Ur Rehman poses a threat to national security and that he should be deported from the UK on the grounds that his presence here is not conducive to the public good for reasons of national security."

21. By his grounds of appeal the Appellant denies that JAH, by whom he is employed as a Minister of Religion, is in any way linked to LT. Further he contends:

1. "The Secretary of State is wrong to assert that the Appellant is the leader of MDI in the United Kingdom. The Appellant did attend the MDI conference in Pakistan and he spoke about the welfare, educational and religious work done by him and the organisation which employs him in the United Kingdom (JAH).

2. The Secretary of State is wrong to assert that the Appellant has raised funds for the Mujahiden or recruited any British Muslims to undergo any militant training in the Indian sub-continent. The only funds that he has raised were for the purpose of supporting educational and welfare projects in Pakistan. The Appellant is not aware that these funds were used for military operations in the Jihad.

3. The Appellant's activities in the United Kingdom do not support terrorism in the Indian sub-continent. He had never been involved in any weapons handling. Neither he nor, to his knowledge, any of his supporters have ever been involved in any weapons training or handling. . . .

4. The Appellant supports the cause of the people of Kashmir but does not and never has supported any terrorist organisation which relies on violence to achieve its aims.

5. The Secretary of State has misconstrued his powers of deportation

on the basis of national security. This should be construed strictly and narrowly.

6.   The Appellant submits that the power to deport is limited to activities which have a direct bearing on the national security of the United Kingdom and not of any foreign government."

The Hearing Before SIAC

22. Part of the hearing before SIAC was open to the public in the normal way. Part was held in private and part was held in closed session. During the hearings in public and in private, Mr Shafiq Ur Rehman was represented by Mr Kadri QC. During the closed session Mr Nicholas Blake QC was the special advocate. SIAC held two hearings of the appeal. At the first the Secretary of State was represented by Mr Philip Sales. At the second the Secretary of State was represented by Miss Sharpston QC and Mr Tam. In their submissions to SIAC there was a difference in emphasis between Miss Sharpston and Mr Sales.

23. Miss Sharpston's submissions were influenced by the traditional approach of the courts to issues as to national security. She with justification submitted that it was well established that the courts have always accepted that what constitutes a danger to national security is a matter for the Government and not a matter in relation to which the courts would intervene. She submitted that it was "quintessentially not a matter for SIAC." SIAC like the courts "may examine the types of activity which the Secretary of State regards as constituting a threat to national security in order to satisfy itself that the policy which has been adopted is not unlawful in the Wednesbury sense" but that is the limit to SIAC's role. The 1997 Act permitted SIAC to review the factual allegations which were made but not the policy aspects of national security with which it was wholly inapt to deal.

24. On the other hand Mr Sales accepted before SIAC, that SIAC was entitled to substitute its own view for that of the Secretary of State, but that "in assessing a risk to national security the views of the Executive (based as they are on detailed expert knowledge of terrorism, derived from study of the problem over many years) are entitled to considerable weight.

25. Both Mr Kadri and Mr Blake submitted that the three reasons for deeming a person's deportation to be conducive to the public good under s.15(3) are mutually exclusive and should be read disjunctively. The Secretary of State had relied solely upon the ground of national security and he could not therefore justify his decision basing himself upon damage which might be done to relations between this country and any other country. Nor had any other reasons of a political nature been asserted.

Mr Blake also submitted that no case had been advanced or even argued that MDI:

1. threatens the economic well being of the State;
2. threatens to undermine Parliamentary democracy in the UK by any means;
3. is itself a foreign power intent on occupation, invasion, espionage, or attack on British interests here or abroad;
4. . . . even if MDI is terrorist there is no terrorism directed at the realm that encompasses the physical safety of all residents of the UK, their property, and their safety and interests abroad;
5. the concept of threat, danger, defence of the realm all require actions to be targeted at the United Kingdom its government and its people, and that expulsion of the appellant would protect against this threat."

26. SIAC rejected the approach of Miss Sharpston. They regarded it as their responsibility to construe the expression national security. They considered that it would defeat the purpose for which SIAC was set up if it was not able to decide both the issues of law and fact which were before them. They also accepted Mr Kadri and Mr Blake's submission that s.15(3) of the 1971 Act should be read disjunctively. They considered that "national security" should be construed narrowly and not in the way contended for by the Secretary of State. They derived assistance from the speech of Lord Diplock in *CCSU v Minister for the Civil Service* [1985] AC 374 at p.410 A-C and the judgment of Lord Denning MR in *R v Secretary of State for Home Affairs ex parte Hosenball* [1977] 1 WLR 766 at p.778 D-H and p.783 F-H. They also "noted" a statement which they recognised was obiter, by Lord Justice Staughton in *Chahal v Secretary of State for the Home Department* [1995] 1 WLR 526 at p.531 H. In his judgment Lord Justice Staughton expressed doubt as to whether supporting terrorism in India could affect the national security of this country.

27. SIAC found a passage in a book by Professor Gtahl-Madsen in his book "The Refugee in International Law" (1966), "particularly helpful." The passage is in the following terms:

"A person may be said to offend against national security if he engages in activities directed at the overthrow by external or internal force or other illegal means of the government of the country concerned or in activities which are directed against a foreign government which as a result threaten the former government with intervention of a serious nature."

28. SIAC concluded:

"In the circumstances, and for the purposes of this case, we adopt the position that a person may be said to offend against national security if he engages in, promotes, or encourages violent activity which is *targeted* at the United Kingdom, its system of government or its people. This includes activities directed against the overthrow or destabilisation of a foreign government if that foreign government is likely to take reprisals against the United Kingdom which affect the security of the United Kingdom or of its nationals. National security extends also to situations where United Kingdom citizens are *targeted*, wherever they may be. This is the definition of national security which should be applied to the issues of fact raised by this appeal." (emphasis added)

29. SIAC indicated that as to issues of fact, their approach was as follows:

". . . we have asked ourselves whether the Secretary of State has satisfied us to a high civil balance of probabilities that the deportation of this Appellant, a lawful resident of the United Kingdom, is made out on public good grounds because he has engaged in conduct that endangers the national security of the United Kingdom and, unless deported, is likely to continue to do so."

30. Applying the standard of a "high civil balance of probabilities" SIAC reached the following conclusion on the issues of fact:

1. Recruitment. We are not satisfied that the Appellant has been shown to have recruited British Muslims to undergo militant training as alleged.
2. We are not satisfied that the Appellant has been shown to have engaged in fund-raising for the LT as alleged.
3. We are not satisfied that the Appellant has been shown to have knowingly sponsored individuals for militant training camps as alleged.
4. We are not satisfied that the evidence demonstrates the existence in the United Kingdom of returnees, originally recruited by the Appellant, who during the course of that training overseas have been indoctrinated with extremist beliefs or given weapons training, and who as a result allow them to create a threat to the United Kingdom's national security in the future.

As to the Appellant's activities in sponsoring Pakistanis to enter the United Kingdom by assisting them to make visa applications, we would say only that nothing the Appellant has been proved to have done in this respect could be said to constitute a threat to national security as defined. As for the Respondent's assertion that the Appellant's future behaviour, if he is not deported, is likely to threaten national security, we have heard and seen no evidence that supports such a prediction. Indeed, if anything, the balance of the evidence has been to the opposite effect. In any case, in view of our findings the Appellant has not been proved to have acted in the past in such a way as to cause a threat or damage to national security. We are not satisfied on the evidence that his future behaviour is likely to constitute such a threat or to cause such damage.

We have reached all these conclusions while recognising that it is not disputed that the Appellant has provided sponsorship, information and advice to persons going to Pakistan for the forms of training which may have included militant or extremist training. Whether the Appellant knew of the militant content of such training has not, in our opinion, been satisfactorily established to the required standard by the evidence. Nor have we overlooked the Appellant's statement that he sympathised with the aims of LT in so far as that organisation confronted what he regarded as illegal violence in Kashmir. But, in our opinion, these sentiments do not justify the conclusion contended for by the Respondent. It follows, from these conclusions of fact, that the Respondent has not established that the Appellant was, is, and is likely to be a threat to national security. In our view, that would be the case whether the wider or narrower definition of that term, as identified above, is taken as the test. Accordingly we consider that the Respondent's decisions in question were not in accordance with the law or the Immigration Rules (paragraph 364 of HC 395) and thus we allow these appeals."

The Secretary of State's Appeal

31. Mr Philip Sales and Mr Robin Tam appeared on behalf of the Secretary of State on this appeal. Mr Kadri appeared on behalf of Mr Shafiq Ur Rehman. As it was possible that part of the hearing would have to be in closed session, Mr Blake appeared at the request of the court. The 1997 Act makes no provision for a special advocate on an appeal. However, it seemed to us that, if it was necessary for the court in order to dispose justly of the appeal to hear submissions in the absence of Mr Shafiq Ur Rehman and his counsel, under the inherent jurisdiction of the court, counsel instructed by the Treasury Solicitor, with the agreement of the Attorney General, would be able to perform a similar role to a special advocate without the advantage of statutory backing for this being done. A court will only hear submissions on a substantive appeal in the absence of a party in the most extreme circumstances. However, considerations of national security can create situations where this is necessary. If this happens, the court should use its inherent power to reduce the risk of prejudice to the absent party so far as possible and by analogy with the 1997 Act, Mr Blake could certainly then have provided assistance.

32. The court also was initially of the opinion that it would be appropriate for Mr Blake to act as an Amicus. Accordingly the Attorney General was invited to appoint him in that capacity. However, for understandable reasons the Attorney General did not feel this would be appropriate because a special advocate is not neutral but intended to advance the case of the absent party. The Attorney General therefore instructed Mr Ian Macdonald

QC to appear as Amicus and we are grateful to the Attorney General for enabling both Mr Blake and Mr Macdonald to appear. We were greatly assisted by Mr Macdonald's argument. In the event we were able to conduct the appeal in public in the ordinary way and so it was not necessary for Mr Blake to address us. We did however have the advantage of his written submissions. Mr Sales arguments before us on behalf of the Secretary of State can be considered under four heads which we will deal with in turn.

National Security

33. The correctness of SIAC's approach as to what is capable of being regarded as a threat to national security is the most important issue on this appeal. SIAC acknowledged they were adopting a narrow interpretation. They were influenced in doing so by the alternative grounds set out in s.15(3) of the 1971 Act. The use by SIAC of the word "targeted" clearly indicates that SIAC considered the conduct relied on had to be directed against the United Kingdom. Mr Macdonald initially in his skeleton argument was minded to accept the correctness of SIAC's approach. However, in the course of this hearing and in his oral submissions he accepted that the approach which SIAC adopted was too restrictive.

34. It cannot be the case that if a course of conduct would adversely reflect on the security of this country, it is not open to the Secretary of State to regard the person's presence in this country as not being conducive to the public good because the target for the conduct is another country. Whatever may have been the position in the past, increasingly the security of one country is dependent upon the security of other countries. That is why this country has entered into numerous alliances. They acknowledge the extent to which this country's security is dependent upon the security of other countries. The establishment of NATO is but a reflection of this reality. An attack on an ally can undermine the security of this country. The evidence before SIAC, by Mr Wrench, a senior civil servant in the Home Office and head of the terrorism and protection unit, in the form of a note, makes the position clear. I refer by way of illustration to three paragraphs of his note in support of what I regard as a justification for a wider approach than that adopted by SIAC:

   1.   "Successive Governments in this country have consistently condemned terrorism in all its forms, wherever, whenever and for whatever motive it is committed. The United Kingdom works in a wide range of international fora—including the United Nations, the G8 and the European Union—to encourage collective condemnation of terrorism and effective practical action against it. The direct threat from international terrorism to the United Kingdom, and to British

interests in other countries, including the millions of British citizens travelling or working abroad, is one reason for that policy. British citizens have been attacked, taken hostage and murdered by terrorists overseas. The objectives of such terrorists may or may not be to damage the national security of the United Kingdom, but the effect is to harm individuals for whom Her Majesty's Government has a worldwide consular responsibility. . . .

2. An important part of the Government's strategy to protect the UK and UK citizens and interests abroad from the terrorist threat is to foster co-operation between states in combating terrorist groups whatever their objectives. The UK can only expect other states to take measures to combat terrorists who target the UK or UK citizens if the UK, for its part, reciprocates by combating terrorists who target states other than the UK. It cannot be predicted when such ties of reciprocity may prove to be critical to protecting national security from, eg, a terrorist bombing campaign. It is therefore essential in the interests of national security that the UK fosters such ties with as many states as possible now, against the day when any of them may be able to act directly to safeguard the UK's security interests (whether by taking measures against terrorists in their own territory, or by providing the UK with intelligence about proposed terrorist activity).

3. In Lord Lloyd's report on the future need for counter-terrorist legislation published in October 1996 (Cm 3420) he said:
"A country which seeks to protect itself against international terrorism will not succeed if its defences are confined to its own soil. The activities of international terrorists abroad, whether or not British interests are directly affected, are of concern to the Government because Government's policy must be, and is, that the UK should take an active part in securing international co-operation in fighting terrorism." (para. 2.4)

35. Mr Sales correctly submitted that "national security" is a protean concept, "designed to encompass the many, varied and (it may be) unpredictable ways in which the security of the nation may best be promoted."

36. Although not binding upon us, we would adopt the approach of Auld LJ on a renewed application for judicial review in *Raghbit Singh* [1996] Imm AR 507 at p.511 when he said:

"As to "national security," as Laws J pointed out in his judgment, all sorts of consequences may flow from the very existence of terrorist conspiracies or organisations here, whether or not their outcome is intended to occur abroad. Who knows what equally violent response here this sort of conduct may provoke?"

37. We would also refer to a short passage in a speech of Lord Mustill in *T v The Home Secretary* [1996] AC 742 761 F-H where he said:

"Not all refugees were worthy of compassion and support. As Article 1F of the Convention recognised, war criminals and offenders against the laws of nations could properly be sent home to answer for their crimes. . . . Another, and rather different, impulse was also opposed to the universal reception of refugees; namely the acknowledgement that terror as a means of gaining what might loosely be described as political ends posed a danger not only to individual states but also to the community of nations."

38. At the conclusion of the argument we invited counsel to submit a definition of national security. Mr Macdonald provided the following definition:

"In alleged terrorist cases, a person may be said to be a danger to the United Kingdom's national security if he or she engages in, promotes or encourages violent activity which has, or is likely to have, adverse repercussions on the security of the United Kingdom, its system of government or its people."

39. We regard this as being a generally helpful approach but it is not conclusive or exhaustive. It first of all recognises that what can be regarded as affecting national security can vary according to the danger being considered. Mr Macdonald wisely confined his definition to cases involving terrorism. We also approve the reference which is made in the definition to there having to be adverse repercussions on the security of this country. The repercussions can be direct or indirect. Mr Macdonald indicated that he considered that the adverse repercussions had to be "likely." We consider that it is sufficient if the adverse repercussions are of a kind which create a risk of adverse repercussions. As long as there is a real possibility of adverse repercussions, then the degree of likelihood only becomes important when the Secretary of State has to weigh up against the risk of adverse repercussions the adverse effect of deportation on the immigrant.

40. As to the three situations referred to in s.15(3) of the 1971 Act, while it is correct that they are alternatives, there is clearly room for there to be an overlap. Here if there were terrorist activities to which Mr Shafiq Ur Rehman was giving encouragement, which were directed against India's links with Kashmir, then the involvement of individuals coming from this country could damage relations between this country and India. However, the fact that the conduct could have an adverse affect on our relationship with a friendly state does not mean that the activities could not also have national security consequences. The promotion of terrorism against any state is capable of being a threat to our own national security. The Government is perfectly entitled to treat any undermining of its policy to protect this country from international terrorism as being contrary to the security interests of this country.

41. It follows that the approach of SIAC was flawed in so far as it required the conduct relied on by the Secretary of State to be targeted on this country or its citizens.

Standard of Proof

42. SIAC were, however, correct to regard it as being their responsibility to determine questions of fact and law. The fact that Parliament has given SIAC responsibility of reviewing the manner in which the Secretary of State has exercised his discretion, inevitably leads to this conclusion. Without statutory intervention, this is not a role which a court readily adopts. But SIAC's membership meant that it was more appropriate for SIAC to perform this role.

43. The fact that SIAC is entitled to determine for itself issues of fact, does not assist as to the standard of proof which it should apply when doing so. SIAC accepted that the views of the Secretary of State as to what was conducive to the public good for reasons of national security should be given considerable weight. It was right to do so because questions of policy in this area must primarily be for the Secretary of State. The Executive is bound to be in a better position to determine what should be the policy to adopt on national security than any tribunal no matter how eminent. However, having acknowledged that the Executive's assessment is entitled "to considerable weight," SIAC then identified five specific allegations made by the Secretary of State and came to the conclusion, applying a high civil balance of probabilities, they were not satisfied that the case against Mr Shafiq Ur Rehman had been made out. On one approach to the issue which was before them, the standard applied by SIAC was perfectly appropriate. In so far as the Secretary of State was relying on specific allegations of serious misconduct by Mr Shafiq Ur Rehman, then SIAC was entitled to say the allegations had not been proved.

44. However, in any national security case the Secretary of State is entitled to make a decision to deport not only on the basis that the individual has in fact endangered national security but that he is a *danger* to national security. When the case is being put in this way, it is necessary not to look only at the individual allegations and ask whether they have been proved. It is also necessary to examine the case as a whole against an individual and then ask whether on a global approach that individual is a danger to national security, taking into account the Executive's policy with regard to national security. When this is done, the cumulative effect may establish that the individual is to be treated as a danger, although it cannot be proved to a high degree of probability that he has performed any individual act which would justify this conclusion. Here it is important to remember that the individual is still subject to immigration control. He

is not in the same position as a British Citizen. He has not been charged with a specific criminal offence. It is the danger which he constitutes to national security which is to be balanced against his own personal interests. There are statements made by SIAC in its decision indicating that even if they had accepted the Secretary of State's submissions as to the correct approach they would have come to the same conclusion, However SIAC's approach in general was so different from that of the Secretary of State and different from that which we have indicated is the correct approach, again we come to the conclusion that SIAC's decision has to be regarded as flawed.

The Reasons

45. Rule 23(1) of the SIAC rules reads:

   "23(1) The Commission must record its determination and, if and to the extent it is possible to do so without disclosing information contrary to the public interest, the reasons for it."

46. The Secretary of State submits that as a matter of law and as a matter of good sense, SIAC should give full reasons why an appeal fails, subject to a reduction in the version given to the appellant to take account of the need to protect sensitive sources of information.

47. Mindful of the need to protect sensitive information, SIAC did not in its reasoning analyse the factual evidence. It considered, however, that it was fairer and more sensible to produce only one version of its decision, a version which could be appropriately shown to Mr Shafiq Ur Rehman. There are obvious disadvantages in having two versions in existence of the decision and having regard to the Rules, we regard the course which was adopted by SIAC as being wholly appropriate. In this case SIAC was able to give a reasoned decision which did not offend Rule 23(1) and which fully explained the basis of the decision. No more was required.

Conduct of the Hearing before SIAC

48. A full consideration of this issue on the appeal would at least have required the Court of Appeal to go into closed session. This would not have been desirable. In any event it is doubtful whether an issue of this sort falls within s.7(1) of the 1997 Act as a question of law material to the determination.

49. Mr Sales, in view of the reluctance of the court to go into private session, did not press this ground of appeal. That was appropriate. While we are not in a position to express any view as to how the case was conducted before SIAC, we do point out the obvious need for counsel appearing

before SIAC to be extremely careful, consistent with their duty to their client, not to ask any questions during parts of the hearing which are open to the public which could directly or indirectly reveal sensitive information. Unless the advocates behave in that way, more of the hearing will either have to be held in private or in closed session than would otherwise be the case and this is not in the interest of justice. Before leaving this subject it is right that we should make clear that we understand from Mr Kadri that SIAC rejected any criticism of the manner in which he conducted the case.

50. For reasons we have indicated, the appeal will be allowed and remitted to SIAC for re-determination applying the approach indicated in our judgment.

DOCUMENT NO 14

Opinions Of The Lords Of Apeal For Judgement In The Cause O'Hara

v

Chief Constable Of The Royal Ulster Constabulary
House Of Lords

December 12, 1996

LORD GOFF OF CHIEVELEY

My Lords,

I have had the opportunity of reading in draft the speeches to be delivered by my noble and learned friends Lords Steyn and Lord Hope of Craighead. For the reasons which they give I too would dismiss the appeal.

LORD MUSTILL

My Lords,

I have had the opportunity of reading in draft the speeches to be delivered by my noble and learned friends Lords Steyn and Lord Hope of Craighead. I agree with both, and would dismiss the appeal.

LORD STEYN

My Lords,

I gratefully adopt the account of the background to this appeal given by my noble and learned friend, Lord Hope of Craighead. The appeal can be decided on narrow grounds. The arrest was prima facie unlawful. At trial the respondent sought to justify the arrest under section 12(1) of the Prevention of Terrorism (Temporary Provisions) Act 1984. So far as it is material section 12(1) reads as follows:

". . . a constable may arrest without warrant a person whom he has reasonable grounds for suspecting to be-. . .

"(b) a person who is or has been concerned in the commission, preparation or instigation of acts of terrorism to which this Part of this Act applies; . . . ."

The constable made the arrest in connection with a murder which was undoubtedly an act of terrorism within the meaning of section 12(1) of the 1984 Act. It was common ground that subjectively the constable had the necessary suspicion. The question was whether the constable objectively had reasonable grounds for suspecting that the appellant was concerned in the murder. The constable said in evidence that his reasonable grounds for suspecting the appellant were based on a briefing by a superior officer. He was told that the appellant had been involved in the murder. The constable said that the superior officer ordered him to arrest the appellant. He did so. Counsel for the appellant took the tactical decision not to cross-examine the constable about the details of the briefing. The trial judge described the evidence as scanty. But he inferred that the briefing afforded reasonable grounds for the necessary suspicion. In other words the judge inferred that some further details must have been given in the briefing. The legal burden was on the respondent to prove the existence of reasonable grounds for suspicion. Nevertheless I am persuaded that the judge was entitled on the sparse materials before him to infer the existence of reasonable grounds for suspicion. On this basis the Court of Appeal was entitled to dismiss the appeal. That means that the appeal before your Lordships House must also fail on narrow and purely factual grounds.

Plainly, leave to appeal was granted by the Appeal Committee because it was thought that the appeal raised an issue of general public importance. It was far from clear from the printed cases of the appellant and respondent what the issue of principle was. But during his oral submissions Mr. Coghlin, Q.C. on behalf of the respondent raised an issue of principle. He submitted that the order to arrest given by the superior officer to the arresting officer in this case was by itself sufficient to afford the constable a reasonable suspicion within the meaning of section 12(1). This point is of continuing relevance in relation to the Prevention of Terrorism (Temporary Provisions) Act 1989 which contains a provision in identical terms to section 12(1)(b) of the Act of 1984. But the point is also of wider importance. In the past many statutes have vested powers in constables to arrest where the constable suspects on reasonable grounds that a person has committed an offence or is committing an offence: see *Moriarty's Police Law*, 24th ed. (1981), pp. 19 et seq. and Appendix 9.2 of The Investigation and Prosecution of Criminal Offences in England and Wales: The Law and Procedure, the Royal Commission on Criminal Procedure, (Cmnd 8092-1), (1981) pp. 135–138. An important modern example of such a power is to be found in section 24(6) of the Police and Criminal Evidence Act 1984. Some of the older specific powers also remain. Moreover, the point is of considerable practical importance since orders to arrest are no doubt routinely given by superior officers to constables. It is therefore necessary to examine the point in some detail.

Counsel for the respondent relied on the decision of the House of Lords *McKee v. Chief Constable for Northern Ireland* [1984] 1 W.L.R. 1358 in support of his submission on the point of principle. The issue was the lawfulness of the arrest of a suspected terrorist. The matter was governed by section 11(1) of the Northern Ireland (Emergency Provisions) Act 1978. It reads as follows:

> "Any constable may arrest without warrant any person whom he suspects of being a terrorist."

Applying that provision Lord Roskill, speaking for all their Lordships observed, at p. 1361H:

> "On the true construction of section 11(1) of the statute, what matters is the state of mind of the arresting officer and of no one else. That state of mind can legitimately be derived from the instruction given to the arresting officer by his superior officer. The arresting officer is not bound and indeed may well not be entitled to question those instructions or to ask upon what information they are founded."

The statutory provision under consideration in *McKee* did not require that an arresting officer must have reasonable grounds for suspicion. Moreover, the legislation was in much wider terms inasmuch as it authorised arrest for the purpose of internment. That statute was repealed in 1987 and your Lordships are concerned with a quite different statutory provision. In these circumstances Lord Roskill's observations throw no light on the proper construction of section 12(1) of the Act of 1984 which in terms provides that the power to arrest under it only arises where the constable has reasonable grounds for the necessary suspicion. Contrary to counsel's submission I would hold that it is misuse of precedent to transpose Lord Roskill's observations made in the context of the subjective requirement of a genuine belief to the objective requirement of the existence of reasonable grounds. *McKee* is irrelevant on the point of principle under consideration in this case. On the other hand, the decision of the House of Lords in *Mohammed-Holgate v. Duke* [1984] A.C. 437 is of assistance. The House had to consider the issue whether an arrest was lawful in the context of a statutory provision which authorised arrest when a constable suspected on reasonable grounds that an arrestable offence had been committed. Lord Diplock made the following general observations, at p. 445B-E:

> "My Lords, there is inevitably the potentiality of conflict between the public interest in preserving the liberty of the individual and the public interest in the detection of crime and the bringing to justice of those who commit it. The members of the organised police forces of the country have, since the mid-19th century, been charged with the duty of taking the first steps to promote the latter public interest by inquiring into suspected offences with a view to identifying the perpetrators of them and

of obtaining sufficient evidence admissible in a court of law against the persons they suspect of being the perpetrators as would justify charging them with the relevant offence before a magistrates' court with a view to their committal for trial for it.

"The compromise which English common and statutory law has evolved for the accommodation of the two rival public interests while these first steps are being taken by the police is two-fold:

a.   no person may be arrested without warrant (i.e. without the intervention of a judicial process) unless the constable arresting him has reasonable cause to suspect him to be guilty of an arrestable offence . . .

b.   "a suspect so arrested and detained in custody must be brought before a magistrates' court as soon as practicable . . . ."

Lord Diplock made those observations in the context of statutes containing provisions such as section 12(1). He said that the arrest can only be justified if the constable arresting the alleged suspect has reasonable grounds to suspect him to be guilty of an arrestable offence. The arresting officer is held accountable. That is the compromise between the values of individual liberty and public order.

Section 12(1) authorises an arrest without warrant only where the constable "has reasonable grounds for" suspicion. An arrest is therefore not lawful if the arresting officer honestly but erroneously believes that he has reasonable grounds for arrest but there are unknown to him in fact in existence reasonable grounds for the necessary suspicion, e.g. because another officer has information pointing to the guilt of the suspect. It would be difficult without doing violence to the wording of the statute to read it in any other way.

A strong argument can be made that in arresting a suspect without warrant a constable ought to be able to rely on information in the possession of another officer and not communicated to him: *Feldman, The Law Relating to Entry, Search & Seizure*, (1986), pp. 204–205. Arguably that ought as a matter of policy to provide him with a defence to a claim for wrongful arrest. Such considerations may possibly explain why article 5(1) of the European Convention for the Protection of Human Rights and Freedoms 1950 contains a more flexible provision. It reads as follows:

"Everyone has the right to liberty and security of person. No one shall be deprived of his liberty save in the following cases and in accordance with a procedure prescribed by law: . . .

"c. the lawful arrest or detention of a person effected for the purpose of bringing him before the competent legal authority on reasonable suspicion of having committed an offence or when it is reasonably considered necessary to prevent his committing an offence or fleeing after having done so; . . ."

It is clear from the drafting technique employed in article 5(1)c., and in particular the use of the passive tense, that it contemplates a broader test of whether a reasonable suspicion exists and does not confine it to matters present in the mind of the arresting officer. That is also the effect of the judgment of the European Court of Human Rights in *Fox v. United Kingdom* (1990) 13 E.H.R.R. 157, 167–169, paras. 33–35. But section 12(1), and similar provisions, cannot be approached in this way: they categorise as reasonable grounds for suspicion only matters present in the mind of the constable. In *Civil Liberties & Human Rights in England and Wales,* (1993), Professor Feldman lucidly explained the difference between two classes of statutes, at p. 199:

> "Where reasonable grounds for suspicion are required in order to justify the arrest of someone who turns out to be innocent, the [Police and Criminal Evidence Act 1984] requires that the constable personally has reasonable grounds for the suspicion, and it would seem to follow that he is not protected if, knowing nothing of the case, he acts on orders from another officer who, perhaps, does have such grounds. On the other hand, under statutes which require only the objective existence of reasonable grounds for suspicion, it is possible that the officer need neither have the reasonable grounds nor himself suspect anything; he can simply follow orders."

Section 12(1) is undeniably a statutory provision in the first category. The rationale for the principle in such cases is that in framing such statutory provisions Parliament has proceeded on the longstanding constitutional theory of the independence and accountability of the individual constable: *Marshall and Loveday, The Police Independence and Accountability in The Changing Constitution,* 3rd ed., ed. by Jowell and Oliver, 295 et seq; Christopher L. Ryan and Katherine S. Williams, Police Discretion, 1986 Public Law 285, at 305. This case must therefore be approached on the basis that under section 12(1) the only relevant matters are those present in the mind of the arresting officer.

Certain general propositions about the powers of constables under a section such as section 12(1) can now be summarised. (1) In order to have a reasonable suspicion the constable need not have evidence amounting to a prima facie case. Ex hypothesi one is considering a preliminary stage of the investigation and information from an informer or a tip-off from a member of the public may be enough: *Hussien v. Chong Fook Kam* [1970] A.C. 942, 949. (2) Hearsay information may therefore afford a constable a reasonable grounds to arrest. Such information may come from other officers: *Hussien's* case, ibid. (3) The information which causes the constable to be suspicious of the individual must be in existence to the knowledge of the police officer at the time he makes the arrest. (4) The executive "discretion" to arrest or not as Lord Diplock described it in *Mohammed-Holgate v. Duke* [1984] A.C. 437, 446, vests in the constable, who is engaged on the decision to arrest or not, and not in his superior officers.

Given the independent responsibility and accountability of a constable under a provision such as section 12(1) of the Act of 1984 it seems to follow that the mere fact that an arresting officer has been instructed by a superior officer to effect the arrest is not capable of amounting to reasonable grounds for the necessary suspicion within the meaning of section 12(1). It is accepted, and rightly accepted, that a mere request to arrest without any further information by an equal ranking officer, or a junior officer, is incapable of amounting to reasonable grounds for the necessary suspicion. How can the badge of the superior officer, and the fact that he gave an order, make a difference? In respect of a statute vesting an independent discretion in the particular constable, and requiring him personally to have reasonable grounds for suspicion, it would be surprising if seniority made a difference. It would be contrary to the principle underlying section 12(1) which makes a constable individually responsible for the arrest and accountable in law. In *Reg. v. Chief Constable of Devon and Cornwall, Ex parte Central Electricity Generating Board* [1982] Q.B. 458, 474 Lawton L.J. touched on this point. He observed:

"[chief constables] cannot give an officer under command an order to do acts which can only lawfully be done if the officer himself with reasonable cause suspects that a breach of the peace has occurred or is imminently likely to occur or an arrestable offence has been committed."

Such an order to arrest cannot without some further information being given to the constable be sufficient to afford the constable reasonable grounds for the necessary suspicion. That seems to me to be the legal position in respect of a provision such as section 12(1). For these reasons I regard the submission of counsel for the respondent as unsound in law. In practice it follows that a constable must be given some basis for a request to arrest somebody under a provision such as section 12(1), e.g. a report from an informer.

Subject to these observations, I agree that the appeal ought to be dismissed.

The same approach has been taken in the context of other statutory powers where the question has been raised whether the constable who exercised the power had reasonable grounds to suspect that an offence had been committed. In *Castorina v. Chief Constable of Surrey*, The Times, 15 June 1988; (unreported), Court of Appeal (Civil Division) Transcript No. 499 of 1988, which was concerned with section 2(4) of the Criminal Law Act 1967, Sir Frederick Lawton said:

"Suspicion by itself, however, will not justify an arrest. There must be a factual basis for it of a kind which a court would adjudge to be reasonable. The facts may be within the arresting constable's own knowledge or have been reported to him. When there is an issue in a trial as to whether a constable had reasonable cause, his claim to have had knowledge or to have received reports on which he relied may be challenged. It is within this context that there may be an evidential issue as to what he believed to be the facts, but it will be for the court to adjudge what were the facts which made him suspect that the person he arrested was guilty of the offence which he was investigating."

In *Dryburgh v. Galt* 1981 J.C. 69, 72, in a case which was concerned with the question whether police officers had reasonable cause to suspect that the appellant had alcohol in his body while he was driving, having received an anonymous telephone message to that effect, Lord Justice-Clerk Wheatley said:

"Suffice it to say that the fact that the information on which the police officer formed his suspicion turns out to be ill-founded does not in itself necessarily establish that the police officer's suspicion was unfounded. The circumstances known to the police officer at the time he formed his suspicion constitute the criterion, not the facts as subsequently ascertained. The circumstances may be either what the police officer has himself observed or the information which he has received."

Copland v. McPherson 1970 S.L.T. 87 shows how the question whether the constable had reasonable cause to suspect may arise in a case where the exercise of the power is the result of co-operation between several police officers. The respondent in that case was driving along a road when he was stopped by two plain clothes police officers. They noticed a smell of alcohol on his breath, so they sent for uniformed police officers and breath sampling equipment for the carrying out of a roadside breath test. The respondent refused to provide a sample of his breath when he was required to do so by the uniformed officers. He was removed to a police station where he again refused to provide a breath sample. He was charged with offences under section 2(3) of the Road Safety Act 1967. He was acquitted by the sheriff on the ground that the uniformed police officers had not seen the respondent driving or attempting to drive before they required him to submit to the breath test. On appeal by the prosecutor it was held that the uniformed police officers had reasonable cause to suspect the respondent of having alcohol in his body and that, as it was conceded that the respondent at the time was a person who came within the category of "a person driving . . . a motor vehicle," they were acting within their powers when they required the respondent to provide a sample of his breath. Lord Cameron, at p. 90, rejected the respondent's contention that reasonable cause could not exist in any case in which the uniformed police officers did not themselves see the person suspected himself driving or attempting to drive the motor car. He pointed out that to hold otherwise would involve that a uniformed constable could never act in such a case on information received, however compelling and reliable in quality and source. He went on to say this:

"The issue then becomes purely one of fact: the findings in the case, in my opinion, clearly support the conclusion that the uniformed police officers who were called to the scene at the request of their plain clothes colleagues had such reasonable cause. No doubt the 'reasonable cause' must have arisen in the mind of the officer before he makes the statutory request of a person in the necessary category but when, as here, uniformed officers are called on by plain clothes colleagues to attend on a driver whose conduct has led to such a call and for so obvious reason as is found in this case, I think that in such circumstances the uniformed officers have in fact very reasonable cause for suspicion that the driver has alcohol in his body."

Many other examples may be cited of cases where the action of the constable who exercises a statutory power of arrest or of search is a member of a team of police officers, or where his action is the culmination of various steps taken by other police officers, perhaps over a long period and perhaps also involving officers from other police forces. For obvious practical reasons police officers must be able to rely upon each other in taking decisions as to whom to arrest or where to search and in what circumstances. The statutory power does not require that the constable who exercises the power must be in possession of all the information which has led to a decision, perhaps taken by others, that the time has come for it to be exercised. What it does require is that the constable who exercises the power must first have equipped himself with sufficient information so that he has reasonable cause to suspect before the power is exercised.

I should add that I see no conflict in principle between the approach which has been taken in these cases and the judgment of the European Court of Human Rights in *Fox v. United Kingdom* (1990) 13 E.H.R.R. 157 to which we were referred by Mr. Kennedy. The applicants had been detained without warrant under section 11 of the Northern Ireland (Emergency Provisions) Act 1978. As has already been noted, this section provided for the arrest without warrant of any person whom a constable suspected of being a terrorist. It was held that as the constable's suspicion had not been shown to be "reasonable," the United Kingdom were in breach of article 5(1) of the Convention, which provides:

"Everyone has the right to liberty and security of person. No one shall be deprived of his liberty save in the following cases and in accordance with the procedure prescribed by law: . . .

c. The lawful arrest or detention of a person effected for the purpose of bringing him before the competent legal authority on reasonable suspicion of having committed an offence . . ."

In that case, as was stated, at p. 169, para. 35 of the judgment, the arrest and detention of the applicants was based on a suspicion which was bona fide or genuine. But the court held that the Government had not provided sufficient material to support the conclusion that the suspicion was "reasonable," and that its explanations did not meet the minimum standard set by article 5(1)c.

for judging the reasonableness of a suspicion for the arrest of an individual. As to what these requirements are, they are to be found in the following passage in the judgment, at p. 167, para. 32:

> "The 'reasonableness' of the suspicion on which an arrest must be based forms an essential part of the safeguard against arbitrary arrest and detention which is laid down in article 5(1)c. The court agrees with the Commission and the Government that having a 'reasonable suspicion' presupposes the existence of facts or information which would satisfy an objective observer that the person concerned may have committed the offence. What may be regarded as 'reasonable' will however depend upon all the circumstances."

What Parliament has enacted in section 12(1)(b) of the Act of 1984, as in the other statutes to which I have referred, is that the reasonable suspicion has to be in the mind of the arresting officer. So it is the facts known by or the information given to the officer who effects the arrest or detention to which the mind of the independent observer must be applied. It is this objective test, applying the criterion of what may be regarded as reasonable, which provides the safeguard against arbitrary arrest and detention. The arrest and detention will be unlawful unless this criterion is satisfied.

My Lords, in this case the evidence about the matters which were disclosed at the briefing session to the arresting officer was indeed scanty. But, as Mr. Coghlin pointed out, the trial judge was entitled to weigh up that evidence in the light of the surrounding circumstances and, having regard to the source of that information, to draw inferences as to what a reasonable man, in the position of the independent observer, would make of it. I do not think that either the trial judge or the Court of Appeal misdirected themselves as to the test to be applied. I would dismiss this appeal.

Judgments—O'Hara v. Chief Constable of the R.U.C

DOCUMENT NO 15

Her Majesty's Advocate

v

Abdelbaset Ali Mohmed Al Megrahi and Al Amin Khalifa Fhimah The High Court Of Justiciary

January 30, 2001

[1] At 1903 hours on 21 December 1988 Pan Am flight 103 fell out of the sky. The 259 passengers and crew members who were on board and 11 residents of Lockerbie where the debris fell were killed. The Crown case is that the cause of the disaster was that an explosive device had been introduced into the hold of the aircraft by the two accused whether acting alone or in concert with each other and others. This device exploded when the aircraft was in Scottish air space thus causing the aircraft to disintegrate. In these circumstances it was originally contended that the accused were guilty of conspiracy to murder, alternatively murder, alternatively a contravention of section 2(1) and (5) of the Aviation Security Act 1982. At the conclusion of the Crown's submissions, however, the libel was restricted to the charge of murder.

[2] It is not disputed, and was amply proved, that the cause of the disaster was indeed the explosion of a device within the aircraft. Nor is it disputed that the person or persons who were responsible for the deliberate introduction of the explosive device would be guilty of the crime of murder. The matter at issue in this trial therefore is whether or not the Crown have proved beyond reasonable doubt that one or other or both of the accused was responsible, actor or art and part, for the deliberate introduction of the device.

[3] After the disaster a massive police operation was mounted to recover as much as possible of the debris in order to ascertain the cause of the crash. Tens of thousands of items were recovered, sifted and recorded, and any that appeared to be of particular interest as indicating a possible cause of the explosion were examined by the relevant specialists.

[4] All the parts of the aircraft that were recovered were taken initially to a hangar in Longtown where they were examined by inspectors of the Air Accidents Investigation Board ("AAIB"). Subsequently the relevant part of

467

the aircraft was reconstructed as far as possible at Farnborough. It was found that the majority of the fractures in the skin of the fuselage were overload fractures consistent with the type of damage to be expected from the airborne break-up of an aircraft structure. There was however an area where the fracture failure characteristics were not typical. This area was on the port side of the lower fuselage in the forward cargo bay area. The basic structure of the aircraft consisted of substantial vertical frames set 20" apart and horizontal stringers about 10" apart, with the fuselage skin being attached to the outside. A small region of the structure bounded approximately by frames 700 and 720 and stringers 38 left and 40 left, thus approximately 20" square, had been completely shattered. The fractures around the shattered area were granular in character, whereas further away the fractures were typical tearing fractures. Around the shattered area there were signs of pitting and sooting. The skin panels in the area immediately surrounding the shattered area had been bent and torn in a starburst pattern and were petalled outwards. From the nature of this damage the conclusion was reached, and it is one which we accept, that the cause of the damage was the detonation of an explosive device within the fuselage, with the initial shattered area forming the focus for the subsequent petalling mode of failure. Further processes led on from that which caused the total disruption and disintegration of the aircraft.

[5] The port side forward cargo bay was loaded with luggage in containers. These containers were approximately 5' by 5' by 5,' with an overhang of approximately 18" angled up from the base on the outboard side designed to make maximum use of the curved space in the cargo hold. Most of the containers were made of aluminium apart from the after side which was open for loading and then covered by a plastic curtain. A few of the containers were made of glass-reinforced fibre. The containers were loaded on to the aircraft through a door in the hold, and then slid on rollers into a prearranged position where they were clamped. As part of the reconstruction process, the recovered pieces of containers were reassembled, principally by Mr Claiden, an engineering inspector with the AAIB. When this was done, it was ascertained that with two exceptions there was no damage to containers other than was to be expected from the disintegration of the aircraft and the containers' fall to the ground. It was however found that there was unusual damage to an aluminium container AVE 4041 and a fibre container AVN 7511. From the loading plan of the containers it was ascertained that AVE 4041 was situated immediately inboard of and slightly above the shattered area of the fuselage, and AVN 7511 was situated immediately aft of AVE 4041. The reconstruction of AVE 4041 demonstrated severe damage to the floor panel and outboard base frame member in the outboard aft quadrant, and also on the internal aspect of that part of the container there were some areas of blackening and pitting. There was also damage to the panels and frame members at the lower aft side of the overhang, and again areas of blackening and pitting. The full

details of the nature and extent of the damage are to be found in the evidence of Mr Claiden, and are confirmed in the evidence of Dr Hayes and Mr Feraday, forensic scientists with the Royal Armaments Research and Development Establishment ("RARDE"). The nature of the damage indicated a high-energy event, and the sooting and pitting indicated an explosion. Mr Claiden, whose evidence was given in an impressively careful and restrained manner, stated "I have no doubts in my mind that such an event occurred from within the container," the only occasion on which he stated an absolutely unqualified opinion. Because of the distribution of the areas of sooting and pitting, and in particular the absence of any such signs on the base of the container, it appeared to Mr Claiden that, assuming that an explosive device was contained in a piece of luggage in the container, the likelihood was that that piece of luggage was not lying on the floor of the container but was lying probably on top of a case on the floor and projecting into the overhang of the container. Ascertainment of the precise location of the explosive device was assisted by consideration of the damage to the adjacent container AVN 7511. The forward face of that container had a hole approximately 8" square about 10" up from the top of the base radiating out from which were areas of sooting extending up to the top of the container. This indicated that a relatively mild blast had exited AVE 4041 and impinged at an angle on the forward face of AVN 7511. Combining that information with the damage to AVE 4041, the likely position of an explosive device was about 13" above the floor of AVE 4041. On that assumption allied to the previous assumption that the piece of luggage containing the device was projecting into the overhang, the position of the device would be approximately 25" from the skin of the fuselage. We found the evidence of Mr Claiden wholly credible, reliable and compelling so far as it went. He was not however an expert on explosives or the effects of explosives. The conclusion reached by Dr Hayes and Mr Feraday as to the position of the explosive device coincided with that of Mr Claiden, and in addition Mr Feraday was present at tests in the USA. These tests involved the use of luggage filled metal containers and the placing of plastic explosives within Toshiba radio cassette players in a garment filled suitcase. The tests confirmed the opinion he expressed as to the position of the explosive device and the quantity of explosive involved.

[6] Technical evidence relating to the effects of explosives was given by Dr Cullis and Professor Peel. Dr Cullis is an expert on the effects of blast and the development of computer codes to simulate the effects of blast in particular different situations, and has been employed at the Defence Evaluation and Research Agency ("DERA") since 1978. Professor Peel is the chief scientist for DERA, specialising in materials and structures used in aircraft, and leader of a team conducting research into *inter alia* the assessment of the effect of detonation of explosives in aircraft. They confirmed that the presence of pitting and carbon deposits which would look like a very fine soot indicated a

chemical explosion. The areas in which this would occur would have to be in line of sight with the explosive, and in particular, as far as pitting was concerned, there would have to be no intervening structure of sufficient mass to prevent explosive fragments impacting on the pitted area. The nature of the cracking in the floor panel of the container is typical of the sort of deformation which would be seen from blast loading, but the absence of pitting or sooting in that area would indicate that there must have been something such as another suitcase situated between the explosive device and the floor panel. On the other hand the pitting and sooting seen on the inner aspect of the horizontal base frame member of the container combined with downward deformation of that member confirms the view that the explosive device was situated above and in direct line of sight of that member and thus was likely to be situated partly at least in the overhang where the presence of a suitcase on the floor of the container would not inhibit the explosive products from striking that member. Further confirmation of the position of the explosive device came from the observation of crushing to the upper surface of the aircraft fuselage frame 700 and pitting and sooting of the two neighbouring frames, this being the area adjacent to the lower after end of the container. Professor Peel's evidence also included a substantial complex section on the nature of impulse loading, the critical level of impulse for failure of aluminium alloy sheet of the type used for the fuselage skin, and the calculation of both the stand-off distance and the size of the explosive charge from the size of the shattered zone and the petalled zone. These calculations indicated a charge of about 450 grammes and a stand-off distance of 610 millimetres, which would take the explosion 200 millimetres inside the container. We do not consider it necessary to go into detail about these complex calculations, as the physical evidence of damage to the hull, the container, and, as we shall see later, the contents of the container satisfies us beyond any doubt that the explosion occurred within the container, and the calculations serve merely to confirm that view. We should add that this section of his evidence also dealt with the effect, if any, of the concept of Mach stem formation, but we do not consider it necessary to go into any detail about that, as we accept his evidence that although that concept was considered as a means of assessing stand-off distance, it was not actually used.

[7] In addition to the evidence of these experts who were all clear that the damage to the aircraft was caused by an explosion, there was also evidence from Dr Douse, who has specialised for many years in the trace analysis of drugs and explosives and in 1988 worked with RARDE. He pioneered the use of capillary gas chromatography, which is now a well recognised procedure. He examined for the presence of explosive residues two pieces of metal (labels 270.1 and 270.3) which had been identified as the two major parts of the outboard base frame member of container AVE 4041. The procedures involved, which were described in great detail in Dr Douse's evidence, ended

with traces on which peaks at particular points may indicate the presence of different types of explosives. These include different variations of nitrotoluene, nitroglycerin, PETN and RDX. There may also be other peaks which result from non-explosive co-extractives. The traces relating to 270.1 and 270.3 indicated the presence of PETN and RDX. These are chemicals used in the manufacture of plastic explosives, including Semtex. In cross-examination it was suggested to him that a report by Professor Caddy presented to Parliament in 1996 on the possible contamination of a centrifuge used at RARDE vitiated his conclusions. However, while that report did indeed suggest that a centrifuge was contaminated with RDX, it also made clear that certain examinations carried out in the period which included December 1988 were not affected, and in the list of such examinations was included the examination of the Lockerbie debris carried out by Dr Douse. It was further suggested to him that the traces disclosed peaks which were consistent with the presence of TNT, DNT and nitroglycerin, but for the detailed reasons which he gave in his evidence he was entirely satisfied that the peaks in question related not to these forms of explosive but to non-explosive co-extractives. We see no reason to doubt the conclusion to which this very experienced expert came. Finally it was submitted that inadequate precautions were taken at the laboratory by way of the use of control swabs of clothing and equipment to prevent the risk of distorted results because of contamination. There was however a description both by Dr Douse and Dr Hayes of the precautions taken to prevent contamination, and we are satisfied that these precautions were adequate to prevent any risk that Dr Douse's tests were vitiated by any contamination.

[8] From this evidence we are entirely satisfied that the cause of the disaster was the explosion of a device which was contained within the aircraft. We would also be satisfied that the device was within container AVE 4041, but any possible doubts about that would be dispelled by the evidence relating to the examination of the apparent contents of that container, to which we now turn.

[9] During the course of the massive ground search, a large quantity of luggage and clothing was collected and labelled. Within a few days of the disaster it was established that an explosion had occurred, and accordingly the searchers were asked in particular to recover any items which appeared to be scorched or blackened or otherwise had the appearance of having been involved in an explosion. Any such items were then submitted to the Forensic Explosives Laboratory at RARDE for detailed examination, the principal forensic scientists involved being Dr Hayes and Mr Feraday. Fifty-six fragments which showed various signs of explosives damage were identified as forming part of what had been a brown hardshell Samsonite suitcase of the 26" Silhouette 4000 range ("the primary suitcase"). The nature of the damage indicated that it had been inflicted from within the suitcase. A further twenty-four items of luggage were identified by their characteristic explosives damage as having

been in relatively close proximity to the explosive device. Within many of these items there were found fragments of what appeared to be parts of the primary suitcase, and also fragments of what appeared to have been a radio cassette player. Other similar fragments were found in clothing which from their charred appearance were considered to have been contained in the primary suitcase. In addition, when examining a data plate which had been attached to AVE 4041, Mr Claiden recovered a piece of debris which appeared to be a small piece of circuit board. The number of fragments associated with the clothing in close contact with the explosion and the extent of the shattering of these fragments indicated that the explosive charge had in all probability been located within the radio. It was known at that time that in October 1988 the West German police had recovered a Toshiba radio cassette player which had been modified to form an improvised explosive device. Mr Feraday visited West Germany to examine this device, and ascertained that the fragments in his possession and in particular the piece of circuit board recovered by Mr Claiden did not originate from the same model. However, he considered that there was a sufficient similarity to make it worth investigating other models of Toshiba players. It was found that there were seven models in which the printed circuit board bore precisely the same characteristics as the fragments. Subsequently, when the blast damaged clothing was examined in detail there were found embedded in two different Slalom brand shirts, a Babygro, and a pair of tartan checked trousers, fragments of paper which on examination proved to be from an owner's manual for a Toshiba RT-SF 16 BomBeat radio cassette player. All the other fragments thought to have originated from the radio containing the explosive were consistent with having come from an RT-SF 16. Other fragments of plastic associated with the radio were found in other items of clothing considered to have been in the primary suitcase, namely a white T-shirt, cream pyjamas, a herringbone jacket, and brown herringbone trousers, as well as in the four items in which the fragments of paper were found. The conclusion reached by the forensic scientists was that the nature of the fragments and their distribution left no doubt that the explosive charge was contained within the Toshiba radio, and we agree with that conclusion. Having regard to the presence of fragments of an RT-SF 16 owner's manual, we also accept that it was that model of Toshiba radio that was involved.

[10] As we have noted, a substantial quantity of clothing was examined at RARDE. The primary concern was to ascertain what clothing showed signs of explosion damage, and then, if possible, to differentiate between clothing likely to have been contained within the suitcase that contained the explosive device and clothing in adjacent suitcases. The method adopted by the forensic scientists was to treat as a high probability that any explosion damaged clothing which contained fragments of the radio cassette player, the instruction manual, and the brown fabric-lined cardboard partition from within the suitcase to the exclusion of fragments of the outer shell, was within the pri-

mary suitcase. Where clothing carried neither fragments of the explosive device nor of one or more of the suitcase shells that would have surrounded it, or where it variously carried fragments of the suitcase shells with or without fragments of the explosive device, its specific location was problematic, although the possibility that it was contained in the primary suitcase could not be discounted. There were twelve items of clothing and an umbrella of which fragments were recovered and examined which fell within the first category and accordingly in their opinion had been contained within the primary suitcase. These items were:—

1. A charred fragment of white cotton material which from the details of the stitching and method of assembly appeared most likely to have originated from a white T-shirt of Abanderado brand. Contained within this fragment there were found a piece of loudspeaker mesh and eleven plastic fragments which could have come from a Toshiba radio, and some blue/white fragments consistent with having come from a Babygro (see item 5).

2. Explosion damaged fragments of brown tartan patterned material two of which still retained parts of labels which identified them as having formed part of a pair of Yorkie brand trousers size 34. Contained within one of these fragments there were found fragments of the lining and internal divider of the primary suitcase, five black plastic fragments which could have come from a Toshiba radio, four fragments of an RT-SF 16 owner's manual, and five clumps of blue/white fibres consistent with having come from a Babygro.

3. Four charred and disrupted fragments of grey cloth which in terms of colour, weave and texture appeared to have a common origin. One of these fragments had sewn on to it a "Slalom" label, and all the fragments were consistent with having come from a grey Slalom brand shirt. Contained within one of these fragments (bearing the police label PI/995) there were found a number of items. We shall return to this fragment later, as the defence contended that there were a number of factors surrounding its finding and examination which affected the reliability of the evidence relating to it.

4. Six charred fragments of white material with a fine blue pin-stripe. Although there were no identifying marks on any of these fragments, their colour, weave, texture and construction indicated that their origin was from a shirt closely similar to a Slalom brand shirt. Contained within these fragments there were found sixteen fragments of black plastic and four fragments of loudspeaker mesh which could have come from a Toshiba radio and fragments of an RT-SF 16 owner's manual.

5. Four explosion-damaged fragments of light brown herringbone woven cloth. Although there were no identifying marks on any of these fragments, their colour, weave, texture and construction indicated that their origin was from a pair of Yorkie brand trousers. Six pieces of black

plastic and a fragment of the divider of the primary suitcase were found contained therein.

6. Three explosion-damaged fragments of herringbone patterned brown tweed cloth. Although there were no identifying marks on any of these fragments, their colour, weave, texture and construction indicated that their origin was from a tweed jacket similar in all respects to a control sample obtained by police officers. These fragments contained fragments of black plastic and suitcase divider.

7. Four fragments of cream coloured material with a pattern of brown stripes. One of these was a substantial item clearly identifiable as the remains of a pair of pyjama trousers. Although there were no identifying marks on any of these fragments, their colour, pattern and construction indicated that their origin was from a pair of Panwear brand pyjamas. They contained fragments of black plastic and fragments of lining from the primary suitcase.

8. Thirteen very severely damaged fragments, many extremely small, of blue fibrous material. One fragment consisted of two overlaid pieces of material, one being a blue fibrous material and the other being knitted white ribbed material. Between these two pieces there was trapped the remains of a label printed in different colours containing information about age, height, composition and "made in Malta." This composite fragment matched closely in all significant respects the labelled neck section of a Babygro Primark brand. The material of the other fragments also matched the material of the same brand. Adhering to these various fragments were fragments of black plastic, wire, paper fragments from the Toshiba owner's manual, and fragments of the divider of the primary suitcase.

9. Three fragments of a black nylon umbrella. The major fragments comprised part of the canopy, ribbing and handle stem, shredded and partly collapsed indicating close involvement with an explosion. Strongly adherent to the canopy material were blue and white fibres, similar in appearance to the Babygro fibres. A second fragment was a piece of silver coated black plastic with fluted surface corrugations similar to part of the locking collar of the umbrella, and this was found in a fragment of the tartan checked trousers (item 2 above).

10. A fragment of an explosion damaged knitted brown woollen cardigan. This item had sewn on to it a label inscribed "Puccini design."

The remaining three items had clearly been very closely involved with the explosion, but there was insufficient material to enable identification to be made of their origin.

[11] The nature and extent of the damage to this clothing together with the items embedded therein confirmed, if confirmation were necessary, that the explosion had occurred within container AVE 4041, and also established beyond doubt that the explosive device was contained within a Toshiba RT-

SF 16 radio cassette player which had been within a brown Samsonite suitcase which also contained the items of clothing enumerated above.

[12] It will be recalled that four of the items identified as having been in the primary suitcase were identifiable by labels as having been of Yorkie, Slalom, Primark and Puccini brands. In August 1989 police officers visited Malta in an attempt to trace the source of these items. After a visit to Yorkie Clothing, on 1 September they went to Mary's House, Tower Road, Sliema. This was a shop run by the Gauci family, Tony Gauci being one of the partners. Mr Gauci's evidence was that he was visited by police officers in September 1989. He was able to tell them that he recalled a particular sale about a fortnight before Christmas 1988, although he could not remember the exact date. His recollection was that the Christmas lights were just being put up. It was mid-week, possibly Wednesday. The time was about 6.30pm. The purchaser was a man, and the witness recognised him as being a Libyan. The conversation with the purchaser was probably in a mixture of Arabic, English and Maltese. Many Libyans visit his shop, and when he hears them speaking he can tell the difference between a Libyan and, say, a Tunisian or an Egyptian. He bought an assortment of clothing, but it did not appear to the witness that the nature of what he was buying was of importance. Amongst the items which the witness remembered selling were two pairs of Yorkie trousers, two pairs of striped pyjamas of the same brand as the Panwear fragment, a tweed jacket, a blue Babygro, two Slalom shirts collar size $16^1/_2$, two cardigans, one brown and one blue, and an umbrella. The order number seen on the fragment of one of the pairs of Yorkie trousers was 1705, and the delivery note for this order showed that it was delivered on 18 November 1988. The police obtained either from Mr Gauci or from the manufacturers samples of all of these items, and these were the samples which were used by the forensic scientists when comparing them with the fragments. It may seem surprising that he was able to remember this particular sale in such detail some nine months afterwards, but he explained that the purchaser appeared to be taking little interest in the items he was buying. We are satisfied, however, that his recollection of these items is accurate. While it was never suggested to him that his recollection might have been assisted by the police officers, it is perhaps a measure of his accuracy that he was clear that the purchases did not include an Abanderado T-shirt, even though he did stock such items and it would be one in which the police were interested. While no doubt individual items could have been purchased in many other shops in Malta, or indeed in other parts of the world as many of them were exported, the exact match between so many of the items and the fragments found at Lockerbie is in our view far more than just a coincidence. We are therefore entirely satisfied that the items of clothing in the primary suitcase were those described by Mr Gauci as having been purchased in Mary's House. We shall return to Mr Gauci's evidence in more detail in connection with the date of the sale and the identification of the purchaser.

[13] We now turn to another crucial item that was found during the search of the debris. On 13 January 1989 DC Gilchrist and DC McColm were engaged together in line searches in an area near Newcastleton. A piece of charred material was found by them which was given the police number PI/995 and which subsequently became label 168. The original inscription on the label, which we are satisfied was written by DC Gilchrist, was "Cloth (charred)." The word 'cloth' has been overwritten by the word 'debris.' There was no satisfactory explanation as to why this was done, and DC Gilchrist's attempts to explain it were at worst evasive and at best confusing. We are, however, satisfied that this item was indeed found in the area described, and DC McColm who corroborated DC Gilchrist on the finding of the item was not cross-examined about the detail of the finding of this item. This item was logged into the property store at Dextar on 17 January 1989. It was suggested by the defence that there was some sinister connotation both in the alteration of the original label and in the delay between the finding of the item and its being logged in to Dextar. As we have indicated, there does not appear to be any particular reason for the alteration of the label, but we are satisfied that there was no sinister reason for it and that it was not tampered with by the finders. As far as the late logging is concerned, at that period there was a vast amount of debris being recovered, and the log shows that many other items were only logged in some days after they had been picked up. Again therefore we see no sinister connotation in this. Because it was a piece of charred material, it was sent for forensic examination. According to his notes, this item was examined, initially on 12 May 1989, by Dr Hayes. His notes show that it was found to be part of the neckband of a grey shirt, and when the control sample was obtained it appeared similar in all respects to the neckband of a Slalom shirt. It was severely explosion damaged with localised penetration holes and blackening consistent with explosive involvement. Embedded within some of the penetration holes there were found nine fragments of black plastic, a small fragment of metal, a small fragment of wire, and a multi-layered fragment of white paper (subsequently ascertained to be fragments from a Toshiba RT-SF 16 and its manual). There was also found embedded a fragment of green coloured circuit board. The next reference to that last fragment occurs in a memorandum sent by Mr Feraday to CI Williamson on 15 September 1989 enclosing a Polaroid photograph of it and asking for assistance in trying to identify it. Again the defence sought to cast doubt on the provenance of this fragment of circuit board, for three reasons. In the first place, Dr Hayes' note of his examination was numbered as page 51. The subsequent pages had originally been numbered 51 to 55, but these numbers had been overwritten to read 52 to 56. The suggestion was put to Dr Hayes that the original pages 51 to 55 had been renumbered, the original page 56 had been removed, and that thus space was made for the insertion of a new page 51. Dr Hayes' explanation was that originally his notes had not been pagi-

nated at all. When he came to prepare his report based on his original notes, he put his notes into more or less chronological order and added page numbers at the top. He assumed that he had inadvertently numbered two consecutive pages as page 51, and after numbering a few more pages had noticed his error and had overwritten with the correct numbers. Pagination was of no materiality, because each item that was examined had the date of examination incorporated into the notes. The second reason for doubt was said to be that in most cases when a fragment of something like a circuit board was found in a piece of clothing, Dr Hayes' practice was to make a drawing of that fragment and give it a separate reference number. There was no drawing of this fragment on page 51, and the designation of the fragment as PT/35(b) was not done until a later date. Finally it was said that it was inexplicable that if this fragment had been found in May 1989 and presumably photographed at the time, his colleague Mr Feraday should be sending a memorandum in September 1989 enclosing a Polaroid photograph as being "the best I can do in such a short time." Dr Hayes could not explain this, and suggested that the person to ask about it would be the author of the memorandum, Mr Feraday, but this was not done. While it is unfortunate that this particular item which turned out to be of major significance to this enquiry despite its miniscule size may not initially have been given the same meticulous treatment as most other items, we are nevertheless satisfied that the fragment was extracted by Dr Hayes in May 1989 from the remnant of the Slalom shirt found by DC Gilchrist and DC McColm.

[14] Over the ensuing months extensive investigations were carried out by CI Williamson and other police officers within the printed circuit board industry in an attempt to trace the origin of the fragment, but these were fruitless. In about June 1990 CI Williamson received information from an FBI officer named Thurman as a result of which he and Mr Feraday visited FBI headquarters in Washington. They were there shown a timing device known as an MST-13 (label 420). On examination it was found that there was an area on a printed circuit board within that timer which was identical to the recovered fragment except that the Washington device had double-sided solder masking whereas the fragment PT/35(b) was solder masked on one side only. Subsequent enquiries led to a commission rogatoire being obtained, which enabled judicial and police authorities in Switzerland to carry out enquiries on behalf of the Scottish police. In November 1990 and January 1991 there were judicial interviews of two persons, Edwin Bollier and Erwin Meister, the partners in the firm of MEBO, a firm which was engaged in the design and manufacture of various electronic items. There was a further interview with Scottish police officers in May 1991. During the course of these interviews, a number of items were handed over including a quantity of documentation, three timers (two MST-13s and an Olympus), and various components of timers including circuit boards. The detailed examination of these items by

Dr Hayes and Mr Feraday and comparison with the fragment of green circuit board left them in no doubt that the fragment originated from an area of the connection pad for an output relay of a circuit board of single solder-mask type of an MST-13 timer. We accept the conclusion to which the forensic scientists came.

[15] The evidence which we have considered up to this stage satisfies us beyond reasonable doubt that the cause of the disaster was the explosion of an improvised explosive device, that that device was contained within a Toshiba radio cassette player in a brown Samsonite suitcase along with various items of clothing, that that clothing had been purchased in Mary's House, Sliema, Malta, and that the initiation of the explosion was triggered by the use of an MST-13 timer.

[16] We now turn to consider the evidence relating to the provenance of the primary suitcase and the possible ways in which it could have found its way into AVE 4041. This involves consideration of the procedures at various airports through which it may have passed.

[17] The Crown case is that the primary suitcase was carried on an Air Malta flight KM180 from Luqa Airport in Malta to Frankfurt, that at Frankfurt it was transferred to PanAm flight PA103A, a feeder flight for PA103, which carried it to London Heathrow Airport, and that there, in turn, it was transferred to PA103. This case is largely dependent on oral and documentary evidence relating to the three airports. From this evidence, it is alleged, an inference can be drawn that an unidentified and unaccompanied item of baggage was carried on KM180 and transferred to PA103A at Frankfurt and PA103 at Heathrow.

[18] When an intending passenger checks in baggage for carriage in an aircraft hold, a numbered tag is attached to each item. Part of the tag is removed and given to the passenger to act as a receipt. The portion attached to the item of baggage bears, ordinarily, the name of the airline, or the first airline, on which the passenger is to travel and the destination. Where the journey is to be completed in more than one leg or stage, the tag also carries the name of any intermediate airport. The purpose of the tag is to enable the baggage handlers at the airport of departure, at any intermediate airport and at the destination to deliver or transfer the item to the correct flight and return it to the passenger at the final destination. In 1988, tags preprinted with the name of the destination airport were sometimes used when the journey was to be completed in one stage. Where there was more than one stage, the names of the destination and of any intermediate airport were normally written on the tag by hand at the time of check-in. Baggage checked in at the airport of departure is referred to as local origin baggage. Baggage which has to be handled at an intermediate airport is generally referred to as transit baggage. A distinction is normally made between two groups of transit baggage. Online

baggage is baggage which arrives at and departs from an intermediate airport on aircraft of the same carrier: interline baggage arrives on an aircraft of one carrier and departs with a different carrier. The terminology is, however, not always used consistently. Baggage is intended to be carried on the same aircraft as the passenger to whom it belongs, but from time to time baggage is misdirected or delayed and has to be carried on a different flight. Such items are identified by an additional special tag, known as a rush tag, and are normally only sent in response to a request from the destination airport, following a claim made by a passenger for baggage which has not been delivered at the destination. The evidence led on this point related only to practice at Luqa airport, but seemed to reflect international practice. A passenger aircraft may also carry items of mail and other freight.

[19] In 1988, and for some time before, airline operators and airport authorities generally were well aware of the risk that attempts might be made to place explosive devices on passenger aircraft and had in place systems intended to minimise that risk. In particular, it was normal to take steps to prevent items of baggage travelling on an aircraft unaccompanied by the passenger who had checked them in, unless there was sufficient reason to regard the items as safe. It was normal to put certain questions to passengers who checked in baggage for a flight and to ensure that every passenger who had checked in baggage at the departure airport had boarded the aircraft, or that safety was otherwise assured, before it was allowed to depart. Similarly, steps were taken to check that transit baggage did not travel without the accompanying passenger. These steps varied between different airports and different carriers. By 1988, PanAm had brought into operation a system of x-raying interline baggage at Frankfurt and Heathrow. The availability of that facility led to changes in the way in which interline passengers and baggage were handled.

[20] PA103 took off from Heathrow shortly before 1830 on 21 December 1988. It was the last transatlantic PanAm flight to depart on that day. Heathrow was therefore the last place at which an explosive device could have been introduced into the hold of the aircraft. Before its departure, the aircraft was parked at stand K14. It had previously been checked and an airworthiness sheet had been completed for it. PA103A arrived at stand K16 and passengers proceeding to New York were instructed to go direct to gate 14. The boarding of passengers, both those originating at Heathrow and those transferring from PA103A, proceeded normally except that one passenger who had checked in two items of baggage at Heathrow failed to appear at the gate. The passenger was an American citizen and a decision was taken that the aircraft could depart despite his non-appearance. It was later found that he had been drinking in a bar at the airport and missed the boarding call. There is no reason to connect that passenger or the items checked in by him with the explosive device.

[21] At Heathrow, as at Frankfurt, PanAm baggage was handled by employees of PanAm. Security duties for PanAm were carried out by employees of Alert Security, an affiliate company of PanAm. Baggage checked in at Heathrow was sent to an area known as the baggage build-up area before being taken to the aircraft when it was ready for loading. The build-up area was adjacent to a roadway extensively used by persons within the airport. In December 1988 it was busier than usual because construction work was in progress at the airport. If, as was the case with a Boeing 747 aircraft, the baggage, or any of it, was to be loaded into containers to be placed in the aircraft, that was done in the build-up area. Interline baggage arriving at Heathrow was unloaded by airport employees and was sent to an area called the interline shed. This shed was a separate building within the airport terminal area. Baggage removed from incoming flights was brought to the outside of the shed by employees of a company called Whyte's, employed by the airport authority, and placed on a conveyor belt, which carried it into the shed. There was no security guard outside the shed, so that the placing of items on the conveyor belt was unsupervised. The interline shed dealt with baggage for other airlines, as well as baggage for PanAm. Within the shed, interline baggage for a PanAm flight was identified and separated from other airline baggage. It was taken to the PanAm x-ray machine, where it was examined by x-ray by an employee of Alert. After x-ray, it was placed in a container or set aside to await the outgoing flight.

[22] On 21 December 1988 the x-ray operator was Sulkash Kamboj. John Bedford, a loader-driver employed by PanAm, and Mr Parmar, another PanAm employee were working in the interline shed. Mr Bedford set aside container AVE 4041 to receive interline baggage for PA103. The container was identified as the container for PA103 by Mr Bedford who wrote the information on a sheet which was placed in a holder fixed to the container. A number of items were placed in that container. Later Mr Bedford drove the container to a position near the baggage build-up area and left it there. From there, the container was taken out to stand K16, and baggage for New York unloaded from PA103A was loaded into it. The incoming plane carried baggage loose in its hold, not in containers. The evidence of Mr Bedford together with that of Peter Walker, a supervisor in the baggage build-up area, and Darshan Sandhu, a chief loader, and with the container build-up sheet (production 1217), shows that container AVE 4041 contained both interline baggage which had been placed in it in the interline shed, and baggage unloaded from PA103A. When it was full, container AVE 4041 was driven directly to stand 14 and loaded into the hold. The evidence of Terence Crabtree, another driver-loader employed by PanAm, who was the crew chief for the loading of PA103, together with the load plan (production 1183), shows that the container was loaded in position 14 left, which corresponds to the position established by the forensic evidence. The plan also shows that container AVN 7511 was

loaded in the adjacent position 21 left, again corresponding to the forensic evidence. There was also some baggage from PA103A which was loaded loose into the hold of PA103.

[23] Mr Bedford said that he recalled that on 21 December 1988 he had set aside container AVE 4041 for baggage for PA103. He recalled also that he had placed a number of suitcases in the container. These cases were placed on their spines in a row along the back of the container. He said that he had left the interline shed to have a cup of tea with Mr Walker in the build-up area. On his return, he saw that two cases had been added to the container. These cases were laid on their sides, with the handles towards the interior of the container, in the way that he would normally have loaded them. The arrangement of these cases was shown in a set of photographs (production 1114) taken in early January 1989 in Mr Bedford's presence. Mr Bedford said that he had been told by Mr Kamboj that he had placed the additional two suitcases in the container during his absence. Mr Kamboj denied that he had placed any suitcases in the container and denied also that he had told Mr Bedford that he had done so. Both witnesses were referred to a number of police statements which they gave at various times and to their evidence at the Fatal Accident Inquiry into the disaster, and it appears that each of the witnesses has consistently given the same account throughout. Mr Kamboj eventually conceded in evidence, in a half-hearted way, that what Mr Bedford said might be correct, but the contradiction is not resolved. Mr Bedford was a clear and impressive witness and he had no reason to invent what he said. Mr Kamboj was a less impressive witness, and he might have been anxious to avoid any possible responsibility. In our view, the evidence of Mr Bedford should be preferred on this point. The difference between the witnesses is not, however, material since for the purposes of this case what is important is that there is evidence that when the container left the interline area it had in it the two suitcases positioned as described above. Mr Bedford agreed that in statements to police officers and in evidence at the Fatal Accident Inquiry he had described one of the two cases lying on their sides as a brown or maroony-brown hard-shell Samsonite-type case. He could not recollect that when he gave evidence in this case, but said that he had told the truth in his statements and earlier evidence. Mr Bedford also said that he had arranged with Mr Walker that because the incoming flight PA103A was a little delayed, and to wait for it would take him beyond his normal finishing time, he should take the container to the baggage build-up area and leave it there, and that he did so before leaving work soon after 5.00pm. Mr Walker could not recall what had happened, but accepted that he had told investigating police officers soon after the event that he recalled seeing Mr Bedford at about 5.00pm and that Mr Bedford had said that he was going home, but that there was no conversation about leaving a container at the build-up area. Mr Walker's evidence at the FAI in regard to whether or not he was aware of a container being brought

to the build-up area differed from his original police statement and he was unable to explain the difference. There is, however, no reason to doubt Mr Bedford's evidence that he did take AVE 4041 to the build-up area and leave it there.

[24] It emerges from the evidence therefore that a suitcase which could fit the forensic description of the primary suitcase was in the container when it left the interline shed. There is also a possibility that an extraneous suitcase could have been introduced by being put onto the conveyor belt outside the interline shed, or introduced into the shed itself or into the container when it was at the build-up area. To achieve that, the person placing the suitcase would have had to avoid being detected, but the evidence indicates that a person in possession of a pass for the airside area would not be likely to be challenged, and there were a very large number of passes issued for Heathrow, a substantial number of which were not accounted for. The person placing the suitcase would also have required to know where to put it to achieve the objective.

[25] It was argued on behalf of the accused that the suitcase described by Mr Bedford could well have been the primary suitcase, particularly as the evidence did not disclose that any fragments of a hard-shell Samsonite-type suitcase had been recovered, apart from those of the primary suitcase itself. It was accepted, for the purposes of this argument, that the effect of forensic evidence was that the suitcase could not have been directly in contact with the floor of the container. It was submitted that there was evidence that an American Tourister suitcase, which had travelled from Frankfurt, fragments of which had been recovered, had been very intimately involved in the explosion and could have been placed under the suitcase spoken to by Mr Bedford. That would have required rearrangement of the items in the container, but such rearrangement could easily have occurred when the baggage from Frankfurt was being put into the container on the tarmac at Heathrow. It is true that such a rearrangement could have occurred, but if there was such a rearrangement, the suitcase described by Mr Bedford might have been placed at some more remote corner of the container, and while the forensic evidence dealt with all the items recovered which showed direct explosive damage, twenty-five in total, there were many other items of baggage found which were not dealt with in detail in the evidence in the case.

[26] At Frankfurt Airport, baggage for most airlines was handled by the airport authority, but PanAm had their own security and baggage handling staff. Frankfurt had a computer controlled automated baggage handling system, through which baggage was passed. Each item of baggage was placed in an individually numbered tray as it was taken into the system. The trays were placed on conveyor belts and instructions were fed into the computer to identify the flight to which the baggage was to be sent, the position from which the aircraft was to leave and the time of the flight. The trays were dispatched

to a waiting area where they circulated until an instruction was fed in to summon the baggage for a particular flight, whereupon the items would be automatically extracted from the waiting area and sent to the departure point. Local origin baggage was received at check-in desks. There was no detailed evidence as to how the check-in staff dealt with it, but such baggage was passed into the system. Transit baggage was taken to one of two areas, identified as V3 and HM respectively, where it was fed into the system at points known as coding stations. All baggage at the airport went through the automated system, with the exception of transit baggage when there was less than 45 minutes interval between flights. In that case, baggage might be taken from one aircraft to another without going through the system.

[27] There were seven coding stations in V3. One such station is shown in photographs in production 1053. The general practice was that baggage from an incoming flight was brought either to HM or to V3 in wagons or containers. On arrival, the baggage from a flight would be directed by an employee called the interline writer to one or more of the coding stations. The proper practice was that each coding station should not deal with baggage from more than one incoming flight at a time. Normally there were two employees at each coding station. One would lift the items of baggage from the wagon or container and place each item in a tray. The other would enter into the computer, in a coded form, the flight number and destination for the outgoing flight, taking the information from the tag attached to the item. There was evidence that from time to time there might be an additional employee at a coding station, who would assist in removing the baggage and placing it in trays, and that the details from the tag might be read out to the coder by the person putting the item into a tray. Rush tag items were dealt with in the same way as other items. Items which arrived at a coding station without a legible tag were sent to an error area to be dealt with there. Records were kept identifying the staff working at particular stations, the arrival times of aircraft, the arrival times of consignments of baggage at HM or V3, and the station or stations to which the baggage from a particular flight was sent. The computer itself retained a record of the items sent through the system so that it was possible, for a limited period, to identify all the items of baggage sent through the system to a particular flight. After some time, however, that information would be lost from the system. The baggage control system contained its own clock, and there was a tendency for the time recorded by that clock to diverge from real time. The baggage control clock was therefore reset at the start of each day, by reference either to the main computer clock or to the employee's watch. The divergence was progressive and by 4.00pm or 5.00pm the discrepancy might be as much as two or three minutes. Times entered in other records were obtained by the staff from the airport clock or from their own watches.

[28] PanAm had x-ray equipment at Frankfurt, which was used to x-ray inter-line baggage. The system was that baggage arriving at the departure gate for a PanAm flight would be separated into categories, according to the flight programme. In the case of PA103A, that meant that the loaders would sepa-rate baggage for London, baggage for New York, and interline baggage. The last category would be taken to the x-ray equipment and examined and returned to be loaded. The practice of PanAm at Frankfurt was to carry out a reconciliation between local origin passengers and baggage and online pas-sengers and baggage, to ensure that every such passenger who had baggage on the flight was accounted for, but there was no attempt to reconcile inter-line passengers and their baggage. Reconciliation of interline passengers would have been difficult because the staff at the gate would not have any knowl-edge of an interline passenger until the passenger appeared to check in at the gate and receive a boarding card there. There was evidence from two wit-nesses, Roland O'Neill, the load master for PA103A, and Monika Diegmuller, a check-in supervisor, that there was a reconciliation of interline passengers and baggage, but there was overwhelming evidence to the contrary and their evi-dence on this point is not acceptable. The evidence that there was no recon-ciliation came from Herbert Leuniger, PanAm's director at Frankfurt, and Wolf Krommes, a duty station manager with PanAm. Further, in March 1988, Alan Berwick, the head of security for a wide area including the Middle East, after discussion with Martin Huebner, the security officer for PA at Frankfurt, sent a memorandum (production 1170) to Mr Sonesen, the company officer in New York to whom he reported, requesting a corporate decision on the ques-tion whether, in view of the existence of the x-ray facility, there should be any reconciliation. The reply (production 1171) emphatically instructed that if bag-gage had been x-rayed, the aircraft should leave, even if the interline passen-ger to whom it belonged had not boarded, and that there should be no reconciliation. In early 1989, Mr O'Neill gave a statement to two FAA inves-tigators in terms which implied that there was normally no reconciliation.

[29] The evidence of Joachim Koscha, who was one of the managers of the baggage system at Frankfurt in 1988, taken with production 1068, shows that flight KM180 reached its parking position at 1248 on 21 December 1988. Since it was not a PanAm flight it was unloaded by employees of the airport authority. According to the record, it was unloading between 1248 and 1300. Andreas Schreiner was in charge of monitoring the arrival of baggage at V3 on 21 December 1988. He made the following record on a document called the interline writer's sheet (production 1092):—

Flug no.	Pos.	ONB	Ank.	DW/V w-Nr.	Anzahl	Wag.	Direkt Pos.	Von V3
KM180	141	1248	1301	146		1		

That bears to record one wagon of baggage from KM180, in position at 1248, arriving at V3 at 1301. Mr Schreiner's evidence was that coding would generally begin three to five minutes after the arrival of the baggage at V3. Mr Schreiner also said that luggage was always delivered from one flight only. Mr Schreiner and Mr Koscha further identified production 1061 as a work sheet completed by a coder to record baggage with which he dealt. The name of the coder in question was Koca, who was not called as a witness. The relevant part of production 1061 is as follows:—

Intestell	Flug Nr.	Kodierzeit Beginn		Cont. Nr. Ende	Wag.	Kodierer Name
206	KM180	1304	1310	—	1	Koca

That record bears to show that one wagon of baggage from KM180 was coded at station 206 in V3 between 1304 and 1310. It was suggested that the figure for the completion of coding might be 1316, but Mr Schreiner preferred the reading 1310, which is more consistent with what can be seen on the document. There is also documentary evidence (production 1062) that the aircraft used for PA103A arrived from Vienna (as flight PA124) and was placed at position 44, from which it left for London at 1653.

[30] Mrs Bogomira Erac, a computer programmer employed at the airport, was on duty on 21 December 1988. She heard of the loss of PA103 during the evening of that day and realised that PA103A had departed during her period on duty. She was interested in the amount of baggage on the Frankfurt flight, and on the following morning she decided to take a printout of the information as to baggage held on the computer in case it should contain any useful information. She did not at once identify any such information, but retained the printout, which later was given to investigators. The printout is production 1060, and includes the following entry:—

Container no.	Flight no.	Counter no.		Time leave store	Time at gate
B8849	F1042	S0009+Z1307	TO	HS33+Z1517	B044+Z1523

The document itself contains no column headings, and those set out above are derived from the evidence showing how the printout is to be interpreted, by reference to the codes in operation at the time. The document therefore bears to record that an item coded at station 206 at 1307 was transferred and delivered to the appropriate gate to be loaded on board PA103A.

[31] The documentary evidence as a whole therefore clearly gives rise to the inference that an item which came in on KM180 was transferred to and left on PA103A. Evidence led in connection with KM180 established that there was no passenger who had an onward booking from Frankfurt to London or the United States and that all the passengers on KM180 retrieved all their checked-in baggage at their destinations. The Malta documentation for KM180 does not record that any unaccompanied baggage was carried. Defence counsel submitted that there was no evidence that baggage sent to the gate was actually loaded onto the flight, nor was there any count of the number of bags loaded. There was however evidence from Mr Kasteleiner that it could be taken from the documents that no baggage was left at the gate and it can be inferred that all items sent there were loaded. It follows that there is a plain inference from the documentary record that an unidentified and unaccompanied bag travelled on KM180 from Luqa airport to Frankfurt and there was loaded on PA103A.

[32] Defence counsel submitted that for a number of reasons that inference could not, or not safely, be drawn. In the first place, it was submitted that there was room for error because the computer time could diverge from real time and because the times entered by the operators could be inaccurate, either because the clock or watch relied on was inaccurate or because the entries were not correctly made. It was further suggested that recording of the place from which an item had come would have been of less importance to the operators than ensuring that it went to the right flight, and that the operators would have an interest to suggest that they had been fully occupied while the accuracy of the records was not a matter of material importance to them. It was also pointed out that the person who made the critical entry in production 1061 had not been called to give evidence, although his name was on the Crown witness list, and that there was no explanation for his absence. We accept that the possibilities of error exist, but the computer clock was reset at the start of each day (although the precise time at which it was reset was not stated) and there was an interest in accurate time-keeping since one of the purposes of keeping records was to be able to trace baggage consignments through the system. The records were records regularly kept for the purposes of the airport business, and can be accepted in the absence of some reason to doubt their accuracy. It was also argued that a very minor discrepancy in the time recording could mean that the inference which the Crown sought to draw would be erroneous, particularly since there might be errors the effect of which was cumulative. Again this is true, but the suspect case was recorded as being coded in the middle of the time attributed to baggage from KM180, so that the possible significance of such errors is reduced.

[33] A further point made by the defence was that the records themselves displayed errors which demonstrated that they could not be relied on. Counsel

for the defence referred to two particular matters. The first concerned entries relating to interline baggage which arrived at V3 between 1221 and 1237 on 21 December 1988. It is recorded that four wagons of baggage came from LH669, a Lufthansa flight from Damascus. The worksheets in production 1061 record that one and a half wagons from that flight were coded at station 202 between 1258 and 1307 and one wagon was coded at station 207 between 1303 and 1309. There is no other record of coding of baggage from that flight, so that on the face of the records one and a half wagons are not accounted for. In view of the timing, it was submitted, it was possible that baggage from LH669 was being dealt with at the same time as baggage from KM180 and that the suspect bag might have come from the Damascus flight. The witness Joachim Koscha, however, referred to notes in the records which indicated that wagons of luggage from that flight had been taken to Customs, as happened from time to time, and gave evidence that wagons taken to Customs might be reloaded in different ways, which might account for the discrepancy. Reference was also made to a number of other instances in which the records showed small discrepancies in the commencing and finishing times entered for coding particular consignments, which on their face seem to show that baggage from more than one flight might have been coded at the same station at the same time. Reference was also made to another item in production 1060. In this instance, the entry is as follows:—

Container no.	Flight no.	Counter no.		Time leave store	Time at gate
B5620	F1042	S0074+Z1544		HV20+Z1546	BO44+Z1549

When interpreted in the same manner as the entry previously referred to, this bears to show that an item coded at a station in HM at 1544 on 21 December also was sent to PA103A, and reference to the coders' records bears to show that baggage from flight LH1071 from Warsaw was being encoded at that station at that time. It was agreed that no passenger from that flight transferred to PA103A, so that the records seem to show the presence of another unaccompanied bag on that flight. In addition it was suggested that the records and other evidence showed, or might show, that additional items of baggage were carried on PA103A, besides those listed on production 1060. The total number of items listed on production 1060 is 111 but production 199, which is a printout of the passenger manifest for PA103A, bears to show that a total of 118 items were checked in. Further, Mr O'Neill spoke of 21 items of online baggage which arrived on a flight from Berlin and it was suggested therefore that there were additional items beyond those listed in the documents. Production 199 was not scrutinised in much detail in the evidence and the discrepancy in numbers was not explored. It can, however, be seen that 21 of the items on the passenger manifest are marked with the letters TXL, and in the course of questions with regard to one of those items, directed to a different issue, Monika Diegmuller read those letters as indicating that the item had come from Tegel Airport, Berlin. It seems likely, therefore, that Mr O'Neill's 21 items are included in the 118 on the passenger manifest. The remaining discrepancy might be accounted for as late arrival luggage which, according to some of the evidence, might not go through the automated system.

[34] There were other comments on the operation of the system to the effect that there were indications that there might be informal working practices, such as one coder giving assistance to another which might lead to inaccurate recording. There was also evidence as to how individual bags which were found in the wrong place were dealt with, which might have the same result. In this connection, emphasis was placed on the evidence of Lawrence Whittaker, an FBI special agent who was present when enquiries were being made at V3, and who observed a person, whom he described as dressed appropriately for the area, bringing a suitcase to a coding station and coding it in, but did not see any record being made. Mr Whittaker could not be absolutely certain that no record was made. Apart from pointing to the possibility of errors in recording, defence counsel drew attention to the fact that the records showed that a consignment of interline baggage for PA103A had been taken to the x-ray machine and examined before loading. If the Crown theory is correct, this consignment should have included the suspect item from KM180. It was submitted that the x-ray would, in all probability, have detected any explosive device in a case, particularly as the staff at Frankfurt were aware of warnings to look out for explosive devices hidden in radio cassette players. One such warning was issued after the Autumn Leaves operation in October 1988. Another, more limited, warning was issued because there was understood to be a threat that a woman from Helsinki would attempt to smuggle a device on board an aircraft. It was submitted that that examination would have revealed the presence of the radio cassette player and its contents, particularly in view of the fact that there had been a warning to look out for explosive devices hidden in radio sets. The x-ray operator, Kurt Maier, was not fit through illness to give evidence, but reference was made to statements by him to the investigators from which it appeared that he had x-rayed the consignment in question. One statement was spoken to by Naomi Saunders, one of the FAA investigators, the other by Hans Fuhl of the BKA. In both, Mr Maier explained that he had had some limited training in the use of the machine, but said that in the course of using it he had taught himself to distinguish various sorts of electrical equipment, and that he knew how to tell if explosives were present, from their appearance. Neither statement directly dealt with the question whether, and if so how, Mr Maier would detect explosives hidden in a radio cassette player. What he said was that the approach in dealing with electrical

equipment was to see whether it presented a normal appearance, for example whether it had a plug. Other evidence, however, particularly that given by the witness Oliver Koch, Alert's trainee manager at the time, shows that the standard of training given to Alert employees was poor. That was also the view of the FAA investigators who visited Frankfurt in 1989. Mr Maier's description of what he looked for does not suggest that he would necessarily have claimed to be able to detect explosives hidden in a radio cassette player. There was no expert evidence as to the ease or difficulty of detecting such hidden devices. The x-ray examination is one of the factors to be taken into account but it is only one factor to be weighed along with the others.

[35] The evidence in regard to what happened at Frankfurt Airport, although of crucial importance, is only part of the evidence in the case and has to be considered along with all the other evidence before a conclusion can be reached as to where the primary suitcase originated and how it reached PA103. It can, however, be said at this stage that if the Frankfurt evidence is considered entirely by itself and without reference to any other evidence, none of the points made by the defence seems to us to cast doubt on the inference from the documents and other evidence that an unaccompanied bag from KM180 was transferred to and loaded onto PA103A.

[36] Luqa Airport was relatively small. The evidence did not disclose the exact number of check-in desks but the photographs in production 871 suggest that there were not very many. Behind the check-in desks there was a conveyor belt, and behind it there was a solid wall, separating the check-in area from the airside area. Behind the check-in desks there were three glass doors, again between the public area and airside, but these were kept locked. There were other doors between the airside and the open area, but at Luqa these were guarded by military personnel, who also dealt with security at other entrances to the airside area of the airport. The conveyor belt carried items of baggage along behind the check-in desks and passed through a small hatch into the airside baggage area. The hatch was also under observation by military personnel and there were Customs officers present in the baggage area. The baggage area was restricted in size. As items of baggage passed along the conveyor belt they were checked for the presence of explosives by military personnel using a sniffer device. The device could detect the presence of many explosives but would not normally detect Semtex, although it might detect one of its constituents under certain circumstances. The only access from the check-in area to the sniffer area was through the hatch or through a separate guarded door.

[37] Air Malta acted as handling agents for all airlines flying out of Luqa. That meant that the check-in desks for all flights were manned by Air Malta staff. There were station managers and other staff of other airlines present at the airport. Some airlines insisted on the use of their own baggage tags, but Air Malta tags could be used for flights of other airlines, in certain circumstances. Whatever

the purpose for which they were to be used, Air Malta tags were treated as a security item. They were kept in a store and supplies were issued to the check-in agents when a flight was due to start check-in. The same applied to interline tags. All remaining tags were returned to the supervisor after the check-in was completed.

[38] Luqa airport had a relatively elaborate security system. All items of baggage checked in were entered into the airport computer as well as being noted on the passenger's ticket. After the baggage had passed the sniffer check, it was placed on a trolley in the baggage area to wait until the flight was ready for loading. When the flight was ready, the baggage was taken out and loaded, and the head loader was required to count the items placed on board. The ramp dispatcher, the airport official on the tarmac responsible for the departure of the flight, was in touch by radiotelephone with the load control office. The load control had access to the computer and after the flight was closed would notify the ramp dispatcher of the number of items checked in. The ramp dispatcher would also be told by the head loader how many items had been loaded and if there was a discrepancy would take steps to resolve it. That might require a check of the ticket coupons, a check with one or more check-in agents or, in the last resort, a physical reconciliation by unloading the baggage and asking passengers to identify their own luggage. Interline bags would be included in the total known to load control, as would any rush items. It was suggested by the Crown that there might at one time have been a practice of allowing the aircraft to leave in spite of a discrepancy, if the discrepancy was less than five items, but the records referred to by the Crown did not bear out that this was a regular practice and the suggestion was firmly denied by the Air Malta and airport witnesses. In addition to the baggage reconciliation procedure, there was a triple count of the number of passengers boarding a departing flight, that is there was a count of the boarding cards, a count by immigration officers of the number of immigration cards handed in, and a head count by the crew. On the face of them, these arrangements seem to make it extremely difficult for an unaccompanied and unidentified bag to be shipped on a flight out of Luqa. It was suggested that there were occasions, particularly when an LAA flight was being checked in, when conditions at the check-in desks were crowded and chaotic because a great deal of miscellaneous and unusual baggage was brought to the desks and because the queues were not orderly. It was therefore suggested that on such an occasion a bag might have been slipped onto the conveyor belt behind the desks without anyone noticing. Again, evidence was led that on occasions airline representatives, such as the second accused, would assist favoured passengers by helping them to obtain special treatment at the check-in and immigration desks and placing baggage on the conveyor. Evidence to that effect was given by Dennis Burke and Nicholas Ciarlo who worked as travel agents at the airport but none of the evidence went further than suggesting that a case might

have been placed on the conveyor belt, from where it would have gone to the explosives check and the baggage area, but not escaping the baggage reconciliation system. The evidence of the responsible officials at the airport, particularly Wilfred Borg, the Air Malta general manager for ground operations at the time, was that it was impossible or highly unlikely that a bag could be introduced undetected at the check-in desks or in the baggage area, or by approaching the loaders, in view of the restricted areas in which the operations proceeded and the presence of Air Malta, Customs and military personnel. Mr Borg conceded that it might not be impossible that a bag could be introduced undetected but said that whether it was probable was another matter.

[39] As regards the flight itself, the check-in for KM180 opened at 0815 and closed at 0915. There were two other flight check-ins open during that period or part of it. Flight KM220 was checking in between 0835 and 0930 and an LAA flight, LN147, was checking in between 0850 and 0950. The records relating to KM180 on 21 December 1988 show no discrepancy in respect of baggage. The flight log (production 930) shows that fifty-five items of baggage were loaded, corresponding to fifty-five on the load plan. There was a good deal of evidence led in relation to the number of items noted on the ticket counterfoils for the flight, and especially in regard to the number of items checked in by a German television crew who travelled on the flight. It does not seem to us to be necessary to examine that evidence in detail. A discrepancy might have masked the presence of an additional item, but the evidence is inconclusive as to whether or not there was any discrepancy and in any event it is difficult to suppose that a person launching a bomb into the interline system would rely on such a chance happening. If therefore the unaccompanied bag was launched from Luqa, the method by which that was done is not established, and the Crown accepted that they could not point to any specific route by which the primary suitcase could have been loaded. Counsel for the defence pointed out that neither the head loader nor the other members of the loading crew were called to give evidence, and submitted that, in their absence, the Crown could not ask the court to draw any inference adverse to them. The absence of any explanation of the method by which the primary suitcase might have been placed on board KM180 is a major difficulty for the Crown case, and one which has to be considered along with the rest of the circumstantial evidence in the case.

[40] We turn now to consider what evidence there is to establish any involvement on the part of either or both of the accused.

[41] In relation to the first accused, there are three important witnesses, Abdul Majid, Edwin Bollier and Tony Gauci.

[42] Abdul Majid in 1984 joined the Jamahariya Security Organisation ("JSO"), later named the External Security Organisation. His initial employment was in the vehicle maintenance department for about eighteen months.

In December 1985 he was appointed as assistant to the station manager of LAA at Luqa airport. This post was one which was normally filled by a member of the JSO. He gave evidence about the organisation of the JSO in 1985. In particular he said that the director of the central security section was Ezzadin Hinshiri, the head of the operations section was Said Rashid, the head of special operations in the operations department was Nassr Ashur, and the head of the airline security section was the first accused until January 1987 when he moved to the strategic studies institute. The second accused was the station manager for LAA at Luqa from 1985 until about October 1988. While Abdul Majid was only a junior member of the JSO, we are prepared to accept that he was aware of the hierarchy and that his evidence on these matters can be accepted. In August 1988 he contacted the US embassy in Malta, and indicated a willingness to provide them with information. His evidence was that he disapproved of Libyan involvement in terrorism, but the final straw was that he had been summoned back to Tripoli in connection with an incident at the airport involving an Egyptian woman. He said that at that stage he wanted to go to America, but he agreed to stay in position to give information to the Americans about terrorist activities. Thereafter he had regular meetings at about monthly intervals with his CIA handlers. Eventually during 1990 he returned to Libya when the Americans stopped making payments to him. In July 1991 however he finally left Libya for Malta from where he was taken on board a US navy ship. Over a period of about three weeks he was questioned by members of the US Justice Department and provided certain information to them. Since then he has been in America on a witness protection scheme. During the period in Malta when he was having meetings with the CIA, his handlers reported by cable to their headquarters the information he provided. These cables also dealt with the financial arrangements. Such information as he provided during that period does not appear to have been of much value, being mainly confined to the comings and goings of various people through Luqa. We do not find it necessary to go into much detail about his dealings with the CIA in Malta. What emerged from the evidence quite clearly in our view was that he endeavoured from the outset to give a false impression of his importance within the JSO in the hope of persuading the CIA that he was a valuable asset who might in the future be able to provide valuable information. Thus he initially told them that when he joined the JSO he was in the secret files section, when in fact he was in vehicle maintenance; he claimed to be related to King Idris, which he was not; he claimed long-standing friendship with Ezzadin Hinshiri and Said Rashid, and acquaintance with Abdullah Senussi, the head of operations administration. We are satisfied that these suggestions were at best grossly exaggerated, at worst simply untrue. It is also in our view clear that whatever may have been his original reason for defection, his continued association with the American authorities was largely motivated by financial considerations. In addition to receiving a monthly salary, initially $1000 increasing to $1500, he also persuaded the CIA to pay for sham surgery to his arm with a view to preventing the risk that he would have to do military service in Libya, and tried to persuade them to finance a car rental business which at one stage he said he wanted to set up in Malta. Information provided by a paid informer is always open to the criticism that it may be invented in order to justify payment, and in our view this is a case where such criticism is more than usually justified. It is in this context that we turn to consider particular items in his evidence upon which the Crown sought to found.

[43] At an early meeting with the CIA in October 1988 he was asked if he knew anything of weapons on Malta. He said that he was aware of eight kilos of explosives which had been stored for months at the LAA office. He understood that they had been introduced some time in 1985 when Abd Al Baset Megrahi was in Malta. They were not kept in a safe, merely in a locked drawer in the desk. He had been asked to help in transferring them to the office of the Libyan Peoples Bureau. A further report shortly thereafter indicated that they were kept in the Valletta office. In July 1991 he added the information that the second accused was the custodian of these explosives, this being the first time the second accused was mentioned in connection with this matter. He further added that it was the second accused who told him that it was the first accused who had brought the explosives. Finally he said that at some stage the first accused told him to 'look after' the second accused, and to take control of the explosives when the second accused left his post as station manager. It is quite clear that the details of this story only emerged some two and a half years after the initial account, and contained a number of inconsistencies with the first account. It is also highly significant that the details only emerged at a stage when it had been made clear to him that unless he came up with some useful information, he was liable simply to be returned to Malta. Even taken at its best, the whole story sounds improbable, and in view of the late introduction of very material detail we are unable to place any reliance on this account. This was the only matter of any significance that was reported to the CIA by Abdul Majid prior to 21 December 1988. Another matter upon which the Crown founded was that in July 1991 Abdul Majid told investigators that he had seen the first accused and the second accused arriving at Luqa off the Tripoli flight some time between October and December 1988. This comparatively innocuous statement gradually enlarged until by the time he gave evidence he said that he saw them at the luggage carousel, that the second accused collected a brown Samsonite type suitcase which he took through Customs, that then he met the two accused who were accompanied by two other people one of whom was introduced to him by the first accused as Abougela Masoud, a technician, that Vincent Vassallo (an associate of the second accused) was also present having arrived in the second accused's new car, and that they then drove off. As other evidence established that the date of

delivery of the second accused's car was 14 December 1988, it follows that if Abdul Majid's story is true this incident must have occurred on 20 December. He maintained that he had told his CIA handlers about this incident at the time. The cables for this period disclose no mention of this incident at all, and the Crown made no attempt to support the proposition that the incident was mentioned at all prior to July 1991. If it had been mentioned, it would be quite inexplicable that the CIA would have failed to appreciate the significance of the information and failed to report it. Furthermore, Mr Vassallo in evidence said that on 20 December he was not at the airport, and that in fact both accused came to his house that evening. We are therefore quite unable to accept the veracity of this belated account by Abdul Majid. A third matter on which the Crown founded was an account given by Abdul Majid of a conversation in about 1986 with Said Rashid in which the latter asked if it would be possible to put an unaccompanied bag on board a British aircraft. Abdul Majid said he would investigate, and asked his assistant Ahmed Salah, also said to be a JSO officer, if it could be done. Ahmed Salah later reported that it could be done, and Abdul Majid wrote a report to Said Rashid to this effect, sending the report through his superior, the first accused. He said that the first accused later visited Malta and this matter was discussed, the first accused saying "don't rush things." In his evidence he accepted that he had never reported this to the CIA even when they asked him if he knew anything about the possibility of the bomb which blew up PA103 being sent from Luqa. He said that his reason for not reporting it was for personal security reasons. Once again, we are quite unable to accept this story when the information was supplied so belatedly. Putting the matter shortly, we are unable to accept Abdul Majid as a credible and reliable witness on any matter except his description of the organisation of the JSO and the personnel involved there.

[44] The next important issue is that relating to MST-13 timers. The evidence relating to this came essentially from Edwin Bollier, Erwin Meister, Ulrich Lumpert and those who supplied the circuit board components of the timers from Thuring AG, Zurich. MEBO AG was formed in the early 1970s by Edwin Bollier and Erwin Meister. In 1985 it had its offices in the Novapark Hotel (now the Continental Hotel) in Zurich. By then it had for some years supplied electrical, electronic and surveillance equipment. At that time, according to Mr Bollier, its principal customer was the Libyan Government and in particular the Libyan military security, and in connection with that business he made fairly frequent visits to Libya. Mr Lumpert was employed by the company as an engineer and in that capacity he was involved in the design and production of such equipment.

[45] We have assessed carefully the evidence of these three witnesses about the activities of MEBO, and in particular their evidence relating to the MST-13 timers which the company made. All three, and notably Mr Bollier, were

shown to be unreliable witnesses. Earlier statements which they made to the police and judicial authorities were at times in conflict with each other, and with the evidence they gave in court. On some occasions, particularly in the case of Mr Bollier, their evidence was self-contradictory.

[46] Mr Bollier gave evidence that one Badri Hassan came to MEBO's offices in Zurich at the end of November or early in December 1988 and asked the firm to supply forty MST-13 timers for the Libyan Army. Mr Bollier checked with Mr Lumpert whether they had sufficient material in stock to make that number of timers. Mr Lumpert, he said, advised that they had not and so, since timers were urgently required by the Libyan Army and Mr Bollier bought timers on the open market. He bought sixteen Olympus timers on 5 December 1988 and the balance of twenty-four such timers on 15 December 1988. On 16 December 1988 he booked his flight from Zurich to Tripoli and back. He flew to Tripoli on 18 December 1988, taking the timers with him. He expected to deliver them to Ezzadin Hinshiri in person on the day of his arrival. Instead, on that day he was taken to Hinshiri's office and left the timers there. On the following day he saw Ezzadin Hinshiri in his office about 10.00am. Hinshiri said that he wanted MST-13 timers and that the Olympus timers were too expensive. Nevertheless, he retained the timers and directed Mr Bollier to go to the first accused's office in the evening in order to get payment for them. From about 6.00pm Mr Bollier sat outside that office for two hours. While he did not see the first accused, he did see Nassr Ashur sitting at a meeting. On 20 December 1988 he again saw Ezzadin Hinshiri who repeated his view that the timers were too expensive, although he wished to keep them and to pay for them later. Mr Bollier however took the timers back and left Tripoli later on the same day, flying by direct flight to Zurich rather than via Malta (as he had expected) where he would have had to spend that night. It was submitted by the Crown that Mr Bollier's visit to Tripoli and particularly his visit to the first accused's office and the presence there of Nassr Ashur provided additional evidence in the case against the first accused. While we accept that Mr Bollier visited Tripoli between 18 and 20 December in order to sell timers to the Libyan army, because that is substantially vouched by documentary evidence and it was not challenged in evidence, we are not prepared to draw the inference that the Crown sought from this evidence. On his return to Zurich Mr Bollier claimed to have discovered that one of the timers had been set for a time and a day of the week which were relevant to the time when there was an explosion on board PA103. He showed this to Mr Meister who agreed that he was able to see a time and even a date which were relevant. We do not accept the evidence of either of these two witnesses about this alleged discovery. It was established, and Mr Meister was forced to accept, that the Olympus timer was incapable of showing a date. Moreover, the evidence of both witnesses about what they claimed to have seen and the

circumstances in which they claimed to have made the discovery was so inconsistent that we are wholly unable to accept any of it.

[47] Similarly, we reject the evidence of Mr Bollier that outside his Zurich office on 30 December 1988 he met a mysterious stranger who Mr Bollier thought was a member of the security services (although of which country he did not specify), who seemed to know a considerable amount about his recent visit to Tripoli, and who encouraged him to purchase a typewriter with Spanish keys on which to type a letter to be sent to the CIA implicating two well known Libyan figures in the bombing of PA103. (Mr Bollier did in fact type such a false letter on a Spanish typewriter which he delivered to the US Embassy in Vienna early in January 1989 on his way to East Germany). This account given by Mr Bollier belongs in our view to the realm of fiction where it may best be placed in the genre of the spy thriller. The notion, also, that a rogue company in Florida was engaged in manufacturing fake MST-13 timers on the instructions of the CIA, to which Mr Bollier spoke in evidence, falls into the same category.

[48] Despite being examined before a Swiss Magistrate and being interviewed by police officers on several occasions before October 1993, it was only then that Mr Bollier admitted that MEBO had supplied any MST-13 timers to the Stasi (the East German intelligence service). At that time he said that in the late summer of 1985 he had taken two prototypes to the Stasi offices in East Berlin where he had delivered them. He accepted in evidence that he had said in a police interview conducted on 26 January 1994 that he had found in his desk drawer in Zurich in late 1993 an invoice dated 18 September 1985 indicating that seven MST-13 timers had been delivered to the Stasi in 1985. Recognising that this was a principal invoice and not, as one might expect, a copy, Mr Bollier sought to account for its presence in the drawer by saying that it had been put there by "the Secret Service." In any event, he said it was typical of the type of false document which he carried with him on his business journeys in order to get through Customs. This was the first time that Mr Bollier mentioned that a delivery of an additional five timers had been made to the Stasi. We do not accept that the invoice which Mr Bollier said he had found was genuine. Indeed, not even Mr Bollier appeared to have acknowledged it to be genuine.

[49] We do however accept certain parts of Mr Bollier's evidence despite finding him at times an untruthful and at other times an unreliable witness. We have done so when his evidence has not been challenged and appears to have been accepted, or where it is supported from some other acceptable source. We accept, for example, that in or about July 1985 on a visit to Tripoli, Mr Bollier received a request for electronic timers from Said Rashid or Ezzadin Hinshiri and that he had had military business dealings in relation to the Libyan Government with Ezzadin Hinshiri since the early 1980s. The potential order

was for a large number of such timers. Mr Lumpert was told of the requirements by Mr Bollier and proceeded to develop two prototypes. There is a dispute in the evidence between Mr Bollier and Mr Meister on the one hand and
Mr Lumpert on the other about the colour of the circuit boards in these pro-
totype timers. Mr Bollier said they were brown, Mr Meister thought they were
grey or brown, whereas Mr Lumpert said that they were manufactured from
the green coloured circuit boards supplied by Thuring. What we do however
accept is that later in the summer of 1985 the two prototypes were delivered
by Mr Bollier to the Stasi in East Berlin, whatever be the colour of their circuit boards. This is consistent with the evidence of Mr Wenzel who at the
material time was a major in the Stasi and with whom Mr Bollier then dealt.
Despite this evidence we cannot, however, exclude absolutely the possibility
that more than two MST-13 timers were supplied by MEBO to the Stasi,
although there is no positive evidence that they were, nor any reasons why
they should have been. Similarly, we cannot exclude the possibility that other
MST-13 timers may have been made by MEBO and supplied to other parties,
but there is no positive evidence that they were. Equally, despite the evidence
of Mr Wenzel that after the fall of the Berlin wall he had destroyed all timers
supplied to the Stasi, we are unable to exclude the possibility that any MST-
13 timers in the hands of the Stasi left their possession, although there is no
positive evidence that they did and in particular that they were supplied to the
PFLP-GC.

[50] The initial order placed with Thuring was for twenty circuit boards, solder masked on one side only, i.e. single sided. In fact Thuring supplied twenty-
four such boards. In October 1985 MEBO placed a further order with Thuring
for circuit boards but it was specified that they should be solder masked on
both sides, i.e. double sided. Thirty-five such boards were ordered, but Thuring
supplied only thirty-four. When the Scottish police visited MEBO's premises
in May 1991, CI Williamson received from Mr Bollier eleven circuit boards,
having been shown twelve. Earlier, on 15 November 1990, following the interview by a Swiss Magistrate of Mr Bollier and Mr Meister, CI Williamson also
took possession of two sample MST-13 timers. It is clear from this, therefore,
that at least twelve of the circuit boards ordered from Thuring were not used
in the manufacture of MST-13 timers. Of the number which CI Williamson
took into his possession, four were single sided circuit boards. Of the circuit
boards in the sample MST-13 timers recovered by CI Williamson, one was
single sided and the other double sided. The MST-13 timer which the US
authorities obtained from the Togo Government in September or October
1986 at Lomé (to which reference will later be made) also had a double sided
circuit board. It follows that some of the circuit boards of these timers were
single sided and some were double sided, and also that a number of the single sided circuit boards supplied by Thuring in August 1985 were not used.

Mr Bollier therefore may well have been correct when he said that the Libyan order was met with the supply of timers which had circuit boards of both types. We also accept Mr Bollier's evidence that he supplied the twenty samples to Libya in three batches. In 1985 he himself delivered five on a visit to Tripoli. In the same year he delivered another five to the Libyan Embassy in East Berlin. In 1986 he delivered the remaining ten personally in Tripoli.

[51] In September or October 1986 the President of Togo asked the US Government to send representatives to examine a cache of arms which had been discovered in that country. Three US government officials attended at Lomé. Amongst the captured equipment there were two MEBO MST-13 timers which interested the Americans because they looked particularly modern and sophisticated compared to the other items which seemed old and worn. The Americans received permission to take one of the two timers back in the diplomatic bag to the US. In June 1990 Mr Feraday attended at the Explosives Unit of the FBI HQ in Washington DC and examined it there. A preliminary examination by him determined that there were similarities between the circuit board of the Lomé timer and the fragment PT/35(b). On later examination he discovered that the Lomé timer had a double sided circuit board, whereas the fragment PT/35(b) came from a single sided circuit board. Further he observed that the board did not have the corners cut out, which indicated that it cannot have been boxed. An attempt had been made to scratch out the letters MEBO on the surface of a smaller circuit board contained within the timer. Counsel for the first accused drew our attention to the fact that amongst the equipment captured there were ammunition pouches which were recognised as pouches of East German design. In fact, there were, in addition, rifles and handguns of East German origin amongst the equipment, but the other items, including detonators, a length of fuse, a detonator box and ammunition, came from several different countries, including Bulgaria, the Soviet Union, France and West Germany. Counsel also reminded us that Mr Wenzel had given evidence that it was his practice to remove the MEBO name from products supplied by Mr Bollier. In these circumstances we cannot exclude the possibility that the source of at least one of the two MST-13 timers found in Togo was East Germany, but on any view there were material differences between these timers and the one used to trigger the explosion on PA103.

[52] The timer recovered in Togo which, as we have said, was one of two, was considered by the witness Richard Sherrow to be identical to one which was discovered in Dakar, Senegal, on 20 February 1988 within a briefcase found on board a passenger aircraft which had arrived at the airport there from Cotonou in Benin. It was recovered in October 1999 by CI Williamson from the French Ministry of Justice in Paris but was not examined forensically. It cannot therefore be said whether its circuit board was single or double sided. In the brief-

case were found also nine metres of fuse, four blocks of TNT, two blocks of Semtex-H, nine electric detonators, a pistol with a silencer, a box of bullets, one empty clip and five discs for the silencer. Three persons were taken into custody from the aircraft—a Senegalese named Ahmed Khalifa Niasse, Mansour Omran El Saber who at the time was a member of the Libyan ESO, and one Mohamed El Marzouk. The evidence did not establish any connection between any of these three arrested persons and the briefcase and its contents.

[53] Mr Bollier gave evidence that he attended tests carried out by the Libyan military in the Libyan desert at Sabha which involved, *inter alia*, the use of MST-13 timers in connection with explosives and in particular air bombs. He said that the timers were brought by Nassr Ashur. Mr Bollier attended there as a technical expert. He thought that this was in 1986 after the last batch of timers had been delivered to the Libyan Government, but later he qualified this by saying that it might be in the middle or the fall of 1987. From the way in which he gave evidence about these tests we are persuaded that he did indeed attend such tests, although it is not clear when they were carried out or what was their purpose.

[54] We also accept Mr Bollier's evidence, supported by documentation, that MEBO rented an office in their Zurich premises some time in 1988 to the firm ABH in which the first accused and one Badri Hassan were the principals. They explained to Mr Bollier that they might be interested in taking a share in MEBO or in having business dealings with MEBO.

[55] The third important witness is Mr Gauci. We have already referred to his evidence in connection with the sale of clothing. Mr Gauci picked out the first accused at an identification parade on 13 August 1999, using the words as written in the parade report "Not exactly the man I saw in the shop. Ten years ago I saw him, but the man who look a little bit like exactly is the number 5." Number 5 in the parade was the first accused. He also identified him in Court, saying "He is the man on this side. He resembles him a lot." These identifications were criticised *inter alia* on the ground that photographs of the accused have featured many times over the years in the media and accordingly purported identifications more than ten years after the event are of little if any value. Before assessing the quality and value of these identifications it is important to look at the history.

[56] In his evidence in chief, Mr Gauci said that the date of purchase must have been about a fortnight before Christmas. He was asked if he could be more specific under reference to the street Christmas decorations. Initially he said "I wouldn't know exactly, but I have never really noticed these things, but I remember, yes, there were Christmas lights. They were on already. I'm sure. I can't say exactly." In a later answer when it had been put to him that he had earlier said that the sale was before the Christmas decorations went up, he said "I don't know. I'm not sure what I told them exactly about this.

I believe they were putting up the lights, though, in those times." He could not say what day of the week it was. He was alone in the shop because his brother was at home watching football on television. When asked about the weather he said "When he came by the first time, it wasn't raining but then it started dripping. Not very—it was not raining heavily. It was simply dripping. . ." As we have previously noted, he said the purchaser was a Libyan. He was wearing a blue suit. When asked about the build of the purchaser, he said "I'm not an expert on these things. I think he was below six feet. . . . He wasn't small. He was a normal stature. He had ordered a $16^{1}/_{2}$ shirt." When asked about age he said "I said before, below six—under sixty. I don't have experience on height and age." He also said the purchaser had dark coloured skin. On 13 September he went to the police station where he assisted in the compilation of a photofit (production 430.1) and an artist's impression (production 427.1). He described the result of both as being 'very close.'

[57] In cross-examination he had put to him a number of statements he had made to the police. He was first interviewed by the police on 1 September 1989. On that date, in addition to giving the police information about the clothing, he also gave information about the circumstances of the sale, the date of the sale, and the description of the purchaser. In the statement noted by DCI Bell on that date, Mr Gauci said that he had been working alone in the shop between 6.30pm and 7.00pm when the purchaser came in. The description of the purchaser as given to DCI Bell was that he was six feet or more in height. He had a big chest and a large head. He was well built but was not fat or with a big stomach. His hair was very black. He was clean-shaven with no facial hair and had dark coloured skin. His overall appearance was smart. He bought an umbrella and put it up when he left the shop because it was raining. Mr Gauci said that he could not remember the day of the week although he thought it was a weekday. In a further statement on 13 September he said that the man was about 50 years of age.

[58] On 14 September 1989 Mr Gauci was taken to police headquarters at Floriana, Malta, where he was interviewed by DCI Bell and Inspector Scicluna of the Maltese police. They took a statement from him and showed him nineteen photographs on two cards. Mr Gauci identified a photograph of a man in one of the cards. He said that he was similar to the man who had bought the clothing but the man in the photograph he identified was too young to be the man who had bought the clothing. If he was older by about twenty years he would have looked like the man who bought the clothing. He signed the front of the photograph of the man whom he identified as similar. He said in his statement that the photograph looked like the man's features so far as the eyes, nose, mouth and shape of face were concerned. The hair of the customer was similar but shorter than that of the man in the photograph. DCI Bell revealed that the person whom Mr Gauci had identified was someone

whom the Maltese Security Branch considered to be similar to the artist and photo-fit impressions which had been composed as a result of the description given by Mr Gauci. The man was later identified as one Mohammed Salem.

[59] On 26 September 1989 Mr Gauci again attended at police headquarters in Malta where he was interviewed by the same two police officers. He was then shown more photographs. He said that he did not see the man to whom he sold the clothing, but he pointed out one photograph of a man who had the same hairstyle. He said that this was not the man he sold the clothing to as the man in the photograph was too young. The person he pointed out, according to the evidence of DCI Bell, was a person called Shukra whose photograph was included at the suggestion of the BKA, the German police force, who suggested that Shukra might be similar to the person whom Mr Gauci had already described.

[60] On 31 August 1990 Mr Gauci gave a further statement to DCI Bell and Inspector Scicluna at police headquarters at Floriana. He was shown a card containing twelve photographs. He examined these photographs and said that he could not see the photograph of the man who had purchased the clothing, and he told DCI Bell that the man's photograph was not present. He pointed out one of the photographs of a man who was similar in the shape of the face and style of hair but it was not, he said, the photograph of the man whom he had described. He informed DCI Bell that three other photographs he was shown were photographs of men of the correct age of the man he had described. DCI Bell then opened another set of photographs, twelve in number. Mr Gauci examined each of these but could not see the photograph of the man who had purchased the clothing. DCI Bell gave evidence that in the first series there was included a photograph of a man Marzouk and in the second series a man named Saber. He could not however say which photographs represented either person.

[61] On 10 September 1990 Mr Gauci again attended at police headquarters. He was shown thirty-nine photographs on that occasion which were contained in an album. He however made no identification of anyone from these photographs which included a photograph of Abo Talb. Mr Gauci had been shown on 6 December 1989 a selection of photographs which included a photograph of Abo Talb, but he made no identification of anyone from these photographs. At about the end of 1989 or the beginning of 1990 his brother showed him an article in a newspaper about the Lockerbie disaster. As he recalled, there were photographs of two people in the article. Across the photograph of the wreckage of Pan Am 103 there was printed the word "Bomber." In the top right corner of the article there was a photograph of a man with the word "Bomber" also across it. Mr Gauci thought that one of the photographs showed the man who had bought the articles from him. When the Advocate Depute put to Mr Gauci in evidence at the trial that the man in the

photograph looked similar to the man who had bought the clothes, Mr Gauci replied that it resembled him and he explained that the man's face and hair resembled the person who had bought the clothes from him. The person whom he identified in that way was Abo Talb. By the time he gave his statement on 10 September 1990 Mr Gauci had been shown many photographs but he said in that statement that he had never seen a photograph of the man who had bought the clothing.

[62] On 15 February 1991 Mr Gauci again attended at police headquarters. He was asked to look at a number of photographs and a card of twelve photographs was put before him. He said: "The first impression I had was that all the photographs were of men younger than the man who bought the clothing. I told Mr Bell this. I was asked to look at all the photographs carefully and to try and allow for any age difference. I then pointed out one of the photographs." He said of the photograph of the person he had pointed out: "Number 8 is similar to the man who bought the clothing. The hair is perhaps a bit long. The eyebrows are the same. The nose is the same. And his chin and shape of face are the same. The man in the photograph number 8 is in my opinion in his 30 years. He would perhaps have to look about 10 years or more older, and he would look like the man who bought the clothes. It's been a long time now, and I can only say that this photograph 8 resembles the man who bought the clothing, but it is younger." He went on further to say: "I can only say that of all the photographs I have been shown, this photograph number 8 is the only one really similar to the man who bought the clothing, if he was a bit older, other than the one my brother showed me." He was asked by DCI Bell if what he said was true and that this photograph was the only one really similar to the man who bought the clothing if he was a bit older, other than the one his brother had shown him, and he said: "Of course. He didn't have such long hair, either. His hair wasn't so large." DCI Bell later gave evidence that the person shown in photograph 8 was the first accused, being apparently the same as the photograph in the first accused's 1986 passport. He also said that before showing Mr Gauci the card of photographs he had all the other photographs dulled down to the same level of brightness as the first accused's photograph. He said that he did that simply for fairness because the rest of the photographs were brighter and sharper than that of the first accused and he wanted them all to look the same. Counsel for the first accused submitted that DCI Bell's attempts to make the quality of all the photographs similar had failed, but in our view this criticism has no validity.

[63] Finally, so far as police interviews were concerned, Mr Gauci was asked about a visit he made to Inspector Scicluna towards the end of 1998 or the beginning of 1999 after another shopkeeper showed him a magazine containing an article about the Lockerbie disaster. Towards the bottom of the page in the article there was a photograph in the centre of a man wearing

glasses. Mr Gauci thought that that man looked like the man who had bought the clothes from him but his hair was much shorter and he didn't wear glasses. He showed the photograph in the article to Inspector Scicluna and, as Mr Gauci recalled it, he said "Well now I said 'This chap looks like the man who bought articles from me.' Something like that I told him." He added that the hair of the man who bought from him was much shorter than that shown in the photograph and he was without glasses. The photograph was a photograph of the first accused.

[64] In cross-examination Mr Gauci was referred to a statement which he had given to DCI Bell on 14 September 1989. In that statement he said that the purchase of the clothing was made on a week day when he was alone in the shop. His brother Paul Gauci did not work in the shop on that particular afternoon because he had gone home to watch a football match on television. It was agreed by Joint Minute that whichever football match or matches Paul Gauci had watched would have been broadcast by Italian Radio Television either on 23 November 1988 or 7 December 1988. Mr Gauci had also said in that statement that the purchaser walked out of the shop with the umbrella which he had purchased and that he had opened up the umbrella as it was raining. In his evidence he agreed that he had said this because it was raining at the time. When the man returned, the umbrella was down because it had almost stopped raining. There were just a few drops coming down. In a later statement he said that it had almost stopped raining when the man came back and there were just a few drops still coming down. It wasn't raining, he said in evidence, it was just drizzling. In a statement dated 10 September 1990 which was put to him in cross-examination he said that just before the man left the shop there was a light shower of rain just beginning. As the man left the shop he opened up the umbrella which he had just purchased. "There was very little rain on the ground, no running water, just damp." He was also asked in cross-examination what he meant when he used the word "midweek" and he responded by saying that he meant a Wednesday. It was put to him that midweek meant a day which was separate from the weekend, in other words that the shop would be open the day before and the day after. To that Mr Gauci said "That's it. Exactly. Tuesday and Thursday." But he then went on to say that for him midweek was Wednesday. It was not put to him that Thursday 8 December 1988 was a public holiday, it being the feast of the Immaculate Conception on that day. That evidence was given on Day 76 by Major Mifsud in the course of evidence led for the first accused. We are satisfied that when Mr Gauci was asked whether the shop would be open the day before and the day after he was being asked what he meant by the word "midweek," and not whether the day after the purchase of the clothing was made in his shop, the shop was open for business.

[65] Major Mifsud was between 1979 and 1988 the Chief Meteorologist at

the Meteorological Office at Luqa Airport. He was shown the meteorological records kept by his department for the two periods, 7/8 December 1988 and 23/24 November 1988. He said that on 7 December 1988 at Luqa there was a trace of rain which fell at 9,00am but apart from that no rain was recorded later in the day. Sliema is about five kilometres from Luqa. When he was asked whether rain might have fallen at Sliema between 6.00pm. and 7.00pm in the evening of 7 December 1988, he explained that although there was cloud cover at the time he would say "that 90% was no rain" but there was however always the possibility that there could be some drops of rain, "about 10% probability, in other places." He thought a few drops of rain might have fallen but he wouldn't think that the ground would have been made damp. To wet the ground the rain had to last for quite some time. The position so far as 23 November 1988 was concerned was different. At Luqa there was light intermittent rain on that day from noon onwards which by 1800 hours GMT had produced 0.6 of a millimetre of rain. He thought that the situation in the Sliema area would have been very much the same.

[66] Counsel for the first accused drew our attention to evidence which Mr Gauci gave that according to an invoice which he received, dated 25 November 1988, he purchased eight pairs of pyjamas about that time. Pyjamas sold well in winter and he used to buy stock "when it finished." According to a previous invoice dated 31 October 1988 he had at that time bought sixteen pairs. Since the purchaser of the clothing had bought two pairs of pyjamas and Mr Gauci had renewed his stock around 25 November 1988, counsel asked us to infer that the purchase of the two pairs must have been made on 23 November 1988. We are unable to draw this inference. In the first place it was not put to Mr Gauci in evidence that this may have been the sequence of events. Secondly, Mr Gauci was not asked what the state of his stock of pyjamas was on or about 7 December 1988.

[67] In assessing Mr Gauci's evidence we should first deal with a suggestion made in the submissions for the first accused that his demeanour was unsatisfactory—reluctant to look the cross examiner in the eye, a strange and lonely man, and enjoying the attention he was getting. We have to say we find no substance in any of these criticisms. We are not clear on what basis it was said that he was strange and lonely, and as far as enjoying attention is concerned, he made it clear that his co-operation with the investigation was a source of some friction within his family. The clear impression that we formed was that he was in the first place entirely credible, that is to say doing his best to tell the truth to the best of his recollection, and indeed no suggestion was made to the contrary. That of course is not an end of the matter, as even the most credible of witnesses may be unreliable or plainly wrong. We are satisfied that on two matters he was entirely reliable, namely the list of clothing that he sold and the fact that the purchaser was a Libyan. On the matter of identification

of the first accused, there are undoubtedly problems. We are satisfied with Mr Gauci's recollection, which he has maintained throughout, that his brother was watching football on the material date, and that narrows the field to 23 November or 7 December. There is no doubt that the weather on 23 November would be wholly consistent with a light shower between 6.30pm and 7.00pm. The possibility that there was a brief light shower on 7 December is not however ruled out by the evidence of Major Mifsud. It is perhaps unfortunate that Mr Gauci was never asked if he had any recollection of the weather at any other time on that day, as evidence that this was the first rain of the day would have tended to favour 7 December over 23 November. While Major Mifsud's evidence was clear about the position at Luqa, he did not rule out the possibility of a light shower at Sliema. Mr Gauci's recollection of the weather was that "it started dripping—not raining heavily" or that there was a "drizzle," and it only appeared to last for the time that the purchaser was away from the shop to get a taxi, and the taxi rank was not far away. The position about the Christmas decorations was unclear, but it would seem consistent with Mr Gauci's rather confused recollection that the purchase was about the time when the decorations would be going up, which in turn would be consistent with his recollection in evidence that it was about two weeks before Christmas. We are unimpressed by the suggestion that because Thursday 8 December was a public holiday, Mr Gauci should have been able to fix the date by reference to that. Even if there was some validity in that suggestion, it loses any value when it was never put to him for his comments. Having carefully considered all the factors relating to this aspect, we have reached the conclusion that the date of purchase was Wednesday 7 December.

[68] Mr Gauci's initial description to DCI Bell would not in a number of respects fit the first accused. At the identification parade the first accused's height was measured at 5'8." His age in December 1988 was 36. Mr Gauci said that he did not have experience of height or age, but even so it has to be accepted that there was a substantial discrepancy. Counsel for the first accused also pointed out that when the witness having pointed to the first accused in court, and asked which of the two accused he was referring to, said "Not the dark one, the other one," and the first accused was the other one. When however he first saw a photograph of the first accused in a montage of twelve, he picked him out in the terms we have indicated above.

[69] What did appear to us to be clear was that Mr Gauci applied his mind carefully to the problem of identification whenever he was shown photographs, and did not just pick someone out at random. Unlike many witnesses who express confidence in their identification when there is little justification for it, he was always careful to express any reservations he had and gave reasons why he thought that there was a resemblance. There are situations where a careful witness who will not commit himself beyond saying that there is a close

resemblance can be regarded as more reliable and convincing in his identification than a witness who maintains that his identification is 100% certain. From his general demeanour and his approach to the difficult problem of identification, we formed the view that when he picked out the first accused at the identification parade and in Court, he was doing so not just because it was comparatively easy to do so but because he genuinely felt that he was correct in picking him out as having a close resemblance to the purchaser, and we did regard him as a careful witness who would not commit himself to an absolutely positive identification when a substantial period had elapsed. We accept of course that he never made what could be described as an absolutely positive identification, but having regard to the lapse of time it would have been surprising if he had been able to do so. We have also not overlooked the difficulties in relation to his description of height and age. We are nevertheless satisfied that his identification so far as it went of the first accused as the purchaser was reliable and should be treated as a highly important element in this case. We should add that we have not made any attempt to compare for ourselves any resemblance between the first accused's passport photograph and the identikit or artist's impression, nor with the first accused's appearance in the video recordings of his interview with Pierre Salinger in November 1991.

[70] Prior to the start of the trial each accused lodged a Notice, in identical terms, which was treated as a Special Defence of Incrimination. The persons incriminated in the Schedule to the Notice were as follows:—

1. Members of the Palestinian Popular Struggle Front which may include Mohamed Abo Talb, Crown witness no 963, Talal Chabaan, present whereabouts unknown, Mohammed Ghaloom Khalil Hassan, present whereabouts unknown, Hashem Salem also known as Hashem Abu Nada present whereabouts unknown, Madieha Mohamed Abu Faja, present whereabouts unknown, Abd El Salam Arif Abu Nada, Magdy Moussa, Jamal Haider all present whereabouts unknown but all formerly directors of the Miska Bakery, Malta and Imad Adel Hazzouri, Gawrha, 42 Triq Patri, Guzi Delia Street, Balzan.

2. Members of the Popular Front for the Liberation of Palestine—General Command.

3. Parviz Taheri, crown witness 996."

[71] As with all special defences, this Notice does not in any way affect the burden of proof. That remains on the Crown throughout the trial and it is therefore for the Crown to prove beyond reasonable doubt that the accused committed the crime charged. There is therefore no onus on the Defence to prove that any of the persons referred to in the Schedule to the Notice were the perpetrators. The sole purpose of the Notice is, as its name implies, to give notice to the Crown prior to the start of the trial as to the possible effect of evidence which the Defence might lead in the course of the trial.

[72] In the event, such evidence was led and in his closing submissions counsel for the first accused made reference to it. In the first place, however, it should be recorded that at the end of his closing submissions counsel said that he was not suggesting that Parviz Taheri may have been responsible for the crime charged. That was in our view an inevitable concession given the evidence that we heard. Counsel for the second accused in his closing submissions did not in fact refer to those mentioned in the Notice at all, preferring to concentrate on the evidence that the Crown had relied on in relation to his client. In these circumstances we need say no more about Parviz Taheri.

[73] We turn next to the evidence in relation to members of the Popular Front for the Liberation of Palestine—General Command ("PFLP-GC"). No member of that organisation gave evidence but it was clear from other evidence that we heard, in particular from officers of the German police force, the BKA, that a cell of the PFLP-GC was operating in what was then West Germany at least up until October 1988. The evidence which we accept showed that at least at that time the cell had both the means and the intention to manufacture bombs which could be used to destroy civil aircraft. On 26 October 1988, after a period of surveillance, the BKA made a series of raids and arrested a number of individuals in an operation code-named Autumn Leaves. In particular they raided premises at Sandweg 28, Frankfurt and the home of Hashem Abassi in Neuss and they seized a car which had been used by Haj Hafez Kassem Dalkamoni, apparently the leader of the cell. In these premises they found radio cassette players, explosives, detonators, timers, barometric pressure devices, arms, ammunition and other items, including a number of airline timetables and seven unused Lufthansa luggage tags. From other evidence it appeared that one of the airline timetables was a PanAm timetable. There was considerable evidence of bombs being manufactured so as to be concealed in Toshiba radio cassette players. The models being used were, however, different from the RT SF-16 used in the PA103 disaster, and the timers were of a type known as ice-cube timers. These were quite different from MST-13s, much less sophisticated and much less reliable, and the intention was no doubt to use them in conjunction with the barometric pressure devices to detonate the explosive.

[74] While all this material was seized by the BKA on 26 October 1988 and the principal members of the PFLP-GC cell in West Germany were arrested on that date, the evidence was that most were released shortly thereafter. Dalkamoni, however, was not, and he was later convicted in relation to bomb attacks on a railway line in Germany in 1987 and 1988 and possession of the weapons found at Sandweg 28. He was sentenced to imprisonment for fifteen years. It is possible, of course, that the cell could have re-grouped and re-stocked with the necessary materials by 21 December. In April 1989 three further explosive devices were recovered at Hashem Abassi's new address in

Neuss, but the indications were that these were items which had formed part of the stock in October 1988. There was no evidence that the cell had the materials necessary to manufacture an explosive device of the type that destroyed PA103. In particular there was no evidence that they had an MST-13 timer. For the reasons given elsewhere, while a small quantity of such timers was supplied by MEBO to the East German Stasi, there is no evidence at all to suggest that any of them found their way into the hands of organisations such as the PFLP-GC. On the evidence which we heard we are satisfied that the explosive device which destroyed PA103 was triggered by an MST-13 timer alone and that neither an ice-cube timer nor any barometric device played any part in it. It is also to be noted that the cell's principal bomb-maker was one Marwan Khreesat who was in fact an agent who infiltrated the cell on behalf of the Jordanian Intelligence Service. His instructions from them were that any bomb he made must not be primed. Moreover, while he himself did not give evidence, there was evidence of a statement given by him to FBI agents (production 1851) in which he said that he never used radio cassette players with twin speakers (such as the Toshiba RT-SF 16 had) to convert into explosive devices.

[75] There was also a suggestion that the PFLP-GC might have infiltrated a bomb on to PA103A in Frankfurt through the medium of Khaled Jaafar, a 20 year old US/Lebanese national who boarded PA103A at Frankfurt and then PA103 at Heathrow with the intention of visiting his father in the USA. He, of course, died in the disaster. The evidence that we accept was that he had come from Lebanon a few weeks before and had been staying in Dortmund with a man Hassan El Salheli, who had himself come to West Germany from Lebanon in 1986 and is now a German citizen. When Khaled Jaafar arrived he had two holdalls with him containing his clothing, and it was these two holdalls that he took with him when he left. El Salheli was present when his bags were packed and they contained nothing but clothing. There was something of a farewell gathering of Arabs at Dortmund train station to see Khaled Jaafar off to Frankfurt on 21 December 1988, but there was no evidence of anything being put in his bags there or of his leaving with an extra bag. At Frankfurt Airport the passenger manifest (production 199) bears to record that he checked in two pieces of luggage. In the queue to pass through passport control he was closely observed by another passenger, Yasmin Siddique (who travelled only to London) and was not seen to be carrying any luggage. The reason for leading the evidence of this other passenger was that she observed him, as she thought, to be acting somewhat suspiciously. The suggestion appeared to be that he was nervous and this might be because he had infiltrated something onto PA103A. We are quite satisfied on the evidence, however, that he only had two bags with him and these were checked into the hold for PA103A at Frankfurt. We are also satisfied that neither of these two

bags contained an explosive device. After PA103 crashed the two bags were found close by one another. Neither had suffered any explosion damage.

[76] It remains to consider those named in paragraph 1 of the Schedule to the Notice. Only one of them gave evidence, namely Mohamed Abo Talb. His evidence was that he was born in Egypt and after a period in the Egyptian army he deserted and went to Jordan and, a few months later, to Lebanon. He said that while in Jordan, in about 1972, he joined the Palestinian Popular Struggle Front ("PPSF") and worked for them thereafter in what he described as military operations, and then security and latterly as bodyguard to the leader of the PPSF. During this period he was mainly based in Lebanon but moved to Damascus in 1982. In 1983 he left Damascus for Sweden where he has lived ever since. He said that after arriving in Sweden he did not belong to any Palestinian organisation and ceased all his activities in relation to Palestine. However, in 1989 he was convicted of a number of serious offences arising out of the bombing of targets in Copenhagen and Amsterdam in 1985 and was sentenced to life imprisonment. He is still serving that sentence.

[77] Abo Talb's wife, whom he married in 1979, and their children also live in Sweden, in Uppsala. So do a number of members of her family and other Arabs with whom Abo Talb associated. In particular, when Abo Talb was arrested in 1989 in connection with the bombings in Copenhagen and Amsterdam (and also one in Stockholm of which he was acquitted) his wife's brothers Mahmud and Mustafa Al Mougrabi were also arrested, as was a friend of Abo Talb's, Martin Imandi (also known as Imad Chabaan). There was also some evidence that some of those in Sweden associated with members of the PFLP-GC cell in West Germany. At that time the PPSF and the PFLP-GC shared the same political objective, namely the complete liberation of Palestine involving the destruction of the state of Israel. They both saw the USA as Israel's greatest ally. In 1988 Mohamed Al Mougrabi visited Hashem Abassi in Neuss and met Dalkamoni at a time when bombs were being manufactured there by Marwan Khreesat. Also there at the same time were two others (a brother and a cousin of Martin Imandi) who were later smuggled into Sweden by Mohamed Al Mougrabi. In addition, Ahmed Abassi, who also lived in Uppsala and knew both Abo Talb and Mohamed Al Mougrabi, was staying with his brother Hashem in Neuss at the time of the Autumn Leaves raids and was with Dalkamoni and Khreesat on an expedition to buy electrical components on 26 October when they were arrested by the BKA. There was also a suggestion that there had been a PFLP-GC cell in Sweden which had been investigated by the Swedish authorities in 1980, before Abo Talb went there, and Abo Talb said that a person called Hamid Al Wani, who owned a café in Uppsala, told him that he was a member of the PFLP-GC. We should also record that when Abo Talb's house was searched by police following his arrest in 1989 a barometric device was found. Abo Talb in his evidence said that

that belonged to his brother-in-law Mahmud Al Mougrabi, who lived in the same house.

[78] Abo Talb gave evidence concerning a number of journeys to various Mediterranean and European countries in the course of the period between the time he was granted right of residence in Sweden and given a Swedish travel document (1984/5) and 1988. He went on a number of occasions to Cyprus where he met other Arabs and relations of his wife. One particular trip was in October 1988. A somewhat strange set of circumstances led him from there to Malta. He was in Malta from 19 October to 26 October 1988 as in effect the guest of Abd El Salam (who is named in the Schedule to the Notice), initially staying at his flat and then in a nearby hotel. Abd El Salam was also known as Abu Nada and his flat in Malta was owned by the Palestine Liberation Organisation. While in Malta Abo Talb said he spent his time with Abd El Salam at the bakery business of which he was a director. This was known as the Miska Bakery, but Abo Talb denied that he knew it by that name and he said that he did not know any of the persons named in the Schedule to the Notice as former directors of the Miska Bakery. He did, however, meet Abd El Salam's brother, Hashem Salem, while he was in Malta and agreed to take some of his clothing merchandise back to Sweden with him to see if he could find sales outlets for it. That came to nothing and the clothing was later found by the police in Abo Talb's home.

[79] When Abo Talb left Malta on 26 October he flew to Sweden on an open return ticket to Stockholm, valid for one month. He explained that Abd El Salam had bought the ticket for him and that it had been a return ticket because that was cheaper than a single. He had no intention of returning to Malta and did not do so. He gave evidence that on 10 November 1988 he visited the Ministry of Labour in Stockholm in connection with his application for Swedish nationality, and on 5 December he consulted a solicitor in connection with the theft of his car, and there was some other evidence which might support that. On 9 December and 16 December he attended for medical treatment in Uppsala. These two appointments were agreed in Joint Minute 11. It was also agreed in that Joint Minute that shortly after midnight on 22 December 1988 his wife's sister gave birth in Uppsala to a child, and Abo Talb said that he was at home looking after his own children at that time. On this evidence, there is some support for Abo Talb when he said that he remained in Sweden and did not return to Malta after 26 October 1988. He did accept, however, that during that period he was in contact with Abd El Salam both by telephone and by post.

[80] As we have said, none of the other persons mentioned in the Schedule to the Notice gave evidence, but certain facts about them and their activities were agreed in Joint Minute 11. These, however, do not in our opinion add anything of significance.

[81] Having considered the evidence concerning these matters and the submissions of counsel we accept that there is a great deal of suspicion as to the actings of Abo Talb and his circle, but there is no evidence to indicate that they had either the means or the intention to destroy a civil aircraft in December 1988.

[82] From the evidence which we have discussed so far, we are satisfied that it has been proved that the primary suitcase containing the explosive device was dispatched from Malta, passed through Frankfurt and was loaded onto PA103 at Heathrow. It is, as we have said, clear that with one exception the clothing in the primary suitcase was the clothing purchased in Mr Gauci's shop on 7 December 1988. The purchaser was, on Mr Gauci's evidence, a Libyan. The trigger for the explosion was an MST-13 timer of the single solder mask variety. A substantial quantity of such timers had been supplied to Libya. We cannot say that it is impossible that the clothing might have been taken from Malta, united somewhere with a timer from some source other than Libya and introduced into the airline baggage system at Frankfurt or Heathrow. When, however, the evidence regarding the clothing, the purchaser and the timer is taken with the evidence that an unaccompanied bag was taken from KM180 to PA103A, the inference that that was the primary suitcase becomes, in our view, irresistible. As we have also said, the absence of an explanation as to how the suitcase was taken into the system at Luqa is a major difficulty for the Crown case but after taking full account of that difficulty, we remain of the view that the primary suitcase began its journey at Luqa. The clear inference which we draw from this evidence is that the conception, planning and execution of the plot which led to the planting of the explosive device was of Libyan origin. While no doubt organisations such as the PFLP-GC and the PPSF were also engaged in terrorist activities during the same period, we are satisfied that there was no evidence from which we could infer that they were involved in this particular act of terrorism, and the evidence relating to their activities does not create a reasonable doubt in our minds about the Libyan origin of this crime.

[83] In that context we turn to consider the evidence which could be regarded as implicating either or both of the accused, bearing in mind that the evidence against each of them has to be considered separately, and that before either could be convicted we would have to be satisfied beyond reasonable doubt as to his guilt and that evidence from a single source would be insufficient.

[84] We deal first with the second accused. The principal piece of evidence against him comes from two entries in his 1988 diary. This was recovered in April 1991 from the offices of Medtours, a company which had been set up by the second accused and Mr Vassallo. At the back of the diary there were two pages of numbered notes. The fourteenth item on one page is translated as "Take/collect tags from the airport (Abdulbaset/Abdussalam)." The word

'tags' was written in English, the remainder in Arabic. On the diary page for 15 December there was an entry, preceded by an asterisk, "Take taggs from Air Malta," and at the end of that entry in a different coloured ink "OK." Again the word 'taggs' (sic) was in English. The Crown maintained that the inference to be drawn from these entries was that the second accused had obtained Air Malta interline tags for the first accused, and that as an airline employee he must have known that the only purpose for which they would be required was to enable an unaccompanied bag to be placed on an aircraft. From another entry on 15 December (translated as "Abdel-baset arriving from Zurich") it appears that the second accused expected the first accused to pass through Malta on that day. In fact the first accused passed through on 17 December and missed seeing the second accused. In his interview with Mr Salinger in November 1991, the second accused said that he had been informed by his partner Mr Vassallo that the first accused had spoken to him and asked him to tell the second accused that he wanted to commission him with something. On 18 December the second accused travelled to Tripoli. He returned on 20 December on the same flight as the first accused. The Crown maintained that the inference to be drawn from this was that on that date the first accused was bringing component parts of the explosive device into Malta, and required the company of the second accused to carry the suitcase through Customs as the second accused was well known to the customs officers who would be unlikely to stop him and search the case. This would be consistent with the evidence of Abdul Majid. Finally the Crown maintained that in order for the suitcase to get past the security checks at Luqa on 21 December and find its way on board KM180, someone would have to organise this who was very well acquainted with the security controls at Luqa and would know how these controls could be circumvented. As someone who had been a station manager for some years, the second accused was ideally fitted for this role. Further, there was a telephone call recorded from the Holiday Inn, where the first accused was staying, to the number of the second accused's flat at 7.11am on 21 December. The Crown argued that this could be inferred to be a call arranging for the second accused to give the first accused a lift to the airport, and also it could be inferred that the second accused was at the airport from the fact that the first accused received special treatment both at check-in and at immigration control before departing on the LN147 flight to Tripoli.

[85] There is no doubt that the second accused did make the entries in the diary to which we have referred. In the context of the explosive device being placed on KM180 at Luqa in a suitcase which must have had attached to it an interline tag to enable it to pass eventually on to PA103, these entries can easily be seen to have a sinister connotation, particularly in the complete absence of any form of explanation. Counsel for the second accused argued that even if it be accepted that the second accused did obtain tags and did supply them to the first accused, it would be going too far to infer that he was

necessarily aware that they were to be used for the purpose of blowing up an aircraft, bearing in mind that the Crown no longer suggest that the second accused was a member of the Libyan Intelligence Service. Had it been necessary to resolve this matter, we would have found it a difficult problem. For the reasons we are about to explain however we do not find it necessary to do so. The Crown attach significance to the visit by the second accused to Tripoli on 18 December 1988 and his return two days later in the company of the first accused. As we have indicated, we cannot accept the evidence of Abdul Majid that he saw the two accused arriving with a suitcase. It follows that there is no evidence that either of them had any luggage, let alone a brown Samsonite suitcase. Whatever else may have been the purpose of the second accused going to Tripoli, it is unlikely that his visit was to hand over tags, as this could easily have been done in Malta. We do not think it proper to draw the inference that the second accused went to Tripoli for the purpose, as the Crown suggested, of escorting the first accused through Customs at Luqa. There is no real foundation for this supposition, and we would regard it as speculation rather than inference. The position on this aspect therefore is that the purpose of the visit by the second accused to Tripoli is simply unknown, and while there may be a substantial element of suspicion, it cannot be elevated beyond the realm of suspicion. The Crown may be well founded in saying that the second accused would be aware of the security arrangements at Luqa, and therefore might have been aware of some way in which these arrangements could be circumvented. The Crown however go further and say that it was the second accused "who was in a position to and did render the final assistance in terms of introduction of the bag by whatever means." There is no evidence in our opinion which can be used to justify this proposition and therefore at best it must be in the realm of speculation. Furthermore, there is the formidable objection that there is no evidence at all to suggest that the second accused was even at Luqa airport on 21 December. There were a number of witnesses who were there that day who knew the second accused well, such as Abdul Majid and Anna Attard, and they were not even asked about the second accused's presence. The Crown suggestion that the brief telephone call to the second accused's flat on the morning of 21 December can by a series of inferences lead to the conclusion that he was at the airport is in our opinion wholly speculative. While therefore there may well be a sinister inference to be drawn from the diary entries, we have come to the conclusion that there is insufficient other acceptable evidence to support or confirm such an inference, in particular an inference that the second accused was aware that any assistance he was giving to the first accused was in connection with a plan to destroy an aircraft by the planting of an explosive device. There is therefore in our opinion insufficient corroboration for any adverse inference that might be drawn from the diary entries. In these circumstances the second accused falls to be acquitted.

[86] We now turn to the case against the first accused. We should make it clear at the outset that the entries in the second accused's diary can form no part of any case against the first accused. The entries fall to be treated as equivalent to a statement made by a co-accused outwith the presence of the first accused. If both accused had been proved by other evidence to have been acting in concert in the commission of the crime libelled, then these entries could perhaps have been used as general evidence in the case as against any person proved to have been acting in concert. As we are of opinion however that it has not been proved that the second accused was a party to this crime, it follows that the normal rule must apply and the entries cannot be used against the first accused. We therefore put that matter entirely out of our minds.

[87] On 15 June 1987 the first accused was issued with a passport with an expiry date of 14 June 1991 by the Libyan passport authority at the request of the ESO who supplied the details to be included. The name on the passport was Ahmed Khalifa Abdusamad. Such a passport was known as a coded passport. There was no evidence as to why this passport was issued to him. It was used by the first accused on a visit to Nigeria in August 1987, returning to Tripoli via Zurich and Malta, travelling at least between Zurich and Tripoli on the same flights as Nassr Ashur who was also travelling on a coded passport. It was also used during 1987 for visits to Ethiopia, Saudi Arabia and Cyprus. The only use of this passport in 1988 was for an overnight visit to Malta on 20/21 December, and it was never used again. On that visit he arrived in Malta on flight KM231 about 5.30pm. He stayed overnight in the Holiday Inn, Sliema, using the name Abdusamad. He left on 21 December on flight LN147, scheduled to leave at 10.20am. The first accused travelled on his own passport in his own name on a number of occasions in 1988, particularly to Malta on 7 December where he stayed until 9 December when he departed for Prague, returning to Tripoli via Zurich and Malta on 16/17 December.

[88] A major factor in the case against the first accused is the identification evidence of Mr Gauci. For the reasons we have already given, we accept the reliability of Mr Gauci on this matter, while recognising that this is not an unequivocal identification. From his evidence it could be inferred that the first accused was the person who bought the clothing which surrounded the explosive device. We have already accepted that the date of purchase of the clothing was 7 December 1988, and on that day the first accused arrived in Malta where he stayed until 9 December. He was staying at the Holiday Inn, Sliema, which is close to Mary's House. If he was the purchaser of this miscellaneous collection of garments, it is not difficult to infer that he must have been aware of the purpose for which they were being bought. We accept the evidence that he was a member of the JSO, occupying posts of fairly high rank. One of these posts was head of airline security, from which it could be inferred that he would be aware at least in general terms of the nature of security precautions at air-

ports from or to which LAA operated. He also appears to have been involved in military procurement. He was involved with Mr Bollier, albeit not specifically in connection with MST timers, and had along with Badri Hassan formed a company which leased premises from MEBO and intended to do business with MEBO. In his interview with Mr Salinger he denied any connection with MEBO, but we do not accept his denial. On 20 December 1988 he entered Malta using his passport in the name of Abdusamad. There is no apparent reason for this visit, so far as the evidence discloses. All that was revealed by acceptable evidence was that the first accused and the second accused together paid a brief visit to the house of Mr Vassallo at some time in the evening, and that the first accused made or attempted to make a phone call to the second accused at 7.11am the following morning. It is possible to infer that this visit under a false name the night before the explosive device was planted at Luqa, followed by his departure for Tripoli the following morning at or about the time the device must have been planted, was a visit connected with the planting of the device. Had there been any innocent explanation for this visit, obviously this inference could not be drawn. The only explanation that appeared in the evidence was contained in his interview with Mr Salinger, when he denied visiting Malta at that time and denied using the name Abdusamad or having had a passport in that name. Again, we do not accept his denial.

[89] We are aware that in relation to certain aspects of the case there are a number of uncertainties and qualifications. We are also aware that there is a danger that by selecting parts of the evidence which seem to fit together and ignoring parts which might not fit, it is possible to read into a mass of conflicting evidence a pattern or conclusion which is not really justified. However, having considered the whole evidence in the case, including the uncertainties and qualifications, and the submissions of counsel, we are satisfied that the evidence as to the purchase of clothing in Malta, the presence of that clothing in the primary suitcase, the transmission of an item of baggage from Malta to London, the identification of the first accused (albeit not absolute), his movements under a false name at or around the material time, and the other background circumstances such as his association with Mr Bollier and with members of the JSO or Libyan military who purchased MST-13 timers, does fit together to form a real and convincing pattern. There is nothing in the evidence which leaves us with any reasonable doubt as to the guilt of the first accused, and accordingly we find him guilty of the remaining charge in the Indictment as amended.

[90] The verdicts returned were by a unanimous decision of the three judges of the Court.

Abdelbaset Ali Mohmed Al Megrahi
V
Her Majesty's Advocate
Appeal Court, High Court Of Justiciary
[2002] Scot CS 68

March 14, 2002
(Edited Text)

Introduction

1. On 31 January 2001 the appellant was found guilty of a charge of murdering 259 passengers and crew on board Pan American World Airways ("PanAm") flight PA103 from London Heathrow airport to New York and 11 residents of Lockerbie on 21 December 1988. This Opinion is concerned with his appeal against conviction, which was heard at Kamp Van Zeist from 23 January to 14 February 2002.

2. In view of the length of this Opinion it may helpful if at the outset we set out a list of its contents, by reference to its paragraph numbers, as follows:

The charge of which the appellant was convicted

3. The charge narrated that the appellant, having formed a criminal purpose to destroy a civil passenger aircraft and murder the occupants in furtherance of the purposes of Libyan Intelligence Services, while acting in concert with others, did certain acts. These included the purchasing on 7 December 1988 of a quantity of clothing and an umbrella in shop premises known as Mary's House at Tower Road, Sliema, Malta; entering Malta on 20 December 1988 at Luqa airport while using a passport with the false name of Ahmed Khalifa Abdusamad; residing overnight at the Holiday Inn, Tigne Street, Sliema, using this false identity; and placing or causing to be placed on board an aircraft of Air Malta flight KM180 to Frankfurt am Main Airport on 21 December 1988 a suitcase containing said clothing and umbrella and an improvised explosive device containing high performance plastic explosive concealed within a Toshiba RT SF 16 radio

cassette recorder and programmed to be detonated by an electronic timer, having tagged the suitcase or caused it to be tagged so as to be carried by aircraft from Frankfurt am Main Airport via London Heathrow airport to New York. The charge went on to state that the suitcase was thus carried to Frankfurt am Main Airport and there placed on board an aircraft of PanAm flight PA103 and carried to London Heathrow airport and there in turn placed on board an aircraft of PanAm flight PA103 to New York; and that the improvised explosive device detonated and exploded on board the aircraft while in flight near to Lockerbie, whereby the aircraft was destroyed and the wreckage crashed to the ground and the passengers, crew and residents were killed. The appellant's co-accused, Al Amin Khalifa Fhimah, was acquitted of that charge.

The general nature of the grounds of appeal

4.   In support of his appeal the appellant has tabled a considerable number of grounds of appeal. At the trial it was not submitted on the appellant's behalf that there was insufficient evidence in law to convict him. In its judgment the trial court rejected certain parts of the evidence relied upon by the Crown at the trial. Nevertheless, it was not contended in the appeal that those parts of the evidence not rejected by the trial court did not afford a sufficient basis in law for conviction. A few of the grounds of appeal maintain that the evidence was not of such character, quality or strength to enable a certain conclusion to be drawn or to justify a particular finding. However, the great majority of the grounds are directed to the trial court's treatment of the evidence and defence submissions. More specifically it is maintained that the trial court misinterpreted evidence, had regard to "collateral issues" and wrongly treated certain factors as supportive of guilt. It is also said that in regard to certain matters it failed to give adequate reasons. In many cases it is maintained that it failed to take proper account of, or have proper regard to, or give proper weight to, or gave insufficient weight to, certain evidence, factors or considerations. It is also maintained that the trial court misunderstood, or failed to deal with, or properly take account of, certain submissions for the defence. In one of the grounds of appeal the appellant seeks to found on the existence and significance of evidence which was not heard at the trial. Before coming to the grounds of appeal in more detail it is convenient for us to deal with two matters of general importance.

The basis of the appeal

5.   Section 106 of the Criminal Procedure (Scotland) Act 1995 ("the 1995 Act") makes provision for a right of appeal against conviction by a jury.

Under subsection (3) an appellant may bring under review of the High Court:

"any alleged miscarriage of justice, which may include such a miscarriage based on—

a.   subject to subsections (3A) to (3D) below, the existence and significance of evidence which was not heard at the original proceedings; and

b.   the jury's having returned a verdict which no reasonable jury, properly directed, could have returned."

In the present case only one of the grounds of appeal seeks to invoke paragraph (a) of section 106 (3). Mr. Taylor, who appeared for the appellant, expressly disavowed any reliance on para (b). Accordingly, with the exception of that one ground, the appeal is based on allegations of "miscarriage of justice" within the generality of that expression in subsection (3).

6.   In this case the trial took place before a court of judges sitting without a jury ("the trial court"), constituted under article 5 of the High Court of Justiciary (Proceedings in the Netherlands) (United Nations) Order 1998 ("the Order in Council"). Article 5(4) provides:

"For the purposes of any such trial, the court shall have all the powers, authorities and jurisdiction which it would have had if it had been sitting with a jury in Scotland, including power to determine any question and to make any finding which would, apart from this article, be required to be determined or made by a jury, and references in any enactment or other rule of law to a jury or the verdict or finding of a jury shall be construed accordingly."

It is clear that for the purposes of an appeal against the verdict of the trial court, the same provisions apply as in the case of the verdict of a jury, subject to the substitution of references to the trial court in place of references to the jury.

7.   Article 5(6) of the Order in Council provides that in the event of a verdict of guilty:

". . . (b) without prejudice to its power apart from this paragraph to give a judgment, the court shall, at the time of conviction or as soon as practicable thereafter, give a judgment in writing stating the reasons for the conviction."

In the case of a jury a miscarriage of justice may arise out of a misdirection of the jury by the judge in regard to a matter of law or a matter of fact (as to the latter, see e.g. *Crawford v HM Advocate* 1999 SCCR 674). The basis for such an appeal requires to be found in the charge to the jury, read along with their verdict. In the case of the trial court there is likewise scope for a conclusion that there has been a miscarriage of justice arising out of a misdirection of law or a misdirection of fact, that is to say a self-misdirection gathered from its written judgment.

8. It is plain that a trial court could include in its judgment more than strictly "the reasons for the conviction." In the present case it is clear that the trial court included in its judgment not only factual findings and reasoning leading to conviction of the appellant, but also an account of evidence which it had accepted or rejected, the weight attached to certain evidence and the submissions made to it. It is thus possible for this court to know the basis on which the conviction of the appellant was arrived at, and hence it can determine, for example, whether or not the trial court has misdirected itself by misinterpreting evidence or failing to take evidence into account in arriving at its conclusions.

9. At the outset, Mr. Taylor submitted that a miscarriage of justice could be based on the failure of the trial court to give adequate reasons for its conclusions, including reasons of adequate clarity. This appeared to be without regard to whether or not the failure was a failure to comply with article 5 (6) of the Order in Council.

10. In our opinion this submission was misconceived. It is not sound in principle or supported by authority. There is no ground for thinking that the perceived inadequacy of the reasons expressed by the trial court, whether performing its duty under Article 5 (6) or otherwise, is to be regarded as of itself establishing that it was not entitled to come to a particular conclusion. Mr. Taylor referred to *Petrovich v Jessop* 1990 SCCR 1, in which a conviction for theft by shoplifting was quashed. It is true that the appeal court stated that the magistrate who convicted the appellant must have "stateable and defensible reasons for drawing the inference of guilt," but the point of the decision was that the meagreness of the reasons which he stated for convicting the appellant indicated that he had failed to consider and assess all the relevant evidence which bore on the question of guilt or innocence, including an alternative to guilt, namely that the appellant had simply forgotten to pay. Likewise in *Ballantyne v McKinnon* 1983 SCCR 97 a conviction was quashed where the sheriff's account of the evidence did not provide a satisfactory basis for conviction. Reference may also be made to *Jordan v Allan* 1989 SCCR 202, in which the appeal court held that the findings in fact made by a justice could not be treated as made on the whole evidence as he had not stated whether or not he believed the appellant or what account he took of his evidence. We do not consider that the decision of the European Court of Human Rights in *Hadjianastassiou v Greece* (1992) 16 EHRR 219 is of assistance. As the Advocate depute pointed out, that case was concerned with a complaint that a denial of access to a finalised judgment within the time limit for the exercise of a right of appeal prejudiced the right of the losing party to "adequate time and facilities for the preparation of his defence."

11. Mr. Taylor also placed reliance on a number of judgments of the Court of Appeal in Northern Ireland dealing with appeals against the decisions of judges sitting without juries in the so-called "Diplock Courts" in criminal trials under section 2 of the Northern Ireland (Emergency Provisions) Act 1973 and similar successive enactments.

12. It is important to bear in mind that the question for the Court of Appeal in these cases was whether the conviction was "unsafe or unsatisfactory" in accordance with section 9 of the Criminal Appeal (Northern Ireland) Act 1968, now section 2 of the Criminal Appeal (Northern Ireland) Act 1980 (applying the explanation of that test in *R v Cooper* [1969] 1 QB 267 at page 271). It cannot be taken that there is a direct correspondence between the result of applying that test and the outcome of applying the Scottish test of a miscarriage of justice. Nevertheless the decisions are of some interest for present purposes since under section 2 (5) of the 1973 Act and the corresponding provisions of succeeding legislation, the judge had the duty to "give a judgment stating the reasons for the conviction."

13. Mr. Taylor founded on the observations of the Court of Appeal in *R v Bennett* and *R v Wilson*, both unreported but accessible in [1975] NIJB. However, an examination of the first of these cases shows that what the appeal court did was to examine the reasons given by the trial judge where there was virtually no evidence other than identification evidence and that evidence was contradictory and inconsistent. The true deficiency in that case did not lie in the judge's reasons but in the evidence which he set out. The Court of Appeal stated (at page 5 of the transcript) that it found the identification evidence to be unsatisfactory in the absence of an adequate explanation by the trial judge. It concluded that it could not accept the evidence of identification as reliable. In the second of these cases the Court of Appeal pointed out that an examination of the reasons given by the trial judge showed that he had simply left out of account a body of exculpatory evidence.

14. We consider that the Advocate depute was well-founded in submitting that inadequacy of reasons, of itself, did not constitute a misdirection and hence potentially extend the scope of section 106 (3). It might, on the other hand, provide the means by which a misdirection was detected, as in *Petrovich v Jessop*.

15. On the same subject of reasons, it is convenient to refer to a number of observations made by the Court of Appeal in Northern Ireland about the extent to which a judge is expected to explain his decision.

16. In *R v Wilson* the court observed (at page 15 of the transcript):

> "He did not give all his reasons nor is he obliged to give detailed reasons and we would deprecate any suggestion that his obligation should be widened in this respect."

In *R v Thompson* [1977] NI 74, in referring to the duty of the judge when giving judgment in a trial under the 1973 Act, the Court of Appeal said at page 83:

> "He has no jury to charge and therefore will not err if he does not state every relevant legal proposition and review every fact and argument on either side. His duty is not as in a jury trial to instruct laymen as to every relevant aspect of the law or to give (perhaps at the end of a long trial) a full and balanced picture of the facts for decision by others. His task is to reach conclusions and give reasons to support his view and, preferably, to notice any difficult or unusual points of law in order that if there is an appeal it can be seen how his view of the law informs his approach to the facts."

17. In *R v Thain* [1985] NI 457 the Court of Appeal was concerned with the conviction of a soldier who had shot a man whom he had been pursuing. It was maintained in his appeal against conviction that, in reaching his conclusion that he had not shot him in self-defence, the trial judge failed to take into account that there was no easy alternative to hand. The Court of Appeal rejected this criticism. At page 478 Lord Lowry LCJ pointed out that in reaching his conclusion the trial judge must have been well aware, since he had so held, that the appellant did not shoot the deceased in order to effect his arrest. He observed on that page:

> "Where the trial is conducted and the factual conclusions are reached by the same person, one need not expect every step in the reasoning to be spelled out expressly, nor is the reasoning carried out in sealed compartments with no intercommunication or overlapping, even if the need to arrange a judgment in a logical order may give that impression. It can safely be inferred that, when deliberating on a question of fact with many aspects, even more certainly than when tackling a series of connected legal points, a judge who is himself the tribunal of fact will
> (a)   recognise the issues and
> (b)   (b) view in its entirety a case where one issue is interwoven with another."

18. In our view these observations are relevant to a written judgment under article 5 (6) of the Order in Council by which, in similar language, the trial court is required to state "the reasons for the conviction." It is plain that reasons do not require to be detailed; that the trial court does not have to review every fact and argument on either side; and that reasons do not require to be given for every stage in the decision-making process.

19. Before leaving this subject we would record that Mr. Taylor founded on the terms of a report which the trial court provided in accordance with section 113 of the 1995 Act. In that report the trial court states:

> "As we have detailed our findings and explained our reasoning in the Opinion of the Court issued at the end of the trial in accordance with the

requirements of the Order in Council, we do not think it appropriate to make any further comment on the evidence or our interpretation of it. We would only say that in order to keep the length of the Opinion within reasonable bounds, we did not attempt to deal with every item of evidence which might be in dispute or with every criticism which was made of the evidence, but confined ourselves to dealing with those items of evidence and those criticisms which appeared to us to be of material importance."

Mr. Taylor maintained that in these circumstances it could be taken that the trial court had taken the view that any item of evidence or criticism which was not mentioned in the judgment had been regarded by the trial court as not being of material importance. Assuming that this report requires to be read along with the judgment of the trial court, we do not consider that this means that items of evidence or criticisms which are not mentioned in the judgment were either ignored by the trial court or were regarded by it as being of no significance whatsoever. The judgment sets out, *inter alia*, the evidence which the trial court regarded as being of material importance in supporting the conviction of the appellant, along with criticisms to which that evidence was subjected. In neither case is the account to be understood as going into every detail.

The function of an appeal court

20. The second matter of general importance is the proper function of an appeal court in a criminal appeal, particularly where, as in the present case, the decision was that of a court of judges which has provided a written judgment giving the reasons for the conviction.

21. Mr. Taylor accepted that this court was not a court of review in the sense in which that expression is used in regard to civil cases. Thus he accepted that it was not open to this court to review all the evidence which was before the trial court in order to determine for itself whether that court had come to the correct conclusion. On the other hand, he submitted that it was open to this court to review the conclusions reached by the trial court in the light of the evidence which it (the trial court) considered to be material. In this connection he referred to a number of decisions in civil cases in which there was a discussion of the role of an appeal court in regard to reliability of evidence or the proper inference to be drawn from evidence. In *Dunn v Dunn's Trustees* 1930 SC 131 Lord President Clyde observed at page 146:

"My opinion is that a Court of appeal in Scotland is still—as it has always been—competent freely to review decisions on fact by judges of first instance, on the ground that the judge of first instance has misapprehended the meaning or the bearing of a piece of evidence, or the relation of one piece of evidence to another, or on the ground that the evidence of a particular witness is unreliable on account of its inconsistency with itself or of any inherent defect in it—no matter how intelligent and honest the witness may have appeared in the eyes of the judge of first instance during the witness's fugitive appearance in the witness-box."

In *Duncan v Wilson* 1940 SC 221 Lord President Normand at page 224 said:

"A court of appeal is certainly bound to respect a finding of fact arrived at on an estimate of the credibility of witnesses made by the judge who saw them and heard their evidence. Yet when a question of fact is submitted for review, the court cannot avoid the duty of considering the material brought before it, and of pronouncing its own judgment upon it."

Mr. Taylor also cited a passage in the speech of Lord Reid in *Benmax v Austin Motor Company* [1955] AC 370 at page 376 where, after referring to the well-known passage in the speech of Lord Thankerton in *Thomas v Thomas* [1947] AC 484 at pages 487–488 (1947 SC(HL) 45 at page 54), he said:

"But in cases where there is no question of the credibility or reliability of any witness, and in cases in which the point in dispute is the proper inference to be drawn from proved facts, the appeal court is generally in as good a position to evaluate the evidence as the trial judge, and ought not to shrink from that task, though it ought, of course, to give weight to his opinion."

22. This raises a fundamental point in regard to the role of the appeal court in criminal cases. It is plain that in the past the appeal court has never taken upon itself the role of resolving issues of fact, any more than the determination of guilt. In *Webb v HM Advocate* 1927 JC 92, more fully reported in 1927 SLT 631 to which we will refer, the Lord Justice-Clerk (Alness) stated at page 631:

"This is not a court of review. Review, in the ordinary sense of that word, lies outside our province. We have neither a duty nor a right, because we might not have reached the same conclusion as the jury, to upset their verdict."

At page 636 Lord Anderson said:

"I express my first general observation in negative form to the effect that this Court will not re-try a case of this nature in the sense in which, in a civil process, a court of review deals with the decision of a judge of first instance. It is not the function of this court, but of the jury, to weigh and balance testimony in an endeavour to ascertain, on quantitative or qualitative grounds, how it ought to preponderate. This court, it is true, in an appeal on fact, is bound to read the evidence, but only for the purpose of deciding whether or not the verdict is unreasonable, or to use a term familiar in civil procedure, perverse."

It cannot be doubted that in the case of an appeal against a jury's verdict of guilty the same applies today. The alterations which have been made in the terms in which the right of appeal is expressed have not changed the role of the appeal court. It is not without significance that what is brought under review by means of a criminal appeal against the jury's verdict is "any alleged miscarriage of justice," and that if the appellant has satisfied the court that there has been such an injustice the court may exercise its power to quash the conviction. So far, this would not be in conflict with Mr. Taylor's submission. However, his argument was that the fact that the decision to convict had been taken by a trial court which had supplied a written account of its reasons for convicting the appellant changed the position.

23. In our opinion this argument is not well founded. The respective roles of the appeal court and the court by which issues of fact are resolved and guilt is determined are not changed by the fact that the normal arrangements have been modified by the Order in Council, and in particular by the requirement that the trial court should deliver a reasoned judgment. While accepting that this court is not a court of review in the sense in which that expression is used in regard to civil cases Mr. Taylor failed to recognise the full implications of that acceptance. Putting the matter the other way round, if he were correct that it was, for example, open to this court to review the inferences drawn by the trial court it would not be possible to stop short of the conclusion that this court could in effect substitute its own view of the evidence which was before the trial court, which is plainly wrong.

24. These considerations are supported by inference from the terms of subsection (3) (b) of section 106 of the 1995 Act. While that provision has not been invoked by the appellant in the present appeal, its terms have a bearing on the scope of review by this court under the section. Subsection (3) (b), where it is invoked, entails that it is for an appellant to show that no reasonable jury could have been satisfied beyond reasonable doubt that the accused was guilty (*King v HM Advocate* 1999 JC 226). Mr. Taylor argued that this provision could not apply to an appeal against the verdict in the present case, because in a jury case, as was plain from the decision in *King*, the appeal court had to consider the whole evidence which was properly before the jury. This did not make sense where the trial court had clearly rejected certain material evidence. We do not accept this argument. If that provision were invoked it would be for the appeal court to consider whether, having regard to the evidence which was not rejected by the trial court, the verdict was one which no reasonable trial court, properly directing itself, could have returned. It is implicit in this exercise that the assessment of evidence may legitimately give rise to differing views, and that evidence may be rejected simply because it is inconsistent with other evidence. That is the responsibility of those who are charged with the task of reaching conclusions as to what facts are proved (*King v HM Advocate* at pages 236 G and 238 B).

25. The Advocate depute submitted, in our view correctly, that if, in order to demonstrate that there was a miscarriage of justice arising from the trial court's verdict, an appellant had to go the length of showing that no reasonable trial court could have reached that verdict, it made no sense if the appeal court could, by applying a lesser standard in reliance on the general power to review any alleged miscarriage of justice, review the inferences drawn by the trial court or could set aside the trial court's assessment of the reliability of evidence. In this respect he drew a parallel with the issue which was the subject of decision in *Elliott v HM Advocate* 1995 JC 95. We have no doubt that, once evidence has been accepted by the trial court, it is for that court to determine what inference or inferences should be drawn from that evidence. If evidence is capable of giving rise to two or more possible inferences, it is for the trial court to decide whether an inference should be drawn and, if so, which inference. If, of course, the appeal court were satisfied that a particular inference drawn by the trial court was not a possible inference, in the sense that the drawing of such an inference was not open to the trial court on the evidence, that would be indicative of a misdirection and the appeal court would require to assess whether or not it had been material.

26. We are satisfied that the fact that the trial court delivered a reasoned judgment does not affect the nature and extent of the role of an appeal court in reviewing any alleged miscarriage of justice. The initial question for this court is whether in arriving at its verdict the trial court misdirected itself either in law or as to a matter of fact so that it took a course which is was not entitled to do or failed to do what it should have done. If and to the extent that this has been shown, the further question would be whether a miscarriage of justice has resulted.

27. As we have already noted, in this appeal it is not maintained that the evidence before the trial court, apart from the evidence which it rejected, was not sufficient as a matter of law to entitle it to convict the appellant. The grounds of appeal, in the main, are concerned with the trial court's treatment of the evidence and defence submissions. We have also noted that in many of the grounds it is said that the trial court failed to take proper account of, or have proper regard to, or give proper weight to, or gave insufficient weight to, certain evidence, factors or considerations. In the course of this Opinion we will discuss each of the grounds of appeal. However, at this stage we would observe that, for the reasons which we have given above, where it is not said that a trial court has misdirected itself by ignoring something, the amount of weight which should be attached to it is a matter solely for the trial court, and not for the appeal court.

The judgment of the trial court

28. The written judgment of the trial court, given in accordance with article 5 (6) of the Order in Council, was extensive. It contained 90 paragraphs. As will be seen, many of the issues of fact which were considered in it were not in dispute at the trial, and many of the trial court's findings in fact are not affected by the grounds of appeal. In order that the matters raised in the grounds of appeal may be understood in their proper context, we propose at this stage to summarise the relevant law and the judgment, with particular reference to the issues with which we are concerned.

29. At the trial, as in all criminal trials in Scotland, the burden of proving the guilt of the accused lay on the Crown, and so remained throughout the trial. In order to secure a conviction against either accused, the Crown had to succeed in proving his guilt beyond reasonable doubt. Corroboration, that is to say, evidence coming from at least two independent sources, was required to prove the essentials of the Crown case. In the present case these were, in relation to each accused, first, that the crime of murder had been committed and, secondly, that the accused in question was criminally responsible for its commission. Applying these tests, the trial court held that the guilt of the appellant had been proved, but acquitted his co-accused.

30. As the trial court explained in para [2] of the judgment, it was not disputed, and was amply proved, that the cause of the disaster was the explosion of a device within the aircraft. Nor was it disputed that the person or persons who were responsible for the deliberate introduction of the explosive device would be guilty of the crime of murder. The matter at issue in the trial therefore was whether or not the Crown had proved beyond reasonable doubt that one or other or both of the accused was responsible, actor or art and part, for the deliberate introduction of the device.

31. Since the Crown case against both accused was based entirely on circumstantial evidence, it is appropriate at this stage to make reference to the requirements of proof by such evidence, and what approach to it was open to the trial court. The rule that proof of guilt requires corroboration was reaffirmed in *Morton v HM Advocate* 1938 JC 50. At page 52 the Lord Justice-Clerk (Aitchison), delivering the opinion of the court, described it as a firmly established and inflexible rule of our criminal law that (with certain statutory exceptions) a person cannot be convicted of a crime on the uncorroborated testimony of one witness however credible. On the same page, passages in Baron Hume's *Commentaries on the Law of Scotland Respecting Crimes*, vol. ii, pages 383–4, were quoted with approval. In these passages Hume spoke of corroboration of the direct evidence of one witness by that of another, or by circumstantial evidence.

He went on to speak of a case where all the evidence was circumstantial. In such a case, he said, it was not to be understood that two witnesses are necessary to establish each particular, "because the aptitude and coherence of the several circumstances often as fully confirm the truth of the story, as if all the witnesses were deponing to the same facts."

32. So it was open to the trial court to hold the guilt of the appellant to be proved on the basis of circumstantial evidence coming from at least two independent sources. Before us, the Advocate depute relied on three cases in support of two further propositions which he advanced. The first proposition was that in a circumstantial case it is necessary to look at the evidence as a whole. Each piece of circumstantial evidence does not need to be incriminating in itself; what matters is the concurrence of testimony. The second was that the nature of circumstantial evidence is such that it may be open to more than one interpretation, and that it was precisely the role of the trial court to decide which interpretation to adopt.

33. The first case relied upon by the Advocate depute was *Little v HM Advocate* 1983 JC 16. At page 20 the Lord Justice-General (Emslie), delivering the opinion of the court, referred to an argument for one of the appellants in that case, that "each of the several circumstances founded upon by the Crown was quite neutral," and said:

"The question is not whether each of the several circumstances 'points' by itself towards the instigation libelled but whether the several circumstances taken together are capable of supporting the inference, beyond reasonable doubt, that Mr.s Little in fact instigated the killing of her husband by MacKenzie."

34. The second case was *Fox v HM Advocate* 1998 JC 94, in which the Crown had relied on circumstantial evidence as affording corroboration of the direct evidence of one witness. In the course of a passage disapproving of the decision in *Mackie v HM Advocate* 1994 JC 132 that circumstantial evidence is corroborative only if it is more consistent with the direct evidence than with a competing account given by the accused, the Lord Justice-General (Rodger) said at pages 100–101:

"[I]t is of the very nature of circumstantial evidence that it may be open to more than one interpretation and that it is precisely the role of the jury to decide which interpretation to adopt. If the jury choose an interpretation which fits with the direct evidence, then in their view—which is the one that matters—the circumstantial evidence confirms or supports the direct evidence so that the requirements of legal proof are met. If on the other hand they choose a different interpretation, which does not fit with the direct evidence, the circumstantial evidence will not confirm or support the direct evidence and the jury will conclude that the Crown have not proved their case to the required standard."

This passage is, in our view, equally applicable where there is no direct evidence and the evidence is wholly circumstantial. In the same case Lord Coulsfield said at page 118:

> "[I]t seems to me to be wrong to try to divide cases into different categories by reference to the nature of the evidence which is relied on, and if there were a rule that each piece of evidence must be incriminating, I would find it difficult to see why that should not apply in every case. I do not, however, think that it is necessary that each piece of evidence, of whatever kind, should be incriminating in that sense. The proper approach, it respectfully appears to me, is already given by Hume, that is, that what matters is the concurrence of testimonies. Whether a single piece of evidence, or a number of pieces of evidence, are incriminating or not is a matter which can only be judged in the whole circumstances taking all the evidence together."

35. Thirdly, in *Mack v HM Advocate* 1999 SCCR 181, the Lord Justice-General (Rodger), in delivering the opinion of the court, said at page 185:

> "There is nothing strange in discovering that circumstantial evidence may give rise to a number of possible inferences since that is one of the characteristics of evidence of that type. When presented with such evidence, the jury have to decide whether they draw the inference that the accused is guilty of the crime."

36. In our opinion these three cases, and the passages from them which we have quoted, support the propositions advanced by the Advocate depute, with which we did not understand Mr. Taylor to take issue. To these passages we would add one from *King v HM Advocate* 1999 JC 226, a case to which we have previously referred in another context. At page 238 C-D the Lord Justice-General (Rodger), delivering the opinion of the court said:

> "[I]t is by no means unusual to find that there is a body of evidence in a case which is quite inconsistent with the accused's guilt. Evidence supporting an alibi defence is necessarily of that nature and, while it is often possible for the Crown to undermine alibi witnesses on the ground perhaps that they are partial or untrustworthy, that is by no means always the case. In such a situation juries may none the less be satisfied of the accused's guilt beyond reasonable doubt on the basis of the Crown evidence and come to the view that they must accordingly reject the alibi evidence as wrong. The jury must consider all the evidence but, having done that, they can reasonably reject the alibi evidence precisely because it is inconsistent with the Crown evidence which they have decided to accept."

The same applies to the trial court, which was entitled to reject evidence which was inconsistent with the guilt of the appellant precisely because it was inconsistent with circumstantial evidence pointing to his guilt which it had decided to accept.

37   Although, as we have said, certain matters were not in dispute before the trial court, nevertheless it heard evidence, and proceeded to make findings in fact, about matters relevant to proof of commission of the crime charged as well as proof of the guilt of the appellant. In paras [3] to [15] the trial court considered the evidence which established that the cause of the disaster was indeed the explosion of a device within the aircraft. It referred to the police operation which led to the recovery of tens of thousands of items of debris which had fallen to the ground, and the examination of some of them by the relevant specialists. It accepted evidence which established that the detonation of an explosive device within the fuselage caused the shattering of an area on the port side of the lower fuselage in the forward cargo bay area, followed by the total disruption and disintegration of the aircraft. The port side forward cargo bay was loaded with luggage in containers. An aluminium container AVE 4041 was situated immediately inboard of and slightly above the shattered area of the fuselage. The trial court accepted evidence that the nature of the damage to the container led to the conclusion that the explosion occurred within the container. There were traces of chemicals used in the manufacture of plastic explosives, including Semtex. Evidence relating to the examination of fragments which showed various signs of explosives damage led to the further conclusion, which the trial court accepted, that the explosion had taken place within a brown hard-shell Samsonite suitcase of the 26" Silhouette 4000 range, which was thereafter referred to as "the primary suitcase." There was evidence also that the primary suitcase had been situated immediately above an American Tourister brand suitcase.

38   Examination of other fragments led to the conclusion, which the trial court also accepted, that the explosive device was contained within a Toshiba RT-SF 16 radio cassette player which had been within the primary suitcase. The suitcase also contained, at the time of the explosion, 12 items of clothing and an umbrella. Some of these items were identifiable by labels. This led to enquiries being made in Malta, and in particular a shop called Mary's House, Tower Road, Sliema, which was a shop run by the Gauci family, Tony Gauci being one of the partners. The trial court accepted evidence from Mr. Gauci that he had sold these items to a man, whom he recognised as being a Libyan, in 1988. This led the trial court to state, in para [12]: "We are therefore entirely satisfied that the items of clothing in the primary suitcase were those described by Mr. Gauci as having been purchased in Mary's House." The trial court also stated that it would return to Mr. Gauci's evidence in more detail in connection with the date of the sale and the identification of the purchaser. These issues are the subject of various grounds of appeal, which we will discuss in due course. As we read para [12], however, the trial court

accepted Mr. Gauci's evidence that the purchaser was a Libyan, and we did not understand that finding to be the subject of any challenge.

39. Another crucial item, as the trial court described it, that was found during the search of the debris was a fragment of green coloured circuit board which was extracted from a remnant of a shirt which had been within the primary suitcase. Subsequent enquiries led to identification of this fragment as coming from a timing device known as an MST-13, of a type which had a single-sided circuit board. The fragment originated from an area of the connection pad for an output relay of a circuit board of this type of timer. MST-13 timers were made by a Swiss company, MEBO AG, which in 1985 had its offices in an hotel in Zurich, and was engaged in the design and manufacture of various electronic items.

40. In para [15] the trial court summarised its findings in fact up to that point in the following terms:

"The evidence which we have considered up to this stage satisfies us beyond reasonable doubt that the cause of the disaster was the explosion of an improvised explosive device, that that device was contained within a Toshiba radio cassette player in a brown Samsonite suitcase along with various items of clothing, that that clothing had been purchased in Mary's House, Sliema, Malta and that the initiation of the explosion was triggered by the use of an MST-13 timer."

No issue was taken with any part of this passage during the course of the appeal.

41. It is convenient at this point to refer to certain findings in fact which were made by the trial court later in the judgment, and which were also not in issue before us. These were derived principally from the evidence of two witnesses, Abdul Majid and Edwin Bollier. Mr. Majid had been a member of a Libyan organisation called the Jamahariya Security Organisation ("JSO"), later named the External Security Organisation ("ESO"). The trial court concluded its discussion of his evidence by stating that it was unable to accept him as a credible and reliable witness on any matter except his description of the organisation of the JSO and the personnel involved there. The trial court accordingly accepted his evidence about the organisation of the JSO in 1985, in particular in a passage in para [42] in these terms:

"He gave evidence about the organisation of the JSO in 1985. In particular he said that the director of the central security section was Ezzadin Hinshiri, the head of the operations section was Said Rashid, the head of special operations in the operations department was Nassr Ashur, and the head of the airline security section was the [appellant] until January 1987 when he moved to the strategic studies institute."

In December 1985 Mr. Majid was appointed as assistant to the station manager of Libyan Arab Airlines ("LAA") at Luqa airport. This post, the trial court accepted, was one which was normally filled by a member of the JSO.

42. Mr. Bollier and Erwin Meister formed MEBO in the early 1970s. The trial court found Mr. Bollier to be at times an untruthful and at other times an unreliable witness. It did, however, accept certain parts of his evidence. In particular, it accepted that in or about July 1985 on a visit to Tripoli Mr. Bollier received a request for electronic timers from Said Rashid or Ezzadin Hinshiri and that he had had military business dealings in relation to the Libyan government with Ezzadin Hinshiri since the early 1980s (para [49]). It also accepted his evidence that he had supplied twenty samples of MST-13 timers to Libya in three batches, and that he may well have been correct when he said that the Libyan order was met with the supply of timers which had circuit boards of both the single-sided and the double-sided types. It accepted that in 1985 he himself delivered five of these samples on a visit to Tripoli, that in the same year he delivered another five to the Libyan Embassy in East Berlin, and that in 1986 he delivered the remaining ten personally in Tripoli (para [50]). It also accepted Mr. Bollier's evidence that he attended tests carried out by the Libyan military in the Libyan desert at Sabha which involved, *inter alia*, the use of MST-13 timers in connection with explosives and in particular air bombs. He said that the timers were brought by Nassr Ashur. Mr. Bollier attended there as a technical expert. The trial court said in para [53]:

"From the way in which he gave evidence about these tests we are persuaded that he did indeed attend such tests, although it is not clear when they were carried out or what was their purpose."

In para [54] the trial court stated:

"We also accept Mr. Bollier's evidence, supported by documentation, that MEBO rented an office in their Zurich premises some time in 1988 to the firm ABH in which the [appellant] and one Badri Hassan were the principals. They explained to Mr. Bollier that they might be interested in taking a share in MEBO or in having business dealings with MEBO."

43. In para [88] the trial court made findings in fact which were based on such of the evidence of Mr. Majid and Mr. Bollier as had been accepted, in these terms:

"We accept the evidence that [the appellant] was a member of the JSO, occupying posts of fairly high rank. One of these posts was head of airline security, from which it could be inferred that he would be aware at least in general terms of the nature of security precautions at airports from or to which LAA operated. He also appears to have been involved in military procurement. He was involved with Mr. Bollier, albeit not specifically in connection with MST timers, and had along with Badri Hassan formed a company which leased premises from MEBO and intended to do business with MEBO."

44. In para [87] findings in fact were also made which, with one exception, were not the subject of challenge in the appeal. The paragraph is in these terms:

"On 15 June 1987 the [appellant] was issued with a passport with an expiry date of 14 June 1991 by the Libyan passport authority at the request of the ESO who supplied the details to be included. The name on the passport was Ahmed Khalifa Abdusamad. Such a passport was known as a coded passport. There was no evidence as to why this passport was issued to him [this sentence is challenged]. It was used by the [appellant] on a visit to Nigeria in August 1987, returning to Tripoli via Zurich and Malta, travelling at least between Zurich and Tripoli on the same flights as Nassr Ashur who was also travelling on a coded passport. It was also used during 1987 for visits to Ethiopia, Saudi Arabia and Cyprus. The only use of this passport in 1988 was for an overnight visit to Malta on 20/21 December, and it was never used again. On that visit he arrived in Malta on flight KM231 about 5.30 pm. He stayed overnight in the Holiday Inn, Sliema, using the name Abdusamad. He left on 21 December on flight LN147, scheduled to leave at 10.20 am. The [appellant] travelled on his own passport in his own name on a number of occasions in 1988, particularly to Malta on 7 December where he stayed until 9 December when he departed for Prague, returning to Tripoli via Zurich and Malta on 16/17 December."

In para [39] the trial court found that the check-in for LAA flight LN147 to Tripoli on 21 December was between 0850 and 0950 hours.

45. The Crown case against the appellant depended on evidence relating to two matters. The first of these was summarised by the trial court at para [17] of the judgment in these terms:

"The Crown case is that the primary suitcase was carried on an Air Malta flight KM180 from Luqa airport in Malta to Frankfurt, that at Frankfurt it was transferred to PanAm flight PA103A, a feeder flight for PA103, which carried it to London Heathrow airport, and that there, in turn, it was transferred to PA103."

The second matter relied on by the Crown, to which we shall return in due course, was the identification of the appellant by Mr. Gauci as the purchaser of the clothing and the umbrella, and the related issue of the date of the purchase.

46. As the trial court explained at para [16], consideration of the evidence relating to the provenance of the primary suitcase and the possible ways in which it could have found its way into container AVE 4041 involved

consideration of the procedures at various airports through which it might have passed. This started with an account of practices relating to baggage checked in by intending passengers for carriage in aircraft holds. Each item of baggage had attached to it a tag bearing, ordinarily, the name of the airline, or the first airline, on which the passenger was to travel and the destination. Where the journey was to be completed in more than one leg or stage, the tag also carried the name of any intermediate airport. This enabled the baggage handlers at the airport of departure, at any intermediate airport and at the destination to deliver or transfer the item to the correct flight and to return it to the passenger at the final destination. Baggage checked in at the airport of departure was referred to as local origin baggage. Baggage which had to be handled at an intermediate airport was generally referred to as transit baggage. A distinction was normally made between two groups of transit baggage. Online baggage was baggage which arrived at and departed from an intermediate airport on aircraft of the same carrier. Interline baggage arrived on an aircraft of one carrier and departed with a different carrier. Baggage was intended to be carried on the same aircraft as the passenger to whom it belonged, but from time to time baggage was misdirected or delayed and had to be carried on a different flight. Such items were identified by an additional special tag, known as a rush tag, and were normally only sent in response to a request from the destination airport, following a claim made by a passenger for baggage which had not been delivered at the destination. It was normal to take steps to prevent items of baggage travelling on an aircraft unaccompanied by the passenger who had checked them in, unless there was sufficient reason to regard the items as safe.

47. Flight PA103 took off from Heathrow shortly before 1830 on 21 December 1988. Before its departure, the aircraft was parked at stand K14. Flight PA103A arrived from Frankfurt at stand K16. Some online baggage was unloaded from flight PA103A, on which it had been carried loose in the hold, into container AVE 4041 at stand K16. The container was then driven directly to stand K14 and loaded into the hold of flight PA103.

48. The trial court considered evidence relating to the placing of baggage into container AVE 4041 and its movements before it was taken to stand K16. At Heathrow there were a baggage build-up area, where baggage checked in at Heathrow was sent before being taken to the aircraft when it was ready for loading, and the interline shed, which was a separate building, where interline baggage was taken after being removed from incoming flights. After being brought to the outside of the shed, it was carried into it by a conveyor belt. In the interline shed, interline baggage for a PanAm flight was identified, separated from other airline baggage and examined by x-ray before being placed in a container or set aside to await

the outgoing flight. On 21 December 1988 John Bedford, a loader-driver employed by PanAm, was working with other persons in the interline shed. He set aside container AVE 4041 to receive interline baggage for flight PA103. The container was identified as the container for that flight by Mr. Bedford, who wrote the information on a sheet which was placed in a holder fixed to the container. A number of items were placed in the container. The trial court considered in some detail evidence from Mr. Bedford and other witnesses, which led them to accept that Mr. Bedford placed a number of suitcases in the container. He then left the interline shed for a time. On his return, two cases had been added to the container. There was a conflict of evidence between Mr. Bedford and the x-ray operator, Sulkash Kamboj, an employee of Alert Security, an affiliate company of PanAm, as to how these two cases had come to be added to the container. The trial court preferred the evidence of Mr. Bedford that he had been told by Mr. Kamboj that the latter had placed them in the container during the former's absence. The trial court also accepted that in his evidence Mr. Bedford adopted a prior statement in which he described one of the two cases as "a brown or maroony-brown hardshell Samsonite-type case." Flight PA103A was a little delayed. Mr. Bedford finished work soon after 1700 hours, which was his normal finishing time. To wait for the incoming flight would have taken him beyond his normal finishing time. It was accordingly arranged that he should take the container to the baggage build-up area. Mr. Bedford drove the container to a position near the baggage build-up area and left it there. It was from there that it was taken out to stand K16. Container AVE 4041 accordingly contained both baggage which had been placed in it in the interline shed, including the two cases referred to by Mr. Bedford, and baggage which was loaded into it from flight PA103A.

49. At para [24], the trial court stated:

"It emerges from the evidence therefore that a suitcase which could fit the forensic description of the primary suitcase was in the container when it left the interline shed. There is also a possibility that an extraneous suitcase could have been introduced by being put onto the conveyor belt outside the interline shed, or introduced into the shed itself or into the container when it was at the build-up area."

50. Before reaching a conclusion about the possibility of the introduction of the primary suitcase into the airline baggage system at Heathrow, the trial court turned to consider the evidence relating to Frankfurt airport. At that airport, PanAm had their own security and baggage handling staff. There was a computer controlled automated baggage handling system. Each item of baggage was placed in an individually numbered tray as it was taken into the system. The trays were placed on conveyor belts and

instructions were fed into the computer to identify the flight to which the baggage was to be sent, the position from which the aircraft was to leave and the time of the flight. The trays were dispatched to a waiting area where they circulated until an instruction was fed in to summon the baggage for a particular flight, whereupon the items would be automatically extracted from the waiting area and sent to the departure point. Local origin baggage was received at check-in desks, and passed into the system. Transit baggage was taken to one of two areas, known as V3 and HM, where it was fed into the system at points known as coding stations. There were seven coding stations in V3. The general practice was that baggage from an incoming flight was brought either to HM or to V3 in wagons or containers and would be directed by an employee called the interline writer to one or more of the coding stations. The proper practice was that each coding station should not deal with baggage from more than one incoming flight at a time. Normally there were two employees at each coding station. One would lift the items of baggage from the wagon or container and place each item in a tray. The other would enter into the computer, in a coded form, the flight number and destination for the outgoing flight, taking the information from the tag attached to the item. Records were kept identifying the staff working at particular stations, the arrival times of aircraft, the arrival times of consignments of baggage at HM or V3, and the station or stations to which the baggage from a particular flight was sent. The computer itself retained a record of the items sent through the system so that it was possible, for a limited period, to identify all the items of baggage sent through the system to a particular flight. The computer controlling the baggage handling system contained its own clock, which had a tendency to diverge from real time. It was reset at the start of each day, but by 1600 or 1700 hours the discrepancy might be as much as two or three minutes. Times entered in records not generated by the computer were obtained by the staff from the airport clock or from their own watches.

51. PanAm had x-ray equipment at Frankfurt, which was used to x-ray interline baggage. The practice of PanAm at Frankfurt was to carry out a reconciliation between local origin passengers and baggage and online passengers and baggage, to ensure that every such passenger who had baggage on the flight was accounted for, but there was no attempt to reconcile interline passengers and their baggage.

52. The trial court considered in some detail documentary and other evidence relating to baggage unloaded from flight KM180, and baggage sent for loading onto flight PA103A. Flight KM180 reached its parking position at 1248 hours on 21 December 1988. It was unloaded by employees of the airport authority. According to the record, the unloading took place

between 1248 and 1300 hours. Andreas Schreiner, who was in charge of monitoring the arrival of baggage at V3 on that day, recorded on the interline writer's sheet (production 1092) that one wagon of interline baggage from flight KM180 arrived at V3 at 1301 hours. A coder, Yasar Koca (who was not called as a witness), was working at station 206 in V3. He completed a worksheet (production 1061) which bore to show that one wagon of baggage from flight KM180 was coded at station 206 between 1304 hours and a later time which the trial court held to be 1310. No passenger on flight KM180 had an onward booking from Frankfurt to London or the United States. All the passengers on the flight retrieved their checked-in baggage at their destinations. The Malta documentation for flight KM180 did not record that any unaccompanied baggage was carried. There was, however, evidence from which the trial court inferred that there was an item of baggage which was neither accompanied nor otherwise accounted for. A computer printout (production 1060) relating to baggage sent for loading onto flight PA103A bore to record that an item which had been placed in tray number B8849 was coded at station 206 at 1307 hours and was transferred and delivered to the appropriate gate to be loaded on board flight PA103A. Discussion of this and other evidence, along with the submissions of counsel, led the trial court to state at paras [31] and [35] that there was a plain inference that an unidentified and unaccompanied bag travelled on flight KM180 from Luqa airport to Frankfurt and there was loaded on flight PA103A. Flight PA103A departed for London at 1653 hours.

53. The trial court then turned to consideration of evidence relating to Luqa airport. After a description of the arrangements for baggage there, it stated, in para [38]: "On the face of them, these arrangements seem to make it extremely difficult for an unaccompanied and unidentified bag to be shipped on a flight out of Luqa." After reference to the evidence of Wilfred Borg, the Air Malta general manager for ground operations at the time, the trial court stated: "Mr. Borg conceded that it might not be impossible that a bag could be introduced undetected but said that whether it was probable was another matter." The check-in for flight KM180 opened at 0815 and closed at 0915 hours, and the doors of the aircraft were closed for departure at 0938 hours. At para [39] the trial court referred to documentary evidence which showed that there was no discrepancy in respect of baggage loaded onto the flight, the flight log and the load plan each showing that 55 items of baggage were loaded. It went on to state:

"If therefore the unaccompanied bag was launched from Luqa, the method by which that was done is not established, and the Crown accepted that they could not point to any specific route by which the primary suitcase could have been loaded. . . . The absence of any explanation of the method by which the primary suitcase might have been placed on board KM180 is a major difficulty for the Crown case, and one which has to be considered along with the rest of the circumstantial evidence in the case."

54. At para [40] the trial court turned to consideration of what evidence there was to establish any involvement on the part of either or both of the accused. In relation to the appellant, it stated that there were three important witnesses, Mr. Majid, Mr. Bollier and Mr. Gauci. We have already referred to the trial court's treatment of the evidence of Mr. Majid and Mr. Bollier. In discussing Mr. Gauci's evidence, at para [55] the trial court referred to an identification by Mr. Gauci of the appellant at an identification parade on 13 April 1999 (not 13 August 1999, as stated by the trial court), using the words as written in the parade report: "Not exactly the man I saw in the shop. Ten years ago I saw him, but the man who look a little bit like exactly is the number 5." Number 5 in the parade was the appellant. In court, Mr. Gauci identified the appellant, saying: "He is the man on this side. He resembles him a lot." The trial court then turned to consideration of various issues bearing on the reliability of these identifications, which included a discussion of statements made and descriptions given by Mr. Gauci on a number of previous occasions, as well as evidence given by him in court. This led in turn to consideration of a number of issues, which included the month in which and the day of the week on which the purchase from Mr. Gauci was made, the weather at the time of the purchase, whether Christmas decorations had been put up in Tower Road, Sliema at that time, and a statement by Mr. Gauci that his brother Paul (who was not called as a witness) did not work in the shop on that particular afternoon because he had gone home to watch a football match on television. After discussion of these issues, the trial court reached the conclusion, at para [67], that the date of purchase was Wednesday 7 December 1988. After further discussion of the reliability of Mr. Gauci's identification of the appellant, including reference to his demeanour when giving evidence, the trial court stated, at para [69], that it was "satisfied that his identification so far as it went of the [appellant] as the purchaser was reliable and should be treated as a highly important element in this case."

55. At para [70] the trial court referred to a notice lodged by each of the accused prior to the start of the trial, in identical terms, which was treated as a special defence of incrimination. As it observed, this notice did not in any way affect the burden of proof. There was no onus on the defence to prove that any of the persons referred to in the schedule to the notice were the perpetrators of the alleged offence. Its sole purpose was to give notice to the Crown prior to the start of the trial as to the possible effect of evidence which the defence might lead in the course of the trial. The

only persons incriminated in the schedule to the notice to whom reference requires to be made were: "1. Members of the Palestinian Popular Struggle Front ["PPSF"] which may include Mohammed Abo Talb. . . . 2. Members of the Popular Front for the Liberation of Palestine—General Command ["PFLP-GC"]." The trial court considered evidence relating to the PFLP-GC and the PPSF, of the latter of which Abo Talb was a member, as part of their consideration of the Crown case against each of the accused. It is clear from the discussion of this evidence that it did not lead the trial court to have a reasonable doubt about the guilt of the appellant (and it was not because of this evidence that the appellant's co-accused was acquitted). No issue arises in this appeal as to the trial court's treatment of this evidence.

56. Because the terms of para [82] of the judgment were subjected to differing interpretations by counsel in the course of the appeal, we think it appropriate to quote it in full:

"From the evidence which we have discussed so far, we are satisfied that it has been proved that the primary suitcase containing the explosive device was dispatched from Malta, passed through Frankfurt and was loaded onto PA103 at Heathrow. It is, as we have said, clear that with one exception the clothing in the primary suitcase was the clothing purchased in Mr. Gauci's shop on 7 December 1988. The purchaser was, on Mr. Gauci's evidence, a Libyan. The trigger for the explosion was an MST-13 timer of the single solder mask variety. A substantial quantity of such timers had been supplied to Libya. We cannot say that it is impossible that the clothing might have been taken from Malta, united somewhere with a timer from some source other than Libya and introduced into the airline baggage system at Frankfurt or Heathrow. When, however, the evidence regarding the clothing, the purchaser and the timer is taken with the evidence that an unaccompanied bag was taken from KM180 to PA103A, the inference that that was the primary suitcase becomes, in our view, irresistible. As we have also said, the absence of an explanation as to how the suitcase was taken into the system at Luqa is a major difficulty for the Crown case but after taking full account of that difficulty, we remain of the view that the primary suitcase began its journey at Luqa. The clear inference which we draw from this evidence is that the conception, planning and execution of the plot which led to the planting of the explosive device was of Libyan origin. While no doubt organisations such as the PFLP-GC and the PPSF were also engaged in terrorist activities during the same period, we are satisfied that there was no evidence from which we could infer that they were involved in this particular act of terrorism, and the evidence relating to their activities does not create a reasonable doubt in our minds about the Libyan origin of this crime."

57. In considering the evidence which could be regarded as implicating either or both of the accused, the trial court bore in mind that the evidence against each of them had to be considered separately, and that before either could be convicted it would have to be satisfied beyond reasonable doubt as to his guilt and that evidence from a single source would be insufficient. After considering the evidence against the second accused, it expressed the opinion that there was insufficient corroboration for any inference that might be drawn from certain entries in his 1988 diary. Accordingly he fell to be acquitted.

58. The trial court then turned to the case against the appellant. Since it had not been proved that the second accused was a party to the crime, it followed that the entries in his diary could not be used against the appellant and the members of the court put that matter entirely out of their minds. The trial court then went on to consider evidence to which we have already referred relating to the appellant's visits to Malta from 7 to 9 December 1988, using his own passport, and on 20 and 21 December 1988, using the passport in the name of Abdusamad. It then referred to the identification evidence of Mr. Gauci, the appellant's position in the JSO, his involvement with Mr. Bollier and a number of other matters. These included the appellant's departure for Tripoli on the morning of 21 December "at or about the time the device must have been planted." It may be noted that elsewhere the trial court found that check-in for flight KM180 was from 0815 to 0915 hours, while check-in for flight LN147, on which the appellant travelled, was between 0850 and 0950 hours. In para [89] the trial court concluded with, *inter alia*, this statement:

"[H]aving considered the whole evidence in the case, including the uncertainties and qualifications, and the submissions of counsel, we are satisfied that the evidence as to the purchase of clothing in Malta, the presence of that clothing in the primary suitcase, the transmission of an item of baggage from Malta to London, the identification of the [appellant] (albeit not absolute), his movements under a false name at or around the material time, and the other background circumstances such as his association with Mr. Bollier and with members of the JSO or Libyan military who purchased MST-13 timers, does fit together to form a real and convincing pattern. There is nothing in the evidence which leaves us with any reasonable doubt as to the guilt of the [appellant], and accordingly we find him guilty. . . ."

* * * * *

Conclusion

59. The Crown case against the appellant was based on circumstantial evidence. This made it necessary for the trial court to consider all the cir-

cumstances founded on by the Crown. In reaching its decision to convict the appellant the trial court found that the evidence fitted together to form a real and convincing pattern.

60. When opening the case for the appellant before this court Mr. Taylor stated that the appeal was not about sufficiency of evidence: he accepted that there was a sufficiency of evidence. He also stated that he was not seeking to found on section 106(3)(b) of the 1995 Act. His position was that the trial court had misdirected itself in various respects. Accordingly in this appeal we have not required to consider whether the evidence before the trial court, apart from the evidence which it rejected, was sufficient as a matter of law to entitle it to convict the appellant on the basis set out in its judgment. We have not had to consider whether the verdict of guilty was one which no reasonable trial court, properly directing itself, could have returned in the light of that evidence. As can be seen from this Opinion, the grounds of appeal before us have been concerned, for the most part, with complaints about the treatment by the trial court of the material which was before it and the submissions which were made to it by the defence.

61. For the reasons which we have given in the course of this Opinion, we have reached the conclusion that none of the grounds of appeal is well founded. The appeal will accordingly be refused.

The Queen (on the Application of the Kurdistan Workers' Party and Others)
and
Secretary of State for the Home Department
The Queen (on the Application of the People's Mojahedin Organisation of Iran and Others)
and
Secretary of State for the Home Department
The Queen (on the Application of Nisar Ahmed)
and
Secretary of State for the Home Department
In the High Court of Justice
Queens Bench Division [2002] Ewhc 644 (Admin.)

April 17, 2002
Crown Copyright (c)
(Edited Text)

Mr Justice Richards:

1. The court has before it three separate claims challenging the proscription of organisations under the Terrorism Act 2000 ("the 2000 Act") and the compatibility of provisions of the Act with the Human Rights Act 1998. In each case I am concerned with whether to grant or refuse permission

to apply for judicial review. The argument before me was far more extended, however, than is usual on a permission application. In the event I have decided to refuse permission in respect of all three claims; but my judgment is likewise fuller than is usual on a permission application, owing to the importance of the issues involved and the likelihood that they will be ventilated further in the Court of Appeal.

2. In brief, the organisations concerned are the People's Mojahedin Organisation of Iran ("the PMOI"), the Kurdistan Workers' Party or Partiya Karkeren Kurdistan ("the PKK") and Lashkar e Tayyabah ("the LeT"). Each was proscribed by virtue of the Terrorism Act 2000 (Proscribed Organisations) (Amendment) Order 2001 ("the 2001 Order"). In each case the claims include a challenge to the lawfulness of the proscription and to the lawfulness of the regime of offences laid down by the 2000 Act.

3. I think it helpful to start with a description of the statutory framework and the factual history, before looking more closely at the individual claimants and their claims and at the specific issues relevant to the grant or refusal of permission. In considering the claimants and their claims, I shall take them in the order in which, by agreement, counsel addressed me at the hearing.

Statutory framework

4. Section 1 of the 2000 Act defines "terrorism" in broad terms:
    "(1) In this Act 'terrorism' means the use or threat of action where—
    - (a) the action falls within subsection (2),
    - (b) the use or threat is designed to influence the government or to intimidate the public or a section of the public, and
    - (c) the use or threat is made for the purposes of advancing a political, religious or ideological cause.
    (2) Action falls within this subsection if it—
    - (a) involves serious violence against a person,
    - (b) involves serious damage to property,
    - (c) endangers a person's life, other than that of the person committing the action,
    - (d) creates a serious risk to the health or safety of the public or a section of the public, or
    - (e) is designed seriously to interfere with or disrupt an electronic system.
    (3) The use of threat of action falling within subsection (2) which involves the use of firearms or explosives is terrorism whether or not subsection (1)(b) is satisfied.

(4) In this section—
    (a) 'action' includes action outside the United Kingdom,
    (b) a reference to any person or to property is a reference to any person, or to property, wherever situated,
    (c) a reference to the public includes a reference to the public of a country other than the United Kingdom, and
    (d) 'the government' means the government of the United Kingdom, of a Part of the United Kingdom or of a country other than the United Kingdom.
(5) In this Act a reference to action taken for the purposes of terrorism includes a reference to action taken for the benefit of a proscribed organisation."

5. Schedule 2 contains a list of proscribed organisations. By s.3 the Secretary of State is given a discretionary power to amend the schedule, subject to approval by affirmative resolution of each House of Parliament. Thus s.3(3)–(5) provides:

"(3) The Secretary of State may by order—
    (a) add an organisation to Schedule 2;
    (b) remove an organisation from that Schedule;
    (c) amend that Schedule in some other way.
(4) The Secretary of State may exercise his power under subsection (3)(a) in respect of an organisation only if he believes that it is concerned in terrorism.
(5) For the purposes of subsection (4) an organisation is concerned in terrorism if it—
    (a) commits or participates in acts of terrorism,
    (b) prepares for terrorism,
    (c) promotes or encourages terrorism, or
    (d) is otherwise concerned in terrorism."

6. The requirements for an Order under s.3(3) to be made by statutory instrument and for a draft of the Order to be laid before and approved by resolution of each House of Parliament are to be found in s.123(1) and (4). There is provision in s.123(5) for an Order to be made without a draft having been approved if the Secretary of State is of the opinion that it is necessary by reason of urgency. In that event the Order shall cease to have effect after 40 days unless by then a resolution approving it has been passed by each House.

7. By s.4 an application may be made to the Secretary of State for the exercise of his power under s.3(3)(b) to remove an organisation from Schedule 2, i.e. an application for deproscription. Such an application may be made by the organisation itself or by any person affected by the organisation's proscription. The Proscribed Organisations (Applications for Deproscription)

Regulations 2001, made under s.4(3), lay down the procedure for applications to the Secretary of State and provide inter alia that he is to determine an application within 90 days from its receipt.

8. By s.5 an applicant whose application under s.4 has been refused may appeal to the Proscribed Organisations Appeal Commission ("POAC"). The powers of POAC and the consequences of its allowing an appeal are set out in s.5(3)–(5):

    "(3)   The Commission shall allow an appeal against a refusal to deproscribe an organisation if it considers that the decision to refuse was flawed when considered in the light of the principles applicable on an application for judicial review.

    (4)   Where the Commission allows an appeal under this section by or in respect of an organisation, it may make an order under this subsection.

    (5)   Where an order is made under subsection (4) the Secretary of State shall as soon as is reasonably practicable—

    (a)   lay before Parliament, in accordance with section 123(4), the draft of an order under section 3(3)(b) removing the organisation from the list in Schedule 2, or

    (b)   make an order removing the organisation from the list in Schedule 2 in pursuance of section 123(5)."

9. The constitution and procedure of POAC are laid down in Schedule 3 and in the Proscribed Organisations Appeal Commission (Procedure) Rules 2001, made under paragraph 5 of Schedule 3. The rules make provision inter alia for the appointment of a special advocate to represent the interests of the appellant in the proceedings, in particular in any proceedings from which the appellant and his representative are excluded (rule 10). They also enable POAC to consider all the evidence upon which the Secretary of State relies in support of his grounds for opposing the appeal, including evidence that by statute or on general grounds of public interest cannot be disclosed to the appellant or his representative, with the POAC sitting in private for that purpose, and evidence that would not be admissible in a court of law (see in particular rules 21–22). By s.18(1)(f) of the Regulation of Investigatory Powers Act 2000 the normal prohibition on the receipt of evidence based on intercepted communications does not apply to POAC.

10. It should also be noted that by the Proscribed Organisations Appeal Commission (Human Rights Act Proceedings) Rules 2001, POAC is the appropriate tribunal for the purposes of s.7 of the Human Rights Act in relation to any proceedings under s.7(1)(a) against the Secretary of State in respect of a refusal by him to exercise his power of deproscription under s.3(3)(b).

11. By s.6 of the 2000 Act, a party to an appeal determined by POAC under s.5 may bring a further appeal on a question of law to the Court of Appeal, but only with the permission of POAC or, where POAC refuses permission, the Court of Appeal.

12. Section 7 deals with the situation where there has been a successful appeal to POAC under s.5 but a person has been convicted in the meantime of an offence under any of ss.11–15, 15–19 and 56. In summary, provided that the activity to which the charge referred took place on or after the date of the refusal to deproscribe against which the successful appeal under s.5 was brought, the person convicted is entitled to appeal and to have his appeal allowed.

13. That brings me to the offences that apply in relation to a proscribed organisation. In brief, and without detailing the various qualifications and defences:

    i)   By s.11 a person commits an offence punishable by up to 10 years' imprisonment if he belongs or professes to belong to a proscribed organisation.

    ii)   By s.12 a person commits an offence punishable by up to 10 years' imprisonment if he invites support for a proscribed organisation; if he arranges, manages or assists in arranging or managing a meeting of three or more persons which he knows is to support a proscribed organisation, to further the activities of a proscribed organisation, or to be addressed by a person who belongs or professes to belong to a proscribed organisation; or if he addresses a meeting of three or more persons and the purpose of his address is to encourage support for a proscribed organisation or to further its activities.

    iii) By s.13 a person in a public place commits an offence punishable by up to six months' imprisonment if he wears an item of clothing, or wears, carries or displays an article, in such a way or in such circumstances as to arouse reasonable suspicion that he is a member or supporter of a proscribed organisation.

14. Further criminal offences, punishable by up to 14 years' imprisonment, exist under s.15 in relation to fund-raising for the purposes of terrorism, under s.16 in relation to the use or possession of money or other property for the purposes of terrorism, under s.17 in relation to arrangements to make money or property available for the purposes of terrorism (funding arrangements), and under s.18 in relation to arrangements facilitating the retention or control of terrorist property by concealment, removal, transfer etc. (money laundering). Those offences are not limited to proscribed organisations, but s.14 defines "terrorist property" as including any resources of a proscribed organisation and, as already mentioned, s.1(5) provides that action "for the purposes of terrorism" includes action

taken for the benefit of a proscribed organisation. Pursuant to s.19 it is an offence to fail to disclose any belief or suspicion that another person has committed an offence under any of ss.15–18 if that belief or suspicion is based on information which comes to a person's attention in the course of a trade, profession, business or employment.

Factual history

15. The 2000 Act came into force on 19 February 2001. It included in Schedule 2 a list of proscribed organisations which are not material for present purposes.

16. On 28 February 2001 the Secretary of State laid before Parliament a draft of the 2001 Order for the purpose of adding 21 organisations, including the PMOI, the PKK and the LeT, to the list in Schedule 2. On the same day he wrote to Members of Parliament explaining the proscription procedure and attaching a background note containing a brief description of the organisations included in the draft Order and of matters relevant to their proscription.

17. The draft Order was debated by the House of Commons on 13–14 March 2001, in a debate lasting 1 1/2 hours, and by the House of Lords on 27 March, in a debate lasting almost 3 1/2 hours. The draft was approved by both Houses and the 2001 Order itself was made on 28 March and came into force on 29 March.

18. In the course of the debates it was stated that in considering which organisations should be proscribed, the Secretary of State took into account a number of factors, including those indicated to Parliament by ministers during proceedings on the Terrorism Bill. Those factors were: the nature and scale of the organisation's activities, the specific threat that it posed to the United Kingdom, the specific threat that it posed to British nationals overseas, the extent of the organisation's presence in the United Kingdom, and the need to support other members of the international community in the global fight against terrorism.

19. By letter dated 4 June 2001 an application for deproscription of the PMOI was made on behalf of the PMOI. The Secretary of State refused the application by letter dated 31 August 2001. The refusal was the subject of an appeal to the POAC. The relevant application for permission to apply for judicial review was lodged in the Administrative Court Office on 8 October 2001.

20. An application for deproscription of the LeT was made on 8 June 2001 by Mr Ahmed, the claimant in the LeT proceedings. The Secretary of State refused the application, again by letter dated 31 August 2001. An appeal to the POAC was lodged on 17 September 2001. The relevant application for permission to apply for judicial review was lodged in the

Administrative Court Office on 21 February 2002, immediately before the permission hearing.

21. Neither the PKK itself nor any of the individual claimants in the PKK case applied for deproscription. They moved straight to their application for permission to apply for judicial review, by a claim form lodged in the Administrative Court Office on 28 June 2001. An application for deproscription of the PKK was, however, made by the Federation of Kurdish Community Associations in Great Britain. It resulted in a decision by the Secretary of State not to deproscribe. There has been no appeal against that decision. It remains open to the claimants to secure an appeal to the POAC either by obtaining an extension of time for appealing the previous refusal or by requesting the Secretary of State to make a further decision and then appealing that decision, if adverse.

22. So far as I am aware, the appeals to POAC in relation to the PMOI and the LeT have been held in abeyance pending the outcome of the judicial review proceedings.

The PMOI claim

23. In the PMOI proceedings, case no. CO/4039/2001, the first claimant is the PMOI itself. The second claimant is an individual member of the PMOI's international relations department who submitted the unsuccessful application for deproscription to the Secretary of State.

24. In his note to Members of Parliament in support of the draft Order, the Secretary of State referred to the PMOI as "Mujaheddin e Khalq," a description which the claimants say is incorrect and is used only by the Iranian Government. The Secretary of State's note describes it as "an Iranian dissident organisation based in Iraq which claims to be seeking the establishment of a democratic, socialist, Islamic republic in Iran." It refers briefly to the organisation's history, states that the organisation undertakes cross-border attacks into Iran, including terrorist attacks, that it has assassinated senior Iranian officials and launched mortar attacks against government buildings in Tehran and elsewhere, and that in June 2000 the Iranian government claimed to have foiled a plot by the organisation to assassinate a former Iranian foreign minister. The note states that the organisation has not attacked UK or Western interests and has no acknowledged presence in the UK, although its publication "MOJAHED" is in circulation here.

25. In his letter of 31 August 2001 refusing the application to deproscribe the PMOI, the Secretary of State stated:

"In the case of Mujaheddin e Khalq, the Secretary of State believes that the nature and scale of the organisation's activities and the need to support other members of the international community in the global fight against terrorism are relevant. Having regard to the statutory criteria that applies [*sic*] to proscription and having considered these additional factors, the Secretary of State believes that proscription of Mujaheddin e Khalq should continue. . . .

In reaching his decision, the Home Secretary has taken full account of the submission made on behalf of your client, including the assertion that Mujaheddin e Khalq is involved in a legitimate struggle against a repressive regime and has no choice but to resort to armed resistance. He notes too the claim that armed resistance is concentrated against military and security targets within Iran only. The Home Secretary does not accept, however, any right to resort to acts of terrorism, whatever the motivation. . . .

The application also seeks to deny that Mujaheddin e Khalq was responsible for attacks on civilian targets and specifically denied a mortar attack on the city of Karaj. However, the Home Secretary notes that, on 10 February 2001, the day following the bomb and grenade attack in the city of Karaj, the office in Paris of the People's Mojahedin Organisation of Iran claimed that the attack was carried out by Mujaheddin e Khalq."

26. The claimants, in extensive evidence filed in support of their claim, take issue with the accuracy and completeness of the Secretary of State's note to Members of Parliament. They describe the PMOI as a broad based popular resistance movement committed to the establishment of a democratic, secular and pluralist government in Iran which would respect human rights and the internationally recognised norms of state behaviour. It has sought to achieve its aims through the political system but it has been denied access to the political system through brutal suppression at the hands of the Iranian regime. It has therefore been driven to resort to armed struggle in Iran. It is not based in Iraq but operates underground in Iran, where all military activity is organised and commanded. According to the claimants, the PMOI's armed attacks have been confined to military targets inside Iran, as permitted within the framework of the Geneva Convention. The organisation has an official or unofficial presence through 170 offices around the world and enjoys extensive political support in Europe and elsewhere. It is not an illegal organisation in the USA, where the only restriction is that it cannot raise funds (the successful challenge, on procedural grounds, to the designation of the PMOI as a foreign terrorist organisation in the USA is referred to below). The only government seeking the banning of the PMOI is said to be the Iranian government itself.

27. The PMOI claimants seek judicial review of the decision of the Secretary of State to lay the 2001 Order before Parliament, the 2001 Order itself

and provisions of the 2000 Act. They seek declarations to the effect that the inclusion of the PMOI in the list of proscribed organisations was unlawful, alternatively a declaration that the relevant provisions of the 2000 Act are incompatible with their Convention rights. In the event that the challenge succeeds, they also seek damages pursuant to section 8 of the Human Rights Act.

28. In common with the other claimants, the PMOI claimants point first to the grave impact of the 2001 Order upon them. The proscription of the PMOI and the consequential criminal prohibitions under ss.11–19 of the 2000 Act give rise to a substantial interference with the right to freedom of expression under Article 10 of the Convention, the right to freedom of association under Article 11 and the right to enjoyment of property under Article 1 of the First Protocol. It is said that the inclusion of the PMOI in a list containing organisations of a wholly different nature, such as Al-Qa'ida, also gives rise to an interference with the civil right to a good reputation under Article 8 and with the right to the enjoyment of Convention rights without discrimination under Article 14.

29. More specifically, the effect of the Order has been to prevent the PMOI from distributing its publication MOJAHED in the United Kingdom otherwise than by postal delivery to subscribers or via the Internet, to prevent the advertising or holding of public meetings in this country, to restrict the holding of property and raising of funds here (though the PMOI had already ceased to maintain an office in this country owing to a concern that a growing rapprochement between the United Kingdom and the Iranian government would lead to its proscription) and to prevent the continuation of previously extensive contacts with humanitarian organisations via the United Kingdom.

30. The claimants emphasise that the Order operates as prior restraint upon the exercise of their Convention rights, as distinct from imposing a penalty for abuse of those rights, and is therefore the most drastic form of restriction, requiring the most compelling justification and the most careful judicial scrutiny.

31. Lord Lester QC has summarised his detailed submissions on behalf of the PMOI claimants under four broad heads: (i) arbitrary and discriminatory treatment, (ii) lack of due process and procedural unfairness, (iii) lack of proportionality and (iv) failure to comply with the requirements of legal certainty and "prescribed by law." Although this does not cover every point included in the claim form and skeleton argument, other points (e.g. that it was unlawful or irrational to include 21 organisations in a single Order) are sufficiently dealt with in the context of submissions for other claimants or do not need to be mentioned in order to give a sufficient indication of the nature of the PMOI claim.

32. As to (i), arbitrary and discriminatory treatment, Lord Lester submits that it is well recognised in domestic as well as in Convention law that like cases should be dealt with in the same way and unlike cases should be dealt with in different ways. In this case the Secretary of State has unfairly discriminated by including the PMOI in a list with organisations such as Al-Qa'ida. Of the 21 organisations in the list, the PMOI is the only one recognised by the Secretary of State to be democratic in its aims. The list also excludes many groups that use or threaten violence for political ends. The list is therefore both over-inclusive and under-inclusive. It is incumbent on the Secretary of State to provide an objective justification for such differences of treatment, which he has failed to do. Moreover this meant that MPs, in considering whether to approve the Order, were faced with a dilemma either to proscribe Al-Qa'ida and all the others in the list or to proscribe none of them.

33. As to (ii), lack of due process and procedural unfairness, the complaint is that the Secretary of State included the PMOI in the list and laid the draft Order before Parliament without first giving the claimants any opportunity to make representations. Reliance is placed on the decision of the US Court of Appeals for the District of Columbia Circuit in National Council of Resistance of Iran v. Department of State (8 June 2001), in which it was held that the designation of two organisations, including the PMOI itself, as "foreign terrorist organizations" violated their due process rights under the Fifth Amendment to the US Constitution by failing to give notice of the intended designation and to afford the organisations an opportunity to respond, at least by way of written representations, to the evidence upon which it was proposed to rely. The court pointed to the serious consequences of designation and to the limited scope of *ex post* statutory judicial review, which related to the adequacy of the record. It held that to give an organisation such as the PMOI notice of proposed designation and of the administrative record to be relied on would not impair the country's legitimate foreign policy goals, subject to the right to withhold classified information and to the possibility of withholding all notice and all opportunity to present evidence where it was shown that harm might otherwise be caused to such goals. Thus the court concluded:

"We therefore hold that the Secretary must afford the limited due process available to the putative foreign terrorist organization prior to the deprivation worked by designating that entity as such with its attendant consequences, unless he can make a showing of particularized need.

. . . We have no reason to presume that the petitioners in this particular case could have offered evidence which might have either changed the Secretary's mind or affected the adequacy of the record. However, without the due process protections we have outlined, we cannot presumed the contrary either" (pages 23–24).

34. So too, it is submitted, the Secretary of State's failure to give the PMOI an opportunity to make representations before laying the draft Order before Parliament was unlawful under the Convention and the common law. There was no pressing reason why such an opportunity should not be given: had there been so, the Secretary of State could have utilised the urgent procedure under s.123(5) of the 2000 Act, which he did not do. It cannot be presumed that the PMOI would have been unable to put forward material capable of causing the Secretary of State to change his mind.

35. As to (iii), lack of proportionality, it is submitted that the proscription of the PMOI lacked an adequate justification and in particular was in breach of the principle of proportionality. In the particular case of the PMOI it is not even accepted that proscription was in pursuit of a legitimate aim: it is said to be unclear what legitimate objectives are pursued by proscribing an organisation which attacks only military and governmental targets in an effort to replace a profoundly undemocratic regime with one which is pluralistic and democratic and which upholds human rights and the rule of law. In any event Lord Lester submits that the Secretary of State, upon whom the burden of justification rests, has presented no evidence that proscription of the PMOI was proportionate, having regard to the nature of the Iranian regime and of the PMOI's activities and the support for the PMOI in this country and elsewhere. It is not suggested that the PMOI poses a threat to UK nationals or that it has attacked British or Western interests. The UK public interest is adequately protected by sections 59–63 of the 2000 Act, which make it an offence to incite terrorist acts overseas or to do anything outside the United Kingdom as an act of terrorism or for the purposes of terrorism or where the action would have constituted the commission of an offence under ss.15–18 if it had been done in the United Kingdom. The case for proscription is not made out on the high level of scrutiny required by the court (as to which, see e.g. R (Daly) v. Secretary of State for the Home Department [2001] 2 WLR 1622 at 1634H-1635B per Lord Steyn).

36. As to (iv), it is submitted that the proscription of the PMOI was in breach of the principle of legal certainty and the requirement that any interference with the relevant Convention rights must be prescribed by law. The definition of terrorism in s.1 of the 2000 Act is sweepingly broad and extraordinarily vague. It covers any foreign government, however oppressive; it potentially covers almost all liberation movements, whether or not fighting against an undemocratic regime which does not respect human rights; it does not distinguish between those aiming only at military targets and those aiming at civilian targets. It is so broad that it was necessary for the Attorney General to clarify in correspondence that the claimants' solicitors would not risk criminal liability under s.1(5) read with s.16(1) by providing legal services for payment to the PMOI. The power

under s.3(3)(a) to proscribe an organisation believed to be concerned in terrorism is by its express terms unlimited. In view of the drastic consequences of proscription, more precise criteria for the exercise of the power to proscribe need to be included in the legislation itself in order to comply with the requirements of the Convention. In any event no criteria exist even by way of administrative guidelines. Moreover the fact that Parliament was required to approve the Order before it came into force did not protect against arbitrary proscription, given the limited information provided to Parliament, the short time given for consideration of the list and the need for an all or nothing decision in relation to the 21 organisations included in the list. Concern about those matters was expressed in the course of the Parliamentary debates. Looking at the procedure as a whole, it lacks the protections against arbitrariness that the Convention requires.

The PKK claim

37. In the PKK proceedings, case no. CO/2587/2001, the first claimant is the PKK. The second claimant is the co-ordinator of two Kurdish campaigning groups in the United Kingdom, edits a magazine called "Kurdish Report" and provides administrative advice and support for the Kurdistan National Congress which maintains an office in London. The third claimant works on a voluntary basis for many Kurdish groups and organisations, including the Kurdistan National Congress; much of his work is with refugees. The remaining claimants are 100 individuals who describe the PKK as their "chosen political organisation." It is said that they are only a small proportion of those who wished to be joined as claimants.

38. In his note to Members of Parliament, the Secretary of State described the PKK as "primarily a separatist movement which has sought an independent Kurdish state in south east Turkey." The note states that the PKK was formed in 1978 but became a significant terrorist threat only upon the formation of the group's military wing in 1984. Since then the PKK has been engaged predominantly in a guerrilla campaign in south east Turkey. The note refers to attacks on British and Western interests in the first half of the 1990s and to threatened attacks against Turkey's tourist resorts until 1999. In relation to the position since then, however, it states:

"In February 1999 the PKK's founder and leader Abdullah Ocalan was captured by Turkish security forces in Kenya. During his subsequent trial in Turkey, in June 1999, Ocalan announced a PKK ceasefire and also that the group intended to seek a peaceful resolution to its aspirations. However, although the group is not believed to have undertaken any offensive action since the ceasefire began on 29 August 1999, previous PKK ceasefires have broken down."

39. In his letter of 5 October 2001 refusing the application for deproscription of the PKK, the Secretary of State stated inter alia:

   "In the case of the PKK, the Secretary of State believes that the nature and scale of the organisation's activities; the specific threat that it poses to UK nationals overseas; the extent of the organisation's presence in the UK; and the need to support other members of the international community in the global fight against terrorism are relevant. Having regard to the statutory criteria which apply to proscription and having considered these additional factors, the Secretary of State believes that proscription of the PKK should continue. . . .

   While recognising comments that the PKK is engaged in a cease-fire, the Home Secretary believes the organisation's recent past involvement in terrorism means it falls within section 3(4) of the Terrorism Act 2000, i.e. that, notwithstanding the ceasefire, it is concerned in terrorism. The Home Secretary would add that the organisation retains its capacity for terrorist acts and has not renounced terrorism. He is aware furthermore of recent statements made by the organisation's Presidential Council and individual members of that Council hinting at a return to armed conflict. On the basis of these declarations, and other information available to him, such as knowledge of fundraising on behalf of the organisation in the United Kingdom, the Home Secretary remains satisfied that as an organisation the PKK is 'concerned in terrorism' as defined by the Terrorism Act 2000."

40. The claimants describe the PKK as a political party committed to the recognition and establishment of Kurdish identity and the rights of Kurdish people. Evidence filed on their behalf in the present proceedings deals further with the factual background, including the PKK's formal abandonment of military action in favour of a non-violent political and democratic agenda in 1999, a point on which the claimants place heavy reliance.

41. The PKK claimants challenge both the making of the 2001 Order, including the decision to lay the Order before Parliament, and provisions of the 2000 Act relating to the consequences of proscription. In presenting his submissions on their behalf, Mr Emmerson QC stresses that the second aspect of the challenge raises distinct issues and that those issues arise even if the proscription of the PKK was lawful.

42. As to the impact of the Order, Mr Emmerson relies on the same general points as those considered above in the context of the PMOI. He submits that proscription is seen by many in the Kurdish community as a victory for the Turkish government and the endorsement of suppression of the Kurds. He points to the depth of support for the PKK as demonstrated by the number of claimants and the thousands more who are

signatories to a petition in support of the PKK. For such people the PKK is the sole means of political expression; yet proscription makes it an offence to invite support for the PKK even if it relates specifically to its commitment to a policy of non-violence. All political debate is suppressed. Members of the Kurdish community will be committing an offence simply by displaying PKK badges or participating in demonstrations of more than three people.

43. Nor are the consequences confined to members or active supporters of the PKK. In a lengthy witness statement the second claimant, Estella Schmid, describes her work for Kurdish organisations in the United Kingdom and states that it would be impossible for these groups to remove the PKK from their contacts or discussions. She expresses the view that "[t]o banish the PKK and those who support it from participation in democratic discussion of the political future of Turkey and the Turkish people is to remove not merely the main nationalistic expression of Kurdish identity of the forty million Kurds world wide, but to make a mockery of any intelligent prospect of democratic debate and permanent peace in Turkey and elsewhere." She refers later to the serious effect of the proscription of the PKK on her journalistic work as editor of the Kurdistan Report and to the impossible choice that she faces of going to the police (and thereby betraying all possibility of future work within the community) if she has knowledge or suspicion of fund-raising activities for the PKK, or of herself committing a crime by failing to do so. The serious impact of proscription of the PKK on the Kurdish community as a whole is also dealt with at some length in the witness statement of the third claimant, Diyari Kurdi.

44. Citing such evidence, Mr Emmerson describes the present case as a paradigm example of the chilling effect of proscription on free speech.

45. Mr Emmerson points to the threefold test for justification of an interference under Articles 10 and 11: the restrictions must (a) be prescribed by law, (b) pursue a legitimate aim and (c) be proportionate to the aim pursued. It is accepted for the purposes of the application that the 2001 Order pursues a legitimate aim. But it is submitted that in order to meet the requirements of "prescribed by law" and proportionality in a case where a discretionary power is conferred on the executive, the law must indicate the scope of that discretion and the discretionary power must be attended by procedural safeguards which are adequate to afford due respect to the interests at stake. Reliance is placed on numerous judgments of the Strasbourg court, including Herczegfalvy v. Austria (1992) 15 EHRR 437, Malone v. United Kingdom (1985) 7 EHRR 14 and Khan v. United Kingdom (2000) 8 BHRC 310. Mr Emmerson submits that the making of an order with such Draconian consequences as apply in the present case engages the highest level of procedural protection under the Convention.

46. There are a number of strands to Mr Emmerson's more detailed submissions. In summarising them I shall concentrate on the emphasis given in oral argument, without seeking to cover the elaboration of the arguments to be found in the claim form and skeleton argument.

47. The starting point is the very broad definition of "terrorism" in s.1 of the 2000 Act and the very broad power of proscription in s.3. The Act permits the proscription of organisations that would never be proscribed in practice, including organisations which are fighting against undemocratic and oppressive regimes and, in particular, those which have engaged in lawful armed conflict in the exercise of the internationally recognised right to self-determination of peoples (where the United Kingdom is bound in international law to recognise the right and to refrain from offering material support to states engaged in the suppression of the exercise of the right by military or other coercive means). The fact that the power of proscription extends wider than the use that Parliament can have intended to be made of it provides the strongest support for the requirement that intelligible criteria be laid down for the exercise of the Secretary of State's discretion and for effective Parliamentary and judicial scrutiny. The explicit assumption on which the legislation depends is that the Secretary of State will not proscribe certain organisations even though they meet the statutory criteria in ss.1 and 3. There is, however, no clear indication in the legislation or in any published policy of the Secretary of State as to the basis on which the Secretary of State is to distinguish between one organisation and another.

48. The principal submission is that in a matter of this nature the criteria for the exercise of the discretion must be enshrined in the law itself. But even on the alternative basis that it was open to the Secretary of State to adopt clear criteria himself, it is submitted that he has failed to do so. The Secretary of State notified to Parliament that certain non-statutory factors would be taken into account (namely the nature and scale of the organisation's activities, the specific threat that it poses to the UK, the specific threat that it poses to UK nationals overseas, the extent of the organisation's presence in the UK, and the need to support other members of the international community). Those do not amount to adequate or intelligible criteria for the exercise of such a wide discretion. They provide no basis for determining which of the organisations meeting the statutory tests will be proscribed and which will not.

49. The second strand in Mr Emmerson's argument is the absence of an opportunity to make representations before the Order was made. It is submitted that a right to make such representations arises under the common law or as part of the requirements of procedural fairness inherent in Articles 10 and 11 of the Convention. It is well settled that an individual directly affected by a proposed administrative act should, as a matter of

natural justice, be given notice of the proposal in advance and an opportunity to make representations: Hoffman La Roche v. Secretary of State for Trade and Industry [1975] AC 295 at 368E. It is submitted that the obligation is capable of applying to an order passed by affirmative resolution (cf. R v. Secretary of State, ex p. AMA [1986] 1 All ER 164) and that, although a right to make representations in advance is not expressed in the 2000 Act, it is to be implied as a requirement of natural justice (cf. R v. Secretary for the Home Department, ex p. Fayed [1998] 1 WLR 763). The right cannot be discharged by the opportunity to apply for deproscription after the event; and no legitimate interest has been identified which would be prejudiced by affording an opportunity to make representations in advance. In common with the PMOI claimants, heavy reliance is placed on the decision of the US Court of Appeals in National Council of Resistance of Iran v. Department of State (8 June 2001). It is submitted that a similar requirement of procedural fairness is to be implied into the present procedure.

50. Thirdly Mr Emmerson submits that the affirmative resolution procedure was inadequate in this case to meet the procedural requirements of the Convention, owing to the inclusion of 21 organisations in a single Order and the limited Parliamentary time available for debate. Parliament was faced with a choice between accepting or rejecting the whole list and it was not possible properly to debate the merits of inclusion of individual organisations. It is submitted that in order to avoid this situation, s.3(3) can and should be read as permitting the Secretary of State to include only a single organisation in any one Order. Only by having a separate Order for each organisation can effective Parliamentary scrutiny of the merits of the decision take place. Such a construction is open on the language of s.3(3), whereby the Secretary of State may by order add "an organisation" to the list, and is supported by the interpretative obligation in s.3 of the Human Rights Act.

51. Finally Mr Emmerson submits that an appeal to POAC is inadequate to provide effective judicial scrutiny of the exercise of discretion. POAC is not concerned with the merits of the inclusion of an organisation in the list. It engages in a process of review which is necessarily limited in scope, given the breadth of the discretionary power and the absence of binding criteria by reference to which the Secretary of State's decision is to be judged. It is required to accord the Secretary of State a wide degree of latitude in the exercise of his discretion. Further, in so far as the challenge is to the compatibility of the 2000 Act with the Convention, it does not lie within POAC's jurisdiction to determine it.

52. Even if the proscription of the PKK was valid, Mr Emmerson submits that the consequences of proscription as laid down by ss.11–19 of the 2000

Act entail a disproportionate interference with the rights of individuals. The essential rationale for the decision to proscribe, namely that the PKK's ceasefire may break down, cannot justify the criminal offences to which proscription exposes the Kurdish community for expressing support for the PKK.

53. The judgment of the Strasbourg Court in Surek & Ozdemir v. Turkey (8 July 1999), in particular at paras 40–64, is relied on in support of those submissions. In that case criminal sanctions under prevention of terrorism legislation had been imposed on a publisher and an editor-in-chief in respect of the publication, in a weekly review, of an interview with a leader of the PKK and of a joint declaration by four socialist organisations. The Court held that the conviction and sentences were not "necessary in a democratic society" since they were disproportionate to the legitimate aim of the protection of national security and territorial integrity and the prevention of disorder and crime. In reaching that conclusion it stressed that freedom of expression constitutes one of the essential foundations of a democratic society and that the need for restrictions must be established convincingly, and that in exercising its supervisory jurisdiction the Court must look at the interference in the light of the case as a whole, including the content of the impugned statements and the context in which they were made. In the particular case the impugned interferences also had to be seen in the context of the essential role of the press in ensuring the proper functioning of political democracy. The Court held that the domestic authorities had failed to have sufficient regard to the public's right to be informed of a different perspective on the situation in south-east Turkey and that the views expressed in the interviews could not be read as an incitement to violence or as liable to incite violence. (The judgment of the Court in Stankov v. Bulgaria (2 October 2001), cited by Lord Lester, contains similar observations.)

54. Adopting the same approach, Mr Emmerson submits that to prosecute a person for inviting support for an organisation which has abandoned violence is disproportionate. Further, the very existence of the criminal law and the prospect of conviction and sentence are sufficient to interfere with the claimants' rights and to render them victims: cf. Bowman v. United Kingdom (1998) 26 EHHR 1 at paras 26–29. The restrictions on freedom of expression by the Kurdish community constitute a restriction of free speech which it is difficult to envisage being justified.

The LeT claim

55. In the LeT proceedings, case no. CO/878/2002, the LeT itself is not a party. The claimant, however, is a supporter of LeT who, as mentioned above, also applied to the Secretary of State for deproscription of the LeT

and is the appellant to POAC from the refusal to deproscribe. The LeT is described in the claim form as a movement committed to the cause of self-determination for the people of Kashmir by means of the holding of a plebiscite as required by UN resolutions.

56. The Secretary of State's note to Members of Parliament, however, describes it as an organisation which seeks independence for Kashmir and the creation of an Islamic state using violent means. It is said in the note to have had a long history of mounting attacks against the Indian Security Forces in Kashmir, to have been blamed for the massacre of 35 Sikhs in Jammu and Kashmir in March 2000 and more recently to have launched attacks in which several people were killed. An LeT leader is said to have recently made a public declaration that he wished to expand the conflict with India beyond Kashmir.

57. In the Secretary of State's letter of 31 August 2001 refusing to deproscribe the LeT, it is stated:

"In reaching his decision the Home Secretary has taken full account of the submission made on behalf of your client. This includes the assertion that Lashkar e Tayyaba is not a terrorist organisation but a legitimate freedom movement. The Home Secretary does not accept, however, that any perceived right to self-determination justifies the terrorist actions of LT, or any other terrorist organisation. The Government condemns all acts of terrorism, whatever the source or motivation. . . .

The Home Secretary has noted furthermore your client's claims in the application that Lashkar e Tayyaba is not involved in violence in the United Kingdom. He is mindful, however, that terrorist action, as defined in section 1 of the Terrorism Act 2000, includes action taken or threatened outside the United Kingdom. But he believes that fundraising and recruitment activities in support of the organisation and its activities take place within the United Kingdom. Such activities are often carried out with a view to supporting terrorist activity, whether here or abroad . . .

. . . Mr Ahmed's letter of 26 March 2001 to the Home Secretary states that Lashkar e Tayyaba was not involved in the murder of 35 people in Jammu and Kashmir in March 2000. The Home Secretary is aware, however, of reports which indicate that Lashkar e Tayyaba was blamed for this attack. He remains satisfied, moreover, that the organisation has been responsible for further acts of terrorism and has noted that, since the proscription powers came into force on 29 March 2001, Lashkar e Tayyaba has continued to carry out and claim responsibility for terrorist attacks that have resulted in civilian casualties. . . ."

58. Mr Ahmed challenges the making of the 2001 Order proscribing the LeT, the refusal of the Secretary of State to deproscribe the LeT and the con-

tinuing proscription of the LeT. On his behalf Miss Mountfield adopts the submissions made by Lord Lester and Mr Emmerson. In the summary of the claimant's grounds it is contended in particular that the making of the Order was unlawful because it included 21 organisations and Parliament was unable to consider the individual merits of proscribing each organisation; it was unfair because no opportunity was given beforehand to make representations; the Order was not "prescribed by law" because the 2000 Act impermissibly leaves to the complete discretion of the Secretary of State which organisations falling within the wide definition should in fact be proscribed; the proscription is not necessary in a democratic society because it is a disproportionate interference with rights under Articles 10 and 11 of the Convention; and the proscription is discriminatory and in breach of Article 14. The same arguments are relied on in relation to the decision not to deproscribe and in relation to the ongoing proscription.

59. The court's special attention is drawn by the claimant to the international law situation and factual circumstances of Jammu and Kashmir, which it is submitted were matters that Parliament was unable properly to consider but which render the proscription of the LeT disproportionate and discriminatory compared with other organisations which have not been proscribed. In particular, it is said that the LeT does not call for the armed overthrow of the Government of India in Kashmir, but campaigns for the right to a plebiscite; this is a campaign for the fulfilment of the international law right to self-determination; the LeT's military activities are directed exclusively against the Indian regime's military/security apparatus and to the disputed territory of Kashmir; they have never targeted civilians and have never posed any threat to the UK or to British nationals overseas; and independent human rights organisations have documented consistent human rights abuses and violations of fundamental tenets of democratic rule in Kashmir. Further, in relation to discrimination in breach of Article 14, it is submitted that the relevant class is of organisations capable of being proscribed as terrorist organisations and that no adequate justification has been advanced for the difference of treatment between the LeT and organisations such as the Northern Alliance in Afghanistan which have not been proscribed.

Arguability

60. It is submitted by Mr Sales on behalf of the Secretary of State that the challenges do not disclose an arguable case. I have come to the view that the challenges are arguable, or at least that they contain a sufficient number of arguable points to get over the threshold in respect of the main

issues. In the circumstances I propose to deal with the topic of arguability relatively briefly.

61. It is convenient to group the claimants' various grounds of challenge into three categories: (1) what may broadly be termed procedural issues relating to the decision to include the claimant organisations in the draft Order and the making of the Order itself, in particular the contention that the Secretary of State's discretion is insufficiently circumscribed to meet the Convention test of "prescribed by law," that the claimants were unlawfully denied the opportunity to make representations in advance, and that it was unlawful to include 21 organisations in a single Order; (2) what may broadly be termed substantive issues concerning the justification for proscription, in particular whether proscription is "necessary in a democratic society" (especially whether it is proportionate to a legitimate aim) and whether it constitutes discriminatory treatment of the claimant organisations; and (3) issues relating to the regime of offences consequential upon proscription, in particular whether it gives rise to a disproportionate interference with the rights of the individual claimants.

62. That is not a clear-cut categorisation. For example, the justification for proscription necessarily engages both "prescribed by law" and "necessary in a democratic society" and it is no doubt an over-simplification to place the first in category (1) as a procedural issue and the other in category (2) as a substantive issue. So too the justification for the regime of offences under category (3) is closely bound up with the justification for proscription under category (2). Nevertheless I think it helpful on balance to categorise the issues in this way. I also note that the PKK case concentrates on categories (1) and (3), whereas the PMOI and LeT also include category (2) as an important aspect of their claims.

63. In relation to the first category, the various procedural issues, Mr Sales submits as follows:
   i) The contention that the discretion to proscribe is too broad to meet the Convention test of "prescribed by law" is misconceived. For the purpose of applying the test, it is necessary to look at the terms of the Order rather than of the enabling legislation, since it is the Order which engages the regime of offences under the 2000 Act and tells individuals what they may or may not do. The Order itself is highly precise, specifically naming the organisations, and meets the requirements of accessibility and foreseeability. The Convention cases relied on by the claimants concerning the need for protection against arbitrary power all relate to decisions taken by officials exercising a broad discretion conferred by legislation. Here, the relevant decision is not that of the Secretary of State under s.3 of the 2000 Act but the decision taken by Parliament in the form of its approval of the Order.

Once the Order was made, the scope of the legal restrictions aris-ing from it was clear and its future application foreseeable. As to the suggestion that there was inadequate Parliamentary scrutiny, there is nothing in the Convention case-law to suggest that any particu-lar legislative process has to be followed in order to meet the test of "prescribed by law"; and in any event the courts do not have authority to scrutinise and criticise proceedings in Parliament.

ii) There is no express requirement under the 2000 Act to give an organisation the opportunity to make prior representations against proscription. Nor is there any general implied right to be consulted or to make objections prior to the making of legislation, whether primary or delegated (see Bates v. Lord Hailsham [1972] 1 WLR 1373), and there could be no sensible implied obligation to con-sult organisations such as Al-Qa'ida. Further, the Convention does not establish any formal or procedural requirements which must be met before legislation is enacted. In a case such as the present "con-sultation" is provided through the democratic process, i.e. the oppor-tunity to make representations to Members of Parliament prior to the debate (as was done in practice e.g. by the PMOI).

iii) There is plainly power to include more than one organisation in a single Order. Although s.3(3) of the 2000 Act refers to "an organ-isation," by s.6(c) of the Interpretation Act 1978 words in the sin-gular are taken to include the plural unless the contrary intention appears. No such contrary intention appears in the 2000 Act. If the Secretary of State was entitled to take the view that each organisa-tion was concerned in terrorism, then it was plainly neither irrational nor otherwise unlawful for him to include them in a single Order.

iv) POAC does provide sufficient procedural guarantees and an effec-tive remedy, notwithstanding that an appeal may arise only after the event. This is covered further below in the context of alternative remedies.

64. It is important to bear in mind that the various procedural issues raised by the claimants are presented not just as discrete points but, especially in Mr Emmerson's submissions, as a package of points in support of the broad proposition that there was a failure to provide the very high level of procedural protection required in the case of an Order giving rise to such serious interferences with Convention rights. In my view that broad proposition is arguable, whatever reservations one may have about cer-tain of the individual points.

65. As to the individual points themselves, I think it arguable that the "pre-scribed by law" requirement applies to the original decision of the Secretary of State to include the organisations in the draft Order rather than to the

terms of the draft Order itself, even though proscription only takes effect through the terms of the Order and following Parliamentary approval. The decision of the US Court of Appeals in National Council of Resistance of Iran v. Department of State provides some support to the argument that the claimants ought to have been given an opportunity to make representations in advance, though there are important differences both in broad constitutional context and in the specific legislative context (including the absence in that case of any equivalent to the right to apply *ex post* for deproscription and the right of appeal to POAC). The specific argument that the Secretary of State has no power to include more than one organisation in a single Order is particularly difficult, but the fact that so many organisations were included in an Order which Parliament had so little opportunity to scrutinise can still be deployed as part of the overall case that sufficient procedural guarantees were lacking.

66. So far as concerns the second category of issues, i.e. whether proscription was "necessary in a democratic society" and was non-discriminatory, Mr Sales submits:

    v)   The restrictions are directed towards the pursuit of a legitimate aim, namely the interests of public safety and/or the interests of national security and/or the prevention of disorder or crime and/or the protection of health and morals and/or the protection of the rights and freedoms of others.

    vi)   The balance to be struck is between democratic society as a whole and the rights of the individual. When, as here, the government decides that it is necessary to prevent particular terrorist groups gathering support and financial aid, the decision is based on the concept that it is better for the interests of democratic society as a whole, and particularly in the United Kingdom, that such organisations do not become more powerful and that terrorism does not become seen as a legitimate tool for altering a nation's policy.

    vii)   The margin of appreciation to be afforded to the State (or, as I think Mr Sales would accept in a domestic context, the decision-maker's margin of discretion or margin of judgment, or the degree of deference to which the decision-maker is entitled) must be determined with due regard to the circumstances, which in the present context includes regard to the potentially serious consequences of terrorist activity and the fact that such activity threatens the collective security of the community of nations. In those circumstances the State is to be afforded a generous margin. The State is also to be afforded a wide margin because it has to strike a balance between competing Convention rights, including the rights of victims of terrorism under Articles 2, 3 and 8 of the Convention.

viii) For the purposes of considering the claim the court must assume that the organisations were concerned in terrorism and the decision to proscribe was warranted on that basis. It follows that the basis of the claim as to discrimination can only be that there are other organisations in precisely the same situation which have not been proscribed. The court is not in a position to determine that question; and in any event, in assessing whether persons are in comparable situations, the State again has a wide margin afforded to it.

ix) Neither in relation to proportionality nor in relation to non-discrimination can it be said that the margin or discretionary area afforded to the State has been exceeded.

67. It seems to me that for the purposes of arguability these issues must be considered on the basis of the evidence at present before the court and without regard to any further evidence, possibly including sensitive intelligence information, that may be available to the Secretary of State in support of the proscription of the claimant organisations. On that basis I am prepared to accept that the PMOI and LeT have an arguable case, given in particular (i) what is asserted in their evidence about the limited aims and activities of their organisations and (ii) the very serious consequences of proscription for rights as important as those of free speech and free assembly. Whether it is a case properly considered by the Administrative Court is a very different question, to which I shall turn in a moment.

68. As regards the third category, the challenge to the regime of penalties, Mr Sales submits inter alia that:

x) Each of the offences is based in law and sufficiently clearly defined.

xi) The offences under ss.11–13 operate by reference to organisations which have been proscribed, and once a particular organisation has been proscribed the requirement of legal certainty is plainly satisfied.

xii) To the extent that the point in relation to offences under ss.15–19 relates to the definition of "terrorism" in s.1, the relevant test for "prescribed by law" (which is substantially the same as the test under Article 7 of the Convention) is whether it is possible to know from the wording of the relevant provision, with the assistance of the interpretation of the courts, what acts or omissions will result in criminal liability. Since laws are of general application it is inevitable that the wording of statutes is not always precise. A State is also entitled to frame laws so that they keep pace with changing circumstances. The fact that in any case there may be a "penumbra of doubt" as to the application of a provision does not render it incompatible provided that it is sufficiently clear in the vast majority of cases. Set against this standard the definition of "terrorism" in s.1 satisfies the test. In the vast majority of cases its application will be certain and predictable.

69. In my view those points do not meet the real thrust of the challenge to the regime of penalties, which is that the circumstances relied on for the proscription of the claimant organisations cannot justify such serious interferences with the Convention rights of the individual claimants, notably the chilling effect on free speech. Again it seems to me that the issue must be considered at this stage on the basis of the evidence at present before the court. On that basis I consider the claim to be arguable, especially having regard to the points made by Mr Emmerson by reference to Surek.

Appropriateness of judicial review

70. The next, and to my mind the most important, question for consideration is whether it is appropriate for the various challenges to proceed by way of judicial review. For the Secretary of State, Mr Sales submits in essence that permission should be refused because POAC can and should determine the substantive issues raised and is the appropriate forum for that purpose. He has an alternative, fall-back position that judicial review should be allowed to proceed on individual procedural issues but not on issues that depend on an assessment of the underlying facts. Counsel for the claimants, on the other hand, submit that POAC cannot review the specific decisions under challenge, cannot consider the full grounds that the claimants wish to raise and cannot give the remedies they seek. By contrast, the Administrative Court can consider the entirety of the claims and can grant the full range of relief and is therefore the appropriate forum.

71. It is common ground that the decision is discretionary. The court's jurisdiction is not excluded by the 2000 Act, by contrast with the position under s.30 of the Anti-terrorism, Crime and Security Act 2001 where certain human rights issues in the field of immigration can be questioned in legal proceedings only before the Special Immigration Appeals Commission.

72. Mr Sales points to statements of principle to the effect that judicial review is a remedy of last resort and that judicial review will not normally be allowed where there is an alternative remedy by way of appeal (see e.g. R v. Panel on Take-overs and Mergers, ex p. Guinness Plc [1990] 1 QB 146 at 177E–178A and R v. Chief Constable of Merseyside Police, ex p. Calveley [1986] QB 424). He also relies, by way of analogy, on statements in R v. DPP, ex p. Kebilene [2000] 2 AC 326 and R (Pretty) v. DPP [2002] 1 All ER 1 to the broad effect that satellite litigation by way of judicial review is to be avoided in relation to issues arising in the context of criminal proceedings. The same principle, he submits, applies in relation to issues that have been or could be raised in proceedings before POAC.

73. The claimants' counsel, in particular Mr Rabinder Singh QC who presented the PMOI's main submissions on this part of the case, submits that the true principle is that an alternative procedure should be exhausted first if it is at least as extensive as judicial review (see generally the discussion at paras 20–018 to 20–021 of de Smith, Woolf and Jowell, "Judicial Review of Administrative Action"), that one potential exception is where the ground of challenge is based on procedural fairness (ex p. Guinness at 184G-185A) and that where the suggested alternative forum cannot consider the entirety of a complaint which can be raised by way of judicial review, the court should entertain a claim for judicial review (R v. Inland Revenue Commissioners, ex p. Mead [1993] 1 All ER 772 at 781–2).

74. All such statements of principle and illustrations of their application provide helpful guidance, but an exercise of discretion in a matter of this kind depends very much upon the particular subject-matter and context of the claim.

75. It is plain that Parliament, although not seeking to exclude the possibility of judicial review, intended POAC to be the forum of first resort for the determination of claims relating to the lawfulness of proscription under the 2000 Act. The procedure established for challenging proscription, whether by inclusion in Schedule 2 as originally enacted or by subsequent addition to the list by means of an order under s.3, is an application to the Secretary of State for removal from the list and an appeal to POAC if the application is refused, with a further avenue of appeal to the Court of Appeal on a question of law.

76. POAC is, as Mr Sales submits, a specialist tribunal with procedures designed specifically to deal with the determination of claims relating to proscription, a context heavily laden with issues of national security: cf. the observations of Lord Steyn in Secretary of State for the Home Department v. Rehman [2001] 3 WLR 877 at 888–9, para 30, in relation to the equivalent composition and procedures of the Special Immigration Appeals Commission under the Special Immigration Appeals Commission Act 1997 (though POAC and SIAC do not have an identical status). The special advocate procedure and the existence of extensive powers in relation to the reception of evidence, including otherwise non-disclosable evidence, place POAC at a clear advantage over the Administrative Court in such an area. In many respects the Administrative Court might be able to devise something equivalent: Lord Lester referred to the observation of the Strasbourg Court at paragraph 78 of the judgment in Tinnelly & Sons Ltd. & Others v. United Kingdom (1998) 27 EHHR 249, that "in other contexts it has been found possible to modify judicial procedures in such a way as to safeguard national security concerns about

the nature and sources of intelligence information and yet accord the individual a substantial degree of procedural justice." But it would be far less satisfactory to go down that route than to utilise the POAC procedure already carefully formulated for the purpose.

77. Moreover proceedings before POAC are expressly excluded from the prohibition on the disclosure of intercepted communications, potentially a very important area of evidence; and although it was submitted for the claimants that the same or a similar result could be achieved in the Administrative Court by a Convention-compliant construction of the Regulation of Investigatory Powers Act 2000, in particular the power under s.18(7)–(8) to order disclosure to a judge of the High Court, this is at best very uncertain and would again be a less satisfactory route than reliance on the clear and general exception under s.18(1)(f) in respect of any proceedings before POAC or any proceedings arising out of proceedings before POAC.

78. POAC has also been designated as the appropriate tribunal for the purposes of s.7 of the Human Rights Act in relation to proceedings against the Secretary of State in respect of a refusal to deproscribe.

79. All those considerations tell strongly in favour of POAC being the appropriate tribunal for consideration of issues falling within what I have previously termed category (2), namely whether proscription was necessary in a democratic society and whether it was non-discriminatory. Those are important parts of the PMOI and LeT claims. They depend heavily on a scrutiny of all the evidence, including any sensitive intelligence information, concerning the aims and activities of the organisations concerned and a comparison between them and other organisations proscribed or not proscribed. I recognise that POAC's appellate jurisdiction relates not to the original proscription but to a refusal to deproscribe, whereas by these proceedings the claimants challenge the original decision to proscribe. But in relation to these substantive issues, at least, I do not think that anything turns on that point. The issues are materially the same whether they are raised in the context of the original proscription or in the context of a refusal to deproscribe. In the case of the PMOI and the LeT, where there have been applications to deproscribe and appeals have been lodged with POAC in respect of the refusal to deproscribe, the issues are already before POAC in materially the same form as they are sought to be raised in this court, as is apparent from a comparison between the written cases in the two fora. If the claimants' arguments are well founded, they will succeed before POAC or on appeal from POAC and this will result in their deproscription. Indeed, it is asserted in the PMOI's amended claim form that "[h]ad the Secretary of State acceded to the Claimants' application . . . it would have been unnecessary to bring legal proceed-

ings of any kind" (para 90). If, therefore, the substantive issues stood alone, there would to my mind be no question but that POAC is the appropriate forum and permission to apply for judicial review should be refused.

80. The problems arise out of the fact that such issues do not stand alone. The PMOI and LeT claimants also raise issues falling within what I have previously termed category (1), i.e. a procedural challenge to the original decision to include the organisations in the draft Order and to the Order itself. Moreover the PKK claimants have not even raised issues within category (2) and have not themselves sought deproscription or appealed to POAC, but have focused their challenge, so far as the proscription of the PKK is concerned, on the broad submission that the original decision and Order are vitiated by a failure to observe the procedural guarantees required by the Convention.

81. In my view it would be possible for those procedural issues, taken by themselves, to be determined in the Administrative Court as effectively as in POAC. Moreover the natural targets of any challenge on those grounds are the original decision and Order, which lie within the jurisdiction of the Administrative Court but not of POAC. If there was a procedural defect as alleged, it occurred at that original stage and not at the stage of the subsequent refusal to deproscribe; and it would generally be considered artificial and inappropriate to challenge a subsequent decision on grounds relating to a defect in the original decision.

82. The present context strikes me, however, as exceptional. The legislative intention is in my view that challenges to an organisation's presence in the list of proscribed organisations should be brought by way of an application for deproscription and appeal to POAC. It is possible to give effect to that legislative intention even in relation to a challenge based on procedural defects vitiating the original decision to proscribe. That is because, as Mr Sales submits, the Secretary of State can be requested to deproscribe on the basis that the original proscription was unlawful on procedural as well as substantive grounds; and if the Secretary of State refuses to deproscribe, an appeal can be brought on the basis that he has erred in law and/or acted in breach of the claimants' Convention rights in so refusing. Mr Emmerson expressed the concern that the Secretary of State might be able to avoid any appealable error by expressing no view one way or the other on the lawfulness of the original proscription. Whatever the theoretical merit of that argument, I cannot see this happening in practice, given the Secretary of State's stance that all matters are more appropriately dealt with on appeal to POAC rather than by way of judicial review. It would be extraordinary if the Secretary of State were to adopt a course that threw the claimants back onto judicial review as the

only means of obtaining an effective remedy, the very thing that the Secretary of State seeks so strenuously to avoid.

83. If the various aspects of the procedural challenge to the original decision can be raised in this way before POAC on an appeal from a refusal to deproscribe, as I think they can, one comes back to whether that is the more appropriate course than to allow a direct challenge to the original decision by way of judicial review. In my judgment it is. That applies with particular force to the PMOI and LeT, since it is much better that their challenge to proscription on substantive grounds be determined by POAC and there is an obvious advantage in all issues being determined by the same tribunal (especially given the inevitable existence of a degree of overlap between what I have termed the substantive and the procedural issues). It is less obvious in the case of the PKK, where there are no proceedings before POAC and the procedural grounds advanced in relation to proscription could all be dealt with as satisfactorily by the Administrative Court. Since, however, POAC is intended to be the forum of first resort and is the appropriate forum for the PMOI and LeT claims, and since there is a heavy overlap between PKK's procedural grounds and the procedural grounds advanced by the PMOI and LeT, POAC is also in my view the appropriate forum for the PKK claim. It is better for all these matters to be determined by POAC, with an appeal if necessary to the Court of Appeal on questions of law, than to allow the claims to be spread between two jurisdictions or to allow the entirety of the claims to proceed in the Administrative Court. As already mentioned, it is still open to the PKK to go down the POAC route even though it has not yet done so.

84. In considering the appropriateness of POAC as a forum for issues relating to proscription/deproscription, I have taken into account the fact that there is no material difference between POAC and the Administrative Court in terms of the legal principles to be applied: by s.5(3) of the 2000 Act, POAC is required to allow an appeal if it considers that the decision to refuse to deproscribe was flawed "when considered in the light of the principles applicable on an application for judicial review." I see no reason why POAC should be any less able than the Administrative Court to provide effective scrutiny of the matters under challenge.

85. I have also taken into account, however, that there is a difference as regards available remedies. The first material difference is that, unlike the Administrative Court, POAC has no power to quash the original decision or Order. By s.5(4)–(5), it may make an order to which the Secretary of State must give effect by means of a further Order removing the organisation from the list in Schedule 2. This means that the proscription remains valid as from the date when the original Order came into effect until the date of the further Order removing the organisation from the list. That

might be relevant if any of the claimants were subject to sanctions dependent upon the validity of the proscription in the interim period (though account would have to be taken of the mitigating effect of s.7). I do not think, however, that this difference in the form of order available to POAC as compared with the Administrative Court would have any practical consequence for the claimants. In particular, I do not think that it would affect the substance of their damages claims, to which I refer below.

86. The second difference as regards available relief is that POAC does not have the power to grant a declaration of incompatibility under s.4 of the Human Rights Act. Such a declaration is sought by the claimants in the alternative to their arguments that proscription is unlawful under the existing legislation when construed compatibly with the Convention. In my judgment, however, POAC's lack of such a power does not render the POAC procedure inappropriate, since there exists an avenue of appeal to the Court of Appeal on a point of law and the Court of Appeal does have such a power. The fact that a declaration of incompatibility cannot be made by an inferior tribunal, but only on appeal to the High Court or Court of Appeal, does not generally render proceedings before the inferior tribunal inappropriate or render an application for judicial review appropriate. The appropriate course is still generally to pursue the proceedings before the inferior tribunal and then on appeal to the High Court or Court of Appeal, rather than to apply for judicial review. An obvious example is that of criminal proceedings in the Crown Court, where a declaration of incompatibility is available only on appeal to the Court of Appeal but the general appropriateness of pursuing all issues in the criminal proceedings instead of applying for judicial review has been stressed in Kebilene and in R (Pretty) v. DPP. Thus in the PMOI and LeT appeals to POAC the incompatibility arguments have properly been advanced with a view to seeking declarations from the Court of Appeal on a further appeal if that becomes necessary.

87. The third difference is that POAC does not have the power to award damages whereas in the present proceedings the claimants, by late amendments, have claimed damages pursuant to s.8 of the Human Rights Act. I do not regard this as telling significantly in favour of the grant of permission for the claims to proceed by way of judicial review. That would be to allow the tail to wag the dog. A claim for damages can properly be made as part of an otherwise appropriate claim for judicial review, but is not in itself a good reason for permitting judicial review. In practice, where there is a claim for damages as part of an otherwise appropriate claim for judicial review, the claim for damages would normally be left over to be dealt with as a discrete issue, if still relevant, after the main issues of public law had been determined. Even if still dealt with under CPR Part 54,

rather than transferred out of the Administrative Court, it would still generally be subject to directions bringing it broadly into line with a damages claim commenced in the normal way. Thus there is no particular reason why the damages claim should proceed by way of judicial review and the claimants would be under no real disadvantage in relation to this part of their claim if they had to bring a separate claim for damages following a successful appeal to POAC for deproscription. Although s.7(5) of the Human Rights Act lays down a basic time limit of one year for the bringing of such a claim, a longer period is permitted where considered equitable and there would be an overwhelming case for allowing a longer period if matters got that far. (In the circumstances I think it unnecessary to decide on a further submission by Mr Sales, that by virtue of the designation of POAC under s.7 of the Human Rights Act, the claimants have no right to bring claims for damages in the High Court until after the proscription issue has been resolved by POAC.)

88. A separate issue arises in relation to the challenge to the regime of penalties under ss.11–19 of the 2000 Act, a point again highlighted by the formulation of the PKK claim. The claimants put the challenge on the basis that the statutory regime infringes their Convention rights even in a case where proscription is lawful. They submit that POAC plainly lacks jurisdiction on that issue and that the Administrative Court must be the appropriate forum, especially given that that a declaration of incompatibility is sought.

89. In my judgment, however, this issue is intimately bound up with those that I have already held appropriate for determination by POAC. The offences under s.11–13 are all direct consequences of proscription. The offences under ss.15–19 are not limited to proscribed organisations, but their true significance for the claimants appears to lie in the definitions in s.14 which bring the resources of a proscribed organisation within the definition of "terrorist property" and provide that action "for the purposes of terrorism" includes action taken for the benefit of a proscribed organisation. Thus the case advanced is in practice concerned with proscription and the consequences of proscription rather than with the possible ambit of ss.15–19 in cases unconnected with a proscribed organisation. It is for that reason that the issues are intimately bound up with those to be determined by POAC. The statutory regime relevant to proscribed organisations must be examined as a whole. The circumstances either warrant the inclusion of an organisation within that regime, taken as a whole, or they do not. There is no half-way house. It follows that in order to determine whether proscription is proportionate, POAC will have to have careful regard to the consequences of proscription, in particular the consequential offences. The fact that proscription gives rise to such a

serious interference with the rights of an organisation and its supporters means that a correspondingly more compelling justification for the proscription will have to be advanced.

90. That is not a complete answer to the claimants' case on this issue. It cannot be right, as Mr Sales appeared at one point to submit, that the existence of even one case where the regime of criminal sanctions would be capable of producing a disproportionate consequence would be sufficient to render proscription disproportionate and unlawful. It must be possible in principle for proscription to be justified but for the regime of offences nonetheless to operate in a particular case in a way that infringes an individual's Convention rights. Moreover cases such as Dudgeon v. United Kingdom (1981) 4 EHRR 149 and Norris v. Ireland (1991) 13 EHHR 186 show that the maintenance in force of legislation containing criminal prohibitions can constitute in itself a continuing interference with Convention rights and that individuals affected by it may be entitled to challenge it without waiting to be prosecuted for an offence. As Mr Emmerson put it, the concern in the present case is with the self-censorship required in order to avoid prosecution, rather than with an actual prosecution; and it is very unsatisfactory if someone who wishes to engage in free speech has to take the risk of committing a criminal offence and asserting Convention rights in defence, rather than being able to challenge the legislation in the first place for interfering with his right to free speech.

91. Nevertheless I am not persuaded that I should allow the challenge to the regime of penalties to proceed in the form of the present claim for judicial review. In my view the question whether the regime of offences consequential upon a lawful proscription gives rise to an unjustified interference with an individual's Convention rights needs to be considered on the particular facts of an individual case as and when it arises. It should not be dealt with as an abstract or generalised issue. Whether there is such an infringement will depend on all the circumstances of the individual case. Alternatively, any challenge should at the very least await the outcome of the appeals to POAC. If the appeals succeed and the claimant organisations are deproscribed, the issue concerning penalties will fall away. If they do not succeed, then consideration could be given to claims advanced at that time on the basis of the circumstances then prevailing. Further, it is better that there should be fresh claims at the right time, rather than adjourning the permission applications in respect of the relevant parts of the present claims.

92. Accordingly I take the view that it would not be appropriate to allow any of the present claims for judicial review to proceed. Most of the issues can and should be canvassed before POAC on an appeal under s.5, and there-

after as necessary in the Court of Appeal on a further appeal on a question of law. To the extent that issues cannot be canvassed in that way, it is inappropriate to allow them to be canvassed now by way of judicial review. They should at least await a determination by POAC of those issues that POAC can deal with. In my view to require the claimants to proceed in this way is to meet the requirement to provide an effective remedy for breach of Convention rights.

Delay

93. On behalf of the Secretary of State, Mr Sales submits that permission should be refused in any event on grounds of delay both in the case of the PMOI and in the case of the LeT. PMOI's claim was lodged in October 2001, well over three months from the date of the Secretary of State's decision to lay the draft Order before Parliament, let alone the date when the 2001 Order came into force (which is the latest date when the grounds for the claim first arose). Let's claim was lodged only in February 2002, far later still. In relation to each case it is submitted that there has been a failure to comply with the time limit laid down in CPR rule 54.5 and no sufficient reason has been advanced to justify an extension of time. It is accepted that no issue on delay arises in the case of the PKK.

94. The PMOI claimants submit that they acted reasonably in seeking first to persuade the Secretary of State to remedy the position by deproscribing the PMOI, in which case legal proceedings would have been unnecessary. The LeT evidence includes an account of the steps taken between the date of proscription and the application for judicial review, but does not begin to offer a satisfactory explanation for the delay. In my judgment in neither case is there a sufficient explanation to justify an extension of time.

95. In each case there is, however, a more general submission that an extension of time is justified by the importance of the issues raised. In each case it is also submitted that the claimants are suffering a continuing interference with their Convention rights and that there has therefore been no undue delay or time should be extended. The claimants would be able to rely on their Convention rights as a defence if prosecuted (cf. Boddington v. British Transport Police [1999] 2 AC 143) and should equally be able to assert their rights by judicial review without waiting to be prosecuted.

96. I should mention that Mr Sales accepted that a challenge to the compatibility of the 2000 Act could be brought at any time but submitted that the substance of the challenges was to the decision to proscribe rather than against the legislation more generally. It seems to me that both are under challenge. But the argument led to an examination of cases such as R v. Secretary of State for Employment, ex p. Equal Opportunities

Commission [1995] 1 AC 1 at 26–27, R (Pearson) v. Secretary of State for the Home Department [2001] HRLR 806 at para 6, and Rusbridger v. Attorney General [2001] EWHC Admin 529. Although the debate was interesting, in my view it does not really assist in the resolution of the issues before me at this stage.

97. In any event, it is unnecessary for me in the circumstances to reach any concluded view on the issue of delay. Suffice it to state that, if and to the extent that I had been of the view that the Administrative Court was the appropriate forum for the issues raised, I doubt whether I would have refused permission on the ground of delay. Given the importance of the issues and the fact that, on this hypothesis, the PKK's claim would have proceeded in any event, I would have been disinclined to shut out the PMOI or LeT.

Conclusion

98. For the reasons given above, permission is refused in respect of each of the three claims.

99. That makes it unnecessary for me to consider a further and somewhat bold submission by Mr Sales to the effect that if I granted permission I should at the same time make a ruling against the Secretary of State on a notional application under CPR Part 24 so as to enable the Secretary of State to challenge my judgment in the Court of Appeal notwithstanding the absence of any right of appeal against the grant of permission.

MR JUSTICE RICHARDS: I am handing down the judgment in these three cases. The judgment relates to applications for permission to challenge the lawfulness of the proscription of three organisations as terrorist organisations under the Terrorism Act 2000 and to the regime of penalties laid down under that Act in relation to proscribed organisations. In each case I have held the claim to be arguable but have taken the view that judicial review is not the appropriate procedure. The right course at this stage is for the claimants to pursue appeals to the Proscribed Organisations Appeals Commission in accordance with the procedure laid down in the Terrorism Act itself and regulations made under it. These and other matters are covered more fully in the judgment handed down.

* * * * *

DOCUMENT NO 18

Nessan Quinlivan
and
Noel Conroy and Hugh Sreenan
The High Court of Ireland [2000] 3 IR 154

April 14, 2000
(Edited Text)

JUDGMENT of Mr. Justice KELLY:

INTRODUCTION

In April 1993 four warrants were issued by Judicial authorities in England and Wales for the arrest of Nessan Quinlivan. He is the Plaintiff in the first of these proceedings in which he seeks relief pursuant to the provisions of Section 50 of the Extradition Act, 1965, as amended. He is the Applicant in the second proceedings which are Judicial Review proceedings. The proceedings were heard together and I will throughout this judgment refer to Mr. Quinlivan as the Applicant.

Two of the English warrants were issued by His Honour Judge Verney, a judge of the Crown Court sitting at the Central Criminal Court in London. The first of them recites that the Applicant stood indicted in the Central Criminal Court on a charge that he with Pearse McCauley and William McKane, on divers days before the 12th day of November 1990, within the jurisdiction of the Central Criminal Court, conspired together and with others to murder Sir Charles Henderson Tidbury and other persons contrary to section 1 of the Criminal Law Act, 1977. The second of Judge Verney's warrants also recites that the Applicant stood indicted in the Central Criminal Court on a charge that with the same persons on divers dates before the 12th day of November 1990 within the jurisdiction of the Central Criminal Court, he conspired with them and with others to cause, by explosive substances, explosions of a nature likely to endanger life or cause serious injury to property in the United Kingdom contrary to section 3(1)(a) of the Explosive Substances Act, 1883.

The two remaining warrants were issued by Mr. Ronald Bartle a Metropolitan Stipendiary Magistrate and Justice for the Inner London area.

The first of these allege that on the 7th day of July 1991 at Her Majesty's Prison, Brixton, the Applicant, whilst in lawful custody on a criminal charge awaiting trial, escaped from that custody contrary to common law. The final warrant alleges that the Applicant on the 7th day of July 1991 at Brixton Hill, London, unlawfully and maliciously wounded Malcolm Hugh David Kemp with intent to do him grievous bodily harm contrary to section 18 of the Offences Against the Person Act, 1861.

All four warrants were backed for execution in this jurisdiction pursuant to the relevant provisions of the Extradition legislation and the Applicant was arrested on foot of the warrants on the 6th day of November 1995.

On the 11th day of December 1995 the President of the District Court ordered that the Applicant be delivered into the custody of a member of the relevant police forces in England for conveyance to the appropriate London Courts which issued the warrants.

In these proceedings the Applicant seeks to be relieved of the consequences of the Orders made by the District Court and asks for his release.

In the course of this judgment I will have to consider the many points which were made by Counsel on behalf of the Applicant but before doing so it is necessary that I set forth the evidence which was adduced on the hearing in some detail. In the course of so doing I will also deal with the legal objections which were taken to the admissibility of such evidence. The proceedings were heard together and it was agreed that the evidence adduced in one of the proceedings could be considered in the other and vice versa.

THE EVIDENCE IN RESPECT OF THE OFFENCES

In his affidavit grounding the application under Section 50 of the Extradition Act, the Applicant says that the conspiracy charges arise out of a campaign of violence which was conducted by the Irish Republican Army (I.R.A.) in England in 1990 during which, *inter alia*, Mr. Ian Gow M.P. was murdered, a former Governor of Gibraltar was shot and wounded and one soldier was shot dead and two others wounded at Lichfield Railway Station. He also says that in the course of their investigations into I.R.A. activities in England the police there had earlier found a list of intended I.R.A. targets, which included Sir Charles Tidbury. He says that Sir Charles Tidbury was a prominent businessman in England. He was a former chairman of Whitbread, the brewers, which under his chairmanship was allegedly a major contributor to the funds of the British Conservative Party.

The Applicant was arrested at Stonehenge in England with one Pearse McCauley on the 2nd October 1990. He says that the police immediately let it be known that they were suspected of the murder of Mr. Gow and of being members of an I.R.A. active service unit that was involved in several serious offences around that time. They were taken to Paddington Green Police Station and were questioned by members of the Anti-Terrorist Branch. He says that the whole tenor of his questioning made it clear that the conspiracy charges relate to the I.R.A. campaign and accordingly they are "political offences." He exhibits extracts from the contemporaneous accounts made by the police during the questioning of the Applicant and Pearse McCauley. The Applicant also exhibited an extract from a contemporaneous record made by the English police of the questioning of his alleged co-conspirator William McKane and his wife. Mr. McKane was tried on the conspiracy charges and acquitted. He says that these extracts further demonstrate the political nature of the alleged conspiracy charges on foot of which his extradition is sought.

The Applicant and Pearse McCauley were held on remand at Brixton Prison. Whilst there, it is alleged they were approached by a named prison officer who encouraged them to attempt to escape and indicated that he would assist them to that end. He says that that prison officer was a former member of the S.A.S. and was working as an informant for a Detective Sergeant of the Staffordshire Police Special Branch. He says that the prison officer was acting as a spy and agent provocateur for the British Anti-Terrorist Police or the Security Services otherwise known as MI5.

The Applicant and McCauley were suspicious of the prison officer when he first suggested escaping. However, the prison officer repeated his suggestion on a number of occasions and went to considerable lengths to gain their confidence. He advised them that the best time to effect an escape would be when returning from Mass on Sunday and he told them of what he believed to be the weakest point of the prison's perimeter wall. He promised to supply them with a map of that section of the prison and to smuggle in a gun which he recommended would be essential to carrying out the plan. He also said that he could arrange for transport to be waiting for them outside the prison when they escaped. This prison officer was transferred from Brixton Prison before the arrangements were completed but it was by utilising the plan suggested by him that they effected their escape on the 7th July 1991. It is that escape that is the subject of the third and fourth charges in respect of which extradition is sought.

The escape resulted in enormous publicity in England. The Home Secretary ordered the Chief Inspector of Prisons to prepare a report. He did so, but the sections of the report dealing with the role of the prison officer were not published. There was also an enquiry into the role of the Detective Sergeant from the Staffordshire Special Branch and indeed of that Branch itself which was conducted by the Deputy Chief Constable of Nottinghamshire. There was also an enquiry into the role of Home Office officials. The reports of these enquiries were not published. Thames Television broadcast two programmes on the matter and the Sunday Express also published material on the topic. It is from the media coverage of these events that the Applicant has formed the belief that the prison officer and the Detective Sergeant were acting throughout on behalf of the S.A.S. or MI5 or some other section of the Security Services. He expresses the belief that the prison officer's task was to persuade them to escape in the hope that they would lead the security services to their alleged confederates in the I.R.A. who at the time were carrying out a campaign of violence in England. He says that the prison officer acted as an agent provocateur in relation to the prison escape and did so with the encouragement and assistance of the British security authorities.

He points out the large amount of publicity concerning all these events and the further publicity which took place subsequent to his arrest in this jurisdiction in April 1993.

The Respondents did not seek to cross examine the Applicant on his affidavits.

The principal replying affidavit to the Section 50 application is sworn by Detective Constable Clive Robinson of the London Metropolitan Police. He was assigned to the Anti-Terrorist Branch of that force and on the 6th March 1995 was appointed as the exhibits officer of the investigation into the matters the subject of the application for extradition. He was cross examined. He made it clear that at the time of the offences he was not involved in the investigation. He subsequently became involved as a result of taking over the position of the exhibits officer who is in control of all of the forensic exhibits in respect of the offences alleged.

In respect of the conspiracy to murder Sir Charles Tidbury and other persons he expressed his belief under oath that there was a conspiracy to murder which created a collective danger to the lives and physical integrity of persons, that it affected civilians and generally persons foreign to any political motives behind it and that cruel and vicious means were to be used. He made a like assertion of belief under oath concerning the conspiracy to cause explosions charges and was cross examined in respect of these assertions of belief.

His affidavit went on to allege that the Applicant and McCauley were members of an active I.R.A. service unit which was intent upon the murder of Sir Charles Tidbury and more than twenty other persons by using under car booby trap bombs and guns to kill them and by causing explosions designed to result in both the indiscriminate loss and endangerment of life and serious injury to property. He says that between January 1990 and October 1990 the Applicant, McCauley and others were variously involved in obtaining and using false identities, obtaining addresses in London, acquiring various vehicles which he listed, preparing lists of those to be murdered and conducting research into them and acquiring, storing and preparing in part an arsenal of terrorist equipment for use when required. He exhibits in his affidavit a list of the persons named in the list of those to be murdered—they include two former Secretaries of State for Northern Ireland, a number of Members of Parliament and a substantial number of Military personnel. The Detective Constable averred that the great majority of the persons on the list had retired by 1990 and that details of their families were included in some instances as were photographs of others. The details recorded about Sir Charles Tidbury included his addresses in Hampshire and London; his telephone number in London; his membership of British United Industrialists and the registration number of two cars. The cars, in fact, belonged to two neighbours of Sir Charles and must have been noted during surveillance of his address. Insofar as James Prior, a former Northern Ireland Secretary is concerned, the details concerning him included the fact that he was a cricket fan who attended cricket matches at grounds open to the public. He says that the Applicant and McCauley took part in the research into those who were to be murdered. This included the use of a 1979 edition of "Who's Who" which contained details of addresses that were deleted from subsequent editions. There was also a 1990 edition of the same book. The Applicant's fingerprints were found on the original list of those to be murdered and numerous pages of the 1979 copy of "Who's Who."

The arsenal of terrorist equipment which was acquired, stored and prepared in part included 54.4 kilograms of semtex high explosive; 8 electric detonators; 6 plain detonators; 4.6 meters of detonating cord. There were also the containers and control units for 5 under car booby trap bombs activated by mercury tilt switches with magnets attached for securing to the under side of cars. There were eight time and power units giving a delay period before activation of up to 60 minutes. Eight more time and power units gave a delay period before activation of about 12 hours. There was also radio control equipment for the detonation of a bomb from a substantial distance. Some of the high explosive was used to make a very large bomb which was hidden in a rucksack. That contained, packed and ready for detonation, over 22 kilograms of semtex high explosive. He says that when detonated it would have caused substantial and indiscriminate loss of life as well as serious injury to property. The 5 under car booby trap bombs were each designed to be loaded with about 1 kilogram of semtex high explosive. One of the bombs was so loaded, ready (with the addition of a detonator) for use. He says that the nature and size of the 5 bombs was such that when detonated they would have been likely to cause loss of life to anyone who happened to be in the relevant car or in its vicinity. In all, therefore, he says there was sufficient explosive equipment for at least one very large bomb, 5 under car booby trap bombs, 1 radio controlled bomb, and 7 other bombs. All of these bombs, he says, would have been capable of causing indiscriminate loss of life as well as causing serious injury to property. With extra detonators, it would have been possible to make more bombs of the same type.

There was also found a Kalashnikov semi-automatic rifle and a repeating shotgun. There was a Browning 9 mm self-loading pistol, a Vzor 7.65 mm self-loading pistol, a Webley revolver, a .38 Taurus revolver and abundant ammunition for use in all these firearms. These firearms were each of a type capable of causing indiscriminate injury. The arsenal was stored at two addresses where the Applicant and McCauley were living in London.

Objection was taken to the remainder of Detective Constable Robinson's evidence concerning the two offences in Judge Verney's warrants on the basis that it was hearsay. Indeed in cross examination the Detective Constable conceded that the material contained in paragraphs 12 to 15 of his affidavit was either second hand or third hand. Such being the case it is, in accordance with the rules of evidence, not admissible and that much was effectively conceded by counsel for the State authorities. In the course of cross examination however counsel for the Applicant accepted that there was no dispute concerning what was sworn to at paragraph 13 of the affidavit. That was to the effect that on the 2nd October 1990 the Applicant and Pearse McCauley were arrested whilst they were in a car parked at the Stonehenge monument in Wiltshire. The Applicant was in possession of false identification papers in the name of Paul Barnes and of keys for two premises where the arsenal already described was stored. The Applicant gave the false name of Connolly and was in possession of a driving licence in the name of Gregory O'Goan. Both the Applicant and McCauley declined to answer questions during subsequent interviews.

Turning then to the escape, the Detective Constable expressed his belief that it involved the taking of a hostage, created a collective danger to the lives and physical integrity of persons and that it affected civilians and generally persons foreign to any political motives behind it. He also expressed the belief that cruel and vicious means were used. He further expressed the belief that there was a malicious wounding of Malcolm Hugh David Kemp with intent to do him grievous bodily harm which created a collective danger to the lives and physical integrity of persons and that it affected civilians and generally persons foreign to any political motives behind it and that cruel and vicious means were used. Insofar as he attempted to describe what occurred on the morning of the escape again objection was taken to this part of the Detective Constable's evidence. It was said, with justification, that this evidence was also hearsay and consequently I decline to take into account paragraphs 18 to 21 of the Detective Constable's evidence. The Applicant did however adduce evidence himself through means of television reports of what went on on the occasion in question which included an interview with the injured party, Mr. Kemp. Whilst the object of this exercise was to adduce evidence of extensive and allegedly prejudicial media coverage of the escape which is the subject of the judicial review application, it was agreed between the parties that the evidence in one application would be admissible in the other. Consequently there is evidence before the court adduced by the Applicant himself demonstrating what occurred on the morning in question. I will summarise that evidence.

On Sunday the 7th July 1991 the Applicant was detained at Her Majesty's Prison at Brixton in London. Following attendance at Mass, the Applicant and Pearse McCauley effected their escape from that prison. They did so by the use of violence and a pistol. In the course of the escape the gun was held to the head of a prison officer and he was used as a hostage. It was also discharged at another prison officer. Having escaped from the confines of the prison to Brixton Hill, the Applicant hijacked a car being driven by a passerby, a Mr. Kemp accompanied by his wife. It is alleged that the Plaintiff discharged the firearm into Mr. Kemp's right thigh, causing him to bleed extensively and to require emergency treatment in hospital. This summarises the evidence in respect of the warrants the subject of the Order of the District Court.

POLITICAL OFFENCE

The first issue made by the Applicant is that the offences to which the four warrants relate were political offences or were offences connected with the political offence.

Section 11 of the Extradition Act, 1965 provides:-

"(1)Extradition shall not be granted for an offence which is a political offence or an offence connected with a political offence."

Section 50 of that Act in so far as it is material provides:—

"(1) A person arrested under this Part shall be released if the High Court or the Minister so directs in accordance with this section.

(2) A direction under this section may be given by the High Court where the Court is of opinion that—

(a) the offence to which the warrant relates is

(i) a political offence or an offence connected with a political offence."

These statutory provisions must now of course be read in the light of the Extradition (European Convention on the Suppression of Terrorism) Act, 1987 in so far as it may be relevant. That Act provides at section 3 that certain offences shall not be regarded as a political offence or an offence connected with a political offence for the purposes inter alia of Part III of the Act of 1965, with which I am concerned. Sections 3 and 4 of the 1987 Act provide for the offences which are not to be regarded as political offences. I will have to consider these statutory provisions when dealing with the offences alleged in the warrants issued by Mr. Bartle.

The offences recited in Judge Verney's warrants are both conspiracy charges. The Applicant contends that the provisions of the 1987 Act must be construed strictly and that the offence of conspiracy is not captured thereunder. Counsel on behalf of the State authorities does not contest that proposition. It was not until the passage of the Extradition (Amendment) Act, 1994 that the offence of conspiracy was brought within the purview of the 1987 Act. As all four warrants in suit in the present case were issued prior to the 5th April, 1994 the 1994 legislation has no application (see section 1(3)(b) of the 1994 Act).

It follows therefore that whatever may be said as to the applicability of the 1987 Act to the offences dealt with in Mr. Bartle's warrants that Act has no application to the offences dealt with in Judge Verney's warrants. The question of whether those offences fall within the political offence exception must therefore be determined in accordance with law excluding the provisions of the 1987 Act.

POLITICAL OFFENCES OUTSIDE THE SCOPE OF THE 1987 ACT

In *Shannon v. Fanning* [1984] I.R. 569 at 579–580 O'Higgins C.J. said:—

"Section 50 of the Extradition Act, 1965, deals with what has come to be known as "the political exception." It empowers the High Court to release a person arrested under its provisions, where the court is of opinion that the offence to which the warrant relates is a political offence or an offence connected with a political offence. Apart from the exclusion in s.3 from the scope of "political offence" of the taking or attempted taking of the life of a Head of State or a member of his family, the Act does not indicate or define what is meant by the expression. In my view it follows that what constitutes a political offence falls to be determined in each case having regard to the act done and the facts and circumstances which surround its commission—the onus being on the person claiming the political exception to establish that the offence, to which the warrant relates, comes within its protection.

It has been submitted in argument on behalf of the plaintiff that the expression should be interpreted in accordance with what has been termed the "political incidence theory," as favoured in British Courts. This is theory or view which found expression in a number of English cases dating from In Re Castioni [1891] 1Q.B. 149 up to recent times and it merely requires that an offence, to be recognised as a political offence, be committed during and as part of a political disturbance. The argument was that, as the political incidence theory represented the prevailing judicial view in Great Britain at the time of the passing of the Act of 1965, and as that Act was intended to be reciprocal with British legislation of the same year, the Oireachtas must be taken to have intended that the term "political offence" would be interpreted in our Courts in the same way as it had always been interpreted in British courts. I do not accept this argument. It seems to me that if such were the intention of the Oireachtas, it would have been a simple matter to specify this intention in words indicating that the term "political offence" should apply to acts done or committed as part of a political disturbance or incident. The Oireachtas, of course, did no such thing. It left the matter open for the opinion of the Courts, thus indicating, in my view, a clear intention that what constitutes a political offence is to be decided on the particular facts and circumstances of each case, viewed in the light of the standards and values which obtain in this country at the particular time."

That statement seems to me to dispose of the argument which was sought to be made concerning where the onus of proof lay in this case. Any doubt which might exist concerning this topic is, it seems to me, finally disposed of by the views of Walsh J. who gave the leading judgment in the Supreme Court in *Maguire v. Keane* [1986] I.L.R.M. 235. He said (at page 237):—

"[t]he burden of proof of establishing political motivation lies upon the plaintiff. The state of the evidence as it was before the learned High Court judge and which contained the contradictions and the omissions which I have set out above could not in law be regarded as acceptably discharging the necessary burden of proof even though the learned trial judge was 'inclined to hold that the applicant had persuaded' him that the crime was for the Provisional I.R.A. organisation."

It follows that the Applicant must satisfy me that the offences in question were political offences or ones connected with a political offence.

The Act of 1965 does not define the term "political offence." This Court must form an opinion on the facts of this case so as to determine whether these offences can properly be so described. Assistance is of course to be gained from the existing jurisprudence on the topic.

In *McGlinchey v. Wren* [1982] I.R. 154 O'Higgins C.J. said (at page 159):—

"The judicial authorities on the scope of such offences have been rendered obsolete in many respects by the fact that modern terrorist violence, whether undertaken by military or para-military organisations, or by individuals or groups of individuals, is often the antithesis of what could reasonably be regarded as political, either in itself or in its connections. All that can be said with authority in this case is that, with or without the concession made on behalf of the plaintiff, this offence could not be said to be either a political offence or an offence connected with a political offence. Whether a contrary conclusion would be reached in different circumstances would depend on the particular circumstances and on whether those particular circumstances showed that the person charged was at the relevant time engaged, either directly or indirectly, in what reasonable, civilised people would regard as political activity.

. . .

As has been already indicated, no offence, regardless of who the perpetrator or the victim may be, can be accounted a political offence or an offence connected with a political offence unless there is evidence to show that it arose, directly or indirectly, out of political activity in the sense already indicated in this judg-

ment. No such evidence has been adduced in respect of those three offences. This court is invited to assume that, because of the existence of widespread violence organised by para-military groups in Northern Ireland, any charge which is associated with terrorist activity should be regarded as a charge in respect of a political offence or an offence connected with a political offence. I am not prepared to make any such assumption.

The excusing per se of murder and of offences involving violence, and the infliction of human suffering by, or at the behest of, self ordained arbiters, are the very antitheses of the ordinances of Christianity and civilisation and of the basic requirements of political activity. Under the Act of 1965 the onus of establishing that the offence in question is either a political offence or one connected with a political offence, as a reason for not handing over a person sought on a warrant properly endorsed under Part III, is upon the person who seeks asylum in our jurisdiction. In my view this plaintiff has singularly failed to discharge that onus."

In the McGlinchey case the offence charged was the murder of an elderly woman in Northern Ireland whose house was attacked by a gang of men firing rifles.

In *Finucane v. MacMahon* [1990] 1 I.R. 165 the Applicant had been convicted at Belfast Crown Court of possession of firearms and ammunition with intent to endanger life or property. He was sentenced to 18 years imprisonment. He subsequently escaped in a mass breakout from the Maze Prison on the 25th September, 1983. A prison officer died during the course of that escape. The Applicant was arrested in County Longford on the 25th November, 1987 on foot of 20 warrants for offences arising from the prison escape. A further warrant was issued seeking the Applicant's arrest with a view to him serving the balance of the prison sentence imposed in Northern Ireland.

A divisional High Court (Hamilton P., Gannon and Costello JJ.) refused to order his release. That decision was reversed on appeal. In the course of his judgment Walsh J. said (at 213–4):—

"Putting it briefly, political offences are defined as offences usually, though not necessarily, consisting of violent crime directed at securing a change in the political order. The effect of the adoption of the Council of Europe Convention was to enable derogation from what the Council of Europe in the report accompanying the Convention called 'the traditional principle according to which the refusal to extradite is obligatory in political matters' in respect of certain acts of violence. It is thus clear that the use of violence does not in itself take an act out of the political exemption, but particular forms of violence such as those already indicated will be grounds for abating the political exemption. This will not effect any change in the distinction between pure political offences and relative political offences, as defined by O'Dalaigh C.J. in Bourke v. Attorney General *[1972] I.R. 36.*

The Extradition Act, 1965, was modelled upon the provisions of the European Convention on Extradition and follows it closely. Article 3 of the Convention prohibited extradition in respect of offences which were regarded by the requested party as political offences or offences connected with political offences. Article 26 enabled parties to make reservations in respect of article 3 but the Government of Ireland made no such reservation either in respect of events in Northern Ireland or elsewhere: and in the subsequent legislation based upon the Convention, namely, the Act of 1965, no such qualification was made. In our domestic law we do not recognise the existence of political exemption to offences committed within the State and triable within the State in respect of offences which are politically motivated. However, the legislative provision for the political exemption does apply in respect of those parts of the national territory which are not within the State, as well as to places outside of Ireland, subject to the qualifications to be found in the legislative provisions already referred to and to others not referred and not relevant to the present case.

It is quite clear that in international law indiscriminative attacks or killing of the civilian population is contrary to the laws of war and can be classed as crimes against humanity even if they have a political objective and are also acts of terrorism whether committed by a state or by those seeking to overthrow a state."

In the portion of his judgment from which I have just quoted Walsh J. makes it clear that violence does not of itself take an act from the political exemption but that particular forms of violence can be grounds for abating the political exemption.

In the present case the first of Judge Verney's warrants alleges conspiracy to murder Sir Charles Tidbury and more than 20 other persons. The method which it is alleged would be used was by placing booby trap bombs under cars and the use of guns. Whilst the lists of persons whom it is alleged were to be murdered include two former secretaries for state for Northern Ireland, a number of members of Parliament and a substantial number of military personnel, there were other persons who did not appear to have any involvement directly or indirectly in political activity. In any event the great majority of the persons on the list regardless of occupation had retired by 1990. Use in particular of the booby trap car bomb must inevitably run a high risk of causing loss of life or serious injury to passers-by with no involvement whatsoever with politics past or present. Bitter experience shows that the use of the booby trap bomb involves indiscriminate death and serious injury to those who are unfortunate enough to be present when it is detonated.

Insofar as the second charge is concerned, it appears to me that, given the arsenal of terrorist equipment including in excess of 50 kg of semtex high explosive, there must likewise be a high probability that use of such weaponry would give rise to loss of life and injury to persons unconnected or associated with politics or military matters. There was therefore in these circumstances a potential loss of civilian lives which in my view denies the applicant a right to avail himself of the political exception as specified under Section 50 of the Act. These activities do not appear to me to fall within what could on any reasonable view be regarded as *"political, either in itself or its connections"* (per O'Higgins C.J. in *McGlinchey v. Wren*). In fact such activities are the antithesis of the *"ordinances of Christianity and civilisation and of the basic requirements of political activity"* (*per* O'Higgins C.J. in *McGlinchey v. Wren*). The booby trap bomb and semtex high explosives do not discriminate as to who they kill or maim when set off. Their use or potential use would constitute *"indiscriminate attacks"* on civilians and would be *"crimes against humanity even if they have a political objective and are also acts of terrorism whether committed by a state or by those seeking to overthrow a state"* (*per* Walsh J. in *Finucane v. McMahon*)

I therefore conclude that the offences charged in Judge Verney's warrent, having regard to the facts of this case, do not fall within the political exception and the Applicant's claim in this regard therefore fails.

THE EXTRADITION (EUROPEAN CONVENTION ON THE SUPPRESSION OF TERRORISM) ACT, 1987

The Respondents contend that the offences specified in Mr. Bartle's warrants fall within the scope of this Act and therefore cannot be regarded as political offences or offences connected with a political offense. The 1987 Act had as its object the giving effect to the European Convention on the Suppression of Terrorism and the amending and extension of the Extradition Act, 1965. The Act applies, except where otherwise provided, in relation to an offence whether committed or alleged to have been committed before or after the passing of the Act (see section 1(4)).

Section 3(1) provides that for the purposes mentioned in section 3(2):—

"(a) no offence to which this section applies and of which a person is accused or has been convicted outside the State shall be regarded as a political offence or as an offence connected with a political offence, and

(b) no proceedings outside the State in respect of an offence to which this section applies shall be regarded as a criminal matter of a political character."

Subsection 2 of section 3, insofar as it is relevant, provides:—

"The purposes referred to in subsection (1) are—

. . .

(b) the purposes of Part III of the Act of 1965 in relation to any warrant for the arrest of a person issued after the commencement of this Act in a place in relation to which that Part applies;"

Subsection 3 of section 3, insofar as it is relevant, provides:—

"(a) This section applies to—

> *(iv) an offence involving kidnapping, the taking of a hostage or serious false imprisonment.*
>
> *(v) an offence involving the use of an explosive or an automatic firearm, if such use endangers persons. . .".*

The term "an offence involving" is defined in relation to kidnapping, the taking of a hostage or serious false imprisonment, as including any offence committed in the course thereof or in conjunction therewith. The term "serious false imprisonment" is defined as meaning any false imprisonment involving danger, or prolonged or substantial hardship or inconvenience, for the person detained.

Section 4, insofar as it is relevant, provides as follows:—

"4(1)(a) For the purposes mentioned in paragraphs (a) and (b) of section 3(2), an offence to which this section applies and of which a person is accused or has been convicted outside the State shall not be regarded as a political offence or as an offence connected with a political offence if the court or the Minister, as the case may be, having taken into due consideration any particularly serious aspects of the offence, including—

(i)   that it created a collective danger to the life, physical integrity or liberty of persons,

(ii)   that it affected persons foreign to the motives behind it, or

(iii) that cruel or vicious means were used in the commission of the offence, is of opinion that the offence cannot properly be regarded as a political offence or as an offence connected with a political offence.

. . .

(2)(a) This section applies to—

(i)   any serious offence (other than an offence to which section 3 applies) of which a person is accused or has been convicted outside the State—

> *(I)   involving an act of violence against the life, physical integrity or liberty of a person, or*
>
> *(II)   involving an act against property if the act created a collective danger for persons*

and

(ii)   any offence of attempting to commit any of the foregoing offences."

The term "serious offence" is defined in section 1 of the 1987 Act as follows:—

"an offence which, if the act constituting the offence took place in the State, would be an offence for which a person aged 21 years or over, of full capacity and not previously convicted may be punished by imprisonment for a term of 5 years or by a more severe penalty."

It is appropriate here to outline the admissible evidence which was given before me concerning these two offences in slightly more detail than the summary which I gave earlier in this judgment. This evidence can be gleaned from the Applicant's own affidavit, the replying affidavits, the cross examination of the witnesses and the evidence submitted by the Applicant in the form of both affidavits and exhibits including the television interview with the injured party Mr. Kemp.

On 7th July, 1991, the Applicant was in custody at Brixton Prison. He along with Pearse McCauley was escorted to Mass in a church at the prison. After Mass they were being escorted back to their wing by four prison officers. McCauley produced a 6.35 mm self-loading pistol which had been hidden inside the trainers that he was wearing. He ran towards the kitchen door where he held the gun close to the head of an auxiliary officer. He then approached Prison Officer Pickford and fired a single shot at him which missed. He then held the gun at Prison Officer Pickford's head and took him hostage. A Prison Officer Eves, arrived at the scene. McCauley pointed the gun at him and fired. As a consequence the bullet tore Mr. Eves' trousers. McCauley then took Prison Officer Pickford's keys and fired a shot in the direction of 'A' wing. The Applicant then used the keys to open the door and both the Applicant and McCauley took Prison Officer Pickford to the outside wall and opened another gate with the keys. They then forced Prison Officer Pickford to climb up onto kennels which were adjacent to the wall and then escaped.

The Applicant and McCauley ran a short distance from the prison. They used a prison officer's car to effect their escape. They later abandoned that. They then hijacked a vehicle belonging to Mr. Kemp and his wife. The car was being driven on the public road by Mr. Kemp accompanied by his wife. The Applicant pointed the gun at the front of Mr. Kemp's car and without further warning pointed the gun at his legs and fired. The bullet passed through Mr. Kemp's right thigh causing a wound which bled extensively and which required emergency treatment in hospital. The Applicant and McCauley thus made good their escape.

The offence of escaping involved the taking of a hostage and serious false imprisonment of the prison officer. This clearly involved danger to that officer who had a gun held to his head. I am satisfied on the basis of the evidence that the escape from Brixton Prison did involve particularly serious aspects. They included the creation of a collective danger to the life, physical integrity and liberty of persons, namely the prison officers or indeed anybody else who got in the way of the Applicant and his accomplice. I am also satisfied that vicious means were used in the commission of the offence. The offence cannot in my view properly be regarded as a political offence or as an offence connected with a political offence. Insofar as it may be said that it was connected with the offences dealt with in Judge Verney's warrants I have already held that they do not constitute political offences or offences connected with political offences. If I am wrong in that view concerning the offences in Judge Verney's warrants and they can legitimately be regarded as political offences then I am satisfied that there is an insufficient causal and factual relationship between those offences and the offence involving the escape from Brixton Prison.

I am satisfied that the offence of escaping from Brixton Prison is captured under section 4 of the 1987 Act. There is no doubt but that the offence of escaping from lawful custody is a serious offence within the statutory definition. The giving effect to this offence involved an act of violence against the life, physical integrity and liberty of the prison officers. It therefore is captured by the provisions of section 4 and cannot in my opinion be regarded as a political offence or an offence connected with a political offence.

The wounding of the unfortunate Mr. Kemp was of course an arbitrary act of violence against a civilian simply going about his lawful business with his wife. In my opinion this offence is likewise within the scope of section 4 of the 1987 Act. It created a collective danger to the life, physical integrity or liberty of persons. Those persons were in particular Mr. Kemp and his wife but also any other person who happened to get in the way of the Applicant and his accomplice. The Kemps were people who were entirely innocent bystanders. The activity of the Applicant clearly affected them and they were entirely foreign to the motives allegedly behind the Applicant. There can be little doubt but that the act was one of considerable cruelty and viciousness. This offence cannot properly be regarded as a political offence or as an offence connected with a political offence.

The provisions of section 4 apply and the political offence exception cannot therefore apply.

Indeed even before the coming into effect of the 1987 Act this offence would not in my view have been regarded as a political offence or one connected therewith. In this regard the views of McCarthy J. in *Shannon v. Fanning* [1984] I.R. 569 at 598 are relevant. He said:-

> *"The argument made on [the Applicant's] behalf involves the proposition that, however revolting the circumstances of a particular crime may be, if the ultimate aim of the criminal, however remote it be from the crime, be truly political, then it is a political offence. I reject such a proposition; on the same basis it could be argued that the murder of a young woman shot down on the public street may be categorised as a political offence because her murder might deter her father, a Belfast Magistrate, from carrying out his duties as such. The mind rebels against such a view."*

The mind equally rebels against the view that what was done to Mr. Kemp could be regarded as a political offence or an offence connected therewith. Even if the offences in Judge Verney's warrants are, contrary to my view, political offences, this offence is neither factually or causally related to them to be treated as an offence connected therewith.

In my view, therefore, the Applicant's claim to the political offence exception in respect of all of these offences fails. I now turn to consider the next submission made on his behalf.

*   *   *   *   *

PUBLICITY

This aspect of the matter falls to be considered both under the application for release under section 50 of the Extradition Act and in the context of the separate judicial review proceedings which were brought by the Applicant but which were tried at the same time.

In essence it is suggested that if the Applicant were to be extradited he would not be able to obtain a fair trial on account of the massive and sustained prejudicial publicity which has been generated in England.

There can be no doubt but that there was huge publicity given to *inter alia* the Applicant's arrest at Stonehenge in October 1990, his charging and Court appearances thereafter, the Brixton escape which took place in July 1991 and the report of Judge Tumin, Her Majesty's Inspector of Prisons, into that escape. Subsequently, between August and November, 1991, there were reports concerning a prison officer who was allegedly working for the Special Branch and who was involved in the escape. There were also television programmes dealing with all of these topics. There was then coverage in January and February, 1992, of the trial of the Applicant's co-accused. He was acquitted and that in turn achieved publicity.

In April, 1993, there was extensive coverage of the Applicant's arrest in Ireland. There was also coverage of the bail applications and trials which followed. There was then speculation in the press in 1994 and 1995 concerning the possible early release and other developments. There was coverage in November and December of 1995 of the Applicant's release and re-arrest. This coverage was not confined to the print media but there was extensive radio and television coverage also and all of these have been deposed to in affidavits and many of the press reports have been exhibited. In addition in the course of the hearing I also viewed a video tape concerning much of this material.

The publicity was universally antipathetic to the Applicant. It would not be feasible to reproduce it here in any extensive fashion since to do so would make an already long judgment unwieldy. However, it can be said that many of the press reports carried headlines which referred to the Applicant as one of "an I.R.A. pair," "I.R.A. escapers," "provos" and even "mad dogs." Posters which were issued by the police showed the Applicant and McCauley under the heading "terrorism—wanted for escaping from Brixton Prison."

In the light of this extensive and sustained prejudicial publicity the Applicant says that it would now be impossible to find a jury in England whose views had not been coloured or influenced by such publicity thereby rendering a fair trial impossible. This publicity he believes assumed and asserted that he was guilty of the charges which had been made against him and upon which he is now sought to be rendered to the United Kingdom authorities. He says that the amount of prejudicial publicity has been so great and damaging and has continued over such a long period of time that it is not capable of being countered by a charge from a trial judge and there is, therefore, a grave risk of a breach of his rights under the Constitution and in particular his right to a fair trial. Indeed in the judicial review application it is asserted that even at the time of the Applicant's initial arrest in October, 1990, there was such extreme and prejudicial publicity concerning him that the then Attorney General in England wrote to the media seeking to restrain the publication of such material lest it might prejudice criminal proceedings against the Applicant.

In pressing this part of his case the Applicant relied heavily upon the judgment of Flood J. in *Magee v. O'Dea* [1994] 1 I.R. 500 at 510–512. There Flood J. in dealing with the question of a fair trial free from bias said as follows:—

> *"The third issue is whether the plaintiff, if required to stand his trial in England, would obtain a fair trial, having regard to the quality and extent of the media publicity which followed the said event and which clearly and unequivocally related to him.*
>
> *In considering the publicity, the standard of proof is laid down by the Supreme Court in* D. v. The Director of Public Prosecutions *[1994] I.L.R.M. 435. That standard is that the court should require that it should be shown that there is a real or serious risk that the trial would be unfair if it were allowed to proceed. That standard is more fully articulated in the judgment of Finlay C. J. at p.436 where he says:—*
>
> *'I am satisfied that, firstly, the right of an individual to a fair trial is of fundamental constitutional importance. Secondly, it is clear that the unfairness which it is suggested would occur in this case would consist of an undisclosed recollection by one or more members of the jury of the material contained in the newspaper; an association of that recollection with the trial before that person and the undisclosed influence upon the mind of that person in regard to the question of guilt or innocence. Such a form of unfairness could not by reason of its nature be subsequently established or corrected either on appeal or by a quashing of the conviction.*
>
> *The fundamental nature of the constitutional right involved and of the incapacity of the court further to intervene to defend it leads, in my view, to the conclusion that the standard of proof which the court should require from the applicant in this case concerning his allegation of the likelihood of an unfair*

trial is that he should be required to establish that there is a real or serious risk of that occurring. Such an approach is consistent with the view taken by this Court in the different context of extradition proceedings in the case of Finnucane v. McMahon *[1990] 1 I.R. 165.'*

Further and later in his judgment at p.437 he goes on to say with regard to the actual publication:—

> *'. . . it is, I think, important to point out its particularly lurid features, the simplicity of identification between it and the actual trial to which the applicant would have been subjected and the number of matters extraneous to any issue arising in that trial which are contained in the article, and all of which would be highly prejudicial.'*

In reviewing the evidence I also have to take into account the views expressed in trenchant form by Denham J. in the same case where at p.442 she says:—

> *'A court must give some consideration to the community's right to have this alleged crime prosecuted in the usual way. However, on the hierarchy of constitutional rights there is no doubt that the applicant's right to fair procedures is superior to the community's right to prosecute.*

If there was a real risk that the accused would not receive a fair trial then there would be no question of the accused's right to a fair trial being balanced detrimentally against the community's right to have the alleged crimes prosecuted.'

The facts underlying this aspect of the matter are that the murder of Sergeant Newman received extensive coverage in the local and national press in England in particular in The Daily Express, The Daily Mail and The Star. The combined circulation of these papers in England would certainly exceed some five million copies."

Flood J. then considered the prejudicial aspect of the newspaper coverage. He then went on to say (at 512):—

"In considering the foregoing evidence which in my opinion is undoubtedly prejudicial one must bear in mind that these headlines and pictures were published in April, 1992, almost two years ago and there must be an element of 'fade' in public recollection of the public from which potential jurors would be drawn.

It must also be borne in mind that there were published with the foregoing headlines, photographs of the plaintiff which effectively accused him as the person who was the cold-blooded murderer of the army sergeant in Derby.

In addition to the 'fade factor' the court must be alive to the fact that a trial judge in England would no doubt strongly and properly charge a jury in a manner which would indicate to them their obligation to try the issues before them only on the evidence adduced and to ignore sensational newspaper articles.

From the plaintiff's point of view there is the very definite photographic identification of him as the murderer. This is a case in which identity must have a major role and certainly the defence would be embarrassed in cross examination by the existence of these photographs or more particularly the captions underlying or noted with the photographs in question.

The question which this court has to address is as the Chief Justice phrased it, the risk of 'an undisclosed recollection by one or more members of the jury of the material contained in the newspaper; an association of that recollection with the trial before that person, and an undisclosed influence upon the mind of that person in regard to the question of guilt or innocence. Such a form of unfairness could not by reason of its nature be subsequently established or corrected either on appeal or by a quashing of the conviction.'

As this is a fundamental constitutional right—the right to a fair trial and to fair procedures—strict construction is the appropriate form of construction to be applied by this court. The onus of proof is one of probability of a serious risk of an unfair trial. The point in time at which this risk is to be considered to exist is now—when the plaintiff on extradition would leave the protection of this court.

I have carefully considered the weight to be given to the lurid and sensational newspaper coverage, the existence of the photograph in the said newspaper and the unvarnished assumption that the person shown in the photograph is guilty of murder, the extent of the newspaper coverage in the national newspaper and the possibility that all or a great part of the foregoing would be rekindled in the mind of a jury trying the plaintiff and I have balanced that against the 'fade factor' and what I accept would be a careful charge by a trial judge to the jury directing them not to permit themselves to be influenced by sensational and lurid newspaper coverage at the time or anything else other than what they hear by way of evidence in the court of trial. In my judgment, on the balance of probabilities, there is a serious risk of the type of unfairness contemplated by the Chief Justice in his said judgment which I have already quoted in D.v. The Director of Public Prosecutions. *[1994] I.L.R.M. 435.*

In the circumstances I would consider that extradition should be refused on this ground also."

There can be little doubt but that the publicity in this case is every bit as lurid if not more so than that which obtained in Magee's case. It was also very extensive and carried on for a long period of time. Much of it was contained in the tabloid press but not by any means all of it.

When looking at this of course I must have regard to the "fade factor" referred to in the judgment of Flood J. Because of the lapse of time many years have passed since this publicity was generated. Furthermore, there is evidence which was placed before me which was not before Flood J. demonstrating the considerable safeguards which exist in English law and practice so as to ensure that the right to a fair trial is preserved. The evidence of Mr. Clive Nicholls Q.C. demonstrates that these take a number of forms. They are:

(a) *Provisions which serve to prevent adverse pre-trial publicity.* This includes a statutory strict liability for publications which create a substantial risk that the course of justice in proceedings in respect of which a warrant has been issued will be seriously impeded or prejudiced. In determining whether a substantial risk was created the courts have regard in enforcing this statutory liability to the imminence of the trial at the time of the publication. Over and above this statutory framework created by the Contempt of Court Act, 1981, there also continues the pre-existing common law of contempt. It is fair to say that these provisions do not appear to have been given effect to in the present case.

(b) *Provisions which serve, once adverse pre-trial publicity exists, to avoid its potentially injurious effect on the trial process.* These fall into three different parts. They are (i) the entitlement to stay proceedings on the grounds of abuse of process; (ii) jury selection; and (iii) the trial judge's directions to be given during the course of the trial and summing up.

Insofar as the first of these is concerned it is open to an accused who alleges that his trial will be unfair because of adverse media publicity to apply to the trial judge for the proceedings to be stayed as an abuse of process. Whilst the jurisdiction is regarded as exceptional and to be used sparingly and only for compelling reasons the fact is that it has been operated in a number of cases of adverse pretrial publicity.

Insofar as jury selection is concerned Mr. Nicholls gave evidence that in certain trials a practice was adopted of providing the jury with a written questionnaire. In cases involving terrorist offences it has been the practice of trial judges to compose a list of appropriate questions and to address them orally to the panel of jurors from which the jury for the case is to be drawn. They are directed *inter alia* to matters which may form the basis of potential bias arising from adverse publicity. In the course of his evidence he gave examples of the sort of questions that are posed to deal with such a risk.

As was recognised by Flood J. judicial directions are given in the course of the trial and in the summing up so as to ensure a fair trial. Just as the Supreme Court here has made clear, it is not to be assumed that jurors would treat such directions lightly or would be incapable of following them. Neither should the ability of a jury to adjudicate solely on the evidence adduced before it be underestimated.

Mr. Nicholls evidence makes it clear that it is open to an accused who alleges that his trial has been rendered unfair by means of adverse publicity either before or during the trial to appeal to the Court of Appeal, Criminal

Division and to have his conviction quashed or to apply for a re-trial. He gave examples of cases where such orders were in fact made.

In the present case, he pointed out that the offences alleged in the warrants include offences in respect of which the Applicant had been committed for trial by a magistrate and stands indicted and offences in respect of which he had not been committed or indicted. If the Applicant is rendered to the United Kingdom authorities he will face committal proceedings before a magistrate and, if committed for trial, be tried in respect of the offences dealt with in Mr. Bartle's warrants. He points out statutory restrictions concerning the reporting of the committal proceedings.

Mr. Nicholls was cross examined by Mr. Forde. I am satisfied on the basis of his evidence that the rights which an accused person has in England and Wales and outlined by him in his evidence are rights of substance which have been enforced by the English Courts in the past. I do not accept that these rights are honoured more in the breach than in the observance or that they pay lip service only to the principles in question. The case law cited by Mr. Nicholls demonstrates the principles being put into action. Indeed it seems to me that the rights in question are broadly similar to the rights which an accused person would have in this jurisdiction.

Finally, it should be noted that notwithstanding the assertions concerning adverse publicity, the Applicant's co-accused was tried and acquitted in respect of the offences dealt with on Judge Verney's warrants.

In these circumstances I have come to the conclusion:
(a) That as years have now passed since the publicity in question, much of its effect would have faded from the minds of any potential jurors.
(b) In any event there are a number of mechanisms available to the Applicant so as to ensure that his right to a fair trial is preserved. These rights are at least as extensive as the rights which exist in this jurisdiction in respect of a forthcoming trial.
(c) His co-accused was in fact acquitted notwithstanding the publicity.
(d) As a matter of probability there is not a real or serious risk of the Applicant not getting a fair trial.

I have therefore come to the conclusion that the Applicant has failed to make out under this heading either exceptional circumstances or circumstances which would render it unjust, oppressive or invidious to deliver him up.

Furthermore, I am satisfied that he is not entitled to the relief claimed in the judicial review proceedings which I have already outlined.

THE GOOD FRIDAY AGREEMENT

The next part of the case which is made by the Applicant relates to an agreement reached in multi-party negotiations at Belfast on 10th April, 1998 (Good

Friday) concerning the situation in Northern Ireland. In that agreement there is a section entitled "Prisoners." It makes provision:

> *"1) . . . for an accelerated programme for the release of prisoners, including transferred prisoners, convicted of scheduled offences in Northern Ireland or, in the case of those sentenced outside Northern Ireland, similar offences (referred to hereafter as qualifying prisoners)."*

The agreement provides for a review process to advance or accelerate the release dates of prisoners who qualify for consideration under the scheme. Such prisoners are those convicted of scheduled offences or their equivalent. The section goes on to provide that:

> *"3) . . . [i] In addition, the intention would be that should the circumstances allow it, any qualifying prisoners who remained in custody two years after the commencement of the scheme would be released at that point."*

The Applicant contends that the offences in respect of which it is sought to extradite him are "similar offences" to scheduled offences and the Plaintiff if convicted of them would be "a qualifying prisoner" under the terms of the agreement.

The evidence is that all qualifying prisoners who formerly resided in the State and who were convicted in England and Wales have been transferred to prisons in the State. Many have availed themselves of the provisions of the appropriate legislation which gave effect to this agreement. That is the Criminal Justice (Release of Prisoners) Act, 1998.

Evidence has been given of a substantial number of prisoners convicted of serious offences in England and Wales who have now been released under the accelerated release scheme contemplated in this Act.

It is said that if the Plaintiff were extradited to England and convicted of the charges against him he would be entitled to apply for transfer to this State. He would expect to be so transferred in accordance with the practice developed in relation to qualifying prisoners. On transfer to the State the question of accelerated release for the Plaintiff would fall to be considered under the statutory provisions. It is for the Minister for Justice, Equality and Law Reform to designate him as a "qualifying prisoner." It is said that the Minister has already accepted the Plaintiff as the equivalent of a qualifying prisoner because he granted him early release from imprisonment in 1995, after he had served just over two years of the four year sentence imposed in October, 1993, by the Special Criminal Court. It is further said that all qualifying prisoners who have not been released under this scheme will be released on or about 13th July 2000. If, therefore, the Applicant is extradited and convicted of the offences for which his extradition has been ordered, he will as a matter of probability be transferred back to the State and would be released on 13th July of this year if not before then. Accordingly, it is said that it is now a fruitless exercise to extradite the Applicant.

It is said on behalf of the authorities that it cannot be anticipated in advance what decision the Minister might make in any particular case or what advice he might receive from the Release of Prisoners Commission. It is for the Minister to specify in any particular case whether a prisoner is to be identified as a "qualifying prisoner" or not. It is submitted that it would not be a fruitless exercise to extradite the Applicant in respect of the offences for which his extradition has been ordered. The person who swore to this latter piece of evidence is Mr. John Kenny, an acting Principal Officer in the Department of Justice, Equality and Law Reform. He was cross examined on his affidavit. The following exchange took place between him and counsel who cross examined him.

> *"Question 117*
>
> *Can I suggest to you then, Mr. Kenny, that it follows from that, that if the Government's belief as to what will happen in all probability with this agreement is correct and if the Plaintiff is extradited and convicted and transferred back to this jurisdiction, isn't it probable that he will be released two years after the commencement of the scheme for the release of prisoners?*
>
> *Answer*
>
> *You are asking me to make a judgment into the future, which I cannot do because I do not know the circumstances which will apply at a future date. I have said quite clearly in my affidavit that I cannot make a statement about a decision the Minister might make in the future in unknown circumstances. If the series of hypotheses you have made come true, if the Plaintiff is extradited, if he is convicted, if he does not appeal or if the appeal is unsuccessful, if he seeks a transfer to this jurisdiction, if the Home Secretary consents to that, if the Minister agrees, if he subsequently transfers, if the Minister considers him to be a qualifying prisoner at that time and if he gets advice from the Release of Prisoners Commission, he may then make a decision. That is a lot of 'ifs' in my view and perhaps too many 'ifs' to say it is probable. It certainly is possible, but probable is too strong a word for me with that number of 'ifs' at this point and time."*

Later in the cross examination these various "ifs" were explored further in order to demonstrate the probability of transfer and release in the event of rendition, trial and conviction for the offences in suit.

For reasons which I will advance in a moment, it does not appear to me to matter much whether the course suggested by the Applicant is a possibility or a probability. First, it is to be noted that the benefits of this agreement are applicable only to convicted persons. Conviction is a prerequisite to the operation of the scheme. It does not seem to me that the scheme attempts to interfere with or dilute the notion that persons accused of offences should be tried for them. Neither does the scheme attempt to interfere in any way with the rendition of persons in respect of whom an extradition request has been made under Part III of the 1965 Act. It would not be appropriate for this court to extend the terms of the 1998 Act and the scheme in effect to persons awaiting trial. The 1998 Act does not provide for this and it should not be expanded so to do by the court.

Even if the benefits of this scheme are applicable and available to the Applicant in the manner suggested, that does not appear to me to be a good reason for refusing rendition. The entitlement of the requesting State to have a person accused of serious criminal offences tried is a benefit which is not to be measured in the context of an application for rendition. If, as a result of arrangements made by the requesting State, the penalty imposed by the courts of that State (if a conviction is recorded) will be foreshortened, is not a reason for ordering release, thus denying to the requesting State an ability to have a trial in respect of the offences. I do not accept the notion that a release should be ordered because any custodial sentence which might be imposed will be served only in part.

In the course of the testimony of Mr. Kenny it was made clear that releases of transferred prisoners pursuant to this agreement and legislation have all been effected under the 1960 Criminal Justice Act. The effect of this is that the prisoners are released subject to conditions. The conditions are that they keep the peace, be of good behaviour and do not in any way cause distress or annoyance to victims of their crimes. A breach of these conditions leaves them liable to immediate arrest and committal to prison. Given that the release is in these terms and not absolute, it seems to me that it cannot be said that the Applicant's extradition would be futile simply because the custodial sentence to be served by him would be likely to be the subject of an early release.

It was also suggested that it would be unjust, unfair, oppressive and invidious to order the rendition of the Applicant in circumstances where as a matter of likelihood he will be remanded in custody in England to await his trial in circumstances where if he is convicted he will be released shortly thereafter. I do not see how it can be said that that is unjust, oppressive, unfair or invidious to the Applicant given his history. Finally there is in my view nothing in the suggestion that is made to the effect that it would be discriminatory to require him to go through a trial process where it is likely that he will be released shortly after conviction (if such occurs) whilst other persons who have actually been convicted are already released on licence. The Applicant will be dealt with in precisely the same way as the other persons if he is convicted. There is no discrimination as between convicted persons. Persons who have not yet been convicted cannot avail themselves of the terms of the agreement but must proceed to trial.

For the reasons which I have already given, I have therefore come to the conclusion that the Applicant is not entitled to his release and has not demonstrated to me that the conditions of Section 50 (2) (bbb) have been made out.

Insofar as the Court has an inherent jurisdiction over and above the statutory provisions I do not here find any circumstances which would render it improper, oppressive, unfair or otherwise inappropriate that the Applicant should not be rendered up to the appropriate authorities. Neither is there anything present which would warrant an order for the release of the Applicant by reference to his constitutional rights. I therefore refuse the reliefs which were sought both in the Special Summons and in the Judicial Review proceedings. These applications are dismissed.

DOCUMENT NO 19

In Re Devine
In the High Court of Justice in
Northern Ireland
Queen's Bench Division (Crown Side)
[1999] NIEHC 7

March 26, 1999
(Edited Text)

1. The applicant in these proceedings, Josephine Devine, seeks a Judicial Review by way of certiorari of the following decisions:

(a) An order of His Honour Judge Russell, dated 6 September 1996, authorising the appointment of a financial investigator.

(b) A decision of Mr Clery, Learned Resident Magistrate, dated 22 September 1997, convicting the applicant of failing to answer certain questions at interview with the financial investigator.

(c) A decision of His Honour Judge Hart dismissing the applicant's appeal against conviction and increasing the applicant's sentence.

(d) A decision of His Honour Judge Hart, dated 14 May 1998, refusing the applicant's application to set aside or vary the ex parte order obtained before His Honour Judge Russell.

(e) A requirement, dated 12 March 1998, that the applicant should attend for interview by a financial investigator in accordance with the provisions of the Proceeds of Crime (Northern Ireland) Order 1996 ("the 1996 Order").

Background to the proceedings

2. The 1996 Order came into operation on 25 August 1996 by virtue of Article 1(2) thereof. Article 49 of the 1996 Order permits an officer of the Royal Ulster Constabulary, not below the rank of superintendent, to apply to a County Court Judge to authorise "a financial investigator" to participate in an investigation by the RUC as to whether a person has benefited from conduct to which the Order applies or the extent of whereabouts of the proceeds

of any such conduct and, for the purposes of the investigation, to exercise the powers conferred by Schedule 2. In accordance with the provisions of Schedule 2, the investigator may, for the purposes of the investigation, require a person to attend before him to answer questions, fairly specified information or to produce specified documents. Failing to comply with a requirement imposed by an investigator under paragraphs 2 or 3, without reasonable excuse, constitutes a criminal offence contrary to paragraph 5 in respect of which a person is liable to be fined or subject to imprisonment for a term not exceeding 6 months on summary conviction. Paragraph 8(1) of Schedule 2 provides that:

> "The Secretary of State shall made a code of practice in connection with the exercise by financial investigators of the powers conferred by the Schedule."

3. A draft code of practice was prepared and, on 19 June 1997, the draft was circulated amongst various individuals and bodies who were required to submit any relevant comments or representations to the Office of the Secretary of State by 30 July 1997. A final draft was ultimately laid before both Houses of Parliament and came into operation on the day of 19

4. On 30 October 1996 the applicant was arrested by the police and taken to Castlereagh Police Office where she was interviewed between 30 October and 1 November 1996 in relation to allegations of her involvement in financially assisting or retaining finances for a terrorist organisation, namely, the IPLO. It appears that the police had arrested a number of male persons, one of whom was the boyfriend of the applicant, who were suspected of having been involved in carrying out robberies on behalf of that organisation and that the police also suspected that the applicant's bank account had been used as a means of retaining the proceeds of those crimes. The applicant was subsequently released without charge.

5. On 6 December 1996 the RUC made an ex parte application to the Learned Recorder of Belfast, for the authorisation of a financial investigator to assist with the police investigation in accordance with the provisions of Article 49(2) of the 1996 Order. The Learned Recorder duly authorised a person known by the pseudonym of John Armstrong to act as a financial investigator and to exercise the powers conferred by Schedule 2 of the 1996 Order for the purposes of the investigation.

6. On 9 December 1996 the financial investigator issued a requirement in writing in accordance with paragraph 2(1) of Schedule 2 of the 1996 Order requiring the applicant to attend for interview by the investigator at Grosvenor Road Police Station on 17 December 1996. The requirement was served upon the applicant on 12 December 1996 and she duly attended for interview on 17 December accompanied by her solicitor.

7. As a result of the applicant's alleged failure to answer certain questions during the interview by the financial investigator on 17 December 1996 a summons was issued in accordance with paragraph 5(1) of Schedule 2 of the 1996 Order and, on the 22 September 1997, the applicant was convicted at Belfast Magistrates' Court by Mr Clery the Learned Resident Magistrate of an offence contrary to paragraph 5(1) of Schedule 2 and was fined [sterling]750. The applicant appealed against the said conviction and the appeal was heard by the Learned Recorder of Belfast, Judge Hart, on 3 March 1998. The Learned Recorder affirmed the conviction made by the Learned Resident Magistrate but substituted for the [sterling]750 fine a term of one month imprisonment suspended for 12 months.

8. On 12 March 1998 the financial investigator issued a further requirement in accordance with paragraph 2(1) of Schedule 2 of the 1996 Order requiring the applicant to attend for interview at Antrim Road Police Station on 1 April 1998 at 2.30 pm and this requirement was served upon the applicant on 27 March 1998. At 2.40 pm on 1 April 1998 the applicant's solicitors telephoned the financial investigator at Antrim Road Police Station to inform him that the applicant was ill and could not attend the interview. Accordingly, the investigator rearranged the interview with the applicant for 10.00 am on Friday 10 April 1998 at Antrim Road Police Station. The applicant's solicitors were duly notified of this further arrangement but, on 7 April 1998, the applicant's solicitors wrote to the financial investigator informing him that Friday 10 April 1998 was a holy day of obligation upon which most offices would be closed and that it was a most unsuitable day to arrange an interview. The applicant's solicitors suggested 17 April 1998 at 11.00 am as an alternative and this was accepted by the financial investigator. At 11.00 am on 17 April 1998 the applicant, together with her solicitor, attended at Antrim Road Police Station but the financial investigator was informed by the applicant's solicitor that the applicant would not be attending any interview or answering any questions in view of her pending Judicial Review application.

9. On 27 April 1998 the applicant applied to the County Court for an Order setting aside or varying the ex parte authorisation obtained by the police in accordance with Article 49 of the 1996 Order on 6 December 1996. This application was heard by the Learned Recorder of Belfast, His Honour Judge Hart, on 14 May 1998 and was refused.

The challenged decisions

10. The proceedings before this court encompass consolidated applications in which the applicant seeks Judicial Review of the following decisions:

(1) The original authorisation of the financial investigator granted ex parte by the then Recorder of the City of Belfast, His Honour Judge Russell, on 6 December 1996.

(2) If the court sees fit to grant an Order of certiorari quashing the original authorisation of the financial investigator, the applicant submits that Orders of certiorari should also follow in respect of the decision of the Learned Resident Magistrate convicting the applicant on 22 September 1997, the decision of the Learned Recorder of the City Belfast, His Honour Judge Hart, dismissing the applicant's appeal against the said conviction and, the decision of the said Learned Recorder of the City of Belfast, dated 14 May 1998, refusing the application to set aside or vary the ex parte authorisation.

(3) An Order of certiorari quashing the requirement issued by the financial investigator in accordance with paragraph 2(1) of Schedule 2 to the 1996 Order dated 12 March 1998.

The parties' submissions

11. On behalf of the applicant, Mr Lavery QC, who appeared with Mr Treacy, submitted that there were two grounds for setting aside the ex parte authorisation of the financial investigator.

12. In the first place, Mr Lavery QC drew the attention of the court to the fact that when the ex parte authorisation of the financial investigator had been authorised by the then Learned Recorder of the City of Belfast on 6 December 1996, in accordance with Article 49 of the 1996 Order, no code of practice, draft or otherwise, had been made by the Secretary of State in accordance with paragraph 8(1) of Schedule 2 to the Order. Mr Lavery QC argued that the scheme of Schedule 2 to the 1996 Order was to regulate the powers which the financial investigator was authorised to exercise as a result of the ex parte Order and that paragraph 8(1) of Schedule 2 clearly placed the Secretary of State under a mandatory duty to bring into operation a code of practice in connection with those powers. Mr Lavery QC accepted that failure to comply with any provision of such a code of practice would not render the financial investigator liable to criminal or civil proceedings but pointed out that, by virtue of paragraph 8(7) of Schedule 2, the provisions of such a code were to be admissible in evidence in both criminal and civil proceedings and could be taken into account by any court or tribunal in so far as they appeared to be relevant to clear the determination of any question arising in such proceedings. Mr Lavery QC suggested that the provisions of such a code might well be relevant to determining whether or not it was reasonable to fail to answer a question or series of questions during the course of an interview by a duly authorised financial investigator. Mr Lavery QC's basic submission in relation to this aspect of the application was that the original authorisation of the financial investigator was ultra vires the 1996 Order because it could not have been the intention of Parliament that the investigator should be autho-

rised to proceed to exercise the Schedule 2 powers without the guidance of a code of practice.

13. Secondly, Mr Lavery QC argued that the ex parte authorisation of the financial investigator should be quashed as being unfair in so far as the investigator was afforded anonymity by use of a pseudonym. He emphasised that this was not a case in which the investigator was referred to by way of a letter or a number, a practice which would clearly indicate that anonymity was being claimed, but that, at all material times, the applicant and her legal advisers had no reason to doubt that the investigation was being carried out by a person whose real name was John Armstrong. Mr Lavery QC argued that such anonymity deprived the applicant's advisers of the ability to independently test whether the investigator complied with the provisions of Article 49(1) of the 1996 Order, whether there were any grounds for believing that he or she might be biased and was in obvious breach of the important general principle of open justice.

14. Mr Lavery QC attacked the requirement of 12 March 1998 as being unfair in that it appeared to have been issued without any real hope or expectation that a further interview would yield additional or fresh information. He submitted that it was quite clear from the first interview with the applicant that she was not prepared to answer questions which she had already been asked by the police and there was nothing to indicate to the investigator that she might have changed her mind. He further argued that the powers of interview should be exercised promptly and that the delay between December 1996 and April 1998 was indefensible, the only excuse offered namely, awaiting the outcome of the criminal proceedings, was, in his view, inadequate and unreasonable. Mr Lavery QC suggested that such a cause of action left the investigator open to the suspicion that his powers were really being exercised punitively or for the purposes of harassing the applicant.

15. In reply, Mr Bernard McCloskey on behalf of the respondent, submitted that the issue of a code of practice by the Secretary of State in accordance with paragraph 8 of Schedule 2 of the 1996 Order was not an essential prerequisite either to the validity of an authorisation of a financial investigator in accordance with Article 49 or to the subsequent issue of a valid requirement in accordance with paragraph 2 of Schedule 2 of that Order. He further argued that, if Parliament had intended a substantial and significant part of this legislation to remain in abeyance pending the promulgation of a code of practice such an intention would have been expressed in clear and unambiguous statutory language. Mr McCloskey contended that, in essence, the submission made by Mr Lavery QC, would entail a fundamental re-writing of the 1996 Order.

16. Dealing with the applicant's criticism of the use of a pseudonym for the financial investigator, Mr McCloskey submitted that the court should be

cautious before making too close an analogy with the criminal and civil cases dealing with the principle of "open justice." In his view, the financial investigator was in a different position from the witness or party required to give evidence during the course of a public hearing. Mr McCloskey submitted that the procedure adopted during the course of the ex parte application before the then Learned Recorder of the City of Belfast provided sufficient safeguards in the circumstances and that there was sufficient material available to the Learned Recorder to justify the making of the authorisation.

17. In relation to the applicant's argument that the imposition of the second requirement was unfair and an abuse of the financial investigator's powers,

18. Mr McCloskey submitted that there was clear justification for this action. In his submission, it was perfectly reasonable for the investigator to await the outcome of the criminal proceedings which might or might not have effected his approach to the issue of any further requirement. He argued that the provisions of Schedule 2 to the 1996 Order clearly contemplated that the powers might be exercised more than once, from time to time and that it might well be necessary to repeat the questions in the course of doing so. Mr McCloskey suggested that the court should be slow to interfere with the judgment of the specialist financial investigator in the course of carrying out his duties.

Conclusions

1. The statutory code of practice

19. The Northern Ireland Order of 1996 repealed and re-enacted, with certain amendments, the Criminal Justice (Confiscation) (Northern Ireland) Orders of 1990 and 1993 relating to the confiscation of the proceeds of drug trafficking and other serious crime and, in doing so, it produced provisions which were generally equivalent to those contained in the Criminal Justice Act 1993 and the Proceeds of Crime Act 1995 in England and Wales. Articles 4–43 of the 1996 Order contain provisions relating to Confiscation and Restraint Orders while part 3, comprising Articles 44–48, deal with offences in connection with proceeds of criminal conduct including failing to disclose knowledge or suspicion of money laundering, assisting others to retain the benefit of criminal conduct, concealing the proceeds of criminal conduct, acquiring or using such proceeds and "tipping off." The investigative powers which are the subject of these proceedings are contained in Article 49, part 4 of the Order, under the heading "Miscellaneous and Supplemental." In 1996 investigative powers of the type contained in Article 49 were not generally available in the other parts of the UK for use in relation to the proceeds of drug trafficking and other crime. However, similar powers did exist to assist investigations into the resources, funding and proceeds of *terrorism* and were contained in Article 57 and Schedule 5 of the Northern Ireland (Emergency

Provisions) Act 1991. Article 57 of the 1991 Order provided for an application in writing to be made by an RUC officer not below the rank of superintendent to the Secretary of State for the appointment of an investigator who was not a constable and who was named in the application. As in the instant case, the powers of the authorised investigator were contained in Schedule 5 which, inter alia, provides at paragraph 7(1), that the "Secretary of State shall make a code of practice in connection with the exercise by authorised investigators of the powers conferred by this Schedule."

20. Essentially the applicant's argument is that, in the context of a mandatory obligation on the part of the Secretary of State to bring into force a code of practice which, prima facie, is likely to provide some degree of guidance and protection for the interviewee, Parliament cannot have intended that the powers of investigation should be exercised until such a code had been published. It seems clear from the provisions of paragraph 8 of Schedule 2 of the 1996 Order that Parliament envisaged that the code of practice would not come into operation until some time after the Order itself in so far as provision was made for the preparation and publication of a draft, consideration of any representations, the drafting of any appropriate modifications and the laying of the draft before both Houses of Parliament. The 1996 Order as a whole was brought into operation on 25 August 1996 in accordance with the provisions of Article 1(2). It would have been a simple and straightforward matter for Parliament to have provided, by way of a subsequent commencement order or other appropriate device, that Article 49 should not come into operation until publication of an appropriate code of practice. No such provision was made and, as I have already noted, Article 49, together with the remainder of the 1996 Order, came into effect on the 25 August 1996. In such circumstances, adopting the applicant's argument, Parliament must have intended to enable the police to secure the appointment of financial investigators whose Schedule 2 powers would be effectively suspended until such time as the Secretary of State effected the publication of a code of practice. The publication of such a code of practice may take place some considerable time after the coming into force of the enabling enactment. For example, the codes of practice in accordance with Section 61(1) (connected with the detention, treatment, questioning and identification of persons detained under the Prevention of *Terrorism* (Temporary Provisions) Act 1989) and paragraph 7(1) of Schedule 5 (connected to the exercise by authorised investigators of the powers conferred by that Schedule) of the Northern Ireland (Emergency Provisions) Act 1991 did not come into force until 1 January 1994 almost two and half years after the original Act. Both the 1991 Act and the 1996 Order were concerned with affording the authorities formidable and extensive powers of investigation and I am satisfied that, if such had been its intention, Parliament would have employed clear and precise words to indicate that such powers should remain in suspension until the relevant code of practice came into operation.

Accordingly, I reject the applicant's submission that the exercise by the investigator of his power to interview the applicant was ultra vires in the absence of the relevant code of practice.

2. The use of a pseudonym by the investigator

21. The second limb of Mr Lavery QC's attack upon the Article 49 authorisation was that the permission for the investigator to use a pseudonym was so unfair as to render the authorisation invalid. While Mr Lavery QC was prepared to accept that paragraph 4(2) of Schedule 2 to the 1996 Order permitted an investigator to withhold his name when producing evidence of his authority, provided that such evidence contained some other means of identification, he submitted that this provision did not, of itself, provide a blanket authority for concealing the identities of investigators. He emphasised the fundamental importance of the principle of "open justice" to which there should be permitted only those exceptions which the appropriate tribunal found to be necessary after carefully balancing the interests of justice. As I have earlier noted Mr Lavery QC also drew the attention of the court to the fact that the use of an apparently ordinary name, such as "John Armstrong," by way of a pseudonym rather than a number or letter not only secured the anonymity of the investigator but also prevented the applicant and her solicitor from being aware that the investigators true identity was being withheld.

22. In the context of the sustained and unremitting campaign of violence to which those institutions that seek to uphold the rule of law in Northern Ireland have been submitted by various terrorist organisations, it is hardly surprising that, in recent times, the principle of "open justice" has been a fairly frequent topic of judicial discussion in this jurisdiction. The subject was fully discussed by Kelly LJ in R v Murphy & Maguire [1990] NI 306 and, in the course of that judgment, at page 333 he cited the well known passage from the speech of Lord Diplock in Attorney General v Leveller Magazine [1979] AC 440 at 449H. The current practice in Northern Ireland was summarised by the then Lord Chief Justice in Doherty v Ministry of Defence [1991] 1 NI JB 68 when he observed, at page 91:

> "In conclusion I add that for many years the courts in Northern Ireland have permitted military witnesses and other witnesses, who would be at risk from terrorist attack if their names were given in open court, not to be named and to give their evidence as soldier A or witness B: see, for example, the report of Farrells case in the House of Lords [1980] NI 78. If there should be any information in relation to the witness which would be discreditable to him or helpful to the other party, counsel who calls that witness furnishes the information to counsel for the other party. This is an entirely properly practice and counsel for the plaintiff in this case

made it clear that he had no objection to the names of the military witnesses not being given in open court but being described by letter."

23. The equivalent considerations to be observed by a judge in a criminal trial were discussed in some detail by Evans LJ in the course of giving the judgment of the Court of Appeal in R v Taylor [1994] TLR 484. In Re Jordan [1996] (unreported) MacDermott LJ dealt with the relevant common law background in the following terms:

"It is a fundamental aspect of jurisprudence throughout the United Kingdom that courts should conduct their business openly and in public. In recent years largely because there have been so many terrorist related cases it has been quite common for applications to be made that witnesses be granted anonymity or be screened when giving evidence. Such applications are founded in the fear of the witness that they or their families might be endangered if they were seen or known to give evidence adverse to some person who has often an allegedly terrorist background. Such fear is understandable and the courts recognise that it is not in the public interest that a suspected terrorist should escape conviction because a witness may be deterred by fear from giving evidence or by giving evidence to be exposed to hostile action or the fear of such action. In every case a judge faced with an application for anonymity (and it is also an aspect of the wider concept of screening) will have to balance between an adherence to the primary requirement for justice to be open and the fears and anxieties of a witness involved in the criminal process."

24. The circumstances in which the investigator was permitted to use a pseudonym have been set out in the affidavits of Miss Hamill, the Assistant RUC Legal Adviser, and Detective Superintendent Lagan in relation to the ex parte application to the then Recorder of Belfast. It is clear from these affidavits that the Recorder was informed of the two identities of the investigators in respect of whom authorisations were sought and that he was also apprised that the reason for the use of pseudonyms was the apprehension of their own personal safety should their true identify be disclosed. The Recorder was also informed that, in the event of granting the application, the orders appointing the investigators would bear their photographs. It appears from the affidavit of Miss Hamill that the Recorder asked a number of questions for the purpose of clarifying the grounds upon which he was being requested to appoint financial investigators who would use assumed names and Chief Superintendent Lagan has averred that he was asked to elaborate on certain aspects of the offences, offenders and investigation with which he was concerned. The Chief Superintendent also gave evidence before the Recorder confirming that he was familiar with the backgrounds and previous experience of the investigators in respect of whom authorisation was being sought and for satisfying that they were fit and proper persons to be appointed. The circumstances of the

ex parte application have also been deposed to by the financial investigator at paragraphs 3 and 4 of the affidavits sworn by him on 22 April 1998.

25. As I have already noted above paragraph 4(2) of Schedule 2 to the 1996 Order contemplates that a financial investigator need not identify himself or herself by name and, having regard to the general principles set out above, I am satisfied that the Recorder had an inherent discretionary jurisdiction to extend anonymity to the financial investigator when granting the relevant authorisation in accordance with Article 49 of the 1996 Order. The affidavits sworn on behalf of the respondent by Ms Hamill, Chief Superintendent Lagan and the financial investigator confirm that evidence was placed before the Recorder indicating that the circumstances of the offenders and offences under investigation were such as to give rise to a justifiable fear for the personal safety of the financial investigator and that the Recorder made appropriate and relevant enquiries for the purpose of arriving at a properly balanced decision.

26. The use of an ostensibly ordinary name by way of a pseudonym, as opposed to a letter or number or some other more obvious means of achieving anonymity, is not a device which I have previously experienced within this jurisdiction but I note that it was recently discussed in the Court of Appeal decision of R v Myles & Anors (unreported: Court of Appeal Transcript 16 June 1998). In that case the defendants had been convicted of involvement in a number of gang related robberies and murders and the trial judge had permitted witnesses not only to give evidence from behind screens but also to use pseudonyms. The fact that the witnesses were using pseudonyms was undisclosed to the jury. On behalf of one of the appellants it was accepted that neither the use of screens nor the use of pseudonyms could, in itself, found a complaint and it was also excepted that the trial judge had scrupulously followed the authority of R v Taylor. Nevertheless, it was argued that, in the context of such crucial witnesses relating to a murder count, the use of pseudonyms was unfair and unjust. In the course of giving the leading judgment the Vice President, Rose LJ, referred to the increasing difficulty in persuading witnesses to come forward, particularly in cases in which gang warfare was involved and went on to observe, at page 13:

> "Trial judges have a difficult balancing exercise to conduct when applications for anonymity or for screens, or for both, are made between, protecting, so far as possible, the interest of the defence and the interest of the public that appropriate prosecutions should be pursued. In the present case, we find it impossible to say that the judge, in carrying out that difficult balancing exercise, in anything other than reach the entirely right conclusion."

27. On behalf of another of the accused in the case of R v Myles & Anors it was argued that the use of a pseudonym was "objectionable in principle." This was not an argument which had been addressed to the trial judge and the issue

was whether, at the appeal stage, it could be argued that the judge, in permitting the use of pseudonyms, not objected to at the time of trial, so unfairly conducted the trial that the verdicts should be regarded as unsafe. In confirming the view of the Court of Appeal that this was "a wholly impossible contention" Rose LJ went on to say:

> "What a case of this kind requires in relation to anonymity, the use of letters, the use of false names, or otherwise, is, again, essentially a matter for the exercise of discretion by the trial judge in the particular circumstances of the case."

28. I fully accept that there may well be significant differences between the circumstances of a full blown criminal trial and the activities of a financial investigator authorised in accordance with Article 49 of the 1996 Order. For example, it is not difficult to understand why those who advised the accused in R v Myles & Anors might not have wished the jury to be alerted to the fact that witnesses had sought the protection of anonymity and, indeed, this appears to have been the view of those advising the defendant Myles. By contrast, the advisers of the applicant in these proceedings have specifically objected that the use of the pseudonym is in conflict with the principle of open justice. However, having given the matter careful consideration, I am satisfied that the existence of such a conflict was fully appreciated by the Recorder of Belfast during the course of the ex parte application and that he conscientiously carried out an appropriate balancing exercise before deciding to authorise the financial investigator to carry out his duties under a pseudonym. Accordingly, I reject the submissions made on behalf of the applicant in relation to this aspect of the case.

* * * * *

32. Accordingly, since none of the submissions advanced on behalf of the applicant have succeeded, this application will be dismissed.

DOCUMENT NO 20

Martin

v

Conroy
The High Court of Ireland [2001] IEHC 87

May 1, 2001
(Edited Text)

Mr. Justice HERBERT:

1. It is alleged against the Plaintiff in these proceedings that in a 47 day period between the 4th November, 1988 and 22nd December, 1988, in England, he had in his possession or under his control an explosive substance, in the form of a movement activated improvised explosive device, with intent to thereby to endanger life or cause serious injury to property in the United Kingdom or to enable any other person so to do. It is further alleged that in the same period the Plaintiff conspired with Nicholas Robert Neil Mullen and others to cause, by explosive substances, explosions of a nature likely to endanger life or cause serious injury to property in the United Kingdom.

2. In giving oral evidence relating to his application for a Certificate under the Attorney General's Scheme, the Plaintiff stated that he returned from London, where he had gone in the summer of 1988, to Ireland, sometime in November 1988. Though no evidence in that behalf was given by the Plaintiff, either orally or on Affidavit, it was accepted by both sides,—or at least the arguments proceeded upon the basis,—that whenever the Plaintiff returned to Ireland he lived here openly. The Plaintiff is now about 35 years of age, he is an unemployed General Operative and is unmarried. His father is living in the greater Dublin area. He has three siblings whose addresses were not given to the Court.

3. In June, 1990 Nicholas Robert Neil Mullen was convicted of offences similar to those alleged against the Plaintiff in these proceedings and was sentenced to a term of 30 years imprisonment. Eamon Wadley was acquitted on related charges.

4. The Plaintiff was arrested in this State on the 29th June, 1994 at Swanlinbar, in the County of Cavan, and was charged with the unlawful possession of firearms contrary to the provisions of Section 30 of the Offences Against the State Act, 1939. He was subsequently convicted of this offence and sentenced to a term of 5 years imprisonment.

5. On the 22nd August, 1994, by Statutory Instrument 220 of 1994, the Extradition (Amendment) Act, 1994, (No. 6 of 1994), became operative in this State. This Act provided that certain offences where no longer to be regarded as 'political offences' or 'offences with a political connection' for the purpose of extradition to territories which included the United Kingdom.

6. In July, 1995 the Crown Prosecution Service for England and Wales received from the Metropolitan Police a file relating to the Plaintiff.

7. In December, 1995 the Crown Prosecution Service for England and Wales determined that there was a realistic prospect of obtaining a conviction against the Plaintiff.

8. On the 18th December, 1995 warrants were issued by Bow Street Magistrates Court in England for the arrest of the Plaintiff pursuant to the provisions of Section 3(a) and Section 3(b) of the Explosive Substances Act, 1883, as amended by Section 7 of the Criminal Jurisdiction Act, 1975, (England), in respect of the aforementioned allegations.

9. On the 22nd March, 1996 an Assistant Commissioner of An Garda Siochána authorised the execution of these warrants in this State.

10. On the 28th March, 1998 the Plaintiff was released from Portlaoise Prison on the expiry of his sentence and was immediately re-arrested on foot of these warrants.

11. On the 10th April, 1998 at Belfast an Agreement was concluded between the Government of Ireland and the Government of the United Kingdom of Great Britain and a Northern Ireland which has become popularly known as the "Belfast" or "Good Friday" Agreement.

12. Consequent upon the provisions of this Agreement, whereby both Governments agreed to enact appropriate legislation to provide for an accelerated programme for the release of certain, *"qualifying prisoners,"* the Criminal Justice (Release of Prisoners) Act, 1998 (No. 36 of 1998), came into operation in this State on the 13th July, 1998.

13. On the 23rd June, 1998, District Judge Malone made Orders pursuant to Section 47(1) of the Extradition Act, 1965, (as substituted by Section 12 of the Extradition (Amendment) Act, 1994), for the delivery of the Plaintiff into the custody of a member of the Constables of the Metropolitan Police for conveyance to Bow Street Magistrates Court, England.

14. On the 24th June, 1998 the Plaintiff issued a Special Summons pursuant to the provisions of Order 98 of the Rules of the Superior Courts, 1986, seek-

ing his release in reliance upon the terms of Section 50 of the Extradition Act, 1965. On the 29th October, 1998 by originating Notice of Motion pursuant to the provisions of Order 84 Rule 18 of the Rules of the Superior Courts, 1986, the Plaintiff sought, consequent upon the leave granted in that behalf by the Order of the High Court, (Mr. Justice McCracken), made the 19th day of October, 1998;

1. An Order of Certiorari by way of an application for Judicial Review of the Order of District Judge Malone made on the 23rd day of June, 1998 directing the extradition of the Applicant to England on a charge of conspiracy with others between the 4th November, 1988 and the 22nd December, 1988 to cause explosions likely to endanger life or property.

2. An Order of Certiorari by way of an application for Judicial Review of the Order of District Judge Malone made on the 23rd day of June, 1998 directing the extradition of the Applicant to England on a charge of possession of an explosive substance with intent to endanger life or property between the 4th November, 1988 and the 22nd December, 1988.

3. An Order consolidating these proceedings with proceedings taken by the Applicant in this Honourable Court seeking his release pursuant to the provisions of Section 50 of the Extradition Act, 1965–1994, which proceedings had been given the Record No. 442 Sp—1998 and are entitled "Between:Andrew Martin, Plaintiff and Noel Conroy and Michael Jones, Defendants."

4. An Injunction restraining District Judge Malone and the Attorney General from delivering up the Applicant for extradition on foot of the Order made in that connection by District Judge Malone on the 23rd June, 1998.

5. Such further and other relief as to this Court may seem meet and just.

15. These reliefs were sought upon the ground that:

"The first named Respondent, Judge Miriam Malone erred in law and exceeded her jurisdiction in ordering the extradition of the Applicant to England in that there was no, or no sufficient evidence, before the first named Respondent that the Applicant was the person described in the warrants dated the 18th December 1995."

16. At the hearing before me, Counsel for the Applicant informed the Court that the Applicant was no longer relying upon this ground and an application was made to the Court, pursuant to the provisions of Order 84 Rule 23(2) of the Rules of the Superior Courts 1986, for leave to amend the grounds upon which relief was sought by the substitution of the following grounds:

"The first named Respondent, Judge Miriam Malone erred in law and exceeded her jurisdiction in ordering the rendition of the Applicant in that:

(i)   *There was no, or no sufficient evidence that the offences specified in the warrants were committed at all or that they were committed by the Applicant.*

(ii)   *The Orders made by the first named Respondent Judge Miriam Malone, are defective on their face in that they fail accurately to set out offences known to the law or which correspond to offences under the law of England and Wales and they fail accurately to describe and identify the Applicant and are not made in accordance with law in that:*

(a)   *There is no Section 3(1)(a) or Section 3(1)(b) of the Explosive Substances Act, 1883;*

(b)   *The Statement of Offence in each case fails to correspond to the wording of the 1883 Act particularly in relation to mens rea;*

(c)   *In the second last paragraph the Applicant is mis-described."*

17. Having heard legal argument by Counsel representing the Applicant and Counsel representing the Respondents, in an *extempore* Judgment delivered on the occasion I refused the relief sought, in summary, upon the grounds that:

1.   The first proposed substituted ground was without substance and was one which would not have been permitted at the stage of seeking leave to apply for Judicial Review as it was not a matter which could properly have been addressed by the learned District Judge in exercise of her Jurisdiction, and further, that insufficiency of evidence before the Inferior Tribunal is not a basis for relief by way of Judicial Review, (*Shannon -v- Ireland* (1984) I.R. 548: *Lennon -v- Clifford*, (1992) 1 I.R. 382).

2.   That there had been substantial delay since the Order of the High Court, (Mr. Justice McCracken), made on the 19th October, 1998 granting leave to seek Judicial Review upon the now abandoned ground.

3.   That no *"exceptional circumstances"* were shown to exist by Affidavit or in Argument before the Court as to why the proposed amendments should be permitted notwithstanding this delay, (*McCormack -v- Garda Siochána Complaints Board* (1997) 2 I.R. 489, per Costello, P., and *O'Leary -v- The Minister for Transport*, (2000) 1 I.L.R.M. 391, per Kelly J.).

18. In these circumstances the only issue remaining to be determined by this Court is the Application by way of Special Summons for relief pursuant to the terms of the Extradition Acts, 1965–1994.

SUBMISSIONS

19. The Plaintiff in seeking his release relies principally upon the passage of time between the date of the alleged offences in November and December 1988 and the date of the execution of the warrants on the 28th March, 1998, a period of 9 ¼ years, which his Counsel submit is contrary to the terms of Section 50(2)(bbb) of the Extradition Act, 1995. His Counsel submit that a delay of this magnitude renders it unjust, oppressive or invidious that he should be delivered up to the Requesting Authority. They further submit that it is a denial of the right of the Plaintiff to fair procedures as guaranteed by Article 40.3.1. and Article 38.1. of the Constitution of Ireland, 1937 and Article 6.1., of the European Convention on Human Rights. They also submit that this Court has an inherent jurisdiction as exemplified by the case of *Quinlivan v- Conroy and Sreenan*, (1999) 1 I.R. 271, (Supreme Court) per O'Flaherty, J., page 280, apart from and in addition to Section 50 of the Extradition Act, 1965, to refuse a request for extradition upon considerations of justice and equity, and that this jurisdiction should be exercised in favour of the Plaintiff.

20. Additionally, the Plaintiff relies upon what he alleges are defects on the face of the Warrants and the Orders of the District Court which have the effect that correspondence is not established between the offences specified in the warrants and offences under the Law of this State, so that he is entitled to be released having regard to the provisions of Section 50(2)(c) of the Extradition Act, 1965.

21. It is submitted on behalf of the Respondents that:—

   1. At the time the warrants were issued by the Relevant Authorities in the United Kingdom, and transmitted to the Authorities in this State the Plaintiff was in custody in the State and remained in custody until the 28th March, 1998 when, upon his release, the warrants were executed. In these circumstances Counsel submitted that there was no *"lapse of time,"* such as to trigger the possible application of Section 50(2)(bbb), of the Extradition Act, 1965.

   2. The requirements of Section 50(2)(bbb) of the Extradition Act, 1965, are cumulative and in addition to establishing *"lapse of time"* within the meaning of the subsection, the Plaintiff must establish the existence of other *"exceptional circumstances"* such that it would, *"having regard to all the circumstances, be unjust, oppressive or invidious to deliver him up under Section 47."*

   3. No *"exceptional circumstances"* are established by the material before the Court. That none of the matters adverted to in the Plaintiff's Affidavits come anyway close to establishing any of the matters recognised as constituting such *"exceptional circumstances,"* nor any other matter or circumstance that would render his return to the United Kingdom *"unjust, oppressive or invidious."*

4. In the case of *Ellis -v- O'Dea*, (1991) I.L.R.M. 346 at 370/72, the Supreme Court had held expressly that the very offences alleged in the instant case, (namely offences under Section 3(a) and Section 3(b) of the (United Kingdom), Explosive Substances Act, 1883 correspond to offences in this Jurisdiction, namely, the equivalent offences under the same Act, which, (as amended) remains in force in this State).

THE LAW

22. Section 50, subsection 1 and subsection 2 of the Extradition Act, 1965, amended with regard to the latter subsection by Section 9 of the Extradition (European Convention on the Suppression of Terrorism) Act, 1987, (No. 1 of 1987), by the insertion of an additional subparagraph, *"(bb),"* and by Section 2(1) of the Extradition (Amendment) Act, 1987, (No. 25 of 1987), by the insertion of a further subparagraph, *"(bbb),"* provides as follows:—

50 (1) A person arrested under this part shall be released if the High Court or the Minister so directs in accordance with this section.

    (2) A direction under this section maybe given by the High Court where the Court is of opinion that—

        (a) The offence to which the warrant relates is—

            (i) a political offence or an offence connected with a political offence, or

            (ii) an offence under military law which is not an offence under ordinary criminal law, or

            (iii) a revenue offence, or

        (b) There are substantial reasons for believing that the person named or described in the warrant will, if removed from the State under this Part, be prosecuted or detained for a political offence or an offence connected with a political offence or an offence under military law which is not an offence under ordinary criminal law, or

            (bb) There are substantial grounds for believing that the warrant was in fact issued for the purpose of prosecuting or punishing him on account of his race, religion, nationality or political opinion or that his position would be prejudiced for any of these reasons, or

            (bbb) By reason of the lapse of time since the commission of the offence specified in the warrant or the conviction of the person named or described therein of that offence and other exceptional circumstances, it would, having regard to all the circumstances, be unjust, oppressive or invidious to deliver him up under Section 47, or

(c) The offence specified in the warrant does not correspond with any offence under the law of the State which is an indictable offence or is punishable on summary conviction by imprisonment for a maximum period of at least 6 months.

23. The provisions of Section 50(2)(bbb) of the Extradition Act, 1965, were subjected to a careful consideration by Denham, J., in the course of her Judgment in *Fusco -v- O'Dea*, (No. 2), (1998) 3 I.R., 470, (Supreme Court), where she held as follows, (page 508 of the report):—

"The section requires that in addition to the lapse of time that there should be "other exceptional circumstances" such as to enable the exemption to apply. It is for the Plaintiff to prove that the exemption applies on the balance of probabilities. The section requires that there be "other exceptional circumstances," not "other circumstances." The fact that the exemption is defined so strongly is in keeping with the nature of extradition where once the executive branch of Government has made a policy decision that extradition or rendition agreements exist between two countries and the legislature has passed the requisite legislation, extradition becomes mandatory subject to the law and the Constitution. Thus, it is understandable that exemptions are so strongly defined in the legislation. However, they must be strictly construed. The word "exceptional" indicates that the exemption will be rare, will be the exception, unusual. The words "unjust, oppressive or invidious" have meanings which overlap to some extent. However, they too are words imbuing a sense of force or power. I do not intend to attempt to give a definitive definition of these terms. However, it appears to me that they suggest certain concepts. Thus, "unjust" suggests, inter alia, unfairness, a lack of fair treatment. "Oppressive" indicates actions that, inter alia, are oppressing a person, or a group of persons, treating them badly, or cruelly, keeping them in subservience. While "invidious" raises the concept of circumstances likely to cause a resentment, anger or envy, such situations may arise if there is, for example, discrimination.

The exceptional circumstances must be identified. It is clear that the learned Trial Judge considered the exceptional circumstances to be: the decision of the authorities in 1981 to prosecute in Ireland on the escape offences and not to proceed with extradition on the murder and other offences, that this had in effect being communicated to the Plaintiff, that the Plaintiff had a belief that he would not be extradited after his term of imprisonment in Portlaoise, that he had relied on it, that he had not been informed that he would be in jeopardy of extradition proceedings after his prison sentence. The High Court held that these circumstances, together with his family circumstances, were exceptional circumstances so as to render his extradition unjust, oppressive or invidious. The learned Trial Judge did not find it necessary to apply the issue of credit being granted in Northern Ireland for the time served in Portlaoise."

24. I adopt this succinct and elegant analysis of the law as expressed in Section 50 subsection (2), (bbb) of the Extradition Act, 1965.

25. In considering whether by reason of the lapse of time since the commission of the alleged offences in November-December, 1988, it would, having regard to all the circumstances, be unjust, oppressive or invidious to deliver up the Applicant on foot of the warrants executed on the 28th March, 1998, in my judgment, I must have regard not alone to the extent of the delay but also to the reason or reasons for it. It could scarcely have been the intention of the Legislature in framing this subsection that this Court should weigh in the balance in favour of an Applicant a lapse of time which was wholly or substantially due to the conduct of that Applicant. In my judgment the only lapse of time to which this Court may have regard in considering the subsection is such as is not attributable to any significant extent to the Applicant or is due to some unnecessary or blameworthy delay on the part of the Relevant Authorities in the Requesting State and additionally or alternatively the Relevant Authorities in this State.

26. In considering the actual 9 1/4 year lapse of time in the present case, I adopt the methodology indicated by Denham J., in *Dalton -v- The Governor of the Training Unit and Others*, (29th February, 2000) (Supreme Court: No. 29/99: unreported/Judgment available), a case of a delay of approximately 2 years and 9 months following the issue of domestic default warrants and their execution, where at page 10 of the Judgment the learned Judge held as follows:—

"The President divided up the delay into . . . periods of time for analysis. This is an appropriate approach to the analysis of an alleged delay. However, in addition, the overall delay may be considered either as a single time frame or in conjunction with an analysis of particular sections of the time in issue. Thus, the learned Trial Judge did not err in his approach to the matter."

27. The Plaintiff, in the verifying Affidavit sworn on the 10th November, 1998 grounding the Special Summons avers that the warrants seeking his extradition were issued on the 18th December, 1995, that is 7 years after the latest date of the alleged offences in respect of which his extradition is sought and 18 months after his arrest at Swanlinbar, County Cavan, on the 29th June, 1994 on charges of unlawful possession of firearms. He states that to his knowledge no attempt was made to execute these warrants in the State until the 28th March 1998. He complains that what he describes as, *"a very lengthy"* delay would seriously disadvantage him in the conduct of his defence against the charges made against him in England.

28. Richard Edwin Glenister, Barrister, of the Crown Prosecution Service in a replying Affidavit sworn by him on the 3rd February, 1999, offers no expla-

nation whatever for this delay of 7 years in issuing the warrants, that is between the 22nd December, 1988 and the 18th December, 1995. I must view this unexplained delay in the context of Mr. Mullen and Mr. Wadley having been brought to trial in England in or prior to June, 1990; in the context of contacts between the London Police and the Zimbabwe Central Intelligence Organisation on the 6th January, 1989 and thereafter to secure the summary deportation of Mr. Mullen from Harare to London and in the context of the conviction of Mr. Mullen on the 8th June, 1990 at the Central Criminal Court. The foregoing facts I have ascertained from the Judgment of Lord Justice Rose, in *R. -v- Mullen*, (1999) 2 Cr. App. Rep 143. It is also averred by the Plaintiff in his Affidavit sworn on the 10th November, 1998 and not controverted, that Mr. Wadley was jointly charged with Mr. Mullen, *"on some counts"* and was acquitted.

29. This delay of 7 years in the issuing of the warrants is the first section of time which requires to be addressed in this case.

30. In his Affidavit sworn on the 3rd February, 1999 Mr. Glenister avers that the warrants were issued by Bow Street Magistrates Court on 18th December, 1995 and delivered to An Garda Siochána, "shortly afterwards" and much in advance of the Plaintiff's release from prison in March, 1998. This is not disputed by or on behalf of the Defendants. Detective Sergeant Michael Heffernan, in an Affidavit sworn on the 4th February, 1999, avers that there was no delay on the part of An Garda Siochána or any other Relevant Authorities in this State in dealing with the request for extradition. He avers that at the time the request for extradition was received the Plaintiff was a convicted person serving a sentence of imprisonment. He further states that notwithstanding the granting of periods of temporary release to the Plaintiff it was the opinion of An Garda Siochána that the warrants could not be executed until the Plaintiff had fully served his sentence and was at liberty.

31. Mr. Forde, Senior Counsel for the Plaintiff, argued at the hearing before me, that this was an error of Law on the part of An Garda Siochána and that the failure to execute the warrants as shortly as possible after they had been received amounted to an unnecessary and blameworthy delay on the part of the Relevant Authorities in this State which was seriously prejudicial to the Plaintiff. This delay of shortly in excess of 2 years and 3 months, between the 18th December, 1995 or shortly thereafter, when the warrants were received by An Garda Siochána and the 28th March, 1998 when the warrants were executed upon the release of the Plaintiff from Prison having served the sentence imposed upon him, constitutes the second section of time to be addressed in this case.

32. The overall delay between the 22nd December, 1988 being the latest date for the commission of the alleged offences charged in the warrants and the 28th March, 1998, the date of execution of the warrants, amounts to a period of slightly in excess of 9 years and 3 months.

33. In my judgment it is not necessary for me to make any determination as regards the second section of time at issue in this case. However, I would not in any event take this period of time into account as a *"lapse of time"* for the purpose of Section 50(2)(bbb) of the Extradition Act, 1965, if it was the only period of delay involved in this case, because the detention of the Plaintiff in prison during this period was a consequence of his own acts. But also, I have not been convinced that the Judgment of Hamilton, C.J., in *Fusco -v- O'Dea*, (No. 2), (1998) 3 I.R. 470 at 501 and 502, is authority for the proposition that extradition warrants may be executed at any time, however remotely, before the actual expiry of a prison sentence. The Plaintiff has failed to satisfy me, the onus being on him, that what Denham, J., at page 525 of the Report in that Case, described as the, *"normal practice to seek extradition of a prisoner at determination of a prison sentence,"* is not also, in the vast majority of cases at least, the correct practice. Indeed, leading Counsel for Mr. Martin accepted in argument that service upon release was the norm, but he submitted that just because it was the norm this could not be used to excuse delay where there was no legal inhibition to a much earlier execution of the warrants and where justice required such earlier execution. In *Ellis -v- O'Dea* (1991) 1 I.L.R.M., 346 at 373, the then Chief Justice records that it was conceded on behalf of the Applicant in that case that the extradition warrants could not practicably have been executed until after the completion of the sentence been served by the Appellant. I also adopt what was held by Denham J., at page 525 of the Report in *Fusco -v- O'Dea* (No.2) (above cited), where she said:—

> *"There is neither injustice, nor oppression nor invidious behaviour in a State not giving notice in advance of an extradition application. The authorities were not obliged to explain that the Plaintiff might be in jeopardy of future rendition."*

34. However, I consider that there is a distinction to be drawn between a lapse of time entirely or substantially occasioned by the deliberate and voluntary actions of a person in seeking to evade discovery and a lapse of time referable to that person serving a term of imprisonment. In my judgment while the former should always be entirely discounted some regard may be had to the latter in looking at the overall lapse of time, provided always that there is in addition a specific and separate particular lapse of time to be taken into account for which the accused is in no manner to blame or which is due to some unnecessary or blameworthy delay on the part of the Relevant Authorities in the Requesting State or in this State.

35. In my judgment there can be no doubt but that the wholly unexplained lapse of 7 years in issuing these warrants, that is between the 22nd December, 1988 and the 18th December, 1995, is the sort of lapse of time envisaged by Section 50(2)(bbb) of the Extradition Act, 1965 as inserted by Section 2(1)

of the Extradition (Amendment) Act, 1987. Such delay is a negation of the right of the Plaintiff to a trial with reasonable expedition. *State (Healy) -v- Donoghue*, (1976) I.R. 325 at 336 per Gannon, J.,: *State (O'Connell) -v- Fawsitt*, (1986) I.R. 362 (Supreme Court).: *P.C. -v- The Director of Public Prosecutions*, (1999) 2 I.R. 25 at 65, 66 per Keane, J., (as he then was),: *B.F. -v- The Director of Public Prosecutions*, (22nd February, 2001), (Supreme Court): (unreported—Judgment available), per Geoghegan, J.,).

36. Despite this finding, the onus remains upon the Plaintiff to establish in addition some, *"other exceptional circumstances,"* which would render it unjust, oppressive or invidious to deliver him up. As was pointed out by Denham, J., in the passage from *Fusco -v- O'Dea* (No. 2), to which I have already adverted, what is contemplated by this requirement of the subsection is something special and unusual.

37. The Plaintiff points to a number of matters which it is submitted constitute such, *"exceptional circumstances."* These matters may be summarised as follows:—

  1. His own difficulty, at such a remove in time, in recalling events in and prior to November and December 1988 and difficulties in tracing and obtaining witnesses, some of whom might now be dead or unavailable, compounded by the vague and unparticularised nature of the charges;

  2. The change effected in the law of this State as of the 22nd August, 1994 by the enactment and coming into force of the Extradition (Amendment) Act, 1994, which removed from the category of non extraditable political offences the offences in respect of which his rendition is now sought;

  3. The terms of the Agreement reached between the Government of the United Kingdom of Great Britain and Northern Ireland and the Government of Ireland on the 10th April, 1998, (commonly called the "Belfast" or the "Good Friday" Agreement), and the provisions of the Criminal Justice (Release of Prisoners) Act, 1998 under which he would probably have been released on or before the 13th July, 2000; and

  4. The probability of a long period awaiting trial in England during which time, he is advised and believes, he would be held in custody as bail is invariably refused in cases involving alleged I.R.A., bomb plots.

38. I reject without hesitation the claim of lack of particularity and want of specifity in the charges preferred against the Plaintiff.

39. Detective Sergeant Heffernan in an Affidavit sworn on the 4th February, 1999 avers that evidence was put before the learned District Judge which established that there was fingerprint evidence to link the Plaintiff with the

offences for which his extradition was sought. At page 10 of the Written Submission filed on behalf of the Defendants it is stated by reference to an Affidavit of Claire Gilligan, sworn on 4th December, 1998, that Detective Garda Kelly, Detective Garda Canning, Detective Sergeant Benton and Mr. Irvine formally of the Metropolitan Police, gave evidence to the learned District Judge that the Plaintiff was fingerprinted and fingerprints found in a premises in London were identified as belonging to the Plaintiff. Apart from this I know nothing of the evidence by which the Crown Prosecution Service would propose to establish its case against the Plaintiff. I want to emphasise, that in referring to these matters I am not seeking to explore or to adjudicate in any way on the merits of the charges against the Plaintiff and I am not drawing any conclusions as to whether the Plaintiff is innocent or guilty in respect of these charges. (*Clarke -v- McMahon*, (1990) 1 I.R. 228 at 235 per Finlay, C.J.).

40. The Plaintiff points to no specific line or lines of defence in the conduct of which he claims to be unfairly prejudiced by the lapse of time in this case. Unlike the situation in *Kakis -v- The Government of the Republic of Cyprus*, (1978) 1 W.L.R. 779, H. of L., to which reference was made by both sides during the course of argument; the *State (O'Connell) -v- Fawsitt*, (1986) I.R. 362, and (though with the material difference that this involved sexual offences against a minor), *M.K. -v- Judge Groarke and The Director of Public Prosecutions*, (13th September, 2000) (Kearns, J.; unreported; Judgment available), the Plaintiff has not identified or sought to identify any particularly essential witness or indeed any witness who is now unavailable. While it is generally true that the ability to recall details of time, place, movement, events and people lessens progressively with the passage of time and that some persons capacity of recall fades faster than others, in the words of McGuinness, J., in *J.L. -v- The Director of Public Prosecutions*, (6th July, 2000), (unreported; Judgment available), *"the right of an accused person to reasonable expedition in the prosecution of offences must be balanced with the communities right to have criminal offences prosecuted,"* as to which exercise the legal principles have been set out by the Supreme Court in *B. -v- The Director of Public Prosecutions*, (1997) 2 I.L.R.M. 118.

In *Kakis -v- The Government of the Republic of Cyprus*, (above cited), Lord Edmund-Davies stated as follows at page 785 of the report:—

> *"The fact that the requesting government is shown to have been inexcusably dilatory in taking steps to bring the fugitive to justice may serve to establish both the injustice and oppressiveness of making an order for his return, whereas the issue might be left in doubt if the only known fact related to the extent of the passage of time, and it has been customary in practice to advert to that factor."*

41. Despite the failure of the Plaintiff to demonstrate with any degree of particularity any actual or probable prejudice to his capacity to defend himself by reason of the passage of 7 years since the date of the alleged offences, in my

judgment, it would still be unjust to deliver him up after such an unexplained delay. In my judgment after such an unexplained delay and in the absence of the sort of special circumstances which arise in cases concerning sexual offences against minors, I am entitled in the words of Finlay, C.J., in *The Director of Public Prosecutions -v- Byrne*, (1994) 2 I.R. 236 at 244, to infer from the excessive length of time itself that the risk of an unfair trial has been established as a reality.

42. In the same case the learned former Chief Justice stated the following principle of Law at page 245 of the Report, a principle which found approval with the present Supreme Court in the case of *B.F. -v- The Director of Public Prosecutions*, (above cited) at page 16, namely:—

"... *I am driven to the further conclusion that, of necessity, instances may occur in which a delay between the date of the alleged commission of an offence and the date of a proposed trial identified as unreasonable would give rise to the necessity for a Court to protect the constitutional right of the accused by preventing the trial, even where it could not be establish either that the delay involved an oppressive pre-trial detention, or that it created a risk or probability that the accused's capacity to defend himself would be impaired. This must lead of course to the conclusion that, on an application to prohibit a trial on the basis of unreasonable delay, or lapse of time, failure to establish actual or presumptive prejudice may not conclude the issues which have to be determined."*

In *P.C. -v- The Director of Public Prosecutions*, (1999) (above cited) it was held by Keane, J., (as he then was), at page 68 of the Report as follows:—

"Manifestly, in cases where the Court is asked to prohibit the continuance of a prosecution on the ground of unreasonable delay, the paramount concern of the Court will be whether it has been established that there is a real and serious risk of an unfair trial; that, after all, is what is meant by the guarantee of a trail "in due course of law." The delay may be such that, depending on the nature of the charges, a trial should not be allowed to proceed, even though it has not been demonstrated that the capacity of the accused to defend himself or herself will be impaired. In other cases, the first enquiry must be as to what are the reason for the delay and, in a case such as the present where no blame can be attached to the prosecuting authorities, whether the Court is satisfied as a matter of probability that, assuming the complaint to be truthful, the delay in making it was referable to the accused's own actions.

If that stage has been reached, the final issue to be determined will be whether the degree to which the accused's ability to defend himself has been impaired is such that the trial should not be allowed to proceed. That is a necessary enquiry in my view, in every such case, because, given the finding that the delay is explicable by reference to the conduct of the accused is necessarily grounded upon an assumption as to the truth of the complaint, it follows that, in the light of the presumption of innocence to which he is entitled, the Court asked to halt the trial must still consider whether the degree of prejudice is such as to give rise to a real and serious risk of an unfair trial."

43. Though these decisions arose entirely within the framework of domestic law where the Court was been asked to stay criminal proceedings against an accused upon grounds of delay, in my judgment the principles of law above stated are equally applicable to extradition cases.

44. In reaching my decision, I am satisfied that the wholly unexplained dilatoriness of the Requesting Authorities in seeking extradition, together with the inferred reality of a real and serious risk of an unfair trial amount to, *"exceptional circumstances,"* within the meaning of Section 50(2)(bbb) of the Extradition Act, 1965. This, in my judgment, is so if one considers only the first period of 7 years, but is overwhelmingly so if in addition one has regard to the overall lapse of time of 9 1/4 years. (*Hogan -v- The President of the Circuit Court*, (1994) 2 I.R. 513). I have noted that in the case of *Kakis -v- The Government of the Republic of Cyprus*, and other leading cases in Britain which have come before the House of Lords, the time lapse element was less than half that of the 7 years delay in the present case.

45. Having so found, it is unnecessary for me to proceed further but as the matters have been extensively argued I propose to deal with each of the other alleged, *"exceptional circumstances."*

46. In my judgment the submission based upon the loss, by the changes effected in the Law in 1994 during the course of the 7 year delay, of the alleged defence that the offences charged were *"political offences"* or *"offences connected with a political offence"* is without merit. No evidence whatever was placed before this Court by the Plaintiff, upon whom the onus lies, from which the Court could be satisfied that either of these offences was a, *"political offence,"* or *"an offence connected with a political offence"* (*Maguire -v- Keane*, (1986) I.L.R.M. 235 at 237.

47. In the course of his judgment in *Kakis -v- The Government of the Republic of Cyprus*, (above cited) at page 785 of the Report, Lord Russell of Killowen said:—

> *"Regard must be had to all the circumstances. Those circumstances are not restricted to circumstances from which the passage of time resulted. They include circumstances taking place during the passage of time which may (as I think here) give to the particular passage of time a quality or significance leading to a conclusion that the result would be unjust or oppressive."*

However, in *Fusco -v- O'Dea*, (No. 2), (above cited), Denham, J., held as follows at page 525 of the Report:—

> *"The developing law on the political offence exemption cannot be called in*

aid by the Plaintiff by way of arguing that in 1981/2 he would have bene-
fited from the common law interpretation of the terms "political offence" or
"connected with a political offence." The applicable law is the current law."

48. And at page 517 of the Report the learned Judge said:—

"The applicable law is the law when the application for extradition has to be
considered.

In Bourke -v- Attorney General, (1972) I.R. 36, O'Dailaigh, C.J., at p. 59
stated:—

"Cassels J., who delivered the first judgment in Kolczynski's Case said a page
549 of the Report:—

"The words "offence of a political character" must always be considered accord-
ing to the circumstances existing at the time when they have to be considered.""

49. He also noted at p. 55:—

"The non-extradition of political offenders is primarily based on the fact that
the criminal nature of the act is relative, depending on the peculiar condi-
tions obtaining in the places and institutions in which the political offences
were committed."

50. The law was restated by Finlay C.J., in *Magee -v- Culligan* (1992) 1 I.R.
223 at 237:—

"The right of the Plaintiff, as of every other citizen, concerning the question
of his delivery into another State for the purpose of serving a sentence law-
fully imposed upon him in that State, was, the Court is satisfied, a right at
any given time to proper, due and fair procedures concerning an investiga-
tion of the validity of the warrant in respect of which he is delivered, and to
a fair, proper and due enquiry into the protections available in law, in paren-
thesis within the State at the time of the application for his delivery, which
may afford him a protection arising from the concept of a political offence
or from any other of the concepts appropriate to prevent such a delivery." (the
emphasis is mine).

51. The application for delivery was made in 1992 so the time to consider
the meaning of *"political offence"* or *"connected with a political offence"* in relation to the Plaintiff's rendition is the current law.

52. The learned Trial Judge stated at p. 479:—

"Nor can the person sought to be extradited be heard to argue that his posi-
tion cannot be altered or disimproved by reason of a change in the law."

"I agree. The applicable law is the current law, the Plaintiff's case is determined
thereon. He cannot rely on the older law or on the fact that it has changed."

53. In my judgment the argument based upon the provisions of the, "Belfast"
or "Good Friday" Agreement and the Criminal Justice (Release of Prisoners)

Act, 1998, cannot succeed for the reasons stated by Kelly, J., in the case *Quinlivan -v- Conroy and Sreenan*, (14th April, 2000) (The High Court: unreported: Judgment available), which I adopt. The learned Judge held as follows:—

> "... It does not appear to me to matter much whether the course suggested by the Applicant is a possibility or a probability. First, is it to be noted that the benefits of this agreement are applicable only to convicted persons. Conviction is a prerequisite to the operation of the scheme. It does not seem to me that the scheme attempts to interfere with or dilute the notion that persons accused of offences should be tried for them. Neither does the scheme attempt to interfere in any way with the rendition of persons in respect of whom an extradition request has been made under Part III of the 1965 Act. It would not be appropriate for this Court to extend the terms of the 1998 Act and the scheme in effect to persons awaiting trial. The 1998 Act does not provide for this and it should not be expanded so to do by the Court.
>
> Even if the benefits of this scheme are applicable and available to the Applicant in the manner suggested, that does not appear to me to be a good reason for refusing rendition. The entitlement of the requesting State to have a person accused of serious criminal offences tried is a benefit which is not to be measured in the context of an application for rendition. If, as a result of arrangements made by the requesting State, the penalty imposed by the Courts of that State (if a conviction is recorded), will be foreshortened, this is not a reason for ordering release, thus denying to the Requesting State an ability to have a trial in respect of the offences. I do not accept the notion that a release should be ordered because any custodial sentence which might be imposed will be served only in part. ... The prisoners are released subject to conditions. The conditions are that they keep the peace, be of good behaviour and do not in any way cause distress or annoyance to victims of their crimes. A breach of these conditions leaves them liable to immediate arrest and committal to prison. Given that the release is in these terms and not absolute, it seems to me that it cannot be said that the Applicant's extradition would be futile simply because the custodial sentence to be served by him would be likely to be the subject of an early release."

54. It was sought to distinguish the present case from that case on the grounds that in the latter case the conduct of the Plaintiff prevented the warrants been executed expeditiously, whereas it was argued that in the present case there was no inhibition to the warrants been so executed. It was argued that if the Authorities here and in the Requesting State so acted the Plaintiff would, on the balance of probabilities, have been eligible for release on or before the 13th July, 2000.

55. The Criminal Justice (Release of Prisoners) Act, 1998, came into force on 13th July, 1998. The warrants were issued on the 18th December, 1995 but for the reasons to which I have already adverted were not executed until

the release of the Plaintiff from a prison in this State on the 25th March, 1998. The warrants were therefore executed prior to the Inter Government Agreement of 10th April, 1998. However, as I understood the argument the Plaintiff contends that if the warrants had been executed, as he says they ought, prior to his arrest, conviction and imprisonment in the State in 1994, and if he had been returned to England and if he had been convicted there, he would probably have been released on or before the 13th July, 2000.

56. In my judgment, the fact that the Plaintiff may have to serve a possibly foreshortened sentence, (should that be in fact the case), now or in the future rather than at some time in the past decade, is no basis for refusing rendition. The decision of the Supreme Court in the case of *Sloan -v- Culligan*, (1992) 1 I.R. 223 at 267/8, was based upon totally different facts and could have no possible application to the facts of this particular case.

57. It was further argued that it would be unjust, oppressive or invidious to permit the rendition of the Plaintiff because it was alleged, he would be remanded in custody in England for more than a year pending trial. The sole basis for this submission is an averment by the Plaintiff in his own Affidavit sworn on the 10th December, 1999, to the effect that he was aware,

> *"That in the case of Nicholas Mullen and of Eamon Wadley who was accused with Mr. Mullen on certain counts, it took 16 months and 17 months respectively for them to be brought to trial and I believe it would take a similar period for me to be brought to trial. I further say and an advised and believe that bail in invariably refused in cases involving alleged I.R.A., bomb plots and that I would have to spend more than a year in custody in England awaiting trial."*

58. The onus lies upon the Plaintiff to establish, to the satisfaction of the Court, on the balance of probabilities, that he would suffer such a period of pre-trial remand in custody. In my judgment, this has not been established by what has been offered by the Plaintiff. Even, however, if I were to proceed upon the basis that these assertions, as not denied in the replying Affidavit of Richard Edwin Glenister, are therefore accepted by the Requesting Authorities as true and accurate, I cannot see how such a delay as this could be said to be an, *"exceptional"* circumstance so as to render it unjust, oppressive or invidious to deliver up the Plaintiff.

59. Finally, on the argument directed to lack of correspondence, in the case of *Hanlon -v- Fleming*, (1981) I.R. 489 and 495, (Supreme Court) Henchy, J., held as follows:—

* * * * *

61. In my judgment therefore the Plaintiff has not succeeded in establishing any other, *"exceptional circumstances"* within the meaning of Section 50(2)(bbb) of the Extradition Act, 1965.

DOCUMENT NO 21

Opinions of the Lords of Appeal for Judgment in the Cause
Regina
v
Director of Public Prosecutions Ex Parte Kebeline and Others [2000] 2 Ac 326 House Of Lords

October 28, 2001
(Edited Text)

LORD SLYNN OF HADLEY:

My Lords,

I have had the advantage of reading in draft the opinion of my noble and learned friend Lord Steyn. The opinion which I intended to write would have been largely repetitious of the views which he expresses. Accordingly and despite the fact that we are differing from forcefully stated conclusions of the Divisional Court I limit myself to saying that for the reasons which Lord Steyn gives I too would allow the appeal.

LORD STEYN

My Lords,

In the Divisional Court the Lord Chief Justice observed that this case raises important issues regarding the impact of the *Human Rights Act 1998* on the exercise of the discretion of the Director of Public Prosecutions during the interim period between the enactment of *the Act* of 1998 and the bringing into force of its main provisions; and about the role and jurisdiction of the court in reviewing that exercise of discretion: [1999] 3 W.L.R. 175.

The Divisional Court held that the DPP had acted unlawfully and granted a declaration to that effect. The DPP now appeals to the House of Lords.

The charges

In 1997 officers of the anti-terrorist squad arrested Mr Kebeline, Mr Boukemiche and Mr Souidi. All three were Algerian nationals. They were charged with offences under section 16A of the *Prevention of Terrorism (Temporary Provisions) Act 1989*. Section 16A of *the Act* of 1989, so far as it is relevant, provides:

1. A person is guilty of an offence if he has any article in his possession in circumstances giving rise to a reasonable suspicion that the article is in his possession for a purpose connected with the commission, preparation or instigation of acts of terrorism to which this section applies.

2. It is a defence for a person charged with an offence under this section to prove that at the time of the alleged offence the article in question was not in his possession for such a purpose as is mentioned in subsection (1) above.

3. Where a person is charged with an offence under this section and it is proved that at the time of the alleged offence—
    (a)   he and that article were both present in any premises; or
    (b)   the article was in premises of which he was the occupier or which he habitually used otherwise than as a member of the public, the court may accept the fact proved as sufficient evidence of his possessing that article at that time unless it is further proved that he did not at that time know of its presence in the premises in question, or, if he did know, that he had no control over it.

Conviction on indictment carries a maximum penalty of 10 years imprisonment plus a fine in an unlimited sum. The particulars of offence against the three men were that they

> "had in their possession chemical containers, radio equipment, manuals, documents, credit cards and sums of money in circumstances which give rise to a reasonable suspicion that the articles were in their possession for a purpose connected with the commission, preparation or instigation of acts of terrorism."

The charges arose from items found during police searches at various addresses in London. The case against the three men was that as members of the Armed Islamic Group they had been engaged in sending equipment to Algeria for use in the civil war in Algeria.

Section 19(1)(aa) of *the Act* of 1989 requires the consent of the Director of Public Prosecutions for proceedings under *the Act* of 1989. In the Divisional Court the Lord Chief Justice explained that section 16A is directed not to unlawful possession of explosives or firearms, which may be the subject of prosecution without resort to section 16A but to the possession of articles and items of information innocent in themselves but capable of forming part of the paraphernalia or operational intelligence of the terrorist. The purpose of requiring the DPP's consent to prosecutions under section 16A is, to ensure that the decision to prosecute is taken at a very senior level in the CPS, following a careful consideration of all relevant matters including the public interest, and to protect defendants from the risk of oppressive prosecutions: see [1999] 3 W.L.R. 175, at 182H-183A. In the present case the DPP gave his consent to the criminal proceedings under *the Act* of 1989.

The trial

The trial commenced on 9 March 1998 but was adjourned on the grounds of late service of evidence by the Crown Prosecution Service. The new trial started on 12 October 1998. Counsel for the three defendants applied for a stay on the ground that it proved impossible to obtain evidence from Algeria. The judge dismissed the application. On 27 October 1998 the jury was empanelled. At the close of the case for the prosecution the defence sought a ruling from the judge that section 16A of *the Act* of 1989 reversed the legal burden of proof and was therefore in breach of Article 6(2) of the European Convention for the Protection of Human Rights and Fundamental Freedoms. Article 6(1) of the Convention contains the general right to a fair trial. Article 6(2) provides: "Everyone charged with a criminal offence shall be presumed innocent until proved guilty according to law." It must be read with Article 13 which requires an effective remedy in national courts for a breach of the rights defined in the Convention. The defence sought this ruling for two reasons. First, in order to persuade the DPP to reconsider his consent. Secondly, as an aid to a renewal of the abuse of process application made at the outset of the trial. On 20 November 1998 the judge ruled that section 16A was in conflict with Article 6(2). He gave the reasons for his decision on 23 November 1998. The solicitors for the defendants then wrote to the DPP requesting him to reconsider his consent to the proceedings. The DPP's view was that section 16A was not inconsistent with article 6(2) of the Convention. But he sought the advice of Mr Rabinder Singh, a barrister with extensive experience in this field. Mr Singh supported the DPP's view. On 26 November 1998 Mr Singh appeared on behalf of the DPP before the judge and attempted to persuade the judge to reverse his earlier ruling. Mr Singh made clear that the DPP did not agree with the judge's ruling. After hearing argument the judge adhered to his earlier ruling. The DPP then sought a further short adjournment after which the DPP indicated that it was his intention to proceed with the prosecution. The defence then placed another argument on abuse of process before the judge but the judge rejected it. On 14 December 1998 the judge discharged the jury because the prosecution had not fully complied with its disclosure obligations and prosecuting counsel required a lengthy adjournment to complete this task. A new trial date had to be fixed.

The application for judicial review

On 18 December 1998 the three defendants applied for leave to move for judicial review. Form 86A described the decision in respect of which relief was sought as being "the continuing decision of the Director of Public Prosecutions ("the DPP") to give his consent pursuant to *section 19*(1) (aa) of the *Prevention of Terrorism (Temporary Provisions) Act 1989* ("the PTA") for the prosecution of the applicants for an offence contrary to section 16A of the PTA." Form 86A sought a declaration that "the decision of the DPP to give his continued consent to the prosecution of the applicants involves an error of law, namely an erroneous conclusion that the prosecution is compatible with Article 6(2) of the European Convention on Human Rights."

On 26 January 1999 Turner J. granted leave to move for judicial review to the three applicants as well as to a fourth applicant (Mr Rechachi).

The Proceedings in the Divisional Court

The importance of the issues led to the matter being heard in March this year by Lord Bingham of Cornhill, C.J., sitting with Laws L.J. and Sullivan J., judges with enormous experience in human rights law and public law issues. The Divisional Court granted a declaration that the DPP's decision to proceed with the prosecution was unlawful: [1999] 3 W.L.R. 175. The Lord Chief Justice took the view that section 16A of *the Act* of 1989 undermines in a blatant and obvious way the presumption of innocence: at 190F. He observed that: "Under section 16A a defendant could be convicted even if the jury entertained a reasonable doubt whether he knew that the items were in his premises and whether he had the items for a terrorist purpose": at 190H: The Lord Chief Justice held that section 29(3) of the Supreme Court 1981 did not preclude the granting of relief. The Lord Chief Justice accepted that it is not for the DPP to disapply legislative provisions which Parliament has enacted. But relying on the judgment of Lord Hope of Craighead (given with the agreement the other members of the House) in *Reg. v. Secretary of State for the Home Department, Ex parte Launder* [1997] 1 W.L.R. 839 at 867 the Lord Chief Justice held that it was appropriate for the Court to review the soundness of the legal advice on which the DPP acted. The Lord Chief Justice explained:

> "Where the grant of leave to move for judicial review would delay or obstruct the conduct of criminal proceedings which ought, in the public interest, to be resolved with all appropriate expedition, the court will always scrutinise the application with the greatest care, both to satisfy itself

that there are sound reasons for making the application and to satisfy itself that there are no discretionary grounds (such as delay or the availability of alternative remedies or vexatious conduct by the applicant) which should lead it to refuse leave. The court will be very slow to intervene where the applicant's complaint is one that can be met by appropriate orders or directions in the criminal proceedings. If, however, strongly arguable grounds for making application are shown, as the single judge rightly held were shown here, and if there are no discretionary grounds for refusing relief, leave to move may properly be granted; and if on full argument grounds for granting relief are established and no discretionary grounds shown for refusing it, such relief may properly be granted even though the consequence is a delay in the resolution of criminal proceedings. Such was, no doubt, the consequence of quashing the applicant's committal in *Reg. v. Bedwellty Justices, Ex parte Williams* [1997] A.C. 225. In the present case I see no discretionary reasons for refusing relief if the applicants establish a ground for granting it": See [1999] 3 W.L.R. 175, at 183G–184A.

Laws L.J. gave a separate judgment. Except perhaps to the extent that Laws L.J. went further than the Lord Chief Justice by observing that the DPP was in law obliged to consider whether section 16A of *the Act* of 1989 was compatible with Article 6(2) of the Convention I have not discerned any material difference between the reasoning in the two judgements. Sullivan J. agreed with both judgments.

The Main Issues

Since the judgment was delivered in the Divisional Court the criminal proceedings against Mr Rechachi have been abandoned. The case against him had required an examination of section 16B of *the Act* of 1989. The appeals before the House are now only by Mr Kebeline, Mr Boukemiche and Mr Souidi. And the focus is only on section 16A of *the Act* of 1989. The principal issues debated before the House were as follows:

1) whether the decision of the Divisional Court failed to recognise the force and effect of Parliamentary sovereignty in the context of unambiguous primary legislation contained in section 16A of *the Act* of 1989;

2) whether, pending the coming into force of its central provisions, the *Human Rights Act 1998* gives rise to a legitimate expectation that the DPP will exercise his discretion to consent to a prosecution in accordance with Article 6(2) of the Convention.

3) whether section 29(3) of the Supreme Court Act 1981 or a common law principle preclude the granting of relief in judicial review proceedings in respect of the DPP's consent to the prosecutions;

4) whether as a matter of interpretation subsections (1) and (3) of section 16A of the Act of 1989 create a reverse legal burden;

5) if question (4) is answered in the affirmative, is the reverse legal burden incompatible with article 6(2) of the Convention?

Issue 1: Parliamentary Sovereignty

My Lords, counsel for the DPP emphasised the principal features of the *Human Rights Act 1998*, which received the Royal Assent on 9 November 1998. The Act of 1998 will, when its substantive provisions come into force on 2 October 2000, give effect to Convention rights in domestic law. *Section 3*(1) enacts a strong interpretative obligation. It provides:

> "So far as it is possible to do so, primary legislation and subordinate legislation must be read and given effect in a way which is compatible with the Convention rights."

Section 4 empowers specific courts to make a declaration of incompatibility where such a court determines, notwithstanding the duty under *section 3*(1), that the statutory provision is not compatible with a Convention right. *Section 4*(5) lists the courts which have this power: they do not include the Crown Court. *Section 4*(6)(a) adds that a declaration of incompatibility

> "does not affect the validity, continuing operation or enforcement of the provision in respect of which it is given."

Section 6(1) states that

> "It is unlawful for a public authority to act in a way which is incompatible with a Convention right."

Section 6(2) adds:

> "Subsection (1) does not apply to an act if
> "(a) as the result of one or more provisions of primary legislation, the authority could not have acted differently; or
> (b) in the case of one or more provisions of, or made under, primary legislation which cannot be read or given effect in a way which is compatible with the Convention rights, the authority was acting so as to give effect to or enforce those provisions."

Section 7(1) identifies the procedural means by which *section 6* may be enforced:

> "A person who claims that a public authority has acted (or proposes to act) in a way which is made unlawful by section 6(1) may—
> a) bring proceedings against the authority under *this Act* in the appropriate court or tribunal, or
> b) rely on the Convention right or rights concerned in any legal proceedings,
> but only if he is (or would be) a victim of the unlawful act.

Section 22(2) states that specified provisions of *the Act* and *section 22* itself come into force on the passing of the 1998 Act. *Section 22*(3) states that the other provisions of *the Act* come into force on such day as the Secretary of State may by order appoint.

Section 22(4) states:

"Paragraph (b) of subsection (1) of section 7 applies to proceedings brought by or at the instigation of a public authority whenever the act in question took place; but otherwise that subsection does not apply to an act taking place before the coming into force of that section."

Section 22(4) is itself already in force as part of *section 22*. But *section 7*, to which it relates, is not yet in force. The Government has announced that it plans to bring the central provisions of *the Act* of 1989 into force on 2 October 2000.

It is crystal clear that the carefully and subtly drafted *Human Rights Act 1998* preserves the principle of Parliamentary sovereignty. In a case of incompatibility, which cannot be avoided by interpretation under *section 3*(1), the courts may not disapply the legislation. The court may merely issue a declaration of incompatibility which then gives rise to a power to take remedial action: see *section 10*.

The Divisional Court was, of course, fully aware of the scheme of *the Act* of 1998 and of the fact that its main provisions are still not in force. Indeed the Lord Chief Justice expressly accepted in his judgment, at p. 186, the following part of the argument advanced on behalf of the DPP:

"Those sections [including section 16A] remain the law of the land. It is not for the Director to disapply legislative provisions which Parliament has enacted. The Convention, despite its recent advance towards incorporation, has not crossed the Rubicon which separates prospective law from binding law. Prospective law cannot override binding law, and the Director would err in law if he treated it as doing so."

Nevertheless, the Attorney-General and Mr Pannick strenuously argued before the House that the judgment of the Divisional Court is in conflict with the principle of parliamentary sovereignty in the context of unambiguous primary legislation, viz section 16A. They submitted that the effect of the judgment was to invite the DPP to disapply primary legislation. In my view this argument is mistaken and fails to do justice to the reasoning of the Divisional Court. The Lord Chief Justice pointed out that in the present case the Director wished to know where he stood on the issue of compatibility of the legislation. The DPP sought and relied on legal advice on that issue. The Lord Chief Justice said that if the advice was wrong, the DPP should have the opportunity to reconsider the confirmation of his advice on a sound legal basis. As the Lord Chief Justice observed this approach is consistent with the judgment of Lord Hope of Craighead in *Reg. v. Secretary of State for the Home Department*,

Ex parte Launder [1997] 1 W.L.R. 839, at 867. In *Launder* Lord Hope observed: "If the applicant is to have an effective remedy against a decision [on extradition] which is flawed because the decision-maker has misdirected himself on the Convention which he himself says he took into account, it must surely be right to examine the substance of the argument." I respectfully agree. There was no infringement of the principle of Parliamentary sovereignty. I would reject this argument of the DPP.

Before I leave this part of the case it is necessary to refer to a sub-issue which arose on this appeal. The Lord Chief Justice adverted to the possibility of the trial resulting in convictions and appeals subsequently being lodged. He then observed [at 187C]:

> "If, at the time of the appeal hearing, the central provision of the 1998 Act had been brought into force, the applicants would on appeal be entitled to rely on sections 7(1)(b) and 22(4) of the Act and the convictions (on the hypothesis of inconsistency between section 16A and the Convention) would in all probability be quashed, at some not inconsiderable cost to the public purse and no obvious advantage to the public weal."

On appeal to the House, but not in the Divisional Court, Mr Pannick argued that *section 22*(4), read with *section 7*(1)(b), is apt only to extend to the trial. It was an argument of some technicality. The language of the statute does not compel its adoption and a construction which treats the trial and the appeal as parts of one process is more in keeping with the purpose of the Convention and *the Act* of 1998. It is the sensible and just construction. I would reject the argument advanced on behalf of the DPP on this point.

Issue 2: Legitimate Expectations

Mr Lords, in their Case the Respondents submitted that in the light of *section 22*(4) read in the context of *the Act* of 1989, the Respondents have a legitimate expectation that pending the coming into force of the central provisions of *the Act* of 1998, the DPP would not give his consent to a prosecution which would violate Article 6. In cogently expressed reasoning the Divisional Court rejected this submission. In a carefully structured oral argument Lord Lester of Herne Hill Q.C., who appeared for the Respondents, did not press this argument. There is a clear statutory intent to postpone the coming into effect of central provisions of *the Act*. A legitimate expectation, which treats inoperative statutory provisions as having immediate effect, is contradicted by the language of the statute. This argument must be rejected.

Issue 3: Section 29(3)

Section 29(3) of the Supreme Court Act 1981 provides:

> "In relation to the jurisdiction of the Crown Court, other than its jurisdiction in matters relating to trial on indictment, the High Court shall have all such jurisdiction to make orders of mandamus, prohibition or certiorari as the High Court possesses in relation to the jurisdiction of an inferior court."

The DPP contends that section 29(3) of the Supreme Court Act 1981 is applicable and that it deprives the Divisional Court of power to entertain the present applications for judicial review. The purpose of section 29(3) was explained by Lord Bridge of Harwich in *In re Smalley* [1985] A.C. 622, at 642–643, as follows:

> "it is not difficult to discern a sensible legislative purpose in excluding appeal or judicial review of any decision affecting the conduct of a trial on indictment, whether given in the course of the trial or by way of pre-trial directions. In any such case to allow an appellate or review process might . . . seriously delay the trial. If it is the prosecutor who is aggrieved by such a decision, it is in no way surprising that he has no remedy, since prosecutors have never enjoyed rights of appeal or review when unsuccessful in trials on indictment. If, on the other hand, the defendant is so aggrieved, he will have his remedy by way of appeal against conviction . . ."

This explanation was approved by Lord Slynn of Hadley (speaking for a unanimous House) in *In re Ashton* [1994] 1 A.C. 9,17. Mr Pannick argues that judicial review of a decision to prosecute is as likely to cause delay to criminal proceedings as judicial review of a decision of the Crown Court. Moreover, he says the decision to prosecute is inextricably linked with the trial itself, the complaint being that the judge will direct the jury in terms about which the Respondents complain. All this is true. But section 29(3) circumscribes the jurisdiction of the High Court. And the plain language of section 29(3) is only apt to exclude the High Court's jurisdiction in respect of orders directed to and affecting the Crown Court's exercise of its jurisdiction in matters relating to trial on indictment. On this point of interpretation I would accept the reasoning of the Lord Chief Justice and of Laws L.J. But Mr Pannick further submitted, that if section 29(3) is not applicable, the matter is covered by a common law principle which limits the High Court's exercise of discretion to entertain judicial review proceedings of a decision to prosecute. He acknowledged that this principle leaves untouched the jurisdiction of the High Court. But he contended that there is a common law principle that, absent dishonesty or *mala fides* or some other wholly exceptional circumstance, the High Court will as a matter of discretion not entertain judicial review proceedings of a decision to prosecute. There are some *dicta* to this effect: *Reg. v. Panel on Takeovers and Mergers, Ex parte Fayed* [1992] B.C.C. 524, at p. 536; *Reg. v. Chief Constable of Kent, Ex parte L* [1993] 1 All E.R. 756, 770–771 and *Elguzouli-Daf v. Commissioner of Police of the Metropolis* [1995] Q.B. 335.

For my part I would not wish to base my decision on these observations. In the opposite case, namely a decision not to prosecute, judicial review is available: see *Reg. v. Director of Public Prosecutions, Ex parte C.* [1995] 1 Cr. App. R. 136. That is, however, a wholly different situation because in such a case there is no other remedy. Counsel for the Respondents also relied on *Reg. v. Bedwellty Justices, Ex parte Williams* [1997] A.C. 225 where the House of Lords quashed a Magistrates Court's decision to commit a defendant on inadmissible evidence. A Magistrates' Court is, however, an inferior court. The present case involves a decision by the DPP in respect of a trial pending in the Crown Court which is a superior court. The decision of the House in *Williams* has no bearing on the problem before the House.

The starting point must be the analogical force of the statute which excludes the High Court's power to review decisions of the Crown Court. Thus section 29(3) would prohibit an application for judicial review of the decision of the Crown Court judge refusing to hold a prosecution to be an abuse of process by reason of an alleged breach of the Convention. It would be curious if the same issue could be raised in the Divisional Court by means of a challenge to the decision of the prosecutor to proceed with the prosecutions. The policy underlying the statute would be severely undermined if it could be outflanked by framing the case as a challenge to the prosecutor's decision to enforce the law rather than as a challenge to the decision of the Crown Court judge to apply the law. It is also noteworthy that it is rightly conceded that once the Act of 1998 is fully in force it will not be possible to apply for judicial review on the ground that a decision to prosecute is in breach of a Convention right. The only available remedies will be in the trial process or on appeal. It would be strange if in the interim period between the enactment of the Act of 1998 and the coming into force of its central provisions defendants in criminal trials were entitled to an additional remedy by way of judicial review. Given that reverse legal burden provisions appear in other legislation, the entertaining of such challenges outside the trial and appeal process might seriously disrupt the criminal justice system. Moreover, when section 6 of the Convention becomes part of our law, it will be the prism through which other aspects of our criminal law may have to be re-examined. If the Divisional Court's present ruling is correct, it will be possible in other cases, which do not involve reverse legal burden provisions, to challenge decisions to prosecute in judicial review proceedings. The potential for undermining the proper and fair management of our criminal justice system may be considerable.

Counsel for the Respondents accepted that there is a common law principle independent of section 29(3) which provides a strong presumption against the Divisional Court entertaining a judicial review application where the complaint can be raised within the criminal trial and appeal process. Counsel persuaded the Divisional Court that section 16A undermines the presumption of innocence in a blatant and obvious way. And that was also his submission before the House. He further submitted that the respondents have no effective remedy in the criminal trial or on appeal. Counsel for the DPP has persuaded me that this complaint is overstated. In the first place counsel for the Respondents are free to submit when the trial against the Respondents is continued that section 16A(1) and (3) should not be interpreted as provisions reversing the legal burden, with the risk of a defendant being convicted even if the jury is in doubt about terrorist intent. This argument involves treating the word "prove" in section 16A (3) as placing only an evidential burden on a defendant. The basis of such an argument was explained by *Glanville Williams, The Logic of "Exceptions,"* [1988] C.L.J. 261 at 264–265. The thrust of the argument is that the real intent of such a provision is to impose on the defendant the burden of neutralising a *prima facie* presumption. That indeed is what counsel for the Respondents argued before the House. This is a respectable argument which is reinforced by the disfavour with which reverse legal burden provisions have been regarded by the Privy Council in *Attorney-General of Hong Kong v. Lee Kwong-kut* [1993] A.C. 951 and leading judgments in other countries: see, for example, *Reg. v. Whyte* (1988) 51 D.L.R. (4th) 481, at 493; *R. v. Oakes (1986) 26 D.L.R. (4th)* 200; *State v. Mbatha* [1996] 2 L.R.C. 208, at 218. If the trial judge rules against the Respondents on this issue, and they are convicted, they will be able to raise this issue on appeal. Moreover, if the Respondents are convicted, they might also be able to challenge the DPP's interpretation by inviting the Court of Appeal (Criminal Division) to interpret section 16A(1) and (3) compatibly with their Convention right under article 6(2). This assumes that the Act of 1989 will by then be in operation. Given that the trial will apparently be a long one this seems a realistic assumption. Secondly, if this is indeed as blatant and obvious a case as counsel for the Respondents contends, it may arguably be open to the Respondents to submit that the prosecution is an abuse of process inasmuch as it is so unfair and wrong that the court should not allow a prosecutor to proceed with it: *Hui Chi-ming v. The Queen* [1992] 1 A.C. 34, at 57; *Attorney-General of Trinidad and Tobago v. Phillip* [1995] 1 A.C. 396, at 417 C-D. I express no view on the likely outcome of any such arguments. But it is not right to say that the Respondents are entirely without remedy in the criminal process.

Looking at the matter more broadly there is also an implausibility at the heart of the Respondents' case. They seek judicial review on the ground that the DPP's consent involves an error of law, namely that the prosecution is compatible with article 6(2) of the Convention. But the DPP may sometimes not have a concluded view of any kind. But he may nonetheless be persuaded that, despite some uncertainty about the law, a prosecution is justified as being in the public interest. There could then be no question of reviewing his decision for error of law. So far as Laws L.J. held that the DPP is at this stage legally bound to form a view on the issue of compatibility I would respectfully disagree: at 197F and 198F. And, if he is not so bound, why should his decision to consent to a prosecution be amenable to judicial review if he arrives at a firm view? After all, such a matter ought not to depend on the degree of confidence in the legal position of the DPP or his counsel. Moreover, it would be odd to allow the possibility of judicial review of the DPP's decision to prosecute to depend on the error being blatant and obvious. That excludes the case where this threshold test is not met. It is difficult to see on what principle such a distinction rests. It gives the appearance of introducing into our public law categories of illegality.

My Lords, I would rule that absent dishonesty or *mala fides* or an exceptional circumstance, the decision of the DPP to consent to the prosecution of the Respondents is not amenable to judicial review. And I would further rule that the present case falls on the wrong side of that line. While the passing of the *Human Rights Act 1998* marked a great advance for our criminal justice system it is in my view vitally important that, so far as the courts are concerned, its application in our law should take place in an orderly manner which recognises the desirability of all challenges taking place in the criminal trial or on appeal. The effect of the judgment of the Divisional Court was to open the door too widely to delay in the conduct of criminal proceedings. Such satellite litigation should rarely be permitted in our criminal justice system. In my view the Divisional Court should have dismissed the Respondents' application.

Issues (4) and (5): Interpretation and Compatibility of Section 16A with Article 6(2)

Given the conclusion I have arrived at it would be wrong to express concluded views on issues (4) and (5). But as I have made clear I regard those issues as arguable. The effect is that those issues are undecided and entirely open at all levels in the criminal proceedings.

The Disposal of the Appeal

My Lords, I would allow the appeal and quash the orders of the Divisional Court.

LORD COOKE OF THORNDON

My Lords,

Having had the advantage of reading in draft the speech of my noble and learned friend Lord Steyn, I am in general agreement with it and can confine my added observations to the following.

As the argument of this appeal developed, the main thrust of the submissions for the appellant appeared to change. In Mr. Pannick Q.C.'s reply the contention put in the forefront was based on the undesirability of satellite litigation attending cases to be tried on indictment. It was said that the present criminal proceedings should not be interfered with by way of judicial review: that the trial and, if necessary, appeal processes should provide adequate remedies for the defendants if their human rights are violated. A risk of imminent violation could no doubt be dealt with similarly at the trial or on appeal.

To that contention I am willing to accede, although other parts of the argument in support of the present appeal appear to me more questionable. There seems to be no sound reason why, in principle, a consent given by the Director of Public Prosecutions should not be open to judicial review—although the concept of a *continuing* consent may want something in accuracy—but, in a case where it is obvious that the Director wishes a charge to go to trial, I think that the courts should be very slow to allow review of a consent to be used as a device for resolving points which would otherwise be dealt with in the ordinary course of the criminal proceedings. As a general rule, proceedings on indictment should not be delayed by collateral challenges. But, as Lord Bingham of Cornhill C.J. [1999] 3 W.L.R. 175, 183–184 pointed out, there are cases where that cannot be avoided. The Lord Chief Justice cited *Reg. v. Bedwellty Justices, Ex parte Williams* [1997] A.C 225, where a committal for trial in the Crown Court was quashed on judicial review. The relevant part of that decision of your Lordships' House was that the indictment process offered no way of curing the breach of the defendant's right to cross-examine witnesses before the examining justices. No equivalent feature is to be found in the present case.

In the present case I am the more ready to apply the general rule because I cannot help thinking that there is a degree of inconsistency in the Divisional Court's approach. They held that section 16A of the *Prevention of Terrorism (Temporary Provisions) Act 1989* is repugnant to article 6.2 of the European Convention on Human Rights, and that in acting on a contrary view the Director had proceeded unlawfully. They had regard to the circumstance that, when the *Human Rights Act 1998* is brought into force, *section 7*(1)(b) will have retrospective effect by virtue of *section 22*(4). But they felt bound in interpreting section 16A of *the Act* of 1989 to adopt the natural and ordinary meaning rather than the new rule of interpretation laid down by *section 3*(1) of the *Human Rights Act.*

My Lords, I see great force in the Divisional Court's view that on the natural and ordinary interpretation there is repugnancy. To introduce concepts of reasonable limits, balance or flexibility, as to none of which article 6.2 says anything, may be seen as undermining or marginalising the philosophy embodied in the straightforward provision that everyone charged with a criminal offence shall be presumed innocent until proved guilty according to law. On its face section 16A of *the Act* of 1989 enables a person to be found guilty of a very serious offence merely on reasonable grounds of suspicion. It may be highly inconvenient that this should not be permissible, an inconvenience brought out by the list of broadly comparable provisions to be given by my noble and learned friend Lord Hope of Craighead, but at best it is doubtful whether article 6.2 can be watered down to an extent that would leave section 16A unscathed. The judgment of the Privy Council delivered by Lord Woolf *in Attorney-General of Hong Kong v. Lee Kwong-kut* [1993] A.C. 951 strongly suggests that it cannot. One cannot exclude the possibility, however, that the European Court of Human Rights, whose jurisprudence in the field is not yet extensively developed, may be prepared to treat terrorism as a special subject or perhaps to found a reading down on "according to law."

But I am constrained to part company with the Divisional Court on their putting aside of *section 3*(1) of the *Human Rights Act*. In my respectful view, it is not altogether logical, nor is it necessary, to consider the likely impact of the other main provisions of that Act on United Kingdom law without taking into account also *section 3*(1), which is a key element in *the Act*.

When the whole Act comes into force, the new canon of interpretation will be that, so far as it is possible to do so, primary legislation and subordinate legislation must be read and given effect in a way which is compatible with the Convention rights. This is a strong adjuration. It seems distinctly possible that it may require section 16A of *the Act* of 1989 to be interpreted as imposing on the defendant an evidential, but not a persuasive (or ultimate), burden of proof. I agree that such is not the natural and ordinary meaning of section 16A(3). Yet for evidence that it is a *possible* meaning one could hardly ask for more than the opinion of Professor Glanville Williams in *The Logic of "Exceptions"* [1988] C.L.J. 261, 265 that "unless the contrary is proved" can be taken, in relation to a defence, to mean "unless sufficient evidence is given to the contrary;" and that the statute may then be satisfied by "evidence that, if believed and on the most favourable view, could be taken by a reasonable jury to support the defence."

I must not conceal that in New Zealand the Glanville Williams approach was not allowed to prevail in *R. v. Phillips* [1991] 3 N.Z.L.R. 175. But, quite apart from the fact that the decision is of course not authoritative in England, section 6 of the New Zealand Bill of Rights Act 1990 is in terms different from section 3(1) of the *Human Rights Act 1998*. The United Kingdom subsection, read as a whole, conveys, I think, a rather more powerful message.

As this case has reached this House, there would appear to be something to be said for a resolution by your Lordships now of the question whether, when *section 3*(1) and the rest of the *Human Rights Act* is in force, it will be possible for provisions such as section 16A of *the Act* of 1989 to be read and given effect in a way which is compatible with the Convention rights. But the possibility of such a resolution had apparently not been foreseen by counsel; the argument on *section 3*(1) was by no means as full as is desirable if the effect of so major a new canon of interpretation is to be settled; and I accept that it would be premature to embark on the question. It should be left to be dealt with in this case, as far as may be found just or expedient, by the trial judge and on any subsequent appeals.

My only reservation is that, as I understood Mr.Pannick to suggest, the question should be treated as truly open to the trial judge on a renewed abuse of process application or otherwise, and thereafter, if necessary, in the Court of Appeal, Criminal Division, and your Lordships' House. That is to say, observations in this case or other cases should not be treated as at all fettering the trial judge or subsequent courts. Otherwise a catch-22 situation could arise in which, although the House allows this appeal on the ground that the defendants have their proper remedy in the course of the trial and appellate process, attempts to obtain any form of remedy or lightening of the defence onus are already destined to failure.

Subject to that caveat, I would allow the appeal.

LORD HOPE OF CRAIGHEAD

My Lords,

These proceedings have been brought to challenge by judicial review in the Divisional Court the decision of the Director of Public Prosecutions to consent to the institution of criminal proceedings against the respondents under section 16A of the *Prevention of Terrorism (Temporary Provisions) Act 1989* which was inserted by section 82 of the *Criminal Justice and Public Order Act 1994*.

When the relevant legislation was being considered in Parliament in 1994 the focus was on familiar problems associated with terrorism in Northern Ireland. Similar provisions had been in force in the Province since 1973. It was also being considered before the initiatives were taken by the present Government which led to the enactment on 9 November 1998 of the *Human Rights Act 1998*. The circumstances in which your Lordships are now being asked to consider the effect of the legislation require it to be subjected to a more exacting scrutiny. We are dealing in this case with allegations that the respondents, who are all Algerian nationals, were involved with terrorism in Algeria. The security situation in that country creates difficulties for the defence in obtaining evidence to rebut these allegations which would not arise if that evidence were being sought in this country or in Ireland. Furthermore, although the 1998 Act is not yet in force, the vigorous public debate which accompanied its passage through Parliament has already had a profound influence on thinking about issues of human rights. It is now plain that the incorporation of the European Convention on Human Rights into our domestic law will subject the entire legal system to a fundamental process of review and, where necessary, reform by the judiciary.

In *Attorney-General of Hong Kong v. Lee Kwong-kut* [1993] A.C. 951, 966 Lord Woolf referred to the general approach to the interpretations of constitutions and bills of rights indicated in previous decisions of the Board, which he said were equally applicable to the Hong Kong Bill of Rights Ordinance 1991. He mentioned Lord Wilberforce's observation in *Minister of Home Affairs v. Fisher* [1980] A.C. 319, 328 that instruments of this nature call for a generous interpretation suitable to give to individuals the full measure of the fundamental rights and freedoms referred to, and Lord Diplock's comment in *Attorney-General of The Gambia v. Momodou Jobe* [1984] A.C. 689, 700 that a generous and purposive construction is to be given to that part of a constitution which protects and entrenches fundamental rights and freedoms to which all persons in the state are to be entitled. The same approach will now have to be applied in this country when issues are raised under the 1998 Act about the compatibility of domestic legislation and of acts of public authorities with the fundamental rights and freedoms which are enshrined in the Convention.

The primary focus of attention in this case is upon the continuing decision of the Director. If the 1998 Act were in force, the appropriate remedy would be to raise at the trial or on appeal under section 7 of that Act the question whether, in terms of section 6(1) of the Act, he was acting or had acted in a way which was incompatible with a Convention right. That in turn would require section 16A of the 1989 Act as amended to be construed, in terms of section 3(1) of the 1998 Act, so far as it was possible to do so in a way which was compatible with Convention rights. But, as the legislation is not yet in force, we have not reached that stage. The procedures which are to be provided under section 7 are not yet available. So the issue as to compatibility was first raised at the trial in the context of an argument that there was an abuse of process. A ruling on the issue was sought from the trial judge. The Director decided to maintain his consent to the prosecutions on legal advice, after the trial judge had ruled that section 16A was incompatible with the presumption of innocence guaranteed by article 6(2) of the Convention. The trial was then adjourned on the grounds of late service of evidence by the Crown Prosecution Service, whereupon applications for judicial review of the Director's decision were made in the Divisional Court.

Among the detailed reasons which Lord Bingham C.J. gave for granting the applications was the following: [1999] 3 W.L.R. 175, 187F:

> "It is, therefore, as it seems to me, appropriate for this court to review the soundness of the legal advice on which the Director has made clear, publicly, that he relied; for if the legal advice he relied on was unsound

he should, in the public interest, have the opportunity to reconsider the confirmation of his consent on a sound legal basis."

I respectfully agree with this observation and with the process of reasoning on which it was based. I also agree that a review of the soundness of the Director's decision would not conflict in any way with the principle of Parliamentary sovereignty. The Director was not being asked to treat section 16A as if it had never been enacted. What he was being asked to do was to reconsider, on a sound legal basis, his decision as to whether prosecutions under that section should be authorised. If the advice on which he relied was unsound, the respondents were entitled to an effective remedy against that decision as soon as this was practicable.

At first sight, the obvious way of achieving this once the trial had been adjourned was to apply for judicial review in the Divisional Court. I am not aware of any other process under English law by which a remedy could be given during the adjournment of a trial. But the fact that it has not been the practice to bring a consent to a prosecution under judicial review means that no example of such an application could be cited to us as a precedent. Furthermore, for all the reasons which my noble and learned friend Lord Steyn has given, there are strong grounds for the view that, in the absence of dishonesty, bad faith or some other exceptional circumstance, the Director's decisions to consent or not to consent to a prosecution are not amenable to judicial review in that court. To this must be added the fact that the process of judicial review could do no more than require the Director to reconsider his decision. It could not require him to change his view. It would fall short of providing a remedy which is as effective as that which could be provided by the trial judge during the trial process or on appeal.

With regret, therefore, I have come to the conclusion that the appeals must be allowed on this ground and that the applications must be dismissed.

Nevertheless I consider that the issues which have been raised in this appeal, and which were fully and ably argued on both sides, are so important to a consideration of the impact of article 6(2) of the Convention upon so many of the statutory provisions which are to be found in our criminal law that the opportunity ought be taken to set out and review the competing arguments on this issue. I have in mind the fact that, while the *Human Rights Act 1998* will not come into force in the United Kingdom until 2 October 2000, the *Scotland Act 1998* is now in force. The Scottish Parliament has already embarked upon its first legislative programme, and members of the Scottish Executive are already taking decisions in the exercise of their functions under *the Act*. Legislation by the Scottish Parliament will be outside its legislative competence if it is incompatible with any of the Convention rights: *section 29(2)(d) of the Scotland Act 1998*. Members of the Scottish Executive have no power to make any subordinate legislation or to do any other act if to do so would be incompatible with any of the Convention rights: *section 57*(2) of that Act.

The Divisional Court held that the provisions of section 16A of the 1989 Act as amended violated the presumption of innocence and that they were thus repugnant to article 6(2) of the Convention. The legislative techniques which these provisions have employed are however not unique to that Act. The implications of that decision do not stop there. It is likely that the compatibility with article 6(2) of a large number of other statutory provisions, both in United Kingdom legislation and in legislation applying only to Scotland, will be called into question as decisions are taken as to whether to prosecute, or to continue to prosecute. Under Scottish criminal procedure these questions can be brought under the review of the High Court of Justiciary and dealt with by providing an effective remedy in the course of the criminal process at any time. A prolonged period of uncertainty as to whether these provisions are enforceable is undesirable.

The Presumption of Innocence

Article 6(2) of the Convention contains this declaration:

> "Everyone charged with a criminal offence shall be presumed innocent until proved guilty according to law."

As a statement of fundamental principle that declaration is wholly consistent with the common law of both England and Scotland. In the well-known words of Viscount Sankey L.C. in *Woolmington v. director of Public* Prosecutions [1935] A.C. 462, 481:

> "Throughout the web of the English criminal law one golden thread is always to be seen, that it is the duty of the prosecution to prove the prisoner's guilt subject to what I have already said as to the defence of insanity and subject also to any statutory exception."

In *Slater v. H.M. Advocate*, 1928 J.C. 94, 105 the High Court of Justiciary took the opportunity, in the first appeal to come before the Court under the Criminal Appeal (Scotland) Act 1926, to say:

> "The presumption of innocence applies to every person charged with a criminal offence in precisely the same way, and it can be overcome only by evidence relevant to prove the crime with the commission of which he is charged. The presumption of innocence is fundamental to the whole system of criminal prosecution, and it was a radical error to suggest that the appellant did not have the benefit of it to the same effect as any other accused person."

The only exception to this rule which the common law has recognised, as Viscount Sankey noted, is in regard to the defence of insanity. The judges throughout the United Kingdom have resisted the temptation to extend that exception to the defence of automatism: *Bratty v. Attorney-General for Northern* Ireland 1991 A.C. 386; *Ross v. H.M. Advocate*, 1991 J.C. 210. In *Hill v. Baxter* [1958] 1 Q.B. 277, 285 Devlin J. said:

> "As automatism is akin to insanity in law there would be great practical advantage if the burden of proof was the same in both cases. But so far insanity is the only matter of defence in which under the common law the burden of proof has been held to be completely shifted."

The reason for the shifting of the burden in the case of the defence of insanity is that, as Viscount Kilmuir L.C. explained in *Bratty's* case at p. 407, normally the presumption of mental capacity is sufficient to prove that the accused acted consciously and voluntarily. The presumption is one of sanity, not responsibility. Although the prosecution need go no further to prove that the accused has mental capacity, it must nevertheless discharge the legal burden of proving mens rea: see *Ross v. H.M. Advocate*, at p. 221. As the presumption of innocence continues to occupy such a fundamental place in the common law, the judges have ensured that all common law presumptions which form part of the law of evidence are subordinated to this principle. An example is the rule of evidence in Scots law that, if the accused is found in possession of recently stolen goods in criminative circumstances, he must displace the inference of guilt raised by these circumstances. These rules do not place a burden of proof on the accused which he has to discharge on a balance of probabilities. All the accused has to do is raise a reasonable doubt as to his guilt. That is not to say that these evidential rules are insignificant. In many cases they can have a vital bearing on the outcome of the trial, depending on how easy or how difficult it is for the accused to rebut the presumption. But the burden of proving his guilt beyond reasonable doubt remains with the prosecution throughout the trial. It has not been suggested in this case that these common law evidential presumptions are incompatible with the presumption of innocence.

The difficulty lies in the area of legislation by Parliament. As Viscount Sankey L.C. noted in *Woolmington v. Director of Public Prosecutions*, it has always been open to Parliament by way of a statutory exception to transfer the onus of proof as to some matter arising in a criminal case from the prosecution to the accused. Glanville Williams, *The Proof of Guilt* (3rd ed., 1963), p. 184 observed that Parliament regards the principle with indifference. That may be overstating the matter; but it is clear that until now, under the doctrine of sovereignty, the only check on Parliament's freedom to legislate in this area has been political. All that will now change with the coming into force of the *Human Rights Act 1998*. But the change will affect the past as well as the future. Unlike the constitutions of many of the countries within the Commonwealth which protect pre-existing legislation from challenge under their human rights provisions, the 1998 Act will apply to all leislation, whatever its date, in the past as well as in the future.

Classification

The first stage in any inquiry as to whether a statutory provision is vulnerable to challenge on the ground that it is incompatible with article 6(2) of the Convention is to identify the nature of the provision which is said to transfer the burden of proof from the prosecution to the accused. Various techniques have been adopted. Some provisions are more objectionable than others. The extent to which they encroach upon the presumption of innocence depends upon the legislative technique which has been used. The field can be narrowed considerably by means of this preliminary analysis.

It is necessary in the first place to distinguish between the shifting from the prosecution to the accused of what Glanville Williams at pp. 185–186 described as the "evidential burden," or the burden of introducing evidence in support of his case, on the one hand and the "persuasive burden," or the burden of persuading the jury as to his guilt or innocence, on the other. A "persuasive" burden of proof requires the accused to prove, on a balance of probabilities, a fact which is essential to the determination of his guilt or innocence. It reverses the burden of proof by removing it from the prosecution and transferring it to the accused. An "evidential" burden requires only that the accused must adduce sufficient evidence to raise an issue before it has to be determined as one of the facts in the case. The prosecution does not need to lead any evidence about it, so the accused needs to do this if he wishes to put the point in issue. But if it is put in issue, the burden of proof remains with the prosecution. The accused need only raise a reasonable doubt about his guilt.

Statutory presumptions which place an "evidential" burden on the accused, requiring the accused to do no more than raise a reasonable doubt on the matter with which they deal, do not breach the presumption of innocence. They are not incompatible with article 6(2) of the Convention. They take their place alongside the common law evidential presumptions which have been built up in the light of experience. They are a necessary part of preserving the balance of fairness between the accused and the prosecutor in matters of evidence. It is quite common in summary prosecutions for routine matters which may be inconvenient or time-consuming for the prosecutor to have to prove but which may reasonably be supposed to be within the accused's own knowledge to be dealt with in this way. It is not suggested that statutory provisions of this kind are objectionable.

Statutory presumptions which transfer the "persuasive" burden to the accused require further examination. Three kinds were identified by the respondents in their written case. I am content to adopt their analysis, which Mr Pannick Q.C. for the Director did not dispute. First, there is the "mandatory" presumption of guilt as to an essential element of the offence. As the presumption is one which must be applied if the basis of fact on which it rests is established, it is inconsistent with the presumption of innocence. This is a matter which can be determined as a preliminary issue without reference to the facts of the case. Secondly, there is a presumption of guilt as to an essential element which is "discretionary." The tribunal of fact may or may not rely on the presumption, depending upon its view as to the cogency or weight of the evidence. If the presumption is of this kind it may be necessary for the facts of the case to be considered before a conclusion can be reached as to whether the presumption of innocence has been breached. In that event the matters cannot be resolved until after trial.

The third category of provisions which fall within the general description of reverse onus clauses consists of provisions which relate to an exemption or proviso which the accused must establish if he wishes to avoid conviction but is not an essential element of the offence. In *Reg. v. Edwards* [1975] Q.B. 27 a provision of this kind was held to impose a burden of proof on the defendant to establish on the balance of probabilities that he had a licence for the sale of the intoxicating liquor. Lawton L.J. said, at pp. 39–40, when giving the judgment of the court, that this exception to the fundamental rule that the prosecution must prove every element of the offence charged was limited to offences arising under enactments which prohibit the doing of an act save in specified circumstances or by persons of specified classes or with special qualifications or with the licence or permission of specified authorities. In *Reg. v. Hunt (Richard)* [1987] A.C. 352, 375 Lord Griffiths emphasised the special nature of these provisions when he said that he had little doubt that the occasions upon which a statute will be construed as imposing a burden of proof upon a defendant which did not fall within this formulation are likely to be exceedingly rare. These provisions may or may not violate the presumption of innocence, depending on the circumstances.

Two further important points need to be made about this classification. The first is that this is not an exact science. The provisions vary so widely in their detail as to what the prosecutor must prove before the onus shifts, and their effect on the presumption of innocence depends so much on circumstances. These matters may not be capable of being fully assessed until after the trial. The best that can be done, by way of a preliminary examination, is to see whether the legislative technique which has been adopted imposes a persuasive or merely an evidential burden, whether it is mandatory or discretionary and whether it relates to an essential element of the offence or merely to an exception or proviso. The second is that, even if the conclusion is reached that prima facie the provision breaches the presumption of innocence, that will not lead inevitably to the conclusion that the provision is incompatible with article 6(2) of the Convention. The European jurisprudence, which I shall examine later, shows that other factors need to be brought into consideration at this stage. In my opinion, for reasons which I shall explain, the Divisional Court did not attach sufficient weight to these factors.

The Discretionary Area of Judgment

This brings me to another matter on which there was a consensus between counsel and which, I believe, needs now to be judicially recognised. The doctrine of the "margin of appreciation" is a familiar part of the jurisprudence of the European Court of Human Rights. The European Court has acknowledged that, by reason of their direct and continuous contact with the vital forces of their countries, the national authorities are in principle better placed to evaluate local needs and conditions than an international court: *Buckley v. United Kingdom* (1996) 23 E.H.R.R. 101, 129, paras. 74–75. Although this means that, as the European Court explained in *Handyside v. United Kingdom* (1976) 1 E.H.R.R. 737, 753, para. 48, "the machinery of protection established by the Convention is subsidiary to the national systems safeguarding human rights," it goes hand in hand with a European supervision. The extent of this supervision will vary according to such factors as the nature of the Convention right in issue, the importance of that right for the individual and the nature of the activities involved in the case.

This doctrine is an integral part of the supervisory jurisdiction which is exercised over state conduct by the international court. By conceding a margin of appreciation to each national system, the court has recognised that the Convention, as a living system, does not need to be applied uniformly by all states but may vary in its application according to local needs and conditions. This technique is not available to the national courts when they are considering Convention issues arising within their own countries. But in the hands of the national courts also the Convention should be seen as an expression of fundamental principles rather than as a set of mere rules. The questions which the courts will have to decide in the application of these principles will involve questions of balance between competing interests and issues of proportionality.

In this area difficult choices may have to be made by the executive or the legislature between the rights of the individual and the needs of society. In some circumstances it will be appropriate for the courts to recognise that there is an area of judgment within which the judiciary will defer, on democratic grounds, to the considered opinion of the elected body or person whose act or decision is said to be incompatible with the Convention. This point is well made at p. 74, para. 3.21 of *Human Rights Law and Practice* (Butterworths, 1999), of which Lord Lester of Herne Hill Q.C. and Mr David Pannick Q.C.

are the General Editors, where the area in which these choices may arise is conveniently and appropriately described as the "discretionary area of judgment." It will be easier for such an area of judgment to be recognised where the Convention itself requires a balance to be struck, much less so where the right is stated in terms which are unqualified. It will be easier for it to be recognised where the issues involve questions of social or economic policy, much less so where the rights are of high constitutional importance or are of a kind where the courts are especially well placed to assess the need for protection. But even where the right is stated in terms which are unqualified the courts will need to bear in mind the jurisprudence of the European Court which recognises that due account should be taken of the special nature of terrorist crime and the threat which it poses to a democratic society: *Murray v. United Kingdom* (1994) 19 E.H.R.R. 193, 222, para. 47.

Section 16A of the 1989 Act

Section 16A creates an offence which is described in the side note as possession of articles for suspected terrorist purposes. It is made up of six subsections, of which those which are relevant to the issues raised by article 6(2) of the Convention are subsections (1), (3) and (4). Subsection (1) creates the offence. It is based on reasonable suspicion. All the prosecution has to do is prove that the accused was in possession of the article in circumstances which give rise to a reasonable suspicion that they were in his possession for a purpose connected with terrorism. Although the essence of the offence is the possession of articles for a purpose connected with terrorism, the prosecution does not have to prove that that was in fact the purpose. There is therefore a presumption that this was the purpose. It takes effect once circumstances giving rise to a reasonable suspicion have been proved.

The severity of this approach is tempered by subsection (3). It provides that it is a defence for the accused to prove that the article was not in his possession for a terrorist purpose. Nothing is said expressly about the burden or standard of proof. But Mr Pannick accepted that, according to the ordinary principles of construction, this provision has the effect of transferring the burden of proof as to the purpose for which the article was in his possession to the accused. Then there is subsection (4). This deals with the question of possession. In the ordinary case knowledge and control are essential elements which the prosecutor must prove in order to show that the accused was in possession of an article. This subsection enables a court to find these facts to been established by evidence that the accused and the article were both present in any premises or that the article was in premises of which he was the occupier or habitual user, unless he proves that he did not know of its presence in the premises or, if he did know, that he had no control over it. The burden of proving lack of knowledge or control is on the accused. But the court is told only that it "may" draw the inference, not that it must do so. In view of the width of the meaning which is given to the expression "premises," the question whether it would be right for the court to rely on the evidence described in subsection (4) as sufficient evidence will obviously vary according to the circumstances.

According to the classification which I have outlined, subsection (3) of section 16A imposes a persuasive burden of proof on the accused, on a balance of probabilities, that the article was not in his possession for a purpose connected with terrorism. If that burden is not discharged, or the accused elects not to undertake it, subsection (1) contains a mandatory presumption that the article was in his possession for a purpose connected with terrorism which is applied if the prosecutor proves that it was in his possession in circumstances giving rise to a reasonable suspicion that it was in his possession for that purpose. Subsection (4) imposes a persuasive burden of proof on the accused that he did not know that the article was in the premises or, if he did, that he had no control over it. If that burden is not discharged, or the accused elects not to undertake it, the subsection contains a discretionary presumption that he was in possession of the article.

Lord Lester Q.C. for the respondents recognised the discretionary nature of the persuasive burden in subsection (4) of section 16A. He also recognised the force of the decision of the Court of Appeal in Northern Ireland in *Reg. v. Killen* [1974] N.I. 220, in which it was held that an identical provision in section 7(1) of the Northern Ireland (Emergency Provisions) Act 1973 placing an onus on the accused to disprove his knowledge of possession should not be used unless, having done so, the court would be left satisfied beyond reasonable doubt of the guilt of the accused. So he did not press the argument which was advanced in the Divisional Court that subsection (4) was in breach of the presumption of innocence. Mr Weatherup Q.C. explained that in practice the application of section 7(1) of the 1973 Act was treated as a discretionary matter in Northern Ireland, with the result that it was not always necessary for the accused to provide an explanation in reply to the Crown case. But Lord Lester maintained his argument that that presumption was breached by subsections (1) and (3). In the Divsional Court Lord Bingham C.J. [1999] 3 W.L.R. 175, 190 said that this section, and section 16B which is no longer in issue as the Director has discontinued proceedings against the fourth named respondent, undermined "in a blatant and obvious way" the presumption of innocence.

These techniques are however not unique to section 16A of the 1989 Act as amended. Section 16B(1) of that Act contains a provision which imposes the persuasive burden of proof of lawful authority or reasonable excuse on the accused. But there are a substantial number of other statutory offences triable in the Crown Court which place a persuasive burden of proof on the accused, coupled with a mandatory presumption of guilt if it is not discharged, in circumstances which fall outside the scope of the exception recognised in *Reg. v. Edwards* [1975] Q.B. 27 and *Reg. v. Hunt (Richard)* [1987] A.C. 352. Your Lordships were provided with an agreed list of these provisions. They comprise the *Prevention of Corruption Act 1916*, section 2; the Sexual Offences Act 1956, section 30(2); the Obscene Publications Act 1959, section 2(5); the Obscene Publications Act 1964, section 1(3); the Misuse of Drugs Act 1971, section 28; the Public Order Act 1986, sections 18(4), 19(2), 20(2), 21(3), 22(3)–(5) and 23(3); the *Criminal Justice Act 1988*, section 93D(6); the *Prevention of Terrorism (Temporary Provisions) Act 1989, sections 10(2)–(3)*, 11(2), 16A(3), 16B(1) and 17(3)(a) and (3A)(a); the *Official Secrets Act 1989, sections 1(5), 2(3), 3(4)* and *4(4)–(5)*; and the *Drug Trafficking Act 1994, sections 53(6)* and *58(2)(a)*. To this list there may be added the *Explosive Substances Act 1883, section 4(1)*: see *Reg. v. Fegan* [1972] N.I. 80; *Reg. v. Berry* [1985] A.C. 246. As Lord MacDermott L.C.J. said in *Reg. v. Fegan* at p. 82, the legislative problem which these provisions seek to address is how to curb a grave evil which postulates a guilty mind or mental element on the part of the offender, when proof of that guilty mind or mental element is likely to be a matter of inherent difficulty.

Compatibility

Mr Pannick submitted that decisions of the European Commission of Human Rights and of the European Court of Human Rights showed that article 6(2) was not seen as containing an absolute prohibition on statutory provisions which imposed a burden of proof on the accused, and that the Convention did not permit the court to review the legality of national legislation in the abstract but only with reference to particular cases after the proceedings are complete. Lord Bingham C.J. recognised in the Divisional Court that there was a measure of truth in this argument: [1999] 3 W.L.R. 175, 189D. But he rejected it, on the view that the court was not precluded from considering the question of compatibility before the completion of the trial and that if, properly construed, a provision of domestic legislation truly infringes the presumption of innocence, any conviction based on that provision is likely, judged by the yardstick of the Convention, to be unsafe: p. 190A. Laws L.J. rejected it for similar reasons, on the ground that the compatibility or otherwise of the impugned legislation with article 6(2) fell to be judged by reference to the statutory provisions irrespective of the facts of the particular case: p. 201G.

I agree with both Lord Bingham C.J. and Laws L.J. that the national court is not precluded from considering the issue of compatibility before completion of the trial. There will, of course, be no question about this once the *Human Rights Act 1998* is brought into force, and issues of compatibility are already being raised before trial in the Scottish courts under the *Scotland Act*

1998. In principle I can see no reason why, in a clear case where the facts of the case are of no importance, a decision that a provision is incompatible should not be capable of being taken at a very early stage. I do however, with great respect, part company with them on the question whether a finding that section 16A is incompatible with article 6(2) is inevitable.

Lord Lester's concession, in the light of the decision in *Reg. v. Killen*, that the discretionary presumption in subsection (4) could not reasonably be objected to at this stage deprives the Divisional Court's reasoning of some of its force. This leaves the more powerful objections to the provisions of subsections (1) and (3). But I think that even in their case there are good reasons for thinking that they may not be as damaging to the presumption of innocence as might at first sight appear. There is also the question of balance, as to the interests of the individual as against those of society. The Convention jurisprudence and that which is to be found from cases decided in other jurisdictions suggests that account may legitimately be taken, in striking the right balance, of the problems which the legislation was designed to address.

In *Salabiaku v. France* (1988) 13 E.H.R.R 379, the Court was concerned with an article in the Customs Code dealing with the smuggling of prohibited goods. Where possession of prohibited goods was established, the person was deemed liable for the offence of smuggling. Read strictly, the provision appeared to lay down an irrebutable presumption. The code did not provide expressly for any defence. But the Court held that there was no failure to comply with article 6(2), because in practice the courts were careful not to resort automatically to the presumption but exercised their power of assessment in the light of all the evidence. At p. 388, para. 28 the Court gave this guidance:

> "Presumptions of fact or of law operate in every legal system. Clearly, the Convention does not prohibit such presumptions in principle. It does, however, require the Contracting States to remain within certain limits in this respect as regards criminal law....Article 6(2) does not therefore regard presumptions of fact or of law provided for in the criminal law with indifference. It requires States to confine them within reasonable limits which take into account the importance of what is at stake and maintain the rights of the defence. The Court proposes to consider whether such limits were exceeded to the detriment of Mr. Salabiaku."

As a matter of general principle therefore a fair balance must be struck between the demands of the general interest of the community and the protection of the fundamental rights of the individual: see also *Sporrong and Lönnroth v. Sweden* (1982) 5 E.H.R.R. 35, 52, para. 69.

The guidance which was given in *Salabiaku* was applied by the Commission in *H. v. United Kingdom*, Application No 15023/89, in which the complaint was that the burden on the accused in criminal proceedings to prove insanity on the balance of probabilities was contrary to the presumption of innocence and in violation of article 6(2); and in *Bates v. United Kingdom*, Application No. 26280/95, in which the complaint was that article 6(2) had been violated by the presumption of fact in *section* 5(5) of the *Dangerous Dogs Act 1991* by which it is to be presumed that the dog is one to which *section 1* of that Act applies unless the contrary is shown by the accused. In the *Bates* case the Commission held that *section* 5(5) fell within reasonable limits, even in the light of what was at stake for the applicant, given the opportunity expressly provided to the defence to rebut the presumption of fact and that *section* 5(5) was applied in a manner compatible with the presumption of innocence. The cases show that, although article 6(2) is in absolute terms, it is not regarded as imposing an absolute prohibition on reverse onus clauses, whether they be evidential (presumptions of fact) or persuasive (presumptions of law). In each case the question will be whether the presumption is within reasonable limits.

Reference was made to cases from various jurisdictions in the Commonwealth, including the decisions of the South African Constitutional Court in *State v. Zuma* [1995] 1 L.R.C. 145 and *State v. Mbatha* [1996] 2 L.R.C. 208 and decisions of the Supreme Court of Canada. The Canadian jurisprudence is to be found primarily in the judgments of Dickson C.J.C. in *Reg. v. Oakes* (1986) 26 D.L.R. (4th) 200 and *Reg. v. Whyte* (1988) 51 D.L.R. (4th) 481. These judgments were carefully analysed by Lord Woolf in *Attorney-General of Hong Kong v. Lee Kwong-kut* [1993] A.C. 951. As Lord Woolf has explained, at pp. 970–971, the Canadian approach when applying the Canadian Charter of Rights and Freedoms is to examine the matter in two stages: to see whether the provision in question has violated the presumption of innocence in section 11(d) of the Charter, and then to apply the limitation set out in *section 1* of the Charter. *Section 1* states that the rights and freedoms which it guarantees are "subject only to such reasonable limits prescribed by law as can be demonstrably justified in a free and democratic society." In *Reg. v. Oakes* at p. 223 Dickson C.J.C. said that it was highly desirable to keep these two sections analytically distinct. In the result a strict approach is adopted to the question as to whether these has been a contravention of section 11(d). A degree of flexibility is applied at the second stage.

In the present case, as I have said, Lord Bingham C.J. reached the conclusion that section 16A undermined "in a blatant and obvious way" the presumption of innocence. In support of this view he quoted a passage from Dickson C.J.C.'s judgment in *Reg. v. Whyte* at p. 493 where he was dealing with the tests to be applied at the first stage. But he did not go on to examine the issues which would have been relevant, under the Canadian jurisprudence, at the second stage. This omission is important because, as Lord Woolf observed in *Lee Kwong-kut*, the Canadian courts, applying the two stage approach, tend to come to the same conclusion as would be reached in other jurisdictions. In my opinion the criticisms which can be made of section 16A in the light of the discussion by Dickson C.J.C. of the tests to be applied to determine whether the provision is in breach of the presumption of innocence do not complete the process of examination which must be conducted in order to determine whether that section violates article 6(2) of the Convention. The better approach to the Convention, as Lord Woolf said in the context of the Hong Kong Bill of Rights, will be to avoid the somewhat complex two stage approach which is involved in the Canadian process of reasoning. But he gave this further guidance at pp. 972–973

> "In a case where there is real difficulty, where the case is close to the borderline, regard can be had to the approach now developed by the Canadian courts in respect of section 1 of their Charter. However in doing this the tests which have been identified in Canada do not need to be applied rigidly or cumulatively, nor need the results achieved be regarded as conclusive. They should be treated as providing useful general guidance in a case of difficulty. This is particularly true in relation to what was said in *Reg. v. Chaulk*, 62 C.C.C. (3d) 193, 216–217, about proportionality since it is the need to balance the interests of the individual and society which are at the heart of the justification of an exception to the general rule."

Mr Pannick suggested that in considering where the balance lies it may be useful to consider the following questions: (1) what does the prosecution have to prove in order to transfer the onus to the defence? (2) what is the burden on the accused—does it relate to something which is likely to be difficult for him to prove, or does it relate to something which is likely to be within his knowledge or (I would add) to which he readily has access? (3) what is the nature of the threat faced by society which the provision is designed to combat? It seems to me that these questions provide a convenient way of breaking down the broad issue of balance into its essential components, and I would adopt them for the purpose of pursuing the argument as far as it is proper to go in the present case.

Striking the balance

Section 16A(1) sets out what the prosecution must prove. It was suggested by Lord Lester that the onus on the prosecution was a light one, because all that had to be established was a "reasonable suspicion" that the article was in the accused's possession for a purpose connected with terrorism. He referred to Lord Devlin's observation in *Hussien v. Chong Fook Kam* [1970] A.C. 942, 948:

> "Suspicion in its ordinary meaning is a state of conjecture or surmise where proof is lacking: 'I suspect but I cannot prove.' Suspicion arises at or near the starting point of an investigation of which the obtaining of *prima facie* proof is the end."

But that was an action for false imprisonment, in which the question was whether a police officer was entitled to arrest the respondents without warrant on the ground that he had a reasonable suspicion that they had committed an offence. Lord Devlin was careful to explain the distinction between reasonable suspicion at the time of arrest and prima facie proof at the trial:

> "Prima facie [proof] consists of admissible evidence. Suspicion can take into account matters that could not be put in evidence at all. ... Suspicion can take into account also matters which, though admissible, could not form part of a prima facie case."

What subsection (1) requires is prima facie proof, not mere suspicion. The prosecution must lead evidence which is sufficient to prove beyond reasonable doubt (a) that the accused had the article in his possession and (b) that it was in his possession in circumstances giving rise to a reasonable suspicion that it was in his possession for a purpose connected with terrorism. Possession may be established with the benefit of the presumption in subsection (4), but the onus is on the prosecution to lead sufficient evidence to establish beyond reasonable doubt that the accused was in possession of the article at the time. Subsection (1) allows for a conviction on reasonable suspicion, but the onus is on the prosecution to lead sufficient evidence to establish beyond reasonable doubt that the circumstances are such that the inference of connection with terrorism is justified. It should not be thought that proof to this standard will be a formality.

Section 16A(3) sets out the defence. The onus is on the accused, but at least it can be said that the matter is not left to inference or to the discretion of the trial court. This is a defence which is provided for expressly by the statute. It has to be seen in the context of subsection (4). If the accused can show that he did not know that the article was in the premises or that he had no control over it, he can by giving evidence to that effect deprive the prosecution of the presumption that he was in possession of the article. He will only need to rely on subsection (3) if he was in possession of the article and the circumstances are such as to give rise to the reasonable suspicion mentioned in subsection (1). A sound judgment as to whether the burden which he has to discharge is an unreasonable one is unlikely to be possible until the facts are known. It is not immediately obvious that it would be imposing an unreasonable burden on an accused who was in possession of articles from which an inference of involvement in terrorism could be drawn to provide an explanation for his possession of them which would displace that inference. Account would have to be taken of the nature of the incriminating circumstances and the facilities which were available to the accused to obtain the necessary evidence. It would be one thing if there was good reason to think that the accused had easy access to the facts, quite another if access to them was very difficult.

Then there is the nature of the threat which terrorism poses to a free and democratic society. It seeks to achieve its ends by violence and intimidation. It is often indiscriminate in its effects, and sophisticated methods are used to avoid detection both before and after the event. Society has a strong interest in preventing acts of terrorism before they are perpetrated—to spare the lives of innocent people and to avoid the massive damage and dislocation to ordinary life which may follow from explosions which destroy or damage property. Section 16A is designed to achieve that end. It would not be appropriate for us in this case to attempt to resolve the difficult question whether the balance between the needs of society and the presumption of innocence has been struck in the right place. But it seems to me that this is a question which is still open to argument.

Had it not been for the fact that the Director's consent is not amenable to judicial review, I would have been inclined to think that the problem of compatibility which is raised by this case would have to await a decision after trial. That also is the consequence of the view which I have reached that, on other grounds, these applications must be dismissed.

LORD HOBHOUSE OF WOODBOROUGH

My Lords,

The circumstances under which these appeals have come before your Lordships' House are exceptional. They arise from the trial of the three Respondents (whom, my Lords, I will refer to as the 'defendants') at the Central Criminal Court on charges under s.16A of the *Prevention of Terrorism (Temporary Provisions) Act 1989*. The indictment particularised the offence as having had "in their possession chemical containers, radio equipment, manuals, documents, credit cards and sums of money in circumstances which give rise to a reasonable suspicion that the articles were in their possession for a purpose connected with the commission, preparation or instigation of acts of terrorism." The prosecution case was that the three defendants had been involved in sending such articles to terrorists in Algeria. The defences of the three defendants were different. Souidi denied being involved with the articles at all. Boukemiche denied having sent to Algeria any material capable of being used in military activity. Kebeline admitted having sent to Algeria at least some of the materials referred to but said that they were not intended for use in connection with terrorism; they were intended for use by members of the Islamic community in the Metidja region of Algeria in defending themselves against unlawful violence by state-sponsored militias.

At the outset of the trial, counsel for Kebeline submitted that the proceedings should be stayed because of the obstacles to obtaining from Algeria evidence to support his defence. The Judge did not accede to that application and the trial proceeded. The Crown opened the case in terms of s.16A(1) and called its evidence. At the close of the prosecution case, counsel for the defendants asked the Judge to give a ruling upon the correct legal construction of s.16A. They asked for this ruling in order to assist them to advise their clients whether to submit no case to answer and whether to give evidence. The type of arguments which were raised at this stage derived from *R. v. Berry (No.3)* [1995] 1 W.L.R. 7, *R. v. Edwards* [1975] Q.B. 27 *R. v. Hunt* [1987] A.C. 352: What did the prosecution have to prove? (*Att-Gen of Hong Kong v. Lee Kwong-kut* [1993] A.C. 951. However the arguments also extended to the consideration of Parliamentary material (purportedly under *Pepper v. Hart* [1993] A.C. 593) and compatibility with Article 6(2) of the European Convention for the Protection of Human Rights and Fundamental Freedoms and whether or not that Article could be used as an aid to construction.

The outcome was that the defendants apparently accepted that their construction argument could not succeed; they took the view that s.16A was irretrievably incompatible with Article 6(1). They asked the Judge to rule that it was incompatible. Their purpose was, they say, to obtain support for a renewed application for a stay on the ground of abuse of process and to assist them to persuade the Director of Public Prosecutions of his own motion to discontinue the proceedings. The Judge made the ruling for which the defendants asked. An adjournment was granted so that both sides could reconsider their position. On the prosecution side, the Director having taken advice from experienced counsel in this field, Mr Rabinder Singh, which suggested that the Judge's ruling was mistaken, instructed Mr Singh to apply to the Judge to reconsider his ruling. Having heard further argument, the Judge maintained his original ruling. The defendants then made an application for the proceedings to be stayed on the ground of abuse of process. The Judge refused this application. The trial then proceeded for a number of days with the defendants calling evidence. However on 14 December 1998, the trial had to be aborted and the jury discharged because of an unresolved problem in connection with the prosecution's compliance with its disclosure obligations.

In the ordinary course, the retrial would have taken place fairly soon after. But, before it could do so, the defendants applied for the judicial review of the Director's decision to continue with the prosecution. Originally they applied upon the basis that they had a reasonable expectation that they would not be prosecuted for an offence formulated in terms incompatible with Article 6(2). They, however, also relied upon the submission that the opinion of Mr Rabinder Singh was erroneous in law and therefore any decision of the Director to continue was vitiated by error of law and should be set aside so that he could reconsider it. It was this alternative submission which the Divisional Court upheld.

One of the features of a prosecution under s.16A upon which the defendants rely is the provision in *s.19* of *the Act* of 1989 that "proceedings shall not be instituted . . . except by or with the consent of" the Director. In relation to other offences under *the Act* the Attorney-General is the relevant person. Such provisions relate to the *institution* of proceedings. Unless the requisite consent has been given at that stage, the court will be acting without jurisdiction and, if convicted, the defendant will be entitled to have his conviction set aside on appeal. (See *R. v. Whale and Locton* [1991] Cr. L. Rev. 692 also *R. v. Cain* [1976] Q.B. 496 and *R. v. Jackson* [1997] Cr. L. Rev. 293.) Having given his consent to the institution of the proceedings, it of course remains the duty of the Director as the person having the conduct of the prosecution to act responsibly; in this, he is subject to the directions of the Attorney-General and can in suitable cases offer no evidence or enter a *nolle prosequi*. This duty exists in all prosecutions, not merely ones which required his consent for their institution. In the present case it must be stressed that there is no suggestion that the Director has acted in bad faith or has abused his position. It is simply said, as evidenced by his acceptance of the advice of Mr Singh and his attempt to persuade the Judge to change his mind, that he has made an error of law and that his failure to discontinue the criminal proceedings by one means or another is accordingly flawed.

This is a remarkable proposition. Disputed questions of fact and law which arise in the course of a criminal prosecution are for the relevant criminal court to determine. That is the function of the trial in the Crown Court and any appeal to the Court of Appeal. Inevitably, from time to time, the prosecutor may take a view of the law which is not subsequently upheld. If he has acted upon competent and responsible advice, this is not a ground for criticising him. Still less should a ruling adverse to the prosecution provide the defence with an opportunity to by-pass the criminal process or escape, otherwise than by appeal, other decisions of the criminal court.

The defendants' case relies upon the provisions of the *Human Rights Act 1998*. *This Act* did not receive its Royal Assent until 9 November 1998. As regards existing law, it provisions do not come into force until a day or days to be appointed by the Secretary of State under *s.22(2)*. No appointment has yet been made although the Government have indicated their intention to bring *the Act* fully into force in October 2000. The Bill was preceded by a White Paper published in October 1997 and was introduced in November 1997. As will be apparent it was the subject of prolonged Parliamentary proceedings before it was finally passed by both Houses. Independently of the *Human Rights Act*, the defendants were and remain able to rely upon established principles of construction in relation to ascertaining the correct effect to be given to s.16A. Thus they can, and have, relied upon cases such as *Berry, Edwards* and *Hunt*. They can pray in aid what was said by Lord Woolf in *Att-Gen of Hong Kong v Lee Kwong-kut* [1993] A.C. 951 and by Lord Hope in

Ex parte Launder [1997] 1 W.L.R. 839. They can use construction arguments based upon a presumption of consistency with international obligations. (*Ex parte Brind* [1991] 1 A.C. 696). In your Lordships' House, Lord Lester QC for the defendants accepted that for the purpose of showing a need to resort to judicial review proceedings as opposed to relying upon the remedies open to them in the Crown Court and in the Court of Appeal (Criminal Division), he had to rely upon some additional legal consideration; he sought to extract that additional consideration from *s.22*(4) of the *Human Rights Act.*

In order to put the present judicial review proceedings in context in relation to the *Human Rights Act*, it is necessary to give some more dates. The offences were alleged to have been committed in May 1997. By early August all three defendants had been arrested and charged. On 13 August 1997 the Director gave his consent to the institution of proceedings against Kebeline and Boukemiche under s.16A and they were committed for trial the following day. For Souidi the corresponding dates were 3 and 16 October 1997. The original trial date was 9 March 1998. There then was a five day hearing of a defence application for a stay on the ground of abuse of process, which was refused and the trial date was re-fixed for October 1998. The trial, interrupted by many applications and submissions, extended between the first half of October and the middle of December when it was aborted. From this it will be appreciated that the Director's consent to institute proceedings was given before any Bill had even been introduced and that by the time that *the Act* received the Royal Assent the trial had been proceeding for some time and the defendants were in the charge of the jury.

The Divisional Court:

Full judgments were delivered by both Lord Bingham of Cornhill LCJ and Laws LJ. Sullivan J agreed with both judgments. The Divisional Court dismissed the case based on legitimate expectation. They were right to do so and there is no need to say anything more about it. They rejected the argument of the Director that s.29(3) of the Supreme Court Act 1981 precluded resort to judicial review proceedings in matters relating to trial on indictment in the Crown Court. They further held that there were no discretionary grounds for refusing relief.

Lord Bingham considered the position of the Director and held that he was amenable to judicial review. He had relied upon the advice which he had been given by Mr Singh. If that advice was wrong, the Director should be told so and, at the least, be given an opportunity to think again, taking into account what would be the consequences which would flow on the correct view of the law from the continuation of the prosecution. One such consequence was, he said, that when the Act had been brought fully into force the defendants would be entitled to rely upon s.7(1)(b) and s.22(4) and the defendants' convictions "would in all probability be quashed, at some not inconsiderable cost to the public purse and no obvious advantage to the public weal": [1999] 3 W.L.R. 175, 187.

He held that s.16A was inconsistent with Article 6(2). (The other case before the Divisional Court concerned s.16B which he also held to be incompatible.) He said, at p. 190:

> "A defendant who chooses not to give or call evidence may be convicted by virtue of presumptions against him and on reasonable suspicion falling short of proof.
>
> . . . .
>
> It seems to me that on their face both sections undermine, in a blatant and obvious way, the presumption of innocence
>
> . . . .
>
> Under s.16A a defendant could be convicted even if the jury entertained a reasonable doubt . . . whether he had the items for a terrorist purpose."

Lord Bingham clearly seems to have been of the view that the Crown's submission on compatibility was not even arguable and this no doubt coloured his decision as well as his choice of language. He however added, at p. 192:

> "I think it undesirable to express any opinion, unauthoritatively, on whether, if s.3 of the Act of 1998 were in force, it would be possible to read and give effect to s.16A and s.16B in a way that is compatible with Convention rights."

Laws LJ rejected the argument of the Director on s.29(3) on the ground that it only applied to orders made by the Crown Court itself; there was a residual discretion to discourage satellite litigation but he did not find it persuasive on the facts of the present case. As to the review of the Director's decision not to end the prosecution, he, like Lord Bingham, attached importance to s.22(4) of the *Human Rights Act* and the provisions which would at some future date come into force. These provisions and their effect were circumstances which, Laws LJ said, the Director was under an obligation to consider:

> "That being so, the Director was bound to consider whether ss.16A and 16B are, without the aid of s.3 of the Act of 1998, compatible with Article 6(2). But that is a question of law. In fact, of course, the Director indeed considered the question; he obtained the opinion of distinguished counsel in the field, Mr Rabinder Singh. . . . Now, if a public decision-maker is obliged to arrive at a conclusion upon a question of law in reaching a decision as to how to exercise the power given him and arrives at an erroneous conclusion, his decision will be vitiated on the ordinary ground of illegality.": pp. 197–198.

Laws LJ accordingly proceeded to determine the question whether s.16A was incompatible with Article 6(2). He agreed with Lord Bingham that it clearly was. "The Act requires the defendant to disprove the offence's principal element." p. 201 He distinguished *Salabiaku v. France* (1988) 13 E.H.R.R. 379, on the basis that the circumstances were irrelevant; the statutory provision should be looked at on its face and was bound to involve the obligation of the defendant to prove lack of terrorist intent. Like Lord Bingham, he declined to express any view upon whether *s.3* of *the Act* of 1998 would, when it came into force, enable s.16A to be reconciled with Article 6(2).

The reasoning of the Divisional Court contains a number of steps. They first reject the argument that under s.29(3) and general principles of judicial review, the remedy was not available, or not appropriate, to challenge the failure of the Director to abandon the prosecution. Secondly, they held that it was necessary that the Director should have formed the correct view in law of the compatibility of s.16A with Article 6(2). Thirdly, they held the opinion of Mr Rabinder Singh was clearly wrong; s.16A was plainly incompatible. Accordingly the Director's decision to continue with the prosecution could not stand.

My Lords, I do not accept the first and second steps in this reasoning. The second step is, on analysis, inconsistent with the structure of the defendants' case in your Lordships' House. As to the third step, I do not accept that the question is as clear as the Divisional Court thought in the light of some of the decisions of the Court and the Commission to which we have been referred. Surprising though it may seem to those trained in the Common Law and the English traditions of statutory construction, there is clearly room for some doubt as to the outcome were the defendants to seek to challenge their convictions in Strasbourg. There is room for more than one view. Insofar as the reasoning and decision of the Divisional Court seems to have been fed by the view that the Director had got the law "blatantly" wrong, I will have to comment shortly on this aspect.

The Divisional Court also seems to have been influenced by the view that *s.19* of *the Act* of 1989 concerning consent to the *institution* of proceedings somehow altered the role of the Director in the conduct of those proceedings at the trial in the Crown Court. However, this error was not essential to their reasoning and *s.19* certainly underlined the importance of not abusing prosecutions of this kind. But it must be appreciated that, if their reasoning is correct in the present case, the same reasoning would be applicable in respect of any prosecution conducted under the control of the Director or Attorney-General. The implications of their reasoning are very far-reaching.

The Availability of Judicial Review:

A number of well established principles are relevant. One involves the relationship between criminal law and procedure and judicial review. Another is the refusal of judicial review where other legal remedies are available. The existence of these principles undoubtedly underlie s.29(3) of the Supreme Court Act 1981. But, even if s.29(3) does not itself preclude the application for judicial review, it will still be necessary to consider whether one of those principles does not do so.

S.29 defines the jurisdiction and powers of the High Court. S.29(3) provides:

> "In relation to the jurisdiction of the Crown Court, other than its jurisdiction in matters relating to trial on indictment, the High Court shall have all such jurisdiction to make orders of mandamus, prohibition or certiorari as the High Court possesses in relation to the jurisdiction of an inferior court."

This is a subject-matter provision. It applies the criterion whether the application for judicial review is "in relation to the jurisdiction of the Crown Court other than its jurisdiction in matters relating to trial on indictment." Guidance on the correct understanding of this provision has been given in a number of cases, particularly by Lord Browne-Wilkinson *R. v. Manchester Crown Court Ex parte Director of Public Prosecution* [1993] 1 W.L.R. 1524 at 1530:

> "In my judgment, the case by case method of elucidating the meaning of s.29(3) has now gone far enough to make it possible to detect a further 'helpful pointer.' . . . It may therefore be a helpful further pointer to the true construction of the section to ask the question: 'Is the decision sought to be reviewed one arising in the issue between the Crown and the defendant formulated by the indictment (including the costs of such issue)?' If the answer is 'Yes,' then to permit the decision to be challenged by judicial review may lead to delay in the trial: the matter is therefore probably excluded from review by the section. If the answer is 'No,' the decision of the Crown Court is truly collateral to the indictment of the defendant and judicial review of that decision will not delay his trial: therefore it may well not be excluded by the section."

So far as their subject matter is concerned, the issues presently raised fell squarely within Lord Browne-Wilkinson's formulation. The validity of the Director's consent to the institution of the proceedings under s.19 was a matter which could have been raised in the Crown Court and, after conviction, in the Court of Appeal. (See the authorities cited earlier.) The question of abuse of process had, in the present case, the same character, as did any question of the construction or effect of s.16A and the question of burden of proof.

The whole purpose of the arguments raised by the defendants in the Crown Court and in the Divisional Court was to bring about the delay or abandonment of the pending trial of the indictment. On the subject-matter test the application was precluded by s.29(3).

The Divisional Court avoided this conclusion by saying that it was the Director's decision which it was sought to review not that of the Crown Court Judge. My Lords, this reasoning places a gloss on the subsection. If the substance of what it is sought to review is the answer to some issue between the prosecution and defence arising during a trial on indictment, that issue may not be made the subject of judicial review proceedings. The issue is within the jurisdiction of the Crown Court judge and (subject to appeal) it is for him to decide it. The argument is that the issue will also affect the assessment of the Director whether to continue the proceedings (and would have affected his decision whether to institute or give his consent to the institution of the proceedings in the first place). Obviously if the Director is acting in bad faith or irresponsibly (which is not alleged in the present case), a cavalier attitude to defects in the criminal proceedings might give rise to scope for such an argument. But all that can be said here is that, having taken competent independent advice upon an issue raised in the course of the trial in the Crown Court, the Director has advanced submissions with which both the Crown Court Judge and the Divisional Court have disagreed. This is not infrequently the fate of litigants. It does not provide a basis for reviewing the decision of the litigator when one is precluded from reviewing the decision of the court. Suppose that the Crown Court Judge had accepted the submission of the prosecution on compatibility: would it be suggested that the defendants could go to the Divisional Court on the basis that the Director had taken a wrong view of the law and so obtain a reversal of the judge's decision? In my judgment, it is not correct either as a matter of the construction of s.29(3) or as a matter of principle to use the device of purporting to review the conduct of the Director to obtain the re-litigation in the Divisional Court of an issue in the criminal trial.

A possible escape from this conclusion is to refine down the issue concerned and say that it was not properly an issue which arose from the indictment, notwithstanding that both parties argued it before the Crown Court Judge and he gave his ruling upon it. I have some sympathy with this approach. Both the Court and the Director were bound by the existing state of the law. As the Divisional Court recognised, the prosecution must present the case upon the basis of the existing law and the judge must direct the jury in the terms of the law as it is. What would be the effect of the *Human Rights Act* when at some later date it came fully into force was irrelevant. Further, even then declaring that a statute was incompatible would not be within the jurisdiction of the Crown Court judge nor would any incompatibility affect the validity of the statute. (ss.3 and 4 of *the Act* of 1998) Indeed, I am at a loss to understand why the Judge allowed himself to be drawn into listening to argument or into ruling upon incompatibility once the construction argument had been abandoned by the defendants: he should have declined to entertain any argument on incompatibility.

However, this was not the way that the defendants put it: they said that incompatibility affected the validity of the Director's consent under *s.19* and whether the continuation of the trial was an abuse of process. It seems that this was also the view of Laws LJ: he said that the Director was *obliged* to consider compatibility and come to the right conclusion in law.

In my judgment the first step in the Divisional Court's reasoning cannot be supported. They should have held s.29(3) to be applicable, either expressly or inferentially. They should have held that judicial review was not available and that the defendants should exercise the remedies open to them within the criminal justice system. The fact that that would lead to the law of the land being applied supports that conclusion and is no reason for finding a way in which to interfere obliquely with the trial of the defendants on this indictment in accordance with *the Act* of 1989.

The Human Rights Act:

Lord Lester made *s.22(4)* the corner-stone of his argument before your Lordships. It is important to understand why he did so. His reason partly recognises the force of the objection in principle to the grant of judicial review in this case. (The same recognition can be observed in the judgments of Lord Bingham and Laws LJ.) He accepts that the trial of the defendants will have to reflect the provisions of s.16A and that the same applies to any appeal heard before the date upon which the *Human Rights Act* comes fully into force. But he submits that the situation will be different once that date has passed. Courts will be required to apply *s.3(1)* and do their best to read and give effect to s.16A in a way which is compatible with the defendants Convention rights. This, he submits would entitle the defendants to invoke *s.22(4)* and *s.7(1)(b)* and obtain the quashing of their convictions on the ground that the Director and Crown Court had acted in a way made unlawful by *s.6(1)*.

This part of Lord Lester's reasoning is radically different from that of the Divisional Court. The Divisional Court founded upon the incompatibility of s.16A and Article 6(2) and declined to express any view upon the *s.3(1)* point. Lord Lester recognised that this was not enough for him; irremediable incompatibility would not assist him. Implicitly, he was rightly recognising that he could not support the reasoning of the Divisional Court as being adequate to justify their conclusion.

The scheme of the *Human Rights Act* is that no decision of the courts can invalidate an Act of Parliament. Under *s.4(2)* a court (being one of those specified in *s.4*(5)) may, if satisfied that a provision of an Act of Parliament is incompatible with a Convention right, make a "declaration of that incompatibility." But, by *s.4*(6), such a declaration "(a) does not affect the validity, continuing operation or enforcement of the provision in respect of which it is given; and (b) is not binding on the parties to the proceedings in which it is made." *S.3*(2)(b) contains a similar reservation of validity. Thus, incompatibility does not found any right under *the Act*. The procedure to be followed after a declaration of invalidity is laid down in *ss.10* and 20 of *the Act* and the second Schedule. Whether the incompatible legislation should be amended so as to confer the relevant Convention right is a matter for the minister and Parliament. Unless and until such an amendment is made, the existing law remains in force notwithstanding the incompatibility and things done in accordance with that law remain lawful. (See also *s.6*(6).) Whether any amendment had retrospective effect would also depend upon the terms of the amendment (Schedule 2 paragraph 1).

Similarly *s.6*(1) and (2) which govern the position of public authorities, which include courts, contain reservations for acting in accordance with legislation which, *ex hypothesi*, cannot be reconciled with the Convention. This creates difficulties for Lord Lester's argument based on *s.22*(4). *S.22*(4), with effect from 9 November 1998, provides:

"Paragraph (b) of subsection (1) of section 7 applies to proceedings brought by or at the instigation of a public authority whenever the act in question took place; but otherwise that subsection does not apply to an act taking place before the coming into force of that subsection."

This therefore refers one back to *s.7*(1)(b) which provides:

"A person who claims that a public authority has acted (or proposes to act) in a way which is made unlawful by section 6(1) may . . . rely on the Convention right or rights concerned in any legal proceedings, but only if he is (or would be) a victim of the unlawful act."

So his submission becomes dependent on *s.6*. The only element of retrospectivity which *s.22*(4) introduces is to allow earlier unlawful actions to be relied upon.

If s.16A is, on the existing principles of statutory construction compatible with the Convention, the defendants' ground for applying for judicial review falls away. The point is fully arguable within the criminal trial and any resultant appeal and the Crown Court or the Court of Appeal will give effect to s.16A so construed. If, on the other hand, s.16A is irretrievably incompatible, as the Divisional Court held that it was, the defendants' application again cannot succeed. Whether the *Human Rights Act* has come into force or not the position remains the same. The incompatibility does not deprive s.16A of its force and validity nor does it affect the criminal trial or any convictions resulting from the application of s.16A. The defendants' guilt or innocence has to be determined in accordance with s.16A. All this Lord Lester had to and did accept.

Lord Lester submitted that once the *Human Rights Act* comes into force, an additional and more potent principle of statutory construction will come into play. *S.3*(1) of *the Act* provides:

> "So far as it is possible to do so, primary legislation and subordinate legislation must be read and given effect in a way which is compatible with the Convention rights."

He submits that this provision will enable s.16A to be construed so as not to impose any burden of proof upon the defendants. This, he submits, will retrospectively render invalid any conviction based upon a direction to the jury that s.16A(3) does impose such a burden and that any convictions would then have to be set aside.

Whether this argument materially advances his submission is clearly open to contrary argument. Neither *s.6* nor *s.7* is retrospective; nor is, for that matter, *s.3*, as Lord Lester's argument recognises. It is therefore difficult to maintain that the prosecution and trial of the defendants in accordance with s.16A has involved any unlawful conduct or will do so or will provide them with any ground for having any convictions resulting from their trial quashed.

There are further arguable points: whether s.16A is incompatible with the Convention and whether all the defendants would properly be described as "victims" of any breach of the Convention. That these are arguable points can be illustrated by reference to the case of *Bates v. United Kingdom* (Application 26280/95) where the Commission declined to admit a complaint that *s.5*(5) of the *Dangerous Dogs Act 1991* infringed the Convention even though it provided that "if in any proceedings it is alleged by the prosecution that a dog is one to which [the Act] applies, it shall be presumed that it is such a dog unless the contrary is shown by the accused by such evidence as the court considers sufficient; and . . . he has given . . . notice of his intention to do so. . . . "This made the mere allegation suffice to impose on the defendant in a criminal trial the burden of disproving the allegation. He was guilty unless he proved his innocence; he might be convicted on the civil burden of proof even though the court was not sure that he might not be innocent. However the Commission following earlier decisions of the Court in *Salabiaku* (A.141-A) and *Pham Hoang* (A.243) did not regard the provision as objectionable. The provision was of a type that fell within reasonable limits. It gave the defendant an opportunity to adduce evidence to disprove the allegation. The defendant had failed at his trial to take advantage of that opportunity.

This case and other similar cases decided under the Convention show that it is necessary to examine each case on its merits. There may be a justification for the terms in which the legislation is drafted even though on its face it would appear to be contrary to the Convention. Similarly, it is necessary to examine whether the relevant provision has in fact resulted in an injustice to the complainant. This last point ties in with the use in *s.7*(1) of the *Human Rights Act* of the term "victim." Criminal statutes which in certain circumstances partially reverse the burden of proof are not uncommon nor are they confined to the United Kingdom. The judgments and decisions of the European Court of Human Rights and the Commission (account of which must be taken under *s.2* of *the Act*) show that they are not necessarily incompatible with the Convention. Such a need to look beyond the bare words of the statute is also borne out by what Lord Woolf said in *Lee Kwong-kut* [1993] A.C. 951, 969 concerning the identification of the essential criminality which the prosecution must prove and the justification for requiring the defendant to prove that he comes within an exception to it. These are difficult concepts and, indeed, his approach may have been more stringent than is required under the European Convention. For myself, I am not presently persuaded that the approach advocated by Professor Glanville Williams in his article at 1988 C.L.J.261 is the right one. Similarly there are clearly arguable questions as to the breadth to be ascribed to the construction of statutes which will be required of the courts by *s.3*(1).

These are not matters which it is necessary or proper to enter upon on the present appeal. If they need at some later stage, in the Crown Court or elsewhere, to be decided in relation to these defendants or any of them under s.16A, that is the time at which they should be decided. The position is not as clear cut as the Divisional Court seem to have thought nor is it right that these proceedings by way of the attempted judicial review of the Director's conduct should be used as a vehicle for their decision now.

I agree that the Appeal should be allowed as proposed by your Lordships.

DOCUMENT NO 22

In Re Hany El Sayed El Sabaei Yousseff [1999] EWCH Admin.185
In the High Court of Justice (Co/706/99)
Queens Bench Division
Crown Office List

March 12, 1999
(Edited Text)

1. MR JUSTICE SULLIVAN: The applicant for habeas corpus in this case is an Egyptian criminal defence lawyer who represented Islamic fundamentalists in Egypt. He was arrested by the Egyptian security forces and it is his case that he has been tortured by them. He arrived in this country in 1994 and claimed asylum on entry. He was not at that time detained.

2. In September last year he was arrested by the Metropolitan Police anti-terrorist branch under the Prevention of Terrorism Temporary Provisions Act 1989 together with five other alleged members of the Egyptian Islamic Jihad. He was released a few days later from arrest under the Prevention of Terrorism Act, but together with four of the other five men who had been arrested under that act was redetained under paragraph 16 of schedule 2 of the Immigration Act 1971. The power to detain under that act is as follows: a person may be detained pending the giving of directions and pending his removal in pursuance of any directions given. A person may also be detained pending a decision to give or refuse him leave to enter.

3. Normally a person in such a position could apply to the Special Adjudicator for bail, see paragraph 22 of schedule 2 to the act, but in this case the detention of the applicant was certified as being in the interests of national security under section 3 subsection 2(A) of the Immigration Appeals Commission Act 1997. The effect of that is to confer jurisdiction to consider applications for bail upon the Special Immigration Appeals Commission which has been set up under the 1997 act.

4. The applicant applied for bail to the Commission in October 1998. His application was heard by his Honour Judge Pearl on 3rd December and

refused. One element of the learned judge's reasoning was that the Secretary of State at that stage intended to reach a decision on the applicant's application for asylum within three weeks or so. The judge regarded that as an important consideration, and bearing mind that a decision on the primary application would be taken in the near future he decided that the right and proper decision was to refuse bail.

5. On 23rd December the applicant was sent a letter refusing his application for asylum. The letter said *inter alia* that the Secretary of State acknowledged that the applicant's case was a case where he might ordinarily have granted asylum, but the Secretary of State then went on to refer to Article 1F of the refugee convention and to the United Nations declaration on terrorism which has reaffirmed that acts, methods and practices of terrorism are contrary to the purposes and principles of the United Nations. So the Secretary of State took into consideration the implications of the applicant's activities in this country on behalf of the Egyptian Islamic Jihad. He formed the view that the applicant was a senior member of that body's constituent assembly and in the light of a security service assessment he was satisfied that there were serious reasons for considering that he had been guilty of acts contrary to the purposes and principles of the United Nations, so the application for asylum was refused. The letter went on to say that consideration would be given to the compassionate circumstances of the case and consideration would also be given to whether the removal of the applicant from the United Kingdom would represent a breach of Article 3 of the European Convention on Human Rights and whether it would be appropriate to seek a safe third country which would be prepared to admit him. The letter also referred to a statement which had been prepared in respect of the bail application by Miss McAlister which said that the Home Office did have the material necessary to enable them to come to a decision on the applicant's asylum application. She gave an indication of the likely gist of the decision by saying that in the light of that material the applicant's case was a case where ordinarily asylum might have been granted, but indicated that consideration was being given as to whether he should be excluded from protection by virtue of Article 1F. She said that if the conclusion was that the application should be refused then the Department would go on to consider the compassionate circumstances and indicated that the Department did not accept that the applicant could not be removed from the United Kingdom in that event. She suggested that there would be a number of options open. Whilst it would be difficult to return him to Egypt, it would be necessary to explore with the Egyptian authorities whether he would be properly treated and whether appropriate undertakings could be given, and then it would also be considered whether it would be appropriate to seek a safe third country which would be prepared to admit him.

6. Since 23rd December last year the applicant has continued to be detained in prison.

7. At the beginning of this year his solicitors wrote to the Home Office saying in substance that in the light of the conclusion that asylum would have been granted but for the exclusion of the applicant under Article 1F, it was impractical to imagine that he could be returned to Egypt without there being a breach of Article 3 of the European Convention. There were letters in January and letters in February. Those letters did not elicit any response, and so the applicant's solicitors set in motion proceedings for habeas corpus.

8. The matter came before me on 2nd March and I adjourned it to today. In response to questions from me it was indicated by counsel who then appeared on behalf of the Secretary of State that matters were going to be put to the responsible minister at the end of that week, in particular assurances from Egypt. That was why I adjourned the matter for two weeks because it was believed at that time that material was being put to the minister concerning those assurances and there should be a clear indication, as I put it, one way or the other as to what view the minister took of that information by today.

9. Subsequently it transpired that that was a misunderstanding and that what was being put to the minister was simply an invitation to agree to a course of action which would involve seeking assurances from the Egyptian authorities in order to decide whether or not return to that country was feasible. So matters are not as far forward as had been indicated at the hearing on 2nd March.

10. Mr Wood, of Treasury Solicitor's Department, has deposed to an affidavit dated 11th March. In that affidavit he sets out the current position. It seems that initially consideration was given to the possibility of returning the applicant to another third country or to Egypt, but the view was taken that removal to a safe third country was not practical and so a submission was put to the Foreign Secretary on 14th January recommending that the possibility of returning the applicant to Egypt be explored and that no attempt be made to remove the applicant to a third country.

11. Later on in January the Foreign Office advised the Home Office it was prepared to seek assurances from the Egyptian Government and asked the Home Secretary whether he wanted to make that approach. Advice was sought from legal advisers and it is that matter which was laid before the Home Secretary on Friday, 5th March.

12. In the meantime the applicant's solicitors had sent a report saying that the applicant had already been sentenced to death in Egypt.

13. Having considered the papers, the Home Secretary authorised officials to attempt to obtain adequate assurances from the Egyptian Government but subject to investigation of the report that the applicant had been sentenced

to death. That matter was investigated and the Egyptian authorities indicated that no death sentence had been passed.

14. Thereafter a draft of the letter to the Egyptian authorities was sent to the British Embassy in Cairo. Their comments were received upon it and in the light of those comments it is envisaged that a formal request will shortly be made to the Egyptian Ministry of Justice. Initially it is proposed that it will be made orally and then it will be followed up with a letter. Mr Wood ends up by saying:

> "I cannot say how long negotiations may take before either a satisfactory outcome is reached or it becomes clear that it will be impossible to remove Mr Yousseff without breaking Article 3 of the European Convention on Human Rights. However, the Egyptian Government is being asked to deal with this matter as swiftly as possible."

15. The final paragraph of the affidavit deals with the number of persons who have to be involved in any discussions concerning the applicant, bearing in mind in particular the security implications of his case.

16. In the light of all that information, Mr Scannell has submitted today that the writ should issue. His submission is based on two grounds: first of all, that there has been inactivity until now, and even now there is no indication when the matter is going to come to a conclusion, so that there has been a failure to comply, or a failure to exercise all reasonable expedition to ensure removal takes place within a reasonable time. As to that he refers me to the decision of Mr Justice Woolf, as he then was, in *R v Governor of Durham prison, ex parte Hardial Singh* [1984] 1 WLR 704.

17. As a second and discrete submission he says in essence that it is pointless for the Secretary of State to seek assurances from the Egyptian authorities. He described it as ludicrous to expect that any such assurances could be capable of being relied on in the light of material that had been sent to the Home Office under cover of a letter from the applicant's solicitors dated 4th March this year. In that material the Egyptian Government is recorded as denying torture exists, and therefore Mr Scannell's submission is that no rational person would see any value in assurances provided by such a Government. Reference is also made in the representations to the decision in *Chahal v United Kingdom* [1996] where the European Court of Human Rights concluded that assurances from India were not an adequate safeguard against torture under Article 3.

18. When the matter was before me on 2nd March it was initially submitted that it was not possible for the court to issue a writ of habeas corpus in a case such as this because the jurisdiction to deal with the matter was conferred upon the Special Immigration Appeal Commission and the applicant was protected by the power of the appeal commission to grant bail.

19. Mr Garnham, who appears this morning on behalf of the Home Office, does not challenge the jurisdiction of the court to grant relief by way of habeas corpus, but he submits that such relief should not be granted as a matter of course and that there is a more appropriate route to giving relief to the applicant; that is to say he should apply for bail to the Special Immigration Appeal Commission which can then take into account all the relevant matters, including the security aspects.

20. I am not persuaded that the power of the Commission to grant bail is an adequate answer to the matter. The question as to whether an applicant should be granted bail by the Commission, or in the normal case by the Special Adjudicator, proceeds upon the basis that the applicant is lawfully detained under schedule 2 to the 1971 act. That is a wholly different issue from the question whether detention under schedule 2 is justified at all; that is to say whether the Secretary of State has power to detain the applicant under schedule 2. Thus I am not persuaded that there is a more convenient alternative remedy, but I think it right to bear in mind the constraints that are necessarily imposed upon this court in considering an application for habeas corpus in a case which raises security implications.

21. Under the 1971 act the Secretary of State, as I indicated, is entitled to detain the applicant pending the giving of removal directions and pending a decision upon his application for leave to enter the country. As Mr Justice Woolf, as he then was, made clear in *Hardial Singh*, that power:

"... can only authorise detention if the individual is being detained in one case pending the making of a deportation order and, in the other case, pending his removal. It cannot be used for any other purpose. Secondly, as the power is given to enable the machinery of deportation to be carried out, I regard the power of detention as being impliedly limited to a period which is reasonably necessary for that purpose. The period which is reasonable will depend upon the circumstances of the particular case. What is more, if there is a situation where it is apparent to the Secretary of State that he is not going to be able to operate the machinery provided in the Act for removing persons who are intended to be deported within a reasonable period, it seems to me that it would be wrong for the Secretary of State to exercise his power of detention."

Then he added:

"I would regard it as implicit that the Secretary of State should exercise all reasonable 'expedition' to ensure that the steps are taken which will be necessary to ensure the removal of the individual within a reasonable time."

22. To avoid any possible misapprehension, it should be made clear that this applicant cannot be detained under schedule 2 to the 1971 act on the ground that the Secretary of State considers that he is linked to international

terrorism. The Secretary of State has other powers to detain suspected terrorists but they are not in issue here.

23. The length of time that a person such as the applicant has been, or is proposed to be kept in detention, is not determinative. It may well be indicative if there is a very long delay that there is no realistic prospect of removal and so detention would not be justified under the enabling power in the act.

24. In deciding whether all reasonable expedition has been exercised one has of course to have regard to all the circumstances of the case. In this case it is right to have regard to the complexity and the sensitivity of the case: for example, it is plain the decisions will not be able to be taken by civil servants. Matters have to be referred up to ministers. There is the problem of ensuring that information on security matters is kept secure, and in terms of liaising with other authorities the liaisons have to be undertaken at the very highest level. Moreover, there is the need to consult with other Government departments who have a legitimate interest, given the security implications.

25. Quite apart from delay, it may of course become clear at a relatively early stage that removal is not a realistic possibility. In such a case continued detention would not be justified.

26. The second limb of Mr Scannell's proposition asserts that this is such a case. He submits that on these particular facts there is no realistic prospect of the applicant being returned to any safe third country, and that much is now accepted in Mr Wood's affidavit. He also submits there is no realistic prospect of him being returned to Egypt otherwise than in breach of Article 3 of the European Convention on Human Rights, because were he returned there he would be exposed to torture or to inhuman or degrading treatment or punishment.

27. It is clear that the Secretary of State is not entitled to keep the applicant in detention under the 1971 act on what might be called the offchance that it might be possible against the odds to return him to Egypt. Nevertheless, the question whether there is or is not a realistic prospect of being able to obtain satisfactory assurances from the Egyptian authorities is for the Secretary of State to decide in the first instance. Potentially, of course, any such decision by him would be susceptible to judicial review on conventional Wednesbury grounds.

28. Whilst there clearly is a difference between the position as it was presented to me in submission on 2nd March and today, whatever criticisms might have been advanced as to lack of activity prior to that date, as things stand at the moment it cannot be said in the light of Mr Wood's affidavit that the Department are being inactive or that they are not taking all reasonable steps and exercising all reasonable expedition, given the particular

difficulties that are inherent in this case. It is understandable that steps were not taken prior to 23rd December. That would have been premature pending a decision on the asylum application.

29. Following 23rd December the possibility of return to a safe third country was examined and that has now been found to be not possible. Therefore, the possibility of returning the applicant to Egypt is under active consideration. The discussions are necessarily complex and delicate and they are bound to take some time. It is understandable that a precise timetable cannot be given. One can well understand, for example, that legal advice was sought before papers were laid before the Home Secretary.

30. Thus I am not satisfied, given the particular difficulties inherent in this case, that the first limb of Mr Scannell's submissions is made out.

31. Turning to his second proposition, I regard that as unduly simplistic. I am simply not able to say that the Secretary of State would inevitably be Wednesbury perverse in concluding that an assurance, the text of which is not yet available, from the Egyptian authorities would in effect be worthless. Nor can I say that the Secretary of State is Wednesbury perverse in adhering to the view that there is some realistic prospect of being able to return the applicant to Egypt. If the assurances are given it will be for the Secretary of State to decide whether they can be relied on. No doubt in doing so he will bear in mind the observations of the European Court of Human Rights in *Chahal*.

32. As I have indicated, if he concludes that the assurances can be relied upon then it may well be that his decision would be susceptible to challenge upon the basis of that it was Wednesbury perverse in the light of the available evidence, but I am not prepared to pre-empt what the Secretary of State's decision might be or what view might be taken about it, given that the approach has yet to be made to the Egyptian authorities, and so we do not know whether they would be prepared to give an assurance and if so what the form of that assurance might be.

33. It is plain, however, that this case should be kept under review by the Department. It is not a normal case where there is no apparently significant obstacle to an applicant's return, save what might be called the ordinary administrative delays and difficulties. Prima facie there is a substantial hurdle that has to be overcome. At the moment the Secretary of State considers that there is a realistic prospect that it may be capable of being overcome. At this stage I cannot say that his conclusion is Wednesbury perverse and, therefore, the detention is still within the ambit of schedule 2 to the 1971 act.

34. I do bear in mind of course that the Secretary of State's hands in this open forum are tied to a degree because he is unable to reveal sensitive

intelligence material. But equally it is right to emphasise that if the prospect of being able to return the applicant to Egypt dims in the light of the discussions with the Egyptian authorities then the Secretary of State will not have power to continue to detain the applicant under schedule 2. There is no power to detain the applicant simply on the basis that the Secretary of State would like to be able to remove him to Egypt but cannot really see any practical means of doing so at the moment. Detention for that purpose would be outside the ambit of schedule 2 to the act. Moreover, I think it appropriate to indicate a note of warning, given the terms of Mr Wood's affidavit. As I have indicated, he says that he cannot say how long negotiations may take before either a satisfactory outcome is reached or it becomes clear that it will be impossible to remove Mr Youssef without breaking Article 3 of the European Convention on Human Rights.

35. In the light of the decision in *Hardial Singh*, the Secretary of State, in order to justify the continued detention of an applicant under schedule 2, must be satisfied at the very least that there is some realistic possibility of his being removed from this country, not that removal would not be impossible. On the basis that anything in life is possible, the test posed in Mr Wood's affidavit is, in my judgment, unduly lax.

36. As I indicated, the Secretary of State must be satisfied there is a realistic possibility of removing the applicant. He cannot be detained until it is clear that it is impossible to remove him. That would be detaining him on the basis that there was merely an offchance that he might be able to be removed. In my judgment, such detention would not be authorised under schedule 2.

37. I should perhaps add this: there was, as I have indicated, detailed correspondence from the applicant's solicitors in January and February of this year. There was no substantive response to that correspondence. I can well understand that this is one of many cases, and it is a particularly difficult case. Nonetheless, it is not surprising that an application for habeas corpus was made, given that the applicant's solicitors had effectively been left in the dark as to what was happening. If information of the kind that is set out in Mr Wood's affidavit had been made available earlier, even on the basis that this is the sort of course that we would be proposing to take, then it might have obviated the need for making this application, because it would have given the applicant's solicitors reassurance that the applicant was not being held in detention simply because the Secretary of State was unable to see any way of removing him from this country and did not really know what to do; but was being held because the Secretary of State considered that there was still some realistic prospect

of removing him and wished to explore that prospect with the Egyptian authorities.

38. I realise that this decision will be disappointing for the applicant, but it does seem that the intervention of the court has at least concentrated minds to a degree, so that action is now being taken to investigate the position with the Egyptian authorities.

39. Mr Scannell suggested that if I was against him on his two submissions, which as I have indicated I am, then I should adjourn the matter for two weeks so that it could be kept under review. I do not think it is necessary to adjourn this application to ensure that the matter is kept under review by the Home Office. I hope I have made it sufficiently clear in this judgment that it would not be acceptable for the applicant to be kept in detention simply on the offchance that he might be able to be removed to Egypt. The Secretary of State has to be satisfied there is a realistic prospect which he wishes to pursue with the Egyptian authorities. Once that prospect ceases in his judgment to be realistic then the applicant should be released.

40. That said, this application for habeas corpus is dismissed.

* * * * *

DOCUMENT NO 23

In the Matter of Ramda, in the Matter of Boutarfa [1997] EWHC Admin.591 In the High Court of Justice (Co/2228/96) Queen's Bench Division (Co/3578/96)

June 25, 1997
(Edited Text)

1. LORD JUSTICE PILL: The applicants Rachid Ramda and Mustapha Boutarfa, who are at present in Bellmarsh prison, each seek a writ of *habeas corpus*. Orders have been made at Bellmarsh Magistrates Court for their return to France following a request by the French Government for their extradition. Boutarfa has dual French and Algerian nationality and Ramda has Algerian nationality. They are accused of criminal conspiracy with the purpose of committing acts of terrorism and of connection with an enterprise the purpose of which is gravely to disturb public order by intimidation or terror. In the second half of 1995 bombings and attempted bombings of a most serious kind occurred in Paris and elsewhere in France. Boualem Bensaid has been arrested and in interview has implicated both applicants. The cases of the two applicants must be considered individually because different considerations to some extent apply.

2. On their behalf it is submitted by Mr Emmerson first that, if they are returned to France, they might be prejudiced at their trial by reason of their race religion or political opinion or, in the case of Ramda, his nationality, within the meaning of those terms in s 6(1)(d) of the Extradition Act 1989 ("the 1989 Act"). Second, their extradition to face trial in France would put the United Kingdom in breach of its obligations under Articles 3 and 6 of the European Convention of Human Rights ("the Convention") and that by virtue of s 4(1) of the Act and the European Convention on Extradition Order 1990 (SI 1990 No 1507) ("the 1990 Order"), s 6 of the Act takes effect subject to Articles 3 and 6 of the Convention (Protection from inhuman or degrading treatment and right to a fair trial). Third, the accusations against the applicants are not made in good faith in the interests of justice and the Court should exercise its power under s 11(3) of the Act because it would, having regard to all the circumstances, be unjust or oppressive to return them to France.

3. S 6(1)(d) of the Act provides, insofar as is material:

"A person shall not be returned under Part III of this Act or committed or kept in custody for the purposes of return, if it appears to an appropriate authority (which includes this Court)

(d) that he might, if returned, be prejudiced at his trial by reason of his race, religion, nationality or political opinions."

4. This paragraph appears to have its origin in international instruments, including the Convention, which set out rights and then provide that they shall be secured without discrimination. Article 14 of the Convention provides:

"The enjoyment of the rights and freedoms set forth in this Convention shall be secured without discrimination on any grounds such as sex, race, colour, language, religion, political or other opinion, national or social origin, association with a national minority, property, birth or other status."

5. To establish that "he might be prejudiced" under s 6 an applicant has only to establish "a reasonable chance," "substantial grounds for thinking," or "a serious possibility," terms approved by Lord Diplock in *R v Governor of Pentonville Prison ex parte Fernandez* [1971] 1 WLR 987 at 994G as describing the degree of likelihood to be established.

6. Mr Emmerson has placed before the Court a body of material which seeks to demonstrate xenophobic attitudes in France and, in particular, hostility towards immigrants from Algeria. It is submitted that there is overwhelming evidence of widespread intolerance and racism in France towards Algerian Muslims. This has been inflamed by the press, it is submitted, both generally and in relation to the applicants and the offences they are alleged to have committed. Terrorism has been linked with Islamic fundamentalism. The applicants rely upon a report from Dr George Joffe, Director of Studies at the Royal Institute of International Affairs, which analyses the history and attitudes of the population towards Algerians in France. It is claimed by Dr Joffe that "racism is now institutionalised within the French state despite strenuous efforts made over the years to counteract it."

7. They also rely on reports of Amnesty International and other organisations. The applicants refer to reports of United Nations bodies including the report of M. Glele-Ahanhanzo, a Special Rapporteur appointed by the Economic and Social Council dated 18 November 1996 upon his mission to France in the Autumn of 1995. He noted (paragraph 45) that "France is being swept by a wave of xenophobia and racism that is extremely damaging to its image as 'the country of human rights'."

8. Mr Emmerson has submitted a large bundle of press reports to support his submission as to the existence of racial intolerance in France and his submission that the guilt of the applicants has been asserted and assumed. By way of example, a newspaper report of 12 December 1996 stated:

> "England, traditionally the welcoming land for political refugees, has become a hub for militant Islam and today it shelters many known terrorists wanted by France, such as Rachid Ramda, the well known financier of the attacks of 1995."

9. Particular reliance is placed upon a statement made by the Minister of Justice, M. Jaques Toubon, on 9 November 1995:

> "He [Rachid Ramda] had played a role that was maybe not exclusive but at any rate essential in the bombing campaign that had struck our country since 25 July."

10. This statement was widely reported. It flouted, Mr Emmerson submits, the decision of the European Court of Human Rights in *Allen de Ribemont v France* [1995] 20 EHRR 557 (February 1995). The Court found a breach of Article 6(2) of the Convention, which provides a presumption of innocence, when police officers, of the highest rank, shortly after the arrest of a suspect, named him as one of the instigators of a murder. The Court found that "this was clearly a declaration of the applicant's guilt which, firstly, encouraged the public to believe him guilty and, secondly, pre-judged the assessment of the facts by the competent judicial authority." The Court stated the principle that "the presumption of innocence may be infringed not only by a Judge or Court but also by other public authorities."

11. Reliance is also placed upon the statement made by M. Toubon on 20 October 1995 after the Swedish authorities refused the extradition of Abdelkrim Deneche, an alleged participant in the bombing campaign, from Sweden where the extradition arrangements are different from those now under consideration. M. Toubon stated:

> "There exists in our country a real solidarity between us, like a political family, however between the different countries, whether in Europe or not, there is not sufficient solidarity. A certain number of countries do not attach the same importance as us to Islamic fundamentalism and seek to protect it."

12. Mr Emmerson emphases the religious basis upon which the objection is put.

13. It is submitted that there is evidence that it is the French Government itself which has disclosed information enabling the press campaign to be sustained. That is denied by the Government. Attention is drawn to the fact that the President of the Republic himself has expressed concern about lack of respect for the presumption of innocence and a Commission has been set up to "examine the best means in order not to let guilt be assumed until the moment it is sufficiently proved" (statement of 21 January 1997).

14. It is against that background, Mr Emmerson submits, that the Court should consider the provisions of s 6(1)(d) of the Act. He submits that the French legal system does not have safeguards to deal with the situation which

has arisen. Trial would be by judges alone at Cour d'Assises Speciale pour les affaires de terrorisme. The Court has no power to stay a prosecution on the ground that pre-trial publicity has rendered a fair trial impossible. It does not give a reasoned judgment and there is no right of appeal save on a point of law to the Cour de Cassation. Moreover, the Conseil Superior De Magistrature, on which the Minister of Justice sits as Vice-President, has a power of veto over the appointment of any judicial magistrate proposed by the President. Mr Emmerson does not attack the Cour d'Assises Speciale as such, (indeed the magistrates who sit in it are senior and experienced judges) but claims that, in the absence of procedural and substantive safeguards, there is a risk of prejudice at the trial in the particular situation which has arisen. Reliance is placed on the analysis of the judicial mind by Viscount Dilhorne in *Attorney General v British Broadcasting Corporation* [1961] AC 303 at 335:

> "Every holder of a judicial office does his utmost not to let his mind be affected by what he has seen or heard or read outside the court and he will not knowingly let himself be influenced by the media, nor in my view will any layman experienced in the discharge of judicial duties. Nevertheless it should, I think, be recognised that a man may not be able to put that which he has seen, heard or read entirely out of his mind and that he may be subconsciously affected by it."

15. In his affidavit on behalf of the French Government, M. Marc Monionard, Director and Head of Criminal Affairs and Pardons at the Department of Justice, states:

> "It also appears that a general allegation is made that the applicants will not get a fair trial or be presumed innocent due to the publicity surrounding the case. That the special court of assize that will try the case is inherently biased. And the magistrates who sit in the special court of assize and who will try the case are unduly influenced by the Minister of Justice.

These matters are unequivocally denied. Publicity will have no effect. The Court of trial will consist of seven full time magistrates who will not be influenced by press reports. The presumption of innocence is paramount in the French judicial system. The applicants will get a fair and public trial. The attack on the French judiciary is unwarranted. The judiciary prides itself on its independence from the Executive."

16. M. Monionard states that Article 64 of the French Constitution confirms the independence of the judiciary from the executive. As to the statement by the Minister of Justice, M. Monionard states that it "reflects his personal view and cannot have any influence on the assessment of the case against Rachid Ramda the professional judges of the special assize court for terrorism will make. The declarations of the Minister do not in any way support a challenge to the guarantee of a fair trial in France. They do not and will not influence

the criminal trial. They cannot bind in any way the court whose independence is guaranteed by the Constitution."

17. I say at this stage I have difficulty with the concept that a public statement made by a Minister of Justice in relation to a major criminal investigation reflects only his "personal view." Even if it does, it appears to me, with respect, no better for that, given the office which M. Toubon held. Indeed the Director's reasoning might bear the implication, though I do not consider the implication was intended, that if it was an official as distinct from a personal view it might influence the judges.

18. In relation to their s 6 claim, the applicants face an obstacle which I regard as insurmountable. The risk of prejudice at the trial must be shown to be by reason of race, religion, nationality or political opinions. Even if it could be shown that a media campaign which followed a serious outbreak of bombing did create a risk of prejudice, I find it inconceivable that a risk could be present for any of the reasons stated is s 6. Mr Emmerson invites the Court to infer on the basis of the material before the Court not only that the judges would be prejudiced against the applicants but also that they would be prejudiced on one or more of the grounds stated in s 6(1)(d). It is submitted that the absence of an obligation to give reasons (which obligation "concentrates the mind wonderfully," Donaldson J in *Tramountana Armadora v Atlantic Shipping Co SA* [1978] 2 All ER 870 at 872) makes it possible to draw the inference. On the material before the Court, I am far from persuaded to make the large leap which the inference would demand in either case. If there were to be potential for unfairness, I could not find that it might arise from the stated criteria as distinct from other possible factors, such as a abhorrence of the dreadful crimes which have been committed in France by some person or persons.

19. However, I do also express the more general conclusion that I do not find a risk of any lack of fairness at the trial or trials of either of the applicants. I accept that the status, abilities and experience of the judges of the Cour d'Assises Speciale are such as will ensure a fair trial. There is no serious possibility, in my judgment, that in performing their duties, they would be influenced by inflammatory press reports or the reported remarks of M. Toubon.

20. That being so, Mr Emmerson's second submission does not arise for decision. The submission is based on the wording of Article 3 of Schedule 1 to the 1990 Order which was made pursuant to s 4(1) of the 1989 Act. There can be little doubt that s 6 of the 1989 Act was enacted to give effect to Article 3 of the Convention.

21. S 4(1) of the 1989 Act provides that:

"Where general extradition arrangements have been made, Her Majesty may, by Order in Council reciting or embodying their terms, direct that this Act $1/4$ shall apply as between the United Kingdom and the foreign

State $^1/_4$ subject to the limitations, exceptions and qualifications, if any, contained in the Order."

22. The European Convention on Extradition ("the Extradition Convention") appears as Schedule 1 to the Order. Article 3 is headed "Political Offences" and provides protection for political offenders and those prosecuted on account of race, religion, nationality or political opinion. Article 3(4) provides:

"This Article shall not affect any obligations which the contracting parties may have undertaken or may undertake under any other international convention of a multilateral character."

23. The submission is that the European Convention of Human Rights is such a convention and Article 3(4) has the effect of incorporating into English law an obligation not to extradite where to do so would involve a breach of Article 3 or Article 6 of the Convention. The effect of Article 3(4) is to give primacy to the obligations which the United Kingdom has undertaken under the European Convention on Human Rights. The 1990 Order imposes a limitation in the s 3(4) sense; extradition in breach of the European Convention on Human Rights is not permissible.

24. If s 4(1) of the 1989 Act does not plainly have the effect for which the applicants contend, it is submitted that at worst from their point of view it is ambiguous. The Convention may be prayed is aid to resolve the ambiguity and reference is made to Article 13 of the Convention which provides that "everyone whose rights and freedoms are set forth in this convention are violated shall have an effective remedy before the national authority." That involves construing s 4(1) of the 1989 Act so as to enable the applicants to rely on Articles 3 and 6 of the Convention in the English courts.

25. Having set out the submission made on behalf of the applicants, I propose to deal with it briefly. The purpose of Article 3(4) of the Extradition Convention is to make clear that the contents of the Article leave intact the international obligations of contracting parties under multilateral conventions such as the European Convention of Human Rights. The Article was not intended to create new rights. It has no bearing upon how those international obligations are treated in the domestic law of a contracting party or whether they are incorporated into that law. It does not have the effect of incorporating the Convention into English law. While the contents of an Order may, by virtue of s 4(1) of the 1989 Act, limit the operation of the procedures in the Act, nothing in the 1990 Order is my judgment achieves that major change in English law.

26. Mr Emmerson's third submission relies upon s 11(3)(c) of the 1989 Act which provides that "the court shall order the applicant's discharge if it appears to the court in relation to the offence, or each of the offences, in respect of which the applicant's right to return is sought that $^1/_4$ because the accusation

against him is not made in good faith in the interests of justice, it would, having regard to all the circumstances, be unjust or oppressive to return him." Mr Emmerson submits first that the maker of the accusation for the purposes of the section is the complainant and that, since the case against the applicants depends substantially upon the evidence of Boualem Bensaid, he should be regarded as the complainant. Second, by reason of the manner in which Bensaid's allegations came to be made and their contradictory nature, they cannot be said to have been made in good faith in the interests of justice. Counsel has analysed the many interviews of Bensaid in support of his submission. Bensaid is not an independent witness and has a strong motive, it is submitted, to implicate others in an attempt to reduce the importance of his own role. Reference is made to the number and timing of the interviews and to allegedly unsustainable allegations against the applicants (though it is not in issue that there is a *prima facie* case). Mr Emmerson also relies on the evidence before the court as to the conduct of the French authorities in the investigation and prosecution.

27. I do not find it necessary to determine whether, for the purposes of s 11(3)(c), the "accusation" is that of Bensaid or the French Government though preferring the view that it is that of the Government of France (Leggatt LJ in *Osman*, transcript 20 June 1990 p 6E) or whose good faith is involved. I apply the test most favourable to the applicants to the material before the court. I am quite unable to conclude that, for s 11(3)(c) reasons and having regard to all the circumstances, it would be unjust or oppressive to return the applicants or either of them to France.

28. When considering this and earlier points, I have borne in mind the fear expressed that, if extradited to France, Ramda might at some stage be sent on by the French authorities to Algeria where it is submitted he could not expect fair treatment. For the purposes of s 2 of the Asylum and Immigration Act 1996, the Court of Appeal in *R v Secretary of State for the Home Department ex parte Canbolat* (The Times May 9, 1997) held that the Home Secretary was entitled to conclude that France is a safe third country. Mr Emmerson referred to more recent cases where, in the light of developments, leave has been granted to applicants for judicial review to test that proposition. I have considered the material before this court. The possibility raised does not in my judgment affect the duties of the court upon the present applications or their exercise. The Government of France is well aware of its treaty obligations.

29. I would refuse these applications.

Astill J:

I agree.

* * * * *

DOCUMENT NO 24

R v Samar Alami Jawad Botmeh [1999] EWCA Crim.1321 In the Court of Appeal Criminal Division

May 10, 1999
Crown Copyright
(Edited Text)

LORD JUSTICE ROCH:

On 26th July 1994 the Israeli Embassy in Kensington Palace Gardens, London, was the target of a car bomb attack. In the early hours of the following morning a second car bomb was exploded outside Balfour House, Finchley, premises occupied by the Jewish Philanthropic Institution for Israel. Happily and miraculously no person was killed or seriously injured, although some 18 persons suffered minor injuries and considerable damage was done to property. These two acts of terrorism were connected, as was demonstrated, by the fact that a group calling themselves the Palestinian Resistance Jaffa Group claimed responsibility for both bombs in letters to two Arab newspapers, those letters being posted on the afternoon of 26th July 1994, that is to say before the second bomb at Balfour House was exploded. On 7th October 1996 at the Central Criminal Court four persons were tried on an indictment containing six counts, the first of which was a charge of conspiracy to cause explosions, the explosions being those which occurred at the Israeli Embassy and Balfour House in July 1994. Two of those four persons, Nadia Zekra and Mahmoud Naim Abu-Wardeh, were acquitted. The applicants Samar Sami Alami, now 32 years of age, and Jawad Mahmoud Botmeh, now 30 years of age, were convicted on 11th December 1996 by majority verdicts of eleven to one. The remaining counts in the indictment were charges against the applicants of possession of explosives and firearms. The jury were directed that in the event of their finding the applicants guilty on count 1, there was no need for the jury to go on to consider the remaining counts against the applicants.

Following the bombing the police made two significant finds which formed a major part of the prosecution's case against the applicants. On 1st February 1995 at 31 Montrose Court SW7 in a flat owned by Samar Alami's uncle, in the ceiling area accessed by a trap door in the roof of a hall cupboard, were found a Cobra .38 revolver and 20 rounds of ammunition, a blue holdall in which, in a plastic bag, was a book entitled "the Engineering of Explosives," in the hall cupboard were found two empty bottles which had contained hydrogen peroxide solution, hydrogen peroxide being an ingredient of an explosive substance TATP. In a refrigerator in the living room there was a briefcase in which were pieces of paper with details of chemical formulae relating to explosives. Jawad Botmeh's fingerprints were found on the book entitled "The Engineering of Explosives" and on other documents in the blue holdall found in the ceiling space. Samar Alami's fingerprints were found on the empty bottles of hydrogen peroxide, on a grey metal container which had contained the pistol and ammunition, on the plastic bag, on the book entitled "The Engineering of Explosives" and on pieces of paper with details of chemical formulae relating to explosives.

On 25th May 1995 a storage unit at the Nationwide Self Storage in Acton was examined by police officers. That unit had been rented by a woman using the name of Miss Alison Conti on 16th July 1994. In the unit was a grey plastic box containing, amongst other things, another plastic box containing a powerful home-made explosive TATP and a Maplin carrier bag inside which were two home-made bombs and spare components. The unit also contained a blue plastic box inside which were two handguns and ammunition, and a box file inside which was a Mercury carrier bag containing a quantity of remote control electrical circuitry and magazines entitled "Combat and Survival" and "Raids." There was also a black bin liner inside which was a two-and-a-half litre bottle of liquid labelled "nitric acid" and four bottles of liquid believed to be sulphuric acid. Both those acids can be used to manufacture TATP. Jawad Botmeh's fingerprints were found on the outside and inside of the Maplin carrier bag which contained the bombs, on the outside of the Mercury carrier bag containing the electrical circuitry, and on five copies of the magazine Combat and Survival. Samar Alami's fingerprints were found on two items in the grey box, on the Helix cash box containing the guns and ammunition from the blue box, and on the outside surface of the dustbin liner that contained the sulphuric acid and the nitric acid.

The prosecution's case was that the motive for the bombings was a desire by those responsible to damage the Israeli/Palestinian peace process. Indeed on the day before the bombing of the Embassy the Prime Minister of Israel, Mr Rabin and King Hussein of Jordan signed a declaration which paved the way to a formal peace treaty between Israel and Jordan. The Crown's case was that the plan to explode these bombs came into existence well before that time.

On 6th April 1994 three timers had been purchased for cash by someone masquerading as a legitimate businessman called Hajjar. Between 12th and 22nd April Miss Samar Alami had received the sum of £6,000 and had opened a mail box at a newsagents under the name S. Allen, Allen being the maiden name of Jawad Botmeh's wife. On 25th April 1994 Jawad Botmeh had purchased at Wimbledon car auction the BMW car of distinctive appearance using a false identity and giving the surname Jaffa and a false address. On 9th May three further timers had been purchased, again in the name of Mr Hajjar. Neither applicant could be connected to the purchase of the timers but three of them were recovered from the Nationwide lock-up unit. On 26th May a person using the name Richard Adams, falsely claiming to represent Geltley and Bates (legitimate chemical wholesalers), ordered by telephone from Hays Despatch at Birmingham an unusual consignment of chemicals consisting of 200 litres of acetone, 240 litres of hydrogen peroxide, five litres of nitric acid and 150 kilogrammes of sodium chlorate. The first three items were capable of producing about 80 kilogrammes of TATP according to a unique formula published by Colonel Abu-Tayeb in a book which Samar Alami possessed. Sodium chlorate could also be used to produce explosive by being mixed with sugar or charcoal. On 2nd June those chemicals were collected by a person signing himself George Davies in a Ford Transit van bearing the registration number G562 YOY—the number of a genuine blue Ford Transit van belonging to the butcher in NW London which on that day was making deliveries in NW London. Two kilogrammes of TATP and five kilogrammes of sodium chlorate together with a small quantity of nitric acid in a carton bearing a label from Hays Despatch were recovered from the Nationwide lock-up. It was the prosecution's case that the items found in the Nationwide lock-up represented the remnants of the chemicals ordered from Hays Despatch, the main part of those chemicals having been used to make the two bombs.

During May 1994 some £4,000 was withdrawn from Miss Samar Alami's bank account. On 13th June George Davies of 12 Church Lane, Wolverhampton purchased a Triumph Acclaim at a car auction in Birmingham. The auctioneer recalled two men, one white, the other Maltese or Egyptian in appearance, inspecting the Acclaim. The Maltese-looking man had bid for it. The auctioneer had retained the purchase documents. Neither the signatures nor the fingerprints on those documents belonged to Jawad Botmeh. It was this vehicle that contained the bomb that was exploded outside Balfour House.

On 15th June at a car auction in Milton Keynes an Audi motorcar was purchased by somebody calling himself "George" of 32 Church Street, Wolverhampton. That Audi was the car used to deliver the bomb exploded in the property next to the Israeli Embassy. Jawad Botmeh admitted being present at that car auction when that car was bought. Jawad Botmeh's case was that the car was bought by a man called Reeda. The Crown had a statement from the person who entered that car in the auction describing the person who bid for the car and who drove the car away in a way which did not fit Jawad Botmeh's description of Reeda but which might have fitted Jawad Botmeh himself. That witness said that he saw the Audi car after its purchase being parked in a public car park next to a BMW car of unusual appearance. The witness' description of the BMW car fitted the BMW car owned at that time by Jawad Botmeh.

On 15th July an Audi car owned by the Alami family was seen in Kensington Palace Gardens, the location of the Israeli Embassy.

On 16th July 1994 Miss Samar Alami rented the lock-up at the Nationwide Self Storage in Acton using the name of a woman whom she knew, Alison Conti, and an address in East London. Miss Samar Alami gave instructions that the unit could be visited by a Zak Allen. Miss Alami was given all three keys to the unit. On 23rd July Jawad Botmeh visited the unit.

Forensic evidence indicated that the bomb at the Embassy was likely to have contained either approximately 50 pounds of a recognised high explosive, or if an improvised explosive had been used it was likely that the weight of the explosive would have been of the order of 150 to 250 pounds. The lack of residue at the scene suggested that it had been a high performance explosive.

With regard to the explosion at Balfour House subsequent forensic scientific analysis revealed that a powerful improvised explosive device had exploded in the boot of the Triumph Acclaim. In both cases the explosive used was not known. In the case of the Embassy there was no trace of any timing or remote controlled device, or of any detonator or other initiating process. In the case of the Balfour House bomb there were two small fragments of a PP 3 Ever Ready battery.

The prosecution case against the applicants was that they were jointly concerned in the manufacture of bombs as the items found at Montrose Court and the Nationwide lock-up with their fingerprints on them proved. Both cars used in the bombings were evidently purchased by the same person or persons as the choice of the name and false addresses demonstrated. Jawad Botmeh was clearly involved in the purchase of the Audi and the irresistible inference was that he was also concerned in the purchase of the Triumph Acclaim. Whether or not the accused had taken part in placing the bombs into position, they were clearly involved in the conspiracy to cause the two explosions.

The defence case was that the applicants, although Palestinians who sympathised with the objectives of the Palestinian Liberation Organisation and the Palestinian Front for the Liberation of Palestine, were adherents to the main policy of those organisations, namely that terrorist acts in western countries were counterproductive to the Palestinian cause. Consequently, they would not have been party to the bombing of the Israeli Embassy and Balfour

House. In any event the sophistication of these acts of terrorism indicated that they had been carried out not as the prosecution suggested by a discontented Palestinian splinter group, but almost certainly by one of the well-established terrorist organisations such as the Iranian-backed Hezbollah. The items found at Montrose Court and at the Nationwide lock-up were explicable. Jawad Botmeh's hobby was the operation of model aeroplanes. He had been contemplating the building of such unmanned air vehicles for use in taking intelligence pictures in Palestine and in Israel and possibly as a means of delivering explosive devices. Such devices would be used by Palestinians as a means of protecting themselves against Israeli aggression. To that end he, a qualified electrical engineer, and Miss Samar Alami, a qualified chemical engineer, had been experimenting in making explosives from easily obtainable substances.

In November 1992 Jawad Botmeh had met Reeda at a lecture at the Arab Club. Reeda was a Palestinian from the Lebanon living in England. They met again by chance in 1993 and on that occasion Reeda had asked Jawad Botmeh to help him buy a mechanically reliable car. To that end they had gone to a car auction in Northampton and had bought a Renault 25. After that they had met again and at one of the subsequent meetings he introduced Reeda to Samar Alami.

Samar Alami's evidence was that she had met Reeda on a few occasions in 1993. In March 1994 they had met at a function and had an important conversation about the Intafada, the peace process, arms, explosives and smuggling weapons. That had developed into a discussion concerning improvised explosives. Her last contact with Reeda had taken place on Wednesday 13th July. He had telephoned her and said he was going away and asked that they should meet. They had met in Baker Street. Reeda told her on that occasion that he had done some experiments and that he had something that might be of assistance to her in the experiments she was performing. As a result two boxes were transferred from Reeda's car to her car. That was the last time she had seen Reeda. She had taken the boxes to Montrose Court. They contained TATP, the timers and other items. Later she had placed some of those items in the Nationwide unit.

Meanwhile Jawad Botmeh's evidence was that he had been contacted by Reeda on 13th or 14th June to help Reeda buy another car. They had gone to the Northampton auctions on the 14th unsuccessfully and then to Milton Keynes car auction on the 15th when the Audi was bought by Reeda.

Neither applicant had any intention of using explosives against persons or property in this country. Their intention was to carry out small experimental explosions in remote places such as the Peak District and to export the know-how that they gained from such experiments to persons living in Palestine.

Following their convictions the applicants applied for leave to appeal. These applications were refused by the single judge. The grounds on which those applications were based were, in the case of Jawad Botmeh:

(1)   the judge erred in failing to discharge a juror who had received an approach from an Israeli journalist during the course of the trial;

(2)   the judge erred in failing to direct the postponement of a television broadcast regarding a terrorist incident in 1977 until after the conclusion of the trial.

Those two grounds were relied on by Samar Alami and in addition in her case there was a third ground, that the judge wrongly directed the jury that they were entitled to draw an adverse inference against her in respect of lies told by her during her interviews.

The applications for leave to appeal were renewed to the full court. Prior to hearing those applications the prosecution sought an ex parte hearing on the question of public interest immunity for certain documents and information in the possession of the Crown. Three such hearings had taken place before the trial judge in connection with the applicants' trial. As a result a considerable body of information had been disclosed, some of it in a redacted form so as to protect either the source of the information or the method by which the information had been obtained. Unhappily not all documents which should have been placed before the trial judge were placed before him and accordingly the trial judge did not rule upon whether disclosure of those further documents should be made or not. Prior to the ex parte hearing regarding public interest immunity before this court on 15th March 1999, a hearing of which the applicants' lawyers were aware, this court received and examined the documents placed before us as being material. Here we use the word "material" as defined by this court in R v Keane 99 Cr App R 1. Having heard the prosecution submissions we decided to invite the applicant's counsel to make submissions. One purpose was to ensure that we understood the applicants' cases and those areas in which the applicants' counsel anticipated that there might be documents which could assist the applicants' cases or undermine the prosecution's cases against the applicants. As a result we received a 33 page skeleton argument prepared by counsel for the applicants and supported by a file of documents which were in the main articles extracted from newspapers. In addition there was a bundle of authorities. The nature of the appellants' cases and of those areas in which counsel anticipated that there might be material documents which could be of assistance to the defence, were developed by Mr Mansfield QC in oral argument. Following Mr Mansfield's submissions we heard submissions on the effect of Article 6 of the European Convention of Human Rights and in particular on the report of the commission in the case of Rowe and Davis v The United Kingdom, a unanimous report, from Mr Emmerson for the applicants and, on behalf of the respondents, from Mr Singh. Whilst we were hearing those submissions the Divisional Court presided over by the Lord Chief Justice handed down their judgments in two cases, R v DPP ex parte Kebilene and others and R v DPP ex parte Rechachi relied upon by Mr Emmerson to support his proposition that although the European Convention of Human Rights is not yet fully incorporated into the laws of the United Kingdom because not all the sections of the Human Rights Act 1998 have been brought into force, courts must nevertheless take heed of the convention and, in particular in this case, of Article 6 of the Convention if decisions are not to be overturned at a later date when the Act does come fully into force, because of the effect of section 22(4) of the Act, which allows the acts of public authorities to be examined whenever those acts were performed.

In the result we were minded to grant leave to appeal on the new issues raised in argument before us, subject to those issues being converted into draft grounds of appeal, so that we could consider whether there were some grounds on which leave should be given and some on which leave should be refused. We also indicated that we would on 10th May (that is today) hear submissions relating to the three original draft grounds on which the renewed applications for leave to appeal against conviction had been based.

Two additional grounds of appeal have been submitted by counsel for the applicants together with a document headed "Submission in support of additional grounds of appeal" which helpfully sets out the essence of the detailed oral submissions we heard from Mr Emmerson. We grant leave to appeal to both applicants against their convictions on the two additional grounds and say nothing further on those grounds.

Turning to the three original grounds, this morning Mr Mansfield helpfully indicated that he did not intend to pursue the third of those grounds which related solely to the case of Samar Alami, namely that the judge wrongly directed the jury that they were entitled to draw an adverse inference against her in respect of lies told by her during her interviews. That concession did not surprise us. The fact is that Miss Alami did, in her first interview, give answers that were not true—those being her assertions that she had nothing to hide whereas she had hidden items both at her uncle's flat and at the Nationwide lock-up—and her account of her own movements on the night of the bombing of Balfour House. In those circumstances the judge was correct to give a Lucas direction. The direction he gave, which is at page 175 of the transcript of the summing-up, was appropriate to the evidence and to the answers given by Miss Alami in interview. Had no such direction been given in a case where the prosecution were relying on those answers as evidence supporting their case that Miss Alami was a conspirator, the summing-up would in our judgment have been defective. For those reasons we would not have given leave on that ground.

Mr Mansfield conceded that the second ground, had it stood alone, would not have represented an arguable ground of appeal but submitted that the second ground taken with the main ground, which is ground 1, is an additional, albeit subsidiary reason why this court should decide that these convictions are unsafe. We say that in our judgment the second ground, the judge's refusal to order an independent television station to postpone the showing of a planned programme for a matter of weeks, was a decision which it was within the judge's discretion to take.

The programme dealt with a hijacking by terrorists of a Lufthansa plane in October 1977 at Mogadishu in Somalia in which the pilot was murdered but the hostages were released after action by special forces from Germany and this country. The programme focused on three persons: the sole surviving hijacker, a member of the SAS who took part in the action which led to the release of the hostages, and the widow of the pilot. The judge before ruling on the matter saw the programme and heard submissions by Mr Mansfield for the applicants and by Mr Rock Tansey QC for the third defendant, who was subsequently acquitted by the jury.

The judge in his ruling expressed his personal view of the programme. He said:

"... my impression—and it is a personal one—was that the programme struck a very good balance between the hijacker, the victims, the hostages, the rescuer and the widow of the murdered pilot."

The judge then set out the eight submissions made by counsel, including Mr Tansey's concern that the name of the leading and most violent hijacker was the same as his client's. Then at page 4 of his ruling the judge observed:

"What has to be borne in mind, of course, is that the programme in no way deals with these proceedings as such or anybody connected with them, nor does it deal with what might be described as the primary issue in the case. It is, as I summarised the arguments, a matter of prejudice of linking the PFLP to the Bader Meinhoff group and matters of that sort."

The judge made the ruling on this application at page 9 of the second of the transcripts:

"I take the view that Mr Caplan is right in his submissions that there is, in aggregate, no substantial risk of serious prejudice. Even if I took the view that there was a risk of prejudice it certainly is not of serious prejudice in the context of this case and the vast amount of background information that has been introduced including the videos we have seen and the very large number of expert witnesses who have been called to describe the Palestinian condition and Middle Eastern politics in general.

Even if I was wrong about that I would certainly take the view that the case fell within section 5. It is a matter of public interest, it has been a matter of public interest for nearly twenty years, and the programme is not, in any way, partizan. It may be emotional. It is, perhaps, my subjective view, but it appears to be a balanced programme looking at the situation from all different view points.

What remains to be done, in my view, is that I should simply remind the jury of what I told them at the outset of the trial, that their jury oath requires them to give true verdicts according to the evidence. What they see on television is not evidence, and I shall remind them of that in my summing-up."

The judge on the jury's return to court gave the jury immediately eminently sensible directions. He accepted that he could not order them not to watch the programme and that if he tried to order them not to watch it, it would simply excite their curiosity. The judge went on:

> "What I can remind you of is the oath you took at the beginning of this case to give true verdicts according to the evidence. If you do feel inclined to watch it remember that it is not and can never be evidence. You try this case on what you hear and see and are told in this court, not what you see on television."

In his summing-up at page 10 the judge again directed the jury that their duty was to try the defendants on the evidence they had seen and heard in court and at page 45 of his summing-up the judge again referred to this television programme and to the expert evidence that the policy of Palestinians who wished to advance the Palestinian cause had changed since 1977 to a policy of confining acts of aggression against Israeli targets to Palestine and Israel. The judge's conclusions about the programme were well within the range of conclusions it was reasonable for him to reach. It is a serious step to interfere with the publication of stories or programmes in the media. The judge was entitled to conclude that there was no interest in the defendants which called for him to take such a step and that the remote risk of bias being created in a juror's mind could be counteracted by directions from him. The directions the judge gave were precisely those necessary in our judgment to achieve that end. The conclusion we have reached is that there is nothing in this ground either as an independent ground or as a support for ground 1.

Ground 1 relates to the judge's refusal to discharge from the jury a juror who had been approached by a journalist during the course of the trial. He was referred to, and we shall refer to him, as Juror A. Juror A was the last to leave the jury box because of the layout of the court. That layout took Juror A past the press bench as he left the jury box. A journalist for the Israeli media was in that press box at the end of the hearing on the afternoon of 19th November 1996. That journalist had, by his body language and by his attempt on one occasion in the previous week to speak to leading counsel for the prosecution and for the applicants, revealed a bias against the defence. The journalist on 19th November 1996 as Juror A was leaving the jury box, offered to supply Juror A with a telephone number if the juror wanted it. Juror A did not reply. That that occurred was confirmed by the juror immediately ahead of Juror A, who we have referred to as Juror B. There was no evidence that any other juror was aware of the incident at the time. Juror B said to Juror A: "What did that guy say?" Juror A says that he replied: "I don't know." Juror A then waited for the other jurors to go before telling the court usher what had occurred. Juror A the next day made a statement to the court clerk, the statement being taken on the judge's direction, which ended: "Nothing like this has happened before." The statement set out the incident in the terms we have described.

On 20th November the journalist was interviewed, again at the judge's direction, by a police sergeant. The journalist twice denied approaching Juror A on 19th November and said that he had not approached any juror on any occasion. It would seem that Juror B was interviewed and there is some suggestion that there might have been a discrepancy between his account of the incident and that of Juror A, in that Juror B may have suggested that Juror A had made some reply to the journalist. We have not seen any statement from Juror B and this suggestion remains speculative.

Mr Mansfield submitted that this approach by the journalist to Juror A came at a critical stage in the trial. The journalist was clearly seeking a gateway into the jury. The concern is how did the journalist feel confident to approach Juror A? The only explanation, argued Mr Mansfield, is that there must have been some understanding spoken or unspoken between them; this juror was a vulnerable point on this jury; there was a real danger that he was biased; the judge should therefore have discharged him as the judge was asked to do so by the applicants' counsel; the judge refused and that ruling was wrong or at least, submits Mr Mansfield, it is arguable that that ruling was wrong. We do not agree. The judge in making his ruling directed himself correctly on the law reminding himself of the principle stated in Gough [1993] AC 646 which are to be found in the current edition of Archbold at paragraph 4–256. It was for the judge to decide if a real danger of bias on the part of Juror A existed. The judge was in a much better position to answer that question than any appellate court would be. The judge made these findings which Mr Mansfield, with his normal realism, accepted he cannot go behind:

> "I take the view that the juror concerned acted with extreme propriety and correctness in the matter. He did report it. The delay was simply to wait until the others had gone. He does not prove an advance reason for that, but one would have thought that it was self-evident to avoid alarm and despondency amongst other jurors. His duty was to report any improper act; he did report it and it has been dealt with appropriately."

Then at page 7B the judge went on with his findings:

"The effect, as I say, of delay, I discount entirely. I am bound to say the suggestion that he only reported it because he thought juror 'B' may have overheard it, I regard as fanciful and scarcely supported on the facts as a matter of inference.

I take the view that everything has been done, as it should have been done. The matter was reported. It has been investigated. It is in my view, not possible to infer that there exists in the mind of that juror or indeed of juror 'B,' a real danger of bias according to the principles which I have outlined from the relevant passage in Archbold. I take the view that the very fact that we spent the greater part of the day investigating the consequences of the account, is demonstrably justice being seen to be done."

On those findings the judge was entitled to conclude that there was no possibility of bias and entitled in his discretion to refuse to discharge Juror A.

After his ruling the judge gave the jury directions. Very sensibly in our view the judge told the jury what had occurred. He told the jury that there had been an approach to a juror from a journalist from the Israeli media; that that journalist denied making such approach; and that that journalist in the course of the case had made no secret as to where his sympathies lay. Then the judge said this to the jury:

"I want to make it absolutely clear that I commend the conduct of the juror who not only reported the incident almost immediately but also had the good sense to wait until the rest of you left, I suspect, so as to avoid any unnecessary anxiety and speculation.

In my view, he did exactly what he should have done.

*   *   *   *   *

DOCUMENT NO 25

Chahal v The United Kingdom European Court Of Human Rights

November 15, 1996
(Edited Text)

PROCEDURE

1. The case was referred to the Court by the Government of the United Kingdom of Great Britain and Northern Ireland ("the Government") on 23 August 1995 and by the European Commission of Human Rights ("the Commission") on 13 September 1995, within the three-month period laid down by Articles 32 § 1 and 47 of the European Convention for the Protection of Human Rights and Fundamental Freedoms ("the Convention"). It originated in an application (no. 22414/93) against the United Kingdom lodged with the Commission under Article 25 on 27 July 1993 by two Indian nationals, Mr Karamjit Singh Chahal and Mrs Darshan Singh Chahal and by two British nationals, Miss Kiranpreet Kaur Chahal and Mr Bikaramjit Singh Chahal.

The Government's application referred to Article 48 and the Commission's request referred to Articles 44 and 48 and to the declaration whereby the United Kingdom recognised the compulsory jurisdiction of the Court (Article 46). The object of the application and the request was to obtain a decision as to whether the facts of the case disclosed a breach by the respondent State of its obligations under Articles 3, 5 §§ 1 and 4, 8 and 13 of the Convention.

2. In response to the enquiry made in accordance with Rule 33 § 3 (d) of Rules of Court A, the applicants stated that they wished to take part in the proceedings and designated the lawyer who would represent them (Rule 30).

3. The Chamber to be constituted included *ex officio* Sir John Freeland, the elected judge of British nationality (Article 43 of the Convention), and Mr R. Bernhardt, the Vice-President of the Court (Rule 21 § 4 (b)). On 5 September 1995, in the presence of the Registrar, the President of the Court, Mr R. Ryssdal, drew by lot the names of the other seven members, namely Mr L.-E. Pettiti, Mr B. Walsh, Mr R. Macdonald, Mr N. Valticos, Mr F. Bigi, Mr D. Gotchev and Mr U. L_hmus (Article 43 *in fine* of the Convention and Rule 21 § 5).

4. On 24 August 1995 the Government informed the Court that there were no immediate plans to deport the first applicant, and undertook to provide the Court with at least two weeks' notice of any intended deportation of him.

The Government had previously been requested by the Commission on 1 September 1994, pursuant to Rule 36 of its Rules of Procedure, not to deport the applicant pending the outcome of the proceedings before the Commission. In accordance with Rule 36 § 2 of Rules of Court A, this request remained recommended to the Government.

5. As President of the Chamber (Rule 21 § 6), Mr Bernhardt, acting through the Registrar, consulted the Agent of the British Government, the applicants' lawyer and the Delegate of the Commission on the organisation of the proceedings (Rules 37 § 1 and 38). Pursuant to the order made in consequence, the Registrar received the Government's and the applicants' memorials on 15 January 1996.

6. On 28 November 1995, Mr Bernhardt, having consulted the Chamber, granted leave to Amnesty International, Justice and Liberty in conjunction with the Centre for Advice on Individual Rights in Europe ("the AIRE Centre") and the Joint Council for the Welfare of Immigrants ("JCWI"), all London-based non-governmental human rights organisations, to submit observations, pursuant to Rule 37 § 2. Comments were received from Amnesty International and from Justice on 15 January 1996, and from Liberty together with the AIRE Centre and the JCWI on 24 January.

7. On 21 February 1996 the Chamber decided to relinquish jurisdiction forthwith in favour of a Grand Chamber (Rule 51 § 1).

8. The Grand Chamber to be constituted included *ex officio* Mr Ryssdal, President of the Court, Mr Bernhardt, Vice-President of the Court, and all the other members and the substitute judges (Mr F. Matscher, Mr A. Spielmann, Mr J.M. Morenilla and Mr E. Levits) of the Chamber which had relinquished jurisdiction (Rule 51 § 2 (a) and (b)). On 24 February 1996, in the presence of the Registrar, the President drew by lot the names of the seven additional judges called on to complete the Grand Chamber, namely Mr F. Gölcüklü, Mr J. De Meyer, Mr S.K. Martens, Mrs E. Palm, Mr A.B. Baka, Mr G. Mifsud Bonnici and Mr P. Jambrek.

* * * * *

AS TO THE FACTS

I. The circumstances of the case

A.   The applicants

12. The four applicants are members of the same family and are Sikhs.

The first applicant, Karamjit Singh Chahal, is an Indian citizen who was born in 1948. He entered the United Kingdom illegally in 1971 in search of employment. In 1974 he applied to the Home Office to regularise his stay and on 10 December 1974 was granted indefinite leave to remain under the terms of an amnesty for illegal entrants who arrived before 1 January 1973. Since 16 August 1990 he has been detained for the purposes of deportation in Bedford prison.

The second applicant, Darshan Kaur Chahal, is also an Indian citizen who was born in 1956. She came to England on 12 September 1975 following her marriage to the first applicant in India, and currently lives in Luton with the two children of the family, Kiranpreet Kaur Chahal (born in 1977) and Bikaramjit Singh Chahal (born in 1978), who are the third and fourth applicants. By virtue of their birth in the United Kingdom the two children have British nationality.

13. The first and second applicants applied for British citizenship in December 1987. Mr Chahal's request was refused on 4 April 1989 but that of Mrs Chahal is yet to be determined.

B.   Background: the conflict in Punjab

14. Since the partition of India in 1947 many Sikhs have been engaged in a political campaign for an independent homeland, Khalistan, which would approximate to the Indian province of Punjab. In the late 1970s, a prominent group emerged under the leadership of Sant Jarnail Singh Bhindranwale, based in the Golden Temple in Amritsar, the holiest Sikh shrine. The Government submit that Sant Bhindranwale, as well as preaching the tenets of orthodox Sikhism, used the Golden Temple for the accumulation of arms and advocated the use of violence for the establishment of an independent Khalistan.

15. The situation in Punjab deteriorated following the killing of a senior police officer in the Golden Temple in 1983. On 6 June 1984 the Indian army stormed the temple during a religious festival, killing Sant Bhindranwale and approximately 1,000 other Sikhs. Four months later the Indian Prime Minister, Mrs Indira Gandhi, was shot dead by two Sikh members of her bodyguard. The ensuing Hindu backlash included the killing of over 2,000 Sikhs in riots in Delhi.

16. Since 1984, the conflict in Punjab has reportedly claimed over 20,000 lives, peaking in 1992 when, according to Indian press reports collated by the

United Kingdom Foreign and Commonwealth Office, approximately 4,000 people were killed in related incidents in Punjab and elsewhere. There is evidence of violence and human rights abuses perpetrated by both Sikh separatists and the security forces (see paragraphs 45–56 below).

C. Mr Chahal's visit to India in 1984

17. On 1 January 1984 Mr Chahal travelled to Punjab with his wife and children to visit relatives. He submits that during this visit he attended at the Golden Temple on many occasions, and saw Sant Bhindranwale preach there approximately ten times. On one occasion he, his wife and son were afforded a personal audience with him. At around this time Mr Chahal was baptised and began to adhere to the tenets of orthodox Sikhism. He also became involved in organising passive resistance in support of autonomy for Punjab.

18. On 30 March 1984 he was arrested by the Punjab police. He was taken into detention and held for 21 days, during which time he was, he contended, kept handcuffed in insanitary conditions, beaten to unconsciousness, electrocuted on various parts of his body and subjected to a mock execution. He was subsequently released without charge. He was able to return to the United Kingdom on 27 May 1984, and has not visited India since.

D. Mr Chahal's political and religious activities in the United Kingdom

19. On his return to the United Kingdom, Mr Chahal became a leading figure in the Sikh community, which reacted with horror to the storming of the Golden Temple. He helped organise a demonstration in London to protest at the Indian Government's actions, became a full-time member of the committee of the "gurdwara" (temple) in Belvedere (Erith, Kent) and travelled around London persuading young Sikhs to be baptised.

20. In August 1984 Mr Jasbir Singh Rode entered the United Kingdom. He was Sant Bhindranwale's nephew, and recognised by Sikhs as his successor as spiritual leader. Mr Chahal contacted him on his arrival and toured the United Kingdom with him, assisting at baptisms performed by him. Mr Rode was instrumental in setting up branches of the International Sikh Youth Federation ("ISYF") in the United Kingdom, and the applicant played an important organisational role in this endeavour. The ISYF was established to be the overseas branch of the All India Sikh Students' Federation. This latter organisation was proscribed by the Indian Government until mid-1985, and is reportedly still perceived as militant by the Indian authorities.

21. In December 1984 Mr Rode was excluded from the United Kingdom on the ground that he publicly advocated violent methods in pursuance of the separatist campaign. On his return to India he was imprisoned without trial until late 1988. Shortly after his release it became apparent that he had changed his political views; he now argued that Sikhs should pursue their cause using

constitutional methods, a view which, according to the applicants, was unacceptable to many Sikhs. The former followers of Mr Rode therefore became divided.

22. In the United Kingdom, according to the Government, this led to a split in the ISYF along broadly north/south lines. In the north of England most branches followed Mr Rode, whereas in the south the ISYF became linked with another Punjab political activist, Dr Sohan Singh, who continued to support the campaign for an independent homeland. Mr Chahal and, according to him, all major figures of spiritual and intellectual standing within the United Kingdom Sikh community, were in the southern faction.

E. Mr Chahal's alleged criminal activities

23. In October 1985 Mr Chahal was detained under the Prevention of Terrorism (Temporary Provisions) Act 1984 ("PTA") on suspicion of involvement in a conspiracy to assassinate the Indian Prime Minister, Mr Rajiv Gandhi, during an official visit to the United Kingdom. He was released for lack of evidence.

In 1986 he was arrested and questioned twice (once under the PTA), because he was believed to be involved in an ISYF conspiracy to murder moderate Sikhs in the United Kingdom. On both occasions he was released without charge. Mr Chahal denied involvement in any of these conspiracies.

24.   In March 1986 he was charged with assault and affray following disturbances at the East Ham gurdwara in London. During the course of his trial on these charges in May 1987 there was a disturbance at the Belvedere gurdwara, which was widely reported in the national press. Mr Chahal was arrested in connection with this incident, and was brought to court in handcuffs on the final day of his trial. He was convicted of both charges arising out of the East Ham incident, and served concurrent sentences of six and nine months.

He was subsequently acquitted of charges arising out of the Belvedere disturbance. On 27 July 1992 the Court of Appeal quashed the two convictions on the grounds that Mr Chahal's appearance in court in handcuffs had been seriously prejudicial to him.

F. The deportation and asylum proceedings

1. The notice of intention to deport

25. On 14 August 1990 the Home Secretary (Mr Hurd) decided that Mr Chahal ought to be deported because his continued presence in the United Kingdom was unconducive to the public good for reasons of national security and other reasons of a political nature, namely the international fight against terrorism.

A notice of intention to deport was served on the latter on 16 August 1990. He was then detained for deportation purposes pursuant to paragraph

2 (2) of Schedule III of the Immigration Act 1971 (see paragraph 64 below) and has remained in custody ever since.

2. Mr Chahal's application for asylum

26. Mr Chahal claimed that if returned to India he had a well-founded fear of persecution within the terms of the United Nations 1951 Convention on the Status of Refugees ("the 1951 Convention": see paragraph 61 below) and applied for political asylum on 16 August 1990. He was interviewed by officials from the Asylum Division of the Home Office on 11 September 1990 and his solicitors submitted written representations on his behalf.

He claimed that he would be subjected to torture and persecution if returned to India, and relied upon the following matters, *inter alia:*

(a) his detention and torture in Punjab in 1984 (see paragraph 18 above);

(b) his political activities in the United Kingdom and his identification with the regeneration of the Sikh religion and the campaign for a separate Sikh state (see paragraphs 19–22 above);

(c) his links with Sant Bhindranwale and Jasbir Singh Rode; (see paragraphs 17 and 20 above);

(d) evidence that his parents, other relatives and contacts had been detained, tortured and questioned in October 1989 about Mr Chahal's activities in the United Kingdom and that others connected to him had died in police custody;

(e) the interest shown by the Indian national press in his alleged Sikh militancy and proposed expulsion from the United Kingdom;

(f) consistent evidence, including that contained in the reports of Amnesty International, of the torture and murder of those perceived to be Sikh militants by the Indian authorities, particularly the Punjab police (see paragraphs 55–56 below).

27. On 27 March 1991 the Home Secretary refused the request for asylum.

In a letter to the applicant, he expressed the view that the latter's known support of Sikh separatism would be unlikely to attract the interest of the Indian authorities unless that support were to include acts of violence against India. He continued that he was:

> "not aware of any outstanding charges either in India or elsewhere against [Mr Chahal] and on the account [Mr Chahal] has given of his political activities, the Secretary of State does not accept that there is a reasonable likelihood that he would be persecuted if he were to return to India. The media interest in his case may be known by the Indian authorities and, given his admitted involvement in an extremist faction of the ISYF, it is accepted that the Indian Government may have some current and legitimate interest in his activities."

The Home Secretary did not consider that Mr Chahal's experiences in India in 1984 had any continued relevance, since that had been a time of particularly high tension in Punjab.

28. Mr Chahal's solicitors informed the Home Secretary that he intended to make an application for judicial review of the refusal of asylum, but would wait until the advisory panel had considered the national security case against him.

3. The advisory panel

29. Because of the national security elements of the case, there was no right of appeal against the deportation order (see paragraphs 58 and 60 below). However, on 10 June 1991, the matter was considered by an advisory panel, chaired by a Court of Appeal judge, Lord Justice Lloyd, and including a former President of the Immigration Appeal Tribunal.

30. The Home Office had prepared statements on 5 April and 23 May 1991 containing an outline of the grounds for the notice of intention to deport, which were sent to the applicant. The principal points were as follows:

   (a)   Mr Chahal had been the central figure in directing the support for terrorism organised by the London-based faction of the ISYF which had close links with Sikh terrorists in the Punjab;

   (b)   he had played a leading role in the faction's programme of intimidation directed against the members of other groups within the United Kingdom Sikh community;

   (c)   he had been involved in supplying funds and equipment to terrorists in Punjab since 1985;

   (d)   he had a public history of violent involvement in Sikh terrorism, as evidenced by his 1986 convictions and involvement in disturbances at the Belvedere gurdwara (see paragraph 24 above). These disturbances were related to the aim of gaining control of gurdwara funds in order to finance support and assistance for terrorist activity in Punjab;

   (e)   he had been involved in planning and directing terrorist attacks in India, the United Kingdom and elsewhere.
         Mr Chahal was not informed of the sources of and the evidence for these views, which were put to the advisory panel.

31. In a letter dated 7 June 1991, Mr Chahal's solicitors set out a written case to be put before the advisory panel, including the following points:

   (a)   the southern branch of the ISYF had a membership of less than 200 and was non-violent both in terms of its aims and history;

   (b)   the ISYF did not attempt to gain control of gurdwaras in order to channel funds into terrorism; this was a purely ideological struggle on the part of young Sikhs to have gurdwaras run according to Sikh religious values;

(c)   Mr Chahal denied any involvement in the disturbances at the East Ham and Belvedere gurdwaras (see paragraph 24 above) or in any other violent or terrorist activity in the United Kingdom or elsewhere.

32. He appeared before the panel in person, and was allowed to call witnesses on his behalf, but was not allowed to be represented by a lawyer or to be informed of the advice which the panel gave to the Home Secretary (see paragraph 60 below).

33. On 25 July 1991 the Home Secretary (Mr Baker) signed an order for Mr Chahal's deportation, which was served on 29 July.

4.   Judicial review

34. On 9 August 1991 Mr Chahal applied for judicial review of the Home Secretaries' decisions to refuse asylum and to make the deportation order. Leave was granted by the High Court on 2 September 1991.

The asylum refusal was quashed on 2 December 1991 and referred back to the Home Secretary. The court found that the reasoning behind it was inadequate, principally because the Home Secretary had neglected to explain whether he believed the evidence of Amnesty International relating to the situation in Punjab and, if not, the reasons for such disbelief. The court did not decide on the validity of the deportation order. Mr Justice Popplewell expressed "enormous anxiety" about the case.

35. After further consideration, on 1 June 1992 the Home Secretary (Mr Clarke) took a fresh decision to refuse asylum. He considered that the breakdown of law and order in Punjab was due to the activities of Sikh terrorists and was not evidence of persecution within the terms of the 1951 Convention. Furthermore, relying upon Articles 32 and 33 of that Convention (see paragraph 61 below), he expressed the view that, even if Mr Chahal were at risk of persecution, he would not be entitled to the protection of the 1951 Convention because of the threat he posed to national security.

36. Mr Chahal applied for judicial review of this decision, but then requested a postponement on 4 June 1992, which was granted.

37. In a letter dated 2 July 1992, the Home Secretary informed the applicant that he declined to withdraw the deportation proceedings, that Mr Chahal could be deported to any international airport of his choice within India and that the Home Secretary had sought and received an assurance from the Indian Government (which was subsequently repeated in December 1995) in the following terms:

"We have noted your request to have a formal assurance to the effect that, if Mr Karamjit Singh Chahal were to be deported to India, he would enjoy the same legal protection as any other Indian citizen, and that he would have no reason to expect to suffer mistreatment of any kind at the hands of the Indian authorities.

I have the honour to confirm the above."

38. On 16 July 1992 the High Court granted leave to apply for judicial review of the decisions of 1 June 1992 to maintain the refusal of asylum and of 2 July 1992 to proceed with the deportation. An application for bail was rejected on 23 July (the European Court of Human Rights was not provided with details of this ruling).

39. The Court of Appeal (Criminal Division) quashed Mr Chahal's 1987 convictions on 27 July 1992 (see paragraph 24 above). The Home Secretary reviewed the case in the light of this development, but concluded that it was right to proceed with the deportation.

40. The hearing of the application for judicial review took place between 18 and 21 January 1993. It was refused on 12 February 1993 by Mr Justice Potts in the High Court, as was a further application for bail (the European Court of Human Rights was not provided with details of this ruling either).

41. Mr Chahal appealed to the Court of Appeal. The appeal was heard on 28 July 1993 and dismissed on 22 October 1993 (*R. v. Secretary of State for the Home Department, ex parte Chahal* [1994] Immigration Appeal Reports, p. 107).

The court held that the combined effect of the 1951 Convention and the Immigration Rules (see paragraphs 61–62 below) was to require the Home Secretary to weigh the threat to Mr Chahal's life or freedom if he were deported against the danger to national security if he were permitted to stay. In the words of Lord Justice Nolan:

> "The proposition that, in deciding whether the deportation of an individual would be in the public good, the Secretary of State should wholly ignore the fact that the individual has established a well-founded fear of persecution in the country to which he is to be sent seems to me to be surprising and unacceptable. Of course there may very well be occasions when the individual poses such a threat to this country and its inhabitants that considerations of his personal safety and well being become virtually irrelevant. Nonetheless one would expect that the Secretary of State would balance the risks to this country against the risks to the individual, albeit that the scales might properly be weighted in favour of the former."

The Home Secretary appeared to have taken into account the evidence that the applicant might be persecuted and it was not possible for the court to judge whether his decision to deport was irrational or perverse because it did not have access to the evidence relating to the national security risk posed by Mr Chahal. As Lord Justice Neill remarked:

> "The court has the right to scrutinise a claim that a person should be deported in the interests of national security but in practice this scrutiny may be defective or incomplete if all the relevant facts are not before the court."

In the absence of evidence of irrationality or perversity, it was impossible under English law to set aside the Home Secretary's decision (see paragraph 66 below).

42. The Court of Appeal refused leave to appeal to the House of Lords, and this was also refused by the House of Lords on 3 March 1994.

43. Following the report of the Commission, the applicant applied for temporary release pending the decision of the European Court of Human Rights, by way of habeas corpus and judicial review proceedings in the Divisional Court (see paragraph 65 below). The Secretary of State opposed the application on the following grounds:

> "The applicant was detained in August 1990 and served with notice of intention to deport because the then Secretary of State was satisfied that he represented a substantial threat to national security. The Secretary of State remains satisfied that such a threat persists. . . . Given the reasons for the applicant's deportation, the Secretary of State remains satisfied that his temporary release from detention would not be justified. He has concluded the applicant could not be safely released, subject to restrictions, in view of the nature of the threat posed by him."

Judgment was given on 10 November 1995 (*R. v. Secretary of State for the Home Department, ex parte Chahal*, unreported). Mr Justice MacPherson in the Divisional Court rejected the application for habeas corpus, on the ground that "the detention *per se* was plainly lawful because the Secretary of State [had] the power to detain an individual who [was] the subject of a decision to make a deportation order." In connection with the application for judicial review of the Secretary of State's decision to detain Mr Chahal, the Judge remarked:

> "I have to look at the decision of the Secretary of State and judge whether, in all the circumstances, upon the information available, he has acted unlawfully, or with procedural impropriety, or perversely to the point of irrationality. I am wholly unable to say that there is a case for such a decision, particularly bearing in mind that I do not know the full material on which the decisions have been made . . . [I]t is obvious and right that in certain circumstances the Executive must be able to keep secret matters which they deem to be necessary to keep secret. . . . There are no grounds, in my judgment, for saying or even suspecting that there are not matters which are present in the Secretary of State's mind of that kind upon which he was entitled to act . . ."

G. Current conditions in India and in Punjab

44. The current position with regard to the protection of human rights in India generally and in Punjab more specifically was a matter of dispute between the parties. A substantial amount of evidence was presented to the Court on this issue, some of which is summarised below.

1. Material submitted by the Government

45. The Government submitted that it appeared from Indian press reports collated by the Foreign and Commonwealth Office that the number of lives lost in Punjab from terrorism had decreased dramatically. In 1992 the figure was 4,000, in 1993 it was 394, and in 1994 it was 51. The former Chief Minister of Punjab, Mr Beant Singh, was assassinated in August 1995; that aside, there was little terrorist activity and only four terrorist-related deaths in the region in 1995.

46. Furthermore, democracy had returned to the state: almost all factions of the Akali Dal, the main Sikh political party, had united and were set to contest the next general election as one entity and the Gidderbaha by-election passed off peacefully, with a turn-out of 88%.

47. The United Kingdom High Commission continued to receive complaints about the Punjab police. However, in recent months these had related mainly to extortion rather than to politically-motivated abuses and they were consistently told that there was now little or no politically-motivated police action in Punjab.

48. Steps had been taken by the Indian authorities to deal with the remaining corruption and misuse of power in Punjab; for example, there had been a number of court judgments against police officers, a "Lok Pal" (ombudsman) had been appointed and the new Chief Minister had promised to "ensure transparency and accountability." The Indian National Human Rights Commission ("NHRC"), which had reported on Punjab (see below) continued to strengthen and develop.

2. The Indian National Human Rights Commission reports

49. The NHRC visited Punjab in April 1994 and reported as follows:

"The complaints of human rights violations made to the Commission fall broadly into three categories. Firstly, there were complaints against the police, of arbitrary arrests, disappearances, custodial deaths and fake encounters resulting in killings. . . . There was near unanimity in the views expressed by the public at large that terrorism has been contained. . . . [A] feeling was now growing that it was time for the police to cease operating under the cover of special laws. There were very strong demands for normalising the role and functioning of the police and for re-establishing the authority of the District Magistrates over the police. The impression that the Commission has gathered is that . . . the Magistracy at District level is not at present in a position to inquire into complaints of human rights violations by the police. In the public mind there is a prevailing feeling of the police being above the law, working on its own steam and answerable to none. . . . The Commission recommends that the

Government examine this matter seriously and ensure that normalcy is restored . . ."

50. In addition, in its Annual Report for 1994/1995, the NHRC recommended, as a matter of priority, a systematic reform, retraining and reorganisation of the police throughout India, having commented:

"The issue of custodial death and rape, already high in the priorities of the Commission, was set in the wider context of the widespread mistreatment of prisoners resulting from practices that can only be described as cruel, inhuman or degrading."

3.   Reports to the United Nations

51. The reports to the United Nations in 1994 and 1995 of the Special Rapporteur on torture and other cruel, inhuman and degrading treatment or punishment and in 1994 of the Special Rapporteur on extrajudicial, summary or arbitrary executions and the Working Group on enforced and involuntary disappearances, recounted that human rights violations on the part of the security forces were widespread in India.

For example, in his 1995 report, the Special Rapporteur on torture commented on the practice of torture in police custody:

"It is apparent that few incidents, in what is credibly alleged to be a widespread, if not endemic, phenomenon are prosecuted and even fewer lead to conviction of the perpetrators. It is to be noted that very many cases that come to the attention of the Special Rapporteur are those that result in death, in other words, those where torture may have been applied with the most extreme results. This must be a minority of cases of torture in the country [India]."

4.   The United States' Department of State reports

52. The 1995 United States' Department of State Report on India told of human rights abuses perpetrated by the Punjab police acting outside their home state:

"Punjab police hit teams again in 1994 pursued Sikh militants into other parts of India. On June 24, Punjab police shot and killed Karnail Singh Kaili, a man they identified as a Sikh terrorist . . . in West Bengal. The government of West Bengal claimed that it had not been informed of the presence of Punjab police in West Bengal, seized Kaili's body and weapons and barred the departure of the police team until the Punjab Chief Minister apologized."

53. In contrast, the most recent Department of State Report (March 1996) declared that insurgent violence had largely disappeared in Punjab and that there was visible progress in correcting patterns of abuse by the police. It continued:

"Killings of Sikh militants by police in armed encounters appear to be virtually at an end. During the first 8 months of [1995], only two persons were killed in police encounters. Attention was focused on past abuses in Punjab by press reports that hundreds of bodies, many allegedly those of persons who died in unacknowledged police custody, were cremated as 'unclaimed' during 1991–1993 or discovered at the bottom of recently drained canals."

5. The Immigration Appeal Tribunal

54. The United Kingdom Immigration Appeal Tribunal took account of allegations of the extra-territorial activities of the Punjab police in the case of *Charan Singh Gill v. Secretary of State for the Home Department* (14 November 1994, unreported), which related to an appeal by a politically-active Sikh against the Secretary of State's refusal to grant him political asylum. The appellant drew the attention of the Tribunal to a story in the Punjab Times of 10 May 1994, which reported the killing by the Punjab police of two Sikh fighters in West Bengal. The Chairman of the Tribunal remarked:

"We should say that we do not accept [the representative of the Home Office's] view of this document, that it was more probably based on imaginative journalism than on fact. In our view, it affords valuable retrospective corroboration of the material set out above, demonstrating that the Punjab police are very much a law unto themselves, and are ready to track down anyone they regard as subversive, as and when the mood takes them, anywhere in India."

6. The reports of Amnesty International

55. In its report of May 1995, "Punjab police: beyond the bounds of the law," Amnesty International similarly alleged that the Punjab police were known to have carried out abductions and executions of suspected Sikh militants in other Indian states outside their jurisdiction. The Supreme Court in New Delhi had reportedly taken serious note of the illegal conduct of the Punjab police, publicly accusing them of 'highhandedness and tyranny' and had on several occasions between 1993 and 1994 ordered investigations into their activities. Following the killing of a Sikh in Calcutta in May 1994, which provoked an angry reaction from the West Bengal State Government, the Union Home Secretary had convened a meeting of all Director Generals of Police on 5 July 1994 to discuss concerns expressed by certain states following the intrusion by the Punjab police into their territories. One of the stated aims of the meeting was to try to work out a formula whereby the Punjab police would conduct their operations in cooperation with the respective state governments.

56. In its October 1995 report, "India: Determining the fate of the 'disappeared' in Punjab," Amnesty International claimed that high-profile individ-

uals continued to "disappear" in police custody. Among the examples cited were the General Secretary of the Human Rights Wing of the Sikh political party, the Akali Dal, who was reportedly arrested on 6 September 1995 and had not been seen since.

II. Relevant domestic and international law and practice

A. Deportation

57. By section 3 (5) (b) of the Immigration Act 1971 ("the 1971 Act"), a person who is not a British citizen is liable to deportation *inter alia* if the Secretary of State deems this to be "conducive to the public good."

B. Appeal against deportation and the advisory panel procedure

58. There is a right of appeal to an adjudicator, and ultimately to an appeal tribunal, against a decision to make a deportation order (section 15 (1) of the 1971 Act) except in cases where the ground of the decision to deport was that the deportation would be conducive to the public good as being in the interests of national security or of the relations between the United Kingdom and any other country or for other reasons of a political nature (section 15(3) of the 1971 Act).

59. This exception was maintained in the Asylum and Immigration Appeals Act 1993, which came into force in July 1993.

60. Cases in which a deportation order has been made on national security or political grounds are subject to a non-statutory advisory procedure, set out in paragraph 157 of the Statement of Changes in Immigration Rules (House of Commons Paper 251 of 1990).

The person concerned is given an opportunity to make written and/or oral representations to an advisory panel, to call witnesses on his behalf, and to be assisted by a friend, but he is not permitted to have legal representation before the panel. The Home Secretary decides how much information about the case against him may be communicated to the person concerned. The panel's advice to the Home Secretary is not disclosed, and the latter is not obliged to follow it.

C. The United Nations 1951 Convention on the Status of Refugees

61. The United Kingdom is a party to the United Nations 1951 Convention on the Status of Refugees ("the 1951 Convention"). A "refugee" is defined by Article 1 of the Convention as a person who is outside the country of his nationality due to "a well-founded fear of being persecuted for reasons of race, religion, nationality, membership of a particular social group or political opinion."

Article 32 of the 1951 Convention provides:

"1. The Contracting States shall not expel a refugee lawfully in their territory save on grounds of national security or public order.

2. The expulsion of such a refugee shall only be in pursuance of a decision reached in accordance with due process of law . . ."

Article 33 provides:

"1. No Contracting State shall expel or return a refugee in any manner whatsoever to the frontiers of territories where his life or freedom would be threatened on account of his race, religion, nationality, membership of a particular social group or political opinion.

2. The benefit of the present provision may not, however, be claimed by a refugee whom there are reasonable grounds for regarding as a danger to the security of the country in which he is, or who, having been convicted by a final judgment of a particularly serious crime, constitutes a danger to the community of that country."

62. Rule 161 of the Immigration Rules (House of Commons Paper 251 of 1990) provides that:

"Where a person is a refugee full account is to be taken of the provisions of the Convention and Protocol relating to the Status of Refugees . . ."

63. In a case where a person to be deported for national security reasons claims asylum, the Secretary of State must balance the interest of the individual as a refugee against the risk to national security (*R. v. Secretary of State for the Home Department, ex parte Chahal* [1994] Immigration Appeal Reports, p. 107: see paragraph 41 above).

D. Detention pending deportation

64. A person may be detained under the authority of the Secretary of State after the service upon him of a notice of intention to deport and pending the making of a deportation order, and also after the making of an order, pending his removal or departure from the country (paragraphs 2 (2) and (3) of Schedule III to the 1971 Act).

65. Any person in detention is entitled to challenge the lawfulness of his detention by way of a writ of habeas corpus. This is issued by the High Court to procure the production of a person in order that the circumstances of his detention may be inquired into. The detainee must be released if unlawfully detained (Habeas Corpus Act 1679 and Habeas Corpus Act 1816, section 1). Only one application for habeas corpus on the same grounds may be made by an individual in detention, unless fresh evidence is adduced in support (Administration of Justice Act 1960, section 14 (2)).

In addition, a detainee may apply for judicial review of the decision to detain him (see paragraphs 43 above and 66–67 below).

In conjunction with either an application for habeas corpus or judicial review, it is possible to apply for bail (that is, temporary release) pending the decision of the court.

E. Judicial review

66. Decisions of the Home Secretary to refuse asylum, to make a deportation order or to detain pending deportation are liable to challenge by way of judicial review and may be quashed by reference to the ordinary principles of English public law.

These principles do not permit the court to make findings of fact on matters within the province of the Secretary of State or to substitute its discretion for the Minister's. The court may quash his decision only if he failed to interpret or apply English law correctly, if he failed to take account of issues which he was required by law to address, or if his decision was so irrational or perverse that no reasonable Secretary of State could have made it (*Associated Provincial Picture Houses Ltd. v. Wednesbury Corporation* [1948] 1 Kings Bench Reports, p. 223).

67. Where national security issues are involved, the courts retain a power of review, but it is a limited one because:

> "the decision on whether the requirements of national security outweigh the duty of fairness in a particular case is a matter for the Government to decide, not for the courts; the Government alone has access to the necessary information and in any event the judicial process is unsuitable for reaching decisions on national security" (*Council of Civil Service Unions v. Minister for the Civil Service* [1985] Appeal Cases p. 374, at p. 402).

See also *R. v. Secretary of State for the Home Department, ex parte Cheblak* [1991] 2 All England Reports, p. 9, where a similar approach was taken by the Court of Appeal.

PROCEEDINGS BEFORE THE COMMISSION

68. In the application of 27 July 1993 (no. 22414/93) to the Commission (as declared admissible), the first applicant complained that his deportation to India would expose him to a real risk of torture or inhuman or degrading treatment in violation of Article 3 of the Convention; that his detention had been too long and that the judicial control thereof had been ineffective and slow in breach of Article 5 §§ 1 and 4; and that, contrary to Article 13, he had had no effective domestic remedy for his Convention claims because of the national security elements in his case. All the applicants also complained that the deportation of the first applicant would breach their right to respect

for family life under Article 8, for which Convention claim they had no effective domestic remedy, contrary to Article 13.

69. On 1 September 1994 the Commission declared the application admissible. In its report of 27 June 1995 (Article 31) it expressed the unanimous opinions that there would be violations of Articles 3 and 8 if the first applicant were deported to India; that there had been a violation of Article 5 § 1 by reason of the length of his detention; and that there had been a violation of Article 13. The Commission also concluded (by sixteen votes to one) that it was not necessary to examine the complaints under Article 5 § 4 of the Convention.

The full text of the Commission's opinion and of the partially dissenting opinion contained in the report is reproduced as annex to this judgment[*fn3*].

FINAL SUBMISSIONS MADE TO THE COURT

70. At the hearing on 25 March 1996 the Government, as they had done in their memorial, invited the Court to hold that the deportation order, if implemented, would not amount to a violation of Articles 3 and 8 of the Convention, and that there had been no breaches of Articles 5 and 13.

71. On the same occasion the applicants reiterated their requests to the Court, set out in their memorial, to find violations of Articles 3, 5, 8 and 13 and to award them just satisfaction under Article 50.

AS TO THE LAW

I. ALLEGED VIOLATION OF ARTICLE 3 OF THE CONVENTION

72. The first applicant complained that his deportation to India would constitute a violation of Article 3 of the Convention, which states:

> "No one shall be subjected to torture or to inhuman or degrading treatment or punishment."

The Commission upheld this complaint, which the Government contested.

A. Applicability of Article 3 in expulsion cases

73. As the Court has observed in the past, Contracting States have the right, as a matter of well-established international law and subject to their treaty obligations including the Convention, to control the entry, residence and expulsion of aliens. Moreover, it must be noted that the right to political asylum is not contained in either the Convention or its Protocols (see the Vilvarajah and Others judgment of 30 October 1991, Series A no. 215, p. 34, § 102).

74. However, it is well established in the case-law of the Court that expulsion by a Contracting State may give rise to an issue under Article 3, and hence engage the responsibility of that State under the Convention, where substantial grounds have been shown for believing that the person in question, if expelled, would face a real risk of being subjected to treatment contrary to Article 3 in the receiving country. In these circumstances, Article 3 implies the obligation not to expel the person in question to that country (see the Soering v. the United Kingdom judgment of 7 July 1989, Series A no. 161, p. 35, §§ 90–91, the Cruz Varas and Others v. Sweden judgment of 20 March 1991, Series A no. 201, p. 28, §§ 69–70 and the above-mentioned Vilvarajah and Others judgment, p. 34, § 103).

The Government contested this principle before the Commission but accepted it in their pleadings before the Court.

B.   Expulsion cases involving an alleged danger to national security

75. The Court notes that the deportation order against the first applicant was made on the ground that his continued presence in the United Kingdom was unconducive to the public good for reasons of national security, including the fight against terrorism (see paragraph 25 above). The parties differed as to whether, and if so to what extent, the fact that the applicant might represent a danger to the security of the United Kingdom affected that State's obligations under Article 3.

76. Although the Government's primary contention was that no real risk of ill-treatment had been established (see paragraphs 88 and 92 below), they also emphasised that the reason for the intended deportation was national security. In this connection they submitted, first, that the guarantees afforded by Article 3 were not absolute in cases where a Contracting State proposed to remove an individual from its territory. Instead, in such cases, which required an uncertain prediction of future events in the receiving State, various factors should be taken into account, including the danger posed by the person in question to the security of the host nation. Thus, there was an implied limitation to Article 3 entitling a Contracting State to expel an individual to a receiving State even where a real risk of ill-treatment existed, if such removal was required on national security grounds. The Government based this submission in the first place on the possibility of implied limitations as recognised in the Court's case-law, particularly paragraphs 88 and 89 of its above-mentioned Soering judgment. In support, they furthermore referred to the principle under international law that the right of an alien to asylum is subject to qualifications, as is provided for, *inter alia*, by Articles 32 and 33 of the United Nations 1951 Convention on the Status of Refugees (see paragraph 61 above). In the alternative, the threat posed by an individual to the national security of the Contracting State was a factor to be weighed in the balance when considering the issues under Article 3. This approach took into account that in

these cases there are varying degrees of risk of ill-treatment. The greater the risk of ill-treatment, the less weight should be accorded to the threat to national security. But where there existed a substantial doubt with regard to the risk of ill-treatment, the threat to national security could weigh heavily in the balance to be struck between protecting the rights of the individual and the general interests of the community. This was the case here: it was at least open to substantial doubt whether the alleged risk of ill-treatment would materialise; consequently, the fact that Mr Chahal constituted a serious threat to the security of the United Kingdom justified his deportation.

77. The applicant denied that he represented any threat to the national security of the United Kingdom, and contended that, in any case, national security considerations could not justify exposing an individual to the risk of ill-treatment abroad any more than they could justify administering torture to him directly.

78. The Commission, with whom the intervenors (see paragraph 6 above) agreed, rejected the Government's arguments. It referred to the Court's Vilvarajah and Others judgment (cited in paragraph 73 above, p. 36, § 108) and expressed the opinion that the guarantees afforded by Article 3 were absolute in character, admitting of no exception. At the hearing before the Court, the Commission's Delegate suggested that the passages in the Court's Soering judgment upon which the Government relied (see paragraph 76 above) might be taken as authority for the view that, in a case where there were serious doubts as to the likelihood of a person being subjected to treatment or punishment contrary to Article 3, the benefit of that doubt could be given to the deporting State whose national interests were threatened by his continued presence. However, the national interests of the State could not be invoked to override the interests of the individual where substantial grounds had been shown for believing that he would be subjected to ill-treatment if expelled.

79. Article 3 enshrines one of the most fundamental values of democratic society (see the above-mentioned Soering judgment, p. 34, § 88). The Court is well aware of the immense difficulties faced by States in modern times in protecting their communities from terrorist violence. However, even in these circumstances, the Convention prohibits in absolute terms torture or inhuman or degrading treatment or punishment, irrespective of the victim's conduct. Unlike most of the substantive clauses of the Convention and of Protocols Nos. 1 and 4, Article 3 makes no provision for exceptions and no derogation from it is permissible under Article 15 even in the event of a public emergency threatening the life of the nation (see the Ireland v. the United Kingdom judgment of 18 January 1978, Series A no. 25, p. 65, § 163 and also the Tomasi v. France judgment of 27 August 1992, Series A no. 241–A, p. 42, § 115).

80. The prohibition provided by Article 3 against ill-treatment is equally absolute in expulsion cases. Thus, whenever substantial grounds have been

shown for believing that an individual would face a real risk of being subjected to treatment contrary to Article 3 if removed to another State, the responsibility of the Contracting State to safeguard him or her against such treatment is engaged in the event of expulsion (see the above-mentioned Vilvarajah and Others judgment, p. 34, § 103). In these circumstances, the activities of the individual in question, however undesirable or dangerous, cannot be a material consideration. The protection afforded by Article 3 is thus wider than that provided by Articles 32 and 33 of the United Nations 1951 Convention on the Status of Refugees (see paragraph 61 above).

81. Paragraph 88 of the Court's above-mentioned Soering judgment, which concerned extradition to the United States, clearly and forcefully expresses the above view. It should not be inferred from the Court's remarks concerning the risk of undermining the foundations of extradition, as set out in paragraph 89 of the same judgment, that there is any room for balancing the risk of ill-treatment against the reasons for expulsion in determining whether a State's responsibility under Article 3 is engaged.

82. It follows from the above that it is not necessary for the Court to enter into a consideration of the Government's untested, but no doubt *bona fide*, allegations about the first applicant's terrorist activities and the threat posed by him to national security.

C. Application of Article 3 in the circumstances of the case

1. *The point of time for the assessment of the risk*

83. Although there were differing views on the situation in India and in Punjab (see paragraphs 87–91 below), it was agreed that the violence and instability in that region reached a peak in 1992 and had been abating ever since. For this reason, the date taken by the Court for its assessment of the risk to Mr Chahal if expelled to India is of importance.

84. The applicant argued that the Court should consider the position in June 1992, at the time when the decision to deport him was made final (see paragraph 35 above). The purpose of the stay on removal requested by the Commission (see paragraph 4 above) was to prevent irremediable damage and not to afford the High Contracting Party with an opportunity to improve its case. Moreover, it was not appropriate that the Strasbourg organs should be involved in a continual fact-finding operation.

85. The Government, with whom the Commission agreed, submitted that because the responsibility of the State under Article 3 of the Convention in expulsion cases lies in the act of exposing an individual to a real risk of ill-treatment, the material date for the assessment of risk was the time of the proposed deportation. Since Mr Chahal had not yet been expelled, the relevant time was that of the proceedings before the Court.

86. It follows from the considerations in paragraph 74 above that, as far as the applicant's complaint under Article 3 is concerned, the crucial question is whether it has been substantiated that there is a real risk that Mr Chahal, if expelled, would be subjected to treatment prohibited by that Article. Since he has not yet been deported, the material point in time must be that of the Court's consideration of the case. It follows that, although the historical position is of interest in so far as it may shed light on the current situation and its likely evolution, it is the present conditions which are decisive.

2. The assessment of the risk of ill-treatment

(a) The arguments

   i.   General conditions

87. It was the applicant's case that the Government's assessment of conditions in India and Punjab had been profoundly mistaken throughout the domestic and Strasbourg proceedings. He referred to a number of reports by governmental bodies and by inter-governmental and non-governmental organisations on the situation in India generally and in Punjab in particular, with emphasis on those reports concerning 1994 and 1995 (see paragraphs 49–56 above) and argued that this material established the contention that human rights abuse in India by the security forces, especially the police, remained endemic.

In response to the Government's offer to return him to the part of India of his choice, he asserted that the Punjab police had abducted and killed militant Sikhs outside their home state in the past.

Although he accepted that there had been some improvements in Punjab since the peak of unrest in 1992, he insisted that there had been no fundamental change of regime. On the contrary, what emerged from the above reports was the continuity of the practices of the security agencies. In this respect he pointed to the fact that the Director General of the Punjab Police, who had been responsible for many human rights abuses during his term of office between 1992 and 1995, had been replaced upon his retirement by his former deputy and intelligence chief.

88. The Government contended that there would be no real risk of Mr Chahal being ill-treated if the deportation order were to be implemented and emphasised that the latter was to be returned to whichever part of India he chose, and not necessarily to Punjab. In this context they pointed out that they regularly monitored the situation in India through the United Kingdom High Commission in New Delhi. It appeared from this information that positive concrete steps had been taken and continued to be taken to deal with human rights abuses. Specific legislation had been introduced in this regard; the National Human Rights Commission, which performed an important function, continued to strengthen and develop; and steps had been taken by both

the executive and judicial authorities to deal with the remaining misuse of power. The situation in India generally was therefore such as to support their above contention.

Furthermore, with reference to the matters set out in paragraphs 45–48 above, they contended that the situation in Punjab had improved substantially in recent years. They stressed that there was now little or no terrorist activity in that state. An ombudsman had been established to look into complaints of misuse of power and the new Chief Minister had publicly declared the government's intentions to stamp out human rights abuses. Legal proceedings had been brought against police officers alleged to have been involved in unlawful activity.

89. Amnesty International in its written submissions informed the Court that prominent Sikh separatists still faced a serious risk of "disappearance," detention without charge or trial, torture and extrajudicial execution, frequently at the hands of the Punjab police. It referred to its 1995 report which documented a pattern of human rights violations committed by officers of the Punjab police acting in under-cover operations outside their home state (see paragraph 55 above).

90. The Government, however, urged the Court to proceed with caution in relation to the material prepared by Amnesty International, since it was not possible to verify the facts of the cases referred to. Furthermore, when studying these reports it was tempting to lose sight of the broader picture of improvement by concentrating too much on individual cases of alleged serious human rights abuses. Finally, since the situation in Punjab had changed considerably in recent years, earlier reports prepared by Amnesty and other organisations were now of limited use.

91. On the basis of the material before it, the Commission accepted that there had been an improvement in the conditions prevailing in India and, more specifically, in Punjab. However, it was unable to find in the recent material provided by the Government any solid evidence that the Punjab police were now under democratic control or that the judiciary had been able fully to reassert its own independent authority in the region.

ii.   Factors specific to Mr Chahal

92. Those appearing before the Court also differed in their assessment of the effect which Mr Chahal's notoriety would have on his security in India.

In the Government's view, the Indian Government was likely to be astute to ensure that no ill-treatment befell Mr Chahal, knowing that the eyes of the world would be upon him. Furthermore, in June 1992 and December 1995 they had sought and received assurances from the Indian Government (see paragraph 37 above).

93. The applicant asserted that his high profile would increase the danger of persecution. By taking the decision to deport him on national security grounds the Government had, as was noted by Mr Justice Popplewell in the first judicial review hearing (see paragraph 34 above), in effect publicly branded him a terrorist. Articles in the Indian press since 1990 indicated that he was regarded as such in India, and a number of his relatives and acquaintances had been detained and ill-treated in Punjab because of their connection to him. The assurances of the Indian Government were of little value since that Government had shown itself unable to control the security forces in Punjab and elsewhere. The applicant also referred to examples of well-known personalities who had recently "disappeared."

94. For the Commission, Mr Chahal, as a leading Sikh militant suspected of involvement in acts of terrorism, was likely to be of special interest to the security forces, irrespective of the part of India to which he was returned.

(b) The Court's approach

95. Under the Convention system, the establishment and verification of the facts is primarily a matter for the Commission (Articles 28 § 1 and 31). Accordingly, it is only in exceptional circumstances that the Court will use its powers in this area (see the Cruz Varas and Others judgment mentioned in paragraph 74 above, p. 29, § 74).

96. However, the Court is not bound by the Commission's findings of fact and is free to make its own assessment. Indeed, in cases such as the present the Court's examination of the existence of a real risk of ill-treatment must necessarily be a rigorous one, in view of the absolute character of Article 3 and the fact that it enshrines one of the fundamental values of the democratic societies making up the Council of Europe (see the Vilvarajah and Others judgment mentioned in paragraph 73 above, p. 36, § 108).

97. In determining whether it has been substantiated that there is a real risk that the applicant, if expelled to India, would be subjected to treatment contrary to Article 3, the Court will assess all the material placed before it and, if necessary, material obtained of its own motion (see the above-mentioned Vilvarajah and Others judgment, p. 36, § 107). Furthermore, since the material point in time for the assessment of risk is the date of the Court's consideration of the case (see paragraph 86 above), it will be necessary to take account of evidence which has come to light since the Commission's review.

98. In view of the Government's proposal to return Mr Chahal to the airport of his choice in India, it is necessary for the Court to evaluate the risk of his being ill-treated with reference to conditions throughout India rather than in Punjab alone. However, it must be borne in mind that the first applicant is a well-known supporter of Sikh separatism. It follows from these

observations that evidence relating to the fate of Sikh militants at the hands of the security forces outside the state of Punjab is of particular relevance.

99. The Court has taken note of the Government's comments relating to the material contained in the reports of Amnesty International (see paragraph 90 above). Nonetheless, it attaches weight to some of the most striking allegations contained in those reports, particularly with regard to extrajudicial killings allegedly perpetrated by the Punjab police outside their home state and the action taken by the Indian Supreme Court, the West Bengal State Government and the Union Home Government in response (see paragraph 55 above). Moreover, similar assertions were accepted by the United Kingdom Immigration Appeal Tribunal in *Charan Singh Gill v. Secretary of State for the Home Department* (see paragraph 54 above) and were included in the 1995 United States' State Department report on India (see paragraph 52 above). The 1994 National Human Rights Commission's report on Punjab substantiated the impression of a police force completely beyond the control of lawful authority (see paragraph 49 above).

100. The Court is persuaded by this evidence, which has been corroborated by material from a number of different objective sources, that until mid-1994 at least, elements in the Punjab police were accustomed to act without regard to the human rights of suspected Sikh militants and were fully capable of pursuing their targets into areas of India far away from Punjab.

101. The Commission found in paragraph 111 of its report that there had in recent years been an improvement in the protection of human rights in India, especially in Punjab, and evidence produced subsequent to the Commission's consideration of the case indicates that matters continue to advance.

In particular, it would appear that the insurgent violence in Punjab has abated; the Court notes the very substantial reduction in terrorist-related deaths in the region as indicated by the respondent Government (see paragraph 45 above). Furthermore, other encouraging events have reportedly taken place in Punjab in recent years, such as the return of democratic elections, a number of court judgments against police officers, the appointment of an ombudsman to investigate abuses of power and the promise of the new Chief Minister to "ensure transparency and accountability" (see paragraphs 46 and 48 above). In addition, the 1996 United States' State Department report asserts that during 1995 "there was visible progress in correcting patterns of abuse by the [Punjab] police" (see paragraph 53 above).

102. Nonetheless, the evidence demonstrates that problems still persist in connection with the observance of human rights by the security forces in Punjab. As the respondent Government themselves recounted, the United Kingdom High Commission in India continues to receive complaints about the Punjab police, although in recent months these have related mainly to

extortion rather than to politically-motivated abuses (see paragraph 47 above). Amnesty International alleged that "disappearances" of notable Sikhs at the hands of the Punjab police continued sporadically throughout 1995 (see paragraph 56 above) and the 1996 State Department report referred to the killing of two Sikh militants that year (see paragraph 53 above).

103. Moreover, the Court finds it most significant that no concrete evidence has been produced of any fundamental reform or reorganisation of the Punjab police in recent years. The evidence referred to above (paragraphs 49–56) would indicate that such a process was urgently required, and indeed this was the recommendation of the NHRC (see paragraph 49 above). Although there was a change in the leadership of the Punjab police in 1995, the Director General who presided over some of the worst abuses this decade has only been replaced by his former deputy and intelligence chief (see paragraph 87 above).

Less than two years ago this same police force was carrying out well-documented raids into other Indian states (see paragraph 100 above) and the Court cannot entirely discount the applicant's claims that any recent reduction in activity stems from the fact that key figures in the campaign for Sikh separatism have all either been killed, forced abroad or rendered inactive by torture or the fear of torture. Furthermore, it would appear from press reports that evidence of the full extent of past abuses is only now coming to light (see paragraph 53 above).

104. Although the Court is of the opinion that Mr Chahal, if returned to India, would be most at risk from the Punjab security forces acting either within or outside state boundaries, it also attaches significance to the fact that attested allegations of serious human rights violations have been levelled at the police elsewhere in India. In this respect, the Court notes that the United Nations' Special Rapporteur on torture has described the practice of torture upon those in police custody as "endemic" and has complained that inadequate measures are taken to bring those responsible to justice (see paragraph 51 above). The NHRC has also drawn attention to the problems of widespread, often fatal, mistreatment of prisoners and has called for a systematic reform of the police throughout India (see paragraph 50 above).

105. Although the Court does not doubt the good faith of the Indian Government in providing the assurances mentioned above (paragraph 92), it would appear that, despite the efforts of that Government, the NHRC and the Indian courts to bring about reform, the violation of human rights by certain members of the security forces in Punjab and elsewhere in India is a recalcitrant and enduring problem (see paragraph 104 above). Against this background, the Court is not persuaded that the above assurances would provide Mr Chahal with an adequate guarantee of safety.

106. The Court further considers that the applicant's high profile would be more likely to increase the risk to him of harm than otherwise. It is not disputed

that Mr Chahal is well known in India to support the cause of Sikh separatism and to have had close links with other leading figures in that struggle (see paragraphs 17 and 20 above). The respondent Government have made serious, albeit untested, allegations of his involvement in terrorism which are undoubtedly known to the Indian authorities. The Court is of the view that these factors would be likely to make him a target of interest for hard-line elements in the security forces who have relentlessly pursued suspected Sikh militants in the past (see paragraphs 49–56 above).

107. For all the reasons outlined above, in particular the attested involvement of the Punjab police in killings and abductions outside their state and the allegations of serious human rights violations which continue to be levelled at members of the Indian security forces elsewhere, the Court finds it substantiated that there is a real risk of Mr Chahal being subjected to treatment contrary to Article 3 if he is returned to India. Accordingly, the order for his deportation to India would, if executed, give rise to a violation of Article 3.

II. ALLEGED VIOLATIONS OF ARTICLE 5 OF THE CONVENTION

A. Article 5 § 1

108. The first applicant complained that his detention pending deportation constituted a violation of Article 5 § 1 of the Convention, which provides (so far as is relevant):

> "Everyone has the right to liberty and security of person. No one shall be deprived of his liberty save in the following cases and in accordance with a procedure prescribed by law:
>
> . . . (f) the lawful arrest or detention . . . of a person against whom action is being taken with a view to deportation . . ."

109. Mr Chahal has been held in Bedford Prison since 16 August 1990 (see paragraph 25 above). It was not disputed that he had been detained "with a view to deportation" within the meaning of Article 5 § 1 (f). However, he maintained that his detention had ceased to be "in accordance with a procedure prescribed by law" for the purposes of Article 5 § 1 because of its excessive duration.

In particular, the applicant complained about the length of time (16 August 1990–27 March 1991) taken to consider and reject his application for refugee status; the period (9 August 1991–2 December 1991) between his application for judicial review of the decision to refuse asylum and the national court's decision; and the time required (2 December 1991–1 June 1992) for the fresh decision refusing asylum.

110. The Commission agreed, finding that the above proceedings were not pursued with the requisite speed and that the detention therefore ceased to be justified.

111. The Government, however, asserted that the various proceedings brought by Mr Chahal were dealt with as expeditiously as possible.

112. The Court recalls that it is not in dispute that Mr Chahal has been detained "with a view to deportation" within the meaning of Article 5 § 1 (f) (see paragraph 109 above). Article 5 § 1 (f) does not demand that the detention of a person against whom action is being taken with a view to deportation be reasonably considered necessary, for example to prevent his committing an offence or fleeing; in this respect Article 5 § 1 (f) provides a different level of protection from Article 5 § 1 (c).

Indeed, all that is required under this provision is that "action is being taken with a view to deportation." It is therefore immaterial, for the purposes of Article 5 § 1 (f), whether the underlying decision to expel can be justified under national or Convention law.

113. The Court recalls, however, that any deprivation of liberty under Article 5 § 1 (f) will be justified only for as long as deportation proceedings are in progress. If such proceedings are not prosecuted with due diligence, the detention will cease to be permissible under Article 5 § 1 (f) (see the Quinn v. France judgment of 22 March 1995, Series A no. 311, p. 19, § 48 and also the Kolompar v. Belgium judgment of 24 September 1992, Series A no. 235–C, p. 55, § 36).

It is thus necessary to determine whether the duration of the deportation proceedings was excessive.

114. The period under consideration commenced on 16 August 1990, when Mr Chahal was first detained with a view to deportation. It terminated on 3 March 1994, when the domestic proceedings came to an end with the refusal of the House of Lords to allow leave to appeal (see paragraphs 25 and 42 above). Although he has remained in custody until the present day, this latter period must be distinguished because during this time the Government have refrained from deporting him in compliance with the request made by the Commission under Rule 36 of its Rules of Procedure (see paragraph 4 above).

115. The Court has had regard to the length of time taken for the various decisions in the domestic proceedings.

As regards the decisions taken by the Secretary of State to refuse asylum, it does not consider that the periods (that is, 16 August 1990–27 March 1991 and 2 December 1991–1 June 1992) were excessive, bearing in mind the detailed and careful consideration required for the applicant's request for political asylum and the opportunities afforded to the latter to make representations and submit information (see paragraphs 25–27 and 34–35 above).

116. In connection with the judicial review proceedings before the national courts, it is noted that Mr Chahal's first application was made on 9 August 1991 and that a decision was reached on it by Mr Justice Popplewell on 2

December 1991. He made a second application on 16 July 1992, which was heard between 18 and 21 December 1992, judgment being given on 12 February 1993. The Court of Appeal dismissed the appeal against this decision on 22 October 1993 and refused him leave to appeal to the House of Lords. The House of Lords similarly refused leave to appeal on 3 March 1994 (see paragraphs 34, 38 and 40–42 above).

117. As the Court has observed in the context of Article 3, Mr Chahal's case involves considerations of an extremely serious and weighty nature. It is neither in the interests of the individual applicant nor in the general public interest in the administration of justice that such decisions be taken hastily, without due regard to all the relevant issues and evidence.

Against this background, and bearing in mind what was at stake for the applicant and the interest that he had in his claims being thoroughly examined by the courts, none of the periods complained of can be regarded as excessive, taken either individually or in combination. Accordingly, there has been no violation of Article 5 § 1 (f) of the Convention on account of the diligence, or lack of it, with which the domestic procedures were conducted.

118. It also falls to the Court to examine whether Mr Chahal's detention was "lawful" for the purposes of Article 5 § 1 (f), with particular reference to the safeguards provided by the national system.

Where the "lawfulness" of detention is in issue, including the question whether "a procedure prescribed by law" has been followed, the Convention refers essentially to the obligation to conform to the substantive and procedural rules of national law, but it requires in addition that any deprivation of liberty should be in keeping with the purpose of Article 5, namely to protect the individual from arbitrariness.

119. There is no doubt that Mr Chahal's detention was lawful under national law and was effected "in accordance with a procedure prescribed by law" (see paragraphs 43 and 64 above). However, in view of the extremely long period during which Mr Chahal has been detained, it is also necessary to consider whether there existed sufficient guarantees against arbitrariness.

120. In this context, the Court observes that the applicant has been detained since 16 August 1990 on the ground, essentially, that successive Secretaries of State have maintained that, in view of the threat to national security represented by him, he could not safely be released (see paragraph 43 above). The applicant has, however, consistently denied that he posed any threat whatsoever to national security, and has given reasons in support of this denial (see paragraphs 31 and 77 above).

121. The Court further notes that, since the Secretaries of State asserted that national security was involved, the domestic courts were not in a position effectively to control whether the decisions to keep Mr Chahal in detention

were justified, because the full material on which these decisions were based was not made available to them (see paragraph 43 above).

122. However, in the context of Article 5 § 1 of the Convention, the advisory panel procedure (see paragraphs 29–32 and 60 above) provided an important safeguard against arbitrariness. This panel, which included experienced judicial figures (see paragraph 29 above) was able fully to review the evidence relating to the national security threat represented by the applicant. Although its report has never been disclosed, at the hearing before the Court the Government indicated that the panel had agreed with the Home Secretary that Mr Chahal ought to be deported on national security grounds. The Court considers that this procedure provided an adequate guarantee that there were at least prima facie grounds for believing that if Mr Chahal were at liberty, national security would be put at risk and thus, that the executive had not acted arbitrarily when it ordered him to be kept in detention.

123. In conclusion, the Court recalls that Mr Chahal has undoubtedly been detained for a length of time which is bound to give rise to serious concern. However, in view of the exceptional circumstances of the case and the facts that the national authorities have acted with due diligence throughout the deportation proceedings against him and that there were sufficient guarantees against the arbitrary deprivation of his liberty, this detention complied with the requirements of Article 5 § 1 (f).

It follows that there has been no violation of Article 5 § 1.

B. Article 5 § 4

124. The first applicant alleged that he was denied the opportunity to have the lawfulness of his detention decided by a national court, in breach of Article 5 § 4 of the Convention, which provides:

> "Everyone who is deprived of his liberty by arrest or detention shall be entitled to take proceedings by which the lawfulness of his detention shall be decided speedily by a court and his release ordered if the detention is not lawful."

He submitted that the reliance placed on national security grounds as justification for his detention pending deportation prevented the domestic courts from considering whether it was lawful and appropriate. However, he developed this argument more thoroughly in connection with his complaint under Article 13 of the Convention (see paragraphs 140–141 below).

125. The Commission was of the opinion that it was more appropriate to consider this complaint under Article 13 and the Government also followed this approach (see paragraphs 142–143 below).

126. The Court recalls, in the first place, that Article 5 § 4 provides a *lex specialis* in relation to the more general requirements of Article 13 (see the De

Jong, Baljet and Van den Brink v. the Netherlands judgment of 22 May 1984, Series A no. 77, p. 27, § 60). It follows that, irrespective of the method chosen by Mr Chahal to argue his complaint that he was denied the opportunity to have the lawfulness of his detention reviewed, the Court must first examine it in connection with Article 5 § 4.

127. The Court further recalls that the notion of "lawfulness" under paragraph 4 of Article 5 has the same meaning as in paragraph 1, so that the detained person is entitled to a review of his detention in the light not only of the requirements of domestic law but also of the text of the Convention, the general principles embodied therein and the aim of the restrictions permitted by Article 5 § 1 (see the E. v. Norway judgment of 29 August 1990, Series A no. 181–A, p. 21, § 49).

The scope of the obligations under Article 5 § 4 is not identical for every kind of deprivation of liberty (see, *inter alia*, the Bouamar v. Belgium judgment of 29 February 1988, Series A no. 129, p. 24, § 60); this applies notably to the extent of the judicial review afforded. Nonetheless, it is clear that Article 5 § 4 does not guarantee a right to judicial review of such breadth as to empower the court, on all aspects of the case including questions of pure expediency, to substitute its own discretion for that of the decision-making authority. The review should, however, be wide enough to bear on those conditions which are essential for the "lawful" detention of a person according to Article 5 § 1 (see the above-mentioned E. v. Norway judgment, p. 21, § 50).

128. The Court refers again to the requirements of Article 5 § 1 in cases of detention with a view to deportation (see paragraph 112 above). It follows from these requirements that Article 5 § 4 does not demand that the domestic courts should have the power to review whether the underlying decision to expel could be justified under national or Convention law.

129. The notion of "lawfulness" in Article 5 § 1 (f) does not refer solely to the obligation to conform to the substantive and procedural rules of national law; it requires in addition that any deprivation of liberty should be in keeping with the purpose of Article 5 (see paragraph 118 above). The question therefore arises whether the available proceedings to challenge the lawfulness of Mr Chahal's detention and to seek bail provided an adequate control by the domestic courts.

130. The Court recollects that, because national security was involved, the domestic courts were not in a position to review whether the decisions to detain Mr Chahal and to keep him in detention were justified on national security grounds (see paragraph 121 above). Furthermore, although the procedure before the advisory panel undoubtedly provided some degree of control, bearing in mind that Mr Chahal was not entitled to legal representation before the panel, that he was only given an outline of the grounds for the

notice of intention to deport, that the panel had no power of decision and that its advice to the Home Secretary was not binding and was not disclosed (see paragraphs 30, 32 and 60 above), the panel could not be considered as a "court" within the meaning of Article 5 § 4 (see, *mutatis mutandis*, the X v. the United Kingdom judgment of 5 November 1981, Series A no. 46, p. 26, § 61).

131. The Court recognises that the use of confidential material may be unavoidable where national security is at stake. This does not mean, however, that the national authorities can be free from effective control by the domestic courts whenever they choose to assert that national security and terrorism are involved (see, *mutatis mutandis*, the Fox, Campbell and Hartley v. the United Kingdom judgment of 30 August 1990, Series A no. 182, p. 17, § 34, and the Murray v. the United Kingdom judgment of 28 October 1994, Series A no. 300–A, p. 27, § 58). The Court attaches significance to the fact that, as the intervenors pointed out in connection with Article 13 (see paragraph 144 below), in Canada a more effective form of judicial control has been developed in cases of this type. This example illustrates that there are techniques which can be employed which both accommodate legitimate security concerns about the nature and sources of intelligence information and yet accord the individual a substantial measure of procedural justice.

132. It follows that the Court considers that neither the proceedings for habeas corpus and for judicial review of the decision to detain Mr Chahal before the domestic courts, nor the advisory panel procedure, satisfied the requirements of Article 5 § 4. This shortcoming is all the more significant given that Mr Chahal has undoubtedly been deprived of his liberty for a length of time which is bound to give rise to serious concern (see paragraph 123 above).

133. In conclusion, there has been a violation of Article 5 § 4 of the Convention.

* * * * *

IV. ALLEGED VIOLATION OF ARTICLE 13 OF THE CONVENTION

140. In addition, the applicants alleged that they were not provided with effective remedies before the national courts, in breach of Article 13 of the Convention, which reads:

> "Everyone whose rights and freedoms as set forth in this Convention are violated shall have an effective remedy before a national authority notwithstanding that the violation has been committed by persons acting in an official capacity."

141. The applicants maintained that the only remedy available to them in respect of their claims under Articles 3, 5 and 8 of the Convention was judicial

review, the advisory panel procedure (see paragraphs 29 and 60 above) being neither a "remedy" nor "effective."

They submitted, first, that the powers of the English courts to put aside an executive decision were inadequate in all Article 3 asylum cases, since the courts could not scrutinise the facts to determine whether substantial grounds had been shown for belief in the existence of a real risk of ill-treatment in the receiving State, but could only determine whether the Secretary of State's decision as to the existence of such a risk was reasonable according to the "Wednesbury" principles (see paragraph 66 above).

This contention had particular weight in cases where the executive relied upon arguments of national security. In the instant case, the assertion that Mr Chahal's deportation was necessary in the interests of national security entailed that there could be no effective judicial evaluation of the risk to him of ill-treatment in India or of the issues under Article 8. That assertion likewise prevented any effective judicial control on the question whether the applicant's continued detention was justified.

142. The Government accepted that the scope of judicial review was more limited where deportation was ordered on national security grounds. However, the Court had held in the past that, where questions of national security were in issue, an "effective remedy" under Article 13 must mean "a remedy that is effective as can be," given the necessity of relying upon secret sources of information (see the Klass and Others v. the Federal Republic of Germany judgment of 6 September 1978, Series A no. 28, p. 31, § 69, and the Leander v. Sweden judgment of 26 March 1987, Series A no. 116, p. 32, § 84).

Furthermore, it had to be borne in mind that all the relevant material, including the sensitive material, was examined by the advisory panel whose members included two senior judicial figures—a Court of Appeal judge and a former President of the Immigration Appeal Tribunal (see paragraph 29 above). The procedure before the panel was designed, on the one hand, to satisfy the need for an independent review of the totality of the material on which the perceived threat to national security was based and, on the other hand, to ensure that secret information would not be publicly disclosed. It thus provided a form of independent, quasi-judicial scrutiny.

143. For the Commission, the present case could be distinguished from that of Vilvarajah and Others (mentioned in paragraph 73 above, p. 39, §§ 122–126) where the Court held that judicial review in the English courts amounted to an effective remedy in respect of the applicants' Article 3 claims. Because the Secretary of State invoked national security considerations as grounds for his decisions to deport Mr Chahal and to detain him pending deportation, the English courts' powers of review were limited. They could not themselves consider the evidence on which the Secretary of State had based his decision that the applicant constituted a danger to national security

or undertake any evaluation of the Article 3 risks. Instead, they had to confine themselves to examining whether the evidence showed that the Secretary of State had carried out the balancing exercise required by the domestic law (see paragraph 41 above).

144. The intervenors (see paragraph 6 above) were all of the view that judicial review did not constitute an effective remedy in cases involving national security. Article 13 required at least that some independent body should be appraised of all the facts and evidence and entitled to reach a decision which would be binding on the Secretary of State.

In this connection, Amnesty International, Liberty, the AIRE Centre and the JCWI (see paragraph 6 above) drew the Court's attention to the procedure applied in such cases in Canada. Under the Canadian Immigration Act 1976 (as amended by the Immigration Act 1988), a Federal Court judge holds an in camera hearing of all the evidence, at which the applicant is provided with a statement summarising, as far as possible, the case against him or her and has the right to be represented and to call evidence. The confidentiality of security material is maintained by requiring such evidence to be examined in the absence of both the applicant and his or her representative. However, in these circumstances, their place is taken by a security-cleared counsel instructed by the court, who cross-examines the witnesses and generally assists the court to test the strength of the State's case. A summary of the evidence obtained by this procedure, with necessary deletions, is given to the applicant.

145. The Court observes that Article 13 guarantees the availability at national level of a remedy to enforce the substance of the Convention rights and freedoms in whatever form they might happen to be secured in the domestic legal order. The effect of this Article is thus to require the provision of a domestic remedy allowing the competent national authority both to deal with the substance of the relevant Convention complaint and to grant appropriate relief, although Contracting States are afforded some discretion as to the manner in which they conform to their obligations under this provision (see the Vilvarajah and Others judgment mentioned in paragraph 73 above, p. 39, § 122). Moreover, it is recalled that in certain circumstances the aggregate of remedies provided by national law may satisfy the requirements of Article 13 (see, *inter alia*, the above-mentioned Leander judgment, p. 30, § 77).

146. The Court does not have to examine the allegation of a breach of Article 13 taken in conjunction with Article 5 § 1, in view of its finding of a violation of Article 5 § 4 (see paragraph 133 above). Nor is it necessary for it to examine the complaint under Article 13 in conjunction with Article 8, in view of its finding concerning the hypothetical nature of the complaint under the latter provision (see paragraph 139 above).

147. This leaves only the first applicant's claim under Article 3 combined with Article 13. It was not disputed that the Article 3 complaint was arguable on

the merits and the Court accordingly finds that Article 13 is applicable (see the above-mentioned Vilvarajah and Others judgment, p. 38, § 121).

148. The Court recalls that in its Vilvarajah judgment (ibid., p. 39, §§ 122–126), it found judicial review proceedings to be an effective remedy in relation to the applicants' complaints under Article 3. It was satisfied that the English courts could review a decision by the Secretary of State to refuse asylum and could rule it unlawful on the grounds that it was tainted with illegality, irrationality or procedural impropriety (see paragraph 66 above). In particular, it was accepted that a court would have jurisdiction to quash a challenged decision to send a fugitive to a country where it was established that there was a serious risk of inhuman or degrading treatment, on the ground that in all the circumstances of the case the decision was one that no reasonable Secretary of State could take (ibid., § 123).

149. The Court further recalls that in assessing whether there exists a real risk of treatment in breach of Article 3 in expulsion cases such as the present, the fact that the person is perceived as a danger to the national security of the respondent State is not a material consideration (see paragraph 80 above).

150. It is true, as the Government have pointed out, that in the cases of Klass and Others and Leander (both cited in paragraph 142 above), the Court held that Article 13 only required a remedy that was "as effective as can be" in circumstances where national security considerations did not permit the divulging of certain sensitive information. However, it must be borne in mind that these cases concerned complaints under Articles 8 and 10 of the Convention and that their examination required the Court to have regard to the national security claims which had been advanced by the Government. The requirement of a remedy which is "as effective as can be" is not appropriate in respect of a complaint that a person's deportation will expose him or her to a real risk of treatment in breach of Article 3, where the issues concerning national security are immaterial.

151. In such cases, given the irreversible nature of the harm that might occur if the risk of ill-treatment materialised and the importance the Court attaches to Article 3, the notion of an effective remedy under Article 13 requires independent scrutiny of the claim that there exist substantial grounds for fearing a real risk of treatment contrary to Article 3. This scrutiny must be carried out without regard to what the person may have done to warrant expulsion or to any perceived threat to the national security of the expelling State.

152. Such scrutiny need not be provided by a judicial authority but, if it is not, the powers and guarantees which it affords are relevant in determining whether the remedy before it is effective (see the above-mentioned Leander judgment, p. 29, § 77).

153. In the present case, neither the advisory panel nor the courts could review the decision of the Home Secretary to deport Mr Chahal to India with

reference solely to the question of risk, leaving aside national security considerations. On the contrary, the courts' approach was one of satisfying themselves that the Home Secretary had balanced the risk to Mr Chahal against the danger to national security (see paragraph 41 above). It follows from the above considerations that these cannot be considered effective remedies in respect of Mr Chahal's Article 3 complaint for the purposes of Article 13 of the Convention.

154. Moreover, the Court notes that in the proceedings before the advisory panel the applicant was not entitled, *inter alia*, to legal representation, that he was only given an outline of the grounds for the notice of intention to deport, that the panel had no power of decision and that its advice to the Home Secretary was not binding and was not disclosed (see paragraphs 30, 32 and 60 above). In these circumstances, the advisory panel could not be considered to offer sufficient procedural safeguards for the purposes of Article 13.

155. Having regard to the extent of the deficiencies of both judicial review proceedings and the advisory panel, the Court cannot consider that the remedies taken together satisfy the requirements of Article 13 in conjunction with Article 3.

Accordingly, there has been a violation of Article 13.

V. APPLICATION OF ARTICLE 50 OF THE CONVENTION

156. The applicants asked the Court to grant them just satisfaction under Article 50, which provides as follows:

> "If the Court finds that a decision or a measure taken by a legal authority or any other authority of a High Contracting Party is completely or partially in conflict with the obligations arising from the present Convention, and if the internal law of the said Party allows only partial reparation to be made for the consequences of this decision or measure, the decision of the Court shall, if necessary, afford just satisfaction to the injured party."

A. Non-pecuniary loss

157. The applicants claimed compensation for non-pecuniary damage for the period of detention suffered by Mr Chahal at a rate of £30,000–£50,000 per annum. The Government submitted that a finding of violation would be sufficient just satisfaction in respect of the claim for non-pecuniary damages.

158. In view of its decision that there has been no violation of Article 5 § 1 (see paragraph 123 above), the Court makes no award of non-pecuniary damages in respect of the period of time Mr Chahal has spent in detention. As to the other complaints, the Court considers that the findings that his deportation, if carried out, would constitute a violation of Article 3 and that there have been breaches of Articles 5 § 4 and 13 constitute sufficient just satisfaction.

B. Legal costs and expenses

159. In addition, the applicants claimed the reimbursement of the legal costs of the Strasbourg proceedings, totalling £77,755.97 (inclusive of value added tax, "VAT").

With regard to the legal costs claimed, the Government observed that a substantial proportion of these were not necessarily incurred because the applicants had produced a large amount of peripheral material before the Court. They proposed instead a sum of £20,000, less legal aid.

160. The Court considers the legal costs claimed by the applicants to be excessive and decides to award £45,000 (inclusive of VAT), less the 21,141 French francs already paid in legal aid by the Council of Europe.

C. Default interest

161. According to the information available to the Court, the statutory rate of interest applicable in the United Kingdom at the date of adoption of the present judgment is 8% per annum.

FOR THESE REASONS THE COURT

1. *Holds* by twelve votes to seven that, in the event of the Secretary of State's decision to deport the first applicant to India being implemented, there would be a violation of Article 3 of the Convention;

2. *Holds* by thirteen votes to six that there has been no violation of Article 5 § 1 of the Convention;

3. *Holds* unanimously that there has been a violation of Article 5 § 4 of the Convention;

4. *Holds* by seventeen votes to two that, having regard to its conclusion with regard to Article 3, it is not necessary to consider the applicants' complaint under Article 8 of the Convention;

5. *Holds* unanimously that there has been a violation of Article 13 in conjunction with Article 3 of the Convention;

6. *Holds* unanimously that the above findings of violation constitute sufficient just satisfaction as regards the claim for compensation for non-pecuniary damage;

7. *Holds* unanimously
    (a) that the respondent State is to pay the applicants, within three months, in respect of costs and expenses, £45,000 (forty-five thousand pounds sterling) less 21,141 (twenty-one thousand, one hundred and forty-one) French francs to be converted into pounds sterling at the rate applicable on the date of delivery of the present judgment;

(b) that simple interest at an annual rate of 8% shall be payable from the expiry of the above-mentioned three months until settlement;

8. *Dismisses* unanimously the remainder of the claim for just satisfaction.

Done in English and in French and delivered at a public hearing at the Human Rights Building, Strasbourg, on 15 November 1996.

Rolv RYSSDAL
President

Herbert PETZOLD
Registrar

* * * * *

DOCUMENT NO 26

R v Secretary of State for Home Department Ex Parte Chahal High Court of Justice Queen's Bench Division

November 6, 1998
Crown Copyright
(Edited Text)

4. MR JUSTICE TUCKER:

This is an Application for Judicial Review made on behalf of Karamjit Singh CHAHAL relating to the question of compensation for detention. The applicant is the longest serving civil detainee in this century, having been detained from 16 August 1990 until 15 November 1996, period of 6 years and 3 months.

5. The applicant is a prominent Sikh separatist, now aged 50. He was detained pursuant to a notice of intention to deport "for reasons of national security and other reasons of a political nature namely the international fight against terrorism." He was released following a Judgement of The European Court of Human Rights who concluded that there had been violations of Articles 3, 5(4) and 13 of the European Convention on Human Rights.

6. Meanwhile, the applicant had applied for asylum, which the Secretary of State had refused. On 25 July 91 Secretary of State signed a deportation order, and set directions for the applicant's removal to India.

7. The applicant, not unnaturally, made strenuous efforts to avoid deportation, to obtain asylum, and to secure his release from detention. On 2 December 1991, on an application for judicial Review, Popplewell J. quashed the decision of the Secretary of State to refuse asylum on the grounds that the decision was flawed because of the Secretary of State's failure to give adequate reasons. In July 1992 Rose J. (as he then was) refused the applicant's application for bail. After a second refusal by the Secretary of State to grant asylum, the applicant again applied for Judicial Review. On this occasion the application was refused by Potts J., who in his turn also refused to grant bail, though like Popplewell J. he expressed anxiety about the case. An appeal from

this decision to the Court of Appeal was dismissed, and a Petition to the House of Lords was refused.

8. Meanwhile, those advising the applicant had made an application to the European Commission of Human Rights, alleging breaches of the Convention.

9. On 14 September 1995, over 5 years after the applicant had first been detained, the Commission released a report unanimously concluding that there had been violations of Articles 3, 5(1), 8 and 13 of the Convention. The matter was then referred by the Commission and UK Government to the European Court of Human Rights. The applicant submits that at that point, if not before, he should have been released from detention, but he was not.

10. There was a third Application for Judicial Review, and for a Writ of habeas corpus, both of which were refused on 10 November 1995 by MacPherson J.

11. As I have said, the decision of the European Court of Human Rights which led to the applicant's release was that the United Kingdom Government had acted in breach of certain Articles of the Convention.

12. The Court made no award of non-pecuniary damages in respect of the period of time which the applicant had spent in detention. The applicant's Solicitors subsequently applied to the Home Office to compensate Mr Chahal for the loss occasioned by the United Kingdom's breaches of the Convention, and in particular the prolongation of his detention caused by the absence of effective judicial remedies in the United Kingdom to vindicate the rights guaranteed by the Convention (See their letter of 19 November 1996). The claim was made under the provisions of Article 5(5) which it was said "requires that there be an enforceable right to compensation in any case of detention which violates Article 5(4)."

13. This application was refused by letter dated 5 February 1997.

14. The reasons given for the refusal were these:

> "With regard to your request that Mr Chahal should be compensated for breaches of the convention, it has been decided that as the Court ordered no compensation other than the payment of Mr Chahal's costs, the Home Office regards itself as being under no obligation to compensate Mr Chahal further."

15. Mr Nicholas Blake QC, who has appeared for the applicant throughout, says that this explanation will not do, given the purposes of Article 5(5). He submits that the right to compensation given by that paragraph may follow a decision by the Court that there has been a breach of another limb of Article 5.

16. It is material to examine the basis of the Court's decision.

17. First. By 12 votes to 7 that there would be a violation of Article 3 of the Convention, in the event of the Secretary of State's decision to deport the applicant to India being implemented.

18. Article 3 provides as follows:

> "No-one shall be subjected to torture or to inhuman or degrading treatment or punishment."

19. Second. By 13 votes to 6 that there had been no violation of Article 5(1) of the Convention. The material part of this Article provides as follows:

> "Everyone has the right to liberty and security of person. No one shall be deprived of his liberty save in the following cases and in accordance with a procedure prescribed by law:
>
> (f) The lawful arrest or detention of a person . . . against whom action is being taken with a view to deportation. . .".

20. Third. Unanimously that there had been a violation of Article 5(4) which provides:

> "Everyone who is deprived of his liberty by arrest or detention shall be entitled to take proceedings by which the lawfulness of his detention shall be decided speedily by a Court, and his release ordered if the detention is not lawful."

21. Fourth. Unanimously that there had been a violation of Article 13, which provides:

> "Everyone whose rights of freedom as set forth in this Convention are violated shall have an effective remedy before a national authority notwithstanding that the violation has been committed by persons acting in an official capacity."

22. As I have indicated, the present application focuses on the finding by the Court of a violation of Article 5(4). There is no doubt that the applicant was deprived of his liberty by arrest or detention. The question before the Court was whether he was entitled to take proceedings by which the lawfulness of that detention, should be decided by a Court. The European Court decided that question in the negative, i.e. against the United Kingdom Government.

23. In other words, the Court found that no procedure existed in the United Kingdom at the material time to challenge in a Court the lawfulness of the Secretary of State's decision that the applicant should be detained.

24. The applicants (i.e. the present applicant and his wife and children) asked the Court to grant them just satisfaction under Article 50, which provides as follows:

> "If the Court finds that a decision or a measure taken by a legal authority or any other authority of a High Contracting Party is completely or partially in conflict with the obligations arising from the present Convention, and if the internal law of the said Party allows only partial reparation to be made for the consequences of this decision or measure,

the decision of the Court shall, if necessary, afford just satisfaction to the injured party."

25. The applicants claimed compensation for non-pecuniary damages for the period of detention suffered by Mr Chahal at a rate of £30,000–£50,000 per annum, i.e. a total of sum of over £300,000. The Government submitted that a finding of violation would be sufficient just satisfaction in respect of the claim for non-pecuniary damages.

26. In view of its decision that there had been no violation of Article 5(1), the Court made no award of non-pecuniary damages in respect of the period of time Mr Chahal had spent in detention. As to the other complaints, the Court considered that the finding that his deportation, if carried out, would constitute a violation of Article 3, and that there had been breaches of Articles 5(4) and 13 constituted sufficient just satisfaction.

27. Therefore the Court did not award the applicant any compensation, though it did award him costs.

28. The applicant recognises that if he were to be awarded compensation by the Secretary of State, it would be by way of an ex gratia payment—i.e. that the decision whether or not to make an award is a matter of discretion. The applicant has no legal entitlement to compensation. There is no cause of action in private law. It is submitted that the exercise of the discretion to refuse any compensation is however susceptible to challenge in administrative law, having regard to the obligations and standards set by the convention.

29. There are, it is submitted, two important and undisputed facts underlying this application.

30. First, at no time during his detention could the applicant have been deported to India without substantial risk of torture, death, or some other form of inhuman or degrading treatment at the hands of the Indian security forces. The Government argued before the European Court that the position was far improved since the nadir in 1992. Nevertheless, the Commission and the Court found that such a risk existed in 1995 and 1996.

31. Second, at no time during that detention was there in existence a UK Court which was able to investigate and evaluate the allegation of a threat to national security that had caused the applicant to be detained during his challenge to the decision to deport him. True, there was an advisory panel procedure, which as the Court accepted, provided an important safeguard against arbitrariness, and an adequate guarantee that there were at least prima facie grounds for believing that if the applicant were at liberty, national security would be at risk. However, as the Court observed the applicant was not entitled to legal representation before the panel, he was only given an outline of the grounds for the notice of intention to deport, the panel had no power of decision, and its advice to the Home Secretary was not binding and was not

disclosed. The Court held that the panel could not be considered as a "Court" within the meaning of Article 5(4).

32. This defect has now been remedied by the introduction, in September 1998, of the Special Immigration Appeals Commission, presided over by a High Court Judge.

33. The Secretary of State submits that even if the obligations under Article 5(4) had been complied with, it is "highly likely" that the applicant would still have been detained for the same period of time. The applicant's challenge to these reasons is on the basis that:

1. A conclusion that the applicant would inevitably have remained in detention is flawed, irrational and inadequately reasoned.

2. The Secretary of State does not recognise that the failure of the Government to provide an effective remedy that might have resulted in the applicant's release was fault for which the Secretary of State was responsible within the meaning of his policy.

34. As to the first of these challenges, it seems to me that any Court or body considering whether or not to exercise its discretion to award compensation would necessarily have to evaluate the chance or prospect that the applicant would have been released, had what is referred to as an Article 5(4) Court been in existence. Such a Court would have had to perform a balancing exercise, based on the information placed before it. Let it be assumed that the Court would have concluded, as did the European Court, that the applicant would have been at risk had he been returned to India. The Court would then have had to balance against that risk, the threat which it was alleged the applicant posed to national security. In Chahal v SSHD (1994) Imm AR 1079 the Court of Appeal considered the judgment of Potts J. in the instant case. In his judgment Staughton LJ. referred to the difficulties which confronted the Court of Appeal. At page 115 he said:

> "I conclude that the Secretary of State has carried out a balancing exercise; or at least it is not shown that he failed to do so.
>
> It is hardly possible for this Court to consider whether, after that exercise, the Secretary of State's decision was irrational or perverse. Whilst we have massive evidence as to whether Mr Chahal's life or freedom would be threatened if he were returned to India, we do not have the evidence on which the Secretary of State considered him a risk to national security. So we cannot balance the threat on the one hand against the risk of the other."

35. The same problem confronts any Court or body which has to consider the question of compensation, and it also to some extent confronts the Court in the present application. Although I have been shown certain information about the applicant, and allegations made against him, which were referred

to the European Commission, which information is said to be erroneous, I do not know, and cannot be told, the full extent of the material placed before the advisory panel, or which would have been placed before an Article 5(4) Court, and I am unaware of the reasons which led the advisory panel to the conclusion which it reached. Their conclusion was that the applicant posed a threat to national security which justified his continued detention. Can it be said that an Article 5(4) Court would have possibly reached a different conclusion, and that the applicant would have been released from detention at some stage during the 6 year period, and if so at what stage?

36. The advisory panel, which I must assume had been given full information about the threat to national security, agreed with the Secretary of State about the action which was intended to be taken in relation to the applicant. Can it be said that an Article 5(4) Court would probably or possibly have taken any different view? I do not have the material before me to entitle me to say that they would, or even that they might have done.

37. I have considered the possibilities that an article 5(4) Court might have released the applicant temporarily or on bail, that they might have considered that the Secretary of State's argument on the core issue would fail, and have decided that issue in favour of the applicant; or that they might have decided on the evidence that Article 3 would be breached if the applicant were deported to India. Again, there is no material before me to enable me to say that any of these eventualities might have occurred.

38. Leave in this case was originally refused on the papers. On a renewed application leave was granted by McCullough J. on 22 October 1997. Following the grant of leave, I accept that the Secretary of State carefully reconsidered the question of the payment of compensation, as appears from the Affidavit of Jeffrey Richard Harmer. It is clear that the Secretary of State recognised that he has a discretion to make such a payment, but that he did not think that it would be appropriate to make a payment unless he was persuaded that there was a compelling case in favour of doing so. Furthermore it is clear that the Secretary of State does not regard the European Court's decision as determinative, though he thinks it is a weighty factor to be taken into account.

39. The nub of the Secretary of State's decision is contained in paragraph 17 of the Affidavit, where it is said that Secretary of State thinks that the discretionary payment of compensation in the absence of any legal liability or Court Order will not normally be appropriate unless there has been some fault or maladministration on the part of the Home Office, and that the lawful detention of the applicant pending the resolution of the Article 3 point does not amount to any such fault.

40. It is submitted on behalf of the applicant that this misses the point. Here the applicant refers to the second of his challenges, which is that there has

been a violation of the Secretary of State's obligation to provide effective machinery to review the applicant's continued detention.

41. It is at this point that the argument seems to me to have come round a full circle. Its begs the question as before—would the outcome have been any different?

42. I agree with Mr Blake's submission that in private law, where damage is contingent upon the hypothetical actions of a third party, the Court will award a measure of damages commensurate with the chance that the third party would have acted in the Plaintiff's favour—see Allied Maples Group Ltd. v Simmons and Simmons (1995) 1 WLR 1602. Stuart-Smith LJ. held at page 1611 that the Plaintiff can succeed provided he shows that he had a substantial chance rather than a speculative one, the evaluation of the substantial chance being a question of quantification of damages.

43. Mr Blake submits that to dismiss the prospects of an Article 5(4) Court admitting the applicant to bail as negligible would be irrational, and to dismiss as of no value independent judicial scrutiny.

44. I disagree with this submission. First, because private law analogies are not entirely appropriate in the present case. What matters here is whether it can be demonstrated that the Secretary of State behaved irrationally, and in a way in which no reasonable Secretary of State would act, when he examined his decision to refuse compensation. Second, even if the private law test was appropriate, it seems to me that the chances of the applicant being released could not realistically be assessed as anything more than speculative. True, the advisory panel did not have the characteristics of a Court, as the European Court found, but it performed an important and useful function in the respects described by that Court. Can it be said that an Article 5(4) Court would, or might, have reached a different decision? In my opinion there is nothing to justify such a conclusion.

45. Accordingly, in my judgment it has not been established that the Secretary of State's discretionary refusal to award compensation was irrational, or that it was in contravention of Article 5(5), or that the Secretary of State fettered his decision in the way complained of.

46. Therefore I refuse to order a Review of the decision, and this application is dismissed.

* * * * *

DOCUMENT NO 27

R v Hugh Thomas Jack [1998] EWCA Crim. 1206 Court Of Appeal Criminal Division (95/1248/Y3)

April 7, 1998
Crown Copyright
(Edited Text)

Lord Justice Kennedy:

1. On 20th January 1995 at the Central Criminal Court, after a two month trial, this applicant was convicted of conspiracy to cause explosions and was sentenced to 20 years imprisonment. Before us he has renewed his application for leave to appeal against conviction and sentence after refusal by the single judge. The application for leave to appeal against conviction we dismissed for reasons which we now give. We also give our decision in relation to the application for leave to appeal against sentence.

Lest it be thought that there has been unreasonable delay on the part of this court in dealing with this matter we set out the history. The perfected grounds of appeal were lodged on the 10th October 1995. The single judge refused leave on 10th November 1995. The proceedings were then delayed whilst Professor Caddy considered the possibility of semtex tracing equipment having been contaminated in relation to this and other cases. On 15th July 1997 this court, differently constituted, acceded to an application by counsel for the applicant that the application should be adjourned for consideration of the papers by Doctor Lloyd. On 24th February 1998 the applicant's solicitors confirmed that they would not be relying on Dr Lloyd, and the matter was listed before us on 17th March 1998. The position therefore is that there is no fresh evidence put forward for our consideration, and we have to consider the matter in the normal way on the basis of the material which was presented to the court below.

2. Facts

In order to set the grounds of appeal in context it is necessary to say something about the structure of the case as put forward by the prosecution and the defence. During the morning of Wednesday 14th July 1993 Robert Fryers was arrested at a bus stop in north London with a bag containing 2^1/$_2$ kilograms of semtex and 2 litres of petrol. The contents of the bag had the hallmarks of an IRA bomb, and Fryers had a piece of paper with a telephone number written on it which was frequently used by the IRA to give warning when bombs were planted. The arrest was no accident, because Fryers had been under observation for some time, and his mainland base was known to be a flat rented by this applicant, **Hugh Thomas Jack**, then a 35 year old agricultural labourer, at 25 Lochbrae, Sauchie, in Central Scotland. The police and the security services had been watching and recording by video the movements at 25 Lochbrae for some time prior to 14th July 1993, and from those observations and from their subsequent enquiries they were able to build up a picture of the activities of the two men who in due course became co-defendants at the Central Criminal Court. The applicant, it seems, spent most nights with his girl friend at a different address, and worked as a casual labourer at Gartmorn Hill Farm, about 5 minutes drive away.

On 27th June 1993, about 2 weeks before the arrest in north London, Fryers was seen to arrive at 25 Lochbrae with a holdall. It was part of the prosecution case that the item of luggage was significant. It was also part of the prosecution case that as Fryers was about to undertake a dangerous mission it was essential for him to have a "safe" house in which to live and that he would not have been sent to 25 Lochbrae unless it was known to be a safe house. Mr Emmerson, for the applicant, contends that as the applicant was known to have a routine pattern to his life he was a perfect host for Fryers who could do what he wished when he knew that the applicant would be away, and who if working near to the kitchen window could observe the applicant's approach should he return.

On 1st July 1993 the applicant applied for a lock-up garage at 96 Greycraigs, near to his home. It was a somewhat surprising application because he had managed for years without a garage. He later said that he made the application because his own car, a Nissan, was "not legal". In fact its tax disc had expired on 31st May and although he was granted the tenancy of the garage on 2nd July his car only spent one night in that garage prior to his arrest twelve days later. On 2nd July Fryers began to buy some of the items which he required to make the bomb.

On 8th July the applicant was enquiring, on behalf of Fryers, about the possibility of renting a unit at Cotton Street, Glasgow. It was the prosecution contention that the applicant was given the task of making that enquiry because he had a Scots accent, whereas Fryers' accent was Irish. The applicant later said that he understood the unit to be required in connection with Fryers' proposal to set up a landscape gardening business. On the same day, the 8th July, the applicant drove Fryers to Glasgow railway station to catch the night sleeper to London, and purchased his ticket for him. The prosecution again suggest that the man with the Irish accent was being kept in the background. According to the applicant he understood that Fryers was going to London to obtain money and possibly to purchase tools and other items he required in connection with his projected gardening business.

On Friday 9th July, while Fryers was in London, he telephoned the appli cant by arrangement at 10 pm. The applicant did not have a telephone in his flat, but there were public telephones nearby, and also nearby was a relation who did have a telephone. None of those facilities were used. This telephone call was made to a telephone box at Bridge of Allan, about 5 miles from the applicant's home. Fryers apparently indicated that he was fed up because his contact had not appeared. The applicant subsequently sought to explain Fryers' use of distant telephone boxes as being attributable to Fryers desire to avoid a money lender who was pursuing him. That would not explain why the appli cant himself was required to drive 5 miles to receive a telephone call, and the prosecution's explanation was that the applicant like Fryers was doing what he could to avoid detection.

Fryers stayed at a hotel in London for the Friday and Saturday nights, and on the Saturday, 10th July 1993, the applicant paid £200 in cash as a deposit for the Cotton Street premises. He explained the cash payment by say ing that he had been in the car trade and become bankrupt. That was a lie, as was the explanation he gave to his girl friend as to what he had done with the £200. He told her that it had been used to pay the deposit on a car. The money had in fact come from Fryers before he had left for London and at 10 pm on that Saturday evening there was a further telephone call from Fryers to the applicant.

On the morning of Sunday 11th July 1993 Fryers was able to take pos session of a Ford Escort which had been left for him to find. It had been bought at Wembley car auctions on 15th June 1993 and thereafter exported to Ireland in the name of Smith. The prosecution contended that when Fryers collected the Escort it was loaded with enough semtex, detonators and time and power units to make seven bombs. Fryers drove the car north arriving back at 25 Lochbrae at about 4.30 pm. At about 9.20 pm that evening the applicant and Fryers went again to Bridge of Allan where Fryers made tele phone calls from the phone box. The prosecution contended that he must have been reporting his safe arrival. The car was not unloaded that evening, but at about 9.35 am the following morning, 12th July 1993, Fryers left 25 Lochbrae in the Escort with the large holdall and went to the garage at 96 Greycraigs. He reversed the car partly into the garage and was then working at the back of the car with the boot open for 20 to 30 minutes. At 10.47 am he returned to the flat carrying the holdall which now appeared to be full. It was the prosecution case that thereafter the holdall remained in the flat for two days. A couple of minutes after Fryers' return to the flat the applicant arrived and stayed for about 20 minutes. The prosecution contended that he was a fellow conspirator checking to see how things had gone on. On that afternoon the applicant took the Escort to the farm. He did some work on it and told a butcher named Drysdale that he had got it from "Jim". As Mr Sweeney, for the respondent prosecutor, points out Jim was not Fryers name. On that Monday evening the applicant and Fryers again went out together and for that one night the applicant's Nissan was housed in his garage. He drove the Escort to his girl friend's home.

On Tuesday 13th July 1993 the applicant called at 25 Lochbrae on his way to work and when he returned at lunch time Fryers was out. The prosecution contend that Fryers would not have risked going out leaving an arsenal in the flat if the applicant was not a full party to the conspiracy. But, as Mr Emmerson points out, whilst the applicant was alone in the flat one of his friends, a man named Collins, called to see him and stayed about 10 minutes. He was not sent away, but when Fryers returned he was introduced to Collins as "Sam". The applicant's explanation for that lie was that it was to protect Fryers from the possibility of his name being made known to the moneylender.

On that Tuesday evening Fryers set off for London in the Escort taking with him a small Premier holdall, and this was the journey which ended at the north London bus stop on the following morning. He had spent a little over a fortnight at 25 Lochbrae, and in that period he and the applicant had spent 41 hours together. The applicant was arrested at 9.11 am on the Wednesday morning, and at 12.11 pm the applicant returned home for lunch as usual, driving the Nissan car. He later accepted that whilst he was in the flat the television or the radio was switched on and by that time the news of Fryers arrest was being broadcast (though there was no direct evidence that he saw or heard it). At 12.55 pm the applicant emerged from the flat and went to his car which was parked about 15 feet away. He drove the car down the street and executed a U-turn. He then drove back and parked the car as close as possible to the flat entrance with the driver's side next to the kerb. He made a quick return visit to the flat and emerged 45 seconds later carrying a bag. It is the applicant's case that he was carrying a binbag into which he had put a pair of wellingtons, a jacket, a bottle of drink and a snack. The prosecution contend that he was carrying the large holdall which had previously been seen in the possession of Fryers and which contained material for the making of a further six bombs. The applicant placed the bag on the back seat of the Nissan and drove off. He did not drive straight back to the farm. That would have been a five minute journey, and his journey took about 17 minutes. It was the prosecution case that he went by way of Gartinny Woods where three days later a holdall containing semtex and other items was found some 37 metres into the wood. The applicant admits that he did go near to the wood, and did stop his car, but not for the purpose of hiding a bag. His case is that he stopped to look for the brother of the farmer who he thought might be able to offer him some casual work. The prosecution contended that on the evidence it was clear that the applicant knew that no casual work was at that time available.

After the applicant returned to Gartmorn Hill Farm he was arrested and taken to Glasgow police station where he was detained. A bottle of drink was found near to where he was arrested and his wellingtons were in the howf of the farm where they were usually kept when they were not required. On the day in question there was no particular need for wellingtons and the applicant was wearing ordinary working boots. His jacket was in the Nissan car where, according to the prosecution, it had been since morning, and the car also contained a black binbag. The farmer indicated that he would only have expected the applicant to bring sandwiches in the afternoon if he was going to do overtime, and no overtime was available.

After his arrest the applicant was interviewed a number of times, and gave the answers which we have indicated in the course of this narrative.

3. General Nature of Defence

It is the applicant's case that if Fryers was a member of the provisional IRA and a bomber he, the applicant, knew nothing of it. All he did was to give Fryers shelter as a friend, who he believed to be trying to start a legitimate business and to be in a little difficulty with a moneylender.

4. Scientific Evidence

The applicant's clothing was examined and no trace of explosive substances was found. Mr Emmerson underlines that fact, pointing out that the outside of the holdall would probably have been quite significantly contaminated. Traces of explosive substances were found in the flat at 25 Lochbrae and on the rear seat of the Nissan car. What was found was consistent with the applicant having placed there a holdall containing explosives. Fibres which matched those in the applicant's trousers were found on the handles of the holdall when it was recovered and fibres matching those in the applicant's clothing were also recovered from a cloth which was found in the Premier holdall which Fryers had with him at the bus stop. There was no holdall left in 25 Lochbrae but there was a rubbish bag which had been used for its normal purpose for a couple of days and which had been torn off the roll before the bag which was found in the Nissan car. There was also displayed at 25 Lochbrae a Republican Resistance Calendar on which the applicant had marked the birthday of his girlfriend. It was some indication of sympathy for the Republican cause, and the applicant lied about it when he was questioned.

5. Grounds of Appeal—General

Mr Emmerson restricted his submissions to three grounds of appeal, which can be summarised as follows:—

(1) that the trial judge was wrong to allow security services witnesses to give evidence screened from the accused, the press and the public. The witnesses were also referred to by letter rather than by name, but no complaint is now made about that:

(2) that the trial judge was wrong not to permit the defence to ascertain the height, angle and distance from the entrance of 25 Lochbrae of the video camera used to film the applicant as he left to return to work at about 12.55 pm on 14th July 1993:

(3) that the trial judge was wrong not to permit cross-examination of security service officers as to the capacity of tracking devices used to monitor the applicant's movements on the journey back to work which began at 12.55 pm.

Mr Emmerson submits that all three grounds of appeal arise out of the tension engendered by the growing practice of using security service personnel for what are in reality routine surveillance tasks. In principle any defendant is entitled to a fair open adversarial trial, but security services, used to working in secret, ask as a matter of routine for protection and, Mr Emmerson contends, on this occasion they got too much. The judge failed properly to protect the interests of the defendant in relation to each of the three matters which now form the grounds of appeal. She should have taken particular care in this case because of the obvious risk of prejudice arising in the minds of the jury from the very nature of the charges. Furthermore, as the trial proceeded it became clear that the issue as to the type of bag which had been carried by the applicant when he left 25 Lochbrae at 12.55 pm was going to be a central issue in the case—whether it was, as the prosecution contended, a holdall or, as the applicant contended, a black binbag. This was an area in which, Mr Emmerson submits, expert evidence by way of imagery analysis would have helped if the defence had access to the information they sought in relation to the video camera. As to the tracking devices, it was the defence case that the secret service surveillance teams were lying when they said that they lost track of the applicant's Nissan on its journey from 25 Lochbrae to Gartmorn Hill Farm by way of Gartinny Wood, a lie invented to explain the failure to search that wood thoroughly so as to find the holdall prior to 17th July 1993. Indeed the defence contention was that the holdall was not in the woods at all until it was planted there shortly before it was found. Mr Emmerson accepts that the judge's ruling in relation to each of the matters now challenged called for the exercise of judicial discretion, but he submits that the interests of justice were such as to dictate the conclusion and that the judge gave far too much weight to the fact that security service personnel were involved. The points now put forward were said to be worthy of consideration separately and cumulatively, and to have had the cumulative effect of preventing the applicant from advancing effectively a serious defence. We turn now to consider the individual grounds of appeal, in the order in which Mr Emmerson invited us to consider them.

6. Ground 2—the video camera.

Mr Emmerson began his submissions in relation to this ground by saying that the case turned on the events of 14th July 1993. That, as it seems to us, was somewhat extravagant. He invited us to look at the public interest immunity certificate of the Secretary of State for the Home Department, which in this case was couched in very general terms, and he submitted, rightly, that the certificate, although material, could not be conclusive.

In fact, as it seems to us, the security service involvement had really nothing to do with the issues which arose in relation to the video camera. It was a fixed camera installed by the police on the 3rd June 1993. Obviously if the defence were informed of its distance from the entrance of 25 Lochbrae, its height, and its angle of view that would be tantamount to disclosing its position, and, as Mr Emmerson recognises, the occupiers of the premises where it was installed did not want its position to be disclosed. Plainly they were entitled to be protected provided that as a result no injustice would be occasioned to the defence, so it is not in any way surprising that prior to the trial the judge ruled that the video film could be used without disclosing technical information in relation to the camera or information as to its position. It is noteworthy that at that stage no request was made for the information which Mr Emmerson now says was needed by the defence, and no evidence has ever been adduced from any expert to say why he or she would wish to have that information. It is easy to see why not. If an expert were to be involved the defence might find it difficult to avoid either calling the expert or allowing the jury to know that he or she had reported and not been called. But it does mean that a complaint made to this court about lack of information when the information was not sought at the normal time is likely to be viewed with some scepticism.

Mr Emmerson submitted, more than once, that without assistance it was not possible for the members of the jury who looked at the video film many times to be sure whether the applicant, who chose not to give evidence, was carrying a black holdall or a black binbag. We saw the relevant part of the film played through about four times, and suffice to say that it would not in the least surprise us if the members of the jury were wholly satisfied that the prosecution were right in their submissions as to what the video film showed. Quite apart from the video film there was observation evidence given by two police officers, Sloan and Telfer, whose car was parked about 100 yards away from 25 Lochbrae. As Mr Emmerson pointed out, the officers may have been looking through wet glass, and neither officer described what he saw as a holdall until Sloan made his statement on 30th July 1993, long after the holdall had been found in Gartinny Wood. Telfer may have seen Sloan's statement before he made his statement next day, but they contemporaneously recorded that the applicant left his home carrying a black bag, and nowhere in what they said or recorded prior to 30th July is there any suggestion of the bag having been a binbag. Only the applicant in interview referred to it as such and, as Mr Sweeney pointed out, the jury had the opportunity to observe on the video film other occasions when the applicant was unquestionably carrying a binbag. They could make the comparison for themselves.

Nothing said by Mr Emmerson has persuaded us that in this case the judge should have ordered further disclosure than was in fact ordered in relation to the video camera. The reality is that except as a matter of speculation the defence is not shown to have been prejudiced at all by the measures understandably taken to protect those who made their premises available, and the judge was at pains to ensure that the jury approached their lack of information as to the position of the camera in a proper way. At Volume 1 page 32 of the summing-up she said:—

"You remember Mr Guthrie, the man who installed the videos . . . . you will notice that no evidence was given as to where they were installed. What he told you was what they could actually pick up . . . again, members of the jury, you do not start drawing inferences adverse to these defendants from the fact that you were not told where those devices were installed. If you think the absence of information about the tracking devices—information about the exact location of the videos—has, in some relevant way, restricted the manner in which questions could be asked of witnesses, then you will take that into account. You will obviously bear in mind Mr Sweeney's comment that actually it applied as much to the Crown as it did to the defence. Just as the Crown could not tell you the full nature of the devices, the defence could not cross-examine at will, so the Crown possibly could not counter what was being said.

So look at what you have got and stick firmly with what you have got. If it is not enough, then you reject that in deciding whether or not certain facts are proved. If it is enough, you do not trouble yourself as to why these restrictions are in place."

In our judgment ground 2 of the grounds of appeal has no substance and must fail.

7. Ground 3: Tracking Devices

We turn now to the restriction imposed by the judge on evidence in relation to the tracking devices. Mr Emmerson submitted that the way in which this topic was dealt with, both during the trial and more particularly in the summing-up, rendered the evidence delphic and contradictory, and prevented the jury from forming a proper judgment as to the veracity of the five teams of secret service personnel who were on mobile patrol on the afternoon of 14th March 1993.

As Mr Sweeney explained, only two cars were actually using tracking devices on that afternoon, and when defence counsel began to cross-examine as to the use of tracking devices prosecuting counsel invited the judge partially to relax her earlier ruling pursuant to which no evidence about tracking devices had been led. The relaxation was made, one witness was recalled, and so evidence was given as to which devices were being used, with what effect. For present purposes suffice to say that the evidence suggested that the devices had their limitations, and after cross-examination of one witness the prosecution sought a further relaxation of the judge's ruling, but that application was refused. So, Mr Sweeney submits, the judge rightly adjusted the ruling as the case developed, as envisaged by this court in *Davis & others* (1993) 97 Cr App R 110 at 115. As a result the defence was not disadvantaged in any way, or at any rate no more than the prosecution, and the disadvantage was minimal. There was an obvious public interest to be protected because tracking devices are clearly a valuable aid in the war against crime, and when the judge came to sum up she reminded the jury not only of the evidence but also of the adjustment of the ruling and the limitations on the questions that had been imposed. She cautioned the jury against drawing inferences adverse to the accused, and said at Volume 1 page 31F:—

> "You recognise that I have considered the extent to which that material can be disclosed, and that is my decision; and what you do is say to yourselves, 'given the evidence that we have, are we satisfied on that evidence?' Do not start speculating about what you have not been told."

Having mentioned the restrictions on evidence in relation to the video camera she repeated her warning in the passage which we have already cited. That seems to us to have been an entirely correct approach, and we can discern no basis on which were leave to be granted the applicant could succeed in relation to ground 3.

7. Ground 1: Screens

Here Mr Emmerson's submission, as we understand it, really amounted to this—that although the relevant authorities were drawn to the attention of the judge and although she apparently had regard to them when exercising her discretion, as can be seen from her reasons for allowing screens to be used, in reality she allowed the assertion that screens were required in the interest of national security to act as a trump card, and did not sufficiently take into account the number of movements of witnesses into and out of the witness box which would result from her ruling. Mr Emmerson also submitted that as the security services are playing a greater part in the investigation of serious crime claims for anonymity are on the increase, and this is a dangerous development liable to disrupt normal trial procedures.

In order to establish the basic principles our attention was invited to *Scott v Scott* (1913) AC 417 and *R v Socialist Worker ex p Attorney General* (1975) Q.B. 637, which show that initially the presumption always is that witnesses will give their evidence in open court without screens. If the prosecution wants screens to be used in relation to any witness the prosecution must persuade the court that it is appropriate to make that order in the instant case. As Lord Lane C.J. said in *R v X, Y and Z* (1990) 91 Cr App **R** 36 at 40:—

> "The learned judge has the duty on this and on all other occasions of endeavouring to see that justice is done. Those are high sounding words. What it really means is, he has got to see that the system operates fairly: fairly not only to the defendants but also to the prosecution and also to the witnesses. Sometimes he has to make decisions as to where the balance of fairness lies. He came to the conclusion that in these circumstances the necessity of trying to ensure that these children would be able to give evidence outweighed any possible prejudice to the defendants by the erection of the screen."

As the quotation indicates, the witnesses for whom a screen was provided in that case were children, but that is not always the position. In *R v Coroner for Greater Belfast*, 22nd April 1993 unreported, the Court of Appeal for Northern Ireland was concerned with an application to the Coroner for the screening of soldiers operating in the area where a death occurred. Lord Hutton CJ said at page 32 that he was satisfied on the authorities that—

> "Where the claim of national security is raised in such a way that it may conflict with the principle of open justice, the courts must balance the claims and decide whether there should be a restriction of the principle of open justice in order to meet the claims of national security."

At page 33 he accepted—

> "That there may be cases where the need to protect national security may be so strong that this prevails over the claims of open justice."

And at page 34 he stated that—

> "Whilst the issue of screening is one to be determined by the court, the court in deciding that issue should pay due regard to the view of the Secretary of State stated in the certificate."

As to what national security meant in the context of the instant case Lord Hutton concluded at page 36 that—

> "The activities of the soldiers do come within the ambit of the term but that, unlike some issues of national security (such as intelligence gathering at GCHQ) which a court is quite unfitted to assess, the activities of

the soldiers are towards the bottom of the scale of matters coming within the concept of national security and are activities which a court is competent to assess and the importance of which a court is entitled to balance against the importance of the requirement of open justice."

He then went on to look at the facts of the case. That approach Mr Emmerson accepts to be correct. Mr Emmerson then invited our attention to part of the judgment of MacDermott L.J., who said at page 4 in the same case that—

"A Certificate founded on grounds of public interest relating to national security should relate with appropriate particularity to the individuals in respect of whom the Certificate is issued."

That is a proposition which we endorse.

The approach adopted in the *Belfast Coroner's* case is materially the same as that applied by the courts in the context of public interest immunity, where it is accepted that a balance must sometimes be struck between, on the one hand, the interests of national security or some other compelling public interest in non-disclosure of documents or in some other departure from the normal procedural rules and, on the other hand, the public interest in the administration of justice (see e.g. *Keane* (1994) 99 Cr. App. **R** 1 at 5–6). Indeed, the use of screens to protect the identity of witnesses could be viewed as an application of the ordinary principles of public interest immunity. There is, however, at least a theoretical difficulty about such an analysis. The authorities tend to suggest that a narrower approach is to be adopted in relation to the principle of open justice, in that a departure from that principle can be justified only in the overall interests of the administration of justice and not, in the absence of express statutory provision, for other reasons of public interest. For example, in *Attorney General v Leveller Magazine* (1979) AC 440, Lord Scarman concluded at page 471 D:—

"(1) that, in the absence of express statutory provision . . . a court cannot sit in private merely because it believes that to sit in public would be prejudicial to national safety, (2) that, if the factor of national safety appears to endanger the due administration of justice, e.g. by deterring the Crown from prosecuting in cases where it should do so, a court may sit in private, (3) that there must be material (not necessarily formally adduced evidence) made known to the court upon which it can reasonably reach its conclusion."

On that basis the balance to be struck is between two aspects of the administration of justice and it is not permissible to balance national security *per se* against the administration of justice. Statute apart, considerations of national security can justify a departure from the principle of open justice only so far as they have an effect upon the administration of justice itself, e.g. by deterring the Crown from continuing a prosecution or, say, by deterring an individual member of the security services from giving evidence out of fear for his own safety.

It is fair to say that in the *Belfast Coroner's* case Lord Hutton does not appear to have understood Lord Scarman's speech in so restricted a way, since it is one of the authorities that he cites in support of the broad proposition that a balance is to be struck between national security and the administration of justice when considering the issue of screens. In any event, however, the problem to which we have referred may be more apparent than real. In the great majority of cases there is likely to be little or no practical distinction between issues of national security *per se* and the impact of national security upon the administration of justice. In the present case, for example, although national security was looked at to some extent as an independent consideration, the matters in question bore directly upon the administration of justice since they concerned the willingness of witnesses to give evidence and of the Crown to call them. As Mr Emmerson accepted before us, the issues of national security and of the administration of justice merged into one. In those circumstances it is unnecessary to decide whether, statute apart, a departure from the principle of open justice could be justified by reference to considerations of national security that had no impact on the administration of justice.

In carrying out the balancing exercise to which we have referred, a vitally important issue is of course that of prejudice to the defendant. In *Cooper v Schaub*, 29th November 1993 unreported, Farquharson L.J. in this court accepted at page 7B that the use of screens is prejudicial to an accused person, even when proper warnings are given, because their use "suggests to a jury that there is a need for the witness to be protected in some way from any contact, even if it is only visual, with the defendant." The court went on to say—

> "In our judgment it should only be in the most exceptional cases that apparatus of this kind should be used when an adult is giving evidence."

We agree with all of that, but it is important to bear in mind that the offence under consideration in that case was rape, and that the trial judge's decision to allow screens to be used was upheld. At 7G the court said:—

> "It is undoubtedly the case, as we have already underlined, that a decision of this kind is very much within the learned judge's discretion. Having regard to the material to which we have briefly been referred, it is not possible in our judgment for this court to say the discretion was exercised unlawfully or in a way which could not reasonably be supported."

Where the charge under consideration is a terrorist offence the prejudice to the accused of allowing screens to be used is likely to be somewhat reduced, because the jury may have to have protection themselves, and will easily appreciate why, if the charge is well-founded, protection should be afforded to a witness. Which all goes to show, as Mr Sweeney submitted and we accept, that each case must be decided on its own facts.

In *Taylor and Crabb*, 22nd July 1994 unreported, Evans L.J. in this court, at page 9, accepted the proposition that except in "rare and exceptional circumstances" a defendant is entitled to see and to know the identity of his accusers, including witnesses for the prosecution brought against him, but whether in a particular case an exception should be made is "pre-eminently a matter for the exercise of discretion by the trial judge". The court then listed five factors which are or may be relevant to the exercise of that discretion, namely—

(1) there must be real grounds for being fearful of the consequences if the evidence is given and the identity of the witness is revealed:

(2) the evidence must be sufficiently relevant and important to make it unfair to the prosecution to compel them to proceed without it:

(3) the prosecution must satisfy the court that the credit worthiness of the witness has been fully investigated and the result of that enquiry disclosed to the defence so far as is consistent with the anonymity sought. This is a factor which, as Mr Emmerson accepts, is of no significance in the present case.

(4) the court must be satisfied that no undue prejudice is caused to the defendant:

(5) the court can balance the need for protection, including the extent of the necessary protection, against the unfairness or the appearance of unfairness in the particular case.

That seems to us to be a useful check list in relation to this type of case.

Here, as Mr Sweeney submits, there were obvious arguments in favour of the limited inroad upon normal procedure which the prosecution sought. They did not seek to screen the witnesses from the jury or from counsel or from the judge, but they did seek to screen them from the defendants. The witnesses were members of the security service, a relatively small group of people doing work in the field. They were comparable, Mr Emmerson submitted to us, to the Anti Terrorist Branch of the Metropolitan Police in respect of whom Mr Emmerson asserts that applications for the use of screens are rarely if ever made. No doubt some of the work being done by the security services was routine work which could easily be done by police officers, but the spectrum of their work is wide, and these witnesses would necessarily be going on to other types of work in which, Mr Sweeney submitted, they might well be at risk if their identities were known. He submitted that members of terrorist organisations and their associates are trained to remember and spread information about any person employed against them. He submitted that if Fryers or the applicant were to obtain their liberty in the near future they might be able to recognise security service officers who gave evidence against them at their trial and, although the position now is that they have both been convicted and sentenced to long periods of imprisonment, that was not the position when the trial judge had to make her ruling in November 1994. Mr Sweeney also pointed out that even without obtaining their liberty the defendants in this case or either of them might, if they saw the witnesses, be able to recognise photographs of them shown to them by persons visiting them in prison, and we see the force of that submission.

The judge gave her ruling in relation to the use of screens on 17th November 1994, and her reasons for that ruling she gave on 19th January 1995. She said at the outset:—

"A fundamental principle of English justice is that it should be openly conducted and courts sit in public other than in exceptional circumstances."

No one quarrels with that, and at page 5C she said:—

"Counsel have set out the applicable principles: and there has been no real dispute about them."

She recognised that in the present case anonymity was being sought for a very large number of witnesses—at that time the number was 84—even though in the end only fourteen witnesses were affected. The judge then reviewed the authorities to which we have referred, and applied the approach suggested by Evans L.J. in *Taylor and Crabb* to the facts of the present case. At page 14 D she said:—

"I am not being asked, in my view, to afford special provisions to the security services as such, but to consider the position of individual witnesses who, because they are members of the security services, are shown by evidence to be at risk. The Certificate of the Secretary of State provides that evidence: and I accept it."

In our judgment that was the right approach. The security services do not have any passport to the use of screens, or to any other form of anonymity. Their position has to be considered as individual witnesses on a case by case basis. The Certificate of the Secretary of State may or may not satisfy the judge that they are at risk. Its chances of doing so will be enhanced if it is tailored to the individuals and the facts of the case, and in this case it can be said that the certificate was not tailored as well as it might have been, but it did provide evidence which the judge was entitled to accept.

The judge accepted that the witnesses concerned would be at risk if they gave evidence and that they might be prevented from giving evidence through fear for their safety. She also accepted that in the absence of steps to protect their identities the Crown would be unable to call any of those witnesses, and that the Crown would be unable to prove the charge of conspiracy without their evidence. After referring to the *Belfast Coroner's* case, she said that she was satisfied that the need to protect the security service witnesses from becoming special targets of the IRA or any other terrorist organisation fell properly within the ambit of national security. She went on:

> "What I have to do is to weigh those interests against the interests of justice in this case—that is to balance the restriction on the public nature of the hearing by anonymity and by screening against the consideration of national security stated in the Secretary of State's certificate and the other reasons advanced by the Crown."

The judge then considered the extent to which each defendant would be prejudiced if she made the order proposed, before carrying out the balancing exercise. Her conclusion in relation to the applicant was:

> "Balancing the effects of a general prejudice which may arise from screens and the specific matter canvassed by the defendant **Jack** against the importance of the evidence overall, the risk to the witnesses and the potential loss of their value in the future, I have concluded protection should be afforded in the manner and to the extent that it is sought."

It is clear that the main focus of the judge's attention was on balancing different aspects of the administration of justice so as to reach an overall view of what justice required. That, in the light of the authorities, seems to us to be an entirely correct approach. For reasons that we have explained, her reference to national security as a separate factor in the balancing exercise may be open to doubt (though supported by the *Belfast Coroner's* case and by the principles applicable to public interest immunity). Nothing turns on it in the present case, however, since the reality is that the issues of national security and of the administration of justice merged into one. It is inconceivable in any event that the outcome of the judge's balancing exercise would have been any different if national security had not been identified as a separate factor.

For those reasons, in our view, the judge's discretionary decision cannot now be impugned, so we find no substance in the first ground of appeal.

8. Finally as to conviction

Even if we had been persuaded of the arguability of one or more of the three grounds of appeal which Mr Emmerson developed before us we would not in this case have given leave to appeal because, in our judgment, the circumstantial evidence against the applicant which we summarised in the earlier part of this judgment was very strong indeed, so strong that, looking at the matter in the round, we find it difficult to see how it can be maintained that the conviction was unsafe. For all of those reasons we concluded that the application for leave to appeal against conviction must be dismissed.

DOCUMENT NO 28

Special Immigration Appeal Commission, Summary Of Conclusions

July 30, 2002

Since the judgment of the Commission, which has been handed down this afternoon, is a substantial document, we thought it would be of assistance to those who might be interested if we gave a brief summary of our conclusions.

The Anti-terrorism, Crime and Security Act 2001 contains in Part 4 provisions which enable the Home Secretary to certify that a person is an international terrorist if he reasonably

a. believes that the person's presence in the United Kingdom is a risk to national security, and

b. suspects that the person is a terrorist threat.

Anyone so certified is described as a suspected international terrorist. He may be detained under powers contained in the Immigration Act 1971 even though he cannot be removed from the United Kingdom because he is a refugee or he would be treated in such a way as amounted to torture or inhuman or degrading treatment if returned or thee is no country to which he could be returned because for example he was stateless or none would accept him. Before the 2001 Act, such people could not be detained since detention could only be pending and for the purpose of removal. If there could be no removal, there could be no lawful detention.

Such detention is also contrary to Article 5 of the ECHR, now incorporated into domestic law by the Human Rights Act 1998. The only way that such detention could be justified was by derogating from the Convention to enable what otherwise would be a breach of the detainee's human rights to be done. On 18 December 2001, the Government did derogate from Article 5 and in particular from the provisions in Article 5 which only permitted detention of aliens against whom action was being taken with a view of their removal.

Article 15 of the Convention, which deals with derogation, is in very strict terms. It only permits derogation if effectively three preconditions are satisfied. These are:

1. There must be a public emergency threatening the life of the nation.

2. The measures, which derogate from any obligation under the

Convention must only be to the extent strictly required by the exigencies of the situation.

3. The measures must not be inconsistent with the United Kingdom's other obligations under international law.

Section 30 of the 2001 Act confers exclusively on SIAC the powers which otherwise would be held by the High Court to consider a challenge to the derogation relating to someone detained by virtue of the powers in the 2001 Act. It was said by the appellants that none of the three preconditions had been met and further that there were breaches of other Articles of the Convention from which there had been no derogation.

Our task under s.30 has been to review the derogation. The Government makes the decision; the court's power is to review it to determine whether it was lawfully made in that the preconditions are satisfied. Since issues of national security arise, we have considered not only the material referred to in open court but also material which could not be disclosed for reasons of national security. We have been able to do that with the assistance of submissions from special advocates appointed to represent the interests of the appellants. The appellants and their advisers cannot see and have not seen the undisclosed material; the special advocates and we ourselves have seen it.

We have decided that the Government was entitled to form the view that there was and still is a public emergency threatening the life of the nation and that the detention of those reasonably suspected to be international terrorists involved with or with organizations linked to al-Qaida is strictly required by the exigencies of the situation. However, there has been no derogation from Article 14, which prohibits discrimination in the application of the ECHR. The Act permits the detention of non-British citizens aloe and it is quite clear from the evidence before us that there are British citizens who are likely to be as dangerous as non-British citizens and who have been involved with al-Qaida or organizations linked to it. It is not only that there is no reasonable relationship between the means employed and the aims sought to be pursued. On that ground, we have decided that that 2001 Act, which is the measure derogating from the obligations under the Convention, to the extent that it permits only the detention of foreign suspected international terrorists is not compatible with the Convention.

DOCUMENT NO 29

A and Others

v

Secretary of State for the Home Department Court of Appeal

October 25, 2002

The detention without charge of non-national suspected terrorists who could not be deported because of fears for their safety was not incompatible with the United Kingdom's human rights obligations since such a measure was objectively justified during a time of public emergency and was proportionate.

The Court of Appeal so held in allowing the appeal of the Home Secretary against the decision of the Special Immigration Appeals Commission (Andrew Collins J, Chairman, Kennedy LJ and Mr Mark Ockelton) on 30 July 2002, on appeals by 11 detainees, to quash the Human Rights Act 1998 (Designated Derogation) Order 2001 and grant a declaration under s 4 of the Human Rights Act 1998 that s 23 of the Anti-terrorism, Crime and Security Act 2001 was incompatible with arts 5 and 14 of the Convention for the Protection of Human Rights and Fundamental Freedoms in so far as it permitted the detention of suspected international terrorists in a way that discriminated against them on the ground of nationality.

The 2001 Order set out the United Kingdom's proposed derogation from art 5(1) of the Convention in s 23 of the 2001 Act, under which the Home Secretary could detain non-nationals who resided in the UK if he suspected that they were terrorists and for the time being it was not possible to deport them because, for example, that could result in treatment contrary to art 3 of the Convention.

LORD WOOLF CJ said that the appeal arose out of the steps the United Kingdom had decided to take in the interests of national security following the attacks in the United States on 11 September 2001. Under art 15 a state could derogate from its obligations under the Convention in time of public emergency to the extent strictly required by the exigencies of the situation. The Commission had concluded that there existed a public emergency threatening the life of the nation within art 15. The Commission was entitled to come to that conclusion. There was no suggestion that the Home Secretary was not perfectly bona fide in coming to the conclusion that the action that was necessary was limited to removing or detaining suspected terrorists who were not nationals who had unconditional rights of abode in the UK. Whether the Home Secretary was entitled to come to that conclusion was an issue on which it was impossible for the court in the present case to differ from the Home Secretary. Decisions as to what was required in the interest of national security were self-evidently within the category of decisions in relation to which the court was required to show considerable deference to the Home Secretary because he was better qualified to make an assessment as to what action was called for. Was the Government entitled to single out non-nationals who could not be deported in the foreseeable future as the subject of the 2001 Order and the 2001 Act? Art 15 restricted the extent of the derogation to what was strictly necessary. No doubt, by taking action against nationals as well as non-nationals the action from a security point of view would have been more effective. Equally, if the non-nationals were detained notwithstanding the fact that they wanted to leave this country, the action would be more effective. However, on his assessment of the situation, the Home Secretary was debarred from taking more effective action because it was not strictly necessary. The Home Secretary had come to the conclusion that he could achieve what was necessary by either detaining or deporting only the terrorists who were aliens. There were objectively justifiable and relevant grounds for selecting only the alien terrorists which did not involve impermissible discrimination—the aliens who could not be deported had, unlike nationals, no right to remain, only a right not to be removed, which meant legally that they came into a different class from those who had a right of abode. The class of aliens was in a different situation because when they could be deported to a country that would not torture them that could happen. It was only the need to protect them from torture that meant that for the time being they could not be removed. In those circumstances it would be surprising indeed if art 14, or any international requirement not to discriminate, prevented the Home Secretary taking the restricted action which he thought was necessary. The approach adopted, which involved detaining the detainees for no longer than was necessary before they could be deported, or until the emergency resolved, or they ceased to be a threat to the safety of this country, was one which could be objectively justified. By limiting the number of those who were subject to the special measures, the Home Secretary was ensuring that his actions were proportionate to what was necessary. Further, the proceedings before the Commission did not contravene art 6 and the scheme of detention adopted by the 2001 Act did not contravene art 3.

BROOKE and CHADWICK LJJ gave concurring judgments.

Selected Bibliography

Alexander, Yonah, ed. *Combating Terrorism: Strategies of Ten Countries.* Ann Arbor, Mich.: The University of Michigan Press, 2002.

———Alexander, Yonah, ed. *International Terrorism.* Praeger Publishers, 1976.

Alexander, Yonah and Brenner, Edgar H., eds. *Legal Aspects of Terrorism in the United States.* Vols. I–IV. Oceana Publications, 2000.

Alexander, Yonah and Brenner, Edgar, H. eds. *Terrorism and the Law.* Transnational Publications, 2001.

Alexander, Yonah and Hoenig, Milton, eds. *Super Terrorism: Biological, Chemical, Nuclear.* Transnational Publications, 2001.

Alexander, Yonah and Letter, Richard. *Terrorism and the Media: Dilemmas for Government, Journalists and the Public.* Brassey's, 1990.

Alexander, Yonah and Musch, David eds. *Terrorism: Documents of Local and International Control-U.S Perspectives: Vol. 15–35,* Oceana Publications, 2001.

Alexander, Yonah and Nanes, Allan S. eds. *Legislative Responses to Terrorism.* Martinus Nijhoff, 1986.

Alexander, Yonah and Noone, Michael F. eds. *Cases and Materials on Terrorism: Three Nations' Response.* Kluwer Law International, 1997.

Alexander, Yonah and O' Day, Alan, eds. *The Irish Terrorism Experience.* Dartmouth, 1991.

Alexander, Yonah and Alan O' Day, eds. *Ireland's Terrorist Trauma: Interdisciplinary Perspectives.* St. Martin's Press, 1989.

Alexander, Yonah and Alan O' Day, eds. *Terrorism in Ireland.* Croon Helm; St. Martin's Press, 1984.

Alexander, Yonah and Pluchinsky, Dennis A. eds. *European Terrorism: Today and Tomorrow.* Brassey's, U.S. 1992.

Alexander, Yonah and Swetnam, Michael S. eds. *Cyber Terrorism and Information Warfare: Threats and Responses.* Transnational Publications, 2001.

Alexander, Yonah and Swetnam, Michael S. eds. *Usama bin Laden's al-Qaida: Profile of a Terrorist Network.* Transnational Publications, 2001.

Alexander, Yonah, and Meyers, Kenneth A. eds. *Terrorism in Europe.* Croom Helm, 1982.

Alexander, Yonah, Carlton, David and Wilkinson, Paul eds. *Terrorism: Theory and Practice.* Westview Press, 1979.

Asmal, Kader. *Shoot to Kill? International Lawyers Inquiry into the Lethal Use of Firearms by the Security Forces in Northern Ireland.* Mercier Press, 1985.

Aston, Clive C. *A Contemporary Crisis: Political Hostage-Taking and the Experience of Western Europe.* Greenwood Press, 1982.

Bassiouni, M. Cherif, ed., *International Terrorism: Multilateral Conventions (1937–2001)*. Transnational Publications, 2001.

Bell, J. Bowyer. *A Time of Terror*. Basic Books, Inc., 1978.

Beresford, David. *Ten Men Dead: Story of the 1981 Irish Hunger Strike*. Grafton Books, 1987.

Bergen, Peter L. *Holy War, Inc.: Inside the Secret World of Osama Bin Laden*. Free Press, 2001.

Bishop, Patrick and Mallie, Eamonn. *The Provisional IRA*. Corgi Books, 1988.

Cline, Ray S., and Alexander, Yonah. *Terrorism and State Sponsored Covert Warfare*. Hero Books, 1986.

Clutterback, Richard, ed. *The Future of Political Violence*. Basingstoke: Macmillan, 1986.

Clutterback, Richard. *Terrorism and Guerilla Welfare: Forecasts and Remedies*, Routledge, 1990.

Clutterback, Richard. *Terrorism, Drugs, and Crime in Europe: After 1992*. Routledge, 1980.

Clutterback, Richard. *Living with Terrorism*. Arlington House, 1975.

Cohen, Susan and Cohen, Daniel. *Pan Am 103: The Bombing, the Betrayals, and the Bereaved Family's Search for Justice*. Signet, 2001.

Conference on the Defense of Democracy Against Terrorism in Europe: Tasks and Problems. Council of Europe (Compendium of Documents), Strasbourg, 1981.

Coogan, Tim Pat. *The IRA*. Fontana Books, 1988.

Cooley, John K. *Unholy Wars: Afghanistan, America and International Terrorism*. Pluto Press, 1999.

Coyle, Dominick J. *Minorities in Revolt: Political Violence in Northern Ireland, Italy, and Cyprus*. Fairleigh Dickinson Press; 1983.

Crenshaw, Martha, ed. *Terrorism, Legitimacy and Power*. Wesleyan Press, 1983.

Dunne, Derek. *The Birmingham Six*. Birmingham Six Committee, 1988.

Emerson, Steven and Duff, Brian. *The Fall of Pam Am 103: Inside the Lockerbie Investigation*. G.P. Putnam, 1990.

Finn, John. *Constitutions in Crisis: Political Violence and the Rule of Law*. Oxford University Press, 1991.

Fletcher-Cooke, Charles. *Terrorism and the European Community*. European Conservative Group, 1979.

Gal-Or, Neomi. *International Cooperation to Suppress Terrorism*. St. Martin's Press, 1985.

Gibson, Brian. *The Birmingham Bombs*. Rose, 1976.

Gill, Peter. *Policing Politics: Security Intelligence and the Liberal Democratic State*. Frank Cass, 1984.

Greer, Steven. *Supergrass: A Study in Anti-Terrorist Law Enforcement in Northern Ireland*. The Clarendon Press, 1995.

Gurr, Nadine and Cole, Benjamin. *The New Face of Terrorism: Threats from Weapons of Mass Destruction.* St. Martin's Press, 2000.

Gurr, Ted Roberts. *Why Men Rebel.* Princeton University Press, 1986.

Hamill, Desmond. *Pig in the Middle: The Army in Northern Ireland 1969–1985.* Methuen, 1986.

Harding, A. and Hatchard, J. *Preventive Detention and Security Law: A Comparative Study.* Martinus Nijhoff, 1993.

Heymann, Philip B., *Terrorism and America: A Commonsense Strategy for a Democratic Society.* MIT Press, 1998.

Higgens, Rosalyn and Flory, Maurice eds., *Terrorism and International Law.* Routledge, 1997.

Hoffman, Bruce. *Inside Terrorism.* Columbia University Press, 1998.

Hogan, Gerard and Walker, Clive. *Political Violence and the Law in Ireland.* Manchester University Press, 1989.

Hogan, Gerard. *Political Violence and the Law of Ireland.* St. Martin's Press, 1989.

Holmes, Jennifer S. *Terrorism and Democratic Stability (Perspectives on Democratization).* Manchester University Press, 2001.

Jackson, Sir Geoffrey. *Surviving the Long Night.* Vanguard, 1974.

Juergensmeyer, Mark. *Terror in the Mind of God: The Global Rise of Religious Violence.* University of California Press, 2000.

Kassimeris, George. *Europe's Last Red Terrorists: The Revolutionary Organization 17 November.* New York University Press, 2001.

Kelly, Kevin. *The Longest War: Northern Ireland and the IRA.* Lawrence Hill, 1982.

Laqueur, Walter. *The Age of Terrorism.* Transaction, 2000.

Laqueur, Walter. *Terrorism.* Little, Brown, and Co., 1977.

Laqueur, Walter, and Alexander, Yonah. *The Terrorism Reader.* NAL Penguin Inc., 1978.

Lee, Alfred McClung. *Terrorism in Northern Ireland.* General Hall, Inc., 1983.

Leventhal, Paul and Alexander, Yonah, eds. *Nuclear Terrorism: Defining the Threat.* Pergaman-Brassey's. 1986.

Leventhal, Paul and Alexander, Yonah, eds. *Preventing Nulear Terrorism.* Lexington Books, 1987.

Levitt, Geoffrey M. *Democracies Against Terrorism: The Western Response to State-Supported Terrorism.* Praeger, 1988.

Livingstone, Neil C. *The War Against Terrorism.* D.C. Heath & Co., 1982.

Lodge, Juliet, ed. *The Threat of Terrorism.* Brighton, Wheatsheaf, 1988.

Matthews, Anthony. *Freedom, State Security and the Role of Law.* University of California Press, 1986.

McArdle, Patsy. *The Secret War: An Account of the Sinister Activities Along the Border Involving Gordei, RUC, British Army and the SAS.* Mercer Press, 1984.

McCreary, Alf, ed. *Tried by Fire: Finding Hope Out of Suffering in Northern Ireland*. Marshall Pickering, 1986.

McGowan, Robert, et al. *The Day of the S.A.S.: The Inside Story of How Britain Ended the Siege of Princes Gate*. Express Newspapers, 1980.

Miller, Judith, et al., *Germs: Biological Weapons and America's Secret War*. Simon & Schuster, 2001.

Mulloin, Chris. *Error of Judgement: The Birmingham Bombings*. Chatto & Windus, 1986.

Netanyahu, Benjamin, ed. *Terrorism: How the West can Win*. Farrar, Straus, and Giroux, 1986.

Netanyahu, Benjamin, ed. *Fighting Terrorism: How Democracies Can Defeat Domestic and International Terrorists*. Farrar, Straus, Giroux 1995.

O'Ballance, Edgar. *Terror in Ireland*. Presidio Press, 1981.

O'Day, Alan, ed. *Terrorism's Laboratory: The Case of Northern Ireland*. Dartmouth Publishing Co., 1995.

Patrick, Derrick. *Fetch Felix: The Fight Against the Ulster Bombers, 1976–1977*. Hamish Hamilton, 1981.

Rapoport, David C., *Inside Terrorist Organizations*. 2nd ed. Frank Cass, 2001.

Reinares, Fernando, ed., *European Democracies Against Terrorism: Governmental Policies and Intergovernmental Cooperation*. Ashgate Publishing Company, 2000.

Rose, Gideon and Hoge Jr., James F. *How Did This Happen? Terrorism and the New War*. Public Affairs, 2001.

Rowe, Peter J. and Whelan, Christopher J. eds. *Military Intervention in Democratic Societies*. Croom Helm, 1985.

Short, Kenneth, R. M. *The Dynamite War: Irish American Bombers in Victorian Britain*. Humanities Press, 1979.

Simpson, Brian A.W. *Holy Terror: Inside the World of Islamic Terrorism*. Adler and Adler, 1987.

Smith, Colin. *Carlos: Portrait of a Terrorist*. Holt, Rinehart, and Winston, 1976.

Sofaer, Abraham D. and Goodman, Seymour E. eds. *The Transnational Dimension of Cyber Crime Terrorism*. Hoover Institution Press, 2001.

Stern, Jessica. *The Ultimate Terrorists*. Harvard University Press, 2001.

Taillon, J. Paul de B. *The Evolution of Special Forces in Counter-Terrorism: The British and American Experiences*. Praeger, 2001.

Tanter, Raymond. *Rogue Regimes: Terrorism and Proliferation*. St. Martin's Press, 1999.

Townshend, Charles. *Political Violence in Ireland: Government and Resistance since 1948*. Oxford University Press, 1983.

Tucker, H.H., ed. *Combating the Terrorist: Democratic Responses to Political Violence*. Facts on File, 1988.

Tucker, Jonathan B., Ed., *Toxic Terror: Assessing Terrorist Use of Chemical and Biological Weapons.* MIT Press, 2000.

Urban, Mark. *Big Boys' Rules: The Secret Struggle Against the IRA.* Faber & Faber, 1992.

Walker, Clive. *The Prevention of Terrorism in British Law.* Manchester University Press, 2nd ed., 1992.

Wallis, Rodney, *Lockerbie: The Story and the Lessons.* Praeger, 2001.

Wilkinson, Paul, ed. *British Perspectives on Terrorism.* Boston Allen & Unwin, 1981.

Wilkinson, Paul. *Terrorism Versus Democracy: The Liberal State Response.* Frank Cass, 2001.

Wilkinson, Paul. *Political Terrorism.* MacMillan and Co., 1974.

Wright, Joanne. *Terrorist Propaganda: The Red Army Faction and the Provisional IRA, 1968–1986.* St. Martin's Press, 1990.

Wright, Robin. *Sacred Rage: The Wrath of Militant Islam.* Simon and Schuster, 1989.

About the Editors

Professor Yonah Alexander is Senior Fellow and Director, International Center for Terrorism Studies, Potomac Institute for Policy Studies, as well as Director, Inter-University for Terrorism Studies and Co-Director, Inter-University Center for Legal Studies. He has published over 90 books in the field of terrorism and international affairs and is founding editor of *Terrorism: An International Journal* and *International Journal on Minority and Group Rights*. He is co-editor, with Professor Edgar H Brenner, of a four-volume set on *Legal Aspects of Terrorism in the United States* (Oceana Publishers, 2000), *Terrorism and the Law* (Transnational, 2001), and *U.S. Federal Legal Responses to Terrorism* (Transnational, 2002).

Professor Edgar H Brenner is Co-Director of the Inter-University Center for Legal Studies in Washington, D.C., as well as Legal Counsel to the Inter-University Center for Terrorism Studies. He is a graduate of the Yale Law School and is a member of the District of Columbia Bar. Professor Brenner has lectured on various aspects of counterterrorism policy at such venues as The George Washington University, Tel Aviv University, Marmara University Law School (Istanbul, Turkey), University of Michigan Law School and Carleton College, Northfield, Minnesota. He is also an advisor to the International Center for Terrorism Studies, Potomac Institute for Policy Studies.